Drawn by Lieut. A. K. Lawrence, 19th Battalion Northumberland Fusiliers, for the "St. George's Gazette," April, 1919.

St. George's Day.—Ypres, 1915.

To fill the gap, to bear the brunt
  With bayonet and with spade,
Four hundred to a four-mile front
  Unbacked and undismayed—
What men are these, of what great race,
  From what old shire or town,
That run with such goodwill to face
  Death on a Flemish down?
    Let be ! they bind a broken line :
      As men die, so die they.
    Land of the free ! their life was thine,
      It is St. George's Day.

Let say whose ardour bids them stand
  At bay by yonder bank,
Where a boy's voice and a boy's hand
  Close up a quivering rank.
Who under those all-shattering skies
  Plays out his Captain's part
With the last darkness in his eyes
  And *Domum* in his heart?
    Let be, let be ! in yonder line
      All names are burned away.
    Land of his love ! the fame be thine,
      It is St. George's Day.

By HENRY NEWBOLT.

THE FIFTH IN THE GREAT WAR.

A History

OF THE

1st & 2nd Northumberland Fusiliers

1914—1918

By

Brigadier H. R. SANDILANDS,

C.M.G., D.S.O.

Dover:
G. W. GRIGG AND SON
"St. George's Press."

1938

FOREWORD.

Fifth Fusiliers—Past, Present and Future.

When honoured in March of this year by an invitation to write a foreword to the History of your 1st and 2nd Battalions in the Great War, my thoughts went back at once to the same month twenty years ago.

Your 1st Battalion had then been with me in the 3rd Division for one and three-quarter years. In 1914-1915 I had served as a junior officer in the same Division as your 2nd Battalion. I had served as a Commanding Officer of a Battalion of the 50th (Northumbrian) Division. As the facts so ably recorded in this History show, I could not as a soldier have felt anything but the deepest admiration for, and complete confidence in, the splendid fighting qualities of your Regiment.

In March 1918 we were awaiting a great German attack, the results of which would inevitably mean so much to the military issue of the War. We had reason to expect that we should be included in the area of the attack. I had addressed the Officers and Non-Commissioned Officers of each Brigade Group of the Division in turn, and had told them clearly that we must expect the greatest strain to which we had yet been subjected, but that in my opinion, though we might bend we should not break. I felt confident that greatly as I respected the fighting qualities and thoroughness of our enemies, yet they had for nearly four years been subjected to an even greater strain than ourselves. In the circumstances I could not believe that they, or any human beings, could carry an offensive against the British Empire Army to such lengths as to emerge victorious. But for our salvation it was essential to toil without ceasing to strengthen our defences, and toil by day and night the soldiers of the 3rd Division did, and none more so than the men of your 1st Battalion. Many of them who were miners by occupation were particularly tried by the reports of the high wages being earned by their comrades at home, but in my daily visits to them in the trenches it was clear to me that they understood the reason for the demands made upon them, and that if the attack were coming their wish was that it would come quickly. This History tells you of the results of their labours, and of the fine defence made, and of the part they played in the subsequent advance to victory, operations in which they were engaged from start to finish.

This story of the 1st Battalion is typical of the whole British Army at its best—gallant and resolute infantry supported by equally gallant and resolute comrades of the other arms, but above all officers and men imbued with an intense pride in their own particular regiment and determined at no matter what cost to themselves that the Regiment and Battalion must not be let down.

In no Regiment was that pride more intense than it was in yours. It existed before the War, it existed during the War, long may it continue to exist, for infantry in a modernized form will remain the backbone of every defence force.

I have written principally about your 1st Battalion, because in the War it was best known to me, but from what I saw in 1915, and from what is told in this

History, all that I have said applies equally to the 2nd Battalion. Indeed, it could not be otherwise for you are one Regiment, and from the day of your raising there has been only one FIFTH.

It was my privilege, when serving in India after the War, to have the 2nd Battalion with me, and I learned to appreciate them in peace as I had learned to appreciate their Regiment in war. I carry with me a very happy memory of the Ceremony of the Trooping of the Colours on St. George's Day at the little hill station of Dagshai, close to Sabathu, where the Battalion spent the summer of 1914—a ceremony carried out with a precision and smartness worthy of the best traditions of the Regiment and in a manner which would have the approval of all those devoted soldiers of the Regiment who fell fighting in the War.

I have addressed this foreword to The FIFTH—Past, Present and Future, for the History will be read principally by them, but it is a history which can be read with interest and profit by all. It is a faithful and graphic account of a Great Regiment in a Great War, and in the first chapter alone there is much for reflection not only for those who are responsible for the organization, training and preparedness of the Army in peace, but also for those who have any interest in it at all. The compilation of such a History is a heavy task, but writing as I do with an intimate knowledge of much of its contents, I congratulate the author, Brigadier H. R. Sandilands, who has written throughout with accuracy, thoroughness and much understanding of human nature. The Regiment has indeed been fortunate in having such an author with ability to produce a History worthy of the Regiment in which he is so proud to have served.

C. J. DEVERELL, *Field Marshal.*

10*th May*, 1938.

PREFACE.

This History has already appeared in the form of a monthly supplement to the *St. George's Gazette*. With its publication as a volume I wish to take the opportunity of acknowledging the help I have received from so many in its compilation. My thanks are due to Brigadier E. E. Dorman Smith, M.C., for preparing the maps for the first ten chapters; to Major B. T. St. John for correcting the printed proofs and assisting in drawing up the Index; to Major G. C. Humphreys and Serjeant Pomfrey for arranging the Appendix; and to Colonel J. A. C. Somerville for reading the several chapters prior to their first publication and offering the most valuable criticism in the kindest way. Space forbids the mention individually of over forty officers and other ranks to whose detailed information regarding incidents in which they were actively concerned the history owes much as an accurate record of events. Mr. A. K. Lawrence, R.A., in reply to my request to be allowed to include as a frontispiece the very fine design done by him in 1919 for the *St. George's Gazette*, offered to design one specially for the book. As the date fixed for publication did not permit of the acceptance of this generous offer, he made the alternative suggestion for the reproduction of a group of figures from his war picture painted in 1923, one of the works submitted in the open competition for the Prix de Rome which he won in that year. I was bold enough to ask if we might have *both*—the picture done by him when serving as a Lieutenant in the Regiment and the section of his later war picture. Thanks to his very kind agreement to this request it has been possible to include the latter at the end of the book.

There are to be found in the *London Gazette* many notable actions by members of the FIFTH during the period 1914-18 of which, owing to no indication being given of the exact occasions on which they were performed, I have been unable to include an account in a general narrative. In these circumstances I feel that those whose names are mentioned in the History as having rendered distinguished service would wish that the record of their actions should stand as testimony to the spirit which inspired the FIFTH as a whole rather than as a tribute to their individual prowess.

Printed and published by Messrs. G. W. Grigg of Dover, who have been associated with the Regiment for the past fifty years, this book, if it has no other merit, can at least claim that of being in every sense a home product.

H. R. SANDILANDS.

CONTENTS.

	PAGE
FOREWORD	iii.
AUTHOR'S PREFACE	v.
INTRODUCTION	1

CHAP.

I. "QUO FATA VOCANT" .. 3

II. ARRIVAL OF THE 1ST BATTALION IN FRANCE .. 9

"Mons"—"Le Cateau"—"Retreat from Mons" (14th Aug.-5th Sept., 1914)

III. "Marne 1914"—"Aisne 1914" .. 30

(6th Sept.-2nd Oct., 1914)

IV. "La Bassée 1914"—Bout Deville—Pont du Hem—Herlies—Neuve Chapelle .. 43

(3rd-30th Oct., 1914)

V. "Messines 1914"—"Armentières 1914"—"Ypres 1914" .. 55

The fighting at Wytschaete and Herentage Chateau.
(31st Oct., 1914-17th Feb., 1915)

VI. THE 2ND BATTALION ENTERS THE WAR—TRENCH WARFARE AT YPRES 69

1st and 2nd Battalion together in the 28th Division.
(July, 1914-7th April, 1915)

VII. 2ND BATTALION—"Ypres 1915"—"Gravenstafel"—"St. Julien"—"Frezenberg"—"Bellewaarde" .. 84

(13th April to 25th May, 1915)

VIII. 1ST BATTALION—The St. Eloi Sector—Attack on Bellewaarde.. 105

(5th April-16th June, 1915)

IX. 2ND BATTALION—In trenches on the Kemmel Front—Fighting in the Hohenzollen Redoubt—Departure from France .. 122

(25th May-24th Oct., 1915)

CONTENTS.

CHAP.		PAGE
X.	1st Battalion—Trench Warfare—The Attack on St. Eloi—The Battalion moves to the Somme (17th June, 1915-2nd July, 1916)	130
XI.	1st Battalion—"**The Battles of the Somme, 1916**"—"**Bazentin**"—"**Delville Wood**"—"**Ancre 1916**" (3rd July-31st Dec., 1916)	146
XII.	1st Battalion—"**Arras 1917**"—"**Scarpe 1917**" (7th Jan.-29th June, 1917)	169
XIII.	1st Battalion—"**Ypres 1917**"—"**Menin Road**"—Actions at Bullecourt and the Apex (30th June-31st Dec., 1917)	182
XIV.	1st Battalion—The Great German Offensive—"**Somme 1918**"—"**St. Quentin**"—"**Bapaume 1918**"—"**Arras 1918**" (1st Jan.-30th March, 1918)	196
XV.	1st Battalion—The Battle of the Lys—"**Lys**"—"**Estaires**"—"**Bethune**" (1st April-8th Aug., 1918)	214
XVI.	2nd Battalion—"**Macedonia, 1915-1918**"—"**Struma**" (25th Oct., 1915—26th June, 1918)	225
XVII.	1st Battalion — The Advance to Victory — "**Somme 1918**" "**Hindenburg Line**"—"**Bapaume 1918**"—"**Canal du Nord**" (9th Aug.-29th Sept., 1918)	251
XVIII.	The Advance to Victory (*continued*)—Return of the 2nd Battalion to France and the Final Phase—"**Hindenburg Line**"—"**Beaurevoir**"—"**Cambrai 1918**" 2nd Battalion (28th June to 11th Nov., 1918) 1st Battalion (30th Sept. to 11th Nov., 1918)	269
APPENDIX		
INDEX		

ILLUSTRATIONS.

"Quo Fata Vocant"		*Frontispiece*
Bridge at Mariette		*Facing* 16
The Aisne, 1914—"Cramped in narrow trenches"		,, 40
"Mud"		,, 67
Defences in the Ypres Salient		,, 81
Hell Fire Corner		,, 101
"All that were Left"—2nd Battalion, 25th May, 1915		,, 104
Earliest Form of Protection against Gas (May, 1915)		,, 110
After the Action at St. Éloi		,, 142
Supports Moving Up—Somme Battle, 1916		,, 148
Trading with the Troops, Vermelles		,, 160
Clearing a Road through a Village on the Somme Battlefield		,, 166
The Arras—Tilloy Road, April 10th, 1917		,, 174
The Cathedral and Cloth Hall at Ypres		,, 184
Ruins of Neuville Vitasse		,, 212
Refugees		,, 216
The Ruined Belfry and Square at Béthune		,, 222
Salonika		,, 227
Nevolyen Village viewed from the Right Bank of the Struma		,, 236
Sentry in a Sap-head		,, 263
A Shell-wrecked House in Le Catelet		,, 274
Casualty Clearing Station		,, 298

Page 72, foot-note—for " page 73 " read " page 71."
Page 144, 1st foot-note—for " page 146 " read " page 139."
Page 184, 2nd foot-note—for " page 194 " read " page 185."
Page 204, 2nd foot-note—for " page 210 " read " page 201."
Page 249, 2nd foot-note—for " page 256 " read " page 246."

MAPS INCLUDED IN THE VOLUME.

			PAGE
Map	2	Position of "B" Company 1/Fifth at Mariette, 22/23 August, 1914	15
,,	9	Attack by Buffs for Capture of O Trench, 15th February, 1915	73
,,	10	2/Fifth Attack on 21st February, 1915	77
,,	19	1/Fifth Attack on Lonely Trench, 18th August, 1916	158
,,	20	Location of 1/Fifth, 30th August–22nd September, 1916	161
,,	21	Trenches held by 1/Fifth during October and November, 1916	164
	24	Attack for Capture of Tilloy, 9th April, 1917	172
	28	German Attack on "The Apex," 12th December, 1917	191
	38	Attack by "W" and "Z" Companies, 1/Fifth, to the east of Noreuil, 2nd September, 1918	261

For remainder of Maps 1 to 43, see the Atlas issued with the History.

ADDENDA AND CORRIGENDA.

On the issue of each of the instalments in which this History first appeared it was necessary to break up the type from which the pages for the present volume had also been printed. The following table is accordingly necessary for the correction of certain errors and omissions which have since been discovered or pointed out. One or two simple misprints which leave the meaning of the words in which they occur unmistakable are not included.

Chapter III. *p.* 36.

Margin— For " 14th September " read " 13th/14th September."
Line 5—For " 14th September " read " 13th September."

Chapter VI. *p.* 75.

Line 4 from bottom—For " 83rd " read " 85th."

Chapter IX. *p.* 122.

Line 23—For " C. A. Steel " read " C. H. Steel."

Chapter XI.

Page 150, *2nd footnote*—For " 15th June " read " 15th July."
Page 159, *2nd footnote*—For " 2nd-Lieutenant Steele " read " 2nd-Lieutenant J. R. Steel."
Page 162, 10 *lines from bottom* } For " Blaney " read " Blayney."
Page 166, *line* 8

Chapter XII. *p.* 179.

Line 24—For " 12th Division " read " 17th Division."

Chapter XIII.

Page 185, *line* 17—For " Lieutenant R. Evans " read " Lieutenant D. Evans."
Page 188, *line* 15 } For " Lieutenant C. H. Steele " read " Lieutenant C. H. Steel."
Page 190, *line* 8

Chapter XIV. *p.* 205.

3rd Footnote—For " Z " Company read " Y " Company.

Chapter XV.

Page 216—Add 3rd footnote, " 2nd-Lieut. D. S. Lee was wounded on the 10th April."

Page 223—Add as a footnote to second para. :—

"It has since been ascertained that the raid on the 30th/31st July, 1918, of which the object was to secure identifications of the enemy on the 9th Brigade front, was carried out by a detachment of " Z " Company, numbering 30, under the command of Captain T. M. Scanlan, M.C. The actual raiding party of 10 other ranks was led by 2nd-Lieutenant T. Sanderson, on whose previous patrol reports the selection of the objective had been based, and was protected by two flanking parties, each of 1 N.C.O. and 8 men. Sanderson was awarded the Military Cross in recognition of the value of his preliminary reconnaissance and the skill and gallantry with which he conducted the subsequent operation.

INTRODUCTION.

Vast as was the growth of the British Army during the Great War, yet even greater in proportion was that of the Northumberland Fusiliers. For, in response to the nation's call to arms, so many sought service in the Regiment that before peace was signed its battalions had increased in number from seven to fifty-two. Following closely on the regular battalions, the four territorial battalions, as a complete brigade, took the field in Flanders in the critical days of 1915, and before hostilities were brought to a close by the Armistice of 1918, Northumberland Fusiliers had been fighting in Flanders, France, Gallipoli, Macedonia, Egypt and Italy. Time and again, during those four crowded years, battalions, in the space of a few hours, were reduced to one quarter of their strength. In the replacement of casualties, the officers commissioned to the Regiment could be numbered in thousands, and the men who passed through its ranks by tens of thousands.

If these facts are considered, it will be realised that for a history of the Northumberland Fusiliers in the Great War comparable in its detail to what has been written of the Regiment's life and achievements in preceding centuries, not one but many volumes would need to be filled. Some have already appeared, relating the deeds by which certain of the Territorial and New Army battalions upheld the great name of their Regiment; but a detailed account of the part played by many others still remains to be written. Among these are the two regular battalions—the parent battalions—to whose officers and N.C.O.'s both from the active and retired list, largely fell the duty of training the earlier battalions of the New Army, and whose traditions acted as an inspiration to all, from the date of their formation till the day of their final demobilisation. It is with the history of the two regular battalions of the Northumberland Fusiliers, which together are more intimately known as "THE FIFTH," that the present volume is concerned.

CHAPTER I.

"Quo Fata Vocant."

In this history of the part played by the FIFTH in the Great War place cannot be found to discuss the origins of that vast conflagration, which, breaking out in Europe in 1914, spread during the following years throughout the world. For those who wish to study a question that is likely to remain for long, if not for ever, a matter of controversy, there is already no lack of literature. But though in a regimental history of this kind we are not concerned directly with the anxieties, anticipations, and preparations of those in the inner councils of the nations of Europe, some account of the life that the subjects of this history were leading during the months immediately preceding the outbreak of war can be regarded as a justifiable, even necessary, preface to the main theme. For from this the reader of a future generation may estimate the extent to which the battalions of the FIFTH, though trained to meet the event of a European war, were unprepared in mind, and in one respect in organisation, for its early occurrence.

In the autumn of 1913, home and foreign service had been exchanged between the battalions of the FIFTH. The 2nd Battalion had moved to Ambala, in the Punjab, and a few months later the 1st returned from India to open its home tour at Portsmouth. It would be wrong to say that at this time the question of a European war was never mooted. It was generally known that in recent years more than one crisis threatening war had arisen in Europe, and the conditions under which the 1st Battalion found they were serving in Portsmouth differed essentially from those that had prevailed when, fourteen years earlier, the 2nd Battalion had taken up their quarters in the same station, just before being mobilised for the South African War. Battalions were no longer, as in those days, mere isolated units destined to be thrown together to form some sort of hotch-potch as occasion might demand. They were now grouped together in formations, under the officers who would command those formations in war, and be responsible for their training in peace. It was so that the 1st Battalion had taken its place as part of the 9th Infantry Brigade (Brigadier-General F. C. Shaw) of the 3rd Division (Major-General Sir H. Rawlinson)* of the British Expeditionary Force—an organisation of which the general purpose was well recognised.

Yet, it had come to seem that these European storm clouds were destined always to clear; and it would be fair, perhaps, to say that the average British regimental officer in 1913, while admitting that war in Europe could not be indefinitely

---

* To be replaced by Major-General Hubert Hamilton, under whose command the 3rd Division entered the War.

postponed, could never in his heart believe that such an event would come within Aug., 1914— his personal experience. It may, perhaps, be judged remarkable that this point of view should have been shared by the officers of the 1/FIFTH, for they had received a more definite warning of what the future held in store than had been given to most. In the winter of 1912 a lecture had been delivered to the officers and N.C.O.'s of the Battalion in the regimental gymnasium at Mhow on the aspirations and intentions of Germany. The lecturer, Captain Reichwald, of the Royal Horse Artillery, had peculiar qualifications to speak on this subject. For, as he contended, the closest friendship between men of different race can never give to either a true understanding of the racial prejudices of the other, personal friendships or dislikes being entirely distinct from national sentiments. It was for this reason that Reichwald, from his descent and early upbringing, claimed to be capable of understanding and even to some extent sympathising with the outlook of Germany. He pointed out how, everywhere in the world, Great Britain stood as an obstacle to what Germany regarded as the legitimate expansion of her empire, and he told of how for years past the German children had been taught in their schools to look upon Great Britain as the arch enemy of their country. He characterised the belief held by many in England that the social democrats in Germany would prevent their country from going to war as a dangerous delusion, and asserted his conviction that in one matter, if in no other, the German people of every class and creed would be found united. There was, he declared, not a man, woman or child in Germany who would not subscribe their last penny in support of war with the British Empire.

While it is true that, for delivering the same prophetic warning at a later date to a more august assembly, Captain Reichwald had been subjected to an official reprimand for talking nonsense, it is equally true that among those of the FIFTH who heard him there had been none who at the time had not been deeply impressed by the strength and sincerity of his convictions. But twelve months had passed since that lecture in the Mhow gymnasium. Much can be forgotten in that period, and it was not till his predictions had been confirmed that Reichwald's warning was to be recalled. To the 1st Battalion once again in England, with leave open and the time-expired men going off light-heartedly to the Reserve, war in Europe seemed, indeed, remote. The general anticipation was rather of a prolonged period of peace soldiering under Lieut.-Colonel H. S. Ainslie who, on the return of the Battalion to England, had taken over command from Lieut.-Colonel D. S. Sapte.

A matter of more immediate concern to the 1/FIFTH was the reorganisation of the Battalion from the eight company system, under which they had returned from India, to the four company organisation, which had recently been introduced at home. The transformation was not in itself an intricate matter, as under this first reorganisation, there was nothing in the nature of the subsequent " Headquarter Company." It was merely necessary to convert by amalgamation eight small companies to four large ones. Still, though the conversion was in itself a simple affair, not requiring any essential change in tactics, time was required for the machine to adapt itself to novel conditions and to run with its customary smoothness. Junior captains, relegated to the position of second-in-command of companies, felt at first that they represented little more than a fifth wheel to the coach ; and company commanders, at the outset, were scarcely less puzzled as to the precise duties of " company serjeant-majors " and " company quarter-master serjeants " than the colour-serjeants themselves who had assumed these novel titles. Fortunately for the 1st Battalion, sufficient time was to be given to shake down to some extent and to become accustomed to the

Aug., 1914— four company organisation before being thrown into war. The 2nd Battalion, as will be seen later, were to be less fortunate in this respect.*

For the adjutant, Captain W. N. Herbert, work in these days lay ready to hand in the preparation of the Battalion Mobilisation Scheme. If his labours were influenced by thoughts of the next General's Inspection rather than of war, it was but natural. At Portsmouth, in the early days of 1914, the robust figure of Brigadier-General Shaw was an object more clearly discernible than the distant phantom of War. Moreover, one could be satisfied that what passed muster with the former would prove adequate to the latter. For the rest, training pursued its normal course. In the early spring, the officers attended a brigade exercise. The subject, the disposition and action of troops in defence, was uninspiring. Yet, close and critical attention was given to the solutions of the various problems by one who was present, the G.O.C.-in-C. Southern Command, General Sir Horace Smith-Dorrien. On that bleak March day at Arundel how little could any foresee that, in the fierce heat of the following summer, they would be engaged under the same great leader in the most critical defensive battle in the history of their country.

During May and June the Battalion was in camp near Wool, in Dorsetshire, where battalion training was, for the first time, carried out under the four company organisation. Simultaneously with their return to Portsmouth came news of the assassination of some Austrian archduke at a place hitherto unknown called Serajevo. A regrettable incident, but one it seemed that could scarcely concern the Fifth Fusiliers. They had more important things to think of. Goodwood races, for instance, represented the next objective for many of the officers, while August Bank Holiday promised relaxation for the other ranks after the strenuous weeks in camp. And so in the *St. George's Gazette* we learn from 1st Battalion Notes dated 23rd July, 1914, that " the month of July has been used as a period of restful repose so far as training is concerned . . . the chance of a fortnight's leave has been seized by all those who could fit it in." In the same number we find that the serjeants are busy competing for a billiard cup, when not engaged in confetti battles on the South Parade Pier.

While the 1st Battalion, after long years of exile, were thus anticipating the full enjoyment of their first summer in England, the 2nd in India were fast settling down to the new conditions under which they had been called to serve. It has been said that the general expectation of the 1st Battalion was of a prolonged period of peace soldiering. Only more certainly can it be asserted that no one in the 2nd Battalion at mid-summer, 1914, foresaw, in his wildest dreams, the return of his unit to England before the close of the year. The " turn over " of personnel left in India by the 1st Battalion had been absorbed, and battalion training under the eight company organisation, which had been retained by British battalions in India, had been completed in the plains. At the end of March the Battalion had moved to the hills, where it was somewhat scattered, Headquarters being stationed at Sabathu, with single company

---

* NOTE.—Earlier in this chapter it was stated that, in one respect, the FIFTH were in their organisation not fully prepared for war. The extent to which British infantry battalions were affected by the introduction of a new organisation so shortly before mobilisation has been generally overlooked. Of the officers and N.C.O.'s who had some slight experience of the four company system, 80% to 90% were to become casualties in the first few weeks of the War. Those who replaced them from depôts, special reserve, or retirement, had had no practical experience of it. The organisation, moreover, was entirely strange to the retired officers and N.C.O.'s who were largely responsible for training the battalions of the New Army. It can, indeed, be said that the four company organisation *in its true intention* was never fully understood or adopted till some years after the War.

detachments at Jutogh and Dagshai. In May new colours were presented to the Battalion by H.E. the Viceroy, Lord Hardinge; and shortly afterwards it was intimated that, in the ensuing cold weather, the Battalion would be stationed at Delhi, where it was to have the honour of furnishing the Viceroy's guard. This would be a welcome exchange for dusty Ambala, and all were looking forward eagerly to the delights of a winter in Delhi. Polo had been taken up with enthusiasm by many of the officers, and the last week of July found a party playing away up in Kashmir. Others had taken shooting leave in the same country, or in other distant parts of India.

Aug, 1914—

This was the situation when, at the close of July, the astounding news reached Sabathu that Europe was on the brink of war, and that developments already threatened to make it impossible for Great Britain to maintain neutrality with honour. To the 2nd Battalion, so recently in England, it was bitter that at such a juncture they should find themselves in India. For should this long talked of but scarcely credible war become at last a reality, it was generally believed that it would be brief. There were many who were confident that if time were but gained for the mighty forces of Russia to be put into motion Germany would be doomed. So, whatever transpired, it seemed that the lot of the 2nd Battalion would lie in India. And here, feverishly awaiting further news from Europe, we must for the time leave them to turn to the events which had provoked these alarming rumours and broken "the period of restful repose" which its correspondent had so recently pronounced that the 1st Battalion was enjoying.

Events in Europe had moved rapidly. With the increasing gravity of the situation, it seemed that at long last a crisis had arisen that was destined to come to a head, instead of "passing" in the customary manner. But it was not, perhaps, till the declaration of a "Precautionary Period" on the 27th July, four days after the optimistic pronouncement of the 1st Battalion correspondent in the *St. George's Gazette*, that a full sense of the realities of the situation came to the Battalion—the first awakening to the fact that the engagement of the FIFTH in a first class European war had grown to something more serious than a matter for academic discussion at the Staff College. By the mobilisation scheme this declaration required the Battalion to despatch "precautionary detachments" for the protection of certain vital points in the neighbourhood of Portsmouth. But it did not, in itself, involve mobilisation. Nor, let it be recorded, did it upset the plans of most for attending Goodwood Races. For those who went racing that day and survived the War, the scene at Goodwood was often to be recalled in later years. The move towards mobilisation that had already been made had left them in no doubt as to the gravity with which the Government viewed the situation, yet, as they listened to the bookmakers shouting the odds and watched the eager backers staking their money, it was clear that the general public were quite oblivious to what threatened their country; and that their concern was still with the chances of the horses rather than with what these officers now knew was the practical certainty of war.

In the 1st Battalion, waiting anxiously on events, tension was extreme. The few days that elapsed before the country's decision was made seemed endless. The time, however, was not spent in idleness. Though mobilisation had not been ordered, the situation was so acute that all preparations that could be made before the calling up of the Army Reserve were undertaken in anticipation of the order. So when, at last, at 6 p.m. on 4th August, the order to mobilise was received, the Battalion was well ahead of its schedule. On the morning of the 6th August the first draft of 420 men from the Reserve arrived from the Depôt, and a further draft of 221 reached Cambridge Barracks late the same night. As recently as the previous winter the

Aug., 1914— annual Army Horse Census had been regarded by farmers and other horse owners as a pleasing farce, and an officer of the FIFTH engaged on it had been subjected by them to much good-natured chaff when classifying horses for mobilisation purposes. Yet, early on the morning of 7th August, the horses earmarked for the FIFTH were no longer in their home stables in Berkshire but in the transport lines of Cambridge Barracks. Mobilisation had been completed, and on the 9th August the Battalion at full war strength paraded for inspection by Brigadier-General Shaw.

But though in numbers the Battalion was complete, its quality was not regarded by the Commanding Officer as entirely satisfactory. It had been anticipated that the first men to arrive from the reserve would be the highly trained men who had but recently left the Colours. But this was not the case. At the close of the South African War, the terms of service for the infantry of the line had been altered to 3 years with the Colours and 9 with the Reserve. This reduced colour service had remained in force for some three years. In 1914 the reserve service of those first enlisted under these terms was approaching its conclusion. The drafts had proved to be composed very largely of these men, who had been in civil life for close on nine years—years, moreover, that had been marked by the great developments in training which had followed the South African War. An urgent call was despatched to the greatly harassed Depôt Commander for one hundred picked, fully trained, reservists, and each commander was instructed to weed out the twenty-five most backward reservists allotted to his company. The hundred men despatched by the Depôt in response to this demand were selected from among those who had received their discharge on the return of the Battalion from India. The arrival of these cheery, confident men, to take their place in the ranks they had but recently left, immensely strengthened the Battalion. None the less, the FIFTH was to go to war with a large proportion of men who for years had had no marching, and who were in sad need of military training in general. Never let it be thought that these older men lacked spirit; they were to give ample evidence of that. But had it been possible on mobilisation to arrange for men to rejoin the Colours in the reverse order to that in which they had gone to the Reserve, opportunity would have been secured for giving training and exercise to those most in need of it, and the Battalion, by the inclusion of men in harder condition and with more recent training, would have been better equipped for the first few strenuous weeks of the War.* In the meantime, Lord Kitchener had embarked on the raising of the New Army, and the 1st Battalion had been required to detail a captain and two subalterns to assist in the formation of the 8th (Service) Battalion. In compensation, four subalterns of the Special Reserve were posted to the 1st Battalion, but one company had to remain short of a captain second-in-command.

The busy days of mobilisation had given relief to the impatience with which the declaration of war had been awaited. But, now that the Battalion stood ready, the days that followed were scarcely endurable to the men, confined to barracks and chafing under the delay which succeeded the rush of preparation. Field operations, carried out among crowds of trippers on Southsea Common, though rudimentary as training for war, served to shake the reservists down in the ranks and filled in some of the time. For the rest there was little that could be done to ease the nervous tension that afflicts most men awaiting participation in some great event, be it a battle or merely

---

* This consideration applied not only to the FIFTH but to all infantry units. The question of whether it would have been sound policy to send out all the most highly trained men at the outset is, perhaps, arguable. That there would have been less suffering during the retreat from Mons had such a policy been followed is, however, indisputable.

a football match. But while this was the atmosphere in barracks, and though guns Aug., 1914— firing shots across the bows of approaching ships by day, and searchlights sweeping the waters by night, proclaimed that war reigned on the Solent, the attitude of many of the civil population gave evidence of how innocent they remained of the realities of the situation. Thousands, it is true, in reply to Lord Kitchener's appeal, were already crowding the recruiting offices throughout the land. But, for some nights following the declaration of war, while the searchlights on the foreshore swept the Solent, the parade at Southsea was thronged with laughing trippers enjoying their August holiday, while a band played merrily on the brightly lit Clarence Pier.* Though, with the wane of illuminations, the trippers gradually dispersed, the calm and almost indifferent attitude of the general public in Portsmouth, that continued to the end, impressed those who had been in the fever of mobilisation as remarkable. Those who, in 1899, had marched to Portsmouth station on their way to South Africa, recalling the cheering masses which had thronged the streets on that occasion were struck by the contrast in the scene when the 1st Battalion, on 13th August, 1914, left barracks to entrain for Southampton. On this occasion there was no great demonstration. Apart from a little cheering, small attention was paid to the Battalion on its march to the railway station, and but for the presence of a few relatives who had come down to see the last of their men folk, an ordinary change of station might have been in progress—an idea that was encouraged by the prominent display of destination boards marked " WOKING " on the coaches of the two trains that were to convey the Battalion to Southampton. The same calm atmosphere prevailed at Southampton during embarkation on s.s. *Norman*, which was to carry the Battalion to France. But this quiet, normal entrainment and embarkation of units represented no anti-climax ; it stood for one of the most remarkable achievements of the War. To those accustomed to the most trivial events being broadcast daily by wireless, or in print and pictures, it may indeed seem incredible that, ten days after the declaration of war, two battalions could march out of barracks through the streets of Portsmouth and vanish, without the news being known throughout England the same evening. Yet, it was to be found that, till certain officers of the FIFTH wrote from " Somewhere in France," their closest relatives believed them to be still in Portsmouth, and it has since been established that the German General Staff was almost equally ignorant of the movements and location of the whole British Expeditionary Force.

At 4 p.m. the s.s. *Norman*, setting sail for an " unknown destination," passed close to the men o' war who were to act as her escort. Then, at last, it was made clear that the FIFTH and other units aboard were bound for some adventure more serious than peace manœuvres, as round upon round of cheers came over from the men of that sister Service which for four long years was to safeguard the passage of hundreds of thousands of British soldiers across the narrow but perilous waters of the English Channel. As the leaders of that great army of Northumberland Fusiliers that was to follow, the 1st Battalion was bound for France.

---

* This is scarcely borne out by the description of Portsmouth and Southsea given in the *St. George's Gazette* of 31st August, 1914. But it is based on a contemporary diary which described such a scene as being witnessed as late as the 10th August. The change in scene, when it came, occurred very suddenly. It was probably the later aspect of the town that was in the mind of the correspondent of *St. George's Gazette*.

CHAPTER II.

Arrival of the 1st Battalion in France.

"Mons"—"Le Cateau"—"Retreat from Mons."

14TH AUGUST—5TH SEPTEMBER, 1914.

14th Aug., 1914   Shortly after sailing it had been disclosed that the "unknown destination"   Map No. 1
of s.s. *Norman* was Havre, which was reached at 3 a.m. on 14th August. Two hours later the Battalion disembarked; and under the guidance of a minute, but very alert, French boy scout, set out for a camp at Eprémesnil, some six miles from Havre. The mobilisation of the British Expeditionary Force had been completed on the seventh day, but it was now shown that with an infantry unit, the completion of its mobilisation does not mean that it is fit for service in the field.

Shortly after the march had started, an early morning mist cleared and the sun beat down fiercely on the column, which before joining the camp, had to negotiate a long, steep ascent by a heavy, sandy road. Industrial life from which the majority of the reservists had been drawn affords few opportunities for marching; the troops had set out with empty stomachs, and many were still suffering from the effects of innoculation for enteric. Consequently a considerable number proved unable to keep their place in the ranks. Reflecting on the ordeal which the Expeditionary Force was shortly to face, one realises how fortunate it was that this opportunity of getting the men fit was afforded before touch was gained with the enemy. Nor is it only Reservists who on mobilisation will be found soft; the requisitioned horses are apt at first to prove unequal to their work.

The steep and heavy road was an even severer trial to the transport of the Battalion than to the troops. As a result the Battalion, pending the arrival of its transport and supplies, remained till late in the afternoon without food or shade in almost tropical heat. At midnight a terrific thunderstorm burst over the camp. Torrential rain throughout the following day converted the stubble field on which the Battalion was camped to a morass. At midnight, 15th/16th August, when the Battalion paraded to march to Havre for entrainment for the front, the rain had ceased, but the condition of the ground and roads severely hampered movement, and the night was pitch dark. The transport preceded the Battalion which, with long halts, crawled behind it. The requisitioned horses jibbed and plunged in their unaccustomed work; both water carts turned turtle in a narrow lane; and there were times when it was feared that the war might be finished before the Battalion reached its entrainment point. It took $3\frac{3}{4}$ hours to cover the distance of $3\frac{1}{2}$ miles. Once arrived, however, entrainment went forward so smoothly and rapidly that it was completed $1\frac{1}{2}$ hours before the time scheduled for departure.

At the railway station two recruits had joined the Battalion—Soldat Simon and Soldat Steinhardt, of 114e Infanterie, appointed to serve as interpreters. In their old-fashioned French uniform—heavy blue coats, red pantaloons, and huge knapsacks—they gave the impression of a most formidable reinforcement. It was not till later that they confessed to having but slight knowledge of the handling of the Lebel rifles and long, wicked looking bayonets with which they were armed. In civil life Simon was the principal of a leading firm of jewellers in Paris; Steinhardt a brilliant young advocate, who in a recent *cause célèbre* had enhanced an already high reputation. As qualified interpreters they had been exempted from the normal term of service. Both were the best of good fellows. Simon, unfortunately, was very shortly afterwards to be lost to the Battalion, but Steinhardt was to share its trials and adventures for close on twelve months.

The first two days in France had been marked by considerable discomfort, but the ensuing week by its very contrast was to remain, perhaps, one of their happiest recollections to those who survived the years of horror and suffering that came after. The brilliant weather, the gay scenes at the halting places in the rail journey, where the brave women and children of France crowded to welcome the British troops ; and to the inspiration of this welcome was added the optimism of French officers, who already spoke confidently of an early and triumphant issue to the War.* On detrainment on 16th August at Busigny the Battalion marched to billets in Landrécies, which was reached shortly before midnight. Here the troops were placed in the local barracks, while a dormitory in the innocent precincts of an empty girls' school furnished the officers each with a bed and demure little washstand. On the following day the Battalion moved to Noyelles in the area of assembly of the 3rd Division. The opportunity was now taken of carrying out brigade route marches for the much needed hardening of the troops. For the rest, the atmosphere in Noyelles was that of perfect peace, leisure hours being spent by the officers in enjoying the hospitality of the kindly curé, and by all ranks in bathing and in mastering the French language. It was in connection with the last that an incident occurred illustrating the advantages of a public school education. The need for soft boots for marching was at the bottom of the trouble. Entering the village shop, an officer found a distracted French woman faced by a number of his men rendered desperate by having reached the limit of vocabulary and gesture. Appealed to by all, the officer was not found wanting. " L'huile pour l'estomac du bébé, madame," he explained. " Ah ! c'est le ricin qu'ils desirent ! " cried the good woman. " Pourquoi n'a-t-on pas dit ça d'abord ? " and a jar of the necessary castor oil was promptly produced. Some time was yet to pass before the development of that strange *lingua franca* by which the troops in later days communicated with the French and Belgian inhabitants. It is interesting to observe that the British soldier on arrival in a foreign country appears to regard a strong negative as the first essential to conversing with the local inhabitants—something to convey the English " nothing doing." The *napoo* that was coined for this purpose in France during the Great War was, in the wide range of its application, almost identical with the Kaffir *Ikona*, which was ever on the lips of the troops in the South African War, and with *Mafeesh*, the first word picked up in Egypt.

The assembly of the British Expeditionary Force was completed by the 20th August. At 3.30 a.m. on the 21st, the FIFTH, leaving the good people of Noyelles sleeping the more soundly for having witnessed the British concentration in their peaceful district, marched east to meet the German forces whose threat against the French left flank had now been revealed. The FIFTH will ever remember the hospitality of the kindly inhabitants of Noyelles, who within a few days of the 1st Battalion's departure were to be called on to endure the bitterness of an enemy occupation for four long years.

A march of 12½ miles brought the Battalion to La Longueville, where it was in billets for the night. Late in the evening officers were summoned to Battalion Head-

---

* Their optimism was based on the initial successes of the French Armies in Alsace and Lorraine.

22nd Aug. 1914 quarters where they were informed that the British Army was to move forward on Map No. 3 the following day with the object of taking the offensive against German forces reported to be advancing through Belgium north of the Meuse. On the 22nd the Battalion paraded before dawn, and set out with the 9th Brigade towards Mons. Shortly after daybreak the battlefield of Malplaquet was passed, and as the sun rose on a perfect summer day, the Battalion crossed the frontier of Belgium. Hitherto, no detail of the destination of units having been given, a halt was now called and orders were issued. *The ultimate object was still to take the offensive*; but as a preliminary to such operations an outpost position was to be taken up for the night 22nd/23rd August. In this the 3rd Division was allotted a very extensive front. Its left section, for which the 9th Brigade was made responsible, extended westwards along the line of the Condé Canal from Nimy due north of Mons, to the bridge of Mariette, a distance of six miles. The 9th Brigade was to hold this front with the 4/Royal Fusiliers on the right, the 1/Royal Scots Fusiliers in the centre, and "B" and "C" Companies of the FIFTH on the left from (excl.) Jemappes to (incl.) Mariette. Further to the left the line would be continued by troops of the 5th Division. The 1/Lincolnshire Regiment and the FIFTH (less 2 companies) were to be held in reserve at Cuesmes, a suburb of Mons situated about 1½ miles south-west of the town. The nature of the country through which the line of the 3rd Division was to run differed completely in the two sections into which its front was to be divided. On the right the line passed through a smiling agricultural country of fields, farms, and pleasant villages. South-west of Mons and south of the canal, in the area allotted to the 9th Brigade, a patch of coal had converted the country to a densely populated tangle of mining villages; familiar and home-like to many of the FIFTH, but as a field of operations as difficult as it was strange to the experience of all. In contrast, again, the country immediately north of the Canal was fair and open. The detail of the orders on which the two companies of the FIFTH destined for the Canal position were to act will be referred to later when the position itself is described.

Very shortly after resuming the march the column entered the maze of streets, railways and coal dumps which characterises a mining district. At the village of Genly, "B" and "C" Companies of the FIFTH, detached under the command of Major Yatman, branched left, and covered by their own advanced guard, took the most direct route to their position on the left of the line. From this moment Yatman's Detachment came directly under the orders of the 9th Brigade. The remainder of the Battalion, moving at the rear of the Brigade, reached Cuesmes at 1 p.m., where they took up billets in brigade reserve, Battalion Headquarters being established in the curé's house on the "Place." The atmosphere of Cuesmes was that of a general holiday. The troops were welcomed as deliverers by joyous, laughing crowds, while children from the local convent with sober piety distributed among the men religious medals bearing the superscription of Ste. Barbe, the patron saint of the miners. The reception of the British troops in Belgium, though no whit less warm than their welcome had been in France, differed markedly in one respect. In France the railway platforms had been crowded with girls and little children, and stern old women in the fields, as the train passed, twirled imaginary moustaches to indicate the Kaiser, and pointing to the frontier, drew their hands across their throats. In Belgium, it was largely strong young men who cried to us " Forward, my brave ones." But, in justice, it should be remembered that at this time there were still many of their age in England whose war effort was limited to similar exhortations, while applying themselves to " business as usual." The attitude of both was due solely to an inability to realise the meaning of war with Germany, but whereas the latter were to be granted the opportunity of proving this, these young Belgians, carefree on the very eve of invasion, were to suffer the humiliation of being held helpless for four long years while their country was ravaged by the enemy.

In the meantime, with gifts of cigarettes, chocolate and cigars pressed upon them by the enthusiastic inhabitants, Yatman's Detachment, footsore from mile after mile of cobbled streets, but cheery and confident, had pursued their way through a succession of mining villages and had reached Quaregnon, the main street of which leads to the bridge of Mariette marking the left flank of the Detachment and of the 3rd Division. The attentions of the populace now proved embarrassing, for on arrival in their position there was much to be done, and done quickly, by the troops, and the curiosity of the people hampered work. Before describing the position that was to be occupied and the arrangements to be made for its defence, we will turn to the orders which were the basis of these arrangements and the mainspring of Major Yatman's action during the next twenty-four hours.

For a proper understanding of the action of the detachment of the FIFTH on the canal it is necessary, in the first place, to understand that, throughout the events later to be narrated, Yatman was to receive no orders of any kind nor to be given any information as to the general situation or what was occurring on his flanks. He was to be guided solely by the verbal orders given to him before leaving the column at Genly, and by such information as could be gained by the local observation of his own troops. We are not, however, dependent only on the recollection of Major Yatman for the substance of the verbal orders issued to him. This can be ascertained from orders and instructions of the 9th Infantry Brigade and the 3rd Division which are to be found in the original among their records. It can be taken that the first of these, a 9th Brigade order, dated 22nd August, was intended merely to confirm the verbal instructions.* This gave the information that heavy infantry columns of the enemy had been reported advancing South on Mons, and the warning that their advanced guards might gain contact with " us "† during the afternoon. After defining the Canal as " the line of resistance," it gave, in detail, the dispositions of units in defence which have been generally described on a previous page. Now, in view of the fact that the bulk of the infantry of the 3rd Division had been ordered to take up a forward defensive position, it is questionable whether the troops in occupation of it could be rightly termed " Outposts." This point cannot be discussed here. But there is ample evidence that they were regarded and referred to as such, and it is essential that Outpost commanders should be instructed as to the degree of resistance they are to put up. No indication as to this is given in the Brigade order referred to, but Major Yatman's impression that he was required to maintain his position " as long as possible " is supported by other instructions and orders that are on record. At 5.30 p.m. on 22nd August, the 3rd Division reported to II. Corps that the two and a half battalions of the 9th Brigade on the canal had orders to hold on if attacked, but that their position was so unfavourable for defence that it was not proposed to reinforce them. If the " outposts " (8th and 9th Brigades) were driven back, the 7th Brigade would take up a position north-east of Frameries. The opening para.

---

* It includes among the addressees Major Yatton (*sic*), but was never received in writing by Major Yatman. The message bears no time.

† It is not clear to whom " us " is intended to apply. British cavalry first engaged the Germans at dawn on 22nd August.

22nd Aug., 1914 of Special Instructions issued by the 9th Brigade at 7.15 p.m. reads "If attacked Map No. 2
outposts are to hold their ground *as long as possible** but will not be reinforced by
units in Cuesmes." These instructions were confirmed and, to some extent, elaborated
by verbal instructions, of which a précis has been recorded, given at 10.45 p.m.,
to the 9th Brigade by a staff officer of the 3rd Division. The substance of these
was to the effect that German pressure against our cavalry was increasing from the
north-east; that attack from that direction was possible, in which event the 3rd
Division would take up a position facing north-east; that the 9th Brigade must
therefore be prepared to collect all troops in the area and to move to Ciply station
as a reserve to the Division. "*Outposts in this case would be relieved by Cavalry
and Cyclists.*" It will be noted that the original idea of the infantry on the canal
maintaining their position as long as possible had now been abandoned in favour
of their relief by mounted troops, in the event of a heavy attack developing. In
fact, it seems to have been realised ever more strongly that the line of the Condé Canal
though a clearly defined feature, and a potential obstacle to the enemy's advance,
as a line of defence had no merit and many defects. Less clearly, it would seem,
was it realised that, failing the destruction of the bridges, the virtue of the canal
as an obstacle would largely be discounted, for no reference to the arrangements
made for their demolition is to be found in the orders addressed to the infantry
units whose action, one would think, should have been ruled and timed by a consideration of this factor.

Now the reader may think that, in much that has been written above, he
has been asked to travel rather widely beyond the limits of a Regimental History.
But it is believed that no point has been put forward that was not intimately to
affect the situation of the Detachment of the FIFTH on 23rd August. It is well
again to emphasise that, of all the orders and instructions that have been mentioned,
none except the first verbal orders was ever to reach Major Yatman. These were
to the effect that he, in common with the commanders of other units on the canal,
was to maintain his position as long as possible, and to exercise his individual discretion as to when his troops should withdraw. We will now return to the position
of Yatman's Detachment in the long line of defence of the Condé Canal.

The vital point in the position was the bridge crossing at Mariette, one of
the five bridges on the front of the 9th Brigade. It was here that the most important
work was to be carried out, and here that the most critical fighting of the detachment was to occur. Some description of this point and of the measures taken to
defend it is therefore necessary. At Mariette there was in addition to the main
canal, itself some 60 feet wide, a flood aqueduct on the Quaregnon side, 15 feet wide
and of great depth. The two were separated by a central bank 45 feet wide along
which ran the southern tow path of the Canal. The bridges across the canal and
aqueduct were in prolongation and connected by a path, on each side of which were
two houses. On the north bank stood the bridge-keeper's house and the winch by
which the lever bridge of the Canal was operated. West of the bridge-keeper's house,
and opposite the left of Yatman's position, some coal sheds on the north bank offered
potential cover from the fire of the defence. The road leading north from the bridge
traversed an open space for a distance of 60 yards, then, leading by a level crossing
over a railway, which ran parallel to the Canal, entered Mariette to turn north-
west as the main street of the village, which extended northwards for about a quarter

---

* Author's italics.

of a mile. For a distance of one mile or more beyond the village the ground was level, though much intersected by deep dykes, when it rose very gradually to a wooded sky line. The houses of the village, while blocking the view from the Canal, completely concealed the Mariette bridges from observation from the north.

The task of holding the bridges was allotted to " B " Company, while " C " Company was placed in position in defence of the line of the Canal to their right. The measures taken for the defence of the crossing were as follows. The bridgekeeper's house on the north bank was placed in a state of defence and garrisoned by a party of twelve men under Serjeant Panter. The duty of this party was to report and delay the approach of the enemy; but they were to fall back south of the Canal if in danger of being cut off. To cover their position the gates of the level crossing were jammed, and connected to the houses beyond by a wire entanglement. In rear of the post a further obstacle constructed from some iron railings was erected at the north end of the bridge, in which a small opening, easily closed, was left for the withdrawal of the serjeant's party. In short, though the assembly of hostile infantry in the village that confronted the defence could not be prevented, any attempt to advance from that covered position and deploy on either side of the main road leading to the bridge would be seriously hampered. Of the buildings on the central bank, one was demolished to clear the field of fire from the southern bank, the other was placed in a state of defence and manned by small parties capable of bringing fire to cover the withdrawal of the advanced post, before themselves falling back on the main defence which was established on the south bank. This main defence relied on fire from a barricade at the southern bridge exit and from loopholes made in the houses that flanked the bridge and in the walls of their adjacent gardens. For a few yards south of the canal the street of Quaregnon ran in direct prolongation of the bridges, then, bearing left, it continued south-east in a straight line for 300 yards. At the end of this stretch, *i.e.* at a distance of some 400 yards from the Canal, " B " Company's support was placed, and yet another barricade was constructed. All houses adjacent to the defences were cleared of their inhabitants. The hardship involved by this temporary eviction was slight in comparison with that endured by people whose life was on the canal. On the following morning it was to be realised that the barges that lay at hand must be sunk. The grief of the barge people in witnessing the destruction of the floating homes in which they took such pride was a sorrowful sight to the troops.

The dawn of a bright summer's day found Yatman's Detachment still busy in completing their defences That they would probably have to be manned very shortly was now brought home to Major Yatman by a warning received in dramatic fashion from an unexpected quarter. He was called to the telephone at Quaregnon railway station, and here found that he was being addressed in perfect English by a voice which was strange to him. The speaker disclosed himself as a British agent, who wished to render a report. Without specifying the exact point from which he was speaking, he indicated that he was in the neighbourhood of the Bois de Baudour, some four miles to the north of Quaregnon. He detailed various German units that he had identified, and was continuing his report when a sudden silence fell: the mysterious voice, speaking from far away among the enemy, abruptly ceased, and no reply could be got to questions from Quaregnon. The report was passed on to Brigade Headquarters; but Yatman was never to discover the identity of his informant, or whether the fate of this brave man, playing a lone hand in the service of his country, was as tragic as that sudden silence portended.

23rd Aug., 1914   In the meantime, the remainder of the Battalion in their billets at Cuesmes   Map No. 3
had awoken to look out on a scene of perfect peace. As the morning drew on, the
church bells rang out, and the " Place " of Cuesmes was soon thronged with people
in holiday attire summoned to their Sunday worship. Gradually the crowd melted
into the church, and silence for a time reigned. But before the church doors again

Map No. 2.

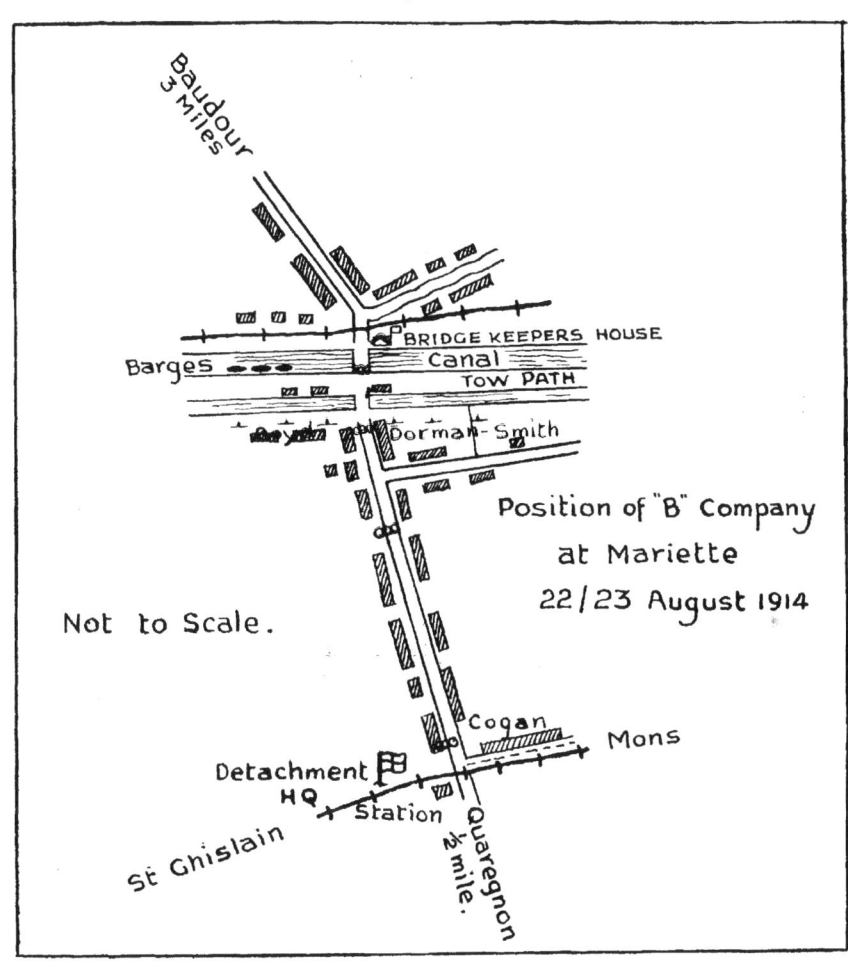

[Map: Position of "B" Company at Mariette 22/23 August 1914. Not to Scale. Shows Baudour 3 Miles, Bridge Keepers House, Canal, Tow Path, Barges, Dorman-Smith, Cogan, Mons, Detachment HQ, Station, St Ghislain, Quaregnon ½ mile.]

opened, the fire of artillery was heard, and, the service over, the congregation poured
out to scatter in terror to their homes.

The German attack, directed from the north-east, had first struck the right
of the 9th Brigade on the canal immediately north of Mons. Thence it spread swiftly
and progressively westwards along the length of the Canal. But the bridges at
Mariette were, perhaps, not regarded by the enemy as holding the same importance
as those on either side at Jemappes and St. Ghislain. At first it seemed to " B "
and " C " Companies of the FIFTH that they were to escape attention, as, undisturbed,
they watched for upwards of an hour the hostile bombardment in progress on the

British positions a mile to the east and west of them. Not a shell had fallen at Quaregnon, when suddenly and unexpectedly Panter's party at the bridge-keeper's house observed German infantry entering the main street of the village in "column of fours." The fire that was at once opened on them inflicted heavy casualties and cleared the street. But their infantry had also gained the houses to the north of the railway, and Panter, having carried out his task, withdrew his detachment without loss. Though at heavy cost to the enemy, Yatman's detachment had been located. This was shortly afterwards signified by a burst of artillery fire directed at the position. The shells, however, passed over the Canal and burst for the most part in the neighbourhood of the railway station and the support barricade. Hitherto, Yatman had been in visual communication with the troops of the 5th Division on his left through a signaller posted on the top of a gasometer. This man was now shelled off his position, and from this time all touch with the troops on this flank was lost. Later, a heavy concentration was directed on the buildings on the central bank. The garrison of one of these effected its withdrawal to the southern bank; in the other the serjeant in command was killed, and the men were forced to find refuge in the cellars.* On the artillery bombardment slackening, the enemy's riflemen still hesitated to advance, and contented themselves with sniping from the houses north of the railway, but with little effect. Any sniper that showed himself, on the other hand, was given so warm a reception that this action was soon discontinued. A lull in the fighting ensued, broken only by an occasional shell. It was now long past noon. A critical situation had already developed on the right and centre of the 9th Brigade, but Yatman with no information of this had every reason to be satisfied with the situation on his front, where for the present a stalemate existed. It was probably about 3 p.m. when, after a long period of this cat and mouse game, some Germans were observed preparing to round the corner of the street in front. To prevent this fire was opened, when, to his alarm, Captain St. John, who had given the order, saw a group of little girls dash across the street, and he immediately ordered his men to cease fire. The children crossed backwards and forwards three times, and could be heard crying in dismay. The incident occupied but two or three minutes but the cessation of fire was sufficient to enable the Germans to cut the wire and gain the shelter of the coal sheds on the western flank.† From this point they were able to bring cross fire on to the bridge entry barricade. Under cover of this fire, a field gun was then brought to within 400 yards and opened at point blank range on the same portion of the defence. Its indifferent field of fire prevented it from doing material damage, but the moral effect of artillery at such a range must always be considerable. Simultaneously a message was received from 2nd-Lieutenant Boyd, in position on the southern bank opposite the coal sheds, that hostile infantry and artillery were assembling on his front, but that the height of the central bank largely defiladed them from his fire. It was now about 3.30 p.m. That the situation of the detachment of the FIFTH had deteriorated will have been clear, but to realise the full danger in which it now stood, it is necessary to consider what had been passing

---

* The three men that constituted this small garrison, unable to withdraw, remained here undetected for 24 hours, during which a continuous stream of German troops crossed the bridge. They ultimately effected their escape and, showing great resource, managed to rejoin the Battalion five days later.

† That the enemy took immediate advantage of the cessation of fire is indisputable, one may say natural. There is no evidence that they deliberately staged the incident, and the Official History acquits them of so inhuman and despicable a ruse.

BRIDGE AT MARIETTE.

In 1927, when the above photograph was taken, the general surroundings had in some respects changed from those of 1914, but a good idea is given of the canal and the lever bridge.

23rd Aug., 1914 in the meantime on the remainder of the 9th Brigade front. About 1 p.m. the Brigade Map No. 3 Reserve had been moved to positions to cover the withdrawal of the right of the line from the canal. The 1/Lincolnshire Regt. had been disposed to guard the southwestern exits of Mons, while, of the FIFTH, " A " Company (less Ovan's platoon), and the M.G. Section had been placed in position half a mile north of Cuesmes, and " B " Company had taken up a position at Cuesmes railway station.†

The 4/Royal Fusiliers, heavily attacked in the salient of the canal north of Mons, had, in accordance with the discretion granted to Commanding Officers, started at 2 p.m. to withdraw in good order. At 2.30 p.m. the 9th Brigade had issued orders for all troops to withdraw from the Canal, and shortly afterwards the 1/R. Scots Fusiliers, hard pressed by the enemy, had fallen back from Jemappes. In the right and centre sectors of the Brigade front two only of the four bridges had been destroyed, and very shortly after the withdrawal of the British troops the enemy had started to cross the Canal by those that remained. Owing to telephone failures the order to withdraw had not reached Major Yatman, who had no information of the situation on the remainder of the Brigade front, and was now placed in a quandary. Though ignorant of the full nature of the precarious situation in which his detachment now stood, he judged that local developments demanded his withdrawal, if he was to carry out the spirit of the only orders he had received. On the other hand the bridges at Mariette still stood intact, and, though their destruction had not been ordered as an essential preliminary to retirement, nor the means of effecting it placed at the disposal of the infantry, it was known they had been prepared for demolition. At 4 p.m. Yatman gave the order to withdraw—action which would have been taken a full hour earlier had the Brigade Order been received. But scarcely had the movement been started when Lieutenant Wright, of the 57th Field Company R.E., arrived to blow up the bridges. This officer gave the alarming news that the Germans had already crossed the Canal on both flanks of the detachment.* It was then found that leads had only been provided for the main canal bridge, the nearer aqueduct not having been taken into consideration. Nothing daunted, Wright went forward from the barricade, and, lowering himself beneath the nearer bridge, dragged himself through the water to the centre bank. Wriggling forward, under fire, he searched in vain for the leads of the main bridge and was at length forced to abandon his task. Though his efforts proved fruitless, the great valour of this young officer's action was recognised by the award of the Victoria Cross.‡ The garrison of the barricade had already been withdrawn with the exception of Captain St. John and C.Q.M.S. Lewis, who delivered what covering fire they could, and then, in company with Lieutenant Wright and his gallant party of engineers, hastily withdrew to join the remainder of the Detachment in its retirement through Quaregnon. Very shortly after it had started the long delayed orders from Brigade were delivered by cyclist orderly, and " B " and " C " Companies, threading their way through the intricacies of the mining

---

† In the 1st Edition of the Official History of the War it was stated, in error, that the whole Battalion was in position on the Canal. In the 2nd Edition, while this was corrected, the further error was made of supposing " A " and " D " Companies to be in rear and in support of " B " and " C." As will be seen above, " A " and " D " at the outset were in Cuesmes and, when sent forward, were directed to positions three miles east of Mariette. No troops from Brigade Reserve were placed in rear of either Jemappes or Mariette.

* It is difficult to determine how far this report was accurate in regard to the left flank. Troops of 5 Division were still in position on the Canal at nightfall.

‡ Captain Theodore Wright, V.C., was killed in action in the following month.

18   THE FIFTH IN THE GREAT WAR.

Map No. 3   area, headed for Frameries. The enemy had not followed closely at their heels, but,   23rd Aug., 1914
before the Detachment reached its destination, a large body of German infantry, who
had come in from the flank, was observed on its direct line of retreat. Unaware of
the approach of the Detachment, they offered a tempting target, but a wise discretion
prompted the companies to hold their fire and to strike west and then south to Paturages. This, while adding to the distance they had to traverse, enabled them to reach
Frameries at dusk unobserved and unopposed.

In the meantime, all units of the 9th Brigade having withdrawn from the
Canal, the troops sent forward from Reserve had been ordered to retire from their
covering positions to Frameries. The Germans following up the 4/Royal Fusiliers had
collided with and been roughly handled by the 1/Lincolnshire, but the position of
neither " A " nor " D " Company of the FIFTH had been approached by the enemy.
The M.G. Section and " D " Company moving east of Cuesmes joined Battalion Headquarters on the Frameries road. " A " Company, withdrawing later through the
centre of the suburb, took up successive rearguard positions along the railway embank-
ments which flank the two bridges that cross the Frameries road south of Cuesmes.
The check experienced at the hands of the 1/Lincolnshire Regt. had imposed caution on
the enemy on this flank, but the Royal Scots Fusiliers, falling back from Jemappes
by the west of Cuesmes, had been closely followed up by the Germans. The two
rear companies of this battalion when about one mile north-west of Frameries were
hotly engaged by the enemy, whose supporting artillery simultaneously opened on
the Cuesmes road, dropping shells unpleasantly close to the Headquarters and M.G.
Section of the FIFTH. Ovans' (detached) platoon of " A " Company, which was at
hand, moved west of the road to the support of the Scots Fusiliers; the attack died
down, and the Germans withdrew, to be located shortly afterwards, as already recounted,
by " B " and " C " Companies in their withdrawal from Mariette. The Battalion
(less " A " Company) was assembled in Frameries by about 7 p.m. During the events
related above, " A " Company had remained in the rear guard position astride the
Cuesmes road, unmolested, but not undisturbed by the rifle fire heard to their left
rear and by the sight of shells bursting to their rear on the road by which they
had planned to retire. Eventually the company, scouting to its flanks, slipped
away under cover of a convenient railway cutting and reached Frameries after dark.

Studying the events of 23rd August, one cannot but feel that fortune favoured
the Battalion. Widely dispersed, it had fallen to the commanders both of the companies on the Canal and of those sent forward from reserve to act almost entirely on
their own initiative, with no information as to what was occurring on their flanks.
The failure of orders to reach Major Yatman placed the companies of his Detachment
in a most perilous position. It is no detraction from the merit of junior commanders
to say that good luck aided sound judgment in enabling the troops of the Detachment to be the last of the 9th Infantry Brigade to leave the Canal and the battalion
to be assembled in Frameries with the comparatively light loss of 8 killed and 11
wounded. But fortune had failed them in the matter of the demolition of the Mariette
bridge. The withdrawal south-east of Yatman's Detachment on the left of the 3rd
Division inevitably left that gap between it and the 5th Division which was later to
cause so much anxiety. But the exploitation of that gap by the enemy would have
been materially delayed, and anxiety lessened, had the gallant efforts of Lieutenant
Wright achieved their purpose. It must, however, be remembered that his attempt
was only made possible by the orders to withdraw not having reached Major Yatman
an hour earlier.

24th Aug., 1914   On the assembly of the Battalion in Frameries orders were received to take   Map No. 3
up positions in defence of the village. No written orders are extant and the exact dispositions of the 9th Brigade, which were taken up in the dark, are difficult to determine from available records. The 4/Royal Fusiliers on their withdrawal from Mons had fallen back on to the 7th Infantry Brigade, to whom for the present they remained attached at Ciply, 1½ miles east of Frameries. Of the remaining battalions of the 9th Brigade, 1/Lincolnshire Regt., on the right, were made responsible for the northern edge of Frameries, the FIFTH for the north-western edge of the village, and the 1/Royal Scots Fusiliers took up billets in reserve. The FIFTH were disposed as follows. " B " and " C " Companies, in some orchards on the outskirts of the village, occupied the forward line ; " A " Company in support, was placed in defence of cross-roads in the centre of the village ; " D " and the M.G. Section* were held in Battalion reserve.

In the withdrawal from the Canal a dangerous gap had occurred between the inner flanks of the 3rd and 5th Divisions. To fill this the 5th Infantry Brigade had been sent forward from the 2nd Division of I. Corps and had occupied Paturages to the west of Frameries. The 2/Worcester Regt. on the right of this Brigade was in touch with " B " Company on the left of the FIFTH. The troops had had an arduous day, but the situation allowed of little rest. The night was spent in intensive work on the defences, " B " and " C " Companies entrenching, " A " Company constructing three strong barricades at the cross-roads. So, in reliefs, they worked without cease through the hours of darkness, the men, between their tasks, sinking to sleep beneath the orchard trees or on the cobbled streets of Frameries, or making the most of such food as could be obtained. Rations there were none, but the evening output of a local bakery supplied a sufficiency of bread to take the edge off the hunger of all.

Frameries on the night of 23rd/24th August constituted a paradise for spies. All inhabitants should have been confined to their houses, but there had been no opportunity for issuing orders for this. Though the people of the village showed sincere and generous hospitality, suspicious characters were found wandering about the streets throughout the night. " Drunken men " whose friendliness was embarrassing, hysterical youths with tales of having run the gauntlet of the German troops ; zealous parties begging permission to retrieve wounded British soldiers, alleged to have been reported in a house on the Cuesmes road. It would, indeed, be underrating the enemy to suppose that, under such conditions, he could not secure a fairly accurate account of the British dispositions. Yet dawn broke and peace still reigned. But not for long, though it was fully light when the first shell burst over Frameries, as herald of the German attack. It was followed by an intense bombardment of the trenches on the whole front of the 9th Brigade. Shells also burst, with all but perfect accuracy, in the houses on either side of the street within twenty yards of " A " Company's main barricade. The men here, however, were well protected and the only casualty was Captain Sandilands, who was wounded but able to remain in command of the barricades. But in other parts of the defence casualties were mounting up, regimental medical officers, as was the custom at this date, were forward with the troops in position, and a hospital to which the wounded were being taken back was hard pressed to deal with the number of cases. This gave rise to an incident that is deserving of record. An elderly Belgian lady, to the consternation of the

---

* At this date 2 guns.

troops, suddenly appeared at "A" Company's position and demanded to be allowed to pass the barricade to call in the assistance of Dr. D—— who lived a short distance down the street. Captain Sandilands told her that the artillery fire might at any moment change to rifle fire and the street be swept by bullets. The old lady was unimpressed. Stern injunctions to retrace her steps and assurances that measures would be taken to procure the doctor proved as powerless to move her as the shells, that were bursting close at hand. She had come to fetch Dr. D—— to attend to the wounded, and she was not going to budge till Dr. D—— appeared. Recourse was had to a megaphone. In response to a call by this, a little man appeared on the doorstep of a house some twenty yards down the street. Simultaneously a shell burst in the roof of a house opposite and the little man popped back to the shelter of his own house. This act was twice repeated before the good doctor took the plunge, and with his black bag gained the shelter of the barricade at a brisk double. At last this stubborn and gallant old lady was satisfied. Having directed the doctor to go with all speed to the hospital, she left the barricade and slowly toddled after him.

The German artillery fire continued for some two hours, not as a continual bombardment, but by intense bursts at irregular intervals. The infantry in their approach to the attack for a brief space had offered good targets to our field guns, which were firing over open sights from positions in a clearing south-west of the village, but on gaining cover from our artillery they made no attempt to advance further against the trenches of "B" and "C" Companies of the FIFTH, though, in this quarter of the defence, their proximity was revealed by the sniping which was drawn by any movement from the cover of the trenches. More determined efforts, however, were made by the enemy further to the right. On the opening of the attack, "D" Company of the FIFTH had been sent forward from reserve east of the Cuesmes road to take up a position in echelon on the right of the 1/Lincolnshire Regt. who, west of the road and north of Frameries, were in occupation of a salient. It was against this salient that the Germans made their main effort, but the Lincolnshire Regt. and "D" Company of the FIFTH, while themselves suffering severe casualties, inflicted far heavier losses on the enemy and completely held up the attack.

It was now past 8 a.m. The British troops at Frameries had no thought of retirement, and, from their purely local outlook, they had every reason to be satisfied with the course of events on the front of the 9th Brigade. Now, readers who are acquainted with the wider aspect of the events of the 23rd and 24th August will know that at the hour mentioned above these troops were, in fact, in a most perilous position, and that orders for their withdrawal had long since been issued by G.H.Q. To these the statement that equanimity still prevailed at Frameries might be surprising until the time necessary for information and orders to reach the fighting troops is taken into consideration. It had been the intention of Sir John French to stand and fight. Orders for this had been issued by G.H.Q. at 8.40 p.m. on the 23rd August, but it was not till five hours later that the 3rd Division conveyed these orders to its brigades. At 1.39 a.m. on the 24th August the following message* had been sent to the 9th Infantry Brigade—"Field Marshal directs that the enemy will be withstood on the ground now occupied and driven back and every effort will be made to strengthen the position and to carry out these instructions whereby great effect will be had on other portions of the campaign." It is probable that the gist of this

---

* 3 Division G. 157.

25th Aug., 1914 order did not reach battalions till an hour or so later, but since, as has been seen, Map No. 3 the action ordered had been anticipated by organising the defence of Frameries, the delay in its transmission had been of no consequence. What was of very grave consequence, however, was that some two hours before the 3rd Division had transmitted the order to stand on the defensive, information had reached G.H.Q. at Le Cateau, 30 miles from Frameries, that the French Fifth Army on the right of the B.E.F. was falling back. This news had forced Sir John French to change his plan and to issue orders at 1 a.m. on the 24th August for the withdrawal of his force. A brief calculation will enable the reader to realise how it was then that at 8 a.m. on the 24th August the FIFTH had received no other order than to stand their ground and fight; were satisfied with the progress of events, and had made no arrangements of any kind for withdrawal. The factor of the time taken in transmission of orders should, too, be considered in reading the lines that follow.

At 6.30 a.m. the 3rd Division, having been, by then, informed of the C.-in-C.'s change in plan, ordered the withdrawal of the 7th and 8th Infantry Brigades, who were to the right and slightly forward of the 9th Brigade. The 9th and 5th Infantry Brigades were to hold on at Frameries till further orders. Now, the 5th Infantry Brigade, it will be remembered, had been lent by I. Corps. But, as an integral part of II. Corps defence, it would reasonably be presumed that the brigade would be acting under II. Corps orders. Yet incredible though it may seem, their withdrawal was ordered by I. Corps and carried out before any orders for retirement had been received by " B " and " C " Companies of the FIFTH, whose left flank was, in consequence, in grave danger of being turned.† At 8.30 a.m. the 9th Brigade received an order to withdraw on Sars La Bruyère as rear guard to the Division. But it was not till close on an hour later that the order to break off the battle and withdraw reached the companies of the FIFTH, who had been detailed to act as rear guard to the 9th Brigade. " A " Company was ordered to hold its barricades at the cross-roads in the centre of the village to cover the withdrawal of the battalion.* Within ten minutes of the order reaching " A " Company, a group of German infantry appeared in the main street, to the north and within a hundred yards of the centre barricade, and opened fire. Their fire, passing harmlessly over the barricade, swept the street which sloped upwards in rear. Reply from the barricade speedily dispersed all but two left lying in the street. The incident had lasted but a few seconds. Some ten minutes later, a group of the enemy who had got round the right flank endeavoured to dash across the road that ran east from the cross-roads. Two were dropped by fire from the eastern barricade, and the remainder fled to cover. Efforts then made to snipe from the cover of the corners of the main street were quickly subdued. In the meantime the bulk of " B " Company had been withdrawing by a street to the

---

† See Vol. I. Official History, Chapter IV. The writer, believing this could only be a misprint, drew the attention of Brigadier-General Edmonds to the point. General Edmonds confirmed that the Brigade retired on orders from *I. Corps.*—H.R.S.

* The confusion caused by taking up positions after dark with the intention of a prolonged and determined defence, and by the sudden unexpected orders to retire, is shown by the misconceptions that have arisen as to what units were covering the withdrawal. The History of the Lincolnshire Regt. shows that they were under the impression that they were acting as Rear Guard to the Brigade on the 24th August. The officers of " B " Company of the FIFTH believed that their company covered the withdrawal of the Battalion from Frameries. My personal recollections, as recorded above, are supported by the War Diary of 9 Infantry Brigade and by the Adjutant 1/FIFTH (now Major-General W. N. Herbert).—H.R.S.

west, covering their own withdrawal by barricades which had been constructed by the Royal Engineers. The remainder of "B" Company and the whole of "C" Company now filed in behind "A" Company's barricades and withdrew unmolested by the street that sloped up in rear of the central barricade. While this was in progress the enemy could be heard hammering at the walls of houses, to which they had gained access, in an effort, it was supposed, to make loop holes. While stragglers were delaying the withdrawal, every moment seemed critical. At last the time came when "A" Company could start filtering away from its barricades in the manner that many had practised from hill tops on the North West Frontier of India. Finally, the four men left at each barricade, south, east and west, together with two officers, slipped away at their best speed without a shot from the enemy, who, had they realised what was in progress, could have swept the whole street by fire. The Battalion was assembled in a street in the southern outskirts of Frameries and, undisturbed by fire of any kind, debouched from the village to move south by the Eugy road as rear guard to the 9th Brigade in its march on Sars La Bruyère. The casualties in the FIFTH had not been heavy. They are shown in the War Diary as amounting to 3 O.R. killed, 2 officers and 32 O.R. wounded, but these totals do not include a considerable number of wounded who, owing to the sudden and unexpected order to withdraw, had to be abandoned in the Convent to which they had been taken. Among those that fell into the hands of the Germans was the medical officer of the Battalion, Captain Malcolm Leckie, who throughout the morning had displayed the most conspicuous gallantry and devotion to duty. Grievously wounded, he died as a prisoner of war five days later.

At the time it seemed miraculous that, within half an hour of its rear party being engaged with the enemy's infantry in the centre of the village, the Battalion should be allowed not only to complete its assembly, but to continue its retirement unmolested. For it is often difficult on the occasion to realise the full effect of one's fire on the enemy, and it was only in later years that one could appreciate, from German accounts, the demoralisation caused by the terrible casualties suffered by the enemy at Frameries.* It is to this that the lack of enterprise shown by his infantry may be attributed, while the presence of their own troops in the village doubtless deterred the German artillery from firing. It is more difficult to understand the failure of the hostile artillery to bring under fire the road by which the long columns of the infantry of the 9th Brigade were retiring.

It was from now onwards that the FIFTH, with but brief snatches of sleep, and rations so rare as to be regarded as manna from Heaven, was to be engaged day and night in that critical and perilous retreat which so narrowly saved the British Expeditionary Force from annihilation. The 7th and 8th Brigades had already withdrawn by the Genly road. The 9th Brigade, on reaching Sars La Bruyère about noon without incident, halted and took up a defensive position, in touch on the right with the 8th Brigade, and on the left once more in contact with the 5th Brigade. The situation of the 3rd Division was satisfactory and a further retirement on Bavay had been ordered. But the 5th Division to the west had been very roughly handled, and there was considerable anxiety at Corps Headquarters concerning the gap that still existed between the inner flanks of the two Divisions. In view of this II. Corps ruled that while the remainder of the 3rd Division might continue to withdraw, the

---

* See Official History, Vol. I., Chapter IV., for "The German Account of Frameries."

24th Aug., 1914 9th Infantry Brigade must be retained at Sars La Bruyère to cover the right flank Map No. 4 of the 5th Division, and to guard the gap as best it could. It was not till 4 p.m., accordingly, that the Battalion, still acting as rear guard to the Brigade, continued its retirement, now moving south-west. The distance to Bavay was only some seven miles, but the heat of a tropical day was still considerable; the troops had been subjected to hours of artillery bombardment, and even the more fortunate had now had little sleep or food for over twenty-four hours. They were, moreover, moving in a direction that must always be dispiriting to a soldier. It was at this juncture, when the men had struggled along wearily for some miles, that a small group of mounted officers rode past. One of these, looking fresh and confident, spoke to the men as he passed, cheering and encouraging them. It was the Corps Commander, Sir Horace Smith-Dorrien. Of the thousands of men under his command there were few that day who did not hear the simple and brave words of this great leader; none who could have realised the weight of anxiety he was being called on to bear at that moment. An infantryman himself, none knew better than he what the men were undergoing, and, as for the troops, already in the FIFTH there was none that did not know and trust the name of "Smith Doreen."† Thus encouraged, the Battalion plodded on till Bavay was reached just after sunset. Troops were streaming in from more than one direction, and the congestion in the main street reduced progress to a snail's pace. Few things are more harassing than this to tired men, and orders were now received for the Battalion to push on a further two miles to Bermeries. It was dark before the Battalion reached its destination, and 10.30 p.m. before it was formed up in bivouac in an open field. The Quartermaster, Captain Landen, who had preceded the Battalion, was waiting with dinners ready cooked—a welcome sight to men who had been without a meal for 36 hours. The sweltering day had been followed by a chill night, but the troops, utterly weary, having taken their meal, sank immediately to sleep on the bare ground. They could get but four hours' rest, however, as the retirement of the 3rd Division was to be continued at 3 a.m. It was to be carried out in two columns, the 9th Brigade being directed by the easterly route on Audencourt, the 8th Brigade by the westerly route on Caudry.* The 7th Brigade was to act as rear guard. Rations were served and the men got some sort of meal before the Battalion moved off at 5 a.m. Throughout the 25th August the heat was intense. Two events only are recalled of the day's march—the one, the first sight of an enemy aeroplane brought down by fire; the other, the cheers that broke spontaneously from the men of "B" Company when they recognised in a young officer who passed, Lieutenant Wright, the hero of the incident at Mariette bridge on the 23rd. Late in the afternoon a thunderstorm broke, and after a march of close on twenty miles the Battalion in drenching rain halted at the village of Inchy. The main body of the 3rd Division had completed its movement undisturbed, but late in the afternoon the enemy had gained contact with its rear guard north of Solesmes. The 5th Division which, on the 23rd and 24th August, had been on the left of the 3rd Division, had in the course of the retirement, fallen back to a position on its right (east) flank. The 4th Division, recently arrived from England, had come up on the left of the 3rd

---

† A few weeks later in conversation with officers belonging to five or six different units of the 3rd or 5th Divisions, I found that there was none who had not seen and been spoken to by the Corps Commander during the withdrawal on 24th August.—H.R.S.

* The terms right and left being in relation to the position facing the enemy are apt to be confusing when employed in connection with a retirement. They will be generally avoided in this History in favour of east, west, etc., when referring to *movements to the rear*.

Division. The line to which II. Corps had now fallen back had been partially prepared for defence by French Territorials. In this the front allotted to the 3rd Division was on the general line Troisvilles—Audencourt—Caudry. The 9th Brigade had been detailed to occupy the right (Troisvilles) section of this front. But it was considered that the situation did not permit of II. Corps standing on the defence. The intention therefore was to resume the retreat after a brief halt. In any case, night had fallen before brigades had reached their destinations and it was too dark to select positions. Orders were received by the 3rd Division shortly after 9 p.m. that the defensive position would not be taken up, and that troops should be prepared to move again on the 26th. The 9th Brigade, accordingly, billeted in Inchy for the night, under cover of outposts. The Battalion, after being given a meal, was billeted by 10 p.m. with orders to turn out at 2 a.m. Soaked to the skin, and without being permitted to remove their equipment, the troops settled down to procure what rest they could during these few hours. But a brief respite was to be granted to them. Severe as had been the ordeal of the FIFTH there were other units who had not only been actively engaged with the enemy on the 25th August, but for whom there would not be the opportunity for the briefest rest if the retirement was to continue as planned. Few commanders can have been faced with a graver situation than that which confronted Smith-Dorrien on that fateful night; fewer still who, with such confidence, could have made the true decision. Convinced that to continue the retreat, without checking the enemy's pursuit, would risk involving his divisions in disaster, he determined to stand and fight on 26th August. So when the Battalion turned out at 2 a.m., companies were ordered to turn in again and stand to arms before dawn. None at that time knew the reason for this change in orders. One gathers that, where a Corps Commander should have been credited with an historic decision, a long-suffering adjutant was blamed for having issued wrong orders in the first place! The pawns in the game know so little of the great issues that influence the small, though to them all important, moves on the chess-board of war.*

Thus it was that at dawn the FIFTH moved out to prepare a position in defence. The front line of the 9th Brigade, on the right of the 3rd Division, was sited on a forward slope some 800 yards south of Inchy. The Battalion was to take position on the right flank of the Brigade, thus again having troops of the 5th Division on its outer flank. At Mons these had been on its left, but now, owing to the change in the relative positions of the 3rd and 5th Divisions, they were on its right. Such trenches as had already been constructed were found unsuitable, and it became necessary to re-dig the whole position. Few heavy tools were available, and the

---

* In view of the controversy which has arisen with regard to the stand at Le Cateau, the following statement, communicated by Brigadier-General C. Yatman (2nd-in-Command of the 1/FIFTH in August, 1914) is of great historical interest :—" On the afternoon of the 25th August Smith-Dorrien was at the side of the road, when I went over to speak to his A.D.C. Smith-Dorrien called me to him and said : ' Come here. I am going to tell you something which you must repeat to none but your C.O. We are going to stand and fight to-morrow. What will your men think ? Are they tired of retreating ? ' I said that the men were certainly tired of retreating and would be delighted. It was some time before I got the opportunity of telling Ainslie, and he was then so harassed by other concerns that I have never been sure that he grasped the significance of what I told him. After the battle I told various folk of the incident. During the controversy which followed the publication of French's book, I recalled the calm and deliberate way that Smith-Dorrien had spoken of what he meant to do on the morrow. He said that he would fight at Le Cateau—and that is a fact."

25th Aug., 1914 work had to be carried out almost entirely with infantry entrenching tools. While Map No. 4 three companies and the machine gun section set to work on the construction of a forward line of defence, " B " Company as Battalion Reserve took up a position with the 1st Line Transport in a sunken road some three to four hundred yards to the rear. Work had not been completed when the enemy's artillery opened to prepare the way for attack. The bulk of the fire was directed to the rear and did no damage to the forward companies, but " B " Company and the transport suffered several casualties, including two officers wounded, Captain Toppin (who remained at duty) and 2nd-Lieutenant Dorman-Smith. The 23rd Field Brigade and 20th Howitzer Brigade, covering this position of the front, immediately replied, and doing splendid work proved more than a match for the German guns. There was little further trouble from this quarter, work was steadily continued and before long good cover had been constructed for the forward companies. In the meantime, though little of it was seen by the FIFTH, fierce fighting had developed on the 3rd Division front at Caudry and the right of the 5th Division was also heavily engaged. Attack, however, was not pressed against 9th Brigade. On the slightest indication of enemy movement in Inchy, the exits from the village were smothered by artillery and rifle fire, and the battalion undisturbed, except for an occasional hostile shell, remained throughout the morning and early afternoon under cover of its trenches in readiness for possible developments. To the FIFTH all seemed to be going well, till suddenly they observed, with surprise and a certain dismay, that troops on their right flank were withdrawing. As early as 1.45 p.m. news had reached H.Q. 3rd Division that the 5th Division was being so heavily attacked that it seemed probable that it would be forced to retire, and at 2.35 p.m. the 3rd Division had issued orders for withdrawal along its whole front. But before these orders reached battalions, the retirement of the 5th Division had already started. It had, accordingly, become more than ever urgent for the 3rd Division to break off the battle. About 3.30 p.m. orders to this effect reached Battalion Headquarters. Simultaneously a forward section of the 107th Field Battery* opened rapid fire on Inchy and shortly afterwards the Brigade Major, Captain Stevens, galloped up and personally conveyed orders to the forward companies of the FIFTH to retire, being immediately afterwards mortally wounded. The position, strong for defence, was most unfavourable for this operation. Retirement from the forward trenches entailed traversing an open slope for some four hundred yards. Had the enemy on this portion of the front been in greater force, or shown more enterprise, the Battalion must have suffered heavy losses during the operation.

As it was, held in check by the fire of the two guns of the 107th Battery, which were sited close in rear of the trenches and maintained fire till the last moment before being perforce abandoned, the Germans did not advance further than to within 1,000 or 1,200 yards of " B " Company, which had taken up a position in rear to cover the retirement of the remaining companies. Having effected its withdrawal without a single casualty the Battalion formed up in the village of Troisville. In the course of the historic battle of Le Cateau, in which the British losses totalled close on 8,000, the FIFTH had sustained the very slight casualties of 3 Other Ranks killed, 2 officers and 15 O.R. wounded. Practically all of these had occurred among the reserve company and transport personnel in the first minute of the battle.

The 9th Brigade now assembled at Clary with orders to march south-west

---

* So given in Map 11, Vol. I. Official History—referred to as 109 Battery in Lieut. Watkins' diary, *St. George's Gazette*.

to Beaurevoir and the FIFTH was detailed to act as rear guard. Owing to the scramble back that had resulted from the 3rd Division having been forced to break off the battle half an hour earlier than had been planned, and on no regular orders, battalions and brigades had temporarily become a good deal mixed up. Many men of the Battalion were, accordingly, still absent when the march started. This proved unimportant, as they were to rejoin the Battalion in due course. A far graver result was that certain of the units of the 8th Infantry Brigade did not receive the orders directing them to retire. Now, while the full force of the enemy's attack was being directed against these unfortunate battalions, the remainder of their Division had been extricated, and undisturbed by shot or shell, was moving ever further from them. It was owing to their gallant stand that the Germans held back from pursuit. Tragic as their fate was, it is not too much to say that the chance that caused their sacrifice saved the British Army on 26th August.

On moving from Clary there were still some hours before darkness would fall. But at dusk a wet mist came down which, though adding to the discomfort of the weary marchers, proved welcome in the concealment it afforded. Over ten miles had been traversed, and darkness had long fallen, when the head of the Brigade reached Beaurevoir. The road here was found completely blocked by transport and further movement was for the time impossible. Still covering the rear, the FIFTH halted in a small village to the north of the town. It is, mercifully, a virtue of the British soldier that it takes much to keep him from sleep when opportunity is offered, and on the soaking ground, beneath a steady drizzle of rain, the bulk of the Battalion rested for three weary hours. At 2 a.m. orders were received to move on to Hargicourt. It was now a column of automatons that dragged along through the darkness of the night. Heedless of the villages they passed through, they just followed on in the ranks. Whither they were bound they knew not, and had ceased to care. Those hallucinations that must be familiar to any who have experienced the torture of the effort to retain consciousness when the brain cries for sleep, are recorded by several of the officers. To one there gleamed a bright light a mile ahead and another a mile to the rear, while the road seemed flanked on either side by a sheet of water, beyond which other troops, mounted and dismounted, appeared to be moving. In the dreams of another, every group of trees was presented as a village. A third, who was mounted, recalls how he spent the night in ducking his head to escape imaginary arches that spanned the road. There was an hour's halt before daybreak, and again the column moved on. Daylight on the 27th August revealed all the depressing sights witnessed by troops bringing up the rear of a retreat—overturned wagons and motor lorries; the roadside strewn with dead horses, with here and there a group of exhausted men who had reached the end of their tether. Hargicourt was reached, but turning south, the column still moved on, and yet another mile was covered before at last at 9 a.m. a halt was made at Villeret. Little respite, however, was to be given to the troops. About noon the enemy was reported to be following up at no great distance, and the 9th Brigade was ordered to take up a position to cover the withdrawal of the Division to Vermand. As the Battalion was deploying for defence in a neighbouring turnip field, shells began to burst about the village of Villeret. Shortly afterwards, our cavalry patrols fell back, and a withdrawal was made to a strong defensive position about a mile in rear of the village. Hitherto, the only evidence of the approach of the enemy had been his artillery fire, but now a detachment, 2 guns and about 200 infantry, was observed on the right flank at a distance of about 1500 yards. As the infantry started to entrench and the artillery to unlimber in

28th—30th Aug., 1914

leisurely fashion, they presented a perfect target for our guns. Alas! none was at hand, and ultimately the Battalion, without having fired a shot, received orders to retire. As the FIFTH moved off shells were being showered on the unfortunate Villeret, and they looked back on the sorrowful sight of the village in flames. The head of the 9th Brigade reached Vermand at 6 p.m. and an hour later the Battalion closed up and halted. In a little over twenty-four hours, acting as rear guard throughout, it had covered a distance of thirty miles. Yet the situation allowed only the briefest rest. The Battalion's rations, dumped by the roadside, had vanished before the arrival of the party sent to collect them. Sheep were procured in the village, but there had barely been time to cut up and cook these when at midnight the 9th Brigade again took the road, still acting as rear guard to the 3rd Division. Dawn of the 28th August found the column still on the move. At 7 a.m. Ham was reached and the 9th Brigade took up a defensive position to cover the crossing of the river Somme. By noon the Brigade itself was across the river and again on the march. The men were now desperately tired. To carry those who were completely exhausted ammunition wagons had to be emptied, and the rear of the Division presented a depressing sight. In the circumstances, however, straggling in the 9th Brigade was remarkably small, and Brigadier-General Shaw recorded his pleasure this day in witnessing the staunchness of his battalions. At 4 p.m. the FIFTH reached Crisolles, where the Brigade was to halt for the night. Over 60 miles had been covered in 48 hours, and at last the Battalion was to get a full night's rest. The troops were billeted, and, supplies having arrived, the men were given a square meal. Battalion Headquarters were accommodated in the cottage of a labourer, a naturalised Belgian who had been called to service by France and was preparing to leave his home next day—" the old woman (his wife) apparently thought we were all deaf . . . but supplied us liberally with cider and two fowls." (Lt. Watkin's Diary.) One could wish that these poor peasants could have known that their simple acts of kindness were to be recorded for all time in the pages of a regimental paper.

Map No. 1

It had been hoped that the enemy had been sufficiently out-distanced to give the troops a full day's rest on the 29th August. But late in the morning reports came in from our patrols of German cavalry, backed by infantry, at Guiscard, some three miles north of Crisolles. On this it was decided that the 3rd Division should continue its retirement, and the 9th Brigade was ordered to take up a position to cover its withdrawal through Noyon to the crossings of the R. Oise. Two battalions were deployed for defence astride the Ham—Noyon road, the FIFTH being east of the road. Though the withdrawal of our cavalry along the road drew the enemy's artillery fire on to this position, no casualties resulted. At dusk the Battalion fell back through troops of the 7th Brigade, who had taken over the duties of rear guard to the Division, and after halting in Noyon, crossed the Oise at 10.30 p.m. and took the road south-east towards Cuts. At midnight, during a two hour halt, distant explosions were heard announcing the destruction of the bridges at Noyon. The march was then continued till Morsain was reached, 10 miles south-east of Noyon, where a halt was made at 10 a.m. for breakfasts. It had been but a week before that at this hour the FIFTH had watched the people crowding to church at the call of the bells in Cuesmes; only a month since, their officers had been backing their fancy at Goodwood races. Yet already those scenes seemed to belong to another age. But, though days of hard marching still lay before them, the worst of the Retreat had passed with the crossing of the Oise. And now with breakfast on the 30th August came the first good news received for days. A great improvement in the situation

was officially announced, and report came of a naval victory in the North Sea.* 29th Aug., 1914
These good tidings, combined with the belief that in a few short hours billets would
be again taken up, set the FIFTH off on the road again in high spirits. These by
6 p.m. had been somewhat dampened when the weary Battalion found itself still
tramping the road in what seemed an endless march. Crossing the R. Aisne at Vic,
anxious inquiry as to where these promised billets would be found elicited the cheering assurance from a Staff Officer, " Just up the road and round the corner to the
left." " Just up the road " proved to be a further two miles, and it was not till
7 p.m., after being on the march for over twenty-four hours, that the Battalion
reached its billets at Resson Le Long. The long march, however, received its reward.
In war one learns that the truest joys are those that brighten the existence of
primitive man—sleep for the weary and the satisfaction of a hungry stomach. The
billets at Resson were the best that had fallen to the lot of the FIFTH since leaving
England, and the officers received their valises which had not been seen since the
22nd August. The generous hospitality of the owners of a local chateau, moreover,
supplied them with an excellent dinner, champagne and cigars. To complete the
content of the Battalion came the first mail received since it had advanced from
Noyelles.

With strength renewed by their night's rest at Resson, the FIFTH set out on
the 31st August for Vauciennes. It was soon found, however, that the enemy had still
to be reckoned with. On entering the forest of Retz, through which the route led,
report was received of German cavalry patrols in Soucy. The Battalion was ordered
to act as rear guard to the Brigade. The dense nature of the forest made these duties
simple. Small parties to block the main road and the glades on the flanks, with a
few patrols detached to give warning of the enemy's approach, provided adequate
protection. It was on this day that von Kluck made the fatal blunder of changing
the direction of the movement of First German Army from south-west to south and
south-east, content, in his belief that the British Army was a beaten force, to ignore
it. On the same afternoon a small, but representative, part of that " beaten army,"
the FIFTH, after nine hours of intense heat and dust, is recorded as moving in good
order into Vauciennes to take up billets for the night. Though General von Kluck
knew it not, conditions for the FIFTH were improving daily, and the 2nd Line Transport, which had been separated from the Battalion since the battle of Le Cateau,
joined up again this day. On the 1st September the march was continued, in great
heat, to Bouillancy. The day passed without incident, but when the Battalion reached
the village all the inhabitants were found vacating it in fear of the approach of the
Germans. A short march of ten miles on the 2nd September brought the Battalion
to billets at Penchard. The hand to mouth existence that had characterised the early
days of the retreat had now ended. Supplies were coming in freely and the troops
were being regularly rationed. The general situation of the Allied Armies, however,
was judged by General Joffre not yet to be so satisfactory as to justify a stand on
the R. Marne. The retreat was, accordingly, continued on 3rd September, and the
FIFTH, crossing the river at Meaux, found the town deserted and the fine old bridge
that spanned the Marne prepared for demolition. Thence, the column after moving
south of Nanteuil turned east to Villemareuil, where the 9th Brigade halted at 4 p.m.
for the night under the protection of the FIFTH, who took up an outpost position west

---

* The improvement had been brought about by the French counter-attack at Guise. The
naval victory was the action off Heligoland on 28th August.

4th Sept., 1914 of the village near Le Moulin farm.* Late in the afternoon there were reports of German cavalry close at hand, and on the following morning (4th September) the outpost mounted troops came into contact with and dispersed hostile cavalry patrols, but the infantry outposts remained undisturbed.† The Battalion was relieved on outpost duty during the afternoon of the 4th September and rested till 10 p.m., when a further retirement was ordered. Leaving their camp fires burning, the FIFTH once again took the road, not knowing that this was to be their last march in a retreat that would remain famous in history. Their goal was Chatres, but a roundabout route was taken to bring them there. South to Sancy, then north-east for a mile before turning south-east to La Haute Maison, thence, completing three sides of a square, south-west to cross the Grand Morin river at Crécy, before turning south again to plunge into the Forest of Crécy. All night long they marched in the bright moonlight, across streams, through sleeping villages, vineyards and forest. Twenty-eight miles had been traversed and the sun had long risen on the 5th September when the Battalion, too weary to have any thought except for sleep, reached Chatres and its longed-for billets. The Retreat from Mons was ended.

Map No. 1

---

* Confusion having occurred in verbal orders between " B " and " D " Companies, companies of 1/FIFTH were this day re-named " W," " X," " Y," " Z."

† These cavalry patrols were the right flankers of v. Kluck in his movement across the British front.

CHAPTER III.

"Marne, 1914" — "Aisne, 1914."

6TH SEPTEMBER—2ND OCTOBER, 1914.

Map No. 1

By nightfall on the 5th September the whole British Expeditionary Force had been withdrawn south of the Marne and Grand Morin rivers, and was in position from between 15 and 30 miles south-east of Paris. I. Corps was on the right, II. Corps in the centre, and III. Corps* on the left. In the course of the retreat from Mons a newly formed French Army, under General Maunoury, had come up on the left of the British, and, in the general retirement, had withdrawn to a position north of the Marne, covering Paris from the north-east. The Fifth French Army was still on the right (east) of the British.

6th Sept., 1914

By the original German plan the First Army (von Kluck), on the enemy's right flank, was to continue its westerly movement with the idea of passing west of Paris. Von Kluck, however, having heavily engaged Maunoury's Army, believed he had so decisively defeated it as to be able to leave it out of serious account. He held a similar view of the condition of the British force, and had been completely misinformed as to the direction of its retirement. As related in the previous chapter, he had, accordingly, decided on 30th August to wheel his Army left, and leaving light protection against Maunoury, to sweep aside the British, and falling on the left flank of the French Fifth Army, roll up the line of the Allies.

This ambitious scheme was, in fact, leading him into the gravest danger. For, by changing the direction of his advance to south-east, he was exposing his right flank and rear to attack by Maunoury, whose Army was not only in itself far from being the negligible quantity of the German commander's estimate, but was to be reinforced by troops from the garrison of Paris. "Von Kluck, therefore, thinking by extraordinary forced marches to outflank the Allies, was actually advancing into the net that Joffre had in preparation for him." (Official History of the War.)

The moment to which General Joffre had so anxiously looked forward had arrived. But were the troops of the Allies in a fit condition to exploit the situation? The trials endured by the FIFTH during the retreat of thirteen days have been related. Weighted with rifle and equipment, sleepless and ill-fed, the men, many of whom had been called from civil life less than a month before entering battle, had toiled night and day through the heat and dust of that terrible march. It can be well imagined that the Battalion was in sore need of a brief respite in which to rest and re-fit, yet the experiences of the FIFTH formed no criterion of what the British Army as a whole had endured. Compared with other units, its casualties at Le Cateau had been negligible. During the days that followed, though constantly acting as rear guard to its Brigade on critical days, the Battalion had not been engaged or suffered a single battle casualty. But few units, outside the 3rd Division, had escaped so fortunately during the Retreat, and many had suffered severely, notably in rearguard actions on 1st September. On arrival at Chatres, moreover, the FIFTH had received its first Reinforcement of 2 Officers and 100 Other Ranks, and, worn though it was, the Bat-

---

* Formed on 30th August of 4th Division and 19th Infantry Brigade.

6th Sept., 1914 talion, both in numbers and general condition, was in better plight than the greater Map No. 1 part of the British units. Sir John French, indeed, some days before the end of the Retreat, had expressed his belief that, unless opportunity were given to withdraw his force for a few days to rest and refit, it could not be considered to be in condition to attack.

But sore as was the need for it, this rest was to be denied to the troops. The enemy was as yet innocent of the danger in which he had placed himself. At any moment this might be revealed to him, and even one day's delay might enable him to extricate himself. It was decided that a further demand must be made on the strength of the wearied troops. The manner in which they were to respond was to justify the faith in their spirit on which this decision was based.

So the pleasing prospect presented to the FIFTH of resting weary limbs, and enjoying for a few days the hospitality of the good people of Chatres, was short-lived. Orders were received to parade at 6 a.m. on the 5th September for yet another move. In truth, this eternal marching had to such an extent become part of the normal existence of the Battalion that few had credited the rumours of a halt. But marching to the men had also become synonymous with retiring. When, on the 6th, they found that, instead of moving back, they were once again actually advancing, and they realised that it was the Allies who were now calling the tune to which the Germans would be asked to dance, resignation to what had been accepted as inevitable, gave place to enthusiasm for the events that the future seemed now to promise. Those who experienced the change that came over the Battalion with this realisation have said that the exultation of that one moment repaid them for the long sufferings of the Retreat.

The Battalion formed the Advanced Guard to the Brigade, whose destination was Lumigny, as the crow flies, only 7 miles north of Chatres, but, by the route allotted to the Brigade, a full ten. Throughout the day the Battalion was in constant expectation of encountering the enemy, but nothing had been seen of the Germans when, the Brigade having reached Lumigny, the FIFTH was withdrawn to billet in the village for the night. The good woman, whose hospitality was enjoyed by Battalion Headquarters in a tiny cottage, is recollected for the stewed rabbit she added to the daily ration—the gratitude of primitive man again ! Though the movement of the 3rd Division had been unchecked, the cavalry covering the British advance had obtained contact during the day with the enemy, who had also been encountered by an advanced guard of I. Corps.

On the night of the 6th/7th September the 3rd Division was disposed in depth, the 7th Brigade being located at Faremoutiers about five miles north of Lumigny, with two battalions on the north bank of the Grand Morin river. In the early morning of the 7th an attack on these two battalions was driven off. Later, the remainder of the 3rd Division moved up on the right, unopposed, and took up a position on the Grand Morin east of Coulommiers. A nine mile march brought the FIFTH to Martroy, where they billeted for the night. Though the cavalry had again been engaged, for the Battalion the day had passed without incident. But everywhere, now, was evidence of the recent presence of the Germans and of their hurried retreat. Houses had been ransacked and were strewn with empty bottles. All telegraph wires had been cut, and wagons were found abandoned on the road. On this day Lieutenant Platt with 97 other ranks arrived as 2nd Reinforcement to the Battalion.

Orders for the 8th September directed the advance of the British Army to the line of the Marne. But to reach this line it would first be necessary to force the crossings of the Petit Morin. This small river, which runs deep between steep, and densely wooded, banks, presented an obstacle of which the enemy was to take full advantage. The events of this day are dismissed in the 1/Fifth War Diary by the brief entry, "Marched 6 a.m.—skirmish at Orly." While that represents a fair and accurate record of the action of the Fifth, history demands some account of the events which led to the Battalion becoming involved in the skirmish. The 3rd Division, with the 8th Brigade as advanced guard, was to cross the river at Orly. Early in the morning the Scots Greys located a force of the enemy taking breakfast at Gibraltar, about one mile S.S.W. of the crossing. Artillery fire was brought to bear, and dispersed the Germans with heavy casualties. The enemy, however, were strongly placed and skilfully disposed on the opposite bank. The 8th Brigade, advancing between 9 a.m. and 10 a.m. to support the cavalry, came up against serious opposition, mainly from machine guns. Nor was this opposition merely local, for the British advance was at the same time held up on the whole line of the Petit Morin. The 9th Brigade, in reserve at Gibraltar, sent forward the Machine Gun Section of the Fifth to assist the 8th Brigade and the artillery in subduing the enemy's fire.* The struggle continued for full five hours without further progress being made. The afternoon was well advanced when 1/Royal Scots Fusiliers were sent forward from 9th Brigade to the right flank, to fill a gap between the 8th Brigade and the 2nd Division of I. Corps who were engaged on the right of 3rd Division. A little later the Fifth, directed still further to the right, were pushed up in support of Scots Fusiliers, with orders to swing left and sweep the valley and hostile entrenchments from east to west. But, before their movement was completed, British troops had at last succeeded in crossing the river above and below Orly ; the enemy's resistance was already weakening, and the 8th Brigade was advancing from the south. When, therefore, the Fifth, after effecting their wheel at 4 p.m., debouched from dense woods to complete the discomfiture of the Germans, they encountered little opposition from an already beaten enemy. It was so that the forcing of the Petit Morin, which had cost the 3rd Division seven hours' fighting, represented to the Fifth no more than "a skirmish at Orly."

With the crossing of the river opposition ceased, and the artillery alone could engage the distant and now hastily retreating enemy. The check had, however, prevented the British from gaining the objective given for the 8th September, and the Battalion took up billets for the night in a foundry at La Fauchère, $2\frac{1}{2}$ miles south of the River Marne.

The river which now lay before the British represented a potential obstacle more formidable even than that which had delayed their advance on 8th September. It was anticipated that strong opposition would have to be overcome before the crossing could be effected. The 9th Brigade had been detailed as advanced guard to the 3rd Division on the 9th September, and at 4.30 a.m. the Fifth moved forward to take up position as van guard. The Marne was to be crossed by the 3rd Division at Nanteuil. It was fully expected that this village would be found strongly held by the Germans, and the 9th Brigade advanced slowly and cautiously deploying before it debouched from the woods that crowned the high ground to the south of the river. The Fifth, in the meantime, having moved forward to cover the Brigade, found themselves most dangerously placed, in full view to observation from the high

---

* An account of the action of these machine guns, and a detailed description of the Petit Morin at Orly, by the late Lieutenant F. E. Watkin, appears in Vol. XXXII. of *St. George's Gazette*, p. 195 (December, 1914).

9th Sept., 1914 ground on the north bank. But there was no sign of the enemy; no sound of a Map No. 5
gun. To the wary the surprise of silence in war is, perhaps, more intense and unnerving than any form of the unexpected. " W " Company was directed to move on Nanteuil, " Z " Company, on its right, to Citry, half a mile south-east of Nanteuil. A thousand yards of open ground lay before them. A single machine gun could have played havoc with their movement. Yet, unbelievably, the companies reached their objectives without a shot being fired, and to the amazement of all the bridge at Nanteuil was found intact. The inhabitants reported that on the previous evening German cavalry, infantry, and guns, their horses showing signs of great exhaustion, had passed rapidly through the village.

" W " and " Z " Companies now joined hands, and together advanced up the steep hill that rose north of the village. The remainder of the Battalion followed in support. Before the summit was gained the arrival of shells, some 800 yards to the left, at last gave evidence of the enemy being still in the neighbourhood. A hostile battery was now observed in action about 1½ miles to the north-west, on the west edge of the Bois des Esserties. Its fire was being directed against the 5th Division, who were operating on the left of the 3rd Division, and whose advance throughout this day was to be seriously hampered by the enemy's artillery fire. A field battery of the Advanced Guard was brought into action against this target, and after a brief halt the FIFTH again moved forward, adopting artillery formation as a precaution against the desultory shelling that was now being directed against their front. The whole country in which II. Corps was now operating was very close, and the road by which the FIFTH led the advance of the 9th Brigade was flanked on either side by dense woods. Passing through Bezu, the Battalion halted ¼ mile south of Ventrelet Farm, while "W" and "X" Companies were sent forward to clear the woods. During this halt the remaining companies watched, with breathless interest, the evolutions of a British aeroplane under heavy fire of German anti-aircraft guns. There are, perhaps, few more beautiful sights than an aeroplane, high in the blue, turning, twisting, diving and rising among the white puffs of the enemy's shells; there is, certainly, none more sudden and terrible than that which follows a hit. When this plane, at length, turned back and sailed to safety, a sense of relief came to all. It would have been even keener had they known at the time what they were to learn later, that the observer in it was an officer of the FIFTH. Lieutenant Cogan's platoon, covering " X " Company, which was moving to the left of the road, after pushing its way with difficulty through blackberry bushes and dense undergrowth, eventually gained a rise which was seen to lead to a clearing in the wood. Moving forward to reconnoitre, Cogan with his field glasses found he could just discern, on the far side of the clearing, a German machine gun and the pickel haubers* of its detachment. The target was invisible to the naked eye, but calling forward six of his men, the officer directed them to fire at the base of a tree that stood behind the machine gun. The gun must have been laid on the exact position they had taken up, for almost instantaneously a burst of fire in retaliation wounded Lieutenant Cogan and every one of the six men he had called forward. Apart from this incident no serious resistance was experienced, and, the woods having been cleared, the Battalion continued its advance to the line of the main Chateau Thierry—Montreuil road. The statement that the woods had been cleared, perhaps needs modification. So close was the country that, unknown to the Battalion, a German battery had been in action in the

---

* The old German infantry helmet. This was long before the days of the steel helmet.

Bois des Esserties to the west of, and in close proximity to, the line of its advance. Brigadier-General Shaw, himself observing this, ordered forward two companies of the 1/Lincolnshire from brigade reserve for the capture of the battery.* Advancing with great skill under cover of the dense woods, these companies effected a complete surprise and captured the battery.

Though the 3rd Division had encountered little resistance to its advance, it had been otherwise with the divisions on its flanks. As a result it had now pushed so far ahead of the general line that a halt was necessary. The position gained by the FIFTH on the Montreuil road not being favourable to defence, the Battalion was withdrawn about half a mile to a stronger position just north of Ventrelet Farm. Trenches were dug, and in these the Battalion spent the night. Rain fell and the night was cold, but the Battalion remained undisturbed by the enemy.

The general situation on the 9th September had been critical. The 5th Division had been held up the whole day opposite Montreuil, and further west the British III. Corps, experiencing even greater difficulties, had only been able to get small elements across the river. The French Sixth Army, holding its own with difficulty against the desperate attacks of von Kluck to free his army from the trap that was closing on him, was calling for relief to its position. It was urgent that the resistance at Montreuil should be overcome, and a combined attack on the place by the 3rd and 5th Divisions was planned for the following day. But when dawn broke on 10th September, it was found that Montreuil had been abandoned by the enemy; pressure against Maunoury's Sixth Army had ceased; and the German armies were streaming north and north-west along the whole front of the Allies' left. The enemy's stand on the Petit Morin and the Marne had not delayed the British advance to the degree they had hoped, and they had realised that immediate withdrawal could alone save them from utter disaster. "The battle of the Marne was over, and with it all the hopes of the rapid knock-out blow with which Germany had counted on winning the War against her unprepared opponents." (Official History.)

Such then was the situation when the 9th Brigade, as Advanced Guard to the 3rd Division, resumed the northward advance at 5 a.m. on the 10th September. The Royal Fusiliers formed the van guard. The FIFTH followed the Royal Scots Fusiliers, who led the main guard. After a short halt to allow the 3rd Cavalry Brigade to pass through to a position to cover the advance, the column moved forward again towards Marigny and Veuilly La Poterie. The enemy's rearguard troops, supported by artillery, were found to be still clinging to positions in the densely wooded country through which the advance was being directed. At about 9 a.m. the van guard became engaged with certain of these at Vinly, $1\frac{1}{4}$ miles north-west of Veuilly. The advanced guard artillery was brought into action, and the Scots Fusiliers were sent forward to support the Royal Fusiliers. These two battalions then struck north-east towards St. Gengoulph and in co-operation with troops of the 2nd Division, directed from the right flank, surrounded and captured 600 of the enemy. But scattered parties of the enemy still remained concealed in the dense woods south of Vinly, and continued to harass the main body of the 9th Brigade by sniping from its left flank. Artillery fire having failed to dislodge the snipers, the guns were ordered to cease fire, and the FIFTH were given the task of clearing the enemy from this quarter.

---

* Actually, the Adjutant, Captain Herbert, drew the attention of the Brigadier to these guns, and begged that the task of capturing them should be committed to the FIFTH.

11th Sept., 1914 The Battalion, with "W" and "X" Companies deployed in line, "Y" échelonned Map Nos. 1 & 5
in rear of their left, and "Z" Company in reserve, advanced through the woods.
Then, fording the Alland stream waist deep, they swept the area clear of the enemy.
Of the few who remained to oppose the advance, twelve were either killed or captured and the task was accomplished without casualty in the Battalion.

Throughout the morning burning wagons and other wreckage abandoned by the Germans had given evidence to the troops of the decisive manner in which the tables had been turned on the enemy. The sight of hundreds of prisoners now being brought in further raised spirits that had already mounted high. Among these prisoners some of the FIFTH discovered an old friend. A few years previously the Regiment had obtained a considerable number of recruits from Nottingham. Many of these men were now with the Battalion. Their amusement and surprise were great when, from the ranks of the German prisoners, they were greeted by a late member of the Nottingham town band, well known to them all. This worthy made it clear that he regarded himself better suited to a bandstand than to a trench on the Petit Morin, and that the sooner he was blowing his trombone again at Nottingham, the better he would be pleased.

It was now past noon. All fire had ceased, and the 9th Brigade, moving forward over ground littered with enemy dead and wounded, passed through Chezy to halt, after an advance for the day of 10 miles, at Dammard, where the FIFTH billeted for the night. During the 10th September 1800 prisoners and a large amount of material had fallen into the hands of the British, and the German rearguards had suffered heavy casualties. But, though the enemy had lost the initiative, it was to be made clear during the next few days that he had succeeded in extricating himself from a situation which had threatened him with a catastrophe of far greater magnitude.

On the 11th September, changing direction to north-west, an advance of 12 miles was made to Rozoy. During the march an aeroplane was forced by weather conditions to land near the battalion. The observer proved to be Lieutenant Bonham-Carter, who had been seconded from the FIFTH for the Royal Flying Corps shortly before the War. It was now found that it was his aeroplane that the Battalion had watched so anxiously from Ventrelet Farm two days before.* At Rozoy the Battalion found outposts to the Brigade during a cold and very wet night.

Fortune, which had recently favoured the Allies, was now to turn against them. News came that, on the 7th September, Maubeuge had fallen, making possible the reinforcement of the retreating enemy. "There were some indications that the enemy might hold the line of the Aisne, but it was impossible to forecast in what strength, and whether as a mere rear-guard or as a battle position. . . . Orders quite appropriate to the pursuit of a broken and disorganised enemy can be wholly unsuited to the very different problem of beating an unbroken foe." (Official History.) In any case there was need for the British advance to be pressed forward as rapidly as possible. But, on the 12th September, heavy rain set in, preventing the Allies from obtaining information from the air, to clear up the situation, and also greatly hampering movement in the pursuit. On this day the 9th Brigade again formed the advanced guard to the Division. On approaching Braine the Brigade was deployed in support of the cavalry, who had gained contact with the enemy, but did not itself come into action.

---

* Formerly Adjutant of 1/FIFTH; later Air-Commodore I. M. Bonham-Carter, C.B., Royal Air Force.

It was ominous that among the prisoners captured by the cavalry many were identified as belonging to a German division known to have been at Maubeuge. Crossing the river Vesle at Braine, the Battalion, together with the remainder of the 9th Brigade, was billeted for the night at Brenelle.

Orders for the 14th September required that the British should cross the Aisne and push northwards to seize the high ground five miles north of the river. The 8th Brigade, as advanced guard to the 3rd Division, was to move by Chassemy and seize the crossing at Vailly. The 9th Brigade, advancing north-west along the Brenelle ridge, was to take up a position about 1½ miles north-east of Chassemy to cover the crossing of the 8th Brigade.

It was a raw, wet morning when at 7 a.m. the troops advanced. Very soon the first experience was gained of the German long range howitzers (5.9 and 8 inch), which outranged all the British artillery except the 60 pdr. guns. From positions north-east of Vailly, they brought fire on the Chassemy—Vailly road, and greatly retarded the advance of the 8th Brigade. In the meantime the FIFTH had been placed in position to command the Vailly crossing, while the remainder of the 9th Brigade was held in reserve on the Brenelle road, under cover of the ridge. At Vailly the Aisne canal runs close and parallel to the river. The 8th Brigade, on arrival at the crossing, found the bridges over the canal intact, but the road and railway bridges that had spanned the river had been destroyed. To start the construction of a pontoon bridge before dark was impossible, and the advance was held up till, at 2.30 p.m., a single plank bridge was found, the removal of which by the enemy had been overlooked. Taking advantage of this, the whole 8th Brigade, moving in single file, completed the crossing of the Aisne by 3.30 p.m. At dusk the 9th Brigade descended to the river, and after dark also started to cross by the plank bridge. On gaining the right bank, the Lincolnshire Regiment and Royal Fusiliers moved forward to gain touch with the 8th Brigade, the former taking up a position east of Rouge Maison Farm, the Royal Fusiliers occupying the farm and continuing the line to the west. At midnight the FIFTH billeted with the remainder of the 9th Brigade in the village of Vailly.

The 1st Line transport of the Battalion, pending the construction of a pontoon bridge, remained at Chassemy. Until this bridge could be completed, the 3rd Division, with a single plank as the sole connection between its forward infantry and its artillery and reserve, remained in a most anxious and unenviable situation. The Royal Engineers, however, got the bridge across before daylight, and at 6 a.m., in pouring rain, the transport of the FIFTH crossed the river to join its Battalion. But on gaining Vailly it found the Battalion had left the village, for events had occurred which had called it to the front line.

In the mist and rain that prevailed the Royal Fusiliers at Rouge Maison had failed to realise that 200 yards beyond the crest of a ridge that confronted them, and only 600 yards from their position, was a German trench. Advancing from this at dawn, the enemy's infantry, supported by artillery fire, had opened a surprise attack on the two forward battalions of the 9th Brigade. To support the defence, the FIFTH had been ordered to move up on the left flank of the Royal Fusiliers. On the Battalion drawing level with them, " Y " Company, on the right of the advance, pushing further forward to the crest of the ridge, came under a devastating fire from the enemy's position on the reverse slope against which further movement became impossible. The company commander, Captain Gatehouse, was killed, and Lieutenant Sutherland, who was with him, fell severely wounded. Sutherland then ordered

15th Sept., 1914 the men to abandon him and withdraw to cover.* The company accordingly retired   Map No. 6
and rallied on the left of Royal Fusiliers. In the meanwhile "W" and "X" Companies under Captain Toppin, advancing through woodland, had engaged in heavy fighting at close quarters, and had come into line further to the left. But a little later the Royal Fusiliers were forced to vacate Rouge Maison Farm and, about noon, both battalions, suffering heavy casualties from artillery and machine gun fire, were compelled slightly to withdraw their line. They still clung, however, to the southern edge of Cils Raies spur, due north of Vailly and south-west of Rouge Maison. While these events were in progress, the Royal Scots Fusiliers had been sent forward from Brigade Reserve to reinforce the line. Two companies had been directed to support the right of the Lincolnshire, and the remainder of the Battalion had later moved to the left of the FIFTH, to connect with the 8th Brigade whose right was at Chateau Vauxelles. Following the loss of Rouge Maison, the Lincolnshire, heavily attacked, and under fire from both flanks, together with the reinforcing detachment of Scots Fusiliers, were driven from their position and forced to withdraw to the south of the Aisne by the partially reconstructed railway bridge, east of Vailly. Somewhat later, a heavy attack to the left of the FIFTH forced back the Royal Scots Fusiliers, who had come up on that flank, and the 8th Brigade from Vauxelles—Jouy ridge to the low hills about S. Pierre north of the river. In the meantime the situation of the 3rd Division, unsatisfactory on the left, had become critical on the right flank. The right flank of the 9th Brigade had become completely exposed, as between the right of the Royal Fusiliers and the left of the 2nd Division (of I. Corps) at La Cour de Soupir there was now a gap of over two miles, and troops of the 7th Brigade sent forward from Divisional Reserve to restore the situation in this quarter, and directed to cross the river by the railway bridge, had found the advance blocked by the withdrawal of the Lincolnshire Regt. Fortunately, either from ignorance of the situation or owing to the severe punishment they had received, the Germans did not take advantage of the opportunity offered to them. Ultimately, the reinforcing troops of the 7th Brigade were pushed up on the right of Royal Fusiliers, who when darkness fell were still alongside the FIFTH in position on the Cils Raies spur, covering Vailly from the north. But the early morning advance, and the stubborn defence of the position later taken up, had cost the FIFTH dearly. Captains Toppin and Gatehouse and 7 other ranks, including Company Serjeant-Majors Longden and Luke, had been killed; Captain Forster, Lieutenants Ovans and Sloper and eighty other ranks had been wounded; and Lieutenant Sutherland had been wounded and captured by the enemy.

An attempt by the Germans to develop an attack at midnight was checked by the fire of the forward trenches, and the trench garrisons, though cramped and weary, were left undisturbed during the remaining hours of darkness. Not so Vailly, which was subjected to desultory shell fire throughout the whole night.

More rain came with dawn on the 15th September to add to the discomfort of the men in the trenches, but on this and the following two days no further attempts were made by the enemy's infantry against the front of the FIFTH. But the untraversed trenches they were holding rendered the garrison very vulnerable to the constant fire

---

* A search party, under the Red Cross, was sent out for these officers when the fighting had died down at the end of the day. It was met by a German officer who showed great courtesy and chivalry. On being informed of the quest he expressed regret that he could not allow the party to proceed, but gave an assurance that every attention would be given to the wounded who fell into their hands.

of the German guns. Suffering continual casualties, the companies laboured incessantly at the improvement of the defences. In particular, guns sited on the Chivres spur on the left flank of the Battalion continually harassed the trenches by enfilade fire. Desperate efforts by troops of the 5th Division on the 15th September to carry this position failed. On the following day Lieut.-Colonel Ainslie, in a report, drew attention to the danger of these guns which were not only inflicting casualties on his battalion but, in the event of a hostile attack, were in a position enabling them to support an infantry advance against the trenches till the last moment before assault. Among the casualties on these days were the last company commander and company serjeant-major remaining of those who had embarked with the Battalion. Captain Matthews, of " Z " Company, was killed on the 15th September, and one of his subalterns, Lieutenant Geddes (attached from the K.O.S.B.) was wounded. On the 16th September three high explosive shells, bursting in the trenches of the same company, killed C.S.M. Wilkinson and wounded eleven others. While any exposure of working parties immediately drew the fire of the enemy's field guns on the trenches, his heavier artillery continued to shell Vailly and the valley in rear of the position. Troops or transport venturing from the village were heavily shelled, and all movement had to be restricted to the hours of darkness, during which water and rations were taken to the trenches by parties sent down by the companies to Vailly.

The situation that confronted the remainder of the British Expeditionary Force and the French Armies on its flanks was similar to that which had developed on the front of the 3rd Division. It had become clear that it was not as a mere rearguard position that the enemy were holding the line of the Aisne, but that, reinforced from the north, they intended to stand and fight in the positions they had taken up. With the armies face to face in trenches at a distance of less than that of effective rifle fire, a situation had developed in which further frontal attacks could prove of little avail. A deadlock had been reached which already marked the beginning of a form of warfare that had not been visualised during training in peace. But so long as the possibility of manoeuvre remained open, the opposing armies were not wholly committed to costly frontal attacks. Though the southern flanks of the armies rested on neutral territory, the opportunity of turning the opponent's other flank was still presented to the side that could forestall the enemy in that direction. It was so that the feverish race to the north was now to start; the race that was to end only when the sea opposed all further effort to manoeuvre against a flank, bringing the armies face to face in the stalemate of trench warfare on a front of 400 miles.

But the Germans were not yet to relinquish their efforts to thrust back the British from the slender foothold they had gained on the right bank of the Aisne, and the next week was to be marked by fierce fighting. That in which the FIFTH was to be engaged was mainly to be concerned with one particular point in their defence. A small detached post had been established at the corner of a wood about 300 yards in advance of the left flank of the Battalion. From this, clear observation of the German trenches could be obtained, and warning could be given of any attempt by the enemy to mass for attack. The value of this post to the Battalion gave the measure of the irritation that its presence caused to the enemy. Except for some sniping and the usual artillery fire that was maintained on Vailly and its approaches, the 17th September had passed without incident. On the 18th the German artillery fire slackened during the morning, but late in the afternoon a surprise attack was made by a strong patrol of the enemy with a view to cutting off the detached post. At the cost of the corporal in command and one man killed, and another wounded,

20th Sept., 1914 the post effected its withdrawal. A strong fighting patrol of the FIFTH was then Map No. 6 immediately sent forward, the corner of the wood was soon in our hands again; and a stronger piquet of 20 men was established at the point under dispute. Early on the following morning an attack by the enemy once again drove in our piquet. Once again counter-attack recovered the position, and a yet stronger piquet of 50 men was detailed to hold it. Later it was decided that, to avoid maintaining a post in this exposed position, other arrangements should be made. For observation purposes a small post was placed at a point 150 yards in rear of the original position, while the bulk of the piquet was withdrawn into the wood to prevent the enemy massing there unseen. During the afternoon hostile shell fire steadily increased, and, at 6 p.m., the enemy opened an infantry attack on the whole front of the 9th Brigade. This was repulsed without serious difficulty. Further efforts made by the enemy late in the evening and during the night met with no better success. On this day the casualties in the FIFTH had amounted to 3 other ranks killed and 14 wounded, while the strength of the Battalion was increased by the arrival of a draft of 103 other ranks under Lieutenant J. Lambert, of the Special Reserve Battalion.

"The Germans were evidently most anxious to hold the Allies to their ground and prevent them from shifting troops to their western flank; for already there were indications of a general movement of German units from east to west." (Official History.)

With this object the enemy delivered vigorous attacks on the 20th September against the Fifth French Army and the right of the British. Though these attacks included the front of the 3rd Division, their full force did not extend to the position of the Fifth Fusiliers. As will be seen, however, the Battalion was not left undisturbed. On its right the Royal Fusiliers at one time were in so critical a situation that it seemed their withdrawal would become inevitable. Under enfilade and almost reverse fire at dawn from machine guns, this battalion's position was later enfiladed by a German field gun brought into position during the night. Ultimately, however, our artillery silenced the German gun, and after troops of the 1/Lincolnshire Regt. had moved up to support, the situation on the right flank of the 9th Brigade was eased. On the front of the FIFTH, in the meantime, it had been discovered at daybreak that the enemy had taken advantage of the withdrawal of the post from the more advanced position on the left flank by establishing themselves in a trench within close range of the Battalion's main position. At first there were indications of an intention to push forward an attack, but this did not develop. Instead, the enemy contented themselves with sniping from the position they had gained. Artillery fire directed against the enemy's position opposite the FIFTH failed to subdue the snipers who had been skilfully placed under cover of the wood. The slightest exposure in the trench covered by their rifles drew immediate fire. Attempts by the garrison to retaliate resulted in certain casualties, and the men of the FIFTH found themselves pinned to the trench in utter impotence. The situation was serious and called for drastic action. At 9.40 a.m. Lieut.-Colonel Ainslie decided to throw in his reserve company to clear the wood. Lieut.-Colonel Smith, Commanding the 1/Lincolnshire Regt., having readily agreed to send forward a company of his battalion as temporary reserve to Ainslie, the company of the FIFTH advanced and swept the wood clear of the enemy. This put an end to the trouble, but not before it had cost the FIFTH very dearly. For although the casualties among the other ranks, 3 killed and 5 wounded, could be counted as light, the already heavy casualties among the officers of the Battalion had been increased by 2nd-Lieutenant Boyd having been killed and Captain Selby and 2nd-

Lieutenant Tottie mortally wounded.* The medical officer of the Battalion, Lieutenant Fisher, was also wounded on this day.

20th Sept., 1914

On the evening of 20th September the Battalion was warned that the 9th Brigade was to be relieved by the 8th Brigade, reinforced by troops of 16th Brigade (temporarily attached to the 3rd Division from the recently arrived 6th Division). The relief of front line battalions was to be carried out on 21st September in two stages. They were, in the first place, to fall back to supporting positions, where they were to remain till 7 p.m., when they would complete their withdrawal after dark. Relief of the FIFTH in the forward trenches passed without incident, but when the hour arrived for the second stage of their withdrawal an attack had developed against the front line, and Lieut.-Colonel Ainslie considered he should remain in support till assured that the services of the FIFTH would not be required. How often during the next few years was the Battalion, with heads turned towards billets and a well-earned rest, to know the disappointment of being called to face about. On this occasion, however, the attack died down and at 8.30 p.m. the Battalion withdrew to join the remainder of the 9th Brigade at Courcelles, where it was to enjoy the first rest granted to it since the advance to Mons just a month before.

From the outbreak of war up till the 14th September, when the Battalion moved into position on the Aisne, the casualties among the officers of the FIFTH had amounted only to the astonishingly light figure of three wounded. In the seven subsequent days no fewer than six officers, including four captains, had been killed, and four had been wounded. With one captain admitted to hospital at the end of the Retreat, the total officer casualties to date amounted to six captains and eight subalterns. With the reinforcements that had arrived only one captain and three subalterns had become available to fill the fourteen vacancies that had occurred. There was, accordingly, already a serious shortage of officers, a difficulty that was continually to beset the Battalion until in 1918 it was to be to some extent remedied by the formation of large pools of officers. Compared with the losses in officers, or with the heavy casualties in the later days of the War, the casualties among the other ranks in the FIFTH during the Battles of the Marne and the Aisne could be counted as light. They amounted only to 22 killed and 136 wounded, a number that had been fully made up by the reinforcements. Yet the conditions under which the troops had been fighting were, perhaps, as trying as any that they were to be called on to experience. Following the fatigue and strain of the Retreat, the opportunity of a brief spell in which to rest and refit had been denied to the Battalion. Packs, greatcoats and other equipment that had been abandoned by order, to ease the overtaxed transport or to lighten the men's burden, could not be replaced before the Army turned to advance. Though little opposition had been encountered by the Battalion in its advance to the Aisne, the mere mileage it covered as measured on the map will give little idea of the fatigue it endured in the scouring of dense woods and the crossing of rivers with the constant expectation of meeting the enemy. Sadly in need of rest, on gaining Vailly, the Battalion had been called on to seize a position in face of the enemy. For the eight ensuing days, in bitter cold and constant rain, cramped in narrow trenches, unable to cook their food, or even to remove their wet boots, the troops, harassed by continual shell fire, and ever expecting hostile attack, had laboured incessantly at the improvement of the defences. But the trials endured and the

---

* A sad coincidence in connection with the death of this young officer was the death on the same day of his brother killed in action with the Fleet in the North Sea.

THE AISNE, 1914.
"Cramped in narrow trenches."

[Imperial War Museum—Crown Copyright.

THE FIFTH IN THE GREAT WAR.   41

26th Sept., 1914 lives lost had not been in vain for, despite the eager desire of the enemy to thrust them   Map No. 6
from their position, the FIFTH had handed over intact the line they had taken up on
14th September.

Four full days were spent at Courcelles. The weather had now cleared, and
in these bright days of early autumn, away from the constant drone and bursting of
shells, taking their meals without fear of interruption, and sleeping through the still
nights undisturbed, the men were completely refreshed when the Battalion was again
ordered forward to Vailly on 26th September. Its ranks, moreover, had been
replenished by the arrival on 23rd September of a fourth reinforcement consisting
of 162 other ranks with Lieutenants Hon. D. Mitford and C. Leather, both of whom
had served with the Battalion in former days previous to retirement.

On relief on 21st September the right of the line held by the FIFTH had been
taken over by the 1/Buffs of 16th Brigade and the left portion by the 4/Middlesex of
the 8th Brigade. It was the latter part of the line for which the Battalion now again
became responsible for holding with two companies. "Y" and "Z" Companies
relieved the Middlesex during the night 26th/27th September. "W" and "X"
Companies were detached under Major Yatman to the 16th Brigade, where they were
held in reserve in a position three miles to the east of the remainder of the Battalion.
Fighting had now died down and the front was much quieter than it had been during
the first strenuous week. On the 28th September one man of the Battalion was killed
and five wounded by shell fire, but the enemy's efforts were clearly slackening, and
on the following day there was but one casualty in the whole of the 9th Brigade. Both
sides were now looking elsewhere for an opportunity of decisive action and on the
Aisne had fallen back on the defensive. Work on the strengthening of the position
was pushed forward vigorously, and an inner line of defence on the outskirts of Vailly
had been completed when orders for the relief of the 9th Brigade by the 16th Brigade
were received on the 1st October.

The FIFTH, relieved by the 1/Buffs and the 1/K.S.L.I., withdrew to Vailly,
which was reached at 8.30 p.m. Crossing the Aisne, they were rejoined by Yatman's
detachment and moved to billets in Augy just west of Braine. After spending the
following day at Augy, the Battalion marched in the evening to Cramaille in the neighbourhood of which the remainder of the 9th Brigade assembled during the night.

The future of the Battalion in the War was to lie far from Vailly and the
Aisne, but the fighting of 14th-20th September, 1914, will ever be memorable in the
FIFTH for the loss of so many whose names had come to stand as household words
in the Regiment.

Of the officers who had fallen, two had met their death on the threshold of
their careers—Boyd, the splendid young athlete, with less than one year's service, and
Tottie, fresh from Sandhurst, killed within four days of joining the Battalion. But
of the others, there was not one who had not long since made his mark in the FIFTH:
Toppin, the hunter, zoologist and explorer, whose report on a South American boundary
dispute had been interrupted by the outbreak of war; Gatehouse, whose skill as a
yachtsman and love of the sea was known to all, though his deep knowledge of
military history was kept concealed from many; the brave and gentle-natured
Matthews, than whom none in the FIFTH has been more greatly loved by brother
officers and men; Selby, small in stature as he was great in heart and in physical
strength. To the loss of these officers had been added that of three company serjeant-
majors, who had given long and faithful service to the Regiment: Longden, whose
stern sense of discipline had made him, as provost-serjeant in former years in India,

the terror of the erring Fusilier, and whose courage and determination in these more recent days had proved an inspiration to all; Luke, the gymnast, with his splendid physique and high spirits; Wilkinson, the senior of the three, who had served in campaigns with the Battalion in the Soudan, South Africa, and the N.W. Frontier, and whose handsome features and soldierly bearing marked him for the model of the Fifth Fusilier that may be seen to-day surmounting one of the silver bells in the Officers' Mess of the 1st Battalion. These who had been killed were all trusted leaders in the prime of life, and there were many others of similar standing who had been wounded and evacuated to England. With such losses in leaders the Battalion, as mobilised, had been shattered. It was natural that anxious friends at home, reading the casualty lists, should question how long the Battalion could continue to exist if the experiences of the first few weeks of war were to be repeated. Those who had been lost were, indeed, hard to replace. Yet, as the following pages will show, their places were to be filled, and again refilled, by others inspired by the same spirit as that in which these first leaders of the FIFTH had fallen, and the 1st Battalion was to maintain its entity and its character to the end.

CHAPTER IV.

"La Bassée, 1914."

Bout Deville—Pont du Hem—Herlies—Neuve Chapelle.

3RD OCTOBER—30TH OCTOBER, 1914.

3rd Oct., 1914.   Moves and counter-moves of the opposing forces, with the object of securing   Map No. 1
an advantage on the still open flank, had been in progress since the 17th September.
The Second and Tenth French Armies had been shifted to the left of Maunoury's
Sixth Army, while, to counter these moves and endeavour to regain the initiative,
the Germans had withdrawn forces from less important fronts. Already, on 2nd
October, when the FIFTH had been withdrawn from Vailly, the northern extension
of the fighting line had so far progressed as to bring the French and Germans face
to face at Arras, some sixty miles north of the River Aisne. Under cover of the French
armies so placed, the British II. Corps and two cavalry divisions were now to be moved
by rail and road to take their place on the northern flank.

A westerly march of four days was made by the 9th Brigade to bring it to
its entraining points, movement being made during the first three under cover of
darkness, to conceal from the enemy the withdrawal of British troops from the Aisne.
Leaving Cramailles on the 3rd October, the FIFTH marched to Troesnes; on the 4th
to Crépy en Valois, on the 5th to Moru. On the 6th October a short march brought
the Battalion to Pont Maxence, where it entrained after dark for Abbeville, which
was reached the following day. On detrainment it moved to billets at Port le Grand,
five miles north-west of Abbeville, where it rested during the 8th October.

The II. Corps, having completed its concentration in the Abbeville area, was
now to move fifty miles north-east to the neighbourhood of Bethune, the 9th Brigade
being directed on Robecq, six miles north-west of that town. Starting shortly after
midnight, the FIFTH marched to Tollent (14 miles) on the 9th October, and in the early
hours of the 10th continued the march to Ste. Austreberthe (7 miles), from which
point they were carried a further 21 miles by bus to Sachin, where they were joined
by officer reinforcements of 1 captain and 8 subalterns. On the 11th October a short
march brought the Battalion with the 9th Brigade to Robecq, where report was
received that the French cavalry, covering the front and left flank of the British II.
Corps, were in close touch with the enemy at Lestrem and Fosse, six miles to the east.
The Battalion was billeted for the night to south of the La Bassée canal, immediately
in rear of Mt. Bernenchon, which was held by the right of the 9th Brigade outposts.

The French were facing the Germans some five miles east of Bethune, their
Tenth Army being south of the La Bassée canal, while two cavalry corps continued
the line for about ten miles to the north of the canal. On the 12th October, II. Corps,
with the 5th Division on the right and the 3rd Division on the left, was to push eastwards to come into line with the Tenth French Army, while the French cavalry was
to side slip to the north to take up position on the left of the 3rd Division.

In accordance with these plans, the 3rd Division advanced at 7 a.m. on the
12th October to force the line of the Lawe canal between La Couture and Fosse. The
7th Brigade was on the right, the 8th Brigade on the left, and the 9th Brigade in reserve.

Map No. 7

The ground on the right, intersected by numerous dykes, greatly delayed the advance on that flank. As a result, the 7th Brigade was still some distance from its objective when the troops of the 8th Brigade found themselves held up by the enemy on the line of the canal. To assist the progress of the 8th Brigade the FIFTH and Royal Fusiliers under Lieut.-Colonel McMahon, of the latter regiment, were ordered forward from Divisional reserve to Vieille Chapelle. On arrival they found the church tower in flames and the village still under the desultory fire of the German artillery; but the 8th Brigade had already succeeded in crossing the canal and was no longer in need of assistance. The FIFTH, however, remained forward till dusk, when they were withdrawn to billets at Paradis.

12th Oct., 1914.

Further south, the 5th Division and the French troops on its right had met with stronger opposition and had been very heavily engaged during the 12th October. To assist the advance of the 5th Division, the 3rd Division, which seemingly was opposed only by cavalry and jäger, received orders to advance on the 13th October to the line of the La Bassée—Estaires road, and so turn the flank of the enemy engaged with the right of the II. Corps. The 3rd Division, disposed as on the previous day, advanced at 5 a.m. over dead flat ground and across the numerous dykes that are found everywhere in this country. The 7th Brigade, on the right, making rapid progress, gained Richebourg St. Vaast, but was here held up by fire from Croix Barbée on their left flank. In the meantime, the advance of the 8th Brigade on the left had been checked short of a general line Croix Barbée—Bout Deville; while the Divisional Cavalry in protection of the northern flank, though in occupation of the latter village, were unable to get further forward. Towards noon, the enemy, advancing from Riez Bailleul, drove back the cavalry from Bout Deville and developed a counter-attack against the Gordon Highlanders, who were on the left of the 8th Brigade. At 3 p.m. the FIFTH were sent forward to support the Gordons. The situation was very obscure. Considerable confusion reigned on the left flank, and they found it difficult to locate the positions in which either our own forward troops or the enemy were placed. Pending further developments, the leading companies established themselves in a line of trenches from which they could resist attack, while the Adjutant, Captain Herbert, went forwards towards the left to secure information by a personal reconnaissance. Herbert had moved but a short distance from cover when he fell severely wounded by an enemy bullet. Two stretcher bearers rushed forward to his assistance, but they had carried him only a few yards when both were hit and the officer wounded a second time. All were ultimately brought to safety, but the Battalion was to lose the services of Captain Herbert for many months. No attempt was made to advance against the position taken up by the FIFTH, and no greater result was obtained by the enemy from the counter-attack than a definite check to the forward movement of our left flank. When darkness fell the 8th Brigade held a general line from a point west of Croix Barbée to one just south of Bout Deville, while the FIFTH and the Divisional Cavalry were entrenched on its left on the line of the Rue de Ponch. The casualties in the Battalion on the 13th October had amounted to 8 other ranks killed, 1 Officer and 18 other ranks wounded. Captain Herbert's place as adjutant was taken by Captain W. Platt.

Operations were to be resumed at dawn on the 14th October in co-operation with an attack by the French cavalry against Riez Bailleul. But shortly after the FIFTH, still acting as the left of the 8th Brigade, moved forward, it was learnt that the French would not be ready to play their part till after 1 p.m. The Battalion was, accordingly, withdrawn again to the line of the Rue de Ponch. On the resumption

14th Oct., 1914 of the attack in the afternoon the FIFTH, advancing with great determination, thrust Map No. 7
the enemy back from Bout Deville, and by 4.30 p.m. were in complete possession of
the village. On other parts of the front, however, things had not gone so well. The
French cavalry, checked by enfilade fire from La Gorgue, had failed to carry their
objective, while, to the south, three further attacks by the 8th Brigade to force the
enemy from Croix Barbée had met with no success. At the close of the day, the right
and centre of the 8th Brigade were back in the positions from which the attack had
started, but the capture and occupation of Bout Deville by the FIFTH had notably
improved the situation on the left flank of the 3rd Division. Four other ranks of the
Battalion had been killed and 33 wounded.

It was on this day that the 3rd Division lost the commander who had brought
them to France, and under whom they had fought at Mons and in the battles of the
Marne and the Aisne—Major-General Hubert Hamilton—who was killed by a shrapnel
bullet close to Bout Deville. He was succeeded in command by Major-General C.
J. Mackenzie who, on being invalided two weeks later, was then replaced by Major-
General F. D. V. Wing.

Shortly after dawn on the 15th October the 8th Brigade once again renewed
the attack. But, though additional artillery support had been given to the attack,
no progress could be made against the obstinate defence of Croix Barbeé. On the
left flank, however, the French Cavalry, supported by the fire of the Fifth Fusiliers,
now succeeded in carrying Riez Bailleul. During the remainder of the morning there
was a lull in the fighting, and the 4/Royal Fusiliers were brought forward from the
9th Brigade to come into line on the left of the FIFTH. At 2.15 p.m. the supporting
artillery, including that of the French, opened on the whole front of the 8th Brigade,
and the infantry once again advanced to the attack. The FIFTH, with the Gordons
on their right and the Royal Fusiliers on their left, reached and fought their way
through the village of Pont du Hem; but the Germans still clung desperately to Croix
Barbée. Having carried Pont du Hem, the FIFTH, among whom Captain Booth
and his company figured prominently this day, swept east of the village and, together
with the Royal Fusiliers, drove back all opposition and simultaneously with the French
cavalry further to the north, gained the line of the Neuve Chapelle-Estaires road about
4.30 p.m. Then at last the enemy, finding his northern flank turned, abandoned his
position at Croix Barbée, though he continued till darkness fell to offer a stubborn
resistance to the right of the 8th Brigade attack. Not till 11 p.m. was the 8th
Brigade in occupation of the line of the Estaires road along its whole front.

For two whole days costly frontal attacks had been delivered in vain against
the German position at Croix Barbée. It can be claimed that it was the capture of
Bout Deville by the FIFTH on the 14th October that had made possible the successful
advance on the left flank on the following day, and that it was the capture of Pont du
Hem and the line of the road to the east of the village which on the 15th overcame
the enemy's resistance opposite the centre of the 8th Brigade. The scene that had
greeted the FIFTH on carrying the line of the Estaires road gave evidence of the confusion into which the enemy had been thrown by the attack of the Battalion. The
road was strewn with equipment, rifles, and ammunition; and an officer enthusiastically
records how "the company commanders took advantage of the many abandoned
bicycles to mount their orderlies." Unfortunately, the company runners have left
no record of the spirit in which these contributions to their mobility were accepted.
Experience of pushing or carrying an army bicycle across country induces doubt as to
their sharing the complacency of this officer.

Map No. 7

The objective given to the 3rd Division for the 16th October was the general 16th Oct., 1914 line Illies-Herlies. During the night of the 15th/16th the 8th Brigade was withdrawn to Divisional Reserve on relief by the 9th Brigade, to which the FIFTH and Royal Fusiliers, already in the forward line, now reverted. The country was shrouded in dense fog when, at 7.15 a.m., the 9th Brigade advanced as the left of the Division. The brigade was formed in two columns, in the left of which the FIFTH moved in support of the Royal Fusiliers. Once again the advance was delayed by what seems to have been a persistent reluctance of the French cavalry at this period to operate before noon. It had been planned that they should move on the northern flank of the 3rd Division, but it was now learnt that they would not be ready to advance till 1.30 p.m. No opposition having hitherto been encountered, it was decided that, rather than incur further delay, the infantry should continue their advance and watch their own open flank. Late in the afternoon the enemy was located holding the general line Halpegarde-Aubers. The Royal Fusiliers, with "Z" and "W" companies of the FIFTH échelonned on their right and left flanks, were deployed for attack. But fog, combined with approaching darkness, decided Brigadier-General Shaw to hold up further advance, and the troops were withdrawn to billets; the FIFTH being accommodated for the night in Fauquissart under protection of their own outposts. Before the action was broken off the forward companies had suffered a few casualties from the enemy's shrapnel fire.

At 7 a.m. on the 17th October the 9th Brigade continued its advance for the capture of Herlies. By 11 a.m. the FIFTH, still moving in support with the left column, had entered Aubers unopposed, and "W" and "X" companies were ordered to take up a position on the high ground to the north, in protection of the left flank of the 9th Brigade. But when these orders were issued it was not known that the French cavalry, in advancing still further to the north against Fromelles, had met with strong resistance and had failed to carry their objective. As a result of this check, the companies of the FIFTH, on gaining the high ground, came under heavy fire from Fromelles. So long as this village remained in the hands of the enemy, further advance by the 9th Brigade against Herlies was impossible. An attempt by the companies of the FIFTH to advance against the village showed that it was held by the Germans in considerable strength, and left them no alternative but to dig in on a line about 500 yards to the south of it and await developments. In the position taken up the companies looked down on Fromelles as the spectators in the upper circle of an amphitheatre might view the stage; nor had they long to wait for the opening of a stirring drama. At about 12.30 p.m. a tornado of fire from the French 75's burst over the village. Scores of Germans driven from cover by the fire of the French guns, fled into the open to fall victims to the rifles of the FIFTH. Simultaneously, the assaulting troops, following close on their artillery barrage, swept through Fromelles. If in previous days the French had been found somewhat dilatory, they were seen in another mood now. While the troops in the centre of their attack were clearing the streets and houses of the village, others were rushed forward on the flanks to cut off the fugitive enemy. For a moment it seemed that the men of the FIFTH, in their unfamiliar uniform, would be called on to defend themselves against a fierce onslaught of their impetuous allies. In an earlier chapter it was related how an officer had come to the assistance of his men in procuring the castor oil they were seeking at a village shop. To-day he was confronted by the more difficult, if less delicate, task of establishing his nationality and dissuading the excited Frenchmen of the right flank from cutting the throats of his devoted company. Fortunately, Captain St. John's early

17th Oct., 1914 grounding in French irregular verbs once again proved equal to the occasion. Convinced of their error, the French flanking troops were persuaded to pursue their way and join their comrades of the centre who had now completed the capture of the village. While the FIFTH remained in position near Fromelles to guard the left flank, the Royal Fusiliers and the 1st Lincolnshire now continued the advance on Herlies, which was carried just before dusk following a brilliant attack by the latter. The FIFTH, relieved by the Royal Irish of the 8th Brigade, were then withdrawn to billets at Bas Pommereau, just south of Aubers, having suffered the comparatively light casualties of three other ranks killed and seven wounded.

Map No. 7

When Bout Deville was captured on the 14th October the FIFTH had represented the extreme left of the British forces in the operations directed to turning the enemy's northern flank. During the following days, with the arrival of the III. and I. Corps from the Aisne and corresponding movements by the enemy, the situation had been rapidly changing. During the 15th October III. Corps, coming in to the north of the French cavalry, who were still on the left flank of the 3rd Division, had extended the line to the north of Armentières; while, north again, General Allenby's Cavalry Corps had gained touch with General Rawlinson's force, which on its failure to relieve Antwerp had fallen back on Ypres. North of Ypres, the Belgians held the line of the Yser. The race to the sea had ended in a dead heat. Already the German and Allied Armies were standing face to face on the whole line from the Alps to the English Channel. But, though an open flank was no longer offered to either opponent, the northern flank of each was still held but thinly, and it seemed that success was promised to the army that could most quickly concentrate force in this quarter. At the same time, neither side could risk weakening its line further to the south, for a breach made by its enemy here would prejudice the success of any attack on the northern flank. Indeed, it had become apparent to the Germans that they must stiffen their opposition against the II. Corps if the progress of the past few days was to be checked. To this end they now substituted their VII. Corps for the Cavalry Corps, with whose troops the 3rd Division had hitherto been engaged. The effect of these changes was to be experienced by the FIFTH during the next few days.

Though, on the 17th October, the enemy had been driven from Herlies, the 3rd Division had failed to capture Illies, and the Germans were now found strongly entrenched on the line of the Illies—Fournes road. They were also in considerable strength in Fournes itself, against which the French cavalry had been unable to progress. In these circumstances further advance by the 9th Brigade was for the present impossible, and it was decided to consolidate the position won at Herlies. The FIFTH were ordered to move forward on the 18th October to the eastern outskirts of the southern portion of the village, where they would take up a position on the right of the Royal Fusiliers, who were to continue the line as far north as Le Riez. On the right of the FIFTH, the Royal Scots Fusiliers were to extend the line south-west to join the 7th Brigade north-east of Illies.

After a good night's rest at Bas Pommereau, the Battalion, further refreshed by a hearty breakfast, set out at 6 a.m. for Herlies. A covered approach had been planned; but the morning was misty and, misled by the map, the Battalion in close formation came under the observation of the German artillery and drew heavy fire on approaching the village. Fortunately, most of this passed overhead, and the Battalion escaped with only a few men wounded by the enemy's shrapnel. "W" and "X" Companies were then placed in reserve west of Herlies, while the remainder of the Battalion took up the front line position and entrenched. Large numbers of the enemy were observed in the small village of Le Pilly, about 800 yards from the position, and throughout the day sniping was engaged in with the Germans entrenched on the line of the Illies—Fournes road. Just before dark the enemy opened heavy artillery fire on the village and on the trenches of the Royal Fusiliers and the FIFTH. An attempt by their infantry to advance under cover of this bombardment was repulsed without difficulty, but the shelling was maintained for a considerable period. Much of the fire enfiladed the trenches of the FIFTH, and little rest was possible either here or in the village throughout the night. To find cover from the shells bursting over Herlies, " X " Company clung to the reverse side of a large slag heap. The experiences of that night are recorded in the diary of an officer, who describes the deafening noise of battle, the blinding flashes of the shells, silhouetting for an instant two solitary fir trees against the sky, before being followed by a deeper darkness and the crashing of the shrapnel bullets on the far side of the slag heap and the roofs of the neighbouring buildings. As is often the case, however, the moral was greater than the material effect of this bombardment. The casualties in the Battalion during the twenty-four hours amounted only to one other rank killed and nine wounded. But already the village had suffered very heavy damage.

On the 19th October there was a change in dispositions, by which the FIFTH, replaced by the Royal Fusiliers, moved to the right to take up a position covering the south-eastern and southern faces of Herlies; " X " and " Y " Companies on the right flank were thrown back to the west to join the Lincolnshire, whose right was in contact with the 7th Brigade at L'Aventure. There was a continuance of shell fire and sniping, whereby the Battalion lost 2 other ranks killed and Lieut. Waddilove and 29 other ranks wounded; otherwise, the day passed uneventfully. But it was becoming ever more apparent that the enemy was being reinforced by fresh troops and was in no mood to give up more ground. If doubt remained as to this, it was dispelled on the following day. At 9 a.m. on the 20th a heavy bombardment was opened on the front of the 9th Brigade, fire being concentrated chiefly on the village and on the position held by the FIFTH. An hour later, the German infantry advanced from their trenches but under the accurate fire of the British artillery the attack dwindled to a half-hearted effort which was easily repulsed by the rifle fire of the FIFTH. At noon the attack was renewed with greater determination. But though it became necessary to throw all the company supports into the firing line, no German succeeded in reaching the Battalion's trenches, and by 1.15 p.m. this second attack had definitely failed. The village itself, meanwhile, was being subjected to pitiless shell fire. Every house was in ruins, many in flames, and the streets were being ploughed by shells. At 2.50 p.m. the enemy were observed again massing for attack opposite the south-eastern quarter of the village, but were dispersed by the fire of our artillery before they could advance from their assembly positions. The enemy's efforts this day on the 9th Brigade front were mainly directed against the trenches of the Royal Fusiliers and of " W " and " Z " Companies on the left of the FIFTH. Here 2nd-Lieut. C. H. Van Neck and 8 other ranks were killed, and Lieuts. Vachell, Buckle, Hobbs and 41 other ranks wounded. There had been no attempt to advance across the very open ground which confronted the right of the Battalion, and an officer of " X " Company records that " except for being occasionally subjected to spells of shell fire from an uncomfortably oblique angle on our left, we were not threatened, and the day was really *almost dull*." But it had been no mere local effort of the enemy. Attacks had been delivered by the Germans on the 20th October along the whole front of the II. Corps, and in the course of the day orders had been issued to the 3rd Division to adopt

THE FIFTH IN THE GREAT WAR. 49

20th Oct., 1914   a defensive attitude. The position now occupied by the Division had been gained in   Map No. 7
the course of an advance in face of the enemy, and had been hitherto held with a view
to continuing the offensive. The French cavalry, directed on Fournes, had, however,
failed to carry their objective. Driven back on Le Riez, they were now resisting
attacks delivered by the Germans against that village. The 2/Royal Irish of the 8th
Brigade, in occupation of the small village of Le Pilly, afforded some protection to
the left flank of the Division, but were themselves in so precarious a situation that
their early withdrawal had become necessary. In short, whatever advantages it might
have held for a renewal of the attack, the salient occupied by the 3rd Division at
Herlies was wholly unsuitable to the defensive attitude now necessitated. It was,
in fact, necessary to withdraw to a position more favourable to defence and at the
same time to shorten the line. As a first step towards this, the FIFTH (less " X " and
" Y " Companies) and one half of the Royal Scots Fusiliers were withdrawn in the
early hours of the 21st October to a line half a mile west of Herlies, astride the Herlies—
Aubers road. " X " and " Y " Companies, who remained in the forward position,
passed a comparatively quiet day, for no serious attack was attempted by the enemy
during the course of it against the 9th Brigade's section of the defence. But on other
parts of the front the 21st October was a critical day for the 3rd Division. On their
right, heavy attacks threatened an enemy penetration at its junction with the 5th
Division, while, to the north, the Germans overran Le Pilly and made strenuous efforts
to drive the French cavalry from Le Riez.* Further to the north, the 19th Infantry
Brigade, which had been sent forward by the III. Corps in rear of the French cavalry
and had occupied Le Maisnil, were forced in the evening to evacuate the position they
had taken up.

    The II. Corps now decided to fall back on a line running south from Fauquissart
and east of Neuve Chapelle. To cover the preparation of this line, a preliminary
withdrawal of about one mile was to be made to an intermediate line, in which the
9th Brigade was to occupy a section from Halpegarde to Le Plouich. At about 10 p.m.
on the 21st the FIFTH (less " X " and " Y " Companies) fell back on La Cliqueterie,
in the centre of this line. It remained to withdraw the troops from the trenches
at Herlies, and this promised to be a more difficult operation. The withdrawal was
planned to be carried out progressively from left to right and to be completed an hour
before dawn on the 22nd. The delays which too often occur on such occasions placed
" X " and " Y " Companies of the FIFTH in the predicament of having to decide
whether to depart from orders or to risk the disaster which would almost certainly
result from a retirement in daylight under observation of the enemy. Dawn was
approaching; the troops on their right, impatient of delay, after repeated messages
urging retirement, withdrew. But the company commanders of the FIFTH deemed
it their duty to stand fast until the troops on their left had got clear. Events justified
their decision. Their withdrawal was ultimately effected in the first glimmer of dawn
and was undetected by the enemy, who two hours later launched an attack against
the vacated position and suffered heavily from our artillery fire. Later in the morning
the whole Battalion was concentrated in divisional reserve at Piètre.

    A brief consideration of the situation that had developed further to the north
is necessary to an understanding of the issues involved in the fighting in which the

---

    * Communication with the Royal Irish Regiment at Le Pilly was severed, and the orders
to withdraw failed to reach them. The battalion, after a most gallant defence in its isolated position,
was annihilated.

FIFTH was to take part during the following week. The I. Corps by the 19th October had moved up behind Ypres, and during the two following days had come into line east and north of that town as the extreme left of the British front. On the 21st October Sir John French, though ordering a defensive attitude on his whole front, was still hopeful that, while the II. Corps stood fast, a successful advance might prove possible to the I. Corps. Of the fierce fighting that had developed opposite Ypres, he reported as late as the 22nd October :—" In my opinion the enemy are vigorously playing their last card, and I am confident they will fail." This estimate was to prove to be unduly optimistic. Long before the fighting on the northern flank died down, the FIFTH, as will be seen later, were to be drawn into the desperate struggle known as the First Battle of Ypres. But, for the present, the Battalion was to stand on the defensive with the II. Corps covering the coalfields of the Bethune district, which represented to the enemy an objective only less important than the Channel ports.

While the withdrawal from Herlies was in progress the enemy had opened a violent attack on the 5th Division. In response to an appeal for assistance, the 3rd Division had ordered its 7th Brigade to despatch its reserve battalion to the threatened sector. Shortly after concentrating at Piètre, the FIFTH were directed to move to the Bois de Biez in replacement of this battalion. Here they remained in support of the 7th Brigade till late in the afternoon, when they returned to Piètre. After midnight the Battalion was moved back as Divisional Reserve to billets in Rue Bacquerot, 1½ miles north-east of Neuve Chapelle ; and by dawn of the 23rd October the whole of the 3rd Division had completed its withdrawal, and was established in the position selected on the line Neuve Chapelle—Fauquissart. The billets at Rue Bacquerot were good, but they were dangerously close to the front line, and the rest granted to the Battalion was brief. As a precaution against shell fire the companies were ordered in the afternoon to construct shelter trenches on the outskirts of the village. A half hour had barely passed when the wisdom of this step was proved. While the companies were at work and the battalion transport being evacuated from the village the German guns opened. A shell burst in the middle of a group of farm buildings where Battalion Headquarters were situated. Fortunately, all but one pair of horses had been already removed, and compared with the heavy casualties that might have occurred, the loss was slight. Lieut. Platt, who was at work in the farm, was wounded ; two other ranks were killed and five wounded. The two horses were also destroyed. Platt's place as acting adjutant was taken by Lieut. L. C. A. Barrett, a young officer who, before his death later in the war, was to attain the high distinction of battalion command in another regiment.

At dusk the companies returned to their billets in Rue Bacquerot, where they were left undisturbed till 2.30 a.m. on the 24th. At this hour, on an alarm of attack, the Battalion was ordered to occupy trenches near the neighbouring village of Rouge Croix. After remaining in these throughout an uneventful day, companies were withdrawn at dark to billets in Rouge Croix itself.

The 3rd Division was now disposed, in order from right to left : 7th, 9th, 8th Infantry Brigades, the FIFTH still being in Divisional Reserve. During the night determined attacks were delivered by the enemy south of Neuve Chapelle and at Fauquissart, against the right and left flanks of the Division. These succeeded in penetrating the line on the left, and the FIFTH were kept standing to arms during the greater part of the night. But counter-attack by the 8th Brigade restored the situation and the Battalion was not called on. In the meantime the 7th Brigade had repulsed the attack against the right flank with heavy loss. A fresh attack against this flank

25th Oct., 1914 during the morning of the 25th, however, was more successful, and at 11.45 a.m. the Map No. 7
FIFTH were ordered forward to support the 2/Irish Rifles, in whose trenches the enemy
had obtained a lodgment. But the captured position was recovered without their
assistance, and the Battalion was ordered back to Rouge Croix. Casualties from
the 21st to the 24th October had amounted to 6 other ranks killed, 1 officer and 13
other ranks wounded. Though these losses were slight, the amount of rest that it
had been possible to give to the men while the Battalion was in reserve had been
negligible.

The FIFTH were now ordered to take over the line in front of Neuve Chapelle
in relief of the 1/Lincolnshire. At 1.30 a.m. on the 26th October the Battalion left
its billets to move forward to the line. Rain was falling, and the night was pitch
dark. The route lay over ploughed fields and ditches, crossed by single, slippery
planks. Sniping was continuous during relief, but by 5.30 a.m. the Battalion was
in position. On its right, separating it from the left of the 7th Brigade, the trenches
were held by two companies of the Royal Fusiliers; on its left were the Royal Scots
Fusiliers. "Z" Company occupied the right trenches of the FIFTH. The trials of
this company were to start early. Shortly after dawn, it lost a very fine officer in
2nd-Lieut. Laws, who was killed by a sniper's bullet. Laws, who had served many
years in the ranks of the FIFTH, had but recently been promoted from company
serjeant-major. His place was filled a few hours later by Captain Barnsley, of the
Lancashire Fusiliers, who had just arrived on attachment to the FIFTH. The morning,
otherwise, passed uneventfully. Except for continual sniping, the front remained
quiet. Suddenly, at 2.50 p.m., the Germans opened a heavy bombardment, concentrating the fire mainly on the positions held by "Z" Company, the Royal Fusiliers,
and the left battalion of the 7th Brigade. At 3.30 p.m. the enemy launched a strong
infantry attack against the same portion of the line. The Royal Fusiliers were forced
from their trenches and Captain Gordon, commander of "Z" Company, was compelled
to throw back his right platoon in order to protect his flank and to cover by fire a
British field gun sited in a forward position some twenty yards to his right. Scarcely
had these dispositions been completed when a German shell burst in the gun emplace-
ment, killing several of the gunners, forcing the remainder of the detachment to
evacuate the position, and disabling one of the wheels of the gun. This was the signal
for the German infantry to swarm into the vacant position. Lieut. Nunneley, commander of the right platoon, immediately called on a party of men to follow him and
led a counter-attack, but within ten yards of the gun this very gallant officer was
killed. Gordon then recalled the survivors of the counter-attack to the trench from
which he was directing the defence, and drove the Germans from the neighbourhood of
the gun by rifle fire, killing many. For a time there was a lull in the fighting, but
thirty minutes later the enemy were observed again advancing to the assault. Gordon
attempted to lead his men forward to charge with the bayonet, but a wire fence
obstructed his advance. Of five men who succeeded in crossing this, three were
killed; and, after receiving a bullet through his cap at a range of fifteen yards, Gordon
withdrew with the survivors and ordered his men back to the cover of the trenches.
Here, opening fire, they once again drove back the Germans with very heavy loss.

In the meantime, the situation further to the south remained serious. On
the left of the 7th Brigade the line had been broken, and, as already related, the two
companies of the Royal Fusiliers between this point and the right of "Z" Company
had been driven back. The enemy, following up this success, had pressed forward
through Neuve Chapelle till held up at the western exits of the village by a reserve

company of the Wiltshire Regiment of the 7th Brigade. The remainder of the Royal Fusiliers had been sent up to the support of their two forward companies, and the Lincolnshire moved to Pont Logy, but no measures had yet been taken to give relief to the exposed flank of " Z " Company of the FIFTH. The German attack had not included the remainder of the front of the Battalion nor that of the Royal Scots Fusiliers on its left, and here the troops were still in their original positions.

As darkness was falling, a party of Germans was detected making a further attempt to destroy the abandoned field gun. One of these, courageously advancing with lighted straw, succeeded in placing this under the gun before he and his companions were shot down. Corporal A. J. Fisk then sought and obtained permission from Captain Gordon to go forward and extinguish the conflagration. Dashing out under the close fire of the enemy, this gallant N.C.O. succeeded in his enterprise and returned unscathed.* The enemy were now established within two hundred yards of the front of " Z " Company, and within sixty yards of its right flank, and could be heard talking and singing. It was clear to Gordon that they were in position to bring both enfilade and reverse fire on his company, and he urged his men rapidly to throw up back cover. While they were employed in this, the enemy once again suddenly attacked, but our men remained steady and behaved magnificently. Firing both to front and rear—for the attack was directed from three sides—they completely repulsed the Germans. But Lieutenant Christopher Leather was killed by the side of his company commander; Captain Barnsley had already fallen, and Captain Gordon found himself the sole surviving officer in the company. Counter-attacks, delivered by troops of the 7th and 9th Brigades, at 8.30 p.m. and again at 1.20 a.m., met with only partial success in Neuve Chapelle, but enabled the Royal Fusiliers once more to gain contact with the right flank of the sorely tried " Z " Company. Twenty-four hours had passed since the company had left its billets at Rouge Croix; for the last twelve it had been engaged in repelling repeated attacks by the enemy. But the worst had now passed. At 4 a.m. on the 27th October " Z " Company, on relief by " Y," was led back to Battalion Reserve by Captain Gordon, who, of the officers, had alone survived the ordeal through which his company had passed. With events still vivid in his mind, moved by the recollection of the manner in which his men had stood by him, Gordon wrote that night:—" Men dog tired but cheery. They are splendid. Often in peace they madden me, but I love them all to-night." Indeed they had deserved well of their commander. Yet there was not one among them that day who was not conscious of what he, on his part, owed to the inspiration of Gordon. For it had been his cool and clear-headed action which had enabled the company to maintain its position, and his determination which had inspired his men to beat back the repeated attacks of the enemy in their endeavour to turn the exposed flank of his company and surround it. The casualties sustained by " Z " Company on the 26th October amounted to 4 officers and 10 other ranks killed; 21 other ranks wounded; 32 other ranks missing, of whom all had, unfortunately, been killed or wounded.

The above account of the action of " Z " Company of the 1/Fifth Fusiliers represents the first public record of the part played by the company in the fighting of the 26th October, 1914. If the situation following the first German assault has been made clear, there is no need to emphasise the immense service rendered by Gordon's stubborn stand. To many, then, it may seem strange that in the Official

---

* Corporal Fisk, who was killed on the 15th November, 1914, was awarded the D.C.M. subsequent to his death.

27th Oct., 1914. History of the War, which refers in generous terms to other less important services Map No. 7 of the Battalion, there is no reference to the action of "Z" Company. Stranger, even, that in the War Diary of the 3rd Division the name of the FIFTH is not mentioned in connection with the critical events of this day. A reasonable explanation of the omission is found in the fact that the Battalion as a whole was not involved in the fighting, as it inevitably would have been had "Z" Company not stood fast in protection of its right flank. The official narrative, as can be understood, presents the events in terms of the larger units and formations whose fronts were included in the enemy's assault, and the part played by a single company has accordingly been overlooked. But in a history of the FIFTH the action of "Z" Company on the 26th October can be recorded as equalling in valour and importance any service rendered by the Regiment in the Great War.

Daybreak on the 27th October found the Germans entrenched in the positions they had gained on the previous day. Preparations were now being made for the relief of the 3rd Division by the Lahore Division of the Indian Corps. The attachment of the 47th Sikhs to the 9th Brigade made it possible to strengthen the line by sending forward the Lincolnshire for insertion between the FIFTH and Royal Fusiliers. Otherwise there was no improvement in the situation. Sniping was continuous throughout the day, and the already heavy loss of officers in the Battalion was increased by the death of Captain J. M. Lambert and 2nd-Lieut. D. M. Coles, who were both killed by snipers. In addition 21 other ranks of the FIFTH were killed and 21 wounded.

On the morning of the 28th October a further desperate effort was made to drive the enemy from Neuve Chapelle. British, Indian and French infantry were engaged in the counter-attack, in support of which French artillery co-operated with our own. The day was memorable for the gallant attack made by two companies of the 47th Sikhs and the 20th and 21st Companies of the Sappers and Miners. Driving back the Germans, they forced their way to the eastern limits of the village. But the attack as a whole lacked co-ordination, and the Indian troops, unsupported on either flank, were unable to hold the position they had captured, and after suffering terrible casualties were forced to withdraw. The FIFTH took no part in this ill fated counter-attack. During the 28th and 29th they remained in occupation of the trenches taken over on the 26th, the forward companies harassed by constant sniping, the reserve company and Battalion Headquarters by shell fire. On the night of the 29th-30th October, the FIFTH were relieved by the 2nd Gurkha Rifles. After relief, which was carried out under continual enemy rifle fire and completed just before dawn, they withdrew to Vieille Chapelle, moving later in the day to find billets in some scattered farms about $1\frac{1}{2}$ miles north-west of Estaires.

From the 13th to the 29th October the Battalion had been actively engaged with the enemy on every day, with the exception of the four days during which it had been in reserve. Such rest as it had then gained had been disturbed by bombardments and by constant calls to stand to arms, followed frequently by orders to move to the support of some threatened front. The casualties during the advance to and withdrawal from Herlies, and in the subsequent stand at Neuve Chapelle, had amounted to :—Killed, 7 officers and 73 other ranks ; wounded, 6 officers and 234 other ranks ; missing, 44 other ranks ; a total of 13 officers and 351 other ranks.

The following passages, which refer to the operations in which the Battalion had taken part, are quoted from the Official History of the War :—

"The fighting on the La Bassée front, so far as the valour and determination of the troops on both sides are concerned, was as desperate as that at Ypres, but it never had the same strategic or sentimental importance. The capture of the Bethune district, with its coalfields and resources, would undoubtedly have been a serious loss to France, but not an irreparable one like that of the Channel ports. Nevertheless, the Germans did confessedly endeavour to break through on the Arras—Armentières front all through October. . . . In the end he (the enemy) abandoned his ambitious scheme and, after 29th October, contented himself with maintaining his position . . . and holding as many of the Allies as possible to their ground. But he failed even in this object, and was unable to prevent the extrication of the II. Corps from the line and the employment of the greater part of it at Ypres."

It was to the Ypres Salient, then, that the FIFTH was now to be directed. The fighting in which the Battalion was to be engaged in the course of its move to the north and on its arrival in the Salient, will be dealt with in the following chapter.

CHAPTER V.

"Messines, 1914. "Armentières, 1914." Ypres, 1914." "Nonnebosschen."

THE FIGHTING AT WYTSCHAETE AND HERENTHAGE CHÂTEAU.

TRENCH WARFARE IN THE KEMMEL SECTOR.

31ST OCTOBER, 1914—17TH FEBRUARY, 1915.

31st Oct., 1914

Before relating the events in which the 1/FIFTH were to be involved in their northward move from Estaires, a brief account must be given of the occurrences which had called it to Ypres, in the neighbourhood of which its future was to lie for the next eighteen months. It may be difficult for those who to-day visit Ypres for the first time to visualise the vast rubble heap of ruins which the name of the town brings to the recollection of the majority of the British soldiers who knew it in the War. Yet, the town as it now stands will give them a close picture of the Ypres of 1914. For, at the date we are now considering, Ypres still stood intact under the shadow of the towers of its Cathedral and Cloth Hall, and its streets were thronged with a civil population. In these early days of the War even more than to-day, it was unimaginable that a town of this size and beauty should ever be reduced to its ultimate state of desolation. True, since the British forces from the south had joined hands with the 7th Division after its westerly withdrawal on the fall of Antwerp, fierce and stubborn fighting had been in progress with the enemy, who had moved parallel with the former and in pursuit of the latter; but none could yet foresee the years of desperate defence that were to save the town from capture. At this time the thought was rather that Ypres and its population would be freed by the repulse of the enemy.

Map No. 8.

The position which had been taken up by the 7th Division to the east of Ypres was greatly in advance of the line of the Yser, on which the Belgians had fallen back, and considerably beyond the line reached by the British cavalry to the south of the town. When the I. Corps arrived on 19th October to take up a position on the left of the 7th Division to connect with the Belgians, the allied line thus already formed a salient about Ypres. In the fighting which had opened on that day, the British, facing greatly superior numbers of the enemy, had been thrown definitely on the defensive. But, on the 23rd October, the French by taking over that portion of the Salient that lay to the north and north-east of the town had greatly strengthened the position of the allies. The optimistic outlook of Sir John French has been referred to in the previous chapter. The consistent failure of the German attacks against the weak British defence encouraged him in the belief that when these had been exhausted it would be possible to drive back the enemy. On the 24th it seemed that the initiative had passed to the allies, and the French commander shared the view of the British Commander-in-Chief that Ypres could now be freed from the German menace.

An allied offensive was opened, and on every day from the 25th October onwards, orders were issued for its continuance. But the attacks of the allies made no greater progress than had those previously delivered by the Germans. On the 29th October, after ten days of continual attacks and counter-attacks, there had been little change in the positions as originally taken up by the opposing forces. On the evening of that day, the British line ran roughly from Messines north-east to beyond

Gheluvelt, and thence north to join the French just east of Zonnebeke. It was known that the 3½ divisions and 3 cavalry divisions of the British had hitherto been opposed by as many as 5 divisions and 8 cavalry divisions of the enemy; and it may well be considered that Sir John French, in ordering a renewal of the attack for the 30th October, was underrating the quality of his enemy. But an even more vital factor had been introduced of which he was still ignorant. On the night of the 29th/30th the enemy had brought up unseen a further five fresh divisions to within a few hundred yards of the British front, and in their support had placed in position as many as 260 heavy guns.

On the 30th October, as the FIFTH, in expectation of a promised ten days' rest, reached Estaires, the Germans had opened an offensive at Ypres, which was to bring the British to what must rank as one of the most desperate and critical battles of their country's history. The main objectives of the German attack were the Messines—Wytschaete ridge and the commanding position at Kemmel. They calculated that by gaining these objectives, they would cut off the troops in and north of Ypres, whom they would then drive against the coast, and in pursuance of this plan, their heaviest attack had been directed against the southern portion of the Salient. The vital sector was held by the Cavalry Corps. Fighting with superb valour, the British cavalry were thrust back west of Zandvoorde, and, further to the south, fell back on Wytschaete, which, on the 31st October, they were defending desperately against overwhelming numbers. Unless they could be supported in good time, a situation, already critical, might turn to disaster. The nearest troops available for their assistance were those of the 9th Brigade who had just been withdrawn to rest from the heavy fighting at Neuve Chapelle. At 6.45 a.m. on the 31st October, Brigadier General Shaw set out from Estaires with the Fifth Fusiliers and the 1/Lincolnshire Regiment to the support of the threatened front. On starting, the men were in high spirits, for rumour had it that the unexpected move was attributable to the billets at Estaires being required for other troops, and that the Battalion, in consequence, was to be taken further to the rear to enjoy in greater comfort and security the rest it so sadly needed. The true situation, however, was soon learnt and was accepted philosophically. They were cheered, too, by the Battalion receiving an addition to its strength in the course of their northward march. The route lay by Steenwercke and Neuve Eglise, and at the latter place Captain Fletcher and Lieutenant Willans with a draft of the FIFTH were found digging trenches with all the zeal of new arrivals, and this obvious keenness made the reinforcement additionally welcome. After a march of 12 miles, the small column halted at Lindenhoek, 2½ miles southwest of Wytschaete. Here the battalions remained in support till the evening, when they were moved to billets in Kemmel.

At 1.45 a.m. on 1st November, sudden verbal orders were received by 9th Brigade Headquarters to support the cavalry, who were being heavily attacked at Wytschaete. The troops were out of billets and formed up within fifteen minutes, and the two battalions, with the Lincolnshire leading, moved up the Kemmel—Wytschaete road for about one mile before halting. The night was dark, but the sky was lit by the fires of burning houses, while in the distance a continual rattle of musketry fire and the crash of bursting shells gave evidence of the fierce fighting in which the cavalry were engaged. Close at hand, cartridges exploding from time to time in a burning limber gave the impression that the supporting troops had already become involved in the battle. In the meantime, Brigadier-General Shaw, on reaching the Headquarters of the 4th Cavalry Brigade, had been informed that the enemy had carried a portion of the cavalry trenches and occupied part of the village. Orders

1st Nov., 1914 were issued for a counter-attack to be delivered at 4.30 a.m. for the recovery of the Map No. 8
lost position. So critical was the situation that it was apparently necessary for anything in the nature of a detailed plan to be sacrificed to the need for immediate support to the hard-pressed cavalry. Only the roughest outline of how the operation should be carried out was given. The Lincolnshire, on the right, and two companies of the FIFTH, on the left, were to carry out the attack, while the remainder of the FIFTH were to act in support. "W" and "X" Companies of the FIFTH were detailed for the attack; but, before the orders reached them, the Lincolnshire had already moved forward and disappeared in the darkness. It was learnt, however, that the battalion was advancing to the south of the road; the two companies of the FIFTH, accordingly, deployed to the north of it and advanced in line of platoons, to draw level with the Lincolnshire. The ground to be crossed, reported as open, was found, in fact, to be very enclosed. Wire hampered the advance, and wire cutters were few. "X" Company, on the left, was confronted by a wood which spread to within a narrow distance of the north-western outskirts of the village; "W" Company had a clearer line of advance between the southern edge of this wood and the road. Touch had not been gained with the Lincolnshire when, on approaching the village in the grey of dawn, the leading platoons of both companies were met by a withering fire from the enemy's rifles and machine guns. Against this, advance across the open space that now intervened was impossible. Captain St. John, the commander of "X" Company, wishing to discuss the situation with Captain Fletcher, of "W" Company, now went across to the road. He found the ground strewn with wounded men of the FIFTH, but he could get no information as to the whereabouts of Fletcher.* To the south of the road, however, he located the Lincolnshire, whose men shouted to him that they were suffering heavily. They were, in fact, in similar plight to the companies of the FIFTH, and it was clear that the counter-attack had been brought to a standstill along the whole front. Report of the situation having reached Brigade Headquarters, General Shaw realised the hopelessness of continuing the attack with the slender resources at his disposal. French troops were now coming forward, and pending the organisation of a heavier attack by these, it was decided to stand on the defensive. The 3rd Hussars, in reserve, already held a position astride the road, about one mile west of Wytschaete; and the supporting companies of the FIFTH ("Y" and "Z") were ordered to move into position on their right, to prolong the line to Point 75. The forward troops were to consolidate on the line they had reached. "Y" Company set out in accordance with these orders; but the full dispositions were not to be carried out. At about 7.15 a.m., Captain St. John, who had not yet been informed of the plan, was making his way back to his company when the enemy opened a very heavy shell fire on the Lincolnshire and the forward companies of the FIFTH, who were simultaneously subjected to a devastating fire of rifles and machine guns from the wood, the village, and the southern flank. Captain St. John fell severely wounded; his subaltern, Lieutenant Everard Lamb, had already been killed, and of the six officers of "W" and "X" Companies but one remained. The position of the forward troops had now become untenable. The projected move of "Z" Company to the right was cancelled, and Captain Gordon, its commander, was ordered

---

* It has never been possible to ascertain the circumstances of the death of Captain Fletcher, who was reported as "missing" at the end of the day. The casualties of the Battalion as a whole, moreover, cannot be accurately determined owing to the relevant Appendix to the Battalion War Diary having been lost.

to stand fast in support north of the road. The Lincolnshire fell back, by order of their Commanding Officer, to a ridge some 800 yards in rear of the line they had gained; and the forward companies of the FIFTH, now leaderless, withdrew in conformity on the north side of the road. Here they were rallied and reformed by Captain Gordon to take up a position with his own company on the left of the Lincolnshire. Against this position the Germans did not venture to advance. Later in the morning, a stronger and more carefully organised attack, delivered by the French in co-operation with the 12th Lancers, swept the enemy from Wytschaete and recovered the trenches that had been lost during the preceding night. About 11 a.m. the FIFTH, on relief by the 16th Lancers, were withdrawn to billets at Kemmel, together with the Lincolnshire, whose strength had been reduced to less than 100 all ranks.

The objective of the Germans had been Kemmel Hill. Following the gallant stand of the British cavalry, the action of the Lincolnshire and the FIFTH had been effective in thwarting the enemy's plans. Referring to the events that have been narrated, the Official History says: "In the few hours' fighting, the Lincolnshire had lost 8 officers and 293 other ranks, and the Northumberland Fusiliers 5 officers and 93 other ranks, totals representing 30 per cent. of the men present; but they had put up a fight worthy of the best traditions of the British Army." With the opportunity for cool reflection, it is possible to be wise after the event, and to derive profit from the experiences of any action. In studying the events at Wytschaete on 1st November, 1914, one is inevitably impelled to consider whether the early attack with its heavy losses was necessary to achieve the results ultimately obtained; and whether casualties might not have been avoided had the troops of the 9th Brigade, pending the organisation of a more deliberate attack, been placed at the outset in the positions taken up later to contain the Germans. It must have been realised from the first that nothing less than incredible good fortune could bring success to an attack in which the troops were to advance in the dark over unreconnoitred ground, on orders that amounted to little more than "go in and win." In so far as the capture of the objective was concerned, the counter-attack by the Lincolnshire and the FIFTH was in the nature of a forlorn hope. But it must be remembered that General Shaw, when called on to assist the Cavalry in their desperate situation, had no expectation of the timely arrival of the French reinforcement. Furthermore, it may well be that, even though it failed, the dawn attack in its very boldness, by creating a false impression of strength, deterred the enemy from taking action that might have prejudiced the success of the Allies' later effort. The following letter, addressed by the G.O.C. Cavalry Corps to General Smith-Dorrien, may be taken as confirming this view :—

> "MY DEAR SIR HORACE,
>
> "I must thank you for the help given me during the past 48 hours by the four battalions* you so kindly sent to our aid, the Lincolns, K.O.S.B., K.O.Y.L.I., and the Northumberland Fusiliers. They arrived at a very critical time and their arrival saved the situation. I fear they have suffered severe loss, but they fought brilliantly. I am deeply indebted to them and to Brigadier-General Shaw.
>
> "Yours sincerely,
> "E. H. ALLENBY."

---

* K.O.S.B. and K.O.Y.L.I. of the 15th Brigade of the 5th Division had been temporarily placed under the command of Brigadier-General Shaw, and had been sent by him on the 31st October to the support of the cavalry engaged at Messines.

The Fifth in the Great War.

3rd Nov., 1914

Except for the few days spent at Courcelles in September, the FIFTH had enjoyed no real rest since the Battle of Mons. They were now to be given their second spell, but it was to prove as brief as that which had been granted six weeks before. After a quiet day at Kemmel, the Battalion marched on the 3rd November to Bailleul, where three nights were spent in comfortable billets. During this period the Battalion was inspected by General Sir Horace Smith-Dorrien, who addressed the troops on parade. To quote a contemporary diary, "The men turned out wonderfully clean and smart which particularly struck Sir H. He spoke of the services of the Battalion in words which will live for ever in the Regiment's History." Smith-Dorrien was not one who lightly lavished praise. It is well that we have this diarist's testimony to the feelings that his address inspired, for, alas, there remains no record of the words he spoke on this occasion.

Map No. 8

But the luxury of hot baths, clean clothing, and full nights' sleep was not to be enjoyed for long. On the 31st October, simultaneously with the attack on Wytschaete and Messines, the Germans had attacked the British troops in position astride the Ypres—Menin road. In the fierce fighting of that critical day Gheluvelt had been lost and retaken, but on the same night the recovered position had been vacated and the line withdrawn west of the village. During the ensuing days the enemy had continued to hammer at the southern and eastern faces of the Salient, while to the north, counter-attacks by the French had failed to progress. With the loss of Messines and, later, of Wytschaete, the enemy had gained a position from which for nearly three years he was to dominate the low-lying ground in the neighbourhood of Ypres, and hourly the situation of the troops in the Salient was becoming increasingly critical. British resources were taxed to the utmost; troops, wherever they could be found, and regardless of the command to which they belonged, had to be thrown into the weakened portions of the line; indeed it had become impossible to maintain formations intact under their own commanders. The II. Corps, as such, had for the time ceased to exist. Of the 3rd Division many battalions were still on the La Bassée front. Of the 9th Brigade, the 4/Royal Fusiliers had now come north to rejoin the FIFTH and the Lincolnshire, who with several battalions of other brigades were to be grouped during the next week or more under Brigadier-General Shaw.

On the 6th November, Shaw's group came under the command of the 1st Division and received orders to take over trenches held by the 6th Cavalry Brigade. A twelve mile march from Bailleul brought the FIFTH to a point one mile south-west of Ypres early in the afternoon. It had been intended that the Battalion should halt here till the time came to carry out the relief in the trenches. But, at 5.30 p.m., on report being received that the enemy had broken through the line south-east of Ypres, the three battalions of the 9th Brigade were moved forward to a position in reserve one mile east of the town. Here they remained till midnight, when they again moved forward to take over the trenches.

During the past few days a further slight withdrawal had been made to the east of Ypres, and the British line now crossed the Menin road about one mile east of Hooge. Just to the south of the road, the line passed through Herenthage Wood, which was situated on the high ground to the east of Herenthage Château. It was here that the FIFTH took up their position, with the Royal Fusiliers continuing the line on their left to the Menin road. The relief had passed without incident, and during the early morning all remained quiet. Suddenly, at 11.30 a.m., the German guns opened with terrific force on the trenches, fire being concentrated mainly on the right of the FIFTH. Hour after hour the bombardment continued without intermission. Except on its right, "Z" Company in position on the left of the Battalion escaped the worst of the enemy's fire. But, on the remainder of the front occupied by the FIFTH, terribly heavy casualties were sustained. The trenches, which had been dangerously undercut, not only provided scant cover from the enemy's fire, but, collapsing under the bombardment, buried many of the unfortunate garrison. At 3 p.m. the German infantry assaulted. "Z" Company repulsed the attack and held fast to its position, but the two right trenches of the FIFTH were carried by the enemy. Later, the remnants of the garrison of the captured trenches were rallied, and, supported by two companies of the Lincolnshire, were led forward by Captain Booth to counter-attack the lost position. As the attack moved forward Captain Booth was wounded; the troops, left leaderless, failed to carry their objective; and the Lincolnshire companies were brought to a standstill on a line about three hundred yards to the right rear of "Z" Company. Captain Gordon then threw back the right of "Z" Company and, by converting a communication trench to a fire trench, provided protection for his right flank. The situation was a repetition of that in which this officer's company had been placed but ten days before at Neuve Chapelle. When darkness fell, the Germans were established some 250 yards to his front and little more than 30 yards from his right flank.

It had been an evil day for the FIFTH. The numbers of the Battalion, already seriously diminished in the fighting at Herlies, Neuve Chapelle and Wytschaete, had been further reduced by 1 officer and 13 other ranks reported wounded, and 1 officer and 140 other ranks missing. The missing officer, Lieutenant Willans, was later found to have been killed; and the remainder reported under this heading represented those killed or wounded by the bombardment who had fallen into the enemy's hands in the captured position. For an appreciation of what the FIFTH was to face in the fierce fighting of the next few days, it is necessary for the reader to realise what was now the strength and composition of the Battalion. Some figures as to officer casualties may convey an idea of this. Of the 26 officers who had sailed with the Battalion from England, only four now remained: Major Yatman, in temporary command, Lieutenant Barrett, temporary adjutant, Lieutenant Gunner, transport officer, and Captain Landen, quarter-master. Of the rest, 5 had been killed, 12 wounded, 1 wounded and captured, and 4 invalided. Of officers sent out as reinforcements or promoted from the ranks, 11 had been killed, 4 wounded, 1 wounded and captured, 3 invalided. Of the regular officers so sent out, who had been on the active list at the outbreak of war, Captain Gordon was the sole survivor.* The casualties among other ranks had been nearly commensurate. It had not been possible for reinforcements to keep pace with these losses, and the standard of training of the men sent out was in no way comparable to that of those who had fought in the earlier weeks. But, as was to be shown in the trench warfare that had developed, where manoeuvre was no longer possible, stout hearts could do much to compensate for lack of experience. The total strength of the Battalion was now little over two hundred in all. The left trench, which had originally been committed to "Z" Company alone, now represented the Battalion front, and to this all available men were sent forward to reinforce Gordon, whose situation was already highly critical.

---

* In the absence of detailed lists of officer reinforcements, it is not possible to determine the actual number of officers present with the Battalion at this date. From what can be gathered, it seems to be generally agreed that the only *company officer* in addition to Gordon was 2nd-Lieut. J. O. Lawson, a very young officer.

8th Nov., 1914   Brigadier-General Shaw, realising that further attempts to recover the lost   Map No. 8
trenches were unlikely to result in anything beyond a further diminution of his rapidly
dwindling numbers, had ordered that the line gained by the Lincolnshire companies
should be consolidated as a new front line, échelonned in rear of " Z " Company of
the FIFTH. Orders were issued that the position thus readjusted should be held at
all costs. The morning of the 8th November was characterised by intermittent shell
and rifle fire. About 1 p.m. an attack by the Germans to the left of the 9th Brigade
met with some initial success, but the situation was restored with the bayonet by the
2/Duke of Wellington's, of Shaw's Group and the 4/Royal Fusiliers. On the front
of the FIFTH the enemy continued to harass the trenches by fire during the early
afternoon, but our men harboured their ammunition, and were not drawn into replying
to the German snipers. These tactics, doubtless, encouraged the enemy to expect
little opposition, when, at 5.30 p.m., their infantry suddenly swarmed from their
trenches and rushed forward to assault the right of Captain Gordon's line. But our
men were ready for them and behaved with great coolness and judgment. From the
hitherto silent trenches a heavy rifle and machine gun fire opened on the attackers.
The Germans displayed great dash and determination; some reached the parapet
before they fell to the fire of the defence; two succeeded in mounting it before they
were killed. The enemy needed only to effect a penetration on this weak and exposed
flank for the whole trench line of the FIFTH to be involved in disaster. But their
most desperate efforts were of no avail against the resistance they encountered, and in
a few minutes some fifty dead and many wounded lay in front of the position as the
only evidence that remained of the attack.

During the next two days, the enemy contented themselves with subjecting
the trenches to intermittent artillery and rifle fire. Retaliation was, however, taken
against the German snipers, Company Serjeant-Major Gillborn, in particular, for long
a noted marksman in the Regiment, taking a heavy toll. But this comparative
inactivity on the part of the enemy was but preparatory to their last supreme effort
in the long drawn out First Battle of Ypres to break the British front and gain the
Channel ports. The 11th November was to prove a critical day in the Great War,
and one in which, it may be said, the fate of the British Empire hung in the balance.
Shortly after daybreak, a very heavy bombardment was opened on the whole British
front. For 1½ hours, without pause, the front line of the FIFTH was severely shelled,
while a constant stream of projectiles searched the woods in rear, where such weak
supports as were available were located. At 8.30 a.m., the German infantry *advanced
to the attack. In front of the FIFTH they were met by the fire of every rifle of Gordon's
slender garrison. Staggered by heavy losses, the attack at this point completely
broke down. But further to the north, the enemy, pushing forward astride the Menin
road against the left of the 9th Brigade, met with better success, and succeeded in
carrying the trenches of the 4/Royal Fusiliers immediately on Gordon's left. The
situation of the FIFTH was thus made most precarious. With their right still thrown
back almost at right angles, they were formed in a narrow salient, with their left flank
completely exposed. The trench facing east was open to enfilade fire from both flanks;
the flanking trench, facing south, was exposed to reverse fire from the recently cap-

---

* The attack against the 9th Infantry Brigade was delivered by the German 4th Guards
Brigade. A German brigade at this date consisted of six battalions and fourteen machine guns.
The strength of a battalion was 26 officers, 1050 other ranks. The 4th Guards Brigade had been
brought up fresh, and in full strength.

62   THE FIFTH IN THE GREAT WAR.

Map No. 8   tured position. A most gallant counter-attack by two companies of the Royal Scots   12th Nov., 1914
Fusiliers* failed to recover the lost position ; and, brought to a standstill, they were forced to dig in on a line about 300 yards to the left rear of the FIFTH. A later effort by a company of the Duke of Wellington's met with no better success. Gordon represented the urgent need for steps to be taken to remedy a situation which threatened momentarily to render his position untenable, but there were no troops available to send to his relief. Lieut.-Colonel McMahon, of the Royal Fusiliers, had been killed, and there remained with that battalion but two subalterns of all its officers ; the Royal Scots Fusiliers had been already exhausted in the counter-attack, and the Lincolnshire, in occupation of the trenches to the right rear, had repulsed the German attack, but needed all their resources to maintain their position. Brigadier-General Shaw, himself wounded, had been compelled to hand over command to Lieut.-Colonel Douglas Smith, of the Royal Scots Fusiliers. Providentially, three companies of the 2/Royal Sussex Regiment now reported to 9th Brigade Headquarters. A direct reinforcement of a position so precarious as that held by Gordon was, however, judged to be merely risking the loss of further troops. So long as the FIFTH could hold their own, they would stand as an embarrassment to the enemy, though it was scarcely hoped that they would not ultimately be overwhelmed. The Sussex companies, accordingly, were held in reserve, while the FIFTH were left to their own resources to fight in a position which events had converted into a detached post in advance of the general line of defence. Captain Gordon had to find what comfort he could in an injunction to "hold on at all costs." Such success as could be claimed by the enemy on the front of the 9th Brigade had been obtained at heavy cost. Their infantry during the afternoon were fully taken up in resisting counter-attack and consolidating the positions gained, and at nightfall the situation on the 9th Brigade front remained unchanged from that which had developed after the German assault of the early morning.

At 1 a.m. on the 12th November, yet another attempt was made to recapture the trenches lost on the left flank, but with no success. Dawn found the 9th Brigade in touch with the 15th Brigade, on the right, and with the 1st Brigade, on the left. A company of the Sussex, pushed up to the right of the Scots Fusiliers, who were now in position immediately south of the Menin road, made the defence slightly more secure to the left rear of the FIFTH, but Gordon's detachment in its isolated position remained a subject of acute anxiety to Brigade Headquarters throughout the day. A renewal of the German attack was expected, and with it its annihilation. In anticipation of this event, the Grenadier Guards, who had been placed at the disposal of the 9th Brigade during the afternoon, were employed with the Royal Engineers in entrenching a second line of defence in rear of Gordon's position. In the course of the day two out of the three machine guns of the FIFTH were put out of action by rifle fire. One, riddled by bullets, was completely destroyed ; the other was temporarily repaired by Serjeant Crouch, who throughout the whole of this period had been rendering splendid services to his commander. At 7 p.m. German machine guns opened from both flanks, in the hope of driving the FIFTH back by fire from a trench that they did not venture again to assault. But the fire, which was high, proved ineffective, and darkness found Gordon's men still firmly holding the position. During the night, which passed quietly, Captain Gordon received the thanks and

---

* This battalion, originally left with the Indian Corps at Neuve Chapelle, had recently rejoined the 9th Brigade.

13th Nov., 1914 congratulations of the Commanders of both the Division and the Brigade. But no way could yet be found to relieve his sorely tried men, whom dawn of the 13th November found still in their isolated position, closely hemmed in on both flanks by the enemy. Throughout the day, the trench was heavily bombarded at frequent intervals by the enemy's artillery, and first acquaintance was made with the deafening detonation and volumes of black smoke of the German close range mortars. The garrison also suffered the demoralising experience on three or four occasions of sustaining casualties from short shells of their own supporting artillery. Yet, when darkness closed on an anxious day, Gordon, himself unscathed, together with those of his men who had escaped injury, still stood firm in the defence of the now shattered trench.

Map No. 8

But there are limits to human endurance. Major Yatman, in forwarding a report from Captain Gordon on the evening of the 13th November, represented that "Captain Gordon and his men have had practically no sleep for five nights. Captain Gordon is quite worn out and his men fall asleep standing under fire." He strongly urged the necessity for their relief. The troops for this could not be found, and it was at last decided that the position must be abandoned, and the line drawn back to pass through Herenthage Château. At 8 p.m. Brigade Headquarters issued orders for the evacuation of the trench and the withdrawal of the garrison, which for six days had resisted every effort of the enemy to oust them from their position. To effect the withdrawal unobserved, with the enemy within thirty yards of either flank, constituted a difficult and delicate operation. Yet, at 11 p.m. that night, it was successfully accomplished without a shot being fired, and the FIFTH were withdrawn to Brigade reserve.

The position now occupied by the 9th Brigade was something as follows. Its left rested on the Menin road, from which the main front line ran south, to pass just east of Herenthage Château, situated 180 yards from the road. Some 80 yards east of the Château, which itself was occupied, a stable building with a short length of trench on either side was held as an advanced post. In rear of the front line, the FIFTH as reserve were placed in a switch trench north-west of the Château. About noon on the 14th November, a determined attack by the enemy carried the advanced position and thrust our troops back from the portion of the main front line to the south of the Château. The loss of the stable buildings was serious, as it gave the enemy command of our trenches in enfilade, a point of which they took immediate advantage by opening a galling rifle fire. The Royal Scots Fusiliers were ordered to counter-attack to recover the lost position, and "W" Company of the FIFTH, about 60 strong, was detailed to support the attack. The front line was recaptured, but the attack failed to eject the Germans from the stables. At 7 p.m. the 2/K.O.Y.L.I., who had now taken over the recaptured line, attempted to recover the stables; the enemy remained immovable. Plans were then made to renew the attack during the night with the support of a field gun, manhandled to within a short distance of the stable buildings. But before the orders for this operation could be issued, report reached Brigade Headquarters that the enemy had again captured the trench to the south of the Château, and had succeeded in carrying the Château itself. The situation was now very grave. At 4 a.m., however, the K.O.Y.L.I., by a brilliant counter-attack retook the Château and the trench, and the operation against the stables could now proceed. The field gun was brought into position, and "Z" Company of the FIFTH was ordered to furnish the assaulting party. At 5.45 a.m. the field gun fired four rounds in rapid succession into the building, and immediately C.S.M. Gillborn of the FIFTH led a party of 50 men to the assault. Gaining his objective, Gillborn fell mortally wounded, and fifty per cent. of his men were put out of action. But his gallant leadership had resulted in the capture of the position, the occupation of which was so vital to the whole of the defence.* Gillborn, at the outbreak of war a young serjeant, had from the first day of entering battle shown such outstanding qualities as a leader as to give promise of a brilliant future had he been spared to wear the D.C.M., which was awarded in recognition of the gallant action that led to his death. Another who fell this day was Corporal Fisk, whose gallantry at Neuve Chapelle on the 26th October has been recorded on a previous page. He also was granted the D.C.M., but the announcement of the award was not made till 3 months later (26th February).

Following the episode of the early morning, the 15th November passed very quietly on the front of the FIFTH, and after dark the Battalion was relieved by the 5th Dragoon Guards and withdrawn to reserve in dug-outs east of Hooge village.* The approximate fighting strength of the Battalion on the 16th November is recorded in the War Diary of the 9th Brigade as 170 all ranks; that of the Brigade, including two attached battalions, was but 1385—an average of less than 300 per battalion.

Though attack and counter-attack had continued at Herenthage and at other points on the British front, they were but local incidents. The vast attack of the 11th November had represented the supreme effort of the Germans in the First Battle of Ypres, and with its failure they had for the time shot their bolt. The war was now to become stabilised on the positions in which the shattered and exhausted units of the opposing forces faced each other. A hard frost had already set in, and the efforts of the opponents were to be directed to securing what comfort they could for themselves, whilst increasing the discomfort of their enemy in the miseries of trench warfare during the fast approaching winter.

Arrangements had now been made for the French to take over the line from the British in the Ypres Salient. The FIFTH, after a further two days' tour in the trenches at Herenthage, were relieved on the night of the 20th November and marched by Ypres and Dickebusch to billets in Westoutre. During the six days' rest accorded to the Battalion two large drafts arrived from home: on the 21st, 5 officers and 295 other ranks; on the 26th, 2 officers and 111 other ranks. These reinforcements were of very good material, and included three experienced officers—Captain Festing, Lieutenant Watkin, who was returning from a few weeks' sick leave, and Lieutenant Dorman-Smith, who had been wounded at Le Cateau. The Battalion had weathered the storm, and with this fresh strength and the rest given to the men who had been in battle, was fit again to take the field. During the rest period, the Battalion was visited by Major-General Haldane, who at this date took over command of the 3rd Division from Major-General Wing, and by the Corps Commander. It was also inspected by Field Marshal Sir John French, who praised its recent conduct and expressed his thanks for the services it had rendered. In anticipation of what lay before them in the winter, the men were practised in the construction of trenches

---

* The Official History credits the field gun with having accounted for most of the enemy's garrison, and dismisses somewhat lightly the part played by the assaulting infantry. Had the casualties suffered by the infantry been known, this view would surely not have been taken. " Z " company suffered 30 casualties on this day, of which nearly all were sustained in the above episode.

* It is recorded that an application was received on this day by the C.O. from 2nd-Lieut. John Lawson (Special Reserve), that he might be granted a commission in the Regular Army on the grounds that " he wanted to go on soldiering "—a naïve and somewhat surprising petition from one who had just returned from the thick of the fighting at Herenthage !

27th Nov., 1914 and breastworks, while for their comfort leather jerkins were issued and various devices for the installation of charcoal braziers in the trenches were studied. Demonstrations of bomb throwing were given; rifles overhauled, and musketry practice carried out. In these activities and the reorganisation of the Battalion the days passed only too quickly, and on the 27th November the FIFTH moved again to the line.

Map No. 8

On the withdrawal of the troops of the I. and II. Corps from the Salient, the British Expeditionary Force had been reorganised, units reverting to their appropriate formations and commanders. The French, who had hitherto stood between the right and left wings of the Expeditionary Force, were to be relieved by the British in the line to the south of Kemmel. By these reliefs a compact British front would be established from La Bassée to a point opposite Wytschaete at the southern shoulder of the Ypres Salient. After its recapture on the 1st November, Wytschaete had again fallen into the hands of the Germans. The trenches just west of this village had been recently taken over from the French by the 2/Highland Light Infantry, who were relieved by the FIFTH on the 27th November. The so-called "trenches" were found to be merely a series of unconnected excavations, between which there was no covered communication, and to which there was no protected approach. Carpeted with layers of straw mingled with mud, they were filthy in the extreme, while the unburied bodies of unfortunate French soldiers which lay around added to the depressing conditions of the position.

The life that the Battalion led during the next few days was but typical of what it was to endure for the greater part of the long drawn out trench warfare that continued for the next four years. It was a life which, between the major events of the War, became so familiar to those who survived for any length of time as almost to be accepted as their normal existence. As the War dragged on, the constant introduction of new weapons of attack necessitated continual developments to meet them on the part of the defence; and the static nature of the fighting became productive of the organisation of an elaborate defensive system with deep timbered dugouts, concrete strong points and covered communications. Improvements, moreover, were not to be concerned only with providing protection to the garrisons, but also with securing for the men such measure of comfort as conditions would allow. But in this winter of 1914/15 trench warfare was in its infancy; and though the men manning the trenches were spared from the terrors of the more formidable weapons of later days, it is unquestionable that the conditions of life in the trenches were more severe during this early period than at any later time. The first tour of the FIFTH in the trenches on the Kemmel front lasted for five days. The weather was bitterly cold, with occasional rain, and sniping was engaged in continuously by both sides. The proximity of the opposing front lines, however, as was the case in many sectors where the trenches could not be taken in enfilade by artillery, largely secured their garrisons from shell fire. The high angle fire, necessary under such conditions for searching the opposing trenches, had already been realised by the enemy with his trench mortars, to which rifle grenades were shortly to be added. But it seems that neither of these weapons were employed on the Kemmel front at this time. Though work could only be carried on after dark, an immense improvement in the trenches was made; lateral communications were dug, and traverses and rear cover constructed. Night patrols found the enemy busily engaged in similar activities. The cover thus secured generally, gave adequate protection against the German snipers, and the casualties had only amounted to 3 other ranks killed and 1 wounded when the Battalion was relieved on the 1st December to return to billets at Westoutre.

Map No. 8   On the 3rd December the King visited the Western Front. At a parade held   3rd Dec., 1914
at Locre His Majesty presented Distinguished Conduct Medals, which had been awarded to the following of the FIFTH :—No. 2558 Corporal Bentley, the particulars of whose action have not been recorded ; No. 8473 Serjeant J. Squires, for exceptional gallantry under machine gun fire at Vailly ; No. 1822 Corporal J. G. Pickering, for gallantry in the attack on Pont du Hem on the 15th October ; and C.S.M. Gillborn, who had met his death in circumstances which have been related. Bentley was the only one to receive the medal in person. Squires had been wounded and evacuated to England, and Pickering had died of wounds received on the 7th December. In the afternoon the Battalion lined the road to cheer His Majesty as he drove slowly past in company with the Prince of Wales and Sir Horace Smith-Dorrien.

During the past two months in which Major Yatman had been officiating in command, the strain of battalion command was, perhaps, as great as at any period of the War. Right well had he stood up to it, when, on the 12th December, he was relieved of the responsible position he had held by the return of Lieut.-Colonel Ainslie from sick leave in England. The Germans shelled Battalion Headquarters the same night with serious results. "W" Company and a platoon of "X," which were located there in reserve, had five men killed and eight wounded.

Reliefs in the 3rd Division at this time were arranged to give 3 days in the trenches, 3 days in immediate reserve at Locre, and 3 days in reserve further back at Westoutre, to each Brigade in turn. The FIFTH had three tours in the trenches during December. The dispositions of the Battalion in defence at this period might astonish those whose experience was limited to the later days of the War, and probably provoke their criticism. A length of 560 yards of front line trench was manned by 395 men ; 130 yards of support trench by 50, and 200 yards of reserve dug-outs were occupied by 180. In the later days of the War it became customary to hold the front line lightly by posts at wide intervals, while the bulk of the garrison was kept further back. But methods of attack and defence develop by continual reaction, the one to the other ; and, before condemning a system of defence in which the front line was crowded with men, the conditions under which this obtained should first be considered. In this first winter, the opposing forces, covered only by the slight obstacle of a weak wire entanglement, were face to face in assault positions. Machine guns were few, and a sudden strong assault could be stopped only by the development of intense rifle fire. Except by maintaining a strong rifle garrison in the front line, this could not be realised ; for, even should time allow of the reinforcement of the front line, covered approaches by which supports could be brought forward were rarely available. Moreover, at this date there were not the same objections as developed later to a thickly held front line. Firstly, as already pointed out, the very proximity of the opponent to his enemy often made it impossible to bring artillery fire on to the front line ; secondly, short-range high-angle mortars had attained neither the numbers nor the efficiency of later years. It was the increase in the number, weight and accuracy of trench mortars, and their power to destroy trenches, that was to compel the thinning out of front line garrisons. Fortunately for the defence, this had by then become possible, as strong belts of wire had grown up which made a sudden surprise assault impossible, and communication trenches had been constructed by which supports could be brought up rapidly under cover to the reinforcement of the front line. On the other hand, the later system, whereby the bulk of the infantry of the defence was withdrawn to rear positions, laid them open to the ever increasing weight of the enemy's artillery, and this again led to the necessity for deep dug-outs

"MULE."

[Imperial War Museum.—Crown Copyright.

12th Dec., 1914 for the protection of the garrison. Later still, the constant destruction of communication trenches by heavy trench mortars and artillery required the construction of underground approaches for supports to reach the forward positions. But these developments in defence were still a long way off when the FIFTH were in the Kemmel sector. They have been referred to here only to emphasise the fact that methods of defence are conditioned solely by those of the particular form of offence which they are designed to counter, and to explain and justify dispositions which, under the conditions of 1914/15, were as sound as those of later years would then have been unsuitable.

Map No. 8

It was believed, however, that the Germans were not holding their front line in the same strength as we were, and this had encouraged the idea that a surprise attack might secure a lodgment in their trenches. The French had accordingly planned an attack for the recapture of Wytschaete and the subsequent clearing of the Germans from the commanding ground of the Messines Ridge. To assist this attack it was desired to obtain a footing in a small wood opposite the left of the 3rd Division. On the 8th December a first attempt by two companies of the Lincolnshire to secure this objective had been repulsed with heavy loss. The element of surprise could therefore no longer be reckoned on. In fact, the bombardment of the FIFTH on the 12th December, which has already been related, was an indication that the Germans were nervous about the intentions of the British in this quarter, for it was there that the Battalion had taken over the line. Nevertheless, it was decided that a second attempt should be made to secure the objective, and a stronger attack by the 2/Royal Scots and 1/Gordon Highlanders was ordered for the 14th. The FIFTH, whose trenches represented the starting line of the Gordons, were ordered to withdraw from the line at 3.30 a.m., after leaving the trenches lightly held by the battalion machine guns and a small detachment of riflemen, and to move to Kemmel. Captain Watkin, the Machine Gun Officer of the FIFTH, who watched the attack delivered by the Gordons at daybreak, has recorded the gallant manner in which they attempted a hopeless task.* Suffering heavy casualties in their endeavour to cross the 250 yards of ground, deep in mud, which intervened between our line and the German trenches, they were brought to a standstill within fifty yards of the enemy's position. Here, throughout the day, they remained pinned to such cover as they could find, under a galling fire. At dusk, perforce leaving their dead and wounded in the terrible territory of No Man's Land, the two officers who had alone survived of the nine that had led forward the attack withdrew the remnants of the attacking troops to the starting line of the early morning. The Royal Scots had succeeded in carrying their objective, but on their left the main attack by the French made little progress, and nothing had been gained to compensate for the heavy losses. On the relief of the Gordons by the 4/Middlesex Regiment, the machine guns and rifle detachment of the FIFTH were ordered to rejoin the Battalion at Kemmel, which they reached at midnight, worn out by the long and anxious hours they had passed in the front line.

Beyond a dismal tale of casualties, there is little to relate of the life of the Battalion during the following six or seven weeks. Each tour in the trenches was but a repetition of that which had preceded it—sniping, desultory shell fire, which occasionally increased to a sharp bombardment, and continual work on the defences in the misery of mud and water knee deep. Christmas Day, brightened by a half-pound of plum pudding for every officer and man, was spent in billets at Locre. On the 30th

---

* *St. George's Gazette*, Vol. XXXIII. p. 36.

December the battalion paraded at a fighting strength of 772 men for inspection by General Smith-Dorrien.* Casualties during December amounting to 8 other ranks killed, Lieutenant Dorman Smith (for the second time) and 11 other ranks wounded, could not be counted as unduly high. The greater number of these occurred during reliefs, or in carrying parties moving by night across the open, which at this period was still the only method of approaching the front line. New Year's Eve found the Battalion once again moving to the trenches. Steadily throughout January the FIFTH did four days' duty in the trenches and were four days in billets at Westoutre or Locre, where on occasion they were held in readiness to move at fifteen minutes' notice. Casualties during this month were heavier, amounting to 1 officer and 28 other ranks killed, and 50 other ranks wounded. The officer included among these was Captain Watkin, who, as M.G. Officer, had rendered splendid service to the Battalion, and to whose diary, which appeared by instalments in the *St. George's Gazette* between August, 1914, and February, 1915,* this History owes a great debt. Sickness also took a heavy toll of the Battalion in January, but drafts from England of 4 officers and 235 other ranks were sufficient to make this good.

After two further tours in the line, during which it lost 5 killed and 14 wounded, the Battalion was again withdrawn to reserve at Locre on the 13th February in expectation of taking over the same trenches after the normal four days' rest. But the stay of the FIFTH in the Kemmel Sector was now to be brought abruptly to an end. At 11 a.m. on the 17th February orders were suddenly received to stand by in readiness to turn out at short notice. At 12.30 p.m. word came to fall in, and at 1.30 p.m. the Battalion marched with the 9th Brigade via Dickebusch to Ypres, where it was quartered in the Cavalry Barracks.

Now, the events which had led to this sudden movement represent an essential part of this History, for they had occurred on the front of the 28th Division, which included the 2nd Battalion of the FIFTH. The 9th Infantry Brigade for a brief period was to be attached to this Division, and for the first time since the Battle of Salamanca the two battalions of the Regiment were to find themselves serving under the same Divisional Commander. Before the close of the next chapter, which at its opening will bring the 2nd Battalion on to the scene, the 1st will again enter, and for a space it will be possible and convenient to deal simultaneously with the actions of both.

---

* " Feeding Strength " was reckoned at " Fighting Strength " plus 101.

* The censorship which permitted publication in these early months was not so rigorous as in the later days of the war.

CHAPTER VI.

The Second Battalion enters the War.

Trench Warfare at Ypres.

1st and 2nd Battalions together in the 28th Division.

JULY, 1914—7TH APRIL, 1915.

5th Aug., 1914

In the opening chapter of this History we left the 2nd Battalion of the FIFTH in the hill station of Sabathu anxiously awaiting news of the critical events which were occurring in Europe. All leave had been cancelled, and the Battalion had been concentrated in readiness for such duties as it might be called on to undertake. The uncertainty in which all at this period were living, and the difficulty of predicting the future, are shown clearly in the Notes of the 2nd Battalion that appeared in the *St. George's Gazette* during the next four or five months. In July, it will be remembered, the Battalion had been "looking forward to a pleasant cold weather in Delhi." The Notes of the next month are written on the 5th August, just after the receipt of news of the declaration of War. In September the correspondent announces the despatch of the Lahore Division to France, and laments that the Battalion, being supernumerary to the strength of the Division, has been split up into detachments to replace the troops who have left for the seat of war. In the next number the Notes, dated 1st October, are written in the same strain. All hope of taking part in the War seems to have been abandoned. It should be remembered that at this date Turkey still remained neutral, and that operations had not yet spread beyond the limits of Europe and the German colonies. On the Western Front, it seemed, the tide had turned against the enemy. Time had been gained to put in motion the "Russian steam roller," and one is led to think that the 2nd Battalion shared the popular belief that the ponderous advance of this monstrous machine would seal the doom of Germany. For we learn that in early October "we had finally made up our minds that we were destined to remain in India and not go to the War, we had settled down to polo, football, etc., as best we could, and were looking forward to being together, and having as good a time as possible later on at Delhi." How many battalions during the next eighteen months were similarly to despair of their services ever being required in the War—battalions whose ranks were to be decimated in battle time and again before the final victory was won ! Yet, there could have been none destined to suffer more devastating casualties than those that the Fates had decreed for the 2nd Battalion of the FIFTH.

On the 16th October, suddenly and unexpectedly, came news that the Battalion was to be sent to England to equip itself for joining the British forces on the Western Front. It was to be in readiness to sail from India within a week. All detachments were immediately called in, private property was stored or sold, and the Battalion hastily packed up. There were still, however, some weeks to wait, and it was not till the 20th November that the 2/FIFTH sailed from Karachi in H.M.T. *Nevasa*, one of a convoy of nine ships, which later joined a larger convoy from Bombay and headed for Europe. The first glimpse of the transformation in scene that had been effected by the War was obtained on passing through the Suez Canal. The peace 16th Oct., 1914 and silence always associated with the passage of the Canal was now broken by the constant whirr of aeroplanes passing overhead, while the desolate banks between which the Battalion had passed but twelve months before were now thronged with troops from the fortified posts that had been established for the defence of this vital artery of communication. At Malta the ships bound for Marseilles parted company from those destined for England, and the latter made the passage to Gibraltar independently, again to form convoy for the last stage of the voyage. Having disembarked at Plymouth on the 22nd December, the 2/FIFTH were moved by rail to Winchester to form part of the 84th Infantry Brigade (Brigadier-General Wintour) of the 28th Division, which was in process of formation under Major-General E. S. Bulfin. The strength of the Battalion on arrival at Winchester was 26 officers and 903 other ranks.

The conditions under which the troops had to live during the next ten days were a severe trial to men who but a week or two before had been sweltering in the heat of the Red Sea. The camp at Hursley Park, in which the Battalion was accommodated, was ankle deep in mud. The bitterly cold and wet weather which prevailed culminated on the 28th December in a violent squall which partially wrecked the camp. Fortunately, on the 4th January, it became possible to move the Battalion to billets in Winchester, where its Headquarters were established in the Workhouse.

It will be remembered that the 1st Battalion, though not fully accustomed to the four company organisation that had been recently introduced in England, had at least had practical experience of it in training before being thrown into war. It is difficult to determine why in India, where an approximate organisation already existed in the Indian Army, British battalions had been made to adhere to the old eight company system. Yet such was the case. The 2nd Battalion had embarked at Karachi under the old organisation, and had been required under the unfavourable conditions of a voyage on a troopship to reorganise into four companies. On arrival in England the five days' leave which was granted in turn to 25% of the Battalion made it even more difficult to accustom those concerned to a new system of organisation and command. In such circumstances, it was not possible to devote to it the same careful consideration as it would have received under peace conditions. For there were other distractions apart from all the work of clothing and equipping the Battalion for war in Europe. On reading the official correspondence and orders that passed at this period, one discerns a very real anxiety at the War Office with regard to the possibility of a raid by the enemy on the coast. One also gains a realisation of the difficulty of finding troops armed and equipped to deal with such a contingency. The 28th Division was required to hold 8000 infantry in readiness for despatch in the event of an enemy raid. General Bulfin reports on Christmas Day that not more than 7000 men armed with the Mark VII. rifle are at his disposal; of these, 5000 would have 100 rounds, and he is "trying to obtain ammunition for the remainder." No artillery or 1st Line transport were yet available, and only one day's rations could be issued.

The necessity for moving the troops from the sodden camps to billets had for the moment checked progress, but the greater facilities afforded by the acquirement of proper store rooms more than counterbalanced the temporary delay, and the first week of the New Year saw mobilisation rapidly approaching completion. On the 12th January, the 28th Division, completely mobilised, was drawn up on Fawley Down for inspection by H.M. The King. On the 16th January, in bright sunshine, the 2nd Battalion of the FIFTH marched with the 84th Infantry Brigade to South-

16th Jan., 1915 ampton, where it embarked at a strength of 25 officers and 970 other ranks on the Map No. 8 s.s. *Australind*. During that night the transport lay off the Isle of Wight before crossing on the following day to Havre, where at 9.30 p.m. on the 18th the 2/FIFTH entrained for Hazebrouck. On arrival at its destination the Battalion marched to billets about two miles west of Strazeele. Here, in preparation for taking their place in the line, senior officers were given short tours in the trenches of the 27th Division, while companies, in the intervals of route marching, were practised in the construction of field works.

There could be no stronger contrast than that between the conditions under which the 2nd Battalion was to enter the War in Flanders and those under which the 1st Battalion had first met the enemy less than six months before. Whereas the senior battalion had first come under fire in the familiar surroundings of the outskirts of a thickly populated mining town, the 2nd Battalion was to suffer its first casualties in the mud and misery of a trench system. While in the opening days of the War the troops suffered from the intense heat of a brilliant summer, the hardships now to be endured were those of cold and wet in the close confines of life in the trenches. The 1st Battalion, after a brief period of suspense, had viewed masses of German infantry shortly after the bursting of the first shell; the 2nd Battalion was to move direct to within a distance of a stone's throw of this same enemy, yet for weeks to get no glimpse of him.

Orders had been issued for the 28th Division to relieve the 31st French Division, which was in occupation of the line astride the Ypres Canal in the southern portion of the Salient. A general description of the Sector and of the dispositions that were to be adopted by the 28th Division for its occupation may make it easier for the reader to follow the events of the next few weeks, as, during this period, both battalions of the FIFTH were to be engaged at various points on the front of the Division. From the right of the Sector, which was situated south-east of St. Eloi, the front line ran east by north for 1000 yards; then, turning north-east, it crossed the Canal d'Ypres 600 yards east of Lock 7 Bis, and continued in the same direction till it reached the Ypres-Courtrai railway just east of Verbrandenmolen; here it turned east to face Hill 60, recently captured by the enemy from the French, and to include Zwarteleen. East of Zwarteleen, the line resumed its general (north-easterly) trend, the left of the Sector being situated about 500 yards from the village.* The 28th Division arranged for the occupation of the line by two brigades, of which the right brigade was to be in position astride the Canal.

Recent attacks and counter-attacks in the neighbourhood of the Canal, which had resulted in the loss and recovery by the French of various portions of the line, left the 28th Division, on taking over, in some doubt as to actual positions to be occupied. This was to lead to the continuation of confused fighting for the capture or recapture of trenches, in this quarter. The FIFTH, however, were not to be involved in this at the outset, as the 84th Brigade had been allotted to the northern section of the Divisional front. The defence scheme for this section placed two battalions in the line, one battalion in support, north and south of Zillebeke, and held the brigade reserve in Ypres. On the 2nd February the 84th Brigade was conveyed by motor transport to Vlamertinghe, whence its battalions, having debussed,

---

* At a later date the front of the 28th Division was to be reduced by S. Eloi and the trenches to the south of it being transferred to the 27th Division. This, however, was not to affect the general dispositions, and does not directly concern the history of the FIFTH.

72   THE FIFTH IN THE GREAT WAR.

Map Nos 8 & 9   moved forward to the line. The 2/FIFTH, as the left battalion of the brigade, relieved   2nd Feb., 1915
the French 95th Infantry Regiment in trenches to the south and south-east of Zillebeke.
The line taken over, 1140 yards in length, extended from opposite Hill 60 to the
left boundary of the 28th Division. To those accustomed to the narrower fronts
allotted to formations in the later days of the War the length of line which the Battalion
was required to hold may seem excessive. But, as explained in the previous chapter,
dispositions in defence at this earlier period were ruled by considerations which differed
from those that in the later phases made depth both possible and desirable. In this
first tour in the trenches, the 2/FIFTH placed 3½ companies and all four machine guns
in the front line. The trenches on the right of the Battalion were held by the
2/Cheshire Regiment of the 84th Brigade, and a squadron of the 2/Life Guards of the
7th Cavalry Brigade occupied the line on their left.

    The main occupation of the Battalion, after taking over, was the repair and
improvement of the trenches, which were found in wretched condition. On the 3rd
February the position was subjected to a sharp bombardment. "B" Company,
situated in a dangerous salient, were the chief sufferers; the machine gun in their
trenches was damaged, and in addition to several other casualties Lieutenant Heyder
and 2nd-Lieutenant Mortished were wounded. On the following day the Battalion
was relieved by the 1/Welch Regiment and withdrawn to the supporting position at
Zillebeke. In this first brief tour in the trenches the Battalion's casualties, 6 other
ranks killed—2 officers and 27 other ranks wounded—had been severe. They had
been for the greater part inflicted by artillery fire, which constituted the main
action of the opposing sides on this portion of the front. It was stated in a
previous chapter that the garrisons of front line trenches in close proximity enjoyed
a certain immunity from artillery fire; and this was true where direct, overhead fire
alone was possible. But in the trenches at Ypres the garrisons in many places were
exposed to enfilade and even reverse fire from the enemy's artillery, a fact which
was largely responsible for the evil reputation gained by the Salient. In the course
of two further short tours in the front line during the next week the Battalion lost a
third officer in 2nd-Lieutenant Corbet-Singleton, who was wounded, but casualties
in general were lighter.

    On the 11th February the Battalion was withdrawn to reserve at Ouderdom,
two miles south-west of Vlamertinghe, where it was accommodated in huts. An
important feature of duty in reserve was the opportunity that was afforded for a bath
and a change of clothing. Advantage was taken of the chance for this on the 14th.
The bulk of the Battalion managed to get through with it, but " D " Company still
remained unwashed and unchanged when sudden orders were received to fall in and
march to Ypres. The events which were responsible for " D " Company's misfortune
were as follows. To the south of the canal an attack had been delivered against the
3/Middlesex, of the 85th Brigade, and one of their companies had been driven from a
position known as O Trench. The right of the battalion still held fast, but a neighbouring trench, which had been garrisoned by troops of the 27th Division,* had also
been captured by the Germans. The 85th Brigade had been ordered to re-establish
the situation before daylight on the 15th, and the 2/FIFTH had been lent to the Brigadier
to support the operation. On arrival at Ypres, the Battalion accordingly was ordered
forward to the section of the 85th Brigade. After spending the afternoon in support

---

    * 27th Division had now taken over S. Eloi and trenches just east of that village—see Note
page 73.

Map No. 9.

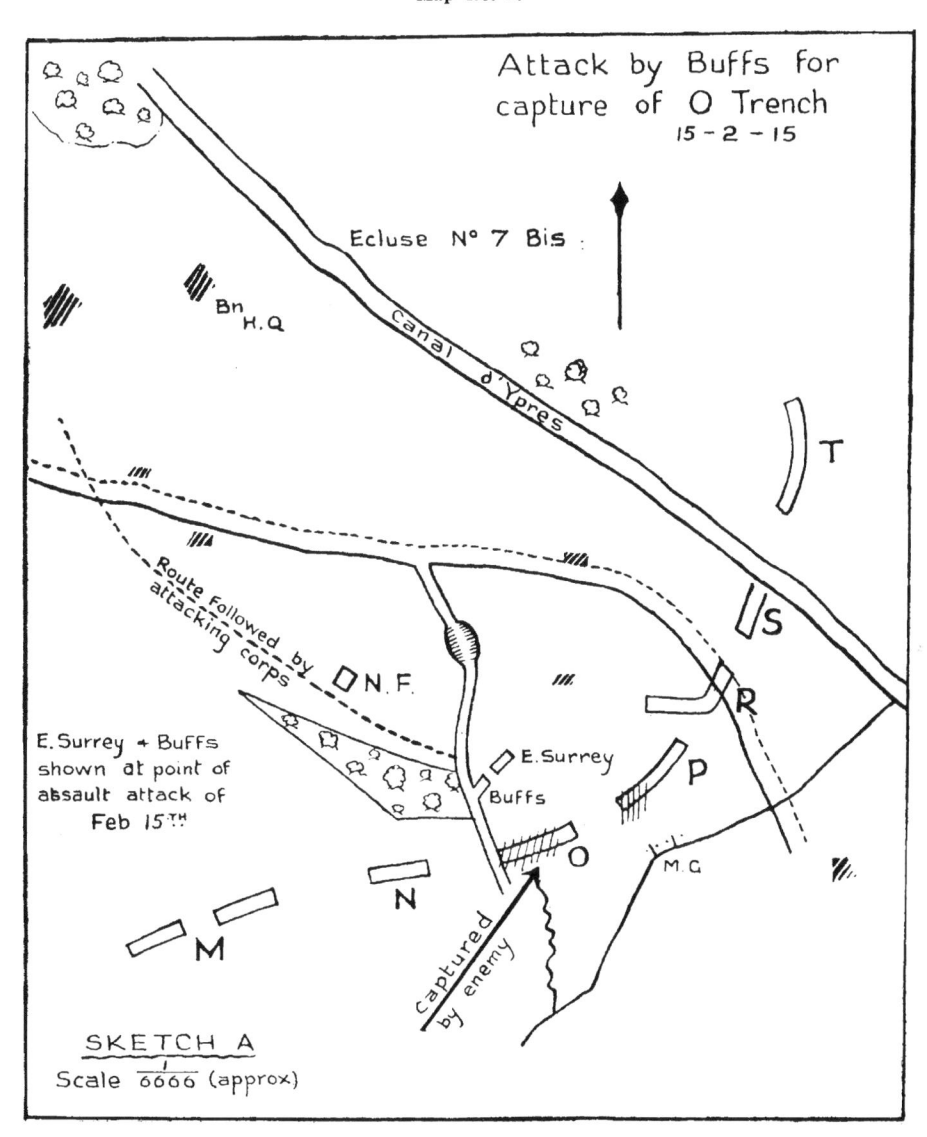

Attack by Buffs for capture of O Trench
15-2-15

SKETCH A
Scale 1/6666 (approx)

trenches about half a mile south of the Canal, the companies were moved after dark to dug-outs on the Canal bank. A counter-attack before dawn, in which the FIFTH were not actively employed, failed to eject the enemy from the captured positions, and the Battalion was retained in support on the Canal bank throughout the 15th February, suffering several casualties from shell fire during the day.

A further counter-attack, to be delivered by the 2/Buffs and 2/East Surrey, under the command of Lieut.-Colonel Geddes of the Buffs, was now planned for the night of the 15/16th. The 2/FIFTH (less two companies) was required to support this operation. "A" and "B" companies, who were not to take part, were moved back after dark to Château Rosendal.* The two attacking battalions assembled on the line of the Ypres—S. Eloi road, from which they moved forward in the pitch dark to deploy in a position about 150 yards north of O Trench. The FIFTH, following in rear, were halted fifty yards from the position of deployment. Here, in ignorance of the progress of the attack, they could but lie down in the open and await events. That the enemy had been alarmed was soon notified by the opening of heavy shell fire on the supporting position. The stoutest troops may well become demoralised in a situation in which they are called on to remain motionless under shell fire from which they can find no protection. Realising this, Lieut.-Colonel Enderby coolly walked down the line of the companies, reassuring the men and foretelling that the bombardment would shortly cease. In this he proved right, the fire gradually slackened ; but not before the Battalion had sustained several casualties, including Enderby himself, who, however, remained at duty.

The events that followed serve to illustrate how rash it is to look for success in an attack of this description, delivered in the dark over unknown ground and without careful arrangements for communication. Reading the reports submitted by the various units after the operation, one finds that the Buffs succeeded in carrying O Trench, but that Lieut.-Colonel Geddes realised that his battalion was too weak in numbers to consolidate the whole position. He desired, accordingly, to reinforce the Buffs from the FIFTH or the East Surrey, but could find no trace of either of these battalions. Now, of this no word came to the FIFTH, who remained in the unenviable position already described, in complete ignorance of what was transpiring to their front. Ultimately, a report came through that O Trench had been captured, and this was followed by orders for the half-Battalion to withdraw and join "A" and "B" Companies at Château Rosendal. One finds, also, that both at Brigade and Divisional Headquarters the impression had been gained that the operation had been entirely successful. As will be seen, this view was to prove unduly optimistic.

On the withdrawal of the FIFTH, both Lieut.-Colonel Enderby and his adjutant, Captain Auld, who had also been wounded, were evacuated to hospital. Major E. M. Moulton-Barrett replaced the former in command, and the duties of adjutant were taken over by Lieutenant Mahon.

On the 16th February, the 1/Suffolk of the 84th Brigade, on moving up to take over the front line, found that two-thirds of O Trench, reported as captured on the previous night, was in fact still in the hands of the Germans. Orders were issued for the FIFTH to complete the capture of the trench during the night. The Battalion

---

* Château Rosendal, in which both battalions were billeted during 1915, had been the residence of Cavaliere Ginistrelli, the owner of Signorinetta, the winner of the Derby, 1908. At a later period of the War, when the château had been reduced to ruins, the dug-outs which marked the site were known as Bedford House.

16th Feb., 1915 was deployed for attack after dark, but, before any further advance had been made, Map No. 9 the orders were cancelled owing to the failure of a preliminary operation on which ultimate success was held to depend, and the Battalion was again withdrawn to reserve. On the following day a report came through to "C" and "D" companies, in position on the Canal bank, that the Germans were believed again to be preparing to attack, and that the garrison of R Trench was short of ammunition. Captain Foster, with great promptitude, loaded a party of men with bandoliers and despatched them to the threatened point. The sequel was dramatic. Scarcely had the ammunition reached the trench and been hastily distributed, when the enemy rushed forward from their trenches to the assault. The garrison, which but ten minutes earlier would have been found with empty rifles, inflicted heavy casualties on the Germans and completely repulsed the attack.

The 84th Brigade had now taken over the right section of the Divisional front, where there had been so much recent fighting, and, on the night of the 17th February, the 2/FIFTH were moved forward to take their place again in the front line, the position allotted to them being north of the Canal. It will be remembered that it was on this day, the 17th February, that the 1st Battalion had moved with the 9th Brigade to Ypres, where we left them in the Cavalry Barracks. On the evening of the 18th they were moved forward to Château Lankhof. From there the left half-Battalion, on attachment to the 84th Brigade, was despatched under Capt. E. L. D. Forster to the forward area in which the 2nd Battalion was in position. "Y" Company took up a position in some dug-outs, about 300 yards south-east of 2nd Battalion Headquarters; "Z" Company was placed in support in some ruined buildings about 100 yards further to the rear. These companies were withdrawn at dawn to Château Rosendal, but not before a rare coincidence had nearly ended in tragedy. In the 2nd Battalion the company commanders had no knowledge of the move of the 1st Battalion to Ypres. In the companies of the 1st Battalion, which had been hustled forward to take up positions after dark, the rank and file, at any rate, were ignorant of the fact that the 2nd Battalion was close at hand. "C" Company of the latter, under command of Capt. Foster, withdrawing to reserve on relief in the trenches, was heard approaching by a piquet of "Y" Company of the former, whose commander was Capt. *Forster*. The piquet of "Y" gave the war-time challenge, "Who are you?" "C" replied, "Fifth Fusiliers." No patrols were out: the thing seemed impossible. Suspecting a trap, the piquet continued their interrogatory: "Who is your officer?" Out of the darkness came the reply, "Captain Foster." This, for Capt. *Forster's* men, clinched matters, for it *was* impossible that the considerable body of men approaching should belong to their company. They ceased to parley and opened fire. An indignant, and unmistakably English, roar, however, induced them to check their fire as the massive frame of Capt. Foster emerged from the darkness. Fortunately, no casualties had resulted and, after an exchange of compliments, the identity of each party was made clear to the other, and it was agreed to regard the incident as closed. It may be opportune to remind the reader that the re-naming of the companies in the 1st Battalion should serve to some extent to save him from the risk of similar confusion when reading the present chapter, which deals with the actions of both battalions of the FIFTH.

The 9th Brigade had now definitely taken the place of the 83rd Brigade in the 28th Division. Later in the morning of the 19th February "Y" and "Z" Companies were moved from Rosendal to Château Lankhof, to replace the right half-Battalion, which with Battalion Headquarters was withdrawn to billets in Ypres,

76   THE FIFTH IN THE GREAT WAR.

Map No. 10 This was the situation of the 1st Battalion up till noon on the 20th. Before dawn 20th Feb., 1915
on the same day the 2nd Battalion was relieved in the trenches by the 1/Suffolk and was
withdrawn to Kruisstraat. During the 48 hours they had spent in the line Lieut.
Rushbrooke had been wounded, but on the whole their tour had passed comparatively
quietly.

The 2nd Battalion, however, was to be given little rest. Hitherto the activities
of the enemy had been mainly directed against our positions to the south of the Canal.
After many conflicting reports had been received at Brigade Headquarters during the
morning of the 20th February, with regard to the situation in two trenches, Y
and Z, in the area of the 1/Welch Regiment to the north of the Canal, it was
established at 1.30 p.m. by the battalion commander, Lieut.-Colonel Marden, that
the Germans had occupied Y Trench. The 2/FIFTH were ordered to send forward
one company to join one and a half companies of the King's Own, which had been
placed under Marden's command. A first attempt to recover the lost position was
made by three platoons of the King's Own. Advancing over terribly difficult ground,
these platoons were held up by fire and failed to reach their objective. In the
meantime, orders had been issued to Brig.-General Wintour by the 28th Division
to despatch all available troops to the assistance of the Welch Regiment. Lieut.-
Colonel Marden on learning this decided to hold up further operations pending the
arrival of darkness and the promised reinforcements. Communication was slow,
but by 5.30 p.m. the 2/FIFTH had reached La Chapelle Farm in the forward area, and
the 2/Cheshire had also come forward from reserve. The situation had now changed.
The Germans were reported to have vacated Y Trench and to be in possession of
Z, which was further to the left. The Brigadier then decided personally to direct
further operations, and at 11.40 p.m. issued orders for the attack. By these, the FIFTH,
having formed up at a distance of 200 yards from their objective, in three lines on
a front of 60 yards, were to advance at 12.30 a.m. for the capture of Z Trench.
On their right the 2/Cheshire were simultaneously to effect the occupation of Y
Trench. By the original plan the attack was to be supported by artillery fire, but
this idea was later abandoned as involving too great a risk of casualties to our own
troops. Both attacking battalions were very weak in numbers. Three companies
of the 2/FIFTH, each at a strength of fifty rifles, were detailed for the attack, and were
formed up in successive lines. Punctually at the hour given they advanced to the
attack ; " A " Company (Capt. Hart) led, followed by " C " (Capt. Foster), followed
by " D " (Capt. Lamb). The advance lay through the remnants of a wood ; the
ground to be crossed had been reduced to a quagmire, which broken brushwood
and shattered tree stumps rendered even more difficult to negotiate in the dark.
Struggling forward, the leading line had succeeded in approaching unperceived to
within a close distance of the objective, when it was held up by an abbatis. An attempt
to charge over this revealed the presence of the attackers to the enemy, who
immediately opened heavy fire. Lieuts. Legard, Brownlow and Jenkins were wounded,
and the leading troops were practically wiped out. The second line, coming forward,
was unable to make any headway against the intense fire which now swept the whole
front of attack, and the attacking troops were forced to fall back. " B " Company
was then sent forward, and with such men of " A " and " D " Companies as were
available to make up the numbers to 150, renewed the attack at 2 a.m. This second
effort, however, met with no better success than the first, and resulted only in further
casualties. In the meantime the Cheshire Regiment had occupied Y Trench without
opposition. Commanded by a German trench within a distance of 30 yards, Y Trench

Map No. 10.

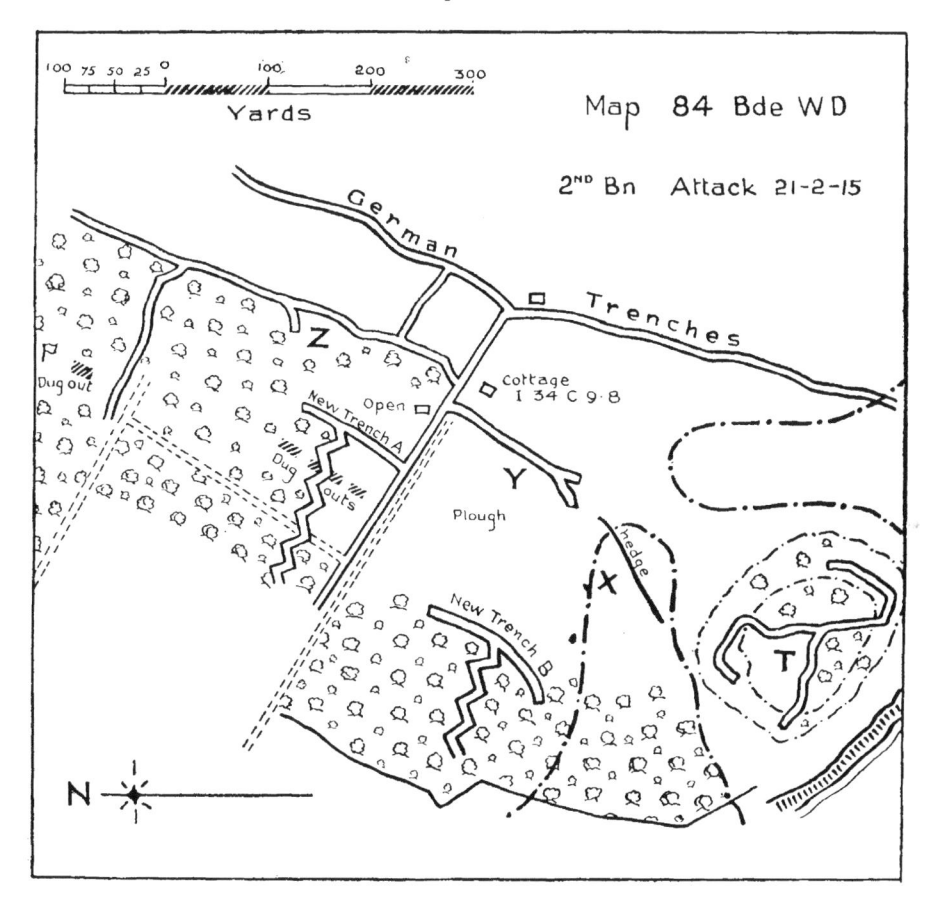

was found, however, to be little better than a ditch filled with water and dead bodies, and capable of accommodating twenty rifles at the most. It represented a position which was not only useless but dangerous to hold. In these circumstances the Brigadier ordered the occupation of positions in rear, and the 2/FIFTH were withdrawn at 5 a.m. to Kruisstraat.

In this disastrous minor operation the Battalion had lost 6 other ranks killed, 3 officers and 61 other ranks wounded, and 40 other ranks missing. In his report on the action, the Brigadier stated that no blame for the failure of the attack could be attached to the troops, who had done their utmost to achieve success. He attributed it to the difficult ground, full of holes, barred by broken trees, interspersed with dense undergrowth, over which the troops were called to advance on a dark night against a well armed and strongly entrenched enemy.* The impression one gains from messages and reports is that the operation was forced on the Brigadier, who, from the outset, regarded its success as more than doubtful, and who did not share with Divisional Headquarters the view that the recovery of the trench was of such importance as to justify the casualties that any attempt to recapture it would inevitably entail. Those who had to decide on the action to be taken in a situation such as that which had developed on the morning of the 20th February were, however, always faced by a difficult problem. Continually to lose trenches without striking a blow for their recovery must inevitably have a bad effect on the morale of one's troops ; but on the other hand, to suffer heavy casualties in attempting the impossible cannot fail to dishearten the men who survive.

Two companies of the 1st Battalion, " Y " and " Z," and two machine guns had been moved up from Ypres on the 20th, and of these " Z " had been in support both of Colonel Marden's early counter-attack and of the later attack in which the 2nd Battalion had been engaged. During the three days that the 1st Battalion had been serving on the front of the 28th Division 3 other ranks had been killed and 2nd Lieutenant Arnold and 16 other ranks wounded.

On the afternoon of the 21st the 2nd Battalion moved to the Infantry Barracks at Ypres, and the 1st Battalion took over the billets they had vacated at Kruisstraat. Both Battalions remained in billets till the 23rd February, when the 1st took over trenches south of the Canal, and the 2nd moved with the 84th Brigade to Bailleul. During the three weeks that had passed since the 84th Brigade had first entered the line, battle casualties had been very heavy, and to these had been added severe losses through sickness among the men who had been transferred from the Indian climate to serve in the trenches under the worst conditions of winter in Flanders. The 2/Fifth had lost 38 other ranks killed, 8 officers and 171 other ranks wounded, and 43 other ranks missing. On the 24th February the Battalion, which had sailed from England a month before at a strength of just under 1000 all ranks, could muster only 14 officers and 510 other ranks ; of the latter, not more than 388 were available for duty in the trenches. The other units of the Brigade had suffered no less severely, and Brigadier-General Wintour himself, whose health had broken down, was at this time invalided, being replaced by Brigadier-General L. J. Bols. It was necessary not only to give the 84th Brigade a few days' rest, but, after this was granted, to employ it on some quiet front till its ranks had been replenished. With this object the Brigade, on arrival at Bailleul, was temporarily attached to the 5th Division. So ended the third of those rare but memorable occasions in the history of the FIFTH

---

*Report by Brigadier-General Wintour.—Appx., War Diary, 28th Division.

THE FIFTH IN THE GREAT WAR. 79

24th Feb., 1915 on which the two Battalions have fought together under command of the same Brigade or Divisional Commander*; nor were they again to come into the close proximity of February, 1915, before the advent of peace brought the more normal distance of 6,000 miles between their respective headquarters.

Map No. 8

Leaving the 2nd Battalion at Bailleul, we will return to the sector of the 28th Division, in which the 1st Battalion was to remain for some weeks longer. The 1/FIFTH War Diary of the 24th February gives a very full description of the trenches taken over on the preceding night to the south of the Canal. Extracts from this will give some idea of the conditions under which the 2nd Battalion had been fighting in this same locality. " All the trenches with the exception of N trench are in very fair condition . . . but P, R, S, and N are all overlooked by German trenches . . . N trench is in an appalling condition . . . thigh deep in mud . . . what there is of parapet not bullet proof and the trench is advanced and isolated. The trenches are not deep dug but the parapets are built up with sand bags . . . the nights are at present so bright that little wiring can be done, work outside N is impossible, and as this trench contains only liquid mud very little can be done to improve it with sand bags. The approaches to all trenches are flat and open, no communication trenches are possible owing to water, thus many casualties occur when working outside the trenches and during reliefs. There are no support trenches, only the one thin line of trench. Material of all sorts is lying about everywhere, and there are many unburied dead. The dead are being buried and material is being collected and sent back or used on the spot . . . " To those who served at Ypres during the first winter of the War, the above extracts from the Battalion War Diary will be reminiscent of the general conditions that prevailed in the Salient. Since no protection was given to the cables, communication between headquarters was constantly cut. The tasks of the linesmen, to whom fell the duty of repairing the cables, and of the orderlies who had to be employed till a line was mended, can be realised from the record, in the Diary of the same month, of a journey made by an orderly bearing a message from the front line to the supporting artillery. Floundering through deep mud and water, fired at by German snipers whenever he rose from cover to pursue his way across the exposed ground, he managed to get through untouched and deliver his message, but it had taken him two hours to cover the first six hundred yards. Though the enemy made no further attempt to attack, the 1st Battalion suffered heavy casualties from snipers, bombs and artillery fire during the brief period they were in this portion of the line. On the 25th February Captain H. L. F. Nicholls fell to a stray bullet just after the relief of his company in the trenches. Captain M. Lloyd, Captain E. L. D. Forster, and Lieutenant J. F. E. Radcliffe were wounded on the 3rd March, the first-named later succumbing to his wounds; and in three short tours in the trenches, prior to the 9th Brigade being withdrawn to Divisional Reserve at Ouderdom, the casualties among other ranks of the Battalion amounted to 45 killed and 164 wounded.

After five days in reserve, the 9th Brigade was again moved up to the line, now taking over the left section of the divisional front, astride the Ypres—Courtrai railway, which, it will be remembered, had been occupied by the 84th Brigade during its first tour in early February. But, whereas the 2/FIFTH had then been placed on the left of the Brigade at Zwarteleen, the 1st Battalion now took over the right of

---

* The previous occasions were in 1779 and 1812.

the Section immediately to the south of the railway. Except on the left of the Battalion, covered approach to the trenches was afforded by wooded slopes which led to the front line, which itself ran through the shattered remnants of trees. The supports on this portion of the front were located among the woods on the reverse slope. The left trench, running south-west from the railway, could not be approached by day; but it was backed by a strong supporting position on "The Dump" which, situated just east of Verbrandenmolen, overlooked both our own and the German front line. The Dump, like Hill 60, on the other side of the railway, was not a natural feature, but had been formed from the excavation of the railway cutting which ran between these two important pieces of high ground. As was the case in the greater part of the Ypres Salient, the digging of trenches had become impossible in the water-logged ground, and the defences consisted of breast-works. To those who in England had heard much of the trench warfare that had developed, the nature of the so-called "trenches" often came as a surprise on their arrival in Flanders. To give some idea of Ypres and life in the Salient at this period, the writer, who rejoined the 1st Battalion at this date, may be permitted to continue the narrative in the first person for a brief space for the purpose of recording his own reminiscences.

"Ypres was no longer the undamaged town which the 1st Battalion had entered five months before. None the less, though the cathedral and cloth hall had been shattered by the enemy's shells; and though, as was to be seen a few weeks later, it was in the power of the Germans to reduce the whole town to ruins, it had not in general suffered much as yet, and the inhabitants were still plying a brisk trade with the troops who thronged the town. I had arrived at Ypres during the afternoon, and found the Battalion due to return to reserve from the trenches the same night. While eagerly awaiting their arrival, I passed the time strolling round the town. In the Infantry Barracks I found the upper balconies, which overlooked the square, crowded with troops watching a party of the Liverpool Scottish sounding retreat on penny whistles and tin cans. The air was filled with the chaff and laughter of the men, and it would have been difficult to believe that a war was in progress had it not been for the continuous desultory artillery fire that could be heard in the distance. I could not but shudder at the thought of the havoc that would be wrought by the arrival of a single heavy shell in the midst of this cheery, light-hearted crowd. As darkness fell there came a striking change. Artillery fire died down and was replaced by a ceaseless rattle of musketry fire from the not very distant trenches; while south, east and north the sky was lit by Verey lights rising incessantly from the opposing lines. To one who, so to speak, had not been behind the scenes to witness the simple methods by which these illuminations were produced, the scene was one of beauty and mystery. But, as I watched this narrow semi-circle of rising lights, there came to me a full sense of the peril in which Ypres already stood. Shortly after midnight the Battalion marched into Ypres, and I made my way to the Headquarter billet to greet the friends from whom I had been so long separated. Such meetings are not soon forgotten; but the incident that remains most vividly in my memory is that of being hailed by a strange individual, smothered in mud from head to foot, and whose face was adorned by a week's beard. It was not till I had looked again that I recognised in this fantastic figure an old friend who, in the happier days of peace, had been noted for being one of the smartest and most immaculate mess waiters that the 1st Battalion had ever known! But my greatest surprise was still to come. Floundering through mud and slush to take over the line a few nights later, in the

DEFENCES IN THE YPRES SALIENT.

"... the so-called 'trenches' were, in fact, breastworks."

[Imperial War Museum—Crown Copyright.

THE FIFTH IN THE GREAT WAR.   81

10th to 21st Mar, 1915

belief that I was to enter 'trenches,' I found myself in a state of complete bewilderment during the remaining hours of a pitch dark night. Dawn revealed to me that the so-called 'trenches' were, in fact, breast-works, which in places had been built up as high as seven feet above the ground and provided with fire steps."

Map No. 8

This was the general character of the front line covering Verbrandenmolen, in which the 1/FIFTH carried out two tours between the 10th and 21st March. At one point in the position the opposing trenches were no more than fifty yards apart. The front line remained fairly immune from the enemy's artillery fire, but his trench mortars were active, and the German snipers proved both vigilant and dangerous. It was by a sniper's bullet that Lieutenant Belchem, who before being commissioned had served in the ranks of the FIFTH, was killed on the 19th March, and during the two tours in this part of the line casualties among other ranks totalled 22 killed and 30 wounded. At this period the German snipers undeniably held the upper hand; for a man to raise his head above the parapet meant almost certain death. As evidence of the accuracy of their aim, the occasion on which a young Belgian artillery officer had come forward to observe the fire of his battery may be recalled. He reported to his commander that his periscope had been broken. Bidden tersely to borrow another from the British infantry, he wrung his hands and wailed down the telephone : "Mais *toutes* les périscopes sont cassées, mon commandant." This was true ; in the course of the afternoon every periscope in the trench, perhaps half a dozen in all, had been smashed by the enemy's snipers within a few seconds of being cautiously raised an inch or two above the parapet. The Battery Commander, however, was not to be deterred by trivial considerations of this kind, and decided to dispense with observation. The excitement of the shoot which followed rendered the occasion doubly memorable to the front line infantry, who for twenty minutes lay prone at the bottom of the trench while the guns fired blindly over them.

On relief in the Verbrandenmolen sector, the 1st Battalion spent five days in reserve in huts at Vlamertinghe. During this period drafts amounting to two officers and 93 other ranks joined from England. On the 25th March, the Adjutant, Captain Herbert, returned to the Battalion. His arrival was signalised by the camp being subjected, for the first time, to a brief but very unpleasant bombardment at the officers' dinner hour. Thirteen shells of high calibre burst in and around the camp, fortunately without causing any casualties.

The 9th Brigade had now once again taken over the right section of the Divisional front astride the Canal, and on the 26th the 1/FIFTH were moved to reserve in Kruisstraat, pending the relief, two days later, of the 4/Royal Fusiliers in the trenches south of the Canal. The defences had been greatly improved, and the enemy was now less active than they had previously been on this portion of the front. None the less, there still remained much work to be done, and in the course of two brief tours in the trenches the Battalion lost 6 other ranks killed and 22 wounded. Intervening days were spent in support at the two châteaux, Rosendal and Lankhof. The latter was still intact, but Rosendal had already been seriously damaged, though in one of its rooms a piano, unharmed if untuned, under the hands of Captain Sidney could for a time make war forgotten. This was to be the end of the attachment of the 1st Battalion to the 28th Division. On relief in the trenches in the early hours of the 4th April, it spent the day at Kruisstraat, marching after dark to Dickebusch. Here, once again with the 3rd Division, we will for the time leave the 1/FIFTH and revert to the doings of the 2nd Battalion.

During the period of the 1st Battalion's attachment to the 28th Division, the 2nd, whom we left at Bailleul with their new Brigadier, had remained detached to the 5th Division, where conditions proved less strenuous than those which they had recently experienced. On the 27th February, after a full week's rest, the 2/FIFTH again moved up to the front line with the 84th Brigade, which relieved the 15th Brigade of the 5th Division in the Dranoutre section, which was situated south-west of Kemmel. The front line of this section ran from a point about one mile east of Wulverghem in a direction N.N.W. and faced the Messines—Wytschaete ridge. The 2/FIFTH Headquarters were established at Lindenhoek. Weather conditions were severe, and work on the defences never ceased, but casualties were slight in this section in which the Battalion, except for one short spell in a still quieter section south of the River Douve, continued to carry out periodical tours in the trenches till the 7th April, when the 84th Brigade reverted to the 28th Division.

During this period the only day on which the Battalion sustained heavy casualties was the 12th March. On this day an attack had been planned by troops of the 3rd Division, which held the line to the north of the 5th Division. In the event of this operation proving successful, the 2/FIFTH, in position on the left of the 5th Division, was to carry the German trenches on its front. Thick fog delayed the attack and severely hampered our artillery in the preliminary bombardment. To quote the report of the C.R.A. of the 5th Division :—" Owing to the error of the gun the operation was extremely risky, but owing to the success of the registration series the chances of risk so far as could be foreseen were reduced to a minimum . . . the periscope of the forward observing officer was broken and his wire cut in several places . . . thick weather made observation from the rear most difficult." The unfortunate result of these conditions was that in " D " Company, which occupied the forward trench on the front of the 2/FIFTH, 5 other ranks were killed and 2nd Lieutenant Cooper and 24 other ranks wounded, almost all the casualties being caused by our own supporting artillery. In concluding his report the C.R.A. states :—" The 5th Divisional Artillery deplore the fact that their comrades of the infantry have suffered casualties from British shell . . . the risks were considerable, and the risk had to be taken for the sake of the infantry." These concluding remarks will be appreciated by all in the FIFTH who have witnessed the splendid devotion of the British gunners in supporting their infantry, and the terrible anxiety that besets an artillery officer when called on to carry out a task of the difficulty of that which has been related. Despite their terrible efficiency, the German gun detachments in the War could be driven from their guns : it was traditional in the British artillery that, so long as their infantry were engaged, our gunners stood to their guns to the last man. To realise the full implication of this tradition it is necessary to have seen a battery position subjected to a concentrated bombardment by the enemy—a sight that many infantrymen have never witnessed and an ordeal as severe as any that a soldier is called on to face in modern war.

Delayed till late in the afternoon, the attack of the 3rd Division failed in the end to carry its objective, and the 2/FIFTH were withdrawn after dark to Bailleul. Apart from the losses sustained on the 12th March, the battle casualties of the Battalion during the six weeks it remained with the 5th Division amounted only to 5 other ranks killed and 18 wounded. When in reserve at this time the Battalion was either in billets at Bailleul or St. Jan Cappel, or in huts near Locre. To be in reserve was by no means synonymous with being at rest. Every night parties were sent forward after dark to carry material to the trenches or to work on the defences. It

THE FIFTH IN THE GREAT WAR. 83

7th April, 1915 is recorded that, towards the end of March, a working party of 500 men of the FIFTH, Map No. 8
starting work after dark, dug a five foot communication trench to a depth of 3½ feet
for a distance of 500 yards, and was back in billets by 3 a.m. This task, which must
have demanded considerable organisation, serves as an example of how the men were
employed while "resting" in reserve.

From the size of the working party on this occasion it will be realised that
reinforcements had arrived for the Battalion. Two strong drafts had come out
early in March; and on the 7th April, when General Sir Horace Smith-Dorrien
inspected the 84th Brigade after its return to the 28th Division, the 2/FIFTH
paraded at a strength of 25 officers and 916 other ranks. A return two days later
shows the total strength of the Battalion as 994 all ranks. However, the intensive
recruiting campaign which had secured for the New Army and Territorial Force the
strongest of the nation's young men had an adverse effect at this time on the reinforcement of the units overseas. In its war diary, a unit of the 84th Brigade describes
a newly arrived draft as made up largely of *spingirai*,* and both battalions of the
FIFTH similarly found their ranks replenished largely by elderly men, some of whom
had fought as reservists in the South African War. But let it be said that the spirit
which had led these men to return as volunteers to their old regiments on the outbreak
of war, went far to make up for physical disabilities, and acted as an inspiration
to the young lads who were fighting by their side.† For the balance of the drafts at
this date was in the main formed of immature lads—boys who had declared a false
age in order to get to the War. Later, steps were taken in the Special Reserve Battalion
of the FIFTH to induce these youngsters to confess to their true ages, and they were
retained at home in a special "boys' squad," under Regimental Serjeant-Major Ouzman,
whose pride in his boys was justified by a proficiency in drill never surpassed and
seldom equalled by any squad in the Regiment. But these wise measures were still
to come, and in 1915 some very young boys were to be seen serving, and, alas, meeting
their death, in the ranks of the old regular battalions, while at home the divisions of
the New Army were being trained for war.

When the reader comes to the events of the late spring and early summer of
1915, which will be related in the succeeding chapters, he must, for a full appreciation
of the actions of the FIFTH, bear in mind this mixture of age and youth which constituted the ranks of the two Battalions. It was the Army Reservists, stiffened by
the men still in their colour service, who had carried the FIFTH through the early
months of the War; it was the young recruits, stiffened by men old enough to be
their fathers, who were to face the heavy fighting that was in store for the Regiment
during the next few months. Nor were the *spingirai* of the FIFTH to be found wanting. There can be none who served as a company commander at this period of the
War who is not conscious of what he owed to these old soldiers—these re-enlisted
men of the FIFTH who took charge of the young lads, their comrades in the ranks, and,
as can be instanced by the present writer, would endeavour at the risk of their own
lives to protect them on dangerous patrols or in battle.

---

* Pushtu for "silver beards"—the name applied to their old men by the Pathans.

† Private J. Comerford, who had enlisted in the FIFTH in 1879 and had served with the
Mounted Infantry at Majuba, was in employment in Malaya at the outbreak of War. He immediately returned to England, joined the 1st Battalion in March, 1915, and was wounded in the
following month. His portrait appears in the *St. George's Gazette* of June, 1915.

CHAPTER VII.

SECOND BATTALION — 13TH APRIL TO 25TH MAY, 1915.

"Ypres, 1915"

"Gravenstafel" — "St. Julien" — "Frezenberg" — "Bellewaarde."

Map No. 11

The 84th Infantry Brigade had now received orders to rejoin the 28th Division. 13th April, 1915 Early in April there had been an extension of the British front at Ypres, by which our troops had taken over from the French in the northern portion of the Salient as far as the Ypres-Poelcappelle road. In this readjustment of the front the 28th Division had been moved north to occupy a Sector to the north of the Menin Road astride the Ypres—Broodseinde road. Preparatory to going into the line on this front, the 2/FIFTH left their billets at S. Jan Capel on the 13th April and moved to a hutted camp near Vlamertinghe. Two days later, the 84th Brigade took over the Zonnebeke Section of the 28th Division front, and the 2/FIFTH relieved the 3/Royal Fusiliers in trenches opposite Broodseinde, about 400 yards east of Zonnebeke. On completion of the relief, " A " Company (Captain Hart), " C " (Captain Foster), and " D " (Captain Baxter), in order from right to left, held the front line, while " B " Company was placed in support. During the night of the 15th–16th April, on which these dispositions were taken up, all had remained quiet. But on the following day the Germans opened a very heavy bombardment on the trenches of " C " and " D " Companies. In anticipation of a hostile attack, three platoons of " B " Company were sent forward to the threatened point; but, though over one hundred trench mortar bombs fell on our front line, obliterating 150 yards of parapet, no infantry assault followed. After dark the platoons of " B " Company were, accordingly, withdrawn again to their supporting position, and the troops in the line set to work in repairing the damage that had been done. By dawn some ninety yards of parapet had been restored, but there still remained an unoccupied gap between "C" and "D" Companies. At 6.30 a.m. it was reported to Captain Foster that a party of from twenty to thirty of the enemy had established themselves in this gap. Foster himself went forward to investigate the truth of this report. He was soon assured of its accuracy by being heavily fired on as he approached the point in question, and immediately ordered a counter-attack for the ejection of the enemy. It was planned that, under cover of the rifle fire and bombs of two rifle sections, two sections of grenadiers should work up the trench and engage the intruders. Captain Baxter was to co-operate by rifle and machine gun fire and by bombing from the left flank, and Captain Hart was asked to assist with the grenadiers of " A " Company. In order to keep down fire from the enemy's main position, it was arranged that the 37th How. Battery R.F.A. should bombard the German front line. On the advance of our grenadiers a fierce bombing fight opened. For twenty minutes, while our men hurled bomb after bomb, the enemy retaliated with grenades of every description. The Germans then decided to abandon the position and regain their own front line. They effected their escape, but only at the cost of heavy casualties inflicted by the fire of the riflemen supporting the operation. In the meantime Captain Hart, constitutionally incapable of keeping out of a fight, had in person brought forward the

17th April, 1915 grenadiers of his company. With these he now pushed up a sap, in the hope of capturing a prisoner. He was forced, however, to content himself with returning after securing no more than a German rifle—and this at the cost of a slight wound.

Map No. 11

Captain Foster received the congratulations of the Brigadier on the prompt and effective action he had taken to expel the enemy from the trenches, and he himself paid a tribute to the efficient manner in which Lieutenants Mahon and Markham had handled their men in this small operation. The remainder of the day passed quietly, and after dark the Battalion was relieved and withdrawn to Brigade reserve. During the two days' tour in the trenches the casualties had amounted to 14 other ranks killed; Captain Hart, Lieutenants Mahon, Markham and Tuke, and 30 other ranks wounded.

The difficulty of observation in the flat or gently undulating country through which the opposing lines ran in the Ypres Salient lent a special importance to certain artificial mounds, which had been formed in the area from earth thrown up from canals, railway cuttings or other excavations. Among formations of this description, reference has already been made to "The Dump" near Verbrandenmolen, and in later chapters something will be heard of "The Mound" at St. Eloi; but there was none that earned in the War a notoriety equal to that of Hill 60, which was destined to be captured and re-captured no less than six times in fierce and bloody contests before the Germans were ultimately driven from the Salient.

Standing as a small eminence some 1,500 yards from Zillebeke and to the north of the Ypres-Courtrai railway, Hill 60 had originally been occupied by the Allies, but in December, 1914, had been lost by the French. After remaining in the hands of the Germans for four months, it had been recovered by troops of the 5th Division on the 17th April, the day on which the FIFTH had been withdrawn to reserve. On the days that followed, however, the beating off of incessant counter-attacks had exhausted the resources of the 5th Division to such an extent that it had become necessary to call in assistance from elsewhere. In response to this appeal, the 2/Cameron Highlanders of the 27th Division had already reinforced the 15th Brigade which held the hill, when the 2/FIFTH, as an additional reinforcement, were placed at the disposal of the 5th Division on the 20th April.* The grenadiers of the Battalion were straightway sent forward, under 2nd-Lieutenant Walton, to join the Camerons on Hill 60, while the remainder of the 2/FIFTH were ordered to take up a position under cover of the bank of Zillebeke Lake, as local reserve to the 15th Brigade. In the fierce fighting which continued during the two following days on Hill 60, 2nd-Lieutenant Walton was wounded, and the conduct of the grenadiers of the FIFTH, among whom Lce.-Corporal M. Turner was conspicuous, earned the thanks and high praise of the G.O.C. 15th Brigade. Though the Battalion as a whole was not actively engaged, the reserve position it occupied was subjected to continual artillery fire by the enemy during this time.

But, while this local struggle for Hill 60 was in progress, a situation of far graver importance had developed to the north. On the 20th April, a heavy bombardment had been opened on Ypres, and throughout the two ensuing days the enemy's shells had continued to rain ceaselessly on the unfortunate town. At 5 p.m. on the 22nd, under clouds of asphyxiating gas, the Germans had delivered a sudden attack

---

* Lt.-Colonel Enderby, recovered from the wound received in February, resumed command of the Battalion on this day.

at the left shoulder of the Salient, where the line was held by French colonial troops. The moral, even more than the material, effect of this new and forbidden form of warfare had been instantaneous against the wholly unprotected and unsuspecting troops. Choking, and stricken with panic, they retired in disorder, and the French front was overwhelmed by the enemy. Their rapid withdrawal had exposed the left flank of the Canadian Division, which, with its 3rd and 2nd Brigades, held the line between the French and the 28th Division; the 2nd Canadian Brigade being in contact with the 28th Division to the north of Berlin Wood, 1000 yards east of the village of Gravenstafel. The threat which had developed against their rear placed the British divisions, at the head of the Salient, in the gravest danger. The 3rd Canadian Brigade had thrown back a protective flank from their left to south-west of St. Julien, and the reserves of the 27th and 28th Divisions, échelonned to the west of their respective divisional fronts, had been faced north and directed to block the gap as best they could. For the time, these measures had served to check the Germans, but only at the expense of denuding the British divisions of reserves intended for the support of their own front line against direct attack. Such was the critical situation when, late in the evening of the 22nd April, the 2/FIFTH were ordered to withdraw immediately from Zillebeke to huts west of Ypres, which were reached just before midnight.

On St. George's Day the Battalion was moved forward to relieve the 1/Welch Regiment in the trenches which it had previously occupied east of Zonnebeke. Ypres was being heavily shelled, and a route was taken through the northern outskirts of the town. Before the Battalion got clear of it, however, a shell burst over the column, killing one man and severely wounding Captain Baxter and five others. But for this unfortunate incident, the relief was carried through without casualty. A heavy attack against the left of the 28th Division had been repulsed during the night, and when the 2/FIFTH came into the line the front of the division was still intact. The 2nd Canadian Brigade and the right of the 3rd also occupied their original positions, but the left of the latter brigade now bent back at right angles, and the situation of the British troops in the eastern quarter of the Salient, under this threat to their communications, was hourly becoming increasingly precarious. Throughout the 23rd April British reserves were thrown in, to deliver desperate counter-attacks against the southern point of the re-entrant created by the Germans. The casualties were appalling, but little ground was gained; and the best that could be said was that the enemy's advance had been checked. Moreover, " this had been achieved at the expense of throwing into the fight every battalion in divisional and corps reserve, and the two brigades, 1st Canadian and 13th, of the Second Army reserve." (Official History—Battle of Ypres, 1915).

Throughout this day and the night that followed, the front of the 28th Division was subjected to spasmodic bursts of rifle fire and to incessant artillery bombardment. Frezenburg, in particular, was made a target for the enemy's shells, and in the afternoon was in flames. Far away, to the north of Ypres, the Belgians, holding the line of the Canal on the left of the French, had put up a fine defence, and held firmly a defensive flank established against the enemy, who had succeeded in crossing the canal to the south of their position. But, though the Germans had been checked in rear of what had been the French front and, as was to be proved, had here reached the high water mark of their penetration, the most anxious and critical time for the 28th Division was still to come.

Hitherto, the fiercest fighting in which the Canadians had been involved had resulted from the break through on their left; the main weight of the attack had not

THE FIFTH IN THE GREAT WAR. 87

24th April, 1915   been directed against their front, and such gas as they had experienced had been only   Map No. 11
that of shells, with its comparatively transitory effect. At 4 a.m. on the 24th April
a heavy bombardment of the Canadian front was followed by the release of cylinder gas,
on a front of 1,000 yards, in the centre of their position. Drifting before a N.N.E.
wind, what appeared as a fog bank, some fifteen feet high, passed over their trenches
to the defensive flank which had been thrown back from the original centre of the
3rd Canadian Brigade. The gas cloud was followed by German infantry in overwhelming numbers. The Canadian 2nd Brigade (5th and 8th Battalions) held fast to
their position, but the 3rd Brigade was forced back towards St. Julien, and a gap
of 1,500 yards was created in the Canadian front. The commanders of 5th and 8th
Battalions were authorised by their brigadier to retire on Gravenstafel should the
situation demand, but they decided to maintain their position after throwing back
the left of the 8th Battalion to cover the open flank by fire as best it could. The
critical point seemed to be St. Julien, and the G.O.C. 27th Division, on his own
responsibility ordered the reserves of the 28th Division, as the only troops immediately available, to Fortuin, south-west of St. Julien. This was an instance of the
departure from the channels of command that, it seems, was frequently made in the
critical days of this battle. Though in the circumstances inevitable, how distracting
it must have been for the commanders of the various detachments thrown in as reinforcements can be easily imagined. Time and again one finds cases of junior officers
having to exercise their own discretion as to whether they should depart from orders
received, at the urgent call of some hard-pressed commander.

While these events were in progress, the 2/FIFTH were still in position east
of Zonnebeke, with 2½ companies in the front line, and "C" company with two
platoons of "A" company in support trenches. About 5 p.m. the 1½ companies in
support were withdrawn, and, with two companies of the 2/Cheshire Regiment and
one company of the Monmouthshire Regiment (T.A.), were formed into a detachment
under the command of Major E. M. Moulton-Barrett of the FIFTH. Orders were
given him to take up a position to the south-east of the cross-roads Zonnebeke-
Langemark—Gravenstafel-Wieltje, about midway between Zonnebeke and St. Julien,
in support of the 2nd Canadian Brigade. Moving by the Langemark road, he reached
the point given without opposition. Finding the front clear of the enemy, he then
struck north and took up a position to the north of the Haanebeke stream,* sending
forward two platoons to reinforce the 8th Canadian Battalion. Those of the Canadians
that still survived were found to be suffering acutely from the effects of gas, and this
strengthening of their line proved opportune. For, scarcely had the platoons of the
FIFTH arrived in the trenches than the Germans delivered an attack against the very
point they had reinforced. This, and a second attack delivered later, were repulsed
with heavy loss to the enemy.

The Canadians were now all but completely exhausted. They had kept in
close touch with the 3/Royal Fusiliers (85th Brigade), who were in position as the
left of the 28th Division, at Berlin Wood, and to this battalion the Canadian battalion
commanders now appealed for further reinforcement. But the O.C. 3/Royal Fusiliers,
owing to his heavy losses and to the critical position in which his own unit itself was
placed, was unable to assist, and suggested application to Major Moulton-Barrett.
About 8.30 p.m. the appeal for assistance came to the latter, who immediately sent

---

* The upper Steenbeke is also named Haanebeke. The stream above referred to is the
northernmost of the two and flows due west to join the Steenbeke at St. Julien.

forward the remainder of the detachment of the FIFTH to the left of the 8th Canadian Battalion. A detachment of the 1/Suffolk Regiment, under Lieutenant Bradley, had already been sent up to strengthen this flank and was found in position at Boetleer's Farm.* The reinforcing platoons of the FIFTH now came in on the left of the Suffolk detachment and extended the line S.S.W. of Boetleer's Farm. The situation after these dispositions had been made was that in the space of close on three miles that intervened between the left of the 2nd Canadian Brigade, whose trenches were crowded with gassed and wounded men, and the right of the 3rd Canadian Brigade, which had been withdrawn to near Wieltje, troops were disposed in two groups, each of which occupied a comparatively short length of front. The first, under command of Moulton-Barrett, consisting of Bradley's Suffolks, the FIFTH and Cheshire detachments, one company of the 1/Monmouthshire, and some reserve troops of the Canadians, occupied about 800 yards. Further to the south-west, and out of touch with the above troops, the second group, composed of the 1/Suffolk (less Bradley's detachment) and the 12/London Regiment, were disposed under command of Colonel Wallace of the Suffolk on a front of about 1,200 yards. In this quarter of the field the night of the 24th/25th April passed without incident.

At dawn on the 25th April, the bulk of the 8th Canadian Battalion was relieved by the 8/Durham Light Infantry. Moulton-Barrett, being thereby freed from the necessity of holding troops in the forward position, then withdrew his detachment south of the Haanebeke to the position which he had originally been ordered to occupy when detached from the Battalion on the previous day. Here, east and west of the cross-roads Zonnebeke-Langemark—Gravenstafel-Wieltje, he established his troops under cover as supports. Throughout the morning, the enemy maintained an incessant artillery fire. In the afternoon an intensified bombardment created some confusion among the forward troops, certain of whom fell back on Moulton-Barrett's supporting position, and for a space the situation threatened ugly developments. But, later, these parties were rallied on the rear line and succeeded in re-occupying the vacated trenches and re-establishing the forward position. At dusk the men set to work improving the trenches and generally strengthening the supporting position. For the detachment, the night passed comparatively quietly.

Now let it not be thought, either from what has been recounted above or from what is about to follow, that the writer has any wider purpose than to record the action of the 2/FIFTH in the Battle of St. Julien. Indeed, the difficulty of giving any detailed and accurate description of the battle as a whole will be evident to anyone who examines the official records. For, the circumstances in which the battle opened, as has been seen, resulted in reserve units being split into fragments and thrown piecemeal into the fight. Moreover, in messages sent during the action, one finds that map references, given by officers in unknown country and under the stress of battle, are often obviously inaccurate. The contradictory nature of many of the reports, in fact, is alone sufficient to give the measure of the task presented to the historian who wishes to compile a true and full narrative of the battle.

In accepting, however, that the intention of the present writer is merely to

---

* 1/Suffolk had been directed on Fortuin. In response to a strong appeal from 2nd Canadian Brigade, the Battalion Commander, on his own responsibility, detached this party. His action stands as an example of the decisions that had to be made by unit commanders in this battle without reference to the superior who had ordered them forward.

25th April, 1915 record those incidents of the battle in which the 2/FIFTH were involved, there may be readers who consider that, for this purpose, too much has already been written of the action and movement of other units. It is claimed, nevertheless, that references of this kind that have already been made, and others that are to follow, are necessary to a proper appreciation of the part played by the 2/FIFTH and, in particular, of the great services rendered by Moulton-Barrett's detachment. While the narrative that follows is based mainly on the reports of officers of the FIFTH who were engaged in the battle, it is necessary that the reader should bear in mind that much that is written with regard to the progressive changes in the general situation has been derived from other records, and that commanders in the position of Major Moulton-Barrett were, at the time of their occurrence, ignorant of the events which produced those changes.

Map No. 11

It has been said that the night of the 25th/26th April passed quietly for Moulton-Barrett's detachment, and from his report on the events of the 25th one can judge how he, with his local outlook, viewed the situation. While he was under no illusion as to its being grave, he was ignorant of the full extent of the gravity. Though he had taken all steps to render his position secure, he had not been given such full information of the movement of neighbouring troops in the defence as would have prepared him for the critical developments which were to take place on the 26th April. For a realisation of the actual position in which his detachment stood at dawn that day, it is necessary to turn to what had been passing on the front of the 28th Division on the 25th, and briefly to study the movements of the Canadians and other troops, who at daybreak had held a line south-west of Gravenstafel, in protection of the left flank and rear of the 28th Division.

Early on the morning of the 25th the German artillery had opened an intense bombardment on the left of the Division, for some four hours sweeping the trenches and searching the ground in rear with shrapnel. Later in the day a heavy bombardment with high explosive shell was directed on the trenches, and extended southwards to the front of the FIFTH. Very shortly, smarting and watering of the eyes indicated to the men that a large quantity of gas was included in the bombardment. At 1 p.m. the German infantry advanced to the attack. Some thirty of the enemy succeeded in gaining a lodgment in our front line trenches on the right of the 2/East Surrey Regiment, whose boundary with the FIFTH represented the junction of the 84th and 85th Brigades. Their success was short-lived. In a counter-attack the East Surrey captured eighteen of the enemy and killed the remainder. On the left flank of this battalion, however, a party of Germans who had obtained a footing in the front line, though unable to penetrate more deeply, successfully resisted all efforts to eject them. Further to the north, the 3/Royal Fusiliers stood firm on the left flank of the Division. Later in the day four successive attacks were delivered by the enemy opposite Zonnebeke. All were repulsed, and when darkness fell the 2/FIFTH still held their position, while, except for the slight penetration on the left of the East Surrey, the 28th Division presented an unbroken front to the enemy forces attacking from the east. But, late in the afternoon of the 25th April, the troops of the 2nd Canadian Brigade on the left of the 28th Division had been withdrawn south of Gravenstafel. During the night of the 25th/26th they were replaced in the position to which they had fallen back by the 1/Hampshire Regiment of the 11th Infantry Brigade. Thus, at dawn on the 26th April the left flank of the 28th Division was situated in a sharp salient, with the 1/Hampshire, some four hundred yards to the south-west, in position south of Gravenstafel and north of the Haanebeke. South-west again, but out of touch with the Hampshire, Moulton-Barrett's detachment was at the cross-roads, while the 8/Durham L.I., who had not retired with the Canadians on their right and left, were still right forward at Boetleer's Farm, some 800 yards north-west of the Hampshire. Units of the 11th Brigade had come into position during the night about Point 37, 600 yards south of Moulton-Barrett.

Now, it will be remembered that after the 8/Durham L.I. had come forward to reinforce the line on the 25th, Moulton-Barrett had withdrawn his detachment in order to take up a position in support in accordance with the original orders he had received. He had had no information of the movements and reliefs which had taken place on the night of 25th/26th. Within his knowledge, nothing had transpired to alter his rôle of being in support to a forward line of defence. But, if the withdrawals which had been carried out have been made clear, it will be realized that, before dawn broke on the 26th April, his detachment had in actual fact become a section of a front line of defence, which was continued on the right by the 1/Hampshire, and by the 11th Brigade in échelon to the left rear; while the 8/Durham Light Infantry, completely in the air, occupied the perilous and unforeseen position of an advanced detached post. The considerable gaps which existed on his right and left found both flanks of Moulton-Barrett's detachment exposed; the left, in particular, being vulnerable, owing to the rearward position occupied by the 11th Brigade.

All troops as far west as the St. Julien—Fortuin road had now been placed under the command of Major-General Bulfin. It would seem that the opposition encountered in the attacks against the front of the 28th Division had discouraged the enemy from making further efforts in that quarter. It was otherwise on the left flank of the salient. The Battalion Diary for the 26th April reads: "A quiet day in the trenches at Zonnebeke but a strenuous day for Major Moulton-Barrett's mixed detachment." To the experiences of this detachment we will now return.

Except for continual shell fire, the night had passed without disturbance by the enemy; good work had been put in during the hours of darkness, and the defence of the position taken up by the detachment had been greatly strengthened by daybreak on the 26th. As is common at this season around Ypres, the country at dawn was shrouded by mist, but all remained quiet. Suddenly, a number of stragglers from the Durham Light Infantry, rushing down the slope from the far side of the Haanebeke, gave the information that the forward trenches were in the hands of the enemy, and that the Germans were concentrating on the left flank. With great promptitude Moulton-Barrett withdrew his detachment some four hundred yards to a position more favourable to meeting the situation, and, realising the danger which threatened his left flank, asked for reinforcements from Battalion Headquarters. In response to this request, Captain Foster was despatched with two machine guns which he succeeded in establishing in a position from which they could bring fire in protection of the threatened flank. In the meantime the Germans had been pushing forward small parties to within 300 to 400 yards of Moulton-Barrett's men, with a view to assembling for a massed attack on the detachment. These, as they were observed, were engaged by rifle fire, and all attempts by them to advance in force were completely checked.

At this juncture, with the Germans brought to a standstill on his front, Major Moulton-Barrett was wounded and placed *hors de combat*. Time and again, in this battle of St. Julien, it fell to regimental officers, acting on their own initiative, to prevent critical and unforeseen situations from turning to disaster. Among the names of those who did great service in this respect that of Moulton-Barrett of

26th April, 1915 the FIFTH will always stand prominent. From the time of his arrival in the danger area he had never hesitated to send support to the points where it was most needed; and, throughout, his example had acted as an inspiration to all under his command. The judgment he had shown in the final dispositions he had made before becoming a casualty was an example of the sound appreciation he had shown from the outset of the measures necessary to meeting unforeseen contingencies. But the task of his detachment was far from ended, and his replacement was no easy matter. Captain Foster, after establishing the two machine guns in position, had returned to the Battalion. Rather than withdraw a senior officer from the companies which, for all that was known, might be involved at any moment in heavy fighting at Zonnebeke, Lieut.-Colonel Enderby decided to send his own adjutant, Captain Auld, to take over command of what figures in the history of the Battle of St. Julien as "Moulton-Barrett's Detachment." Captain Auld, setting out along the Zonnebeke—St. Julien road, "found a mixed detachment of 2/FIFTH and 2/Cheshire Regiment with two French soldiers holding a hedge facing roughly north and engaging the enemy at a range of 300 to 400 yards.* It was now reduced to about 70 men, was out of touch with the troops on its flanks and appeared to be isolated. The machine guns, though prevented by dead ground from giving complete protection to the left, afforded a measure of security on that flank. But on the right, high ground, on which stood some farm buildings among scattered trees, offered to the enemy a position from which the detachment could be brought under deadly enfilade fire. From his slender resources Auld detached a small party, under a Company Serjeant-Major of the Cheshire, for the occupation of the farm buildings. A heavy shrapnel fire was now opened by the enemy, but their range was faulty, and little harm resulted. More effective was the oblique rifle fire that was simultaneously opened from both flanks. By this the Company Serjeant-Major in command of the farm buildings was killed. The situation appeared so serious to Captain Auld that he was convinced that a determined attack by the enemy would annihilate the detachment. He realised that such an event would inevitably result in the 1/Hampshire on his right being taken in reverse, and he sent an urgent appeal to Battalion Headquarters for further reinforcements. All was still quiet at Zonnebeke, and, in response to this request, Captain Foster was again sent to strengthen the position of the detachment, bringing with him six more machine guns and a company of the 1/Welch Regiment. On his arrival, Foster took over command from Auld, who returned to his duties at Battalion Headquarters. Captain Hart, with "A" Company (less the two platoons already with the detachment) was ordered to take up a position to the rear in support. These measures proved adequate to make the defence secure. Here, as elsewhere on the 26th April and during the preceding night, the Germans had missed their opportunity of breaking through the thinly held line which ran west from south of Gravenstafel to south of St. Julien.† It can only

Map No. 11

---

* Report by Captain R. Auld.

† While, on the right of this line, the British were defending their positions against German attacks during the 26th April, costly but fruitless counter-attacks were being delivered against the enemy further to the west. Notable among these was that of the 149th (Northumberland) Brigade (4th, 5th, 6th and 7th Northumberland Fusiliers), the first Territorials to go into battle as a brigade. Their gallant attacks towards St. Julien, unsupported by artillery and in face of a devastating machine gun fire, can find no place within the narrow limits of this History, but so outstanding an episode in the history of the Regiment cannot be allowed to pass unnoticed. It was on this occasion that Brigadier-General J. F. Riddell, late of the FIFTH, one battalion of which he had commanded, met his death.

be supposed that the resolute stand made by Moulton-Barrett's detachment had led the enemy to believe that it was in far greater strength than was actually the case, and so saved it from being surrounded and overwhelmed. The crisis of the battle had passed. During the 27th and 28th April reinforcements were pushed forward, filling up the gaps which had hitherto existed, and gradually consolidating the defence of the northern flank of the Salient. The Germans during these days maintained a continuous artillery bombardment, but no attempt was made by their infantry to renew the attack. On the evening of the 28th "Moulton-Barrett's Detachment" was withdrawn from the flank on which it had faced and held the enemy for five days, and, under command of Captain Foster, rejoined the Battalion.

Though the following few days passed uneventfully for the FIFTH at Zonnebeke, their position, equally with that of all troops of the 27th and 28th Divisions, was extremely precarious. For they stood at the head of a salient so narrow as to bring their communications under the observation and close artillery fire of the enemy. This situation, which led to an ever increasing toll of casualties, could only be remedied in one of two ways—recovery by the French of the ground lost on the northern flank, or a substantial reduction of the Salient by a westerly withdrawal. The latter course had been planned and prepared by Sir John French, but during the next few days it was, at the instance of General Foch, twice postponed. Ultimately, no progress having been made by the French, the withdrawal was carried out during the night of the 3rd/4th May bringing the British line from east of Hooge to Frezenberg, and thence north-west to join the French on the Ypres—Langemark road. On the front of the 2/FIFTH, "B" and "D" Companies evacuated their trenches at 9 p.m. The route, to be followed in the dark, lay across country pitted with shell holes, where the shattered stumps of trees, and the dead and decaying bodies of animals which littered the ground gave terrible evidence of the fighting that had followed the German gas attack. At 10.30 p.m., "A" and "C" Companies, leaving rear parties in the trenches, withdrew in their turn. Simulating the full garrison, the rear parties, under Lieutenants Legard and Tuke, each of 30 N.C.O.'s and men, remained in the position till midnight, when they slipped away without their movement being detected by the enemy. After its withdrawal the Battalion was ordered to reserve, and moved back to hutments north of the Ypres—Vlamertinghe road, which were reached at daybreak on the 4th May. The withdrawal of the British troops in the Salient marked the close of the Battle of St. Julien. Between the 21st April and the 4th May, the casualties in the 2/FIFTH, slight though they were in comparison with those sustained by other units of the 28th Division, had totalled 35 other ranks killed, 6 officers and 149 other ranks wounded, and 17 other ranks missing.

Hitherto we have been considering only the troops in the forefront of the battle. It is right that we should now turn for a space to those who had been responsible, under the Quartermaster and the Transport Officer, for feeding the men in the line, and for keeping them supplied with ammunition and material for the maintenance of the defences. For, without the great services of these, the staunchest garrison could not have held out against the enemy.

It is, perhaps, fair to say that the men in the trenches during the War generally believed that their life compared unfavourably with the "comfortable

23rd April, 1915 existence" enjoyed by their comrades of the Battalion Transport. Whatever justification there may have been for this theory during the quieter periods of trench warfare, there was little enough when a battle was in progress; and perhaps least of all during the Battle of St. Julien. On the 22nd April, the 1st Line Transport of the 2/FIFTH was located in a field just west of Ypres and to the north of the Vlamertinghe road. On that night, it fell to them to carry forward supplies to the Battalion at Zillebeke Lake. News of the French débâcle had reached the transport lines, and it was known that, with darkness falling, there was nothing to prevent the Germans pushing straight through to the Menin road. It was not, however, known that they themselves had not foreseen the overwhelming effect of their gas attack, and were unprepared to exploit its success. It was in these circumstances that Lieutenant The Hon. D. Mitford, the Transport Officer, on setting out, bade farewell to Captain Allan, the Quartermaster, in the certain anticipation that the Germans would shortly be in Ypres, and that he would never regain the transport lines. On his way forward he called at Divisional H.Q. to inform the G.O.C. of what he had learnt of the situation. Later, having succeeded in reaching the Battalion and off-loading supplies, he turned about to lead his wagons back, fully expecting to meet the Germans face to face before he passed through Ypres. Unprepared though they were, had the enemy had an accurate knowledge of the situation, Mitford's anticipations would, undoubtedly, have been realised. Mercifully, they failed to seize their golden opportunity, and in due course the empty convoy safely reached its lines. "Never was I more surprised in my life," Lieutenant Mitford has recorded, "than when I found myself back in the transport lines with Allan." Map No. 11

The anxiety of that night, however, was but a foretaste of what the 1st Line Transport was to experience night after night during the ensuing fortnight. On the Battalion moving up to the Zonnebeke sector, the transport lines were withdrawn to Poperinghe. From there, after dark—sometimes even twice in the same night— the wagons had to make the perilous journey to an off-loading point just west of Zonnebeke. As was well known to the enemy, all approaches led through Ypres; and the town was kept under a ceaseless and heavy bombardment. There were two alternate routes; a longer, but less heavily shelled one, by which a way could be found through the northern outskirts of the town * and another and more direct route, which, entering Ypres by a level crossing, led through the town square, past the Cloth Hall and out by the Menin Gate. Mitford as a rule chose the latter route. His method was to quicken pace on approaching the town, and then to lead his wagons at full gallop through the death-trap of Ypres, never drawing rein till the Menin Gate bridge was passed. On one occasion, however, a heavy shell burst just as they were approaching the exit, blowing a huge crater in the road on the near side of the bridge. As a rule such a shell was followed by a second of the same type. By ill luck a G.S. wagon had been included in the transport that night. To turn was impossible, and it seemed doubtful whether it could be got past the crater. While the transport officer went forward to investigate matters, the wagons were stationary in the last place that would have been chosen for a halt. Fortunately, no second shell followed; and by inches the wagon was got safely through. This was but typical of nightly experiences, of which space does not admit record. The return journey was even more hazardous, for halts had often to be made to pick up the "walking wounded" who were making their painful way through Ypres.

---

* It will be remembered that the Battalion had taken this northern route on the 23rd April.

Maps 11 & 12

The N.C.O.'s and men worked in two reliefs, doing duty on alternate nights; 23rd A[p] but no such respite was possible for Lieutenant Mitford, who had to accompany his wagons on every one of these perilous journeys. Fortune favoured him; but it was primarily due to his fine leadership that, while the Battalion never failed to receive its supplies, there was, miraculously, not a single casualty among the transport personnel during these critical days. The spirit which reigned in the Transport Lines at this time can best be gauged by quoting Lieutenant Mitford's reference to Captain Allan, with whom he worked in such close association: "Allan, always cheerful and in good spirits, did everything. He was for ever offering to take a turn at my job. He was a wonderful companion and made everything easy for everybody." *

In the War, everyone was so intent on his own particular business that the troops in the line were apt to take such matters as supplies for granted, without bothering to inquire into the machinery that produced them—unless, by chance, they failed to materialise! The smooth working of the Quartermaster's department and the transport in both battalions of the FIFTH, itself tended to obscure the difficulties and anxieties connected with ensuring that the forward troops should lack nothing. In a history of this kind, reference cannot be made to all the services rendered in this respect. What has been related above of the supply of the 2nd Battalion during the Battle of St. Julien may stand as an example of the manner in which the FIFTH were served throughout the War by their Quartermasters and 1st Line Transport.

By the fresh dispositions that had been taken up following the withdrawal in the Salient, the 27th Division astride the Menin Road held the line from Hill 60 to just south of the Roulers railway. From that point the 28th Division continued the line by Frezenberg to Mouse Trap Farm. Between the farm and the right of the French a comparatively short length of line was held by the 12th Brigade of the 4th Division. The British front line, sited for the greater part on a forward slope, was greatly exposed throughout; and the positions of the 83rd Brigade on the right of the 28th Division were open to enfilade fire from the enemy's artillery. The hastily constructed trenches, narrow and but three foot deep, afforded little cover and had no revetment. Such wire as existed formed but a slight obstacle. There were no communication trenches and little in the nature of overhead or splinter proof cover.

It will be realised that, both in its siting and in the nature of the defences, the line was ill calculated to withstand a heavy attack. Nevertheless, the Allies' plans

---

* Lieutenant Hon. D. Mitford (later Lord Redesdale) had been invalided from the FIFTH on account of the effect of wounds received in the South African War. Rejoining the Regiment in 1914, he served for a brief period with the 1st Battalion, but his health proved unequal to the strain of work as a company officer, and he was invalided to England. Having induced a medical board once again to pass him fit for service, he joined the 2nd Battalion shortly before the second Battle of Ypres. He was appointed Transport Officer in the belief that he would be subjected to less physical strain in that capacity than with a company. Unfortunately his health again broke down under the terrible exertions of the days of the Battle of St. Julien, and he was unable again to serve at the front with the FIFTH. It may be interesting to recall that this officer, the equal in age and the superior in experience of many who were at this time serving at home with the rank of major in the New Army, was refused a temporary rank above that of subaltern, despite the repeated representations of his Commanding Officer.

4th May 1915., required that it should be held tenaciously by the troops allotted to its defence for the reason that, further south an offensive was being staged by the First Army in co-operation with the French. The success of this operation would be gravely prejudiced by the development of a situation which might demand the despatch of reinforcements to the Salient. The Battle of St. Julien, however, represented merely the first phase of the Germans' second great effort to reach the channel ports. They had by no means abandoned their intention of breaking the Salient and carrying Ypres, and with this object in view, they now proceeded to mass three corps against the 27th and 28th Divisions. Two thirds of this vast force was being concentrated opposite the 83rd and 84th Brigades, who held the line of the 28th Division.

After thirty-six hours' rest in the hutments to which they had been sent in reserve, the 2/FIFTH were ordered forward at 9 p.m. on the 4th May to take up a position in the G.H.Q. line north-east of Wieltje, where they were held in support of the 2/Cheshire. Two days later the Battalion relieved the 1/Welch in the front line on the extreme left of the 84th Brigade. Its front extended from the Wieltje—Gravenstafel road across the Wieltje—St. Julien road to join the right of the 12th Brigade near Mouse Trap Farm.*

From the 5th May onwards the enemy had been keeping the British trenches under continuous shell fire. On the 7th the bombardment increased in intensity and did great damage to the trenches, the exposed positions of the 83rd Brigade, in particular, suffering very severely. On the night of the 7th/8th May units of the German Marine Division delivered a determined assault against the trenches of the FIFTH and on Mouse Trap Farm. The attack was repulsed with heavy loss to the enemy. 2nd-Lieutenant Tuke and Sergeants Taylor and Spencer of the FIFTH were killed, but, strange to say, these were the sole casualties in the Battalion.

At 5.30 a.m. on the 8th the enemy started to shell the whole front of the 28th Division very heavily, giving particular attention to the 83rd Brigade, which had already suffered so severely on the previous day. At 7 a.m. the shelling intensified, and a terrific bombardment was put down on the left of the 27th Division, the whole front of the 28th, and the right of the 12th Brigade. At 8.30 a.m. an infantry assault was launched against the 83rd Brigade, north and south of Frezenberg, but was driven back. Following a further bombardment of half an hour, a second attack against the same front also failed. By now the trenches had been completely destroyed and the front line garrison all but annihilated, but the open, exposed slope in rear of the position made reinforcement impossible. At 10 a.m. a third attack broke the shattered front of the 83rd Brigade, and the Germans simultaneously began to press forward against the whole line from the Menin Road to Mouse Trap Farm. The 84th Brigade section of the front was held, from right to left, by the 1/Suffolk, 2/Cheshire, 1/Monmouth, 2/FIFTH. Though not exposed to enfilade fire in the same manner as the 83rd Brigade, they had suffered heavily from the enemy's artillery. None the less, they had hitherto succeeded in holding up the continual attempts of the German infantry to develop an attack against their trenches, but with the vast gap which now lay open to the enemy on the right flank of the 84th Brigade it was clear that its battalions stood in imminent danger of being overwhelmed. Reinforcements sent forward to fill this served to check further penetration by the enemy by frontal advance, but they were unable to get sufficiently far forward to secure the right flank of the

Maps 11 & 12

---

* This may be better remembered by its original—and more appropriate—name of Shell Trap Farm.

Maps 11 & 12   84th Brigade. The 12/London Regiment, barely 200 strong, were ordered up by   8th May, 1915.
Brigadier-General Bols at 11.15 a.m. to reinforce the 1/Monmouth on the right of the
FIFTH, but before reaching their destination they were annihilated by a tornado of
shell fire.

The Germans who had penetrated the 83rd Brigade position, finding themselves
checked in front, now directed their efforts to rolling up the 84th Brigade, and so
enlarging the gap in the British line. At 1 p.m. the front of the 2/Cheshire was
broken, their Commanding Officer was killed, and three companies were wiped out.
A similar fate then befell the 1/Suffolk; and of this battalion, only 29 men remained
to report on the following day. The O.C. 1/Monmouth, finding his position turned,
now informed the 2/FIFTH that he proposed wheeling back his battalion to form a
flank. Lieut.-Colonel Enderby requested that, in carrying out this intention, he would
occupy some high ground that occurred on the right of the FIFTH, in order the better
to guard that flank. It was too late: the Germans were already round the flank and
in rear of the line. At about 5 p.m., as the 1/Monmouth were endeavouring to carry
out the manœuvre they were enveloped, their Commanding Officer and 2nd-in-Com-
mand killed, and a mere handful of the battalion escaped death or capture. Of the
84th Brigade there now remained only the FIFTH, still holding stubbornly to their
position, and the 1/Welch, reduced to the strength of less than one company, in
Brigade reserve. All four companies of the FIFTH were in the line. The position held
by " B," " C " and " D " Companies consisted of a single length of trench on the
forward slope, with no support or communication trenches in rear; the trench they
occupied had already been so severely damaged by the enemy's artillery that it was
blocked in many places, and covered communication between companies, and even
between platoons, had become impossible. " A " Company on the left was better
placed; its front line was situated on more level ground and was approached by communication trenches which made the organisation of all round defence possible.
Battalion Headquarters were, unfortunately, situated in rear of the right flank of
the Battalion. Between the FIFTH and the left flank of the 27th Division there was
now a gap of over two miles; and such troops as had been sent forward from reserve
to restore the situation had been directed to the front of the 83rd Brigade, where
disaster had first overtaken the 28th Division.

The full force of the enemy's artillery was now concentrated on the FIFTH.
Under the fearful bombardment to which it was subjected, the Battalion clung
obstinately to its position and held off the German infantry concentrating for attack
from the front and flank. Lieut.-Colonel Enderby managed to get a message through
to Brigade Headquarters, representing the desperate situation in which the Battalion
was placed. He was informed that the 85th Brigade from Divisional Reserve had
started a counter attack, and was ordered to maintain his position unless he deemed
this impossible, in which case he should withdraw to the G.H.Q. line. A small parapet
had been thrown up at right angles to the main line, and had been manned for the
protection of the exposed right flank. On receiving the above orders, Enderby determined to remain in position till the promised relief came to save his battalion from
the disaster that threatened ever more imminently. There were, however, no signs
of the eagerly awaited counter-attack. As already indicated, the 85th Brigade was
advancing far away to the right, in a quarter of the field where, if its action could
give relief to the FIFTH, it would not be for some hours. Lieut.-Colonel Enderby at
length realised that he had no alternative but to retire to the G.H.Q. line, which he
decided to do after dark. At 6.15 p.m. he went forward to the front line trenches to

8th May, 1915. arrange for this. At 7 p.m., while he was still in process of issuing orders to his company commanders, a sudden intense bombardment opened on the position. A rocket rose from the enemy's lines, and the bombardment as suddenly ceased. Immediately, the German infantry swarmed in overwhelming numbers from the trenches vacated by the 1/Monmouth on the right flank, while, simultaneously, rifle and machine gun fire was opened from the rear on the stretcher parties which, in preparation for retirement, were already evacuating the wounded. The FIFTH were surrounded on three sides. The headquarters of " B," " C " and " D " Companies were rushed by the enemy, and in the desperate and confused fighting which ensued both Lieut.-Colonel Enderby and his Adjutant, Captain Auld, were captured. Auld was not with his commanding officer at the time, as he had gone forward to deliver orders to another part of the line, and the assault found him alone with one private soldier, a stretcher bearer, in an isolated fire bay of the ruined trench. The stretcher bearer was immediately bayoneted by the Germans, who were rushing forward to deal similarly with the officer, when his life was saved by a serjeant-major who cried out—" Nein, nein. Das ist der Commandant ! " Mercy was not the consideration on which Captain Auld was spared, but his potential value to the enemy's intelligence branch. Attacked from every side by overwhelming numbers, the shattered remnants of the three companies were completely wiped out. No. 4 Platoon on the right of "A" Company suffered the same fate, but the remainder of the Company continued to hold out behind traverses and hastily constructed blocks. Placing himself on the exposed flank, Captain Hart, the company commander, called on his men to stand to the last. In the days before the War, Hart, greatly loved by all, had been noted for his physical strength, his toughness, his obstinacy, and his complete disregard for danger. In this, his first campaign, his zest for fighting and his absolute fearlessness had already become a tradition among his men ; but they had never seen him with a fiercer determination than that which now possessed him in the most terrible ordeal they had faced under his command. Surrounded on all sides, the situation seemed so hopeless as to justify capitulation. A German officer called on him to surrender, but for reply, Hart shot him dead with his revolver, and called on his men to renew their efforts. Then the inevitable happened, and this very gallant officer was killed. But the spirit inspired by his influence and example survived his death and brought great glory to the FIFTH this day. 2nd-Lieutenant Watson, though wounded, assumed command of the company ; his place in command of No. 1 Platoon being taken by Serjeant Hague. The only other officer, 2nd-Lieutenant Lord, had been wounded and was *hors de combat*, and his place had been taken by Serjeant Lane. No. 2 Platoon was under the command of Serjeant Halliday. While these N.C.O.'s by their demeanour set a splendid example, the situation was such that the men themselves had frequently to act on their own initiative to meet the dangers by which the gallant remnant were being unceasingly menaced. It was thus that Private Ives, in order to extend a traverse and secure further flank protection to the garrison, built up a block under heavy rifle fire and with bombs bursting on every side. Checked at this point, the Germans resorted to hurling bombs over the traverse. Privates Bell and Joyce rushed forward and counter-attacked with bombs to such effect that the enemy were driven back and abandoned their attempts at this point. Private Logue made his way back to a support trench in order to borrow a machine gun from a neighbouring unit. Having secured one, he carried it forward single handed for forty yards across the open and rejoined his hard pressed comrades, only to find that it had been damaged and rendered useless. These few acts which remain on record give evidence of the

Maps 11 & 12

Maps 11 & 12   spirit which inspired all who were engaged in this gallant stand, and of the manner 8th May, 1915.
in which Hart's men obeyed the injunctions given by him before he fell. Darkness
had long fallen before the enemy at length admitted defeat and abandoned their efforts
to overcome the resistance of these platoons of the FIFTH.

In the meantime troops of the 10th and 11th Brigades of the 4th Division
had been directed on Wieltje. A counter-attack had been planned to sweep obliquely
from Mouse Trap Farm across the space that intervened between the FIFTH and the
G.H.Q. line, and to take the enemy in flank. Had this operation been carried out as
planned, the FIFTH would have been saved from the heavy losses they had suffered.
Unfortunately the troops detailed for this counter-attack had not arrived at the G.H.Q.
line till 7.30 p.m., and by that time the approach of darkness made attack over
unknown ground impossible, so that all that could be accomplished was a short advance
beyond that line.

Though the positions of the 28th Division had not been recaptured, reinforcing
troops were now available to form a retrenchment across the gap that had been laid
open by the shattering of its brigades. The line taken up ran behind the Verlorenhoek
ridge, ¾ mile west of that held when the attack had opened, and passed thence by
Wieltje to join the 12th Brigade at Mouse Trap Farm. Just east of the farm "Company 'A' of 2/Northumberland Fusiliers remained unconquered in its original position."
(Official History.) At 4 a.m. on the 9th May the company, reduced to a strength
of 65 N.C.O.'s and men, was relieved by the 1/East Lancashire and led back to reserve
by 2nd-Lieutenant Watson, who on arrival at Brigade H.Q. was immediately placed
in an ambulance and despatched to hospital. Of the other companies there remained
but two 2nd-Lieutenants and 51 other ranks.

The casualties which had been sustained by the 2/FIFTH during the fighting
on the 8th May are found recorded as under:—

OFFICERS.

Killed ..	Captain A. C. Hart.
	Captain G. K. Molineux.
	Lieutenant G. P. Legard.
	Lieutenant A. B. Cramsie.
	2nd-Lieutenant K. Shann.
	2nd-Lieutenant J. K. Manger.
Wounded ..	Lieutenant W. Watson.
	2nd-Lieutenant R. Lord.
	2nd-Lieutenant R. A. Taylor.
Prisoners of War ..	Lieut.-Colonel H. S. Enderby.
	Captain R. Auld.
	Lieutenant B. E. S. Mahon.
	2nd-Lieutenant B. C. Hardy.
	2nd-Lieutenant W. Taylor (wounded).

OTHER RANKS.

Killed 12.   Wounded 126.   Missing 284.

The total of other ranks reported as killed includes only those who had belonged
to the three platoons which had survived the attack. A considerable proportion of

9th May, 1915. those under the heading of " wounded " also were men of these platoons, though this total would include the casualties of the other companies whom it had been possible to evacuate before the final assault. Captain Auld estimated the number of other ranks who were taken as prisoners to Germany at not over eighty, and the mournful conclusion is that of the total of those recorded under the ominous heading of " missing " some two hundred must have met their death in the fierce hand to hand fighting that ensued when the three companies were overwhelmed and now lie in nameless graves.

Maps 11 & 12

Of the disasters that had overtaken the 2nd Battalion on the 8th May, not the least was the loss of their Commanding Officer, Lieut.-Colonel H. S. Enderby. Enderby was the classic type of regimental officer, full of *esprit de corps*, whose highest ambition was to command a battalion of the FIFTH. From the day on which he had first taken it into action he had demonstrated a courage and an unshakeable imperturbability in the face of danger which had secured the confidence of his entire command. Now, following the climax of the fighting of the 8th May, he was taken to the headquarters of the German commander. He was well received by the General, who, after a brief conversation, protested : " But why look so depressed about it all ? " Enderby represented that the almost complete annihilation of one's battalion was sufficient excuse for such an attitude. To this the General replied : " Maybe so. But you may reflect that had it not been for the resistance of that battalion I should not now be here. I should have been in Ypres to-night." A generous utterance, and, it may be hoped that this high tribute, given in all sincerity, served in after years to solace the commander of the Battalion to which it was paid.

Captain H. C. Stephen, who had arrived from England on the eve of the Battle of Frezenberg, had been left at the transport lines. He now assumed command of the Battalion, while Captain Allan took over the duties of Adjutant in addition to those of Quartermaster. Drafts from home brought the strength of the Battalion up to 9 officers and 457 other ranks. But the officers who came with the reinforcements were all very young 2nd-Lieutenants, a large proportion of the N.C.O.'s needed both training and experience, and the men themselves were still very raw. The strength and composition of the other battalions of the 84th Brigade were similar to those of the 2/FIFTH, and to stand again as an efficient fighting formation, the Brigade as a whole required some weeks, at least, of rest for training and reorganisation. The situation, however, did not allow of this. The offensive operations further south, to which reference has already been made, had now been opened by the First Army, and it had become more than ever necessary for the Second Army to rely on its own resources in standing on the defensive in its position covering Ypres. So, weak and half trained as it was, the 2/FIFTH, with the remainder of the 84th Brigade, had to be kept well forward in reserve, with the ever present prospect of being thrown into battle.

During the 9th, 10th and 11th of May the British positions east of Ypres were subjected to terrific shell fire and to repeated, though ineffectual, attempts by the Germans to develop an infantry attack. A lull on the 12th was followed by a heavy attack on the 13th, which again failed to get home. On the 14th the

Germans massed for attack opposite Hooge and Bellewaarde, but their concentrations were broken up by our artillery fire. Then the fighting died down, and but for some desultory shell fire nine days passed uneventfully. The allied attacks to the south were evidently taking effect in relieving the pressure against the Second Army, and this cessation of activity encouraged the belief that "Second Ypres" was at last at an end. But, as will be seen, the enemy, before abandoning their 1915 offensive on this front, were to make one last desperate effort to break the British line that covered the mass of ruins that now stood for the town of Ypres.

In the meantime further reinforcements of officers and men had reached the 2/FIFTH. On his arrival at a base hospital after Frezenberg, 2nd-Lieutenant Watson had met Captain Wreford Brown, to whom he recounted the sad plight to which the Battalion had been reduced. This officer, who had never fully recovered from wounds received seven years before on the North-West Frontier, was quite unfit for active service and had been admitted to hospital a few weeks before after a brief tour of duty with the 2nd Battalion. On learning the sore need for officers, he succeeded in obtaining his discharge from hospital and rejoined the Battalion on the 22nd May, taking over command from Captain Stephen. By that day the strength of the 2/FIFTH had been increased to 15 officers and 608 other ranks. Among the officer reinforcements, Captain Booth, who had been wounded in the previous October with the 1st Battalion, was an experienced leader; the remainder, with the exception of Lieutenant Buckle of the Special Reserve, averaged less than 20 years of age.

The Vth Corps, of which the 28th Division formed part, at this time held a line from Hill 60, on the right, by Hooge, to Turco Farm, due north of Ypres. The centre of this line, occupied by the 1st Cavalry Division and the 85th Infantry Brigade, crossed the Menin road just east of Hooge and thence ran by the west bank of Bellewaarde Lake and Bellewaarde Farm to cross the Roulers railway east of Railway Wood. At dawn on Whit Monday, the 24th May, a very heavy gas attack was opened by the Germans, and was followed by an infantry assault against the whole front of the Vth Corps. The attack failed completely except in one portion of the line—between the Menin Road and the Roulers railway—where the 2nd Cavalry Brigade and the right of the 85th Infantry Brigade were thrust back. Here, the enemy sweeping forward from the Bellewaarde Ridge, effected a serious penetration. On the flanks, however, the 1st Cavalry Brigade, at and south of Hooge, and the 83rd Infantry Brigade, north of the Roulers railway, held fast.

The 84th Brigade represented the nearest available reserves, and at 5.45 a.m. the 2/Cheshire Regiment was sent forward by the Brigadier to take up a position in the G.H.Q. Line, which crossed the Menin road at Hell Fire Corner and ran north to Potijze. At 9.45 a.m. the 2/FIFTH with the other battalions of the brigade assembled east of Vlamertinghe to await orders. It was at first planned that the 84th Brigade should counter-attack for the recovery of the ground lost in conjunction with the 80th Brigade of the 27th Division, which would be moved up from a position some miles further to the west. Fresh rations had been issued, and the troops were ordered to cook and take dinners before moving forward. At 12 noon, however, before the dinners had been cooked, the situation in the fighting line threatened such serious developments that the 84th Brigade was ordered to move forward forthwith. As the FIFTH, who were to lead in the approach march, were moving off, Captain Allan, who

HELL-FIRE CORNER.

"How aptly this point had been named ..."

24th May, 1915 as acting adjutant had gone forward to report at Brigade Headquarters, had a happy encounter. A party composed of newly arrived drafts was halted by the roadside; the officer in command of the party proved to be none other than Captain Salier of the FIFTH, a close friend and former subaltern of Captain Wreford Brown. But recently returned from West Africa, he had not served with Wreford Brown since the day, seven years before, when the latter had been wounded by his side on the Mohmand frontier. Immediately he heard of the task which lay before the Battalion and of its lack of senior officers, he handed over charge of his party to the senior N.C.O. and reported to Captain Wreford Brown. He was straightway appointed adjutant, and Captain Allan was able to resume his position as quartermaster. Perhaps only those who knew the two can realise all that it was to mean to Wreford Brown this day to have Salier by his side.

Maps 11 & 12

With the 2/FIFTH leading, units on approaching Ypres struck right in succession to follow the railway which curved round to the south of the town before running north-east to cross the Menin road at Hell Fire Corner. How aptly this point had been named was illustrated when the Battalion, halting under the treacherous cover of a railway cutting just to the south of it, immediately came under a heavy and devastating artillery fire. The companies were hurriedly moved forward, but already many casualties had been sustained before they were assembled well to the east of this death trap and south of the Menin road. It was now about 2.30 p.m., and it was at this time that a message was received by the G.O.C. 84th Brigade ordering him to attack without waiting for the arrival of the 80th Brigade.* On receipt of this message the Brigadier issued orders to Battalion Commanders for the counter-attack. The attack was to be carried out by the 2/FIFTH and the 2/Cheshire in the 1st line, the centre of the FIFTH being directed on Wittepoort Farm, the Cheshire, with their left on the railway, advancing against Railway Wood. In the 2nd line, the 1/Welch were to support the attack, while to the south of this battalion the 1/Suffolk were to be directed in an independent attack against a body of the enemy which had penetrated our Cavalry position to the south of Bellewaarde Lake and was reported to be established north of Hooge. The 1/Monmouth in reserve were to reinforce the G.H.Q. Line. In short, it had fallen to the weak battalions of the 84th Brigade, led for the most part by young officers whose gallantry could not compensate their inexperience, to undertake on empty stomachs a task which might be deemed to represent a severe test for fresh and seasoned troops under experienced leaders.

The Battalion was to attack in three lines on a one company front; "A" Company (Captain Stephen) leading, followed by "C" Company (Captain Booth), with "D" Company (2nd-Lieutenant Freeman) in the third line. "B" Company (Lieutenant Buckle) was to be held in battalion reserve. As there seemed no immediate task for the machine guns, these were left with 2nd-Lieutenant Gilchrist at the assembly position when, at about 2.45 p.m., the Battalion advanced to the attack. After advancing some 300 yards, companies were ordered to move to the north of the Menin road, in order to face their objective. Having been formed accordingly, the

---

* War Diary 84th Inf. Bde. The Official History suggests that this order was received at 12 noon, *i.e.*, before moving from west of Ypres. The war diary of the 84th Brigade seems to leave no doubt that the order did not reach the Brigadier till he was in the neighbourhood of Hell Fire Corner.

advance was resumed, the centre of the leading company being directed on Wittepoort Farm.*

While Wittepoort Farm had been named in orders as a directing point, it had not been given as an objective to be captured, and there is no indication that it was known to be held by the enemy. Scarcely, however, had the Battalion moved forward than the companies came under heavy machine gun fire from the farm, and almost immediately Captain Stephen was wounded, 2nd-Lieutenant Sellars killed, and many casualties inflicted among the other ranks. It seems that Wittepoort Farm was not held in great numerical strength by the enemy, but that a machine gun nest had been established there as an advanced post in front of the main position. As such it commanded the line of advance of the Battalion, and it was not till late in the afternoon, and at the expense of heavy casualties, that the FIFTH succeeded in driving back the enemy from this position and occupying it. From here a further slight advance was made to the line of the Cambridge Road, but already the losses in the Battalion had been so heavy that mere shattered remnants remain of its companies and platoons. At an early stage Lieutenant Buckle had been wounded and 2nd-Lieutenant Hobbs killed. Later in the afternoon Captain Booth and both his subalterns had been wounded. As darkness was falling, Booth, before being evacuated, saw and spoke to Captain Wreford Brown; but, though the circumstances of his death are now unknown, it must have been shortly after this that Wreford Brown was killed. 2nd-Lieutenant Freeman relates that, on crossing the Cambridge Road just after dark to take up a position for the night in an open field, " Salier (in command), O'Dowd and I were the only three officers left, with as far as I could see a mere handful of men." Here, isolated and completely exhausted, this little band remained throughout the hours of darkness, firing at the flashes of the enemy's rifles.

In the meantime, the attack of the remainder of the 84th Brigade, to the south, had been delayed, and no advance had been made till 5 p.m. In this quarter, it seems, no progress was made at all. At 8.30 p.m. troops of the 80th Brigade at last began to arrive, and it was decided to renew the attack at 1 a.m. The conditions under which this second attack was to be undertaken can best be judged from extracts from the War Diary of the 84th Brigade:—

---

* The events of the 24th May from this time forward must always remain to some extent a matter of conjecture. The Official History, it would seem, relies on the narrative given in the War Diary of the 84th Brigade. But the degree to which this can be accepted as an accurate account can be judged from the admission in the War Diary that Brigade Headquarters remained till 7 p.m. in complete ignorance of what was transpiring in the front line of attack, and from the fact that after the battle no officer of the FIFTH, and few, if any, of other units, were left to report on the details of the action. In so far as concerns the 2/FIFTH, the narrative which follows is based mainly on what has been communicated by officers of the Regiment who took part in the action and are still living—Lieut.-Colonel R. M. Booth, Majors H. C. Stephen, J. H. Hogshaw and C. R. Freeman. While considerable discrepancies are found in their statements, these officers are in general agreement on such points as are included in the narrative given in this history. One point alone is sufficient to support the contention that the "official narrative" cannot be taken as reliable. The line which is said to have been reached by the FIFTH on their front of attack was one which had been given in a first report by Salier; which represented the one small measure of success that could be claimed for the attack of the 84th Brigade. But a *second report* by the same officer stated that the map had been wrongly read, and that it had since been realised that the Battalion was not within half a mile of the line first given. In confirmation of this correction, Freeman, who had discovered the original error, wrote to Brigade Headquarters from hospital a few days later to direct attention to the mistake that had been made. But it seems that these corrections were either not received or were ignored.

24th May, 1915 "Two battalions of the 80th Brigade were to attack between Bellewaarde Lake and Eclusette, while the 84th Brigade pushed on on their former line backed by two battalions of the 80th Brigade. The 84th Brigade was by this time somewhat muddled —the inexperienced company commanders had been unable to keep touch or direction, N.C.O.'s were insufficient to control untrained troops. The men had had no food since the early morning, and were completely exhausted. The G.O.C. saw the O.C. Welch and Suffolk and a representative of the Cheshire. *The Northumberland Fusiliers appeared to have been so heavily punished in the first attack that as a battalion they were a negligible quantity.* The Monmouth, sent for at 11.30 p.m., did not arrive till 2.30 a.m.—too late to use (it was getting light at 2.30 a.m.)."

Maps 11 & 12

Having read the above, one is prepared for the sequel; for what result could be expected from an attack opened under such conditions, apart from further heavy casualties? It is related that the attack was launched at 1 a.m., that very heavy rifle and machine gun fire was heard shortly after, and that very shortly after this the whole of the 3/K.R.R. and 4/Rifle Brigade (of the 80th Brigade) came back to the G.H.Q. Line. It was then decided that the considerable losses already incurred did not warrant further effort.

It is true, as stated in the Brigade War Diary, that the 2/FIFTH as a battalion had ceased to exist, and it might be concluded that it was not represented in this last fruitless attack. But the orders for the attack had reached Salier just before dawn, and he with 2nd-Lieutenants Freeman and O'Dowd faithfully led forward the handful of men that remained. Just on the far side of the ridge on which they had lain during the night ran a hedge. Immediately on passing through this, Salier was wounded, and O'Dowd (on this the eve of his 18th birthday) was killed. Freeman, the sole surviving officer, dropped to the shelter of a shell hole together with a serjeant. He relates:—" It was beginning to get light enough to see around and, apart from the one serjeant in the shell hole with me, there were as far as I could see about half a dozen of us in shell holes with the Germans in holes or a trench not very far from us. On the right and left of us we had no flank troops at all. I saw the men on either side of me shot, and I had a few rounds duel with a tin helmet in front of me. I never knew more of the outcome of this than that my opponent gave up plugging the parapet of my shell hole." Recognising the hopelessness of his position, he signalled to the men to withdraw through the hedge to the cover of the ridge from which they had advanced, and ordered the serjeant to follow them. Then, making a dash back himself, Freeman, who had hitherto miraculously escaped injury, fell shot through the shoulder and back. "I crawled back over the ridge, to find a remnant of some seven of the Battalion digging in with entrenching tools between Cambridge Road and Wittepoort Farm. There were also a few of some other battalion, which had presumably come up overnight, but no-one seemed to know what was on the flanks. The farm building was shelled off and on throughout the morning, but we were left comparatively quiet in front of it. . . . . I sent one of our fellows with a message addressed to 'General Bols' (I had not the faintest notion of the number of the brigade), reporting that we were "in the air" and without water or rations; most of my own iron ration had been shot through my back! Later, whether it was morning or afternoon I knew not, I went back with an orderly (also wounded) to try to find Brigade Headquarters." On reaching the back area, it seems that he was conducted to a casualty clearing station, without being permitted to pursue his search, and his last recollection is of a night-mare journey to hospital. So ends the story of a young officer, 22 years of age, who, after two months' training with the Special Reserve Battalion, had joined the 2/FIFTH on the eve of battle, and, ignorant even of the brigade to which he belonged, had been left with the terrible responsibility of being the last of the officers of his battalion to survive this ill fated counter-attack.

The following were the casualties sustained by the 2/FIFTH on the 24th/25th May 1915 :—

OFFICERS.

Killed .. Captain C. Wreford Brown, D.S.O.
2nd-Lieutenant H. E. Hobbs.
2nd-Lieutenant M. O'Dowd.
2nd-Lieutenant J. H. Sellars.

Wounded .. Captain R. M. Booth, D.S.O.
Captain H. C. Stephen.
Lieutenant E. H. Salier.
Lieutenant D. F. de C. Buckle.
2nd-Leiutenant C. R. Freeman.
2nd-Lieutenant J. H. Hogshaw.
2nd-Lieutenant W. H. C. Bucknall.
2nd-Lieutenant W. G. B. Garrard.

Missing .. Lieutenant J. M. Gillespie, R.A.M.C.

OTHER RANKS.

Killed 29.   Wounded 133.   Missing 188.

In Claude Wreford Brown the FIFTH had lost an officer who, with the 1st Battalion, had served with distinction in campaigns in the Soudan, South Africa, and on the North-West Frontier of India. To "Wreford" the one thing in life was his Regiment; it had been his almost fanatical devotion to the FIFTH which had called him from hospital, where he should rightly have remained, to meet his death where he would have wished, at the head of one of its battalions. The 2/FIFTH, reconstituted but a week before, after the fearful casualties sustained at Frezenberg, had once more been reduced to a strength at which it could not put even a weak company into the field.

If all the circumstances in which this counter-attack was thrown in are considered, it is difficult to believe that, from the outset, there can have been any very great hope of it ending other than it did. But one must remember that a critical situation had demanded urgent action, and there were no other troops available to employ. It is impossible to judge of what might have resulted had action been delayed; and to estimate the true and ultimate achievement of an apparent failure in war, it is necessary to look at that other side of the picture which is seldom revealed till long after the event. For this we may turn to the Official History of the War, which tells us :—" On the evening of the 24th May the German Fourth Army issued orders that operations should be stopped. The German battalions were quite worn out and had suffered nearly as many casualties as the British."

The 24th May, 1915, marked the close of the Second Battle of Ypres, and one may justly believe that the sacrifice of the young and inexperienced lads who lost their lives with the FIFTH that day had not been in vain, but had served towards preventing the enemy from exploiting the initial success of the early morning and so continuing an effort which by the evening he had been forced to abandon.

"ALL THAT WERE LEFT."—(2nd Battalion, 25th May, 1915.)

MACHINE GUNNERS.
Serjts. Musgrove and Hastwell, Ptes. Lawlor, Brough and Wheatley.

OFFICERS.
Capt. W. M. Allan, 2nd-Lieuts. C. H. Steel and J. H. L. Gilchrist.

STRETCHER BEARERS.
Cpl. Lowe, Lce.-Cpls. Carter, Elvin, Cunningham, Wilson and Brielly, Ptes. Mill and Crann.

CHAPTER VIII.

1st Battalion.

The St. Eloi Sector—Attack on Bellewaarde.*

5TH APRIL—16TH JUNE, 1915.

5th April, 1915

As the opposing armies settled down to trench warfare, conditions underwent a great change from those that had prevailed in the opening months of the War. We have seen how the 1/FIFTH for three months after the Battle of Mons, with a steadily mounting toll of casualties, were from day to day engaged almost continuously in attacking or repelling attack. For them, though not yet for all, these experiences ended with the first Battle of Ypres. Thereafter, until the German lines were broken in the final phase of the War, the 1/Battalion was to do duty in the trenches for long periods during which the casualties sustained were slight as compared with those of the early months. For instance, in the trenches on the Kemmel front during the three months following the first Battle of Ypres, battle casualties among officers had been but $\frac{1}{11}$th, and among other ranks only $\frac{1}{8}$th of those suffered between the 23rd August and the 21st November, 1914. In this second phase of the War, however, occasions were to arise on which in a single day the Battalion was to suffer losses almost equalling the total of the first three months. Thus, in the present chapter, we shall see a period marked by few incidents culminate in an action in which the 1/FIFTH were to sustain far heavier casualties than they had hitherto experienced in any one day.

Map No. 11

It will be remembered that on the 4th April the Battalion, with the 9th Brigade, had rejoined the 3rd Division, which now occupied a sector in the southern quarter of the Ypres Salient. The front line of the Division ran from the Vierstraat—Wytschaete road, opposite Hollandscheschuur Farm, in a generally north-easterly direction to a point just south of the Ypres-Comines Canal. The general run of the line was, however, deflected at St. Eloi, whence for a distance of a thousand yards it turned slightly south of east before resuming its general north-easterly trend. The re-entrant thus formed in the British line had recently been accentuated by the capture by the Germans of a mound which formed a prominent feature on the southern outskirts of St. Eloi, and as a result our line had been withdrawn to pass through the village immediately south of the cross roads Voormezeele-Warneton—Ypres-Messines. In this re-entrant the FIFTH, as the right battalion of the 9th Brigade, took over on the 5th April the defences of St. Eloi and the trenches on either side of the village.

The details of the Battalion's dispositions are necessary to an understanding of an event which was shortly to occur here. Three companies were placed in the

---

* There may be some who wonder why the battle honour " Bellewaarde " was shown at the head of the preceding rather than of the present chapter, for it is commonly believed in the FIFTH that the honour was awarded in respect to the attack in which the 1st Battalion took part with the 9th Brigade on the 16th June, 1915. This action, officially named " First Attack on Bellewaarde," has, however, no relation to the battle honour, which was granted in respect to the action in which the 2nd Battalion was engaged on the 24th and 25th of May with the 84th Brigade, and which represented the last battle of " Ypres 1915."

front line, while the fourth occupied support trenches some three hundred yards in rear of the centre and left. The centre company held the village and a line of trench to the left of it. On the other side of the village, the right company occupied a somewhat isolated trench, known as Q1. On the left of this trench, and connected to it by a short length of communication trench, stood a small fortified building, below which a mine shaft had been sunk, garrisoned by a detachment of the right company of the FIFTH and some sappers. In rear of Q1, a support trench, Q2, was held by a company of the Liverpool Scottish, who had recently joined the 9th Brigade. Nowhere on the front of the Battalion could access be gained to the front line during daylight, as between this and the support line the ground was fully exposed to the view of the enemy, and there were no communication trenches connecting the two lines. But in rear of the support line the ground sloped somewhat steeply, giving covered approach to Battalion Headquarters, which were situated in Voormezeele, some 1200 yards in rear of the front line.

The enemy's snipers were always on the alert, but in spite of this the first tour in the trenches passed quietly, and when the Battalion was withdrawn on the 7th April to Brigade Reserve at Dickebusch, the few casualties that had occurred had been mainly caused by stray bullets among parties moving across the open by night. On the 11th the Battalion again went into the line. On the evening of the 13th there was some slight shelling by the enemy, but no damage was done. The following day passed very quietly; but the somewhat perfunctory bombardment of the previous day was repeated just before sundown, when peace again reigned.

With the fall of darkness the trench garrisons as usual got to work in strengthening the defences, while carrying parties went back to Battalion Headquarters to bring forward rations and stores. Q1 was garrisoned on this night by "Y" Company (Captain Roddam), the trench being held by 60 men, while 20 men of the same company with 11 Royal Engineers occupied the fortified house. Suddenly, at 11.15 p.m., rapid rifle fire was opened on Q1, and was shortly followed by a heavy bombardment by shrapnel, which included "W" Company's position in and on either side of the village. Trench mortars were also brought to bear on Q1, and almost simultaneously a mine was exploded just short of the house on the left of the trench. All telephone lines were cut by the shell fire, and at Battalion Headquarters there was considerable anxiety as to what was happening in the front line, but our artillery were quick in replying to the enemy's bombardment. On "W" Company's front the bulk of the enemy's fire was passing overhead, and here the men quickly manned the parapet and stood with fixed bayonets, only too eager for the German infantry to advance to the assault. In "Y" Company, however, the situation was very different. In Q1 the greatest confusion reigned, and had the enemy acted promptly and with boldness they could not have failed to carry the trench. Though the mine had been blown short of the position, the fortified house had been completely wrecked by the concussion, and the parapet on the left of Q1 had collapsed, blocking all communication between the trench and the house. Fifty per cent. of the garrison had been more or less seriously injured, and a certain number had fallen back on Q2.

Captain Roddam, severely shaken, and his subaltern Lieutenant Roderick who was more seriously injured, started to make their way along the trench towards the scene of the explosion, but the latter soon collapsed. Roddam found that rifles had been buried or choked with earth and that the majority of the men shaken by the sudden explosion, and stupefied by the deafening noise and blinding flashes of the shells, seemed incapable of action. He could muster only twelve men with their wits

14th April, 1915 about them and with serviceable rifles. With these he manned the parapet and opened rapid fire. The German artillery had now lengthened its range presumably to clear the way for assault. By this time, however, our own shells were bursting with great accuracy over the opposing front line trench and over " The Mound " in rear; and this, combined with the evidence given by Roddam's fire that the garrison was still capable of resistance, defeated the enemy's plans. The flashes of the shells revealed his infantry quitting their front line and running to the shelter of a trench in rear, and simultaneously rifle fire from the opposing line almost entirely ceased. A message from Captain Roddam had, in the meantime, reached the Liverpool Scottish in Q2, who immediately sent forward a working party and stretcher bearers. Little more than half an hour had elapsed since the opening of the enemy's bombardment before all was quiet again and work started on clearing the trench. An approach to the house was dug round the blocked portion of the communication trench, but it was not possible to clear the debris of the house itself till daylight.

Map No. 11

By 9 a.m. all still living had been rescued and the dead removed from the ruined building. A crater seventy-five feet in diameter was found within five yards of the house, but our mine shaft was fortunately undamaged. The casualties in " Y " Company had amounted to five other ranks killed, including Company Serjeant-Major R. Simpson, who had commanded the detachment in the house, and one officer and 37 other ranks wounded. In bringing to notice the manner in which Captain Roddam by his influence and example, had restored confidence among his men, Lt.-Colonel Ainslie added :—" It is not the first time this officer has shown great coolness and courage in the trenches under nerve-racking conditions." For their gallant conduct on this occasion Roddam was later awarded the Military Cross, and Serjeant J. Clarkburn the Distinguished Conduct Medal. The former, alas ! was to be killed before he had been informed of the award.*

Apart from the incidents of the night of the 14th/15th April, there is little to relate of the remaining six weeks spent by the Battalion on this front. Each succeeding tour in the trenches was but a repetition of the previous one ; the days being given up mainly to rest, broken from time to time by a few rounds of artillery fire or trench mortars or by a sharp hail of the even more dangerous rifle grenades ; the nights being spent in watching and in work. Both sides had early learnt the useless and often fatal risk of exposing themselves to the enemy's snipers, and the rifle grenade accordingly represented the sole means by which the trench-bound infantryman could employ his own weapon against an enemy who never showed himself above his parapet. Against the high-angle fire of the grenade there was scant protection in the open trenches, and if casualties from this source were to be prevented it could only be by a prompt return of the enemy's fire in such volume and with such accuracy as should cause him to regret having started a fight of this description and to refrain accordingly from again courting the punishment he had earned by his action. Accuracy was dependent on skill, and in this the FIFTH by long practice had acquired a high standard ; but, ultimately, superiority was offered to the side with the most plentiful supply of grenades, and here the Germans at this period were known by us to hold the advantage. In these circumstances the FIFTH could only hope to find safety in a bluff which might keep the enemy in ignorance of the advantage he held. A notable

---

* Captain R. C. Roddam M.C., who had joined the Special Reserve Battalion on the outbreak of war, was the only son of the late Colonel R. J. Roddam, who before the War had commanded that battalion, and during the War Commanded the 15th Reserve Battalion of the Regiment.

instance of this occurred in the trenches of "Z" Company when they were in occupation of a position to the north-east of St. Eloi.

Map No. 11

April and May, 1915

Rather unwisely, perhaps, in view of our inferior supply of ammunition, the company for some days had been provoking the Germans in the opposing trenches by a policy of continual grenade sniping. The failure of the enemy to make any very vigorous reply had induced a belief that he was content indefinitely to submit to being harassed in this manner. But, in the peaceful hours of a perfect spring afternoon, when the men were sitting idly in the trenches, this illusion was rudely shattered. Suddenly and unexpectedly, a hail of grenades came over from the German line, to burst with terrible accuracy in three salient bays of the trenches occupied by the offending company. The garrison was speedily withdrawn from the position which had been made the target of the enemy's fire, but not before some twenty men had been killed or wounded by this opening volley of a bombardment which threatened to extend to other parts of the company's parapet. The only hope of checking fire delivered in such volume lay in vigorous and immediate retaliation; a reply in the form of weak and desultory fire, which at the time seemed the most that could be produced by the weakened and disordered garrison, far from quelling the enemy, would serve only to encourage him to further efforts. "Z" Company was placed in a serious predicament, from which in the circumstances there seemed to be no escape. Credit for the solution of the problem lay with Captain Sloper, the Machine Gun Officer, who happened to arrive on the spot at this critical juncture. He ordered twelve rifles to be immediately loaded with grenades and, himself carrying six of these into the fatal bays, called on Lieutenant Dorman-Smith to follow him with the remainder. From this position—the main target of the enemy—the two officers fired twelve grenades in rapid succession, then, having reloaded, they sent over a second salvo. The ruse proved completely successful. To the enemy it appeared that the trench-bays were still fully manned, and convinced of the ineffectiveness of their own fire, of which the sole result seemed to be to bring retaliation and casualties, they at once closed down their bombardment.*

The rifle-grenade fight recounted above, was, however, unusual in its severity at this period. The days on the whole passed fairly quietly and allowed of rest in preparation for the heavier work which started at nightfall. It was then that double sentries, at intervals along the parapet, strained their eyes to detect any movement of the enemy under the illumination of the Very lights, which from the fall of darkness till the break of dawn were sent up by both sides except when patrols crept out to the narrow strip of No Man's Land which separated the opposing lines. Now and again, from one side or the other, a sharp burst of rifle fire would break out, and spreading right and left would continue perhaps for five minutes or so before it was realised that a false alarm had been given. While sentries and patrols thus watched the front, the remainder of the garrison would be employed by reliefs throughout the night ceaselessly repairing and improving the defences. Though on the surface this life in the trenches at St. Eloi was comparatively quiet, the knowledge that mining and countermining was in progress was a disturbing factor. Mysterious underground noises always called for investigation, and on one occasion, a nest of rats, only less unpleasant than the human miners for whom they had been mistaken, was responsible for creating some alarm!

Generally speaking, throughout the War, hard work left little time for the

---

* The action of Captain Sloper on this occasion was an example of the cool and quick judgment and complete disregard of personal danger which were the marked characteristics of this very fine officer. For the circumstances of his death, see note at the end of this chapter.

April and May, 1915

regimental soldier to speculate on what the future might hold in store, or to concern himself very deeply with what was happening outside his own immediate surroundings. In the days of late April, 1915, the vague rumours which reached the 1/Fifth of the German attack at Ypres brought little realisation of the critical situation that had arisen within a few miles of them. While the 2nd and Territorial battalions of the Regiment were engaged in the desperate fighting at St. Julien, the men of the 1st, in the comparative peace of the trenches at St. Eloi, sat listening to the distant bombardment and the moaning of the mighty shells travelling in endless procession towards Ypres; watched the black smoke clouds rise from the stricken town; and " Phew ! That was *some* crump ! " would be the detached comment of the watchers at St. Eloi, when a dull roar announced the arrival of some huge projectile at its destination.

Map No. 11

Only in certain minor ways was the 1st Battalion itself directly affected by the opening of the Second Battle of Ypres. On the afternoon of the 22nd April a curious smell was noticed in the trenches, and many of the men complained that their eyes were smarting. Company commanders were completely non-plussed, though not seriously disturbed, by this phenomenon. Among the more intelligent suggestions put forward was the idea that something had gone wrong with the chlorate of lime, used as a disinfectant in the trenches. Not till the following day, with the news of the German gas attack, was the true significance of what had been observed revealed.* Another way in which the great battle that had broken out to the north interfered with the Battalion lay in the cancellation of its relief on 22nd April, which resulted in its spending St. George's Day in the trenches, instead of in reserve as had been promised. From this day forward, moreover, the extension of the 3rd Division front brought longer spells in the trenches and briefer periods in reserve. The work on a rear switch line, on which large parties were employed nightly while in reserve, was a direct result of events in the north, but little did any in the Battalion know at the time that the trench was being constructed in anticipation of the collapse of the Ypres Salient !

The Battalion remained on the St. Eloi front till the 26th May, when, on the relief of the 9th by the 13th Brigade, it was withdrawn to huts at Ouderdom. Casualties during this first tour at St. Eloi totalled 1 officer and 27 other ranks killed, 1 officer and 107 other ranks wounded. 2nd-Lieutenant H. A. Jung, after having been slightly wounded during his first tour in the trenches, had been mortally wounded while in charge of a working party at night. The wounded officer was Lieutenant B. E. Hervey-Bathurst, who had recently joined the Battalion as machine gun officer.† While at Ouderdom the 1st Battalion was visited by 2nd-Lieutenant Gilchrist and Captain Allan, at that time the sole surviving officers of the 2/FIFTH; and from them details were now first heard of what had occurred at Frezenberg and Bellewaarde on the 8th and 24th May.

On the 28th May, the 9th Brigade was again attached for a few days to the

---

* One finds that, at the time, it was thought by the 3rd Division that gas shells had been employed on their front, but there is little doubt that the gas had come from the St. Julien front. As illustrating the unpreparedness of the British for this form of warfare, it may be interesting to record that, among the desperate expedients advised for protection, was the recommendation that men should use their woollen caps or scarves as respirators after soaking these in their own urine.

† At the outbreak of war Lieutenant Hervey-Bathurst, who had previously served in the FIFTH, was on the Reserve of Officers. He had already once been wounded while serving in the early weeks of the War with a battalion of another Regiment to which he had been posted.

28th Division, the 1/FIFTH occupying support trenches near Potijze Chateau. On the 30th May the chateau was set on fire by an artillery bombardment, but otherwise the four days spent in these trenches passed quietly. At this time, live stock from the deserted farms was still roaming in the neighbourhood of the support line, and two homeless dogs, a very large Belgian " wheel dog " (christened " George ") and a little white mongrel (" Whizz-bang ") took refuge in the trenches of the Battalion. It was with the greatest difficulty that " George " could be persuaded ever to leave the shelter of the dug-out he shared with young John Lawson, and at the sound of artillery fire it was pitiful to see the frantic efforts of the poor creature literally to " dig himself in." Later, " George " found a home at the transport lines, where he was transformed to a " different dog "; but, even there, on the faintest sound of distant gun fire, his terror would return with the recollection of the destruction of the farm where, in more peaceful days, he had worked the churn wheel. " Whizz-bang " was made of sterner stuff, for on relief in the trenches he deserted the FIFTH and joined a battalion bound for the front line !

On the 29th May, Lt. Colonel Ainslie, on appointment to command the 18th Infantry Brigade, left the Battalion to which his leadership in the early weeks of the War had meant so much. Unfortunately it was evident that the labours and anxieties of battalion command had undermined a constitution never too robust, as very shortly after he left the Battalion a breakdown in health was to rob him of the still higher promotion for which he had seemed destined. He was replaced in battalion command by Bt.-Lt.-Colonel C. Yatman, who had already officiated in command during the periods of Lt.-Colonel Ainslie's absence on sick leave in the previous autumn and winter.

On the 2nd June, after two days in reserve, the FIFTH, on temporary attachment to the 13th Brigade, relieved the 2/K.O.Y.L.I. in the front line just south of Hooge. On the 6th, the Battalion was again withdrawn to reserve and took up bivouac at a farm near Ouderdom. On the 12th, the G.O.C. 3rd Division presented the ribbon of the Distinguished Conduct Medal to the following :—

>No. 6931 Serjeant Clarke.
>No. 7309 A/Serjeant Clarkson.
>No. 8528 L/Serjeant Dawson.
>No. 2162 Bandsman Kelly.
>No. 1352 Private Ellingham.

No. 1629 Serjeant Thompson, who had also been awarded the medal, was absent owing to wounds received on the 4th May.

In the seven months which had passed since the First Battle of Ypres the Battalion had sustained over 600 battle casualties, yet, since the storming of the stables of Herenthage Chateau on 15th November, no man of the FIFTH had seen a German soldier face to face. A periscope may have given a fleeting glimpse of a head above the opposing parapet; field glasses had once secured a momentary view of a German officer entering a dug-out behind the mound at St. Eloi, but for the rest the enemy had remained invisible. The experience of the majority of the Battalion as now constituted was limited to the routine of trench warfare, the daily toll of casualties in the trenches, and the despatch into space of projectiles, the effect of which on the enemy had never been seen, and could only be imagined.

One saw in the War that such conditions of fighting, if experienced for long, were apt to induce in most men a certain nervous restlessness, which made them eager to cross the narrow track of desolation which ran between their front line and the

EARLIEST FORM OF PROTECTION AGAINST GAS.
(May, 1915.)

[Imperial War Museum—Crown Copyright.

15th/16th June, 1915

opposing parapet, and to meet this unseen enemy lurking in the trenches beyond. The news that an opportunity for this was now to be given to the 1/FIFTH was, accordingly, welcome to all.*

Map No. 13

In the fighting in which 2nd Battalion had been engaged on the Bellewaarde Ridge, the British line had been thrust back between the Menin road and the Roulers railway. The 3rd Division had now been given the task of reducing the salient which had thus developed by the capture of the German positions between the south-west corner of Bellewaarde Lake and the Roulers railway to the north of Railway Wood. The 8th Brigade was to take over the portion of the line from which the attack was to start; the 9th Brigade to carry out the assault, and the 7th Brigade (less one battalion) to stand in reserve in trenches west of Cambridge Road. The date of the operation had been fixed for the 16th June.

The attack of the 9th Brigade was organized for the capture of three successive objectives. The first of these was the edge of the wood Y16—Y15, and the German front line as far as the north-east corner of Railway Wood; the second, the line of the road from a house one hundred yards south of Y17, through Y17 to Bellewaarde Farm, and thence, through Y14 and Y11 to Y7; the third was the final objective of the operation, which has been described above. Preliminary to the infantry assault, an artillery bombardment of the enemy's trenches and wire was to be opened at 2.50 a.m. and, with three pauses of ten minutes at 3.10 a.m., 3.40 a.m. and 4 a.m., to continue till 4.15 a.m., when the guns would lift from the German front line, and the infantry advance to the capture of the first objective. Thereafter, the artillery support to the attack would be by observation. To facilitate this, distinctive screens were to be carried by infantry units to indicate to the gunners the progress of the attack.

The 4/Royal Fusiliers, 1/Royal Scots Fusiliers, and 1/FIFTH, in line from right to left, were detailed to capture the first objective. These battalions were to assemble for attack after dark on 15th June, partly in the British front line, partly in specially constructed assembly trenches. Following the capture of the first objective, the 1/Lincolnshire, on the right, and the Liverpool Scottish, on the left, advancing from assembly trenches further to the rear and leapfrogging over the leading troops, were to seize the second objective. On the accomplishment of this second phase, the first three battalions were in their turn to pass through the Lincolnshire and Scottish and capture the final objective. On the right of the 9th Brigade, a battalion of the 7th Brigade was to co-operate by an advance from the Menin road; on the left, where the FIFTH were placed, troops of 6th Division were to support the attack by covering fire.

In the light of later experience gained in the Great War, one can see in the artillery arrangements the weak point of this plan of attack. The creeping barrage had not yet been introduced. Only later was it realised that for the artillery in an attack of this nature to support advancing infantry by observation, and without the help of a time table, was a task nigh impossible to accomplish.

A rough map showing the enemy's trench system had been issued. Armed

---

* Apart from the fact that lack of material makes it impossible, the scope of this History does not permit of every action in which the FIFTH were engaged being related in as great detail as that which is to follow. But it is thought that a full account of one attack, as being to some extent typical of many, may be of interest to the reader. In selecting the attack on Bellewaarde of the 16th June, 1915, for this purpose, the writer has been influenced, not by any special importance attaching to the operation, but by the fact that treatment in detail has been made possible to him by the fuller records available, which include a narrative of the events of the day written by himself within a week of the battle.

with this and with periscopes, company commanders went forward on 13th June to the front line to reconnoitre the front of attack. Following this reconnaissance the final orders for the attack were issued. A hedge about 125 yards south of Railway Wood, marked on the map, and plainly recognisable on the ground, was selected as the boundary between the FIFTH and the Royal Scots Fusiliers. North of this the attack of the FIFTH would be delivered astride a sunken road situated immediatly south of Railway Wood. This road had been observed to be full of British dead, and was noted as a place to be avoided.*

The Battalion was to attack with three companies in the front line, "X" Company (Captain Bagshawe) on the right; "W" (Captain Sandilands) in the centre, and "Y" (Captain Roddam) on the left. "Z" Company (Lieutenant Dorman-Smith) was to be held in reserve during the first assault. "X" and "W" Companies were to assemble for attack in specially constructed trenches to the south of the sunken road; "Y" Company to the north of the road, in the British front line on the west side of Railway Wood. At the east corner of Railway Wood was a triangle of trenches, the west side of which, representing the German front line, was to be avoided in the first assault. It would fall to "W" Company, after carrying the front line south of the wood, to push a party north to Point Y 13 and clear the west and east faces of this triangle.

"Y" Company, advancing through Railway Wood, was to direct the right of its attack on the junction of the northern and western faces of this triangle, and then to push forward to gain contact with "W" Company at its eastern apex. "Y" Company was also to direct bombing parties north to clear the trench towards Y7. All companies, on carrying their objectives, if not in touch with those on their flanks, were to push bombers right and left to clear the trench of the enemy and gain contact. They were also to gain ground by bombing up communication trenches on their front.

The number of officers available did not allow of a Second-in-Command remaining with Battalion Headquarters. To anticipate the event of Colonel Yatman becoming a casualty, when command would fall to Captain Sandilands, Lieutenant Heyder, the senior subaltern, and two others were allotted to "W" Company, as against two only to each of "X" and "Y" and but one to Lieutenant Dorman-Smith, the commander of "Z."

At 4.45 p.m. on the 15th June, the Battalion paraded in its bivouac area in readiness to move forward to its assembly trenches. The dress was marching order, without packs. Each man carried two extra bandoliers of S.A.A., one day's rations (in addition to the iron ration); two empty sand-bags (for consolidation), and one water-proof sheet. Four hundred grenades (mostly Mills pattern) were distributed among companies to be carried in canvas carriers. Two platoons of "Z" (Reserve) Company carried shovels, slung on the back.

A march of 8 miles was needed to reach the assembly positions. Moving off just before 5 p.m., the Battalion marched by Vlamertinghe towards Ypres. After a two hour halt just west of the town, they passed through Ypres to debouch by the Menin Gate. It was nearing the shortest night of the year, and it was important that before the few remaining hours of darkness were past, the companies should be established in their assembly trenches. Marching by the Menin Road, the Battalion at length reached Hell Fire Corner,† the point at which the road is crossed by the Roulers

---

* It was later found that many of these were men of the 2nd Battalion who had fallen in Wreford Brown's attack on 24th May.

† See Chapter VII. for the experiences of the 2nd Battalion at this point on 24th May.

16th June, 1915 — railway, whence companies were to turn north-east and move independently at intervals of ten minutes across country to their assembly positions. But at this point, the last in the Ypres Salient at which one would choose to tarry, the progress of the Battalion, which had hitherto proceeded smoothly, was checked by the movement across its front of other troops of the Brigade. Fortunately on this night the German guns were exceptionally inactive, and after fifteen minutes of anxious waiting the companies got on the move without mishap; but when the assembly trenches were ultimately reached little time remained in hand. Owing to some misunderstanding about the allotment of trenches, a serious hitch now occurred, causing some confusion and delay. As a result, the first glimmer of dawn was already in the sky as "W" Company moved to its position. The movement was observed by the enemy, whose front line was less than 100 yards distant, and a sharp bombardment was opened by his field guns. Fortunately, after some fifteen minutes he seemed to become reassured and the fire ceased, but not before several casualties had been sustained.

Map No. 13

The companies were to advance to the attack in company column, leaving their trenches platoon by platoon. But for the troops, now cramped in the narrow assembly trenches, which in places were but $3\frac{1}{2}$ foot deep, there still remained long hours of waiting before the hour of assault. Punctually at 2.50 a.m., our field artillery opened. Thin and weak at the outset, it was disappointing to the infantry. But, gradually, it intensified, and as the heavier guns joined in, the terrific "crumps" of the heavy howitzer, known as "Mother," were heard, as her shells burst at Bellewaarde Farm. The German guns made little reply; but our own bombardment was in itself a trying ordeal for the men crouching in the assembly trenches. Though a slight slope towards the German position eased the delicate task of our field artillery, shells were bursting and shrapnel whistling close overhead during the long hours of bombardment, and occasional casualties among the assembled infantry from short shell were inevitable. During the first two pauses in the bombardment there was almost complete silence on the front of attack. It was now broad daylight, and when, at 4 a.m., our artillery ceased fire for the third time, the enemy's nerve broke. Manning their parapet they opened an intense rifle and machine gun fire. Whilst they were in this position, our guns, at 4.10 a.m. suddenly crashed down a terrific bombardment, and the word was given by company commanders to prepare for the assault. Eagerly, after the long strain of waiting for this moment, the men got ready, and five minutes later the leading platoons sprang from the trenches and rushed forward, followed at intervals of a few seconds by the remaining platoons, whom it was difficult to restrain. Though our artillery had lifted, the smoke of the shells still hung over the front line, but through this the Germans could be seen firing over their parapet; and all along the front men of the FIFTH were falling as the assaulting lines moved at the double across No Man's Land. The distance was short, but before it was covered the casualties were heavy. Four Officers were killed; on the right, Captain Bagshawe;[*] on the left, Captain Roddam and 2nd-Lieutenant Carter;[†] in the centre, 2nd-Lieutenant Dalbiac, whose platoon led the attack of "W" Company: and, as the rear platoon of "W" rose to advance, its commander, Lieutenant Heyder, was shot through the chest. Among the other ranks who fell in this narrow stretch of No Man's Land were many senior N.C.O's. Yet the remainder of the three companies, with the five officers that were all that were

---

[*] Captain L. V. Bagshawe was attached from the Special Reserve of the K.O.S.B.

[†] 2nd-Lieutenant Carter had been recently commissioned to the FIFTH from the Essex Regiment, in which he had served many years.

now left with them, stormed and carried the German front line. As our men leaped into the trench, the greater part of the garrison fled up communication trenches to the rear. A few who had been unable to effect their escape were too demoralised to offer further resistance; for the rest, there remained of the enemy only dead or desperately wounded men. It had been believed that the Battalion was opposed by Saxons, but two unwounded officers, captured in the front line, now declared themselves to be Wurtembergers.

Map No. 13   *16th June, 1915*

That dangerous phase in an attack had now been reached when the men, in the exultation of finding themselves still alive in the captured position among a demoralised enemy, are apt to believe that the battle is over and the victory won. The hostile artillery was still in ignorance of the situation, and for the moment there was no place in the field so immune from fire as the trenches from which the enemy had been driven. Littered with German helmets, gas respirators, and scraps of equipment, the trenches offered a paradise for the souvenir hunter. Officers and N.C.Os. had to exert all their authority to bring the wildly excited men to the important task of consolidating the position and re-organising against an immediate counter-attack, for which this was the supreme moment. But, though the loss of the front line was not yet known to the enemy's headquarters, the British attack had been signalled at the moment the assaulting infantry advanced, and a tremendous barrage had been opened on the assembly positions. On " Y " Company moving forward to the attack, "Z" Company, in reserve, had been sent forward to the vacated trenches, and suffered considerable casualties from this artillery fire, till they in turn were pushed up into the captured position.

Air photography was in its infancy, and the map that had been issued was a poor guide to the labyrinth of trenches in which the attacking troops now found themselves. The main lines of the German system, however, were fairly accurately shown, and the triangle of trenches east of Railway Wood, which it was the duty of " W " Company to clear, was clearly identifiable. Unfortunately the serjeant to whom this duty had been allotted had been wounded; his party had scattered, and the work remained undone. Thus, while the inner flanks of " W " and " X " Companies were in touch, " W " and " Y " were not in contact. The clearing of the triangle was urgent, and Captain Sandilands, arriving at the spot, started to organise a party for the purpose. Before the necessary men for the purpose could be collected, however, an event occurred that upset all pre-arranged plans. All along the battalion front the companies had occupied the enemy front line; had pushed parties forward up communication trenches, and had everywhere planted artillery screens to indicate the positions they had reached. But the smoke of our own shells and the dust they raised floating back over the position, combined, with that made by the German barrage, to obscure the view of our artillery observers, still uncertain as to the success or failure of the first phase of the attack. The gunners, accordingly, hesitated to lift their barrage. At this juncture, the Liverpool Scottish, eager to play their part, charged forward. Held up by the fire of their own artillery, they were unable to sweep forward to the second objective as planned, and became inextricably mingled with the FIFTH in the trenches of the captured position.

From this time forward pre-arranged plans had to be abandoned, and it was left to company officers to improvise methods for carrying the main objective of the attack. There could have been no finer material with which to co-operate in this than the Liverpool Scottish, who to a man showed the keenest readiness to fulfil any demand made of them. It was so that Sandilands now, with a mixed party of the Scottish and his own men, cleared the triangle east of Railway Wood. Failing still

16th June, 1915 to gain touch with " Y " Company, they consolidated the position against counter-attack, and, the artillery barrage having at length lifted, proceeded to bomb their way eastwards towards Point Y 11. The German counter-bombing, by which the advance was opposed, was fortunately wild and erratic; the enemy were slowly but steadily driven back, and our party eventually succeeded in establishing itself at Y 11. In the meantime " X " Company on the right, together with parties of the Liverpool Scottish, who had become mingled with them, had cleared the communication trenches on their front and had pushed forward to the second objective, occupying the trench west of Bellewaarde Farm, north and south of Point Y 14. 2nd-Lieutenant Fearnley-Whittingstall had been wounded, and the only officer remaining now with " X " Company was 2nd-Lieutenant John, a young officer attached from the Special Reserve of the York and Lancaster Regiment. The left flank of the company was in touch, between Y 14 and Y 11, with a party of Liverpool Scottish, which, after accompanying " W " Company to Y 11, had been directed to occupy the trench running south from that point.

Map No. 13

While the FIFTH on the left had thus fought their way forward, in the centre and on the right of the 9th Brigade the Royal Scots Fusiliers and Royal Fusiliers, together with parties of the Liverpool Scottish and Lincolnshire, had succeeded in carrying the second objective; and the Wiltshire Regiment—the battalion of 7th Brigade detailed to support the right flank of the attack—had also made considerable progress by bombing up communication trenches from Y 20 to Y 16. It was now about 5 a.m. Though the plan of attack had been upset, and units considerably disorganised by the slow advance of the artillery barrage, the results of the 9th Brigade's attack at this time could be judged as satisfactory, except on the left flank of the FIFTH. A considerable number of prisoners had been taken, and the second objective had been occupied as far north as Y 11. But between this point and the railway, except for the portion of the line carried by " Y " Company in the first assault, the trenches were still full of Germans.

Captain Sloper, Battalion M.G. Officer, now arrived at point Y 11. He reported that, from what he had seen, he was convinced that though the enemy was in strength between Y 11 and Y 8, the trench further east, —which represented a portion of third objective—was unoccupied. There were, however, insufficient troops at hand both to clear the left of the second line and to push forward for the occupation of the third. Captain Sandilands went back to report the situation to the Commanding Officer, who, with the adjutant, was now in the original German front line. On his return he found that Lieutenant Scrutton, his face covered with blood from a slight wound, had arrived with his platoon of " Y " company at point Y 11. It then transpired that, following the deaths of Captain Roddam and Lieutenant Carter, and the loss of two other platoon commanders and the company sergeant-major, the remainder of the company had lost direction in the maze of trenches, and had drifted to the right. Hence the difficulties now being encountered on the left flank. In the meantime, Sloper had pushed forward with a small reconnaissance party to the third objective, whence on the receipt of reinforcements he was to clear the line northwards towards point Y 8, while Sandilands undertook the clearance of the second objective between Y 11 and the same point. These reinforcements now arrived, in the form of a strong party of Liverpool Scottish, and were sent forward to join Sloper. A fierce bombing fight now ensued in the trench between Y 11 and Y 8. The FIFTH drove back the Germans some sixty yards, and planted an artillery screen to indicate their progress. But they were run out of bombs; enemy reinforcements were observed streaming up by the line of the railway, and the men of the FIFTH were forced to withdraw. A further supply of bombs having been brought forward, a second attack once again drove the enemy back towards Y 8; but, again the supply of bombs being exhausted, the FIFTH were forced back to Y 11 by an enemy counter-attack. The trench junction at Y 11 was now barricaded, and a machine gun mounted on the parapet of the communication trench to the west of the junction. Three times the Germans, shouting as they came, their numbers clear from the helmets and bayonets seen above the parapet, charged up the trench against the barricade; three times they were driven back by the fire of rifles and of the machine gun, which Private Marsden, though wounded, continued to serve with great coolness. It was then that Private Homer, apparently courting certain death, suddenly sprang up, climbed the barricade, and dropped on to the enemy's side of it. He had observed a wounded man, abandoned as dead during the bombing attacks and counter-attacks, dragging himself towards the barricade. Homer was followed by a lance-corporal. Together they lifted their helpless comrade to the top of the barricade, and together they stood on guard while he was being drawn into safety. The lance-corporal then returned. Finally, Homer, as a gallant rear-guard, coolly climbed back and regained the cover of the barricade. Fortunately the Germans had for the time withdrawn, though a renewal of their attempts to storm the barricade was momentarily expected. No man ever saved the life of a comrade at the risk of his own more certainly than Homer, for had the rescued man been abandoned he could not have survived the terrible wounds he had sustained. But, beyond this, any who have been in command of men wearied and shaken by heavy fighting, and still in imminent danger of death, will appreciate the inspiring effect of such an action carried out before their eyes with the cool and determined demeanour observed by this gallant soldier.*

"Z" Company had now reinforced the forward companies, Lieutenant Dorman Smith leading the bulk of his company to the support of "X" Company, while 2nd Lieutenant Lawson led his platoon over the open to where "W" Company held the trench south of point Y 11. Just as he was leaping to the cover of the trench, Lawson was dangerously wounded through an artery in the wrist, and after receiving first aid, had to be evacuated.

It was now about 6.30 a.m. In the centre and right of their front of attack the FIFTH were established in the second objective. The trench representing this, while affording fair cover in the centre, on the right was barely three foot deep and not continuous. It was, moreover, partially open to enfilade machine gun fire which was causing many casualties. On the left, as already related, the attack had lost direction, and all efforts to carry Y 8 from the flank had failed. It seemed that the only possibilty of remedying the situation in this quarter lay in a renewed frontal attack acros the open.

---

* Homer's was but one of many gallant actions that remained unrecognised in the Great War. But there are special reasons for the writer's welcoming an opportunity, to which he has looked forward for twenty years, of placing this incident on record. Homer, whose action he witnessed, was a man of "X" Company, and until this day unknown to him. A few days later the writer was officially required to submit the names of any whose outstanding conduct had come to his notice. It is not customary in the FIFTH to submit long lists on such occasions but Homer's was among the few names sent in. Though none was more deserving, he was the only one of those whose names were submitted who received no recognition. On the matter being represented to them, both Colonel Yatman and Lt. Colonel Wild endeavoured to have rectified what undoubtedly was an omission due to an oversight, but in vain. Homer was one of the few who came unscathed through the operations of the 16th June. For a subsequent act of gallantry he was, at a later date, awarded the Military Medal.

16th June, 1915   In the meantime, Captain Herbert, the Adjutant, had been wounded, and the   Map No. 13
situation as regards officers was as follows. Lt. Colonel Yatman, without either adjutant or 2nd-in-command, was at Battalion Headquarters; forward, apart from Captain Sandilands, who held the additional responsibilities of Battalion 2nd-in-command, there was but one officer with each of the companies viz: " W," 2nd-Lieutenant Cunningham; " X," 2nd-Lieutenant John; " Y," 2nd-Lieutenant Scrutton; and " Z," Lieutenant Dorman Smith. In addition, there was Captain Sloper, the M.G. Officer, who had assumed command of a mixed party of the FIFTH and Liverpool Scottish. All these officers were with the forward troops in the second objective, beyond which advance was held up by fire from the opposing trenches which were being steadily reinforced. Supporting troops of each company were still in the original German front line, but many of these had been wounded, and, owing to heavy casualties among N.C.Os., they were to a large extent leaderless.

    Leaving Cunningham in charge at Y 11 and Scrutton in command of the trench to the south of that point, Sandilands again went back to report the situation to Lt.-Colonel Yatman. The old No Man's Land, where many of the wounded in the first assault were still lying, and the area to the rear were now being very heavily bombarded by the enemy's artillery in order to check the advance of reinforcements from Divisional Reserve.* The 2/Irish Rifles of the 7th Brigade had, however, got forward. The officer commanding this battalion had taken over the original Battalion Headquarters of the FIFTH, but was ignorant of the present location of Lt.-Colonel Yatman.† He was, however, in communication with the 9th Brigade. To him, therefore, Sandilands delivered his report before going forward to the right of " X " Company, just south of Y 14. A terrible proportion of the men here had been killed or wounded, but those that remained were holding out manfully in isolated lengths of trench, under self-constituted leaders where for the most part N.C.O's. had ceased to exist. So shallow were these trench elements that, in order that the officer might gain the cover of the low parapet as he moved to the left, the men, wounded and unwounded alike lay prone in the trench and urged him to crawl over them. Gradually, as it ran north, the trench deepened and grew continuous, and here 2nd-Lieutenant John, wounded in the arm, had been joined by Lieutenant Dorman Smith and Captain Sloper. Sloper, who had reached the third objective east of Y 11 unopposed, had been unable to make any progress towards Y 8, but had succeeded in maintaining his position at, and south of, the trench junction for nearly an hour till, on a threat developing against his right flank, he had withdrawn his party to the portion of the second objective occupied by the left and centre of " X " Company. He himself had been slightly

---

    * The clearing of the wounded from the ground over which the first assault had passed was a very difficult and hazardous task. Despite the gallant work done by the stretcher bearers, many could not be brought in before dark. The generous assistance volunteered by Lt.-Colonel Shoolbred's Battalion of the Queen's Westminster Rifles (T.A.) on this day must always stand prominently in the records of the FIFTH. Of the eight stretcher bearers of this battalion who were engaged on the work two lost their lives and four were wounded in rescuing men of the FIFTH from the ground where they lay helpless under the fire of the enemy's guns.

    † Lt.-Colonel Yatman, in his intense anxiety to learn how things were going, and without any adjutant to send forward, had at this time himself gone up for a brief period to " X " Company's position. He has since condemned his own action in thus leaving his headquarters; but, if it was an error, there are few who would not condone it. He was conscious of the extreme youth and inexperience of the majority of his officers, and his presence among them could not fail to give them fresh confidence.

wounded in the face, and, though still capable of exerting active control, was suffering considerable pain. Here, as further to the right, the slightest exposure drew heavy rifle and machine gun fire from the opposing line, which was now strongly manned by the enemy. Our infantry were pinned to the position. Only following a heavy artillery bombardment might it be possible for the exhausted men of the FIFTH to get forward: lacking artillery co-operation, further advance would mean certain annihilation and useless sacrifice. For the present, nothing could be done but cling to the position gained.

Having viewed the situation on the right, Sandilands moved on to rejoin Scrutton and Cunningham on the left. But before he could reach their position he was hit by a sniper's bullet and had to be evacuated. Sloper, unaware of the fact, was now the senior officer with the forward troops of the FIFTH.

In the meantime, much of the ground gained at the outset on the right and in the centre of the 9th Brigade had been lost. The Royal Fusiliers, supported by the Lincolnshire Regiment, had gained the west bank of Bellewaarde Lake, and a party of the Royal Scots Fusiliers, supported by Liverpool Scottish, had secured a footing in the third objective to the south of the position reached by Sloper's detachment. These troops, however, owing to the artillery screens having again failed to indicate the progress of the attack, had been heavily shelled by their own as well as the enemy's guns, and had been forced to retire, thus exposing Sloper's right flank and compelling his withdrawal, as already related. Further to the right again, the Wiltshire Regiment, whose early progress by bombing has already been referred to, had been forced through lack of bombs to withdraw in face of an enemy counter attack. At this time the enemy seems to have been in doubt as to the situation on the British left. For, though the positions gained by the FIFTH were continually harassed by the fire of the German forward troops, they were for some hours spared by the enemy's artillery. Further to the right, however, The Royal Fusiliers and Scots Fusiliers were so heavily bombarded in the line to which they had withdrawn, that they were again forced to retire, and fell back on the original German front line. Units of the 7th Infantry Brigade were now ordered forward to re-occupy the line between point Y 17 and Bellewaarde Farm; but their attempts to carry this out broke down under heavy artillery fire. Thus, with Germans in the still uncaptured trenches north-east of Railway Wood, the FIFTH in occupation of the line between Y 14 and Y 11 now had both flanks exposed.*

The bombardment which, at the start of the attack, had been opened by the German artillery on Railway Wood, the old No Man's Land, and the assembly trenches, had never ceased. So intense was it that it remained impossible for the stretcher bearers to rescue many of the wounded who lay on this ground throughout the day and, extending far to the west, greatly impeded the advance of the reinforcements that were ordered forward from Ypres during the afternoon. The Battalion Headquarters in Cambridge Road, first occupied by the FIFTH and later by the Irish Rifles, had now been obliterated; and Lt.-Colonel Yatman had been compelled to seek the

---

* 9th Brigade War Diary states that at 9.20 a.m. the enemy were reported massing in Dead Man's Bottom, and that shortly after that, owing to intense artillery fire, the units withdrew to the German 1st Line. Later, it states: "Situation now is that units of various regiments are holding the line Y13—Y15—Y16—5th Fusiliers still working towards Y7 and Y8." From this the fact may not be clear that 5th Fusiliers, mainly of "X" and "Z" Companies, and parties of Liverpool Scottish, with Sloper, Dorman Smith and John, were still in occupation of Y14 and the trench leading north from that point *till late in the afternoon*. This fact, which is stated in the Battalion War Diary, has been confirmed by Lt.-Colonel E. E. Dorman Smith, M.C.

16th June, 1915 hospitality of the headquarters of 1/West Yorkshire Regiment, of the 6th Division, which were situated in a dug-out at the point where the Cambridge Road crossed the Roulers railway.

Map No. 13

As hours passed, the situation of the FIFTH in the forward positions they had gained was growing ever graver and more difficult. 2nd-Lieutenant Scrutton and 2nd-Lieutenant Cunningham, the last remaining officers of " Y " and " W " Companies had been wounded and evacuated. Of the officers with " X " and " Z " Companies, Captain Sloper, now shot through the lungs, and 2nd-Lieutenant John, grievously wounded, could not be moved back; and Lieutenant Dorman Smith alone remained still capable of action. While the enemy had been strongly reinforced, and was now massed for attack in the trenches east and north-east of Bellewaarde Farm, there were of the FIFTH and of the Liverpool Scottish, who had been fighting alongside them, but a handful left who were in condition to handle a rifle. About 2.30 p.m., a devastating fire of rifles and machine guns was opened on the whole line of trench between Y 14 and Y 11. Every foot of the parapet was subjected to a continuous stream of bullets, and simultaneously, the enemy charged up the communication trench leading to Y 11, bombing as they came. In vain our men, manning the barricade, endeavoured to stem the rush by hurling bombs at the attackers. Every bomber of the FIFTH was killed, and the trench junction was carried by the enemy. On the right flank, the Germans were pushing up east of Bellewaarde Farm towards Y 14. Dorman Smith relates that of the men in his immediate neighbourhood all had now become casualties, and most of them had been killed. He thought he was the sole survivor till a young soldier of the Liverpool Scottish came from the direction of Y 14 to tell him that the Germans were working up the trench within 60 yards of where they stood. Barely had this lad delivered his report than he too was shot dead. Though circumstances demanded it, there was now no question of *ordering* a withdrawal, for where the one remaining officer was placed there were none left who could act on the order; elsewhere there was none left to give it. Blocked by the destructive bombardment, the communication trenches no longer provided a covered passage to the rear, and to the scattered remnants of the FIFTH and Liverpool Scottish, still capable of action, it was evident that if they were to escape capture or annihilation at the hands of the enemy who were fast surrounding them, it could only be by risking immediate retirement across the open. It was thus in fact that Dorman-Smith and a mere handful of other ranks escaped from the position, which their companies had captured and held for nine hours, and made their way back to the shelter of the old German front line. Here, where the position had been consolidated for defence, 2nd Lieutenant-Scrutton, after having his wounds dressed, had taken charge of the groups of leaderless men who represented the supports of the FIFTH and the Liverpool Scottish, together with fragments of the Scots Fusiliers.

The other battalions of the 9th Brigade, equally with the FIFTH, had been denuded of officers and were now completely exhausted. A fresh attack by troops of the 7th and 42nd Brigades was ordered for 3.30 p.m. with objective the line Y 18—Y 8. Those of the 42nd Brigade, moving forward from Ypres, were so heavily shelled that they failed to reach the assembly trenches at the appointed hour. The two weak battalions of the 7th Brigade, which alone advanced to the attack, were swept away by shell fire. At 3.50 p.m., it was decided to discontinue the offensive and to consolidate a line Y16—Y15—Y13 and thence to the railway.

So at the close of twelve hours' fighting, and at the expense of very heavy casualties, all that remained in the hands of the British of the positions they had

120   THE FIFTH IN THE GREAT WAR.

Map No. 13   captured was the first objective of the attack. Undoubtedly, the failure to obtain   16th June, 1915
better results was due to the method of artillery support that had been employed. In the War Diary of 1/FIFTH one finds a warm tribute to the gallant and desperate efforts of the forward observing officers to locate their infantry and give them the support they so sorely needed. But the artillery had been set an impossible task. Though casualties, particularly in officers, were heavy in the first assault, the first objective had been captured without difficulty. Had troops of the high mettle of the Liverpool Scottish and Lincolnshire Regiment then been able to pass through, according to plan, there is little doubt that the second and final objectives would have fallen equally easily before a rapid advance.

The casualties suffered on the 16th June by the three companies of the FIFTH in the front line of attack amounted to almost exactly 75 % of their strength. The losses in the Battalion as a whole, which had gone into action at a strength of 15 officers and 645 other ranks, totalled 15 officers and 386 other ranks. Of these, two officers, Lt.-Colonel Yatman and Lieutenant Dorman-Smith, and 20 other ranks had been only slightly wounded and remained at duty. The casualties in detail are shown by the War Diary to have been as under :—

	Officers.			Other Ranks.			Total.
	K.	W.	W. & M.	K.	W.	M.	
Battalion H.Q.	—	2	1	—	—	—	3
" W " Company	1	3	—	11	48	61	124
" X " Company	1	1	1	6	34	65	108
" Y " Company	2	1	—	10	52	56	121
" Z " Company	—	2	—	8	23	12	45
	4	9	2	35	157	194*	401

* See Note 1 at end of Chapter.

All four machine guns had been knocked out during the day. The casualties among machine gunners, who at this date were still held on the strength of companies, are included in the figures given above.

Late in the afternoon the hostile fire died down, but it was not till after dark that many of the men who had been wounded in the first assault, and had lain all day under heavy shell fire, could be got in. During the night, the Battalion was relieved by the 2/Royal Scots of the 8th Brigade, and moved back to the bivouac from which they had set out on the afternoon of 15th June.

It might be thought that the heavy losses sustained by the Battalion had depressed its spirit. But this was far from being the case. After months of trench warfare the men had been brought face to face with the Germans, had entered their trenches, and had driven them back. The inspiring effect of the success of the initial assault survived the later disappointments of the day. On the occasion of a visit by the Brigadier on 18th June, those that remained with the Battalion were further heartened by the warm appreciation he expressed of the manner in which 1/FIFTH had acquitted themselves on the Bellewaarde Ridge. But, stripped of officers, and reduced to skeleton strength, the Battalion needed time now to refit and replenish its ranks. It was not to take the field again for close on four weeks.

16th June, 1915   For conspicuous gallantry on the 16th June, 2nd-Lieutenant Scrutton was   Map No. 13
awarded the D.S.O. and Lce.-Corporal A. Joynson the D.C.M. Lieutenant Dorman-Smith's services were recognised by the award of the Military Cross in the following New Year's Honours List.

NOTE 1.—The number shown as " missing " represents the number who did not answer the roll call on the night of 16th June, and could not otherwise be accounted for. Though, unfortunately, the bulk of these were those killed or wounded who had to be abandoned in the second objective, a large number of wounded were shown under this heading owing to their having been evacuated through the aid posts of other units. Of 33 men of " W " Company located in hospitals in various parts of England in July, 1915, no fewer than 14 had been reported as " missing," and are so shown in the Battalion War Diary. Based on the above, it can be estimated that of the 194 shown as missing in the Battalion, one-third were wounded who were evacuated through the aid posts of other units; of the remainder it is probable that an approximately equal number were killed or too severely wounded to get back. This would bring the casualties in other ranks to 97 killed and 289 wounded, *i.e.* the normal proportion of killed to wounded in an action of this kind in the Great War; of which 62 dead and 66 wounded would have fallen into the hands of the enemy.

NOTE 2.—The fine qualities possessed by Captain Gerard Orby Sloper, to which reference was made in the early pages of this chapter, were never more apparent than during the Battle of Bellewaarde, though from the day on which he had won the Military Cross by leading his platoon to the charge against a superior force of Germans during the fighting on the Aisne in 1914, he had given constant evidence of his indomitable courage and genius for leadership. To fall helpless into the hands of the enemy must indeed have been bitter for one of his character. In the years that followed, his refusal to submit to the life of a prisoner of war, and his several attempts to escape, led to constant terms of confinement in punishment cells. On repatriation to England in December, 1918, he immediately volunteered for service with the North Russian Expeditionary Force. The hardships he had endured in Germany, however, had combined with the wounds he had received, first on the Aisne and later at Bellewaarde, to undermine his constitution, and on the 8th February, 1919, this gallant officer of the FIFTH succumbed to an attack of pneumonia in Russia.

CHAPTER IX.

2ND BATTALION—25TH MAY—24TH OCTOBER, 1915.

In Trenches on the Kemmel Front.

Fighting in the Hohenzollern Redoubt.

Departure from France.

24th May/10th June, 1915

Throughout the Great War there was no one to whom the FIFTH owed more than to their Quartermasters; the 1st Battalion to Captain Landen and, later, Lieutenant Myers; the 2nd to Captain Allan, who served with it from the outbreak of war till the Armistice. On the exertions of these officers, who were responsible for the supply of food, ammunition and material, the companies in the fighting line depended for their very existence; and on withdrawal to reserve it was to them that all looked for those minor comforts which meant so much to the refreshment of men wearied by long days under fire in the squalor of the trenches. But, while it might be said that the services they rendered in this respect formed but a part of their plain duty, there was a greater, though less clearly recognised, purpose which these officers served—not in the special capacity of Quartermasters, but in the general character of officers of the FIFTH. Time and again, after anxious and weary hours, they saw the shattered remnants of their battalions return from battle; and in the continual replacement of officers and replenishment of the ranks they found that they stood for the one constant factor that remained in their units throughout. As such, they became in a special degree the guardians of the traditions of the FIFTH, which served to maintain the high spirit of the Regiment throughout the War.

We have seen how, from the 9th to the 24th May, Captain Allan had been called on to act as Adjutant. He had now to undertake a still heavier responsibility. On the 25th May there remained with the 2/FIFTH, in addition to himself, but two officers—2nd-Lieutenant I. H. L. Gilchrist, 18 years of age, and the Transport Officer, 2nd-Lieutenant C. A. Steel, who had been recently commissioned from the ranks of the cavalry. Thus, pending the arrival of reinforcements, it fell to Captain Allan to assume command of the Battalion, to hearten the men who had lost their leaders, and to reorganise what remained of the 2/FIFTH after the heavy losses of the 24th May.

Four days later, however, he was relieved by Captain Rushbrook, who brought with him a small draft and temporarily took over the Battalion pending the arrival of Major C. A. Armstrong, who had been appointed to command. The Battalion had now been moved to Schipman's Farm, near Herzeele. Here it was reinforced by a steady flow of drafts, and when Major Armstrong arrived on the 10th June to assume command, the strength had been increased by 11 officers and 270 other ranks and was sufficient for the Battalion once more to undertake duty in the trenches. But of the small complement of officers now with it, three only were above the rank of Lieutenant, and more than half were young 2nd Lieutenants; while, of the other ranks who had joined, only thirty had before seen service. If, therefore, the Battalion was to regain

THE FIFTH IN THE GREAT WAR.   123

11th June/20th Sept., 1915

its normal standard of efficiency it required some breathing space before being again exposed to the shattering casualties endured during April and May, so that officers and men should gain experience together before being again engaged in further strenuous fighting. Fortunately, an opportunity for this was to be granted. For the next three months the 2/FIFTH were to do duty on what in the War was regarded as a " peaceful front," and to make such good use of this period as to stand again as a fully trained and well organised unit before entering the last ordeal that they were to pass through before leaving the Western Front.

Map No. 8

On the 11th June the Battalion took over trenches at Vierstraat, north-east of Kemmel, two companies being placed in the trenches, while the remainder were held in reserve, with Battalion Headquarters at Pioneer Farm, south-east of Dickebusch. Apart from occasional shelling, the month during which the Battalion occupied this position passed quietly enough. Casualties averaged little more than one a day, though those among officers were proportionately high : 2nd Lieutenant J. C. Watmough and six other ranks killed, Lieutenants Barkworth and Hopkinson, 2nd Lieutenant Pollock and thirty-two other ranks wounded, and 2nd Lieutenants Walton and Craig injured in a bomb accident. The posting of Captain Lamb and eleven subalterns during the same period, however, increased the number of officers with the Battalion, and the arrival of twenty-seven other ranks from hospital saved it from any serious diminution in strength. There was at this time plenty of work for all, both in and out of the line. Digging in the back area, however, was not without its rewards ; and the unearthing of three bottles of brandy and eighteen of wine by a party employed on the excavation of a refuse pit for a time lent to this form of labour all the excitements of a treasure hunt among the ever hopeful troops.

On withdrawal to reserve on the 12th July the Battalion was accommodated at " Kemmel Shelters," where it enjoyed a fortnight's rest before taking over trenches east of the village. A strongly held front line was still the fashion at this period ; in the section now taken over, while the Battalion reserve consisted of no more than a single platoon held at Kemmel School, all four machine guns were placed in the front line, and the four companies (less the above platoon) were disposed in the front and support lines. With brief periods of rest at Kemmel Shelters, or further back at Locre, the 2/FIFTH held this front till the 20th September. The usual artillery fire continued, and mining and counter-mining were in active progress. An enemy mine, blown under " B " Company's trenches on the 17th August, wounded three men but otherwise did little damage ; apart, however, from his underground operations, the enemy showed little activity till just before the close of the Battalion's tour on this front. During the last three days, the 18th, 19th and 20th September, the German artillery fire greatly increased ; many 8-inch shells were included in the bombardment, and on the 19th a trench was blown in, a number of men being buried. Of the total casualties, 11 killed and 31 wounded, sustained by the Battalion in the eight weeks it spent in this part of the line, no fewer than 7 were killed and 16 wounded in the course of these three days.

The 28th Division had now been ordered back to Second Army Reserve in the neighbourhood of Bailleul. On the 20th September the 2/FIFTH, on relief by the 16th Canadian Regiment, moved to billets at Locre, and on the following day marched with the 84th Brigade to take up billets at Rouge Croix, midway between Bailleul and Hazebrouck. Four months had now passed since the Battalion, after the terrible casualties which had twice depleted its ranks, had been withdrawn from the Ypres Salient. During this period the New Army had made its appearance on the

Western Front, and by mid-September sixteen of its divisions had crossed to France to reinforce the Allies, who it was deemed were now in a position to proceed with the combined French and British offensive which had long been planned for 1915. In these operations the First Army was to carry out the British task, *viz.*: the capture and penetration of the German positions from the town of Loos, in the south, to the La Bassée Canal, in the north. The date of the attack had been fixed for 25th September. Except for a subsidiary attack in the Salient, the Second Army, which was now holding the 28th Division in reserve, was to stand on the defensive. The 2/FIFTH, accordingly, remained quietly at Rouge Croix, filling in the time till the 26th September by general training.

In the meantime the British attack, which had opened with brilliant success at many points, had by the evening of the 25th encountered difficulties which prevented the exploitation of these initial gains. A full account of the Battle of Loos can find no place in this History, but the local events which were to bring the 2/FIFTH to the fighting in the Hohenzollern Redoubt may be briefly recounted. On the extreme left of the attack, immediately south of the La Bassée Canal, the 2nd Division had had the misfortune to be overwhelmed by their own gas, which a change in the wind had carried over the attacking battalions. As a result of this, the attack here had completely failed. On the right of the 2nd Division, however, a remarkable success had been achieved by the 9th Division against one of the most formidable positions on the whole front of attack. Here, in rear of the German front line, the mining works and buildings of the pit known as Fosse 8 were flanked by a huge, flat-topped slag heap, twenty feet high. From this "dump" the enemy had obtained observation over the whole of the Le Rutoire plain, which lay between the British line and Vermelles. In protection of The Dump, which itself was strongly fortified, the enemy had constructed in advance of their original front line—here represented by Dump and Fosse Trenches—an enclosed and strongly wired work known as the Hohenzollern Redoubt. The face of the Redoubt, three hundred yards long and slightly convex, following generally the contour of the ground, was prolonged to join up with Dump and Fosse Trenches by two arms known as "Big Willie" and "Little Willie."* Two communication trenches, named "North Face" and "South Face," ran respectively from Fosse Trench to the centre of the Redoubt and from Dump Trench to Big Willie.

In the early morning of the 25th September, the 26th Brigade of the 9th Division had carried the Hohenzollern Redoubt, Fosse 8, and The Dump, and had later even pushed forward some 1200 yards further east to the outskirts of Haisnes. Before the end of the day, however, these advanced troops had to be withdrawn owing to the situation on their flanks. During the night of the 25th/26th September the 73rd Brigade of the 24th Division, already greatly exhausted, had come forward to relieve the 26th Brigade, and early on the following morning succeeded with remnants of the 26th Brigade in repulsing a German counter-attack against the captured position of Fosse 8. But on the 27th a fresh counter-attack against the troops of the 73rd Brigade, who had by then been without food or rest for 48 hours, had forced the British back from Fosse 8 and The Dump to the Hohenzollern Redoubt.

While these events had been occurring, the 2/FIFTH on the 26th September had marched with the 84th Brigade to Quentin. Embussing the following day at

---

* Much of the description of the Hohenzollern Redoubt has been taken verbatim from the Official History.

28th/29th Sept., 1915

Paradis, they were carried to Béthune, whence they marched to billets at Sailly Labourse, 2½ miles south-east of Béthune and some 3½ west of Fosse 8. Here the Battalion for the present remained in reserve with the 84th Brigade, while heavy and incessant fighting continued for the recovery of The Dump, the occupation of which was considered essential to the renewal of the main attack by the British and French as planned. A first attempt, in the early morning of the 28th September, reached the objective but was later driven back by furious bombing. In the afternoon the 85th Brigade, who had now come forward, made a second attempt, but with no better success; and at nightfall, though the British front line was still in the Hohenzollern, the enemy had obtained footings in " Big Willie " and " Little Willie."

Map No. 14

The close and desperate fighting on this day and those that were to follow can be taken as an outstanding example of trench warfare methods, which before the War had formed no part of the training of the British Army, and for which the Germans at this date were far better equipped than their adversaries. The enemy's bombs were both more plentiful and more effective than those of the British, and his more numerous machine guns gave him a further advantage. It may be said here, too, that it was a type of warfare which makes any accurate description of the progress of the battle well nigh impossible. In the close, almost hand to hand, fighting which it involved, the local situation, by dint of attack and counter-attack, was changing momentarily. Reading the reports that reached, and the orders that were issued by Divisional Headquarters, one realises that before orders had reached the fighting troops for a fresh attack to be delivered " with the utmost determination," the position in question had often already been carried, but at such heavy sacrifice that it had again been lost before the reported success had brought back the congratulations of the higher command.*

Fighting continued without cease throughout the 29th September. In the trenches, which incessant bombardments had rendered unrecognisable, the Germans attacked time and again with bombs, but the 85th Brigade held fast to their position. During the afternoon of this day the FIFTH were moved forward to Annequin, about one mile nearer to the front, where they were kept throughout the night in readiness to move at half an hour's notice. On the following day, which passed more quietly, orders were received for the 84th to relieve the 85th Brigade in the trenches before dawn on the 1st October: in this relief the FIFTH, as the right battalion of the Brigade, was to take over " Big Willie " and a frontage of about 150 yards in the Hohenzollern Redoubt. A vivid idea of the general confusion which attended reliefs carried out in these days is obtained from a report by Brigadier-General Pereira, written in hospital, in which he describes the circumstances in which his brigade (the 85th) had relieved the 73rd Brigade on the 28th September. He relates that, on moving forward to the relief, the only assistance to getting the troops to unreconnoitred positions lay in *one* map and *two* guides for the whole brigade ! Three different reports came to him, viz. :

(i) that the German positions had been captured,
(ii) that the British were back in the old front line,
(iii) that the Hohenzollern was held.

---

* The injunction, so frequently found in orders, that troops should attack " with the utmost determination " is surely redundant. Commanders and troops know well that an attack for the capture of a position, if not delivered with determination, is foredoomed to failure, and the inclusion of such phrases, besides wasting valuable time, is calculated to irritate rather than encourage the recipient of the order.

Map No. 14

The communication trenches, by which his men were to get forward, at this moment were choked with wounded or leaderless men coming back.

1st Oct., 1915

The conditions under which the FIFTH relieved the 1/York and Lancaster Regiment in the early hours of the 1st October, were scarcely more satisfactory than those related above. It had not been possible to reconnoitre the positions before taking over, and the guides supplied were insufficient both in numbers and in their knowledge of the trenches.* As a result, confusion came early. On arriving at the position by the one communication trench by which all four companies had to move forward, a part of the troops had to be led to the one flank and the remainder to the other, so as to bring " C " and " D " Companies on the right and " A " and " B " on the left. By an error of the guides these positions were reversed, and the companies found themselves placed in order, from right to left, " A," " B," " C," " D " ; the three first being in " Big Willie," while " D " Company took over the portion of the Hohenzollern Redoubt which had been allotted to the Battalion. Rather unwisely, it would seem, the entry of the communication trench, South Face, which ran from the German position, had been indicated as the point of junction of the two left companies. Dawn was just breaking, the relief was hurried through, and a party of the relieved troops, impatient to get back, instead of moving by communication trenches, rashly withdrew across the open. This movement, undoubtedly, was observed by the enemy, to whom it gave the clue to what was in progress. Before the relief had been fully completed, and while the men of the FIFTH were still in process of taking up their positions, the Germans, approaching unseen by South Face, suddenly attacked with bombs. The inner flanks of both " C " and " D " Companies were driven back, and the enemy secured a footing of about one hundred yards in the Hohenzollern and " Big Willie." Further progress of the enemy was checked and a barrier was constructed by each company to protect its flank and contain the enemy; but they found themselves completely separated. On report of the situation reaching Brigade Headquarters, orders were issued that the enemy was to be driven from the position at all costs; but though it was simple enough to issue such orders, the manner in which they should be carried out was quite a different matter. Major Armstrong had gone forward to the scene of the trouble before the orders from the Brigade had reached his headquarters, with the intention of organising a counter-attack, the necessity for which was, in truth, quite obvious. But to form any plan without more accurate knowledge of the general situation than could be obtained from the bottom of a trench was impossible. In order to secure a view of his surroundings, he raised himself above the parapet and was immediately shot through the head and killed. On news of this tragic event reaching Battalion Headquarters, Captain Lamb, to whom command now fell, went forward with 2nd Lieutenant Gilchrist, the Adjutant, to " D " Company's position. He found that already many casualties had been sustained; bombing and counter-bombing were in progress; and considerable confusion reigned in the trench. Any attempt to attack across the open would have been swept away by the fire of machine guns from the enemy's rear positions, and the only hope of dislodging the Germans lay in bombing them from the section of trench in which they had secured a footing. But in this crude form of fighting, in which the Germans were certainly

---

* No one with experience of the appalling difficulties of finding the way through the intricacies of a strange trench system, battered to bits by a continuous bombardment, would venture to lay serious blame on a private soldier for failing in the duties of a guide, for which as likely as not he had been selected for no better reason than that he was at the moment the only man available.

2nd/3rd Oct., 1915

as well trained as our own men, the ultimate advantage lies with the side with the most plentiful supply of bombs; and in this respect the enemy held a marked superiority. Throughout the day vain efforts were made by both "C" and "D" Companies to drive the enemy from the trench. As bombs became available, party after party was organised to advance up the narrow trench and hurl their bombs across the barrier. Time and again, as the supply of these gave out, our men were driven back with ever increasing casualties by the heavier bombing of the enemy. At last, late in the evening, an attack by " D " Company succeeded in driving back the enemy some fifty yards and advancing their barrier by that distance. Fifty yards of trench gained after twelve hours of fighting !

Map No. 14

The 2/Cheshire, who were on the left of " D " Company, had assisted in this last attack; while on the left of the Cheshire, the 1/Welch in " Little Willie " had been heavily engaged all day. In " Big Willie," on the other hand, " A " and " B " Companies of the FIFTH, on the right of the 84th Brigade front, had passed a comparatively quiet day. The outer flank of " A " Company, on the extreme right, curled round to join an old trench in the German position at a point called " The Window "; and at this point, which faced the enemy's line opposite " Big Willie," a block had been constructed. There were no troops, British or German, on the right of " A " Company, but their flank was well protected by the fire of a machine gun of the 83rd Brigade in position to their right rear. The trenches of these two companies were subjected to artillery fire throughout the day, but there were few casualties on this portion of the Battalion's front.

The struggle for the Hohenzollern Redoubt and " Little Willie " continued throughout the 2nd and 3rd October. No improvement was effected in the situation of " C " and " D " Companies, between whom the Germans stubbornly clung to the position they had captured, though their efforts to extend their hold on the trench were as vain as ours to drive them from it. Desperate attempts made by " D " Company after dark on the 2nd resulted only in further casualties: from the several attacks that were made few returned, and those for the most part grievously wounded. Captain Lamb, hit in the head, was evacuated; and shortly afterwards Gilchrist, the nineteen year old adjutant, was killed. By the morning of the 3rd every Officer with " D " Company had been killed or wounded, and the Officer Commanding the 2/Cheshire Regiment, having been informed of this, sent Captain Freeman of his battalion to take over command of the company. Very shortly after he had taken over, the Germans, opening a surprise attack against the left flank of the 84th Brigade, drove through the 1/Welch, swept the 2/Cheshire from the trench, and fell on the flank of the sorely tried " D " Company of the FIFTH.* Those of the company who still remained were forced back under a storm of bombs against their barrier, and only twenty-six survived, to escape death by withdrawing with Captain Freeman across the open to the shelter of a support trench in rear. Continuing their way through the Hohenzollern Redoubt, the enemy reached " C " Company's barrier; here they were at last definitely stopped and all their efforts to penetrate to " Big Willie " were

* Any attempt to discover from records what the situation in " Little Willie " was at any given time while the struggle for the Hohenzollern was in progress, becomes quite bewildering. One gains the impression that the position of companies and platoons was changing hourly. As regards its final loss one may quote the War Diary of the 2/Cheshire : " The enemy broke through part of the trench occupied by the 1/Welch on our left flank and advanced with great rapidity throwing hundreds of bombs, their bombers being supported by machine guns and riflemen. The attack came as a complete surprise."

repulsed. "C" Company held fast to its position until, on the relief of the 84th by the 85th Brigade in the afternoon, it was withdrawn with the remainder of the Battalion to reserve.

The total casualties sustained by the 2/FIFTH between the 1st and 4th October amounted to 253 all ranks, and are recorded as follows :—

OFFICERS.

Killed	..	Lt.-Colonel C. A. Armstrong.
		Captain W. E. Jenkins.
		2nd-Lieutenant I. H. L. Gilchrist.
		2nd-Lieutenant G. Wilkins.
		2nd-Lieutenant R. B. Howell (4/N. Staff. attd.).
Wounded	..	Captain R. M. Lamb.
		Captain R. H. Hoffman.
		Captain F. C. Longden (4/D.L.I. attd.).
		Lieutenant A. J. Hopkinson (4/D.L.I. attd.).
		2nd-Lieutenant D. F. C. Bacon (4/D.L.I. attd.).
		2nd-Lieutenant H. A. Fordham.
		2nd-Lieutenant G. Sweet.
		2nd-Lieutenant B. Grew.
		2nd-Lieutenant S. A. Rose.
		2nd-Lieutenant H. J. Holmes.

OTHER RANKS.

Killed 23.   Missing (believed killed) 100.   Wounded 115.

On the 4th October Captain E. C. Maxwell, of the 2/Cheshire Regiment, took over temporary command of the 2/FIFTH. On the following day the Battalion was withdrawn to billets in Bethune, and on the 7th October it marched with the 84th Brigade to Lablette, near Busnes. On the 8th, Major B. Bogle, of the 2/East Yorkshire Regiment, relieved Captain Maxwell, but his tenure of command only lasted four days, and on the 12th October he handed over to Major B. Cruddas of the FIFTH, who had been sent down from the 1st Battalion.* Changes in the command of the 28th Division and the 84th Brigade were also made about this time; Major-General C. Briggs replacing Major-General Bulfin in the former, and Brigadier-General G. A. Weir relieving Brigadier-General Pearce in the Brigade.

Officer reinforcements to the total of eleven subalterns having now joined, the Battalion on the 18th October marched to Mont Bernenchon, and on the following day to Béthune, where billets were found in a tobacco factory.† On the same day a reconnaissance was made of a supporting point in the Cambrin section of the line. It is difficult to determine what the purpose of this could have been, unless to provide the opportunity to the party engaged on it for a formal farewell to the trenches in France. For, on the following day, the 20th October, the Battalion received orders

---

* Major Cruddas had first come to France as Adjutant of the 4th (Territorial) Battalion.

† Though not recorded in the Battalion War Diary, it is thought the reinforcements of other ranks must also have reached the Battalion at this time.

23rd Oct., 1915 to entrain for Marseilles, with a view to embarking for an unnamed destination. Map No. 8 Having entrained at Fouquereuil station, near Bethune, the Battalion travelled by Amiens, Paris and Lyons, to arrive at Marseilles on the afternoon of the 23rd. Here 2nd-Lieutenant Gardner with 39 men and 40 horses were taken aboard H.M.T. *Shropshire*, 2nd-Lieutenant Steel and 33 other transport men were left to follow later, and the remainder of the Battalion, 20 officers and 657 other ranks, embarked on H.M.T. *Invernia*. The following were the officers who accompanied the main body of the Battalion:—

        Headquarters: Major B. Cruddas (Commanding).
                                   2nd-Lieutenant P. M. Johnston (4/D.L.I.) (Adjutant).
                                   Captain and Qrmr. W. M. Allan.
                                   Lieutenant H. Bourne Taylor, R.A.M.C. (Medical Officer).
                                   Captain T. A. Royce (Chaplain).
                                   2nd-Lieutenant G. G. Shiel (Machine Gun Officer).
    "A" Company: Lieutenant N. J. Allgood.
                                     2nd-Lieutenant T. C. L. Redwood.
                                   2nd-Lieutenant K. D. Woodroffe.
    "B" Company: Lieutenant G. Fenwick.
                                   2nd-Lieutenant C. C. G. Wright.
                                   2nd-Lieutenant F. A. Price.
                                   2nd-Lieutenant B. C. Woodroffe.
                                   2nd-Lieutenant J. Dingle.
    "C" Company: Lieutenant C. R. Freeman.
                                   2nd-Lieutenant F. V. Carpenter.
    "D" Company: Lieutenant O. Carr-Ellison.
                                   2nd-Lieutenant H. U. Scrutton.
                                   2nd-Lieutenant G. Clarke.
                                   2nd-Lieutenant Clive Smith.

At 4 p.m. the *Invernia* sailed from Marseilles, and the 2/FIFTH then learnt that their ultimate destination was to be Salonica.

It was but one year before that the 2nd Battalion of the FIFTH had received orders at Sabathu to prepare for transfer to Europe; ten months only had passed since it had arrived in France. Yet in that brief period its battle casualties alone had totalled 62 officers and 1649 other ranks. There is no record of the number of other ranks that remained of those who had landed in France with the Battalion on the 18th January, 1915; of the officers there remained but one—Captain Allan, the Quartermaster.

NOTE.—There is no record in the War Diaries of either Battalion of the dates on which Lewis Guns were issued or Vickers guns withdrawn to form Brigade M.G. companies. When first received Lewis Guns were not allotted to companies, but being regarded as replacing Vickers guns, they were formed as these had been into a separate "section." There is evidence that they are often referred to as "machine guns," and the officer in command of them retained at first the title of Machine Gun Officer (*e.g.*, 2nd-Lieutenant Shiel, who is thus shown above). The term "Lewis Gun" is first mentioned in the War Diary of the 2nd Battalion on 17th October, 1915, but in that of the 1st Battalion it is not found till as late as 7th January, 1916. It has been established that the 2nd Cheshire Regiment received Lewis Guns just before the fighting at the Hohenzollern, and the presumption is that they were issued to the 2/FIFTH at the same time.

CHAPTER X.

FIRST BATTALION—17TH JUNE, 1915—2ND JULY, 1916.

Trench Warfare—The Attack at St. Eloi.

The Battalion moves to the Somme.

Map No. 15

17th June, 1915

When a battalion took part in an attack for the capture of a limited objective such as that which had been given at Bellewaarde, there was seldom reason for any change in the position of its transport lines; and accordingly the details of the 1/FIFTH which had not been taken into battle on the 16th June, e.g., the transport drivers and personnel of the Quartermaster's department, had remained at Ouderdom bivouac. As rumours of the fighting came down, these men had begun to feel the keenest anxiety, and were eagerly awaiting news of what had befallen their comrades in the battle. On the 17th, the first to return from the front was Lieutenant Dorman-Smith, who, being but slightly wounded, had left the lorry by which he was being evacuated and made his way on foot to Ouderdom. He describes his arrival at the bivouac as the most poignant incident among his experiences in the War. He was immediately surrounded by the officers' servants, each of whom clamoured for news of his own particular officer. As one by one they received his reports, and learned that none but the Commanding Officer would return, and that some would never be seen again, their dismay and grief gave touching evidence of the loyalty and devotion of these men of the FIFTH to the officers they served so well.

The difficulty of replacing officer casualties had long since become acute. In the unpreparedness of Great Britain for a land war of the magnitude of that in which she had become involved, little discrimination had been observed in the hasty recruiting of volunteers to fill the ranks of the greatly expanded Army. As a result, thousands of the keenest and best of her young men, who by education and unbringing were well qualified for leadership, had been allowed to enlist in the ranks; and in the early months of the War hundreds who might have been trained to replace casualties among officers had been killed as private soldiers. Special Reserve Battalions had striven manfully to fill the gaps, but, crowded though they were with young officers under training, they had proved incapable of providing by themselves the full requirements, and it had been realised that it was necessary to organise additional sources of recruitment for the commissioned rank.

Among the expedients adopted was the conversion of the Artists Rifles, one of the earliest of the territorial battalions to join the British Expeditionary Force, to an Officers' Training Corps. Several officers from this Corps had been posted to the 2nd Battalion in replacement of the casualties of the 24th May, and the first two to join the 1st Battalion—2nd Lieutenants Barber and Partington—were now awaiting its return from the fighting at Bellewaarde. One cannot but wonder what the sensations of these young subalterns were when, on seeing a few score weary men led back by Lt.-Colonel Yatman, they realised that this small band represented the Battalion to which they had been posted, and that they themselves constituted two-

14th/15th July, 1915

thirds of the present total of its company officers.* Barber and Partington were, however, only the first arrivals of a steady flow of reinforcements. In the course of the next four weeks, during which the Battalion remained in reserve, the following additional officers joined it together with 244 other ranks :—

Captain H. H. Prideaux	North'd. Fusiliers (S.R.).
Captain G. E. B. Waddilove	,,
2nd-Lieutenant G. H. Allgood	,,
2nd-Lieutenant C. S. Bowman	,,
2nd-Lieutenant H. B. Fisher	,,
2nd-Lieutenant B. C. Burton	,,
Lieutenant Burdon	Durham L.I. (S.R.).
2nd-Lieutenant Cooper	,,
2nd-Lieutenant Lynch	,,
2nd-Lieutenant W. E. Harper	,,
2nd-Lieutenant N. Bastow	West Yorks R. (S.R.)
2nd Lieutenant Hartley-French	,,
2nd-Lieutenant P. H. Downing	,,
2nd-Lieutenant J. P. White	,,

Map No. 8

Thus reinforced the Battalion, with the remainder of the 9th Brigade, was sufficiently strong to take its place again in the line, and on the night of the 14th/15th July, it relieved the East Surrey Regiment in trenches on the right of St. Eloi.†

Some attempt has been made in previous chapters to give a picture of the life led by a battalion on a defensive front in these early years of the War, with its alternating periods of duty in the trenches and rest in reserve. But for a single interruption the existence described was to be the lot of the 1/FIFTH during the next twelve months; on one occasion only were they to be allowed to break from the cover of their trenches before being sent south to take part in the great battles of the Somme. Although it brought a severe strain on the morale of the troops, this life in the trenches, when led as close to death as was that of the men on the Western Front, was never one of merely dull routine: in the incidents that broke the monotony of the days spent by the men in the front line there was, however, a sameness which would make a detailed record of such periods tedious to the general reader. In the pages that follow, therefore, this history will pass more rapidly over the months during which the FIFTH were employed in what was little more than passive defence, recording only their general experiences and the casualties sustained on the various fronts they held, and reserving a more detailed narrative for the description of events that were outside the normal, day to day, life in the trenches.

---

* Lieutenant B. G. Gunner, hitherto Transport Officer, now replaced Captain Herbert as Adjutant.

† The G.O.C. 3rd Division had remained in command of the Hooge Sector after the Battle of Bellewaarde, and the St. Eloi Section did not revert to his command till the 23rd July. Till then the 9th Brigade was under the 5th Division.

Map No. 8

24th July, 1915

Mining was now in more active operation than it had been during the Battalion's first tour on the St. Eloi front in April and May. Camouflets were blown on the 17th and 26th July by the Germans, and on the 24th by ourselves. Little damage, however, was done by these, and the casualties sustained during a sixteen days' tour —9 other ranks killed, 2nd Lieutenant Harper and 33 other ranks wounded—were mainly caused by artillery or trench mortar fire. Further reinforcements had in the meantime reached the Battalion. Captain W. H. Wild (of the FIFTH), 2nd Lieutenants A. J. Roberts and E. G. Passingham (both from the Artists Rifles T.C.) and 2nd Lieutenant M. G. Jones (from the Army Service Corps), together with 175 other ranks, had joined on the 22nd, and with a later draft of 109 other ranks the losses of the Battalion at Bellewaarde had been more than made up by the end of the month.

As related in the previous chapter the divisions of the First New Army were at this time arriving on the Western Front ; and in a general relief of the 3rd by the 17th Division * that was now ordered, the 52nd Brigade was to take over from the 9th. Prior to assuming full responsibility for the line, the battalions of the new brigade, as was customary, had undergone a brief period of attachment to the units they were to relieve. It was so that, by a happy coincidence, the 9th Northumberland Fusiliers, who formed part of the 52nd Brigade, had been placed under the tutelage of the 1/FIFTH preparatory to taking over the St. Eloi trenches. The 9th Battalion was commanded by Colonel H. St. G. Thomas, formerly of the 84th Punjabis, his adjutant being Captain J. F. Chenevix-Trench who had been doing duty at the Regimental Depôt at the outbreak of war.

Among those with the Battalion who had served in the FIFTH previous to retirement were Major G. R. Westmacott, Captain C. B. L. Dashwood, Serjeant-Major F. T. Poulter,† Quartermaster-Serjeant J. Hutton, and Serjeant Armitage as well as many other N.C.O.'s and private soldiers ; in truth, there were many more old fusiliers in the new than there were in the old battalion which had been made responsible for instructing the " young idea." On the 31st July the Regiment's oldest battalion, which had been the first to enter the War, was relieved by the first of its new battalions to be sent to the Western Front.‡

The 9th Brigade had now been ordered to take over a section of the line to the north-east of Ypres, and the FIFTH, after spending two nights in billets at Ouderdom, relieved the 2/Sherwood Foresters of the 18th Brigade in trenches near Potijze. At this time heavy fighting was in progress on the 6th Division's front near Hooge, and a certain proportion of the enemy's artillery bombardment extended to the Potijze sector. As a result the Battalion experienced some fairly heavy shelling for the twelve

---

* Commanded by Major-General T. D. Pilcher, formerly of the FIFTH.

† Frank Poulter may be held as typical of those old soldiers of the FIFTH whose immediate response to the call for recruits for New Armies was a source of great pride to their Regiment. He had served with the 2/FIFTH in the Black Mountain Campaign (1888), and in the South African War had been awarded the D.C.M. for distinguished service as Company-Serjeant-Major of the Mounted Infantry Company of the same battalion. Later in March, 1916, this gallant old Fifth Fusilier was to be awarded the Military Cross " for conspicuous gallantry on several occasions during operations. He rescued five men from a blown-in dug-out under heavy shell fire, led stretcher bearers with great bravery, and brought in many wounded." (Quoted from Official Despatches.)

‡ The senior of the New Army battalions, the 8th commanded by Lt.-Colonel C. E. Fishbourne of the FIFTH, had been sent to Gallipoli

16th Aug., 1915 days during which they occupied this portion of the line before being withdrawn once Map No. 8
more to Ouderdom, together with the remainder of the 9th Brigade, which now reverted
to the 3rd Division.

Though the Battalion had now about three-quarters of its full establishment
of officers, the length of service of the greater number of these could be reckoned only
in months. The arrival on the 16th August of Captain Cruddas, an officer of fifteen
years' service, who had hitherto been doing duty as adjutant of the 4th (Territorial)
Battalion, provided a company commander of quite exceptional experience.*

The 3rd Division was now moved north again to take over the Hooge Sector,
in which the 9th Brigade was detailed to hold a line running from a point 1200 yards
north-east of Zwarteleen to a point 500 yards S.S.E. of Hooge. The FIFTH, who were
at first in Brigade reserve, relieved the Lincolnshire in trenches in Maple Copse on
the 23rd August. On the day following this relief Lt.-Colonel Yatman handed over
command of the Battalion to Major Wild, and left for England to take over the 96th
Infantry Brigade, to which he had been appointed. There can have been none who
had better earned such promotion. Just twelve months had passed since the detachment of the FIFTH under his command had first encountered the enemy on the line of
the Mons Canal. Throughout the whole of the strenuous, and often critical period
that had followed, Yatman had served continually, as second-in-command or in command, with the Battalion. He now disappears from this history, and it may here
be said that, after serving throughout the War, he was to emerge from it as strong and
self-reliant as in August 1914, but, as will be later learnt, with the lasting sorrow of
the death in action of his only son as an officer of the FIFTH.

The last week of August passed comparatively quietly on the Hooge front,
but with the opening of September the artillery of both sides became more active, and
on the 4th, the last day of the Battalion's tour, some twenty casualties were suffered
in the course of an exchange of bombardments between our own artillery and the
enemy's guns and trench mortars. A week was spent in the trenches in the middle
of the month, when bombardments and counter-bombardments occurred almost daily.
On the 25th September the 3rd Division delivered an attack on the enemy's position
about Hooge and east of Sanctuary Wood. The operation was carried out by the
7th and 8th Brigades and a part of the 9th. The FIFTH, however, who were in reserve,
partly in the Zillebeke Switch and partly in dug-outs at the west end of Zillebeke Lake,
were not actively engaged in this attack, which is known in history as " The Combat
of Hooge." Their return to the line was marked, on the 29th, by the explosion of a
mine by the enemy and an attempt by his infantry to occupy the mine-crater after a
two hours' bombardment of our trenches. The efforts of the Germans were, however,
repulsed with heavy casualties, though at the cost to the FIFTH of 8 other ranks killed
and 2nd Lieutenant Fox and 14 other ranks wounded.

On the 7th October Captain B. G. Gunner, who had succeeded Captain Herbert
as adjutant, was killed. He and Major Cruddas had been sitting in a sunny spot a
considerable distance in rear of the front line, where they had regarded themselves
as safe from all but the enemy's shell fire. Suddenly a stray bullet was heard to pass
close at hand, and they decided that it would be wiser to move to the shelter of a wood
near by. They had barely risen to carry out this intention when Gunner caught his
breath and fell. Major Cruddas relates : " I thought he had merely slipped. I looked

---

* As recorded in the previous Chapter, Captain Cruddas was shortly to be transferred to
the 2nd Battalion.

back; he was quite still. I turned him over and found that he had been shot straight through the head." Thus in the service of the 1st Battalion of the FIFTH died a direct descendant of the sister of Henry Ridge, who a little more than one hundred years before had fallen when leading the 2nd Battalion to the storming of Badajoz.*

During August and September the following additional officers had joined:—

    2nd-Lieutenant W. A. Rochell.
    2nd-Lieutenant J. H. Somerset, from Artists Rifles T.C.
    2nd-Lieutenant D. C. Fox (now wounded), from Artists Rifles T.C.
    2nd-Lieutenant E. L. Linzell.
    2nd-Lieutenant B. Watson.
    2nd-Lieutenant H. A. C. Marr-Baker.
    2nd-Lieutenant R. Potts.

But, with the death of Ben Gunner, who before being appointed Adjutant had served as Transport Officer, there remained now with the 1st, as with the 2nd Battalion, but one officer of those who had accompanied it to France—Captain Landen, the Quartermaster.

Early in October a chance encounter between an enemy's patrol with one of our own resulted in the capture of two prisoners, who are described as " decent looking fellows, quite young." Under the examination of a trained intelligence officer, even a single chance prisoner would on occasion prove of inestimable value. But the record of the preliminary and unofficial examination of these two is of interest only in giving the methods by which the inquiry was conducted by a serjeant of the FIFTH. This worthy N.C.O., who it seems had some reputation as a linguist in his platoon, bombarded the bewildered youths with questions in a jargon composed mainly of Hindustani and pigeon English, following each separate interrogatory with a brisk " No compree." Ultimately, convinced that nothing short of the rack or thumbscrew could succeed where he had failed, he permitted the *recalcitrant* captives to be removed, trusting, no doubt, that these sterner measures would be applied at Divisional Headquarters!

Daily artillery and trench mortar bombardments continued during the early months of October. Generally speaking, however, things were quieter and the rate of casualties lower than in the preceding months. On the 13th, Lieutenant G. H. Allgood was wounded, and on the same day, in addition to 3 other ranks being wounded, 1 officer and 5 other ranks reported sick. From this and similar entries in the War Diary on succeeding days one learns that at this time wastage through sickness at least equalled that caused by battle casualties. While these particulars are derived from official sources, private records serve to remind us that, for a fastidious officer, the horrors of war in this trench life were not confined to those for which the enemy or the climate were alone responsible. In one such private journal it seems that the diarist, after writing a vivid description of the manner in which a German aeroplane had been brought down by rifle and machine gun fire during the afternoon, looked up from his work, for he adds a final entry for the day : " My servant has just removed my dinner. He cleaned the knife and fork by sticking them in his puttees !" How vividly that entry brings recollection of the somewhat startling originality shown on occasion by the officers' servants in the days of the War ! Yet it recalls much else, for there can be none among the officers of the FIFTH who served in those days who

---

* Ben Gunner was one of seven brothers. His elder brother, Thomas Ridge Gunner, died in India while serving with the 1/FIFTH; his youngest brother, Sub-Lieutenant Geoffrey Gunner, perished in the explosion of H.M.S. *Bulwark* in 1914.

22nd Oct., 1915 does not remember with gratitude all he owed to his servant. These men, it seemed, regarded it as part of their common duty to maintain the morale of their officers—and how much they really did in this respect ! There may still be some who, with the writer, recollect the preposterous yarns which the servants brought up with the officers' rations every night in early 1915. The first night it would be said that there was every reason to believe that " the Kaiser is suing for peace " ; next night the tale would be that " the Battalion is shortly to go home to re-fit at Shorncliffe " ; on the third that " it seems certain that the 1/FIFTH are to be sent to Gallipoli " (this, with every other theatre of war, being regarded by them as a haven of rest as compared with the Western Front) ; and so on. And who will deny that these outrageous " canteen rumours " *did* serve to raise the spirits of an officer who was a bit down on his luck, even though he knew well that they had no sounder foundation than the fertile imagination of the particular one among these optimists who had issued the " nightly lie " to his fellows, before they set out from the transport lines to cross a bullet swept area on their hazardous journey to the trenches?

Map No. 8

On the 22nd October the 3rd Division, on relief by the 17th, was withdrawn to rest in the Steenvoorde Area, the FIFTH being billeted with the 9th Brigade in farms near Godaersvelde. In the period of just over three months which had passed since the re-organisation of the Battalion after the action at Bellewaarde, battle casualties had amounted to 1 officer and 25 other ranks killed, 2 officers and 170 other ranks wounded. Despite the arrival of drafts totalling 154 other ranks, the total strength of the Battalion, owing to losses through sickness, had been decreased by 165 and now amounted only to 666 all ranks. At the end of October, however, the officer strength stood at 23, having been made up during the month by the arrival of the following :—*

2nd-Lieutenant A. Richardson.
2nd-Lieutenant C. Rutlege.
2nd-Lieutenant F. Raynor.
2nd-Lieutenant F. Rea.
2nd-Lieutenant A. F. Ware.
2nd-Lieutenant J. F. Howgill.
2nd-Lieutenant H. Green.

If it be remembered that for some portion of the period referred to above the Battalion had been doing duty in reserve, it will be realised that though little has been recounted of their experiences in the trenches, scarcely a day had passed in the line on which casualties had not occurred. Even during the first three weeks of

---

* The posting of these officers, as in the case of many others, though recorded in the *St. George's Gazette*, is not mentioned in the War Diary. The names of officers who were posted and of those who became battle casualties are given as far as possible, but changes were continual and, owing to there being no record of those admitted to hospital through sickness or returning after a short period of detention there, it is impossible to discover the names of all who were serving with the Battalion on any given date. When this History appears in volume form it is hoped to add appendices giving the names of all officers who served with the 1st and 2nd Battalions of the FIFTH during the War.

October, when the weekly reports of the Division state that there was "little incident"—as indeed was the case from a divisional point of view—men of the FIFTH had been killed or wounded on nine out of the fifteen days spent in the line, and on a single day the Battalion had suffered as many as thirteen casualties. The form of protection afforded against artillery fire was still of a somewhat primitive nature as the following entry in a diary of the period will show: "After breakfast found that the top of my 'dug-out' had been blown off. The tin is there, the sand bags gone." While the overhead cover of a few sand bags on a sheet of corrugated iron gave effective protection against shrapnel bullets, a direct hit by a trench mortar bomb on a fragile structure of this kind might, as one learns from another entry in the same diary, result in terrible disaster. As to wastage through sickness, one marvels only that this had not been greater when reading this brief account of a return from the trenches on relief: "The men very tired. The mud was awful all the way. Half way up one's shins and liquid mud everywhere. Sometimes a shell-hole underneath and then disaster. I was covered with yellow mud up to my waist, spotted with black. My arms and sides were also yellow." This was trench warfare—daily casualties inflicted by the enemy—daily losses through sickness—the "process of attrition," which some believed might of itself bring an end to the War.

The Battalion, first at Godaersvelde and later at Winnizeele, spent a whole month in rest billets. The only notable event during this period was a visit by the King to the V. Corps Area on the 27th October, when Captain H. H. Prideaux of the FIFTH commanded a composite company paraded by the 9th Brigade, to which each of its battalions contributed 20 rank and file. For the rest, time was spent in training and recreation.

In the early autumn of 1915 a policy had been introduced by which brigades and battalions were exchanged between certain of the divisions of the Old and New Armies. In pursuance of this, the 7th Infantry Brigade had left the 3rd Division early in October in exchange for the 76th Brigade of the 25th Division. On the 13th November an alteration in the composition of the Division was made by which the FIFTH were more intimately affected; the 1/Lincolnshire Regiment, who had been their neighbours in Portsmouth before the War, and who had fought alongside them in the 9th Brigade since its outbreak, being transferred to the 62nd Brigade in exchange for the 12/West Yorkshire Regiment.

On the conclusion of its month's rest the 3rd Division was to relieve the 24th in the trenches from south-west of St. Eloi to opposite Verbrandenmolen; and on this front the 9th Brigade was to occupy the right section from a point 800 yards south-west of St. Eloi to a point 500 yards north-east of Shelley Farm. Preliminary to going into the line, the FIFTH were moved on the 19th November to Dickebusch. Shortly after their arrival here an unusual event occurred: a German aeroplane, which had lost its way, made a forced landing within 300 yards of Battalion Headquarters and its crew, an officer and a N.C.O. were captured. On the following day a working party of the Battalion was heavily shelled in a back area, two men being killed and one wounded. On the 23rd November the FIFTH, as left battalion of the 9th Brigade, took over trenches immediately south of the Ypres—Comines canal. Except for some slight artillery fire, by which 7 other ranks were wounded, the tour passed quietly, and at the end of a week the 9th Brigade was withdrawn to reserve, the FIFTH being billetted in Poperinghe.*

---

* 2nd-Lieutenants Miller, Carrick and Phelan joined the Battalion during this tour.

13th Nov., 1915 to 6th Feb., 1916

There is little to relate of the next three months. Week after week one finds that the entries in both the Division and Brigade war diaries are confined to such reports as "uneventful and quiet" or "no incident." The diary of the Battalion, which spent the time in alternate periods of 8 days in the trenches and 8 in rest at Poperinghe or Reninghelst, though fuller, contains little of general interest, and battle casualties were almost negligible. Christmas was passed in the trenches; one reads in the *St. George's Gazette* how, undefeated by mud and water, the FIFTH kept the day in a "truly Christmassy manner," and of how Holy Communion was celebrated in a dug-out. At the New Year they were in the more comfortable surroundings of Poperinghe, which, though occasionally shelled by the Germans, was preferred for rest in reserve to "D" Camp in Reninghelst, where the men in good huts had the better of the officers, who were accommodated in tents. In the former, too, the divisional concert party, "The Fancies," with two famous beauties, Miss Lanoline and Miss Marjorine, proved a great attraction after the mud and misery of trench life, whereas at Reninghelst the battalion band had to do all the work of entertainment. A word should be said about the origin of this unofficial band. To the disappointment of many, all regimental bands had been left in England when the British Expeditionary Force sailed in 1914. The justification of this was soon realised, for though the bands might have played their battalions forward to the Mons Canal in August, it is inconceivable that the big drums, or those imposing brass instruments which grunt so pleasingly in the rear rank of a military band, would have ever reached the Marne in September. Nor in the months that followed, when battalions were almost continuously engaged, and their bandsmen fully taken up with their war-time duties as stretcher bearers, were there opportunities for the men to benefit by music, or the musicians available to provide it. But, when with the development of the more static trench warfare, periods of rest in huts or billets became possible, bands and the refreshment that can be found in music were sadly missed. Accordingly in March 1915, a group of the bandsmen still left with the 1/FIFTH, assisted by some of the officers, procured instruments and music from home and organised their own band. A notable reinforcement to these public spirited musicians, who elected their own "bandmaster," was found in Regimental Serjeant-Major Crabtree (formerly Drum-Major), who undertook the rôle of flute and piccolo player. The first performance, given at Dickebusch, will always be remembered by those who heard it. What Kneller Hall might have thought of it is of no consequence: judged by the standard of the pleasure it gave to the audience, few performances can have ranked higher than this opening programme of the FIFTH's volunteer band. And here let the splendid devotion and self-sacrifice of the bandsmen of the FIFTH, when carrying out their grim duties as stretcher-bearers, be recorded. No regiment was better served in this respect than that in which many of these men had lived since boyhood.

Map No. 8

Generally speaking, the average man in the War was wont to think that the other fellow's lot compared favourably with his own. The impressions formed of trench life by two petty officers and a marine of the Grand Fleet, who spent twenty four hours with the Battalion in December, are, therefore, interesting. They are recorded as follows in the Battalion War Diary:—"Although they enjoyed their visit and were thoroughly interested in everything they saw, they informed us that sea life was 'more agreeable' to them than winter in the trenches."

On the 6th February the whole 3rd Division was again withdrawn to rest, being now located in an area near St. Omer, in which the FIFTH occupied billets at Ruminghem. In the ten weeks that had elapsed since they had taken over trenches

138   THE FIFTH IN THE GREAT WAR.

Map No. 8   on the 23rd November, the casualties of the FIFTH amounted only to 1 officer* and   14th
2 other ranks killed, and 14 other ranks wounded. On the other hand, strong drafts
had arrived during the same period bringing the fighting strength of the Battalion to
the high total of 27 officers and 941 other ranks.

The 3rd Division enjoyed a full month's rest in reserve before again being
moved up to the line. The sector taken over was the same as that which it had previously occupied; but the 9th Brigade was now placed on the left, with the FIFTH, as
its right battalion in trenches at "The Bluff," immediately north of the canal."†
The Brigade held this section of the front for only four days before being relieved on
the 11th March and withdrawn to reserve in Poperinghe. During the tour Brigadier-
General Douglas Smith, on appointment to command the 20th Division, had been
replaced by Brigadier-General H. C. Potter, who was to remain in command of the
9th Infantry Brigade till the end of the War.

On the 14th, the 9th Brigade took over the right section of the divisional
front, and the FIFTH found themselves once again in the familiar surroundings of the
St. Eloi trenches. Five days passed very quietly, and the total casualties of the
Battalion had amounted only to one man wounded when, on the 19th March, it was
withdrawn with the Brigade to reserve and moved into "D" Camp at Reninghelst.
Snow had fallen early in the month, but more recently bright sunny days had given
promise of better weather for an event that was now foreshadowed.

It may be remembered that, when referring to the first occasion on which
the 1/FIFTH took over the St. Eloi trenches in April, 1915, it was explained how,
opposite the village, a salient in the German position, which included what was known
as "The Mound," broke the general run of the line. Beneath the ground which
separated the opposing front line trenches in this neighbourhood both sides had
developed extensive mining systems. An operation had now been planned for the
reduction of this salient, with the dual object of destroying the enemy's mine shafts
which it was known to contain, and of securing the observation which was afforded
to the side which held the ground in question. Our own mines, as will be seen later,
represented an important factor in the plan of attack. The infantry detailed for the
operation consisted of the 9th Brigade and three battalions of the 8th Brigade. The
bulk of these, however, were to be employed in a defensive rôle, and the actual
assault and capture of the enemy's positions to be allotted to two battalions—the
1/FIFTH and the 4/Royal Fusiliers.

At 4.15 a.m. on the 27th March, which was fixed as zero hour for the attack,
a heavy bombardment was to be opened on the German position, and five mines were
simultaneously to be exploded at close intervals under the front line of the salient.
As a precaution against injury to our own men from the falling débris of the mines,
the infantry were to allow a half minute to elapse after their explosion before advancing
to the attack, when the FIFTH would be directed against the western, and the Royal
Fusiliers against the eastern flanks of the salient. Having carried the enemy's front
line, both battalions were to push forward to his support line and join hands at Point
33. On gaining this final objective, five specially organised bombing parties with each
battalion were to push forward up each of ten communication trenches, and there

---

* 2nd-Lieutenant Miller had fallen to the bullet of a sniper three days before the Battalion
was relieved.

†The feature known as "The Bluff" had been formed from the earth excavated from the
Canal.

26th Mar., 1916 take up positions to resist counter-attack by the German reserves and cover consolidation.

To bring them square to their objectives, the two battalions were to be assembled during the night of the 26th-27th March on either side of St. Eloi; the FIFTH being formed in four lines to the west of the village, facing south-east; two companies of the Royal Fusiliers in Shelley Farm, and the remainder of the battalion in rear of the parados of R.1 trench.

Following the opening bombardment, the artillery were to continue to support the attack by progressively advancing their fire. Further support was to be given by the machine guns and trench mortars of the 9th Brigade;* 3 guns only were to accompany the infantry, of which one, under Lieutenant Burdon, was to advance with the FIFTH; 8 guns to be posted well to the left, with the special rôle of guarding against counter-attack from that flank; and the remaining five to be distributed with the trench mortars in positions on either flank to keep down the enemy's fire.

Preparations for the attack were to include the placing of scaling ladders and bridges to facilitate the crossing of our own trenches, the cutting of our own wire on the front of attack, and the formation of advanced dumps of S.A.A., grenades, and other material. A replica of our own and the enemy's trenches had been marked out in the reserve area, and here in very wet and cold weather—for the promise of finer days had not been fulfilled—the attack was carefully rehearsed by the two battalions between the 20th and 24th March.

The FIFTH and the Royal Fusiliers were moved up to the forward area after dark on the 26th, and at 4 a.m. on the following morning both battalions were reported assembled in readiness for attack. In the meantime all troops had been silently withdrawn from the trenches in the danger area of the mines, without any apparent signs that the enemy had noticed that unusual movement was in progress on our side of No-Man's Land.

Punctually at 4.15 a.m. the first heavy shell of the bombardment came over, and following it at intervals of a few seconds the mines were blown along the whole front. For a moment the explosions exercised a curious, paralysing effect on the attacking troops, but this quickly passed. In the FIFTH it was realised that fear of damage to our own men from falling débris had been greatly exaggerated and that the sooner the assault could follow the exploding of the mines, the less chance would there be of opposition; so, without waiting for the half minute as ordered, the companies, with " W " and " Y " leading, climbed their scaling ladders, crossed the bridges which spanned the front line, and advanced to the attack. It proved fortunate that they had acted so promptly, for they thus escaped the enemy's artillery barrage, which burst on the front line a few seconds after the rear troops had cleared it, and gained the line of the enemy's wire with the loss of only one man wounded. This, however, formed a fairly strong obstacle; the leading companies were checked, and for a time became mixed up with the rear troops, who had continued to advance; and to add to the confusion, a machine gun at this moment opened fire from the German front line. Fortunately, the fire of the gun was wild, and before it could be steadied, 2nd-Lieutenant H. J. Holmes and Lce.-Corporal M. Keirsey, who had succeeded in crossing the wire, gallantly attacked the gun with bombs and put it out

Map No. 15

---

* Machine gun sections had at this date been taken from battalions and united to form Brigade Machine Gun Companies. The later organisation of M.G. Battalions as part of the Machine Gun Corps was not introduced till 1918.

of action by killing the whole of its team of five men. The momentary disorganisation, into which companies had been thrown by the check to the advance, had now been remedied, and " W " and " Y," having cut their way through the wire, charged and carried the German front line ; then, wheeling half left, they swept straight forward to complete their task. " The interior of the salient, over which our men now swarmed, was a complete ruin. The dead were everywhere, and the living kept swarming out of the ground, where they had been buried in dug-outs, with their hands up."* The demoralisation caused by the sudden explosion of the mines had been completed by the rapidity with which the infantry assault had followed. Little resistance was encountered, and by 4.45 a.m. " W " and " Y " Companies had captured the final objective of the FIFTH's attack. In the meantime " X " Company, as planned, had followed in support, clearing communication trenches and dug-outs of such of the enemy as had escaped the leading line of attack. After this duty had been completed, two platoons were sent forward to reinforce the leading companies, while the remainder of the company consolidated a second line in front of Nos. 2 and 3 craters. " Z " Company, the last in the order of the advance, took up and consolidated a position in the old German front line from Point 96 to Point 73. The bombing parties, which had followed close on the heels of " W " and " Y " were now sent forward to establish blocks in the communication trenches in accordance with the plan of attack. Covered by these parties the front of the Battalion was well secured.

We will now turn to the situation on the flanks. While, on the front of the FIFTH, the attack had achieved complete success, the Royal Fusiliers had been less fortunate. Owing to a strict adherence to the order which had required a half minute to elapse after the exploding of the mines before the infantry advanced, they had been caught by the artillery barrage, which the FIFTH had escaped, and had been met by heavy machine gun fire whilst crossing their own parapet. At the outset they had suffered very heavy casualties, and at an early stage 8 out of their 14 officers had been put out of action. Two platoons had succeeded in reaching the line of the mine craters and in consolidating an enemy trench to the south of it, but these platoons were neither in touch with each other nor with the FIFTH, and the line gained represented no more than that designated in the plan of attack as a position to be consolidated in support of the final objective. An isolated bombing party, which succeeded in getting forward to Point 33, for a time gave rise to a report that the Royal Fusiliers were in line with the FIFTH. Actually the battalion, after the heavy losses it had sustained, was unable to gain ground beyond the line of the craters, which was ultimately consolidated as the front line of the captured position in this quarter of the attack.

Though not in touch with the FIFTH, the Royal Fusiliers, thus échelonned to their rear, seem to have been in position to give protection to their left, for no attempt was made by the enemy to counter-attack against this flank. It was otherwise, however, on the right flank, against which the Germans at 8 a.m. started to make heavy and persistent bombing attacks, while snipers from their rear positions were responsible for causing many casualties. The manner in which the stubborn resistance of a small party of the FIFTH not only defeated the efforts of the enemy, but compelled a large number to surrender, can be best told by quoting the account given of the affair by 2nd-Lieutenant C. B. Carrick, who was in command at the threatened

---

* Press article quoted in the *St. George's Gazette* of March, 1916.

27th Mar., 1916 point:—"I went forward with the Right company ("W") and eventually found myself with ten to fifteen men on the right of our objective (*i.e.* the German Second Line). I was not in touch with anybody else at the time, either on my left or in rear, and almost immediately we were subjected to bombing and rifle fire from our right. The trenches were at this stage and at this point still in a moderately good state of repair, but a natural block had been effected on my right by shell-fire, and the enemy were attacking us from the cover afforded by this block, and the continuation of a trench beyond. The German bombs did not do a great deal of damage, but the enemy were in a higher position than ourselves and caused us heavy casualties by sniping. We attempted to do likewise, but obtained only very occasional targets and had to rely chiefly on our own bombs, the supply of which was naturally very limited, as they had been carried on the men during the attack and no further supplies were then available. Eventually we found a store of German bombs, which we used against the enemy, and this action continued for about $2\frac{1}{2}$ hours. The situation was looking pretty desperate when there were only four of us left alive, two of whom were wounded, but at that moment a German officer jumped up into the open, waving a white handkerchief as a token of surrender. I signalled to him to come forward, and he did so, followed by another officer and 35 other ranks. They of course came forward in file, one at a time, and after searching each man I ordered him to walk off in the direction of our lines. Finally I sent the one unwounded man I had after them and shortly afterwards obtained touch with some of our own troops on my left, and the position was finally consolidated, the time then being, I think, about 9 a.m."*

Map No. 15

Though the FIFTH had carried their objectives with very slight loss, they were not to come through the day without heavy casualties. As related above, the enemy's snipers were responsible for many of these, but it was from his artillery fire that more still were inflicted. In an attack of this nature, the troops on carrying the hostile position will for an appreciable time be spared from artillery fire, for without definite knowledge of the situation the enemy's guns dare not shell their own trenches. On the other hand it will often be from the latter, when once assured that their infantry has been driven back, that the attackers, in the long hours following a successful assault, will suffer the heaviest casualties of the day. It was so on this occasion. It was not long before the German guns shortened their range from the starting line of the British attack to the trenches that were being consolidated in the captured

---

* Major C. B. Carrick, M.C., now serving with the 6th (Territorial) Battalion, in forwarding this account of the incident, at the writer's request, adds: "On reading the above it seems to make much more of the incident than it deserves, but I have tried to describe the facts exactly as they occurred. I may say we had no idea how many of the enemy there were until they surrendered, and had I known they so greatly outnumbered us I undoubtedly would have been even more alarmed than I was!" The general opinion will be that, had the affair been described by anyone else, more would have been said of the example set by a young officer, whose gallantry and leadership on this occasion was recognised by the award of the Military Cross. It has, however, been decided to give the simple, straightforward account of the incident verbatim as submitted, since it not only gives a very clear idea of what occurred, but also brings out a point which is seldom apparent in "official" narratives of these attacks, viz. the difficulty of maintaining touch when involved in the maze of a trench system, which resulted in the most junior officers and N.C.O.'s being left to act entirely on their own initiative. As to "time," anyone who has taken part in an attack of this description or read reports by others who have, will know that all sense of time is lost, and that the actual hour which is guessed as that at which an incident occurred, or the period during which an action lasted, are alike often very wide of the mark.

142   THE FIFTH IN THE GREAT WAR.

Map No. 15   position. Throughout the day the shelling was continuous, and between 1 p.m. and   27th Mar., 1916
3 p.m. intense. Yet when darkness fell the FIFTH still held fast to the trenches they had captured, and it was on the final objective which they had carried that they were relieved during the night by the 13/King's Regiment and withdrawn to reserve. " The appearance of the Fusiliers when they came out would have surprised their friends, and perhaps even have shocked them. They had no apparent reason for cheerfulness, but merry they were, though plainly tired out. They were disguised in mud from their boots to the crowns of their steel helmets. Their faces were swathed in ragged scarves, and the ironmongery on their heads was wrapped in canvas. They carried German helmets on their rifles and shuffled along to absurd songs. They looked more like the veterans of Agincourt come to life again, and glad of it, than any likeness their homefolk could call to mind. And their eyes, though red-rimmed, were impudent and gay."* It was so that those who had fallen would have had their comrades return from battle.

The following casualties had been sustained by the 1/FIFTH during the action:

OFFICERS.

    Killed .. Lieutenant C. J. McK. Thompson.
                    Lieutenant F. M. Rea.
    Wounded .. Lieutenant M. G. Jones.
                    Lieutenant R. D. Vernon.
                    Lieutenant A. F. Ware.
                    Lieutenant S. A. Rose.

OTHER RANKS.

Killed 29.   Wounded 125.   Missing 21.

The total of the prisoners captured amounted to 5 officers and 195 other ranks. The losses of the 4/Royal Fusiliers totalled 264 all ranks.

In comparison with the great battles of the War, the action at St. Eloi, in which only two battalions were actively employed, must rank as a minor affair. From the point of view of the Battalion, however, it required as careful organisation and as skilful leading as any part played by the FIFTH in the greater battles whose names are borne on their Colours. In the precision with which the attack was carried out and the objectives secured, it may stand, perhaps, as the most completely successful of the actions in which the 1/FIFTH were engaged during the Great War. Just as their success had been largely due to their prompt advance after the exploding of the mines, so had the misfortunes of their friends, the Royal Fusiliers, been attributable to the delay that had resulted from a strict adherence to orders.

If the whole cost of the operation of the 27th March is to be estimated, to the 500 casualties sustained by the two battalions must be added the heavy losses

---

* *St. George's Gazette*, March, 1916: from the article before quoted.

THE 1/FIFTH AFTER ST. ELOI, 27TH MARCH, 1916.

[Imperial War Museum.—Crown Copyright.

4th April, 1916 inflicted by the enemy's bombardment on the troops holding the old British line. Map No. 15 The total, high as it was, could not be regarded as greater than experience would have anticipated, and there might be some who would question whether the small gain of ground which was the object of the operation justified such heavy losses. But, while it may be admitted that frequently during the War attacks were ordered for the capture or recovery of trenches without due regard to the value of the objective in relation to the cost involved in gaining it, and that the cultivation of an offensive spirit, which was sometimes held to justify such costly enterprises, would have been more wisely reserved for an operation which aimed at more far-reaching results, the action of St. Eloi is to be judged, not by the size of the salient which was the objective of attack, but by what that salient contained. Its ultimate object may be said to have been a defensive one, since it was directed solely towards the protection of the British positions by securing the Mound, from which they were under observation, and the shafts of the mines, by which they were continually threatened.

In a letter written by Major-General Haldane about this time, some interesting figures are found supporting his representation of the urgent need of the 3rd Division for reinforcements and also for a period of rest for the purpose of training and refitting. Casualties between the 2nd March and the 3rd April had totalled 128 officers and 2,759 other ranks, and the shortage in infantry personnel amounted to 51 officers and 2,789 other ranks. The average length of service of Commanding Officers was 13 years, of Officers Second-in-Command 5 years, of Company Commanders and Company Officers 1 year and 2 months !

The rest requested had already been granted to the 1/FIFTH, who following their exploits at St. Eloi had been moved on the 4th April to billets at Boeschepe, and thence on the following day to others near Meteren.* It was here that three days later the FIFTH received the congratulations of one whose praise never failed to bring fresh inspiration to them. On reading of the recent action, Sir Horace Smith-Dorien, now in England, had addressed the following message to the G.O.C. 3rd Division :—

"I gather that the success achieved by the 3rd Division at St. Eloi has been a very real one, and has brought great credit to the troops engaged, especially to the Northumberland Fusiliers, Royal Fusiliers and to their Brigade Commander. This news has given great pleasure to one who owes so much to the 3rd Division, and I write a brief note to convey my heartiest congratulations to you and the 3rd Division —May all good luck continue to attend you !"

The Battalion was still in billets on St. George's Day, which this year fell on a Sunday. After Divine Service, with the many greetings from old officers of the Regiment and from sister battalions there came the announcement of the following awards for distinguished service on the 27th March :—

The Distinguished Service Order.

Lieut.-Colonel W. H. Wild.

---

* " Y " Company and 3 Lewis Guns (half the existing complement) were at this time moved to the Kemmel Defences.

The Military Cross. 26th April, 1916

Captain J. P. White (3/W. Yorks Regt., attd.).
Lieutenant J. H. Hogshaw (L.G. Officer). *
Lieutenant C. B. Carrick.
2nd-Lieutenant H. J. Holmes.
2nd-Lieutenant M. G. Jones.

The Distinguished Conduct Medal.

C.S.M. T. F. Cooper.
Serjeant W. P. Carlin.
Lce.-Corporal M. Keirsey.
Private H. Trobe.†

In the record of the festivities which marked the occasion one finds an echo of the South African War in the playing of the final of the Paget's Horse Football Cup; and there is mention again of the band (total 12 men), which played a programme of music in the evening.

At a parade held on the following day for the presentation by the Divisional Commander of the ribands of the decorations that had been granted, an award was made which brought great gratification to the FIFTH. Captain the Reverend E. Noel Mellish, who as Church of England chaplain of the 9th Brigade had long since won the great affection and respect of all in the Battalion, received the riband of the Victoria Cross, in recognition of the gallant and devoted services he had rendered to the men among whom he served. At St. Eloi, during the 27th, 28th and 29th March, Noel Mellish had constantly gone forward under heavy machine gun and artillery fire to the succour and rescue of the wounded.

The 3rd Division had now taken over the Kemmel Sector, facing Wytschaete, in relief of the 50th (Northumbrian) Division (Major-General P. S. Wilkinson).‡ On the 26th April the 1/FIFTH were moved forward to R.C. Farm at La Clytte, near Kemmel, where they relieved the 4th (Territorial) Battalion of the Regiment in Brigade Reserve, and on the next day took over front line trenches in the section allotted to the 9th Brigade. The Battalion remained on the Kemmel front for the greater part of May; tours in the trenches alternating with periods in Brigade Reserve at R.C. Farm or in Divisional or Corps Reserve at Locre. The direction of the wind at this season was "dangerous" for the British, and there was always some anxiety about the enemy employing gas. These expectations were not fulfilled, but the bad condition of the trenches was responsible for heavy casualties, mainly from trench

---

* Lieut. Hogshaw was mentioned in despatches for conspicuous gallantry and ability in handling "his machine guns." Actually, they were Lewis Guns (see Notes p. 146 and at the end of Chapter IX.).

† At a later date the following were awarded the Military Medal for their conduct at St. Eloi:—Serjeants Sockett, Tedstill, S. Wilkinson, Knox; Corporals Day and Iveson; Private McQuade.

‡ Major-General Wilkinson had been appointed Colonel of The Northumberland Fusiliers on the 29th January, 1915.

The Fifth in the Great War. 145

25th May to 1st July, 1916

mortar fire, and also for necessitating the relief of battalions in the line every four days. During the Battalion's tour on the Kemmel front, 12 other ranks were killed, and Captain Hoffman, Lieutenant Bucknall, Lieutenant Lynch and 45 other ranks wounded.*

Map No. 8

On the 25th May the 9th Brigade was withdrawn to Corps Reserve, and the FIFTH were billeted at Locre. At this time the Canadian Corps was holding a front between St. Eloi and Hooge. On the 2nd June the Germans delivered a heavy attack against the left sector of this front and succeeded in forcing back the British line north of Hill 60. The Canadians' resources were insufficient unaided to hold the $5\frac{1}{2}$ miles of line which they occupied and at the same time deal with the serious situation which had arisen on their left, and on the 5th June the 9th Brigade was placed at their disposal. On the 7th, the FIFTH were temporarily attached to the 2nd Canadian Division and took over the front line to the north of the Ypres–Comines Canal. This arrangement however, could only be made as a brief emergency measure, as the 3rd Division was shortly to engage in other operations, and it was desired that the FIFTH, together with the other units of the Division, should undergo training for the task which it was anticipated might lie before them.

The great battle of the Somme was to open on the 1st July, and the 3rd Division, though not destined to take part in the first attack, was required as part of the General Reserve. If the opening phase resulted, as was hoped, in the penetration of the trench system which had been laboriously constructed by the enemy in course of the past two years, the nature of the War would undergo a complete change, and the reserves who would exploit such a success needed to be trained for the open warfare which would follow.

The FIFTH, accordingly, were relieved on the Canadian front on the 11th June, and, after a few days at Locre, were moved by rail to the Second Army Training area, west of St. Omer. Here, with the remainder of the 3rd Division, they were engaged till the end of June in training for a task far different from the trench warfare to which they had become accustomed. During this period the Battalion was billeted at Mentque and Nortleulinghem, 8 miles from St. Omer.

On the 1st July, the 3rd Division entrained at Audricq for its southward move to the Fourth Army area. At 7 a.m. the following morning the 1/FIFTH detrained at Candas, 5 miles south-west of Doullens, whence they marched *via* Bernaville to billet for the night at Prouville.

In the meantime the great British attack had opened, with what results and what influence on the immediate future of the FIFTH will be learnt in the following Chapter.

---

* The monthly nominal roll of casualties is now not attached as before to the Battalion War Diary, which in its day to day records shows considerably fewer casualties than the above, which are based on the totals shown for the Battalion by the 9th Brigade War Diary.

CHAPTER XI.

The Battles of the Somme, 1916.

"Bazentin"—"Delville Wood"—"Ancre, 1916"

3RD JULY TO 31ST DECEMBER, 1916.

Map No. 16
It is not possible within the limits of a regimental history to deal with the origin of the great offensive which had been planned by the Allies for 1916 or to recount the events which, by forcing a modification on the original scheme, had led to the British being called on to play the principal part. Here it must suffice if the threefold object of the operations which had been opened on the 1st July is given in the words of Sir Douglas Haig's despatches :— 3rd July, 1916

"They had been undertaken,
(i) To relieve the pressure on Verdun.*
(ii) To assist our Allies in the other theatres of war by stopping any further transfer of German troops from the Western Front.
(iii) To wear down the strength of the forces opposed to us."

Although the 1/FIFTH were not present at the opening of the offensive, a brief account of the events of the 1st and 2nd July is none the less necessary to explain the circumstances in which they were first to be engaged in the Battles of the Somme. For, the manner in which the Battalion was to be employed resulted directly from the varying failure and success which marked the initial British attack.

On the 1st July, in the area with which we are concerned, the Fourth Army (General Sir H. Rawlinson) had delivered its main attack on a front of some ten miles on either side of the Fricourt Salient; from Maricourt, on the right, to the River Ancre in front of St. Pierre Divion, in conjunction with a simultaneous attack by the French astride and to the south of the Somme. The XIII. Corps, on the extreme right of the British, advancing against the southern flank of the salient, had captured all its objectives and carried the line to the north of Montauban; and, on its left, the XV. Corps, also advancing north, had overrun the German front line and carried the village of Mametz. Troops attacking eastwards between Fricourt and La Boisselle had also obtained considerable success and penetrated to a depth of 2,000 yards. From La Boiselle northwards, however, the attack had failed to progress at any point, in spite of the fact that, on the 2nd July, the capture of Fricourt, which had held out during the first day, confirmed the success of the British attack in the southern quarter.

This, then, was the situation on the battle front when, on the arrival of the 3rd Division in reserve to the Fourth Army, the FIFTH, as related in the previous chapter, had taken up billets in Prouville during the afternoon of the 2nd July. The resistance encountered by the easterly attack to the north of Boiselle made it clear that the best promise of breaking the German defence on the whole front lay in

---

* In February the Germans had forestalled the Allies' offensive by an attack on Verdun, where the French had been engaged for months in a desperate and heroic defence.

3rd July, 1916 exploiting the success gained on the right, by a continuation of the northerly advance. It was to this quarter of the field, accordingly, that the 3rd Division was now directed, with orders to join the XIII. Corps. On the 3rd July the FIFTH were moved to Vignacourt,* whence, marching with the 9th Brigade, mostly under cover of darkness, and staging at Poulainville,* La Houssoye, and Morlancourt, they reached the battle area on the 8th and went into bivouac in the old British front line at Carnoy.

In preparation for an attack in which the 3rd Division was shortly to take part, the Battalion during the next three days was employed in furnishing carrying parties, while company commanders reconnoitred the front. In the course of these duties the FIFTH suffered somewhat severely from the fire brought by the German guns in retaliation for a bombardment which had already been opened by our artillery on the wire on the front of attack, 11 other ranks being killed by shell fire and 2nd-Lieutenant Dodd and 27 other ranks wounded. In the meantime a series of minor operations had succeeded in considerably improving the British position to the north of Fricourt and Mametz and to the north-east of Montauban, and by the 12th July the line had been carried forward to run east from Ovillers, by Contalmaison and Mametz Wood, to the west edge of Trônes Wood, where it bent south to join the French at Hardecourt.

To the north of Montauban, the ground fell steeply to Caterpillar Valley, from which it rose more gently to the flat-topped Bazentin Ridge. The German Second Line, which now faced the right of the Fourth Army, ran from west to east along the far edge of this ridge in front of the villages of Bazentin-le-Grand and Longueval, before turning south at the latter point to cover Guillemont, a village situated in a commanding position at the head of Caterpillar Valley. British posts had already been established on the northern slope of the Valley, but, owing to the contour of the ground, the enemy's trenches covering Bazentin could not be observed either from these or from the high ground at Montauban.

The 14th July was now fixed for an attack which had been planned for the capture by the 9th, 3rd and 7th Divisions, of the German positions from Longueval to Bazentin-le-Petit, a village 1,200 yards north-west of Bazentin-le-Grand. In this operation the objective allotted to the 3rd Division, in the centre of the attack, extended from a point in the enemy's support line 800 yards west of Longueval to and inclusive of the village of Bazentin-le-Grand. For the capture of this objective, the 8th and 9th Brigades were to advance, on the right and left respectively, with their inner flanks directed on a communication trench just east of the village, the 8th Brigade being made responsible for clearing the communication trench itself. The 76th Brigade was to be held in reserve.

In the 9th Brigade, the 13/King's Regiment, on the right, and the 12/West Yorkshire Regiment, on the left, were to lead the attack and, after carrying the enemy's front and support trenches, to continue the advance for the capture and consolidation of Bazentin-le-Grand. The 1/FIFTH were to act in support of the two assaulting battalions, and the 4/Royal Fusiliers to be held in Brigade Reserve. A sunken road about 250 yards distant from the enemy's front line had already been occupied by a screen of piquets and was selected as the general line of deployment for the leading battalions, who were to move forward under cover of darkness and deploy in readiness to attack at 3.25 a.m. The FIFTH, with " W " and " Y " Com-

---

*Not shown on Map 16. Vignacourt is roughly 7 miles N.W. and Poulainville 3½ miles N. of Amiens.

panies in front and " X " and " Z " in rear, were to take up a position on the reverse slope between the Montauban—Bazentin-le-Grand road and Marlborough Wood. The Battalion was to be in readiness to reinforce the leading troops in the attack and, alternatively, in the event of the 7th Division failing to get forward, to form a defensive flank to the north of Marlborough Wood in protection of the left of the 3rd Division.

On the night of the 13th/14th July, the attacking troops moved forward from Montauban. Caterpillar Valley, which lay between them and their assembly positions, had for days past been made a constant target for the German guns, and throughout the preceding night had been raked by shell fire. But on this night of assembly for attack the enemy's guns were strangely silent; the advance was almost undisturbed, and the leading infantry were deployed in readiness for the assault with the loss of but one man in the whole of the 3rd Division.

At 3.20 a.m. our artillery opened an intense bombardment on the whole front of attack, and five minutes later, as the King's and West Yorkshire advanced to the assault, the two leading companies of the FIFTH moved up to the positions vacated by these battalions in the sunken road, in order to watch the progress of their attack and reinforce it as circumstances might require. On the right, the King's, on gaining the ridge which faced the enemy's front line, came under heavy rifle and machine gun fire, and also suffered considerable losses from the German artillery. The battalion, none the less, though heavily punished, succeeded in carrying the front and support lines, and some of its platoons, in their eagerness, rashly overran their objective and entered the village before their supporting artillery had lifted its barrage. On the left, the West Yorkshire, meeting with less resistance, carried their objective with slighter loss. In the course of the assault, however, each battalion had slightly lost direction, and a dangerous gap had developed between their inner flanks. Lieutenant Taylor, commanding " W " Company of the FIFTH, quick to notice this, immediately led forward his company and carried the portion of the front and support lines which had escaped the first assault.

In the meantime, Lieutenant Cooper, commanding " Y " Company, had been awaiting report of the progress of the attack. As to this he could get no definite information, but seeing large numbers of wounded men coming back from the direction of the Bazentin trenches he concluded that the forward troops must be in need of assistance, and at 4 a.m. led forward two platoons of his company to what had been the German front line. This he found to be very sparsely occupied by the 13/King's, who had now suffered further heavy casualties and become greatly scattered. The attack of the troops on their right had been held up by uncut wire, and as a result they had come under a galling fire from the houses in the eastern quarter of the village and from the communication trench which represented the boundary between them and the left battalion of the 8th Brigade.

Lieutenant Cooper now ordered the remainder of " Y " Company to come forward, and disposed his men in the German front and support trenches. As these rear platoons moved up, " X " Company (Captain Rutledge) advanced to the line they had vacated in the sunken road. Casualties among the officers of the King's had been particularly heavy and included their Commanding Officer, Lt.-Colonel Gibbon. Of the men who had advanced prematurely from the 1st objective, it had been possible to withdraw a certain number to the support line, but many still remained forward in the western outskirts of the village. Shortly before 5 a.m. Cooper received orders from Lt.-Colonel Gibbon, whom he had found lying grievously

SUPPORTS MOVING UP—SOMME BATTLE, 1916.

[Imperial War Museum—Crown Copyright.

14th July, 1916 wounded, to take over command of such men of his battalion as were at hand and lead them forward with "Y" Company of the FIFTH to complete the clearance of the village.*

Map No. 17

In the meantime good progress had been made on the left of the 9th Brigade, where the 12/West Yorkshire, whose advance was covered by troops of the 7th Division moving through Bazentin-le-Grand Wood, had got well forward. Thus Cooper, on advancing, found his left flank secured and was able to request a party of the West Yorkshire to occupy a hollow road to the north of the village in protection of his front, while he directed his attention to clearing the eastern portion of the village, where the enemy's snipers in occupation of the shattered remains of houses were causing many casualties.

Information of the general situation had now reached Lieut.-Colonel Wild, who still held "Z" Company in Battalion Reserve in its original assembly position. On learning that the enemy were still in occupation of the village, and that the advance of the 8th Brigade had been held up, he ordered Captain Rutledge to advance with "X" Company from the sunken road to the assistance of "Y," and Captain White to lead forward "Z" Company to the right and, after ascertaining the situation, to take measures for the protection of that flank, where the enemy were reported to be massing to the east and north-east of the village.†

All four companies of the FIFTH were now engaged, of which "Y," "X," and a portion of "W" were employed in clearing the village. The searching of the houses and cellars was at the best a difficult task, and their ruined condition made it in some cases impossible. None the less the enemy's snipers were steadily dislodged, though the work was greatly hampered by rifle and machine gun fire from a fortified "keep" in the eastern quarter of the village.‡ Both "Y" and "X" Companies, on first entering the village, had suffered severely from fire directed from this point. Ultimately on the orders of Captain Rutledge, Lieutenant Lynch led a bombing attack against the "keep," and succeeded in driving the enemy from the position and capturing 20 prisoners and 4 machine guns. The Germans, however, still clung obstinately to some trenches to the east and to a gully to the north-east of the village. All efforts to oust them from these positions for long proved vain, and cost the FIFTH dear. Captain Holmes and Lieutenant Carrick—both of whom, as the reader may remember, had been called on to deal with critical situations on former occasions—now came on the scene. Holmes, who was in command of a detachment of the 9th Brigade Stokes guns, brought these into action, and, under cover of their fire, Carrick led forward the Grenadiers of the FIFTH, who stormed the positions and drove the enemy first from the trenches and later from the gully. Seventy more prisoners were captured, but, owing to the 8th Brigade not having yet got forward, a large number of the enemy succeeded in making good their escape and withdrawing to High Wood.

By 9.30 a.m. the capture of Bazentin-le-Grand had been completed. Later in the morning, after an intense bombardment by heavy artillery, the 8th Brigade

---

* Lt.-Colonel Gibbon later died of his wounds.

† The 9th Brigade narrative states that the fourth company of the FIFTH reinforced the 12/West Yorkshire. This is not borne out either by the narrative of the 1/FIFTH or that of the 12/West Yorks. The movements related above are based on a contemporary report written by Lieut.-Colonel W. Wild.

‡ In reports this is referred to by Lieut. Cooper as "M. le Marcheaux's stronghold"; by Captain Rutledge as "a large farm." According to Lieut.-Colonel Wild it had been a brewery.

was at last able to gain ground on the right, and by 1.30 p.m. the 3rd Division could report that all their objectives had been carried. In the meantime Major Smythe * had been sent up to organise the defence of the village against counter-attack; " W," " X " and " Z " Companies were disposed in defence of the north, east, and west sides of the village respectively, and " Y " was withdrawn to reserve in the old German front line.

The capture of Bazentin-le-Grand had cost the FIFTH the following casualties :—

OFFICERS.

Killed	..	2nd-Lieutenant H. E. Redpath.
Wounded	..	Captain J. P. White.
		Captain R. V. Taylor.
		Lieutenant R. C. Hill.
		Lieutenant A. C. Lynch.
		2nd-Lieutenant J. Bateman.

OTHER RANKS.

Killed 23.   Wounded 148.   Missing 40.

Of the Officers, White and Lynch, attached from the Special Reserve of the West Yorkshire Regiment and Durham Light Infantry, had served with the FIFTH continuously for over twelve months. The services rendered by the latter at Bazentin have been recounted; of Captain White, Lieut.-Colonel Wild says there was no officer under his command in whom he had learnt to place greater trust. With the certain prospect of further fighting in the near future the Battalion could ill afford the loss of officers known and trusted alike by their commander and their men.†

In the attack of the 14th July the British right had advanced due north against Longueval and Delville Wood; but, apart from the clearing of Trônes Wood, there had been no corresponding attack eastwards towards Guillemont. As a result, the salient which, before the attack, had occurred in the British line at Trônes Wood, instead of being flattened, had, so to speak, been carried forward to Longueval, there to become more acute and dangerous. The whole of the ground contained by it was open to view from Guillemont and High Wood, and so subject to observed artillery fire from both the east and north. The capture of Guillemont could alone free the British from this cramped and dangerous situation, and till this was accomplished it was vital that Longueval should be held. These considerations were to

---

* Major R. C. Smythe, Inniskilling Fusiliers, had joined the 1/FIFTH during June, and was acting as 2nd-in-Command of the Battalion at this date. He was given command of the 12/West Yorkshire Regiment in August, 1916.

† Since the above account of the Battle of Bazentin was written an interesting incident, which does not appear in either his own or other contemporary reports, has been related by Lieut.-Colonel Wild to the writer. At dawn on the 15th June some cellars, which had till then escaped notice, were located below the ruins of the " keep." Here it was found that the Colonel of the Bavarian Regiment which had held the Bazentin position had remained concealed together with his staff, a telephone, and some thirty men. The Colonel is described by Lieut.-Colonel Wild as a fine type of stern old " ironside," whose diary read like pages from the Old Testament. Lieut.-Colonel Wild further states that the greater number of the enemy succeeded in escaping to High Wood, and that in his belief the majority of the prisoners reported as captured were in fact taken in these cellars.

19th July, 1916 lead to weeks of desperate fighting and heavy losses, of which the FIFTH, as will be seen, were to bear their full share. Maps 16 & 18

After being employed for five days in holding and consolidating the positions captured at the Battle of Bazentin, the 9th Brigade was withdrawn on the 19th July to Divisional Reserve, the FIFTH taking up bivouac in the old British front line at Talus Boisé, where, except for some slight shelling, three days passed quietly enough. But, though the week following the attack on Bazentin had passed uneventfully for the 9th Brigade, it had not been so with all in the 3rd Division. Counter-attack against the positions captured by the 9th Division on the 14th July had secured for the enemy a footing in the northern parts of Longueval and Delville Wood, and on the 18th the task of clearing the village and ground to the north-west of it had been committed to the 76th Brigade (3rd Division), who after three days of fierce fighting had succeeded in accomplishing this, but only to be driven back later by renewed counter-attacks.

Lieut.-Colonel Wild was now ordered to report to Brigadier-General Kentish, the commander of the 76th Brigade, with a view to the FIFTH taking part under his command in yet another attempt to carry the position. Hitherto the attacks made against Longueval had been directed from Pont Street, which was situated to the west of the village. Brigadier-General Kentish had arrived at the conclusion that further efforts from this direction would be of little avail, and that the best promise of success lay in an attempt from the south. On his instructions, accordingly, Lieut.-Colonel Wild with his company commanders reconnoitred the ground to the south-west of the village in the early hours of the 22nd July. Owing to a dense mist, which shrouded the whole country, little could be seen of the ground, but the reconnaissance in any case was to be rendered valueless by a change in plan.* Wild had been awaiting further instructions from the 76th Brigade when, late in the evening of the 23rd July, he was informed that Kentish was no longer to be responsible for the task of recapturing Longueval and Delville Wood, and that this was to be undertaken on the following morning by the G.-O.-C. 9th Brigade, to whose Headquarters at Montauban he was summoned in order to receive fresh orders for the operation. He then found that the plan of the 9th Brigade attack, which was to be carried out simultaneously with an advance by the 30th Division against Guillemont, and by the 8th Brigade against a line of railway to the south-west of Longueval, reverted to the idea of an advance from the west which had been abandoned by Brigadier-General Kentish.

For the purpose of the operation the Brigadier had at his disposal, in addition to three of his own battalions—the 1/FIFTH, 12/West Yorkshire, and 13/King's—the 8/King's Own, of the 76th Brigade, and the 17/West Yorkshire attached from the 35th Division. The three battalions of the 9th Brigade, each with two machine guns and two Stokes mortars attached, were to assemble in Pont Street, a hollow road which was held as the front line of the British position; the 8/King's Own, together with the remainder of the Brigade machine guns, were to take up a position

---

* Though it is admitted in official records that no battalion that was to take part in the attack, *except the 1/Fifth*, was given the opportunity for reconnaissance, the fact that Wild's reconnaissance was based on a totally different plan is not mentioned. It would have been truer to say that *no reconnaissance* was carried out. It is only in order to make this point clear that reference has been made to the first orders, by which the FIFTH were placed under Brigadier-General Kentish.

in Sloane Street, a support trench to the south-west of the village; the 17/West Yorkshire would be held in Brigade Reserve at Montauban. Lieut.-Colonel Wild's Headquarters* were to be established just south of the village with those of the 4/Royal Fusiliers; the latter battalion was not to be actively engaged, but its companies would support the attack by fire from a line they held through the southern quarter of Longueval and along the edge of Delville Wood. At 3.55 a.m. an intense bombardment was to be opened on the enemy's positions; and the FIFTH, creeping forward under cover of this artillery barrage as close as possible to Piccadilly, a sunken road 450 yards east of Pont Street and 150 yards on the near side of the village, were to assault and carry Longueval at 3.40 a.m. The 12/West Yorkshire would then move forward to the left of the FIFTH, and the two battalions, supported by the 13/King's, would sweep forward in line and clear Delville Wood. The 8/King's Own and other troops assembled in Sloane Street were to remain in that position and "await orders."

Now, though this plan was in itself simple and straightforward, it relied for success on the assumption that, prior to the advance of the 9th Brigade, troops of the 9th Division operating on their left would have carried certain positions on that flank. Hitherto, in the attacks which had been made against Longueval, the chief trouble experienced had been from fire from two German strong points which had been established to the north of the village. Though the village itself had been cleared more than once, the westerly of these two points had never been captured, and on the single occasion on which the easterly point had been carried, our troops had almost immediately been driven out by counter-attack. It had at length been realised that there could be little hope of capturing, let alone holding, the village while these positions remained in the hands of the enemy. It had accordingly been arranged that the 95th Brigade (9th Division) should attack at 10 p.m. on the 22nd (i.e. 5¾ hours before the main operation) with the object of clearing some orchards which lay to the north of Longueval and capturing these two vital points.

It was not till the hour at which this preliminary attack was due to be launched that the FIFTH left their bivouac and moved up to Montauban, where guides were collected to lead them to their assembly position. Lieut.-Colonel Wild, who had awaited the arrival of the Battalion at Montauban, now issued his attack orders. His plan was as follows:—" Y " and " Z " Companies were to lead the attack in half-company column on a front of 250 yards. The leading half-companies, to each of which a bombing squad was attached, were given two objectives in the first phase of the attack: (i) Piccadilly; (ii) the east side of the village street. The rear half-companies were to occupy Piccadilly as the leading troops vacated it, and later to move forward to join them on the second objective. In the second phase, " W "

---

* These were not, properly speaking, the H.Q. of the FIFTH. Although in no way responsible for the initial attack orders to any unit other than his own battalion, Wild was directed to take over command of the three attacking battalions on arrival at the Assembly Position and exercise a general supervision over the attack, and he alone of the battalion commanders was given the means of direct telephonic communication with Brigade Headquarters. The introduction of this dual command was later to be responsible for considerable confusion and misunderstanding. Wild had not the machinery to exercise command over so many units, and on more than one occasion reports by runner, instead of being passed through him, were sent direct to Brigade Headquarters. It is necessary to mention this point, which is not referred to in the official reports; but, as the action of the FIFTH was not affected, it has been considered best to deal with it in a note rather than in the general narrative.

23rd July, 1916 Company, following in support of "Y" and "Z," would draw level and prolong the right to gain touch with the Royal Fusiliers in their position to the south of Delville Wood; then, as "Y" and "Z" swept forward through the wood to gain the final objective, "X" Company, in reserve, would be moved up to a position on the east side of the village. Such was Wild's plan of attack, though, as will be seen, it was never to mature.

Map No. 18

It was a bright moonlit night, but the advance of the Battalion from Montauban to its assembly position was made under great difficulties. Considerable casualties were sustained from shell fire, the officer commanding "W" Company being wounded, one complete squad of bombers wiped out, and many other men put out of action. At one time, too, "W" Company, together with its attached machine guns and trench mortars, was completely cut off by an artillery column which crossed the line of advance. None the less the Battalion by midnight was assembled in its proper order in Pont Street. The enemy's artillery maintained a continuous fire, and the men were dangerously crowded, but fortunately the hollow road afforded protection, and few casualties were suffered by the Battalion while awaiting the hour of attack.

In these trench to trench attacks there was no greater strain than that experienced by infantry, cramped, silent and motionless, in a narrow assembly position, waiting through the long hours of darkness for the moment of assault. As time drew on they would listen ever more eagerly for the quickening of their artillery fire, which would shortly be followed by the streaming of shells overhead to tell them that the long period of suspense was over and the moment for action at hand. 3.30 a.m. on the 23rd July found the companies of the FIFTH, who lay opposite Longueval, in this state of expectancy. The desultory shelling, which had been maintained by the covering artillery throughout the night, was still in progress, but with the approach of zero hour the officers, watch in hand, and the men, keyed up by a whispered warning, were anxiously awaiting the moment to move forward. Slowly the hands of the watch crept forward to 3.40, the time appointed for the bombardment to crash down on the enemy's position and the forward companies to advance—and then came anti-climax ! At the given hour no signal came from the guns, there was no appreciable increase in their rate of fire, no suggestion of the opening of the promised bombardment. Conceiving that orders might have been misunderstood, Lieutenant Cooper, the commander of "Y" Company, which was to lead the attack, sought instructions from Lieut.-Colonel Wild as to whether he should go forward. The situation demanded an immediate decision. Wild had gone forward to supervise the advance, he was not in a position to communicate with Brigade Headquarters, and to refer to them would have meant delay. Having received no information to the contrary, he believed that the 95th Brigade had long since carried the strong points and orchards to the north of the village. Realising that in such case, if the FIFTH failed to advance, the right flank of these troops would be exposed to attack, he ordered Cooper to lead forward the attack immediately. There had been but a few minutes' delay, and the leading troops of the FIFTH now started to move forward, in order to gain the line of Piccadilly, from which the assault on the village was to be delivered.

Now, it had been reckoned that should the first phase of the 9th Brigade's attack for which the FIFTH had been made responsible prove successful, and the village be swiftly cleared of the enemy, the advance through Delville Wood would present comparatively little difficulty. But, as has been pointed out, it had been regarded as essential to the success of the assault on Longueval that the 95th Brigade, in its preliminary operation, should have carried their objectives. Though the weakness of the artillery bombardment, on which the FIFTH depended for the subdual of the enemy's fire from the front, had filled Lieut.-Colonel Wild with grave misgivings, he had every reason to believe that at least his left flank had been secured. This, however, was far from being the case. Though he had received no information of the fact, the attack against the strong points on the left flank, launched five hours earlier, had completely failed. Had he been acquainted with the true situation, he would on his own responsibility have cancelled the advance of the FIFTH.* Subsequent events went to show how fully justified he would have been in taking such action.

As the leading companies of the FIFTH advanced from their assembly positions it seemed at first that they were to meet no opposition, and they had covered nearly half the distance to Piccadilly before a shot was fired by the enemy. Then, suddenly, they came under heavy machine gun fire from the front and left flank, and it was realised that Piccadilly was strongly held. The left and centre of the attack was completely held up. Lieutenant Cooper, with "Y" Company, succeeded in getting forward to within thirty yards of Piccadilly, but here they were forced by a galling fire from rifles and machine guns and showers of bombs to take such meagre shelter as could be found in shell holes. They were joined by men of "W" Company, who having lost all their officers, had pressed forward on their own initiative in the brave hope of being able to help on the advance. In such a situation, however, more men could only mean more casualties; for as any who were in the front line of an attack in the Great War will tell, except by surprise no position was ever carried in daylight by infantry assault unless the enemy garrison had been previously decimated or utterly demoralised by artillery fire or, in the later years, by tank action. Incendiary bombs were used by the Germans in considerable quantities; one man, who mercifully had already been shot through the head, was completely burned by one of these, and in the shell holes in which the troops had found some scant cover and concealment "no man could move a finger without being shot at or bombed." †

Lieut.-Colonel Wild could get no news from his right, but still hoped that the attack on that flank might have found it possible to work round by the south of Piccadilly. In any case it was clear to him that it was only from that direction that the attack could now hope to succeed. At 5 a.m. he left the assembly position and set out for the Headquarters of the 4/Royal Fusiliers; but, owing to the distance to be traversed and telephone communication having broken down, it was not till 5.40 a.m. that he could make an urgent appeal to Brigade Headquarters for reinforcing troops to be thrown in from the south side of Longueval. If immediately taken, such action, which was calculated to ease the situation of the troops whose easterly advance had been held up, might well have succeeded even now in clearing the northern quarter of the village. But, as was so often the case in these actions, the difficulties of communication led to fatal delay. It was not till 7.25 a.m., 1¾ hours after the application had been made, that Wild was authorised by Brigade Headquarters to employ a company of the 8/King's Own to reinforce the attack from the south. It was too late. The 12/West Yorkshire and 13/King's had gone forward with the intention of assisting the FIFTH to force an entry to Longueval from the east, but had alike been held up opposite the line of Piccadilly, and the enemy had now had close on four hours to prepare stronger measures to free his front

---

* Official Report by Lieut.-Colonel W. Wild on the operations of the 23rd July, 1916.

† Report by Lieutenant Cooper.

23rd July, 1916 from the pressure of an attack which he had hitherto held in check but been unable to drive back. Before Lieut.-Colonel Wild could put the action into effect, which even one hour earlier might have saved the situation, he received a report from 2nd-Lieutenant Phelan, his Intelligence Officer, that the Germans had opened a terrific enfilade fire with machine guns from the left flank, simultaneously with very heavy machine gun fire and showers of bombs from Piccadilly, and that the troops were being forced back to Pont Street. At 8.30 a.m. Wild returned to Pont Street to find that all three battalions had been driven back and that none of the attacking troops were in advance of their original assembly positions. At 8.55 a.m., he for the first time received information of the failure of the 95th Brigade's attack, on which so much had depended, and which had been delivered nearly eleven hours earlier.

Map No. 18

On receipt of the report of his Intelligence Officer, Lieut.-Col. Wild had reported the situation to Brigade Headquarters. At 9.20 a.m. he received the following message : " You must collect in Pont Street and attack again." Two companies had now lost all their officers, and but three officers in all were left with the other two ; of N.C.O.s and men, Wild could count only about 120. A conservative estimate placed the casualties in the FIFTH at 50% of its strength. Wild reported that in such circumstances his battalion was unfit for further offensive action.

Even where troops have a thorough knowledge of the ground and a perfect system of communication, it is always difficult, during an attack, for Brigade Headquarters to secure an accurate idea of the situation in the fore front of the battle. An incident now occurred to exemplify how, in the absence of preliminary reconnaissance and of a soundly organised system of communication, a false report may reach the Brigade Commander and completely mislead him as to the result of an attack. Scarcely had Lieut.-Colonel Wild's report of the failure of the attack been despatched than a large body of men was seen approaching from the rear. On arrival at Pont Street, this was found to be a party under 2nd-Lieutenant Young of the FIFTH, who had been sent up to consolidate the captured position ! More men in Pont Street at that moment could only mean a risk of more casualties, and Wild told the subaltern that he had better lead his men back to Brigade Headquarters. Young, however, replied that the Brigadier had been informed that the 13/King's had carried their objective and had given him definite orders, which he must obey. Ultimately Wild found that nothing short of a direct order to withdraw at once could dissuade this staunch and determined young officer from acting on his instructions and so leading his men to certain destruction. It was not till later that the origin of the false report was discovered. A detachment of the King's, having lost direction, had advanced *in rear* of the line held by the Royal Fusiliers, and, somewhat naturally meeting no opposition, had occupied a position which they took to be their final objective, but which actually was an old trench line from which they faced the Headquarters of the 9th Brigade, where their optimistic message had been received with so much satisfaction and acted on with such promptitude ! *

---

* It is in no spirit of criticism of the 13/King's, the comrades of the 1/FIFTH in so many fights, that the above episode is related. After fierce and confused fighting, such as had been for so long in progress at Longueval, it is no easy matter to ascertain the exact positions in which one's own and the enemy's troops were placed. Officers of far greater experience than was that of the majority of those with battalions this day could not have been blamed for making the slight loss of direction sufficient for an error of this kind, in leading their men over unreconnoitred ground,

At about noon Brigadier-General Potter himself came forward and, appreciating that further efforts could only result in useless sacrifice, directed Lieut.-Colonel Wild to select a position in rear to which to withdraw the Battalion. The position chosen was the line of a sunken road about one mile south-west of Longueval, where the Battalion provided protection to the right flank of the gun positions in Caterpillar Valley. Here the FIFTH remained throughout the 24th and 25th July, under the considerable fire of the German heavy guns, which continuously shelled the whole locality.

Thus yet another attempt to drive the Germans from Longueval and Delville Wood had failed. In his report on the action Lieut.-Colonel Wild summed up the causes of failure as follows :—

1. Insufficient reconnaissance before the operations and ignorance of the enemy's position and strength.
2. Failure of the attack on the left and the fact not being communicated.
3. A totally inadequate artillery preparation and support during the action.
4. Bad communication from the front to the rear.

He adds : " Even with careful preparation the task set to this Battalion would have been colossal. From the German Order of Battle dated 22/7/16 it appears the Germans had in the vicinity of Delville Wood three regiments—the 12th I.R., 52nd R.I.R., and the 107th R.I.R."* The report of the G.O.C. 3rd Division confirms that the first two factors named by Lieut.-Colonel Wild contributed to the failure of the operation, and, though not so definite with regard to the insufficiency of artillery fire, it mentions that " the actual shelling of the enemy's position is stated to have been the reverse of intense."

There is no record in the Battalion War Diary of the casualties sustained on the 23rd July, but from the 9th Brigade Diary and other sources they appear to have been as shown below :—

OFFICERS.

Killed .. 2nd-Lieutenant P. C. Fraser } both of " W "
2nd-Lieutenant D. C. Fox } Company.
Wounded .. 2nd-Lieutenant W. H. Salt
2nd-Lieutenant W. Dining.

OTHER RANKS.

Killed 17.   Wounded 89.   Missing 55.

2nd-Lieutenant F. I. Young was killed on the following day while on duty at an ammunition dump.

The 3rd Division was now to be granted a period of rest for the purpose of recuperating, and receiving and training reinforcements. How greatly these were needed can be judged from the losses of the 1/FIFTH, which, from battle casualties alone, had amounted to 12 officers and 448 other ranks. On the 26th July the Battalion was withdrawn to bivouac near Albert, and two days later moved with the remainder of the 9th Brigade to billets in Ville-sur-Ancre.

On the 7th August, in relief of Major-General Haldane, who had been appointed to command the VI. Corps, Major-General C. Deverell came to the 3rd Division, which he was to command till the end of the War. The numbers of the FIFTH had by now

---

* 3 Regiments = 9 Battalions.

26th July, 1916 been partially made up by the arrival of drafts totalling 4 officers* and 356 other ranks, but the 3rd Division as a whole was still 3,000 under strength when, on the 9th August, the news came that a situation had arisen which demanded that its rest should be cut short and that it should again take the field. It has already been shown how essential to securing the positions won on the Bazentin Ridge was our hold on Longueval, and how relief to the critical situation at the latter point could only be found in an advance further to the south and the capture of Guillemont. Fierce but fruitless attacks to this end had been made, and the 55th Division, on the extreme right of the British, had been exhausted in a vain effort to carry the position of Cochrane Alley and gain touch, on the north bank of the Maltz Horn Ravine, with the French, who, further to the south, were endeavouring with no better success to push forward to Maurepas. An important factor in the failure of the 55th Division's attacks had been the opposition encountered from an irregular line of trench in advance of the German main position. Another attempt was to be made by them to capture this line, known as Lonely Trench, and generally to secure a straight and regular starting line for an advance to deeper objectives. The 55th, however, were in no condition to undertake more than this, and were accordingly to be relieved on the 13th August by the 3rd Division, who would then become responsible for resuming the attack to the south of Guillemont, with objectives Falfemont Farm and Wedge Wood. In conjunction with this, renewed operations were to be made by the French against Maurepas and by the 24th Division against Guillemont. Such was the plan; but unfortunately it proved later that the strength of the 55th Division had been so greatly reduced as to render them incapable even of undertaking the preliminary operation. As a consequence, the 3rd Division, on carrying out the relief on the 13th, found that their first task would be to secure the jumping off line necessary for the deeper attack which had been allotted to them by orders.

Maps No. 16 and 19

In the meantime the 9th Brigade had been moved forward to bivouac astride the Bray–Albert road at Sand Pits, and on the night of the 14th/15th August relieved the 166th Brigade in the left section of the Divisional front, with orders to attack on the 16th. The FIFTH, who were in Brigade Reserve at Great Bear, furnished a working party of 400 men on the 15th in preparation for this attack, and in the early hours of the following day were moved up *via* Carnoy to the old German front line about 1,000 yards to the north-east of Maricourt, in order to be in position to support the operation if required. The attacking troops, however, could make no headway against fire directed on them from Lonely Trench, and the FIFTH were not called on. The 17th was characterised by considerable artillery fire by both sides, and there were several casualties from the German shells in the Battalion during the day. After dark a further effort to capture Lonely Trench, made by the 12/West Yorkshire, failed to carry the objective.

Orders were now issued for the FIFTH to assault this isolated length of trench, which had been the cause of so much trouble, simultaneously with an attack by the 8/East Yorkshire Regiment (attached from the 8th Brigade) against the enemy's positions between the Hardecourt–Guillemont road and Arrow Head Copse. The combined operation was to be carried out on the afternoon of the 18th. At 5.45 a.m. of that day, " W " and " X " Companies, which had been detailed for the FIFTH's attack, moved forward and occupied " T " Trench; " Y " and " Z " remained in rear

---

* Captain O. G. Blayney, 2nd-Lieutenants B. R. Newstead, J. R. Steel and D. F. de R. Martin.

Maps No. 16 and 19

positions till 1.15 p.m., when they advanced to take up a position in Assembly Trench. The communication trenches allotted to the latter companies for this movement were very narrow and gave little cover; Maltz Horn Trench, which crossed high and very exposed ground, was so shallow as to be said to deserve the name of "track" rather than "trench." The companies were heavily shelled on their way forward, but, despite

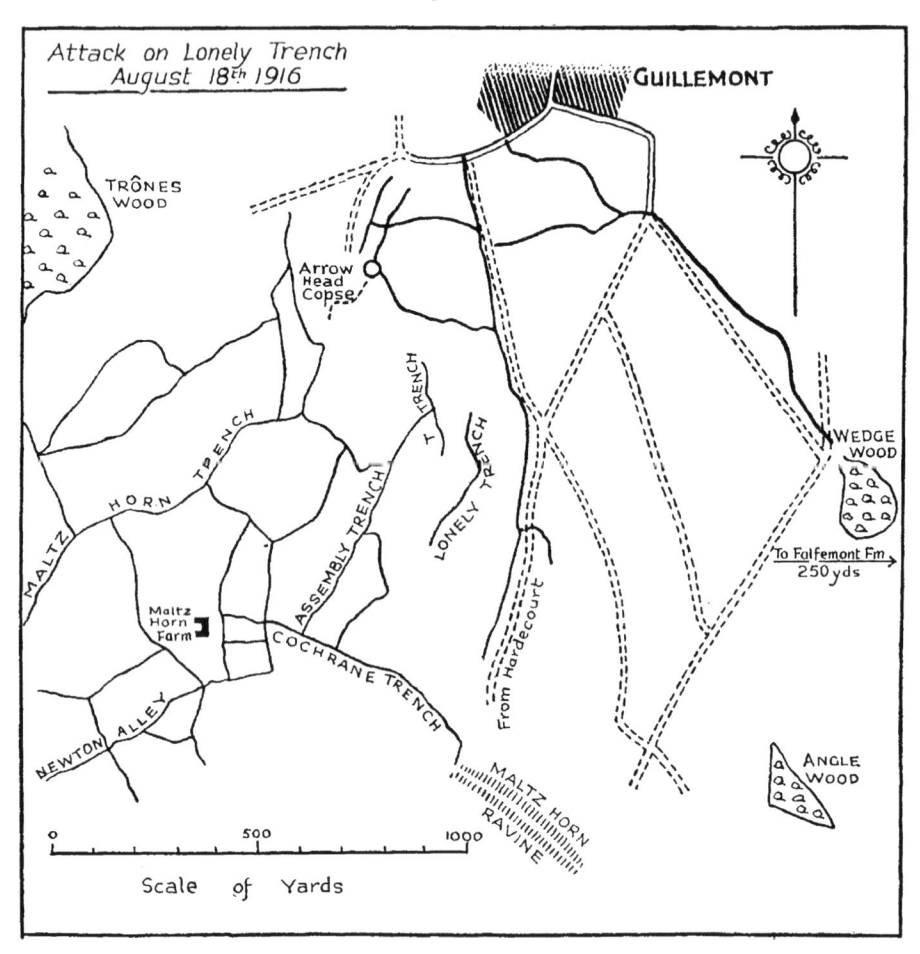

14th Aug., 1916

Map No. 19.

Attack on Lonely Trench August 18th 1916

the great difficulties of their approach movement and the casualties sustained, they were established in Assembly Trench before the hour fixed for the attack. At 2.45 p.m. "W" and "X" Companies, supported by special bombing squads and Lewis Gun detachments, advanced to the assault of the German position. Scarcely, however, had they gained the open ground when they came under heavy rifle and machine gun fire from Lonely Trench, which forced the broken and disorganised troops to fall back again to the shelter of the starting line. Here the survivors of the two companies

19th Aug., 1916 were at once reformed and again led forward over the parapet against the enemy's position. In face of a repetition of the fire which had met their first effort they could, however, make no headway. Later, an attempt was made by the regimental bombers to enter the north end of the trench, but with no better success than had been achieved by direct frontal advance, and at 5.30 p.m. Lieut.-Colonel Wild reported to the Brigadier that further attack by daylight was out of the question. A night attack was then planned, but subsequently cancelled. In the meantime, the north-easterly attack carried out by the East Yorkshire had made no better progress than that of the FIFTH, and the sole result of the day's fighting had been the reduction of our trenches, already shattered by the enemy's artillery, to a still more terrible condition. The whole of the following morning was spent by the Battalion in endeavouring to repair and strengthen the defences. At 2.45 p.m. " T " Trench was temporarily cleared of its garrison, in order to enable our heavy artillery to bring a $3\frac{1}{2}$ hour bombardment on to Lonely Trench. Then, at dusk, 2nd-Lieutenant Martin led forward a patrol of " Z " Company to see what this had effected. They found that, at last, the enemy had vacated the position, and immediately dug back a communication trench to connect it with " T." The remainder of " Z " Company were then led forward by Captain Blayney to occupy the northern half of Lonely Trench and to join hands with the 7/K.S.L.I. of the 76th Brigade, who had already secured a footing in the southern portion.

Maps No. 16 and 19

It became apparent on occupying this isolated length of trench, which had been held in advance of the enemy's general front line, that its strength had lain in its siting, which had enabled the garrison to bring grazing fire over the whole of the ground to be covered by an infantry attack. Only by closely following an intense artillery barrage could infantry have hoped to escape the devastating effect of this fire and gain the enemy's line, and it was in this that an additional difficulty had been presented to the British attacks. To gain full protection from a creeping artillery barrage infantry must advance on a straight and regular front, and for this a straight and regular starting line is essential. The trenches from which the attacks of the 3rd Division had to be delivered, in their irregular alignment and varying distances from the objective, had made it impossible for the field artillery to maintain a close barrage in front of all sections of the infantry advance.* Yet, when full weight has been given to all these factors, it must, in justice to the Germans, be added that none but a staunch and courageous garrison could have held out, as they had, against the repeated attacks against Lonely Trench until blasted out by a prolonged bombardment by heavy artillery. Before it was ultimately occupied, the attacks on this position had cost the FIFTH alone over 200 casualties.† The 3rd Division as a whole had suffered equally heavily. Their losses had not, however, been entirely in vain. As has been pointed out, the main difficulty with which the attacking troops had had

---

* Attacking troops, on whose reports the higher command is dependent for information on such matters, are apt to believe that casualties are being inflicted by fire from the position which is the objective of their assault. Lieut.-Colonel Wild, contrary to official narratives based on company and platoon reports, has always believed that enfilade machine gun fire from Guillemont was responsible for more casualties than frontal fire from Lonely Trench. Study of a layered map gives support to this view.

† Killed—19 other ranks ; wounded—2nd-Lieutenants Newstead and Steele and 162 other ranks ; missing—36 other ranks. Captain H. J. Holmes (attd. 1/9th T.M. Battery) and Captain A. S. Glynn, R.A.M.C., M.O. of the Battalion, were also wounded during these operations.

to contend was the irregular front from which they had been called on to advance. By straightening out the British line they had remedied this, and, when relieved on the 20th August, were able to hand over a regular starting line for future operations.

On relief of the 3rd Division, the FIFTH, after one night in Citadel camp, returned to their former billets at Ville-sur-Ancre. On the 23rd August, the Battalion entrained at Méricourt for Candas, whence it marched to take up billets at Fienvillers, where it was joined by Lieutenant Lord* and 2nd-Lieutenant Wilkinson, who had been posted from England.

With the concentration of the main forces of the opposing armies on the Somme, the War on the remainder of the Western Front had of necessity become stagnant. As division after division was withdrawn exhausted from the fierce struggle that was in progress in the main theatre, they were sent by both sides to find what rest they could in the more peaceful sectors, where ammunition had to be economised, and troops faced each other on the defensive, making it their duty to watch and harass their opponents rather than to engage in more active operations. The 3rd Division, accordingly, was now ordered to join the First Army, on whose front such conditions had replaced those of the previous autumn.

On the 25th August, the FIFTH marched to Bonnières, and, after further halts at Ternas and Eps, reached Marles-les-Mines, near Bruay, on the 30th, where on the following day they were inspected by General Horne, the Commander of the First Army. In the meantime, the 3rd Division had begun taking over the Hulluch sector of the First Army front, and on the 2nd September the 9th Brigade was moved, in Divisional Reserve, to Noeux-les-Mines and Mazingarbe. The latter village, in which the FIFTH were billeted, was at this time still noted for having been spared from serious damage, although within easy range of the enemy's guns. Very different was the condition of the mining village of Philosophe, to which the Battalion was moved on the 9th, as reserve to the 9th Brigade, which had on this day taken over the left section of the divisional front. Here there was scarcely a house that had escaped damage from shell fire, and the neighbouring mine works had also suffered. None the less a fair number of inhabitants, including women, remained, trading with the British troops when things were quiet, and seeking shelter in cellars during a bombardment. An incident, though it occurred at a somewhat later date than that which we are considering, is interesting as indicating the attitude of the people of Philosophe towards the war in general. It had been decided to attempt the destruction of a high water-tower, situated at Wingles, a considerable distance in rear of the German front line, from which the enemy could get observation over our defences and communications, and a 14-inch howitzer was brought forward for the purpose. As the great piece lumbered majestically through Philosophe, the people of the village, who had lined the street to watch it pass, far from welcoming it as a deliverer, greeted it with hoots and hisses, for to them it represented merely an instrument for attracting more shells from the Germans, to the disturbance of their trade. The sequel was so remarkable as, perhaps, to deserve record. The first shell, fired at a range of over 8,000 yards, hit the target, Wingles water-tower collapsed, and, to the relief of the inhabitants, the howitzer packed up and made a stately exit !

Eleven months had now passed since the 2nd Battalion of the FIFTH had

---

* Wounded with the 2nd Battalion at Frezenberg in May, 1915.

Maps Nos. 16 and 19

19th Aug., 1916

VERMELLES NEAR PHILOSOPHE.

". . . trading with the British troops when things were quiet. . . ."

[Imperial War Museum—Crown Copyright.

25th Aug., 1916 been engaged in the fierce and confused fighting for the Hohenzollern Redoubt on the front now held by the 9th Brigade, and, as both sides settled down to the defensive, there had been considerable changes in the method of holding the line. The strongly held front line of former days had been replaced by posts at wide intervals, which could be reinforced from a lightly held support line some two hundred yards in rear, while a reserve line eight hundred yards or so further back constituted the main line of resistance. Except for a few forward guns the great bulk of the machine guns were now sited in the reserve line. On certain portions of the 3rd Division front gas attacks were being carried out at this time. The projectors, by which a large number of containers could be hurled into the enemy's trench, had not yet been introduced, and the gas cloud was still produced from cylinders, for the installation

Maps No. 14 and 20

Map No. 20.

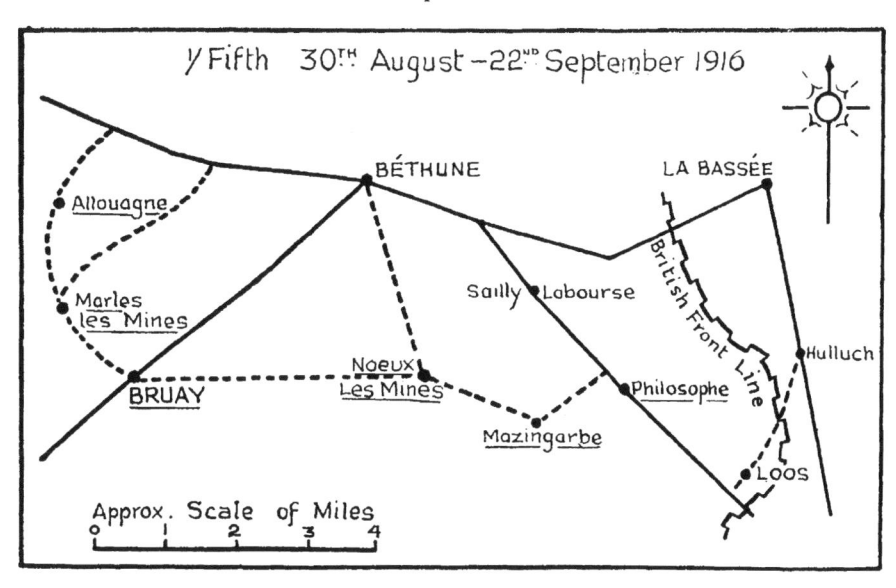

of which a continuous front line trench was necessary. Apart from any question of ethics, the infantryman held the gas cylinder in a more bitter hatred than the enemy against whom it was directed. For it fell to the infantry in reserve to carry these heavy and cumbersome implements forward to be installed, and to toil back with them after the gas had been discharged; while the men in the front line lived in hourly dread of an enemy shell bursting one of these undesirable neighbours and spreading its noxious contents among them. The release of the gas, moreover, was dependent on the wind, and this fickle ally of the cylinder had on occasion been known to turn traitor. In fact, there can have been few duties less popular during the War than "Rat fatigue," the code name given at this period to the task of carrying gas cylinders to the trenches.

On the 14th September the 1/FIFTH moved up from Philosophe to take over the left sub-section of the 9th Brigade front, where they found themselves opposite

162   THE FIFTH IN THE GREAT WAR.

Maps Nos. 14 and 20

the Hohenzollern Redoubt, which, following the fighting in which the 2nd Battalion 14th Sep., 1916
had been engaged in the autumn of 1915, had been finally re-occupied by the Germans.
Here, except for an occasional exchange of artillery and trench mortar fire, a week
was passed fairly quietly.

With the arrival of drafts, and the comparative freedom from casualties enjoyed on a defensive front, the strength of the 3rd Division had now been made up, and it was required again for the Somme battle. The duties carried out during the past few weeks, however, had given little opportunity for training the large number of officers* and other ranks who had recently joined for large scale attack. To provide this, orders were issued for the Division, on relief in the trenches, to spend a brief period in the First Army Training Area before being sent south. On the 21st September, the FIFTH were moved back to Noeux-les-Mines, and, after spending the following night at Allouagne, marched on the 23rd to Beaumetz-les-Aires, 20 miles west of Béthune. Here, technically, the Battalion would have been described as "resting," though the manner in which the following twelve days were spent might scarcely coincide with the peace-time soldier's ideas of repose; for into this brief period it was necessary to cram battalion, brigade, and divisional training! In truth, however, rest is derived from change of scene and occupation rather than from idleness; and withdrawal from the hideous desolation of the forward area to a quiet, untouched countryside in itself provided very real refreshment to the troops during the War.

While at Beaumetz-les-Aires, Lieut.-Colonel Wild received orders to hand over command of the 1/FIFTH and return to England in order to take up training duties at home. The period of over twelve months during which Wild had performed the arduous duties of command had been marked by two outstanding successes—the brilliant action at St. Éloi and the capture of Bazentin-le-Grand. On both of those occasions he had had the satisfaction of seeing the strong battalion, which he had trained, achieve in the most perfect manner a stern, but not impossible task. Later, he had experienced what fell to most battalion commanders in the War who held their position for a prolonged period, the ordeal of undertaking a hopeless enterprise with a battalion whose ranks were but half filled and that largely by men without adequate training, led by a handful of officers, of whom some had never been in battle before. The heavy weight of responsibility which fell on a commanding officer in such circumstances brought an ever increasing strain, and Lieut.-Colonel Wild had fully earned the respite that was now granted to him.

On the 5th October, two days after Lieut.-Colonel Wild's departure, the 1/FIFTH, under the temporary command of Captain O. G. Blaney, left the First Army Training Area and marched to St. Martin Église. Here they were joined, on the following day, by Major W. N. Herbert, the former Adjutant, who had now been appointed to command. At midnight the Battalion set out for St. Pol, where in the early hours of the 7th it entrained for Puchevillers, whence on arrival it marched to billets in Bertrancourt.

The 3rd Division, in preparation for the part it was to play in the last great attack that was to be launched before the winter set in, was now ordered to take over a Sector opposite the village of Serre. The narrow front to be taken over, which extended from Flag Avenue to John Copse, represented that on which the Division

---

* 2nd-Lieutenants Hardy, Thorp, Greener (A. S.), Greener (H.), Douglas, Schofield, Jeffreys, Pattenden, Wooldridge, Twigge, Nichol, Finch. Lieutenant Raynor (invalided in January) rejoined in September.

7th Oct., 1916 was to attack ; and in defence could be adequately held by one brigade, with two battalions in the line and the remainder in reserve. The first brigade to be detailed was the 9th, who went into the line on the 8th October, when the 1/FIFTH were moved up to a supporting position at Maily-Maillet. Early on the morning of the 12th, the Battalion relieved the 4/Royal Fusiliers in the left sub-sector—Southern Avenue to John Copse.

Maps Nos. 16 and 21

In view of the forthcoming attack, it was desired to ascertain the line on which the enemy's defensive artillery barrage would fall, and for this purpose a feint attack was made shortly after the FIFTH had taken over the trenches. Our guns opened a heavy bombardment of the opposing wire, and a smoke barrage was put up from the front line. The enemy's reply, however, was not in sufficient volume to provide the indication required, though one man of the FIFTH was killed by the fire that was brought in retaliation—the only casualty suffered by the Battalion during the day. Intermittent artillery fire continued during the following day, our guns being employed on wire cutting, and the enemy's in shelling our trenches by way of reply. Except for seven other ranks of a Lewis Gun team being wounded by a single shell, the FIFTH sustained no casualties, though considerable damage was caused to the trenches. The attempt to clear up the first point on which information was required, the line of the enemy's defensive barrage, had not been very successful, as the German artillery had declined to be drawn. There were other matters, which could only be discovered by a closer investigation, and the task of securing information as to these had been allotted to the FIFTH. It now fell to them to investigate the nature and condition of the enemy's trenches on the front of the proposed attack, and to procure an identification of the troops in occupation of them. In order to get this information it had been arranged that on the 14th October, at 7.15 p.m., the darkest hour of the night, a party of 2 officers and 47 other ranks of " Y " Company should raid the enemy's trenches at a point opposite Luke Copse. In support of the operation, the field artillery were to put down a shrapnel barrage on the German support line and H.E. shell on all communication trenches leading to the area to be raided ; medium artillery were to engage the enemy's batteries ; and Stokes guns were also to co-operate.

During the afternoon of the 14th a medium trench mortar battery was engaged in cutting gaps in the enemy's wire, one opposite the raiders' point of entry, and one on either flank of this point. At 5.15 p.m. " Y " Company's party, under command of Lieutenant D. P. Hadow, with faces and bayonets blackened, and all badges and other identification marks removed from their clothing, were assembled in a dug-out near the junction of Rob Roy and Northern Avenue trenches. The plan had been worked out in the closest detail, and every man knew exactly the particular part that he had to play. The party had been organised in six squads, and as zero hour approached, filed into Northern Avenue to move up to the front line in the following order : (i) A covering squad of 1 N.C.O. and 6 men, under Lieutenant Hadow, carrying blankets, ladders and tapes ; (ii) Right, centre and left blocking squads, under command respectively of Serjeant Cockburn, Corporal Wanless, and Corporal Heathcote, each of whom had with him 2 bayonet men, 2 bombers, and 2 bomb carriers ; (iii) Right and left " souvenir " squads, led by 2nd-Lieutenant R. O. V. Thorp and Serjeant Thompson, each of 1 N.C.O. and 8 bayonet men. All men of the party carried two bombs in their pockets.

At 7.10 p.m., the head of the party having reached Point D, Lieutenant Hadow, as planned, led forward the covering squad, in order to lay tapes for the

Map No. 21 guidance of those who were to follow, and to examine and make good the gap in the 14th Oct., 1916
wire, placing blanket bridges where necessary. Having done this, their duties were
to lie close under the enemy's parapet, and, after the remaining squads had passed
through them, to guard against counter-attack from the flanks across the open
ground of No Man's Land; to take charge of any prisoners passed back; and, finally,
having placed ladders and assisted the raiders to climb back over the enemy's parapet,
to cover their withdrawal. At 7.15 p.m., the artillery supporting the operation opened
fire. With the first salvo, the remaining squads rushed forward towards the gap in

Map No. 21.

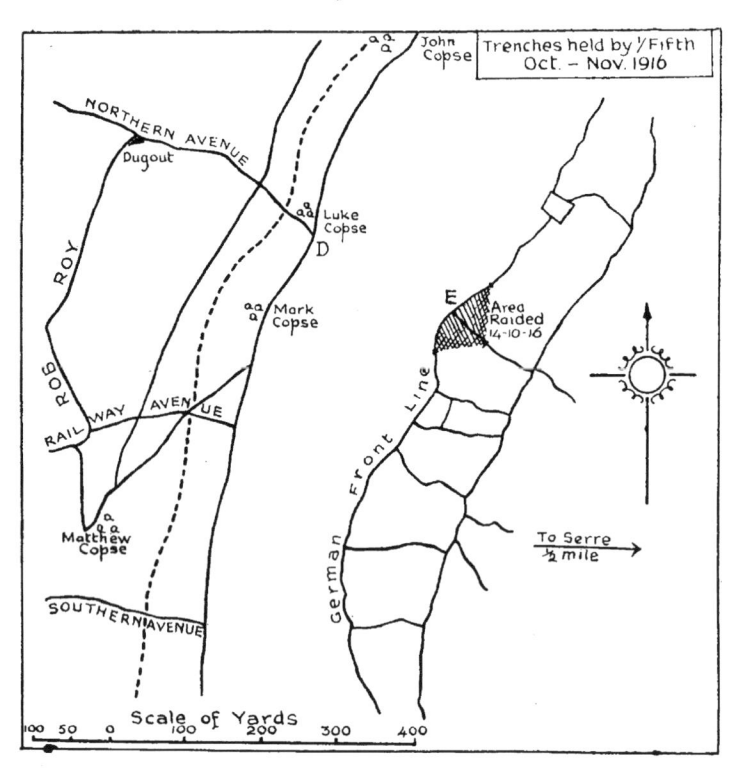

the wire, which had been well cut over a space of some twenty feet and was plainly
visible to the raiders against the flash of the bombs of the Stokes guns fired to direct
the advance. Though some of the men were hindered by loose wire, which had not
been cleared, the bulk of them were over the parapet and into the trench before a shot
had been fired by the enemy. Two German sentries were encountered at the point
of entry, of whom one stood to his post and was wounded and taken prisoner by
2nd-Lieutenant Thorp, and the other, who bolted, was shot as he dived into a
dug-out. The blocking squads, with orders to clear away all opposition with the
bayonet, now advanced forward, right and left, to take up positions fifty yards from
the point of entry and cover the operations of Thorp's and Thompson's squads.

14th Oct., 1916 Everywhere, dark though it was, glimpses were caught of men running up the trenches or plunging into dug-outs. In such circumstances, as had been foreseen, it was no easy task to distinguish friend from foe, and a means to this end had been provided by the issue of a pass-word, "Charlie," to be answered by "Chaplin." The main purpose of the raid was to bring back prisoners. Two other Germans were now seized and disarmed, but in their violent resistance to being passed back from the trench they were unfortunately killed. Ten minutes only had been allowed for the raid, and the trenches were still being explored and dug-outs bombed, when the field artillery, by ceasing fire for half a minute, gave the pre-arranged signal that this period had elapsed, and white bouquet rockets started to rise from the British trenches to guide the raiders back. "Durham," the code word for withdrawal, was given, the raiders scrambled back over the German parapet, the artillery re-opened fire, and the whole party safely regained the British line, bringing in their prisoner and having themselves suffered no casualty.

Map No. 21

When reading of a raid which has been so completely successful as that which has been recounted above, one is apt perhaps at first to underrate the performance of those who took part in it. But when one reflects on the difficulties of maintaining direction and exercising command in some peace-time practice, carried out on a moonlit night and with time in hand to rectify mistakes, one realises that for a raiding party to enter unknown trenches on a pitch dark night, carry out specified duties, and withdraw in ten minutes, not only good leadership was required but self-reliance, determination and intelligence of a high order in every man taking part. On this night 2nd-Lieutenant Thorp, whose conduct throughout had been admirable, had been given a first opportunity of showing the high qualities of leadership which were to distinguish him on many later occasions.* The absence of casualties, however, must be placed to the credit of the supporting artillery, whose protective barrage had been so effective that the raiders had been subjected to no rifle or machine gun fire from close range. As a result of the raid, the presence of the XIV. German Corps had been verified through the prisoner, who was identified as belonging to the 169th Regiment; and the enemy's trenches been reported to be in good condition, seven foot deep, with hurdle revetment and fire steps, and provided with deep dug-outs, approached by wooden stairs.

In the last of the great battles of the Somme seven divisions were to attack on a front from just south of the River Ancre to north of Serre. All were now in complete readiness, but in the second week of October heavy rain had set in, and it was decided to postpone operations in the hope that an improvement in the weather might produce conditions more favourable for attack. On the 19th October, the 9th Brigade was withdrawn to Divisional Reserve, the FIFTH, on relief, being moved to billets at Louvencourt, about seven miles west of the front line, where they were given a week's rest. Owing to the narrow front held by the Division, it was possible at this time to reduce the front line tours of battalions to 48 hours, and during this period two companies only were in the trenches, the remainder being in reserve in

---

* Robert Dakley Vavasour Thorp, M.C., was killed on the 22nd March, 1918, at which time he was attached to the 64th Trench Mortar Battery.

Courcelles. This was fortunate, for, though casualties were not heavy, there was an incessant exchange of artillery fire, and the enemy's guns and trench mortars combined with the incessant rain to reduce the whole sector to a terrible condition, the trenches in many places being now knee deep in mud. 2nd-Lieutenant A. S. Greener was wounded towards the end of October, but there had been no other casualties in the FIFTH when the Battalion found itself in rest again at Louvencourt at the end of the month. Here, Captain H. I. Powell reported to take over command of " Z " Company from Captain Blaney, who had been appointed to the staff of the 9th Brigade.

If it was important for the British to secure information concerning the troops and defences by which they were opposed, the Germans can have been no less anxious to discover the extent of the attack, which from day to day they must have been expecting, and the date on which it was to be delivered. A prisoner might prove to be the means of procuring the desired information. One side of the picture of a trench raid has been given on a previous page, and the above considerations doubtless were responsible for the reverse side of a similar operation being presented to the FIFTH, shortly after taking over the front line on the 8th November. It can be understood, however, that those in the trenches invaded could never give the same accurate account of the sequence of events as the raiders. Conditions had been normal during the first few days of the Battalion's tour, and there had been nothing to suggest the occurrence of any unusual event, when at midnight of the 10/11th the enemy suddenly opened a heavy bombardment on Rob Roy trench and neighbouring communication trenches. This was maintained for a period of twenty minutes, when all fire ceased. After a pause of ten minutes, however, the bombardment reopened with its former intensity. In the first five minutes all communications had been cut, and Battalion Headquarters remained in ignorance of what was occurring; on the renewal of the enemy's fire, however, our artillery were called on to retaliate. In the meantime, two sentries forming a front line post had detected a party of the enemy approaching at a distance of twenty yards and opened fire with a Lewis gun and rifle. The gun jammed, and as the Germans rushed their position they took refuge in a neighbouring Russian sap, where they not only escaped capture but were uninjured by four bombs which the Germans hurled into the sap before pushing forward to Rob Roy trench. Challenged by a sentry at the door of a dug-out, they replied with a bomb, which wounded this man and two others who were behind him on the dug-out steps, and then vanished in the dark. Later an officer in a neighbouring front line post observed a small party of the enemy withdrawing, but, uncertain at the time as to their identity, he dared not open fire. Apart, however, from their success in entering and escaping from our trenches, the raiders had accomplished nothing.

With the continued postponement of the Fifth Army attack in the hope of an improvement in the weather, the ground over which the troops were to advance was becoming progressively worse under an incessant bombardment, and it was at last decided that nothing could be gained by further delay. On the 11th November orders were issued for the attack to be launched on the 13th. The 9th Brigade, which had originally been cast for the front line of the attack, were by these orders relegated

CLEARING A ROAD THROUGH A VILLAGE ON THE SOMME BATTLEFIELD, 1916.

[Imperial War Museum—Crown Copyright.

13th Nov., 1916 to the part of Divisional Reserve, and the FIFTH were, accordingly, relieved on the 12th by troops of the 76th Brigade and withdrawn to Courcelles.

Maps Nos. 16 and 21

Only a brief account is here necessary of the operations of the 13th November, in which the FIFTH were, perhaps, fortunate in not being called on to take an active part. The attack as a whole, both south and north of the River Ancre, was marked by considerable success, but that of the 3rd Division, on the left of the V. Corps, failed completely. The task set to the Division was, indeed, well nigh hopeless from the start. Serre was, perhaps, the most formidable position in the whole area of the Fifth Army attack. Situated on high ground and strongly fortified, it may be claimed that its capture could only have been effected, if at all, by an attack delivered under the most favourable conditions. Yet on no part of the British front had the weather conditions of the preceding weeks had a more disastrous effect than in the area of the 3rd Division's attack, where the advance lay over clay soil, as distinct from the chalk over which the remainder of the divisions had to operate. While hampering the infantry, the state of the ground at the same time deprived them of the co-operation of tanks, whose movement had been rendered impossible. Major-General Deverell estimated that the troops would not be able to advance at a faster rate than 100 yards in 10 minutes, and had made urgent representation that this should be taken as the basis of artillery support. The rate proposed was, however, regarded as dangerously slow for the troops attacking on the right, and, in the interests of the operation as a whole, he had had to consent to the infantry of the 3rd Division endeavouring to struggle forward at just twice the rate he desired. On the morning of the attack fog had been added to the difficulties of the ground, which in themselves were sufficient to break up the cohesion of the attack. It can be truly said that no troops could have made more valiant efforts than those of the infantry brigades of the 3rd Division in the advance against Serre. Under the conditions that have been described, success was impossible.

The FIFTH, who had been moved up to bivouac at Colingcamps before dawn on the day of attack, had remained there till 11 a.m., when orders were received for them to push forward to Northern Avenue with a view to supporting the 8th and 76th Brigades, who, having failed in their first efforts, were to attempt a second attack. An hour after arrival in this position the Battalion, together with the 13/King's, had been placed at the disposal of the G.O.C. 76th Brigade, to whose headquarters Lieut.-Colonel Herbert had gone forward to report. By then, however, it had become clear that further efforts could lead only to useless sacrifice, and at 8.15 p.m. the Commanding Officer came back with orders for the Battalion to return to bivouac at Colingcamps, where, on arrival half an hour later, "hot tea was served to the men and they were told to get what rest they could." (*Battalion War Diary*.) Here the FIFTH remained till late in the following afternoon, when they were moved back to Louvencourt.

It seems that at this time there was still some thought of renewing the offensive on the 3rd Division front, as on the 15th the Battalion was sent forward to Bus-en-Artois, and the receipt of orders for an attack by the 9th and 76th Brigades is recorded in the Battalion War Diary of the following day. On the 18th, however, the Battles of the Somme, 1916, definitely came to an end.

"The three main objects with which we had commenced our offensive in July had already been achieved. . . .

"Verdun had been relieved; the main German forces had been held on the Western front; and the enemy's strength had been very considerably worn down." (*Haig's Despatches*.)

Map No. 16 The few weeks during which the 3rd Division was to remain in occupation of 31st Dec., 1916
the Serre Sector were mainly taken up with repairing and improving the defences, and endeavouring to make the trenches habitable for the winter. After three brief tours in the trenches, alternating with longer spells in reserve, the FIFTH were finally relieved in the front line of the Serre Sector on Christmas Day, and on the last day of the year marched at a strength of 28 officers and 883 other ranks from Couin Camp, where they had been accommodated on relief, to Bus.

Thus another year had closed, and the War was seen dragging through a third winter. Most readers of this history will have learnt from other sources how the situation at the end of 1916 was viewed by the Governments of the belligerent powers, but here we are concerned rather with the outlook of those in the fighting line, who had nothing beyond their own immediate experience and high hopes on which to base an estimate of the general situation, of which, in truth, they were quite ignorant. Officers and men passed through the ranks of the Regiment in quick succession, but mercifully they inherited the same optimism. Throughout, no one in his heart felt doubt as to the ultimate issue of the war; and it can in all probability be truly said that for the average officer or man in the fighting line, never a year had yet opened but with the certainty of the end coming before its close. In starting the next chapter, therefore, subsequent knowledge should be disregarded, and it should be understood that the FIFTH throughout are confident of victory being achieved by Christmas, 1917, at the latest.

CHAPTER XII.

First Battalion—7th January—29th June, 1917.

"Arras 1917"—"Scarpe 1917."

7th Jan., 1917
to
18th Mar., 1917

As a result of the success obtained in the Somme Battles the Germans to the north of the area of the Allies' advance found themselves in a dangerous salient between the River Ancre and Arras. Sir Douglas Haig's intention was to open a simultaneous offensive in the spring of 1917 against each shoulder of this salient. He foresaw that the enemy, in anticipation of such an attack, might voluntarily withdraw from their unfavourable position—a forecast which was to be realised later by their withdrawal to the Hindenburg Line—but he rightly judged that any deep retirement would not extend as far north as Arras, and it did not therefore seem that the attack planned for the Third Army on the northern flank would require much modification. Actually, owing to considerations with which we are not here concerned, the strategy of the Commander-in-Chief was to be subjected to drastic alterations, but it was in the plans that have been briefly outlined above that the next great battle in which the Fifth were to be engaged had its origin.

Map No. 23

Some months were yet to elapse before the opening of the Battle of Arras; the period, however, was comparatively uneventful and can be dealt with very briefly. On the 7th January the 3rd Division, on relief in the Serre Sector, was withdrawn to rest in the Canaples area, the Fifth being billeted in Beauquesnes for three nights before marching eight miles further West to Montrelet, near Candas. On the 28th, the Division, which was now transferred from the Fifth to the Third Army, moved North. The Battalion, marching with the 9th Brigade, was billeted successively at Neuvillette, Croix (just west of St. Pol) and Beugin, in the Diéval area. Here it was detached from the 9th Brigade on the 1st February and sent to Arras to assist the Royal Engineers in burying cable. During the nine days that were spent on this work the weather was intensely cold, with persistent hard frost, but the billets in Arras were good and provided reasonable comfort for the men when off duty. The town, though less than one mile from the front line, had hitherto escaped the fate which had long since overtaken Ypres. The large number of cellars and underground chambers—a feature of the town of which more will be said later—provided cover from occasional artillery fire, and many of the civil inhabitants still remained in their homes. The death of a man of the Fifth, and the wounding of 2nd Lieutenant Bradford and five others by a chance shell, which burst as they were leaving their billet, shows, however that these civilians were risking grave danger at this period in refusing to leave the town.

On the conclusion of cable-burying duties, the Battalion moved to Berlencourt, 16 miles west of Arras, where they completed five weeks' training. In the meantime the 3rd Division had joined the VI. Corps and, in preparation for the part it was to play in the forthcoming attack, had taken over its battle front of 1000 yards immediately to the south of the Arras—Cambrai road. One infantry brigade had been judged sufficient for the defence of this narrow front, and on the 18th March the 9th Brigade moved up to the line in relief of the 8th, and the FIFTH took over the right sub-sector, in touch on their right with troops of the 14th Division.

18th Mar., 1917

Maps Nos. 22 and 23

Shortly before this relief, as a sequel to the Somme battles, the Germans opposite the Fifth Army to the south of Arras had begun their retreat to the Hindenburg Line, which at its northern extremity entered the old German front line at Tilloy-les-Mofflaines, about half a mile east of the centre of the 3rd Division's sector. They had already succeeded in extricating themselves from the salient, and warning had been received that there were indications of the withdrawal spreading further north towards the area opposite Arras. On the morning on which the FIFTH had completed their relief, information came from the troops on their right that the Germans opposite them had vacated their forward trenches. 2nd Lieutenant Tait, of " X " (the right) company, was immediately ordered to take forward a fighting patrol and reconnoitre the situation in front of the right of the FIFTH. On receipt of his report that the front line had been vacated, the whole of " X " Company and two platoons of " Y " were pushed forward, and, at the loss of one man killed and 10 wounded, succeeded in occupying the third line of the German forward system, in touch with troops of the 14th Division. Opposite the left of the Battalion, however, the enemy still held fast to their front line, and it seemed that the withdrawal had been carried out beyond the northern limit that had been intended ; for, on the 19th March they delivered two counter-attacks under heavy artillery barrages for the recovery of the positions they had vacated. Both attacks were repulsed by rifle fire, but not without casualties to the FIFTH ; " X " Company, in particular, suffering somewhat heavily.

The FIFTH were now ordered to attempt the identification of the German troops opposite the 3rd Division. The raid that was carried out for this purpose was planned on lines identical with those of the one that had been so successful in October in the Serre Sector,* but it was organised on a smaller scale, the leader, 2nd Lieutenant Passingham, being the only officer included, and the six squads reduced to a strength of 1 N.C.O. and 4 men each.

At 1.30 a.m. on the 21st, when the raiders left their trenches, the darkness was intense, and though Passingham had made a very thorough reconnaissance of the ground on the previous night, he was unable to get his men forward at the pace required by the scheme. As a result, they were still some twenty yards from the German wire when the supporting artillery opened. But, though premature, the bombardment actually proved of great service ; for, the enemy, alarmed by the fire of our guns, sent up a shower of Very lights. To the raiders, groping their way through the inky darkness, this illumination was a godsend. Their objective was revealed to them, and they immediately rushed forward at top speed. Almost at once, however, they were checked by the enemy's wire, which was found intact. Fortunately it was rather low, and, though the Germans were throwing bombs before our men had torn their way through half of it, the bulk of these, gallantly led by Passingham, succeeded in gaining the enemy's front line, a trench ten feet deep and eight wide, which was found to be strongly held. In clearing three fire bays against stout resistance, eleven or twelve of the enemy were killed, and the ten minutes allowed for the raid had almost passed before its chief object, a live German prisoner, was secured. At the last minute, in a desperate search for a wounded man capable of

---

* See Chapter XI.

being taken back, one of the enemy was found to be feigning to be dead in the hope of escaping capture. Actually the man was unhurt, and, realising that the game was up, surrendered without resistance. The code word for withdrawal was now given, and the party, guided by Very lights from their own trenches, regained the British line together with their prisoner.

    Every man who took part in these night raids knew that he must give his whole attention to his particular task, and that if wounded there would be no one to come to his aid, for there could be no pause for any purpose. On withdrawal every effort was always made to bring in casualties; but the chances of a severely wounded man being found on a very dark night were tragically slight. On this occasion the bodies of a serjeant and one other man, killed during the passage through the wire, were not recovered. Of the others who had been hit by bombs or rifle fire during the check to the advance, fortunately none had been seriously wounded, but the condition of Passingham and his men on their return, gashed and torn by the wire through which they had forced their way, gave evidence of the determination that had been required to bring success to the operation. In the official notification of the award of the Military Cross, which was made at a later date to 2nd Lieutenant Passingham for his conduct on this occasion, it was stated that ; " He led a raiding party with great courage and determination through uncut wire, and succeeded in entering the enemy's front line trenches, where he personally shot three of the enemy." No. 16709 Serjeant Mantle was awarded the Military Medal for gallantry on the same occasion.

    As a sequel to the raid, the enemy at 5 a.m. opened a heavy artillery bombardment on our front line, and there were indications that they were preparing for an assault on the left company of the FIFTH. A prompt counter-barrage by our artillery, however, prevented the German infantry from leaving their trenches. On the following day, the 22nd March, the battalion was relieved in the trenches and withdrawn to billets in Arras, where Battalion Headquarters and two companies remained till the end of the month. The other companies garrisoned support trenches and the defences of St. Sauveur, an eastern suburb of the town. On the 31st March, 2nd Lieutenant Grantham, a young officer who had joined in the previous January, was mortally wounded just before the relief of the Battalion, which was withdrawn on the same evening to Wanquetin. After three days' rest here in good billets, the FIFTH were again moved forward, in order to engage in the final preparations for the great attack, which had now been fixed for the 9th April.

    Reference has already been made to the underground quarries and cellars which represented a peculiar feature of Arras and its suburbs. During past months very extensive mining operations had been carried out, by which these caves and cellars had been linked together by tunnels, and the whole connected by subways with our trench system east of the town. Electric light had been installed and everything possible had been done to provide secure and comfortable accommodation for the troops in this subterranean system, which was to be utilised in the forthcoming battle as a preliminary assembly position for the attacking troops. The FIFTH were now billeted in this " cellars area," and during the next few days were busily employed in digging their assembly trenches and reconnoitring the underground routes by which companies would move up to these before the attack.

    The British attack was to be delivered by the Third and First Armies on a front of 15 miles north and south of the River Scarpe, from the village of Croisilles in the south to the Vimy Ridge in the north. In the centre of the attack the 3rd Division, advancing from the line which it had already taken up south of the Cambrai road, was to form the right of the VI. Corps. It was to attack on a one brigade front for the capture of three successive objectives:

The First, represented by the enemy's front line system, was to be carried by the 76th Brigade.

The Second, known as the Blue Line, which, 1,000 yards to the east of the

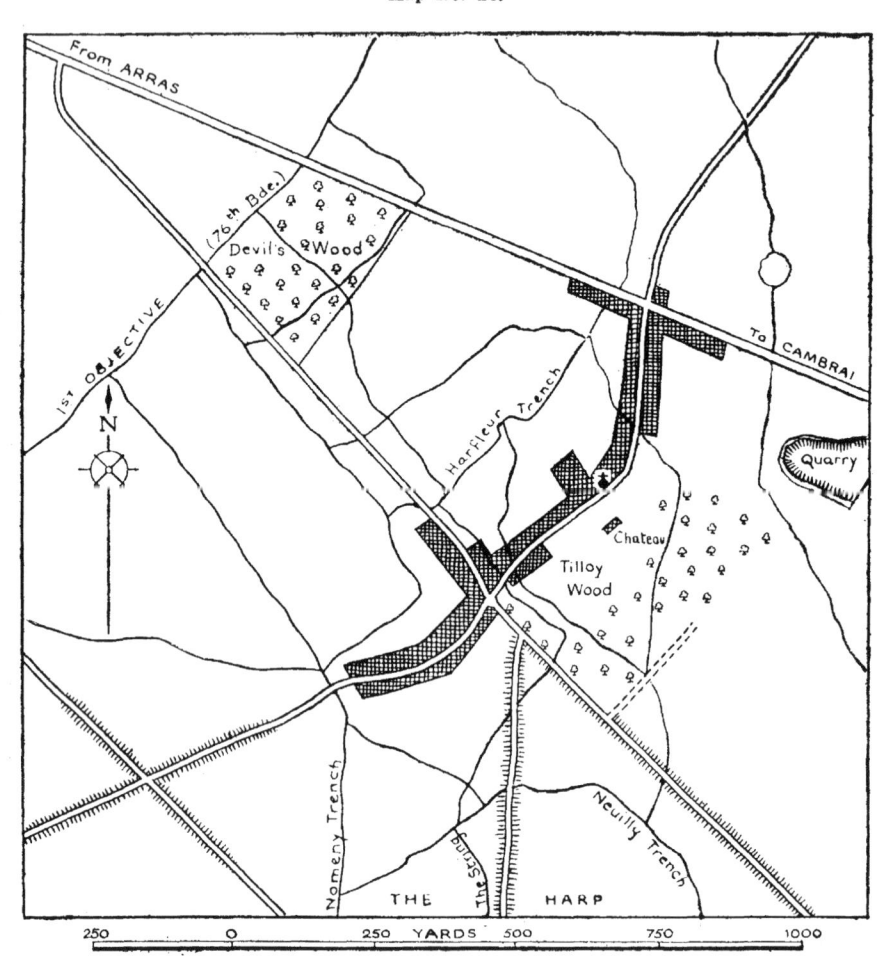

Map No. 24.

First, included the village of Tilloy and the defensive work named " The Harp," was allotted to the 9th Brigade.

The Third, the Feuchy-Wancourt (or Brown) Line, which, 2,500 yards further to the east, formed the third main line of defence, was to be captured by the 8th Brigade.

The 9th Brigade attack was to be carried out by the 4/Royal Fusiliers, 12/West Yorkshire, and 13/King's (right, centre and left respectively) supported on the right by the 2/Suffolk (attached) and on the left by the 1/FIFTH.

9th April, 1917

At 11.30 p.m. on the 8th April, the FIFTH, who earlier in the day had been concentrated in the Arras cellars, moved up by the Crichon sewer and other underground routes to their assembly trenches, which were reached about 2.30 a.m. At 5.30 a.m., the hour fixed for the initial attack, the intense artillery barrage which was to cover the advance opened. Eight minutes later the German retaliatory barrage was brought on to the British front line, but did little harm as the newly dug assembly trenches were well to the rear. Over two hours still remained before the 9th Brigade was to be called on to play its part in the attack, and while the struggle for the capture of the German front line system was in progress, the men of the FIFTH, thanks to their ever faithful Quartermaster's department, were able to make profitable use of the time by regaling themselves with hot tea and rum.

The 76th Brigade's attack was completely successful, and had already carried four lines of trench when, at 7 a.m., the three leading battalions of the 9th Brigade advanced from their assembly positions to close on the barrage and pass through the 76th Brigade for the capture of the second objective. A half hour later, the FIFTH left their assembly trenches to move forward in support. The companies on advancing immediately came under heavy shell fire, but formed as they were in column of sections in file, suffered comparatively few casualties, though " Y " was unfortunate in losing most of the personnel of its headquarters at this time. At 7.42 the barrage lifted for the Brigade to advance to the assault. On the right, the Royal Fusiliers made steady progress, and the Suffolk, passing through them, had carried Neuilly trench, the right of the objective, by 8.30 a.m. In the centre, the 12/West Yorkshire, directed against the south of Tilloy, were reinforced as they gained its western outskirts by the right companies of the FIFTH, and together the troops of both battalions swept forward through the village to the Blue Line.* The King's, on the left of the attack, experienced more serious opposition. Despite considerable casualties from shell fire, their right assaulting company succeeded in carrying Harfleur trench, to the west of the village; but the left of their attack was held up by machine gun fire directed from the north side of the Cambrai road and from Tilloy Wood. Reinforced by the left companies of the FIFTH, and assisted by enfilade fire from troops who had gained the objective in the centre, the left of the King's gradually succeeded in working a way through the northern part of the village. Progress, however, was very slow. The Germans put up a stubborn resistance, and heavy casualties were sustained from the accurate fire of their snipers, many of whom, having eluded the attackers, maintained their fire after our men had overrun their concealed positions.

The 8th Brigade was due to move forward at 10.40 a.m. in order to pass through the 9th for the third phase of the Division's attack; but at this hour fighting was still in progress in the northern quarter of Tilloy, where parties of the enemy established in a strong point and a quarry at the north-eastern exit from the village were still giving trouble. Rather than upset the programme of attack it was decided that the 8th Brigade should advance from its assembly positions without waiting for the complete clearance of Tilloy. In the meanwhile 2nd Lieutenant H. M. Greener of the FIFTH, having collected all the rifle grenadiers that he could find at hand, had opened an attack on the quarry. While this was in progress the troops of the 8th Brigade entered the village. On their appearance the enemy, already badly shaken, abandoned the strong point and quarry and fled, offering a good target

---

* 9th Brigade Narrative. Captain Carrick, whose company was operating on this flank, was under the impression that this line was carried by the troops of the FIFTH alone.

to our riflemen, to whose fire they fell in large numbers. The capture of the second objective on the whole front of the 3rd Division was then completed, and at 12.10 p.m. the 8th Brigade, unchecked and punctual to the programme, continued the advance. The companies of the FIFTH were now collected and re-organised, and the Battalion was ordered to consolidate the Blue Line on a frontage of 300 yards immediately to the north of the Tilloy-Wancourt road.

The advance was carried forward by the 8th Brigade for a distance of over a mile to the east of Tilloy, but two separate attacks failed to drive the enemy from the Feuchy-Wancourt line, and darkness found the forward troops of the 3rd Division dug in at a distance of about 600 yards from their final objective, and the rear brigades in occupation of the positions they had captured and consolidated.

Of the fifteen company officers who had gone into battle with the FIFTH this day, the following nine had become casualties :—

Killed .. Lieutenant H. S. Barnes.
           2nd Lieutenant F. Twigge.
Wounded .. Captain C. B. Carrick.
           Lieutenant C. J. R. Rutledge.
           2nd Lieutenant J. R. Potts.
           2nd Lieutenant S. V. Bradford.
           2nd Lieutenant J. T. Tait.
           2nd Lieutenant R. F. S. Pattenden.
           2nd Lieutenant R. E. D. O'Dowd.*

The casualties among other ranks amounted to 25 killed, 72 wounded, 42 missing.

Serious as were the losses among officers, they did not cripple the Battalion to the same extent as would have been the case earlier in the War; for it had long since been realised that, providing the total number of officers permitted, it was wiser to avoid the risk of sending the whole complement into battle. On this occasion five company officers had been left at the transport lines at Wanquetin and were now available to replace to some extent the casualties that had occurred.

On the 10th April, the 8th Brigade successfully renewed their attack on the Feuchy-Wancourt line, and nightfall found them firmly established on the captured objective, with the 9th and 76th Brigades still in occupation of Tilloy and the old German front line respectively. During the night the 76th Brigade was moved forward with orders to attack for the capture of Guémappe. This village, 2,000 yards east of the Feuchy-Wancourt line, lay in a valley, from which the ground rose on the north to Monchy-le-Preux and on the south to high ground on which stood the ruin of Wancourt tower. Two attacks delivered on the 11th broke down under fire directed from the high ground on the flanks of the village and from Spear Lane, a sunken road running north-east from Wancourt at a distance of 500 yards in front of Guémappe; and the end of the day found the troops of the 76th Brigade brought to a standstill on a line parallel to and 500 yards west of this. At 9 p.m. orders were issued for the 9th Brigade (less two battalions) to relieve the 76th on this line; the remaining two

---

* Younger brother of 2nd Lieutenant M. V. O'Dowd, whose death with the 2nd Battalion in the attack at Bellewaarde in May, 1915, was recorded in Chapter VII.

THE ARRAS-TILLOY ROAD, APRIL 10TH, 1917.

[Imperial War Museum—Crown Copyright.

12th/13th April, 1917 — battalions were to be held in a reserve position in the Bois des Boeufs, near Tilloy. The FIFTH, having been detailed as the right forward battalion, took over trenches from the 1/Gordons and 2/Suffolk before dawn on the 12th. The remainder of the day, during which Battalion Headquarters were heavily shelled by 5.9's, was spent in improving the trenches that had been taken over and digging new ones.

Map No. 25

Plans were now made for a renewal of the attempt to capture Guémappe, in co-operation with simultaneous attacks by troops of the divisions on either flank. From the description that has been given of the situation of the village, the extent to which its capture was dependent on the occupation of the Wancourt Tower Spur and the high ground south of Monchy will be realised. The problem was one which in many respects differed essentially from that which had been presented on 9th April, when a continuous and solid system of strongly held trenches demanded a massed attack by divisions on a narrow front, supported by a heavy concentration of artillery. Manoeuvre had now become to some extent possible; but to secure the advantage which this offered to the attack it was necessary that there should be the closest co-ordination between the movement and action of all units concerned. The advance along the valley and the capture of the high ground which flanked it could be regarded only as component parts of a single operation requiring the central control of an individual commander. Unfortunately, divisions were still operating on the narrow front fixed for the conditions of the 9th April, with the result that, although the distance from Wancourt Tower to Monchy was no more than 3,500 yards, the comparatively few troops disposed on this two mile front belonged not only to three different divisions, but to two separate Corps. In other words there was no authority below that of the G.O.C. Third Army to place the few battalions concerned under a single central command. In these circumstances, it seems, it was left to the three divisional commanders whose troops were involved, to organise an attack by agreement, and later to attempt to control the operation from their separate headquarters, which were a considerable distance from each other and some miles from the scene of action. It could scarcely be expected that delay, postponement, and misunderstanding would not arise from such an arrangement.

To turn now to the plans that were made and the attack which followed. Originally it was arranged that the battalions of the 9th Brigade should advance at 2 p.m., simultaneously with troops of the 50th Division on the right and of the 29th Division on the left. Shortly before this hour, however, information was received from the 29th Division that they would not be able to advance. Though there were features on this flank from which fire could be brought on to the approaches to Guémappe, the Cambrai road, which was to mark the left of the 9th Brigade's advance, crossed high ground to the north of the village, and possibly it was considered that troops moving by this would be sufficient to protect the left. However this may be, it was decided to carry on the attack without the co-operation of the 29th Division, but the hour at which it should be opened was put back to 5 p.m. Now, whatever influence the cancellation of this advance on the left might have, it could only be slight as compared with a failure to occupy the Wancourt Tower Spur, which was the most important factor in an attack on Guémappe. The 50th Division, however, reported that their troops already occupied this feature, and it was now agreed that at 7 p.m. their 151st Brigade should descend northwards from there to the line of railway above the Cojeul River,* simultaneously with an attack by the 9th

---

* Erroneously described in the official narrative as the Sensée, of which the Cojeul is a tributary.

Brigade on Guémappe from the west. It was further arranged that the 50th Divisional Artillery should cover the advance of the 9th Brigade by a creeping barrage, while the guns of the 3rd Division performed a similar service for the 151st Brigade.

13th April, 1917

The attack of the 9th Brigade was to be carried out by the FIFTH on the right, directed between the southern and northern limits of the village, and the 12/West Yorkshire on their left, with a line between the village and the Cambrai road as their objective; the 13/King's and the 4/Royal Fusiliers were to support the right and left respectively. In the FIFTH, "W" Company (Lieutenant Allan) and "X" Company (Captain Hogshaw) were to lead the attack, supported respectively by "Y" Company (Lieutenant Bucknall) and "Z" Company (Captain Powell). The three last named companies were in occupation of the newly dug trenches they had taken over on the 12th. "W" Company, however, was 1,200 yards in rear in the Feuchy-Wancourt Line, and, in order to draw level with the remainder of the Battalion, moved forward at 6.10 p.m., directing its advance towards the southern outskirts of Guémappe. By 6.40 they had come into line with "X" Company, who then quitted their trenches and advanced on the left against the northern section of the village; "Y" and "Z" Companies followed at a distance of 200 yards. To come up to their artillery barrage, which now opened on the western edge of the village, an advance of 1,000 yards was necessary, and on leaving their trenches the companies, silhouetted against a still bright western sky, came under very heavy fire from the enemy's guns. Though efforts to avoid the heaviest concentrations of fire resulted in some loss of direction, both companies succeeded in gaining and crossing Spear Lane, but here "W" Company came under heavy machine gun fire from Wancourt Spur, where instead of seeing, as had been expected, the 151st Brigade attacking down the northern slope, German riflemen were viewed standing on the crest and firing on the troops advancing in the valley below.* Heavy casualties were sustained, and "W" Com-

---

* On the orders for attack being first issued, Hogshaw had reported that he was convinced that the troops that could be seen on the Wancourt Tower Spur were Germans, and at his request Lt.-Colonel Herbert went forward, and, having formed the same impression, communicated the fact to the 9th Brigade. It is believed that this report was in part responsible for the second postponement of the attack. It seems, however, that on the matter being referred to the 50th Division an assurance was received that their forward troops were on the Spur, and that the G.O.C. 3rd Division considered that in such circumstances there could be no justification for cancelling the attack. How vague was the situation on Wancourt Tower Spur may be gathered from the following extracts from the War Diary of the 151st Brigade for the 13th April:—

- 12.55 p.m. Reported to Division that 9/D.L.I. had reached Wancourt Tower and that a patrol was digging in 50 yards east of the Tower. Two companies moving up to continue the line northwards.
- 1.00 p.m. These two companies of 9/D.L.I. failed to reach Tower as they came under heavy M.G. fire during daylight. They, however, got up at dusk and dug in 50 yards W. of the Tower and *not* E.
- 7.55 p.m. 50th Division order an attack by 151st Inf. Bde. on morning of 14*th inst*.

N.B.— (i) The reference to "dusk" in the entry under 1 p.m. shows that it cannot have been made at that time.

(ii) The entry under 7.55 p.m. is the first mention that appears of "an attack." Even more puzzling is the fact that the orders for the attack on the 14th show that it was to be made for the capture of the very objective which, according to the 3rd Division narrative, the 151st Brigade should have carried on the 13th.

13th April, 1917   pany's attack was brought to a standstill. " X " Company on the left, however, succeeded in closing on the artillery barrage and in following its first lift. But as the barrage lifted a second time, and the troops attempted to continue their advance, they came under a withering machine gun fire from the high ground to the south, north, and north-east of the village and from the edge of the village itself. Second Lieutenant Martin, struck by three bullets, was killed, 2nd Lieutenant Nichol, hit twice, was mortally wounded, and many of the men they led became casualties. The barrage put down by the 50th Division to cover the advance of the 9th Brigade, though accurately placed, had not been of sufficient intensity to subdue the enemy's fire from the village; that of the 3rd Division directed on the slopes to the south, in the belief that the 151st Brigade held the ground above, left the enemy's machine guns and riflemen undisturbed on the west of the Wancourt Tower Spur; to the north the troops of the 29th Division, who could have given valuable support by rifle and machine gun fire, had no idea, as it later transpired, that the attack was being made. Captain Hogshaw, realising that his company had been thrust into a death trap, asked permission to withdraw to a line where his men could dig in, and Lt.-Colonel Herbert, in reply, ordered him to act accordingly. Collecting what men he could, Hogshaw then withdrew north-west to the junction of Spear Lane with the Cambrai road, and dug in to the south of the latter in continuation of a line held by the 29th Division to the north of it. " W " Company was ordered to consolidate a line, on which work had been started on the previous night, which placed them in échelon on the right and about 200 yards in rear of " X " Company. Though the supporting companies had to some extent been immune from the rifle and machine gun fire which had played havoc with those that led the attack, they had suffered many casualties, including Captain Powell, from the heavy shell fire to which they had been exposed. The total losses of the Battalion this day, including the three officers already mentioned, amounted to 6 killed, 40 wounded, and 13 missing.   Map No. 25

The difficulties which in the Great War so often hindered the exploitation of a successful attack by which the enemy's forward defences had been pierced, were exemplified in this disastrous affair at Guémappe. On the 9th April, in addition to giving weight to the attack, the disposition of the Division in depth on a one brigade front had greatly facilitated communication and control during the operations of the first day. But with the effort to push further forward, units and formations had become strung out from front to rear, and with the lengthening of the channels of communication between Divisional and Brigade Headquarters, and between the latter and their forward troops, control became increasingly difficult. By the original project for the capture of Guémappe no more than six battalions acting on a front of 3,000 yards would have been required for the operation; yet, as already pointed out, no fewer than three divisions were concerned in planning and attempting to co-ordinate the attack. In his report on the action, Lt.-Colonel Herbert, after pointing out that on the 13th April the 3rd Division was engaged in a manoeuvre battle on a four company front, referred to the hampering effect of the long communications through which all information had to travel, and urged that in the event of a similar operation being undertaken in the future, special arrangements should be made for some more direct central control.

178   THE FIFTH IN THE GREAT WAR.

Map No. 22   At 4 a.m. on the 14th the FIFTH were relieved, and moved back to billet in cellars beneath the Grand Place of Arras. Here, during the next few days, 2nd Lieutenants A. L. Moore and H. A. Bending and 96 other ranks joined as reinforcements. On the 20th, the Battalion was moved to more comfortable quarters in the village of Duisans, 4 miles west of Arras.

In accordance with Sir Douglas Haig's plans, the Arras offensive should now have been broken off. It had never been his intention to push it very far. The immediate objects of his attack had been achieved, and had he been free to do so he would now have diverted troops to Flanders, where the position held by us since the Second Battle of Ypres had been far from satisfactory, and where he always considered the most far reaching results could be obtained from a successful offensive. It had been his intention that the attack at Arras should lead up to these operations in Flanders, but through a revision of the Allies' plans, it had taken the character of one preparatory to a more decisive operation by the French. The postponement of the French attack, which, instead of following within two or three days of the opening of the Arras battle as planned, was only now about to start, demanded that the full pressure of the British offensive east of Arras should be maintained.*

Justification for this reference to the wider aspects of the War may be found in the fact that they profoundly affected the 1/FIFTH. For it was nothing less than the strategical considerations which have been briefly outlined above that prevented the Battalion from completing the celebration of St. George's Day at Duisans. The Fates had called them to a sterner task; and true to their motto, the FIFTH, wearing the customary roses in honour of their Patron Saint, were found late on the afternoon of the 23rd April moving up again to Arras.

In a large scale attack, which was to be carried out on the 3rd May by the Fifth, Third and First Armies, the 3rd Division had been detailed for the capture of the enemy's trenches east of Monchy-le-Preux. In the 9th Brigade, which was to form the left of the 3rd Division, a first objective was to be carried by the 4/Royal Fusiliers and the 13/King's advancing on the right and left respectively; the FIFTH, in support of the King's during the first phase, were later to pass through them and, together with the 12/West Yorkshire, who at the outset would be acting similarly in support of the Royal Fusiliers, to capture a second and more distant objective. The FIFTH, who remained in Arras till the eve of the attack, started moving up to their assembly trenches after dark on the 2nd May. There were soon signs that the enemy had information of what was afoot. The leading company had barely got half way to Monchy when the German guns opened a heavy bombardment, and the whole Battalion had to struggle through an intense barrage of gas shells mingled with shrapnel and H.E. The advance was seriously disorganised, but ultimately it reached Monchy with a loss of only 20 men, though of the remainder there were few who had not suffered from two or three fits of vomiting. The guides of the King's Regiment, who were to have led the FIFTH forward from here, could not now be found; and further delay was caused by the necessity for procuring others in Monchy. Companies were, however, finally assembled in their positions by 2 a.m., though, owing to the intense darkness, platoons and sections had become to some extent mixed up. The attack opened at 3.45 a.m., and from the outset made little progress. Our own artillery barrage, though punctual, seemed in parts to be very thin. The enemy's artillery, on the other hand, immediately replied by bringing an intense bombardment on the

---

* The above is based on "Haig's Despatches."

3rd May, 1917 position of the support battalions. The leading companies of the Royal Fusiliers and the King's succeeded in getting forward a short distance in the woods through which their advance lay, but in the darkness touch with the 8th Brigade on their right was lost. A determined counter-attack by the Germans was repulsed, but heavy casualties were sustained, and on a second counter-attack being delivered the leading lines of the attack were driven from the positions they had gained. In the meantime, the two forward companies of the FIFTH, "Y" and "Z," had suffered many casualties from the enemy's barrage, and to escape this, had been led forward by Captains Bucknall and Passingham to the British front line. The trench, however, was found still to be occupied by the rear companies of the King's, and all but a few had to find what cover they could in shell holes. It was clear that the attack of the leading battalions had broken down, and it fell to company officers to act on their own initiative. The rear companies of the King's now advanced, and with them went "Y" and "Z" of the FIFTH. The situation, however, was hopeless. By this time the whole front was being swept by rifle and machine gun fire from the left flank, and after advancing forty or fifty yards the reinforcing companies found the front waves of the attack still held up on the line to which they had been withdrawn. A vain attempt was made by Captain Bucknall, the only officer now left with the two companies of the FIFTH, to lead his men further forward. He, however, was killed and an advance proved impossible in face of the intense fire. Although but ten minutes had passed since the opening of the attack, casualties had already been terribly severe when "W" Company (Captain Allen) and "X" Company (2nd Lieutenant Edgeworth-Johnstone) moved up in support to the British front line. They found it filled now with men of the 12th Division, who, attacking on the left of the 9th Brigade, had lost direction in the dark and, to add to the general confusion, believed themselves to be in the enemy's position! The trench was under enfilade machine gun fire, anyone attempting to advance from it was immediately shot, and here the FIFTH lost the remainder of their company officers, one of whom was hit three times by three separate bursts of machine gun fire. Sufficient has been said of this disastrous attack, of which, owing to all company officers having become casualties, the full details were never known to the 9th Brigade. The several causes to which failure was attributed seem alike derived from two main factors : (i) The difficulties inseparable from operating in intense darkness ; (ii) The absence of the one advantage that might have been expected from attacking in the dark, viz : surprise. Though the attack opposite Monchy had failed, one learns from Sir Douglas Haig's despatches that he was well satisfied with the operations on the 3rd May as a whole. The casualties sustained by the FIFTH on this day were as follows :— Map No. 22

OFFICERS.

Killed .. Captain W. H. Bucknall.
Captain E. G. Passingham.
Wounded .. Lieutenant Phelan.
2nd Lieutenant Edgeworth-Johnstone.
2nd Lieutenant Yates.
2nd Lieutenant Dent.
Missing .. 2nd Lieutenant Bending.

OTHER RANKS.

Killed 29. Wounded 133. Missing 34.

Following the attack the Battalion, greatly reduced in strength, remained in the trenches east of Monchy for just over a week. On the 5th May, Battalion Headquarters were heavily shelled, two direct hits being registered on the cellar which they occupied, but fortunately no casualties resulted. On the same day twenty men, who had become separated from the Battalion on the 3rd May, rejoined, thus reducing the number reported above as "missing" to 14. In the early morning of the 7th two stretcher bearers brought in 2nd Lieutenant Bending, whom they had found lying wounded in a shell hole in which he had sought cover during the attack four days before. On the 10th May the Battalion was relieved in the trenches, and after three days in bivouac at St. Sauveur was moved to billets in Simencourt. Here, and later in Manin, they remained till the end of the month.

On the 1st June, Major Landen, on appointment to the Royal Flying Corps, left the 1/FIFTH, who had benefited so greatly from his devoted work as Quartermaster during close on three years of war. He left a gap that was hard to fill, but fortunately the right man to succeed him was at hand in 2nd Lieutenant W. Myers. In common with Landen, Myers, who had served many years with the 1/FIFTH, was one of the very few left who had been with the Battalion at the outbreak of war. Before being commissioned, and posted as 2nd Lieutenant to his old battalion in the previous month, he had rendered it distinguished service, firstly as Regimental-Quartermaster-Serjeant, and later as Regimental-Serjeant-Major.*

At the beginning of June the FIFTH moved up again to Arras, and on the 5th of the month took over trenches to the north of Monchy, with their left flank resting on the Scarpe. The following fortnight was spent in these trenches or in Brigade Reserve in the Feuchy-Wancourt Line. During this period constant minor attacks and counter-attacks were in progress, but the FIFTH were not involved in these, nor were they seriously disturbed. Casualties none the less had totalled 5 other ranks killed and 13 wounded before the Battalion was withdrawn with the 9th Brigade to Divisional Reserve. On relief, after two nights in Arras, the FIFTH for the last time turned their backs on the town through which in recent months so many of their comrades had passed forward never to return, and on the 20th June were moved to rest billets at Gouy.

---

* In recognition of their services, Major Landen was awarded the Distinguished Service Order, and 2nd Lieutenant Myers the Military Cross in June, 1917. Though Myers took over the duties of Quartermaster to the 1/FIFTH, and continued to perform them till seconded to the Royal Air Force in January, 1918, the authorities consistently declined to accede to Lt. Colonel Herbert's repeated requests that he should be confirmed in the appointment. In September, 1917, Lieutenant and Quartermaster A. L. Short was posted to the Battalion from England, and for the following four months, it seems, there were two Quartermasters in the 1/FIFTH, the one official and the other unofficial.

NOTE.—During the period dealt with in the above Chapter the Battalion lost 21 officers killed and wounded, and received the following reinforcements :—

January.
    2nd Lieutenant R. E. Johnstone, W.
        ,,   E. R. H. Grantham, K.
        ,,   H. S. Barnes, K.
        ,,   T. F. Ellison

February.
    Lieutenant W. R. Allen.
    2nd Lieutenant T. Tait, W.

March.
    2nd Lieutenant R. E. D. O'Dowd, W.

April.
    Lieutenant W. H. C. Bucknall, K.
    2nd Lieutenant H. Donald.
        ,,   H. A. Bending, W.
        ,,   A. L. Moore.

May 7th.
    2nd Lieutenant T. F. Routledge
        ,,   J. J. Simpson.
        ,,   G. Grant-Ross.
        ,,   C. B. Haworth.
        ,,   N. R. Travell.

May 7th (continued).
    2nd Lieutenant H. P. Mullen.
        ,,   J. H. N. Apps.
        ,,   H. Smith.
        ,,   R. H. Archer.
        ,,   E. Harland.
        ,,   D. Pilling.

June 4th.
    2nd Lieutenant R. M. Hall.
        ,,   L. A. Taverner.
        ,,   D. Evans.
        ,,   W. E. Dwelley.

June 21st.
    2nd Lieutenant S. A. Rose.
        ,,   F. C. Bullen.
        ,,   G. M. Lamb.
        ,,   J. W. Brew.
        ,,   D. S. Rowe.
        ,,   L. G. Marrs.

June 28th.
    Capt. D. E. G. Waddilove.
    2nd Lieutenant H. F. Colling.
        ,,   P. S. Cull.
        ,,   J. Jaques.

K. or W. = Killed or Wounded later in the same period.

Strength of Battalion, 30th June, 1917 = 39 Officers, 973 Other Ranks.

CHAPTER XIII.

"Ypres, 1917"—"Menin Road."

Action at Bullecourt and The Apex.

FIRST BATTALION—30TH JUNE TO 31ST DECEMBER, 1917.

Map No. 22

30th June to 10th Aug., 1917

The Hindenburg Line, on which the Germans had fallen back in April, ran roughly N.W. and S.E. midway between Bapaume and Cambrai. The 3rd Division was now to take over a sector astride the Bapaume—Cambrai road on a front of five miles, from a point about 1,200 yards east of Hermies to just east of Lagnicourt. In preparation for this relief, the FIFTH, together with the remainder of the 9th Brigade, moved by bus on the last day of June to Achiet-le-Petit. In the very wet and cold weather that had set in, snug billets would have been very welcome. But in the course of their retreat the enemy had systematically devastated the whole country through which they passed, and the Battalion on arrival at its destination found that the best had to be made of a very crowded camp. On the 1st July the FIFTH were moved forward to bivouac in Vélu Wood, and on the following night relieved a battalion of the 145th Brigade east of Hermies on the extreme right of the Divisional front. In contrast to the frontage of 1,000 yards allotted to the whole 3rd Division in January east of Arras, that for which the Battalion was now alone responsible, extending from the Canal du Nord on the right to just north of the Hermies—Graincourt road, was over one mile in length. The front line, which had no continuous trench, was held by two companies disposed in eleven posts. With intervening periods in reserve at Vélu, the FIFTH remained in occupation of this position till the 7th August, when they were withdrawn to Frémicourt.* Throughout the tour there had been intermittent artillery fire by both sides and occasional discharges by gas projectors from our trenches. The greater number of the casualties which had occurred had been caused by shell fire, an exception being 2nd Lieutenant Hall, who had been wounded by machine gun fire when inspecting the wire. Casualties among other ranks had totalled 7 killed and 25 wounded. On the 29th July Lieutenant-Colonel Herbert had had a fortunate escape when a shell passed between him and 2nd Lieutenant Harland, bursting a few feet away and slightly wounding them both.

After three days at Frémicourt, the FIFTH on the 10th August took over the line in the left sub-sector east of Lagnicourt village. It was during this tour in the trenches that an unsuccessful attempt against a German advanced post was the occasion of a gallant action for which the Military Cross was awarded to 2nd Lieutenant Joss, a young officer who had only joined the Battalion in the previous month. In the raid that was planned two parties were to co-operate. The first, a small patrol consisting of a corporal and five men under 2nd Lieutenant Joss, was to crawl forward at dusk to within close distance of the objective, hurl bombs into the enemy's trench, and immediately withdraw at top speed. The second, a strong fighting patrol under 2nd

---

* Two miles N.N.E. of Bapaume.

Lieutenant Brew, having simultaneously moved forward some distance to the flank, was then to sweep round to the rear of the post with the object of capturing any survivors of its garrison who might attempt to escape. At the appointed hour the two patrols crept forward into No Man's Land and began to move towards the German line. When rather more than half way to his objective, Joss, observing a strong enemy patrol advancing towards him, hastily withdrew his men some fifty yards to a position on some high ground. His movement, however, had been detected by the enemy, who, uncertain as to the strength of their opponents, halted. For a considerable time the two parties lay motionless, watching each other. At length the Germans, deeming discretion to be the better part of valour, withdrew. Now, Brew had also observed the hostile patrol, and on being wrongly informed by a N.C.O. whose duty it was to maintain touch between the two parties that Joss had abandoned the enterprise, ordered the withdrawal of his men. Unaware of this, Joss, though with considerable misgiving, judged that he must go through with the task allotted to him and resumed his advance. The enemy had now, of course, been warned that something was afoot and were on the alert. None the less it seems that the approach of the patrol was not detected, as they succeeded in getting to within striking distance of the post and throwing their bombs. The bursting of the bombs, however, was the signal for the immediate outbreak of fierce retaliation from every part of the German position. In describing what ensued the patrol leader says, " Up went the S.O.S., machine-guns, rifles, artillery of all calibres, Very lights, and God knows what all ! " and he adds, " I still wonder to this day how any of us got back at all." He tells vividly of how every man, dodging for cover from shell-hole to shell-hole, eventually reached his own front line, but he fails to recount how two of these were only brought to safety by the gallant efforts of their young leader, who " carried one wounded man to a shell-hole 100 yards away, and another from a shell-hole 600 yards to his own lines, being all the time under heavy artillery, machine-gun, and rifle fire. His gallant behaviour undoubtedly prevented an identification being obtained by the enemy." (*London Gazette*, 7th March, 1918.) Actually, the corporal of the patrol was found to be missing when the remainder reached their lines, but after spending 24 hours in No Man's Land he returned at dusk on the following evening, just after 2nd Lieutenant Joss had gone out again to search for him. But for the above incident the time spent on this part of the front, which was divided between duty in the front line or support, and in reserve in Frémicourt, passed quietly, and the total casualties had amounted only to 3 other ranks killed and 11 wounded when, on the 4th September, the Battalion was withdrawn, for a course of training, to camp near Transloy, 5½ miles south-east of Bapaume. A change in the Battalion Staff had occurred during this period, when Lieutenant T. F. Ellison took over the duties of Adjutant from Captain E. G. Pease, M.C., on the appointment of the latter to the Royal Flying Corps. Pease, who had been commissioned from the ranks of the FIFTH, had served the 1st Battalion as Adjutant for nearly two years, and during this period, the longest for which the appointment was held by any officer during the Great War, had been a constant source of strength to his two Commanding Officers, Lieutenant-Colonels Wild and Herbert, and of help to all in the Battalion.

The intensive training which now began was something quite different from the normal routine exercises which were carried out by a battalion when withdrawn to rest, and if doubts remained in the minds of any as to its object, they were speedily dispelled by the Divisional Commander who, in a lecture, outlined the operations which lay before the 3rd Division and the tactics to which training should be directed.

Secrecy, doubtless, prevented him from dealing with future plans in close detail, but here we are not bound by the same considerations.

Sir Douglas Haig's campaign in Flanders on which he had at last been able to embark, had been in progress now for some two months. At the Battle of Messines, fought on the 7th June, the British, between dawn and sundown of a summer's day, had swept the Germans from Hill 60 and the Messines—Wytschaete Ridge. Ypres having been thus freed from the enemy who had for so long threatened it from the southern quarter of the Salient, a second offensive, representing the first phase of the "Third Battle of Ypres," had been opened on the 31st July, and by this the Germans had been thrust back to the S.E., East and N.E., of the town. Rain, which throughout this campaign was to prove the curse of the British operations, had then set in, and the condition of the ground had forced a postponement of the renewal of the attack. Early in September, however, the weather improved, and it had been decided that, after allowing a brief period for the ground to dry, the offensive could be resumed. An attack by the Second and FIFTH Armies, on a front of 8 miles astride the Ypres—Roulers railway, had accordingly been planned for the 20th September. The 3rd Division, which was to be allotted to the V Corps (right of the FIFTH Army), was to be held in reserve in this opening attack, in readiness, should it prove successful, to carry forward the advance at a later date.

On the 17th September, the FIFTH entrained for Flanders, and by the 19th the whole 3rd Division was concentrated as Corps Reserve in the Watou area, to the west of Poperinghe. On the afternoon of the same day the 9th Brigade was moved forward to Brandhoek, just west of Vlamertinghe, to stand in immediate reserve to the 9th Division. This division, as the right of the V Corps, was to advance from the Frezenberg Ridge astride the Ypres—Roulers railway and attack north-east towards Zonnebeke. The FIFTH, who had been detailed as first reinforcement, stood by throughout the 20th in readiness to move forward if called upon. Their services, however, were not required. In the British attack, which proved a complete success, the 9th Division by their own efforts captured the Langemarck—Gheluvelt line on a front of 1,600 yards, and thus established a position some 1,400 yards to the south-west of Zonnebeke. The 3rd Division was now ordered to relieve the 9th in this position, preparatory to carrying forward the advance for the capture of Zonnebeke. It so came about that the 1st Battalion of the FIFTH was to be concerned in operations for the recapture of the very position from which their 2nd Battalion had been withdrawn over two years before, after the Battle of St. Julien.*

On the night of the 22nd/23rd the 9th Brigade. which was to be held in reserve to the attack, began to take over the battle front of the 3rd Division, the FIFTH and 13/King's relieving the 27th Brigade (9th Division) in the right section, on a frontage of 800 yards from a point just north of the railway south-east to the right boundary of the Division. The relief of troops in a recently captured position, before it had been possible to carry out a full consolidation or complete the organisation of the defence, was always a difficult operation and one which might be expected to lead to casualties. On this night, however, there was no hitch in the relief; no fewer than ten guides had been supplied to lead the FIFTH to their positions, and by midnight "Z" and "Y" Companies had been safely disposed in the new front line, with "X" and "W" in a supporting position some four hundred yards in rear.† So far they had been fortunate, but shortly after day-

---

* See Chapter VII. and Map 12.

†Note that these are not the positions shown on Map No. 26, which are those to which companies were withdrawn on the night before the attack as explained on page 194.

THE CATHEDRAL AND CLOTH HALL AT YPRES.

[Imperial War Museum—Crown Copyright.

23rd/26th Sept., 1917

light their troubles began. At 6 a.m. a sharp bombardment inflicted 18 casualties on the Battalion, whose companies found little protection in the trenches, which had been battered by the British bombardment of the 20th and since but partially repaired in their conversion for defence. Nor was it only to artillery fire that the garrison was dangerously exposed. Later in the morning 2nd Lieutenant J. F. Routledge, the commander of " Z " company, was hit by a German sniper and died before he could be conveyed to the Regimental Aid Post. Very shortly afterwards, 2nd Lieutenant G. M. Lamb, hearing that Serjeant Banks of his company had been sniped while reconnoitring in front of the line, crept forward to search for and bring him in. Finding the serjeant dead, Lamb turned back, but before he could regain the trenches was himself hit three times and rendered helpless. His life, however, was saved by Corporal Rolph of " W " who went to his assistance and carried him back to safety. The remainder of the day passed fairly quietly till 6.15 p.m., when artillery again opened on the position, wounding Captain Darley-Waddilove and 2nd Lieutenant G. I. Brew, both of " W " Company. After a brief bombardment the German guns remained silent till midnight, when the area around Battalion Headquarters was heavily shelled. 2nd Lieutenant R. Evans, the transport officer, who by ill luck had just brought the pack ponies up to Headquarters, was mortally wounded and many of the ponies killed. Thus within twenty-four hours of taking over the trenches the FIFTH had lost five officers. There must in all probability have been proportionately heavy casualties among other ranks, though, beyond the 18 that had occurred at dawn, no others are recorded in the War Diary. The German aircraft were very active during the 24th and 25th; otherwise, except for the usual morning and evening bombardments, which seemed to have become a matter of routine with the enemy, and against which the garrison was now better protected, these two days passed uneventfully.

Map No. 26

The trenches occupied by the FIFTH were to be taken over by the attacking troops of the 76th Brigade as their assembly positions on the night of the 25th/26th. The Battalion, however, was not to return to the 9th Brigade, as it had been placed at the disposal of the 76th Brigade as a reserve to its attack on the 26th. The night was clear and the enemy very quiet when these arrangements were carried out, and the relief was completed without incident. On withdrawal the companies of the FIFTH were disposed as follows : " Z " occupied a blockhouse in Hanebeke Wood, with " X " immediately in rear in the " Old British Line ;" " Y " occupied two blockhouses north and south of the railway and just west of the Hanebeke ; one section of " W " manned a strong point right forward in the Langemarck—Gheluvelt Line, from which the attacking troops were to advance, and the remainder of the company occupied a position on the left of " X."

As the right of the 3rd Division's attack, the 76th Brigade, advancing to the south of and parallel to the railway, was to capture three successive objectives. Two battalions were to be responsible for carrying the first two of these, and, on the completion of this first phase of the attack, the remaining two were to pass through and capture the village of Zonnebeke, which represented the Brigade's final objective. At 5.50 a.m. the two leading battalions (1/Gordons and 8/K.O.R.L.), covered by a creeping barrage, advanced to the attack, and by 7 a.m. were reported to have captured the 2nd Objective without great difficulty. On receipt of this information, " Z " and " Y " Companies of the FIFTH, in accordance with the plan of attack, were moved forward to the Langemarck—Gheluvelt Line, and a platoon of " W " was ordered to man a blockhouse at Charing Cross. The remainder of " W " and " X " Company stood fast in the positions to which they had been withdrawn overnight. The second

186   THE FIFTH IN THE GREAT WAR.

Map No. 26   phase of the 76th Brigade's attack now opened. Immediately on advancing, the   26th Sept., 1917
2/Suffolk and 10/Welsh Fusiliers, the two battalions engaged in this, encountered
very stiff resistance. The former, on the right, none the less succeeded in carrying their
objective and establishing themselves in the southern quarter of Zonnebeke. The
right of the Welsh Fusiliers also secured a footing in the village, but the left of their
attack, checked by fire from the railway station and Hill 40, and hampered by marshy
ground*, could gain little ground beyond the line from which the attack had been
launched, while the troops of the 8th Brigade on their immediate left, experiencing
similar difficulties, made no better progress. At 10 a.m., therefore, the line gained by
the 3rd Division on the right and centre ran back obliquely from Zonnebeke to the
2nd Objective.

At 2.30 p.m. Germans collecting for counter-attack behind the station were
dispersed by the fire of artillery, rifles and Lewis guns, and there was little cause
for anxiety in this quarter. It was otherwise, however, on the front of the 8th
Brigade, where the situation was far from satisfactory, and the whole of the
Divisional Reserve, 9th Brigade (less two battalions†) was now placed at the disposal
of the G.O.C. 8th Brigade, who was ordered to attack again at 6.30 p.m. for the
capture of Hill 40 and his final objective. By a coincidence this hour had also been
fixed by the enemy for a further counter-attack, covered by a triple barrage. Attack
and counter-attack opened simultaneously, and in the confusion that ensued, though
the Germans were repulsed, a number of British stragglers were observed withdrawing. This gave rise to a report that the 8th Brigade had broken, and action
as follows was taken by the FIFTH to protect the left flank of the 76th Brigade; two
platoons of " Y " Company were immediately moved to the north of the railway to
take up a position facing N.N.E.; " W," advancing from the old British Line, also
crossed to the north of the railway and swept all the ground on the left flank up to
the 1st objective, where they took up a position on the left flank of the Gordon
Highlanders in occupation of this line between the railway and St. Joseph's Institute;
" X " moved forward to join " Z " in the Langemarck-Gheluvelt Line, and the
Headquarter Company was placed in position astride a railway embankment 100
yards east of Battalion Headquarters. At the time it had seemed that the whole
position of the 76th Brigade was in grave jeopardy; but it transpired later that the
rumour of the collapse of the 8th Brigade was unfounded, and nightfall found the
3rd Division on its final objective in and to the south of Zonnebeke, with its centre
and left on, or just in advance of, the second objective. The dispositions taken up
by the FIFTH strengthened the position as a whole, and the companies remained in
occupation of the various points to which they had been ordered on the alarm of an
enemy penetration.

During the day 2nd Lieutenant J. Jaques had been killed—the fourth officer
casualty in " W " Company since coming into the line—and 2nd Lieutenant N. E.
Travell wounded.

On the 27th September orders were issued for the 9th Brigade to relieve the

---

* Though lower down, where it joined the Steenbeek, the condition of the Zonnebeke had
led the 3rd Division to hope that it would not prove an obstacle to the advance, here in its
upper reaches, it had overflowed its banks, which had been broken by shell fire.

† The 12/West Yorkshire had been attached to the 8th Brigade in the same manner as
the FIFTH had been to the 76th.

8th, with a view to completing the capture of the final objective at an early date, and for the detached battalions—the FIFTH and 12/West Yorkshire—to rejoin the Brigade for this attack. But on the same day, and before the FIFTH had acted on these orders, the Germans, after a very intense bombardment, delivered a determined attack against the positions held by the 4/Royal Fusiliers and 13/King's, the two battalions which had been detailed for the principal part in the 9th Brigade's operation. The enemy's attack was beaten off, but at such heavy cost to these two battalions as to render them incapable of offensive action. The relief of the 3rd by the 3rd Australian Division was accordingly ordered, and the FIFTH remained with the 76th Brigade until this was carried out on the 30th September, when they reverted to their own Brigade and returned to camp at Brandhoek.* The casualties in the Battalion between the 22nd and 29th September had amounted to :

KILLED—3 officers and 33 other ranks ;
WOUNDED—4 officers and 108 other ranks.

On relief the 3rd Division was concentrated to the west of Poperinghe in the Winnezeele area, preparatory to being transferred to the Third Army. On the 4th October, the FIFTH were moved by lorry to Wizernes, south of St. Omer, where they entrained with the 9th Brigade for Bapaume. On arrival here the Battalion marched to Ytres, a village some six miles E.S.E. of Bapaume.

The sector of the front in which the 3rd Division was now ordered to relieve the 62nd Division was immediately on the left of that which they had occupied in early September before being moved to Ypres. From a point about 1 mile E.N.E. of Noreuil the front line ran roughly north for a distance of some 2,400 yards, when it turned sharply west at a point named " The Apex " to pass in front of the northern outskirts of Bullecourt, giving a total frontage of roughly 4,500 yards. The sector was divided into the Right (Noreuil) Section and the Left (Bullecourt) Section, each of which was occupied by one Infantry Brigade. Each of these brigades held two battalions in the line and two in reserve, reserve battalions of the right brigade being placed in the Noreuil and Vaulx—Vraucourt areas, and those of the left brigade at Mory. A full description of the infantry dispositions has been given, as during the next two months the 3rd Division was to experience heavy fighting in this sector, and the FIFTH were to do duty in one or other of the places which have been named.

Relief started on the 9th October, when the 9th Brigade was moved into Divisional Reserve, the FIFTH being placed at Favreuil. On the following day the Battalion took over the front line of the Noreuil Section. There is little to relate of this first tour of the 9th Brigade in the new sector. Except for some intermittent artillery fire, things were quiet, and the FIFTH had the usual alternate spells in the line and in Brigade Reserve. Casualties had amounted only to one man killed and three wounded when, on the 30th October, the Battalion was withdrawn with the Brigade to Divisional Reserve and moved to Mory.

At this time secret preparations were being made for the opening of an offensive a few miles to the south of the position held by the 3rd Division—preparations which were to culminate on the 20th November in the Battle of Cambrai, the most complete,

---

* On the 17th November, 1917, Brigadier-General Porter, the commander of the 76th Brigade, visited the 1/FIFTH and, in addressing the Battalion, said that he had come on behalf of his brigade personally to thank the FIFTH for the services they had rendered first at Monchy on the 14th June and more recently at Zonnebeke. There is no record in the *War Diary* of the action of the Battalion on the 14th June to which the Brigadier referred on this occasion.

188   THE FIFTH IN THE GREAT WAR.

Map No. 27   if not the only true surprise effected in the War. With a view to improving the position   20th Nov., 1917
of the 3rd Division to the north of Bullecourt, plans were now made for an operation to be carried out by the 9th Brigade simultaneously with the big attack to the south. Two battalions, the 12/West Yorkshire and the 1/FIFTH, were to attack for the capture of 500 yards of the German front line (Bovis Trench)* which faced the village at a distance of some 300 yards, while the 4/Royal Fusiliers on each flank of the attack were to detail two companies to join up the right and left of the captured position with the British front lines east and west of Bullecourt. In preparation for this operation the 9th Brigade relieved the 76th in the left of the Bullecourt Section on the 18th November. The 19th passed quietly, and shortly after midnight the FIFTH, who were to form the left of the attack, moved up to their assembly positions. These had been marked by tapes in No Man's Land, and one gathers from the record of a precautionary issue of cough lozenges to the troops that they must have been in fairly close proximity to the enemy's front line ! By 3.30 a.m., " W " Company (Lieutenant C. H. Steele) and " X " (Lieutenant A. E. Phelan), the two companies detailed for the assault, were in position on the tapes, the former being on the right. Their flanks were protected by detachments thrown forward by " Y " and " Z " Companies, which had been assembled in the front line in support of the attack.

At 6.20 a.m. the artillery barrage which was to cover the attack opened, and the assaulting companies advanced, each with two platoons leading and two in close support. Eight minutes later, as the barrage lifted from the objective, the troops rushed forward to the assault. " W " Company, on the right, carried their objective without great difficulty. But, after gaining the position, they suffered considerable loss from fire directed from a sunken road to their left front, and before they had consolidated the captured trench the enemy launched a counter-attack. That this was foiled was mainly due to the prompt action of 2nd-Lieutenant Finch, who turned a captured machine-gun on to the Germans, inflicting very heavy casualties on them with this weapon that they had abandoned. Very shortly afterwards Lieutenant Steele was wounded and command of the company fell to Finch.† " X " Company also succeeded in gaining the position, but at heavier cost, for before the enemy's trenches were reached, their commander, Lieutenant Phelan, and 2nd-Lieutenant Apps, were both killed. In this first rush of a trench to trench attack the loss of an officer was not felt, for the spirit of the troops was sufficient to carry them forward. It was otherwise in the period which followed, when it became

---

   * This was actually a portion of the Hindenburg Line, in which the British had already secured a footing to the east of Bullecourt.

   † The statement of service for which the Military Cross was awarded to 2nd-Lieutenant P. G. Finch, as announced in the *London Gazette*, will be found in the July, 1918, number of the *St. George's Gazette*. But, as was usual, no mention is made of the date or place at which the service was performed. It was only by chance, and after this Chapter had gone to press and the first proofs been printed, that the writer secured a letter addressed in May, 1919, to the father of this young officer by Captain T. F. Ellison (Adjutant) relating the incident recorded above, of which there is no mention in the Battalion War Diary or narrative report. It has been possible to insert a brief reference to the incident, but had the information contained in Captain Ellison's letter with regard to the general action of " W " Company during the 20th and 21st November, 1917, been earlier available, more would have been said of the manner in which his men were inspired throughout by the splendid example set by 2nd-Lieutenant Finch, whose death in the following March will be found recorded on a later page. In this case the writer has been fortunate in having been able, to some extent, to rectify an omission, but fears that there must be many other notable actions by individuals which remain unrecorded in this History.

20th Nov., 1917 necessary to secure the captured position against counter-attack. It was then that the need was felt for a commander like Phelan, whose courage, coolness, and resource had in the course of two years of war proved him the perfect leader. The situation on this occasion, indeed, was one which called for the initiative of an experienced commander, who would not hesitate to depart from orders if satisfied that they had been based on a misapprehension. Owing to the inaccuracy of the map which had been relied on in planning the attack,* it was found that, while "W" Company's position in the captured trench lent itself to strong defence, that occupied by "X" had every disadvantage. Not only was it overlooked by a ridge to the north-west, but the ground in this direction had been so cut up by shells that it gave no field of fire. Though, in such circumstances, the position could not, perhaps, have been made actually tenable, some departure from the dispositions which had been ordered would have strengthened it against counter-attack. As it was, however, the trench was occupied in accordance with the original plan, with bombing posts established at points A, B and C.

Map No. 27

In the meantime the West Yorkshire had carried their objective on the right of the FIFTH, and the supporting companies of both battalions had been moved up to the line from which the leading companies had launched their attack. Owing to the fire of German snipers, communication with the troops in the captured position proved very difficult, but on the whole the morning passed quietly, and it seemed for a time that the enemy had accepted the situation. As to this, it will be seen that the FIFTH were soon to be disillusioned.

At 3.25 p.m., "W" Company reported that they had opened fire on parties of the enemy seen moving by Beef Alley towards the left flank. The sequel to this movement came at 4 p.m., when, following a very heavy bombardment of the blocks which had been constructed and manned by the forward platoons of "X" the enemy assaulted the whole company front and drove the garrison from the trench. The supporting platoons now advanced, and with these the subaltern on whom command had devolved on the death of Phelan attempted to restore the situation by immediate counter-attack. Of those who engaged in this not more than twenty reached the trench; but these, fighting with great determination, succeeded in driving a party of the enemy back to a point where they came under the fire of "W" Company and suffered heavy casualties. None, however, returned; for they were later attacked from the flank and overwhelmed by the Germans, who recovered and retained their hold on the position. In the meantime an enemy counter-attack against the West Yorkshire had been repulsed, and the forward platoons of "W" Company of the FIFTH still stood firm with their left flank at a point just east of Block "C." Lieut.-Colonel Herbert now decided to establish a line running from this point roughly parallel to the lost trench to join the Royal Fusiliers south west of Block "A." This line was occupied by the supporting platoons of "W," whose original position was taken over by "Y" Company, and the remnants of "X" were withdrawn to reserve. On being informed of these dispositions, the Divisional Commander gave orders for this new line to be consolidated; for the weakness of the position captured at dawn by "X" Company had long since been realised, and it was recognised that the ground lost possessed no advantage which could justify further effort to recover it.

In his report on the action, Lieut.-Colonel Herbert stated: "The death of Lieutenant Phelan . . . was a very serious loss. Had he remained in command of the

---

* Authority—Major-General W. N. Herbert.

company it is possible that advantage might have been taken of the initial demoralisation of the enemy to establish strong posts well forward, though it is doubtful if this would have averted the successful counter-attack by the enemy unless the ground to the north-west had also been taken."

In addition to the two officers whose deaths have already been recorded, the losses of the Battalion during the day had been as under :—

Killed	..	16 other ranks.
Wounded	..	Lieutenant C. H. Steele.
		2nd-Lieutentant H. Donald.
		75 other ranks.
Missing	..	18 other ranks.*

Except for intermittent shell fire, the night had passed quietly when, at 6.37 a.m. on the 21st, a party of about fifty Germans was observed advancing against " W " Company's position. The S.O.S. signal was immediately sent up, and the prompt reply of our machine guns and Stokes mortars, combined with rifle and Lewis gun fire, broke up this isolated attack with heavy loss to the enemy. It proved to be the last effort made by the Germans against the trenches they had lost, and though the FIFTH were unfortunate in losing another officer in 2nd Lieutenant M. E. Marjoribanks, who was killed in one of the forward posts which had been established by " Y " Company, there was little serious interference with the consolidation of the line, which occupied the remainder of the 21st and the two following days.

On the 24th, in broad daylight, a party of five men of the FIFTH raided a small advanced post, which the Germans had established opposite our left. A sentry was seized, but before he could be removed, warning of the approach of the enemy forced the raiders to abandon their prisoner and to content themselves with returning with his shoulder strap as an identification. On the next day there were indications of a withdrawal of the enemy from the high ground on the left flank, which had been the source of so much trouble. Orders were accordingly issued for the Royal Fusiliers to advance after dark and seize this position, while the FIFTH co-operated by re-establishing the block at point " B." Such of the Germans as were encountered when these orders were put into execution fled, without attempting any resistance, and dawn of the 26th November found British troops in occupation, not only of the whole position which had been the objective of the attack of the 20th, but also of the ground on the left flank from which the enemy had hitherto rendered it untenable.

On the 26th November, the 9th was relieved by the 76th Brigade, and the FIFTH returned to the camp at Mory. They were, however, to be given little rest. The Germans had by now recovered from the first shock of the Battle of Cambrai, the initial stages of which had been marked by such overwhelming success, and in the counter-attacks which had now started, the tide was turning against the British. To reduce the front of the 56th Division, whose right had become engaged on the left of the great attack, the 3rd Division was required to extend southwards to take over the Lagnicourt Section. This necessitated the 9th Brigade being moved up to the line

---

* These figures are taken from the Battalion *War Diary*. A later entry in the Brigade Diary puts the wounded at 84 and the missing at 10; the discrepancy is probably due to 9 men having been evacuated through the R.A.P. of another unit. The difficulty of accurately recording casualties may be judged from the fact that those that occurred among officers this day were not officially published by the War Office till seven months later and did not appear in the *St. George's Gazette* till June, 1918.

THE FIFTH IN THE GREAT WAR. 191

29th Nov. to from reserve, and on the 29th the FIFTH relieved the 1/London Regiment in the new   Map No. 28
11th Dec., 1917 front. This arrangement, by which all three infantry brigades of the Division were
in the line, was, however, only a temporary measure introduced till the situation on the
Cambrai front had been stabilised, and on the 9th, after ten uneventful days in the
line, the FIFTH were again withdrawn with the 9th Brigade to Divisional Reserve at

Map No. 28.

German Attack on "The Apex," 12th December, 1917.

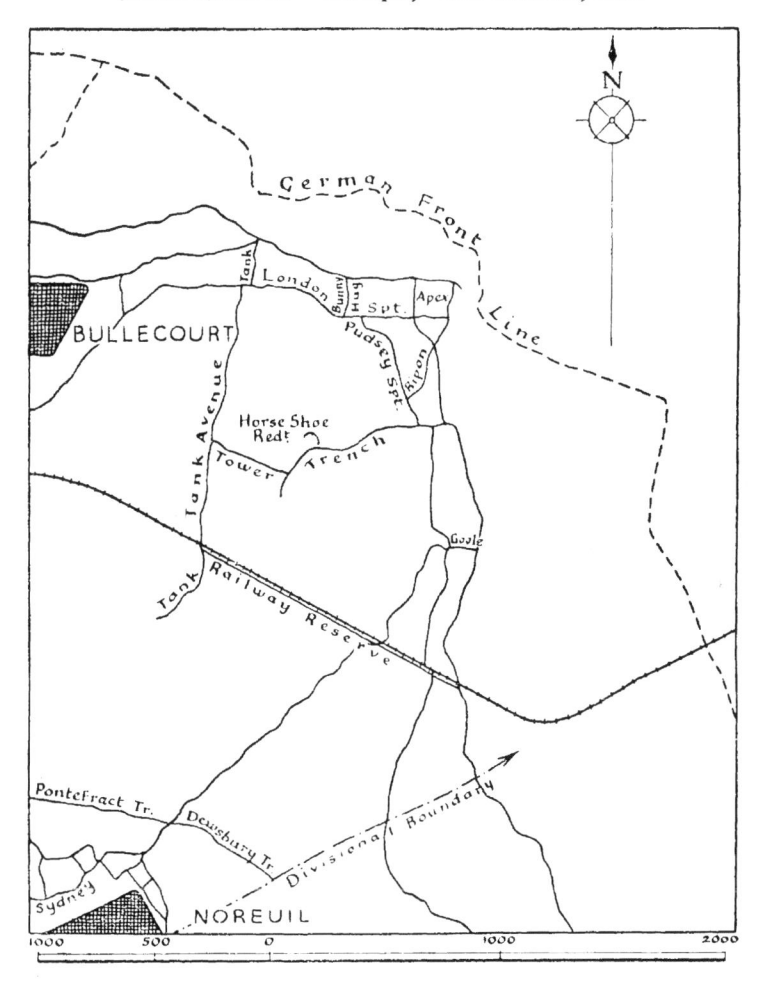

Mory. Here, however, they had time only for baths and an issue of clean clothing—
both sadly needed—before being moved forward once again with the 9th Brigade, which
had now been ordered to relieve the 8th in the Noreuil (right) Section of the 3rd Division
front.

For a clear understanding of the manner in which the FIFTH were to be drawn
piecemeal into the confused fighting of the next few days, it is necessary for the reader
to be acquainted with the dispositions of the 9th Brigade after completion of this relief
on the 11th December. Three battalions—from right to left, 4/Royal Fusiliers,

13/King's, 12/West Yorkshire—held the line, each finding its own supports, the right of the last named battalion being in occupation of "The Apex" salient, to which reference has already been made. The FIFTH (less "W" Company) was held in Brigade Reserve in the Intermediate Line, covering Noreuil village, while "W" Company, under the O.C. West Yorkshire, was placed in the trench known as Railway Reserve.

The night following the relief passed quietly, but at 6.35 a.m. on the morning of the 12th December, a very heavy bombardment was opened on the front and support lines of the centre and left battalions, being most intense on The Apex, where it was thickened by the fire of numerous trench mortars. Without waiting for the S.O.S. signal our artillery and machine guns at once put down a defensive barrage. At 7.15 a.m., the enemy's artillery lifted and his infantry advanced against the trenches held by the King's and West Yorkshire. All telephone communication between the latter battalion and Brigade Headquarters had been cut, but at 8 a.m. a report was received from the King's that, after having repulsed two determined attacks, they were now firing at the enemy across what had been the forward position of the West Yorkshire, who, it seemed, had been driven from the Apex. It was not till an hour later that the Brigade could get any accurate information as to the situation on the front of the left battalion. It was then learnt that, on their right, The Apex had been lost, but that the enemy had been held up by a block which had been established in Ripon Lane; their centre company had given ground, but had constructed a block 100 yards west of Bunny Hug; and their left company still stood fast in its original position. It was further reported that two platoons of "W" Company of the FIFTH had been sent up as reinforcements. On receiving this information, the Brigadier gave instructions for the remainder of "W" Company to be pushed forward, and it was then replaced in Railway Reserve by "Y."

Fierce and confused fighting continued in the forward area during the whole morning. At Brigade H.Q., anxiety as to the situation was not relieved by a report from the King's that a party which had worked up the front line to its junction with Ripon Lane had been shot at from behind from the latter trench. At the same time information was received from the Air that the enemy's trenches, from opposite Bullecourt to the Bapaume—Cambrai road, were full of troops. To enable the O.C. King's to make his position more secure, "Z" Company of the FIFTH was now sent forward to Railway Reserve and placed under his orders. No further news came from the West Yorkshire front till 12 noon, when it was reported that the enemy had penetrated to Pudsey and London Supports. Some two hours later it was learnt that 2nd Lieutentant Colton of the FIFTH had led forward his platoon and bombed his way from south to north right through these trenches, clearing them of the enemy and capturing five prisoners. Subsequently, however, it seems that the Germans regained a footing in these positions, though at what time or in what manner is not made clear by the reports which are still available.

The afternoon was now drawing to a close, and the Brigadier, foreseeing a renewal of the attack at dawn on the 13th, issued orders at 3.30 p.m. to Lieut-Colonel Herbert, as Commander of the Brigade Reserve, to move his headquarters up to those of the West Yorkshire in Railway Reserve, and to place two companies in occupation of Tower Trench with two platoons garrisoning Horse Shoe Redoubt.* But in issuing

---

* For Lieut.-Colonel Herbert to carry out these orders it was necessary that the companies placed at the disposal of the W. Yorks and King's should revert to his command, though this is not made clear in the official narrative.

12th/13th Dec., 1917

these orders the Brigadier was ignorant of the fact that, after "W" Company of the FIFTH had been used up, the platoons of "Y" had one after the other been drawn into the fight as reinforcements to the West Yorkshire.† Herbert, who on receipt of the Brigadier's instructions, had issued orders for "Y" and "Z" Companies to take up the positions designated, was told when he arrived at the headquarters of the West Yorkshire that it would be quite impossible to extricate "Y" Company, and that three platoons of "W" and one of "X" were also too closely involved in forward positions to be withdrawn. In fact the FIFTH (the one time Brigade Reserve) had by now become hopelessly scattered. Of "W" Company, one platoon was in Horse Shoe Redoubt, the remainder in London Support; of "X" (a two platoon company) one platoon was in London Support and one in Railway Reserve; of "Y," one platoon was in Tank Avenue, one in Pudsey Support, one in London Support, and the fourth in Railway Reserve; while "Z" Company, with the 13/King's, was under orders to move to Tower Trench east of Horse Shoe Redoubt. Herbert, accepting the situation, made the best of it. He gave orders for the platoon of "W" already in Horse Shoe Redoubt to remain there, for the one platoon of "X" still at his disposal to move up to Tower Trench to the west of the Redoubt, and confirmed the orders already given to "Z." The remainder of his Battalion (less H.Q.) he placed at the disposal of the O.C., 12/West Yorkshire.

Map No. 28

Thus, when darkness fell, no troops remained under the immediate control of the G.O.C. 9th Brigade. During the night, however, two companies of the Royal Fusiliers on the right of the Brigade were relieved by troops of another Division and brought into Reserve, and the O.C. West Yorkshire was ordered to deliver a frontal attack with his own troops and those of the FIFTH at his disposal, for the recovery of the lost portions of Pudsey and London Supports. Bunny Hug was to be simultaneously cleared of the enemy by bombing. A heavy concentration of gas shells, however, disorganised the assembly for this attack, and at 6.30 a.m. on the 13th, report was received at Brigade Headquarters that, owing to the exhaustion of the troops, the operation had been cancelled. It was also reported that the enemy had opened a very heavy artillery bombardment shortly after daylight.

When acquainted with this situation, the Divisional Commander gave orders that Pudsey Support must be retaken and occupied. Brigadier-General Potter, considering that the frontal attack planned for the previous night would be impracticable by daylight, now arranged for a bombing attack to be delivered from both flanks, following a thirty minutes bombardment by artillery. To assist in this fresh attack "Z" Company of the FIFTH, which hitherto had not been seriously engaged, was placed at the disposal of the O.C. West Yorkshire. It seems that, owing to the battered condition of the trenches, the assembly of the troops for this operation was observed by the enemy, for at 3.30 p.m., when our infantry were ready to advance, the Germans themselves opened a bombing attack. In the confusion that ensued our troops, driven from the blocks they had established in Pudsey and Ripon, fell back on Tower Trench,

---

† In his report on the action the Brigadier stated :—" The O.C. West Yorkshire, in response to appeals from subordinate commanders, frittered away the reserves." Though this criticism is, perhaps, just, it seems doubtful whether, in the situation which had developed, the throwing in of reserves to strengthen threatened points could have been avoided except by the Brigadier himself keeping a tighter hand on them. The Brigade Reserve itself, in fact, was thrown piecemeal to Battalion Commanders to employ as they thought fit. The break-down of communications might be pleaded as excuse for this action, but such plea would be equally valid for the O.C. West Yorkshire.

but later succeeded in forcing the Germans back 30 or 40 yards to the north of this position and in gaining 150 yards of London Support. In the meantime Lieut.-Colonel Herbert, of whose whole Battalion, except for his headquarters, there remained with him only one platoon of " W " Company and one of " X," had ordered the latter to extend its right to the junction of Tower Trench and Sheffield Avenue. The confused nature of the fighting, with constant attack and counter-attack, which continued for the rest of the day, similarly to that in which the 2/FIFTH had been engaged in the Hohenzollern Redoubt in 1915,* defies any attempt at accurate description. By 7 p.m., however, the situation had to some extent been stabilised. It was definitely known that all efforts to recover Pudsey Support had failed, and Herbert, satisfied that fighting had died down, had withdrawn his two platoons to his headquarters in Railway Reserve. Shortly afterwards, he withdrew his headquarters to Noreuil, leaving the platoons at the disposal of the O.C. 4/Royal Fusiliers, who had now come forward with the remainder of his battalion after being relieved on the right of the Brigade.

The 4/Royal Fusiliers were under orders to deliver a frontal attack at dawn on the 14th, but owing to the exhaustion of their men, the operation was cancelled and they were directed instead to relieve the West Yorkshire and the scattered companies of the FIFTH on the left of the 9th Brigade. On the completion of this relief, the fighting which had followed the German attack on The Apex was, so far as the FIFTH were concerned, at an end.

In the period 12th/14th December the Battalion had sustained the following casualties :

        Killed   ..   13 other ranks.
        Wounded   ..   Lieutenant R. H. Archer.
                                  2nd Lieutenant R. Alexander.
                                  32 other ranks.
        Missing   ..   11 other ranks.

Companies on relief were withdrawn independently, and it was not till the 16th December that Lieut.-Colonel Herbert had his battalion complete at Noreuil. From there they moved on the following day to Courcelles-le-Comté, where, the War Diary records, they were fairly comfortable, though " baths were impossible owing to frost." Mercifully, it seems, a thaw must have set in later, as under the date of the 19th one finds the single, triumphant entry " Baths for the whole Battalion (*less transport*)." From Courcelles the Battalion was moved to Mory, where on Christmas Day it was visited by Major-General Deverell ; and the last day of the year found the 1/FIFTH at Mercatel.

Thus a fourth Christmas had passed and another year of war ended. It has been said that, hitherto, as each successive year closed, the regimental soldier had always looked forward with confidence to the War being over by " next Christmas ;" and it may be remembered that at the opening of this history it was related how the 2/FIFTH at Ambala based similar anticipations largely on the part that would be played by the " Russian steam-roller." That monstrous machine, which had long since given evidence of serious mechanical defects, had now finally broken down. At the close of 1917, more, perhaps, than at any previous time, the troops became conscious of the magnitude of the task of beating Germany ; and, though there had been no change in their optimism as to the final issue of the War, it would probably be just

---

* See Chapter IX.

to say that now, when that well-worn prophecy would at last have been a true one, few would have been found in the ranks of the FIFTH rash enough to make it.

NOTE.—During the period 30th June—31st December, 1917, the Battalion lost 16 officers killed or wounded, and received the following reinforcements :—

July.	September.
2nd Lieutenant J. W. Walker.	2nd Lieutenant D. H. Yatman
,, W. F. B. Joss.	
,, A. S. Greener.*	November.
,, B. R. Newstead.*	Lieutenant E. Lawrence, M.C.
Lieutenant C. H. Steel.	
,, C. B. Carrick, M.C.*	December.
	2nd Lieutenant T. Sanderson
	Lieutenant A. Rochell.
August.	2nd Lieutenant R. Alexander, W.
2nd Lieutenant L. Partington.*	,, J. E. Colton.
,, D. S. Marjoribanks, K.	Lieutenant C. E. Hamilton.
,, A. M. Porter-Hargreaves.	2nd Lieutenant C. H. Strong.

* = Re-joining.   K. or W. = Killed or wounded later in the same period.

Strength of Battalion, 31st December, 1917 = 36 officers, 719 other ranks.

CHAPTER XIV.

The Great German Offensive.

"Somme 1918"—"St. Quentin"—"Bapaume 1918"—"Arras 1918."

FIRST BATTALION—1ST JANUARY TO 30TH MARCH, 1918.

Map No. 22.

28th Dec., 1917 to 31st Jan., 1918.

On the 28th December Lieut.-Colonel Herbert had been granted leave to England. Severely wounded in October, 1914, and again in June, 1915, he had returned to the Western Front as a brigade major in the 60th Division early in the summer of 1916, before relieving Lieut.-Colonel Wild in command of the 1/FIFTH in October of that year. He had now borne the strain of battalion command for over twelve months, and the authorities, having decided that he would benefit by a spell in England, appointed him as an instructor at the Senior Officers' School at Woking. Thus temporary command of the 1/FIFTH now fell to Major D. F. de C. Buckle.*

During the first few weeks of January the Battalion was resting and training at Mercatel. On the 14th of the month it was inspected by Lieut.-General Haldane, Commander of the VI. Corps, in which the 3rd Division was now included. The Corps at this time held the line to the south of the Arras-Cambrai road, as the right centre of the Third Army, and orders had now been issued for its left sector, from east of Guémappes southwards to a point east of Croisilles, to be taken over by the 3rd from the 34th Division. To hold this extent of front it was necessary for all three brigades to be in the line, and on the 26th January the 9th relieved the 102nd Brigade in the centre section, opposite Fontaine-les-Croisilles. In this relief the 1/FIFTH as left Battalion took over trenches from the 20th Northumberland Fusiliers. On the following morning an encounter by a dawn patrol with a party of the enemy resulted in a serjeant being killed and 2nd-Lieutenant J. Hornby, the patrol leader, wounded. For the rest, the few days during which the Battalion remained in the line before being withdrawn to Brigade support passed fairly quietly.

Though the Germans opposite the 3rd Division were to show little activity during the next six or seven weeks, the FIFTH were fully alive to what might be expected in the near future. With Russia withdrawn from the War, and some months still to elapse before the United States' Army could be brought to anything approach-

---

* Major Buckle had started his soldiering with the 3rd (Militia) Battalion of the Northumberland Fusiliers in 1896, with the intention of obtaining a commission in the Regular Army. Despite a powerful physique, he had, however, been rejected under the height standard in force at that time. Returning to the 3rd Battalion at the outbreak of War, he had been wounded in October 1914 shortly after being sent out to the 1st Battalion. On rejoining in January 1915, he had been invalided after serving only a few days. Posted to the 2nd Battalion four months later, he had almost immediately been again wounded at Bellewaarde on the 24th May. He returned to the 1st Battalion on the 18th October, 1915, and from that date served with it continuously till the 27th May, 1918, mostly as 2nd-in-command, when he was sent to England for six months' rest and attached to the Hants Yeomanry. On the 24th April 1919 he died of heart failure.

1st/28th Feb., 1918

ing its full strength, the Germans' one hope of securing a favourable decision lay in opening an offensive at the earliest opportunity, before the advantage of superior numbers, which they now held, passed to their adversary. In anticipation of such an event, the whole energy of the 3rd Division was to be directed during the coming weeks to strengthening the defences. As will be seen later, the ceaseless work on this which now started was in due course to stand units in good stead.

Map No. 29.

Early in February the Battalion was again in the line. On the night of the 6th, the last of their tour, a post at Lone Sap was raided by the enemy. The night was pitch black, and no glimpse was caught of the raiders either during their approach or withdrawal. Four revolver shots gave the alarm, but before assistance reached the sap, one of the two sentries posted there had been wounded and the other captured. On the withdrawal of the Battalion to Brigade Reserve next day, command was taken over by Lieut.-Colonel E. M. Moulton-Barrett, who had recently been in command of the 25th Battalion of the Regiment, in the 34th Division.

There is little to be related of the remainder of February. Casualties, which during the whole month amounted to 7 killed and 19 wounded, could be reckoned as comparatively light, but the men got little rest, as during the periods in reserve which alternated with tours in the trenches, large parties for work on the defences were in constant demand. While the Battalion was out of the line towards the end of the month a raid was rehearsed under the direction of Captain Carrick. The operation itself, which took place on the night of the 3rd March, was disappointing. The two platoons, under 2nd-Lieutenants E. I. Lawrence and Williams, which carried it out, played their parts to perfection, but on entering the enemy's trench they found it had been evacuated—a not unusual anti-climax to raids in these days.

As a result of a re-organisation, by which infantry brigades had been reduced from four to three battalions, the 12/West Yorkshire, who had been the comrades of the FIFTH in many a battle, had now been broken up. This reduction in the infantry strength of divisions necessitated a re-adjustment of frontages. The right section of the 3rd Division had accordingly been taken over by the 34th Division, and the 8th Brigade, which had hitherto held it, was now interposed between the 9th and 76th. By these adjustments the front of the 3rd Division was reduced to 4,300 yards, and that of the 9th Brigade, which now held the line from Pug Avenue to Foster Avenue as the right of the Division, to about 1,400 yards. The events which are shortly to be related will be made clearer to the reader by an explanation of the general scheme of defence, and of the manner in which the three brigades were disposed in depth on the divisional front. Each of these had one battalion in occupation of the Front and Support Lines of a First System of Defence, one in Brigade Support in a Second System and its third battalion in Brigade Reserve in hutted camps in Boisleux-au-Mont, Mercatel, or Beurains.* A Third System of Defence, represented by two lines of trench, of which the more forward ran roughly north and south through Hénin-sur-Cojeul, was not permanently occupied and a single line covering the villages in which the battalions in brigade reserve were situated formed a Fourth System. In the defence scheme the 1st System was known as the " Forward Zone." Troops in occupation of this were to do their utmost to maintain their position against attack, but in the event of an enemy penetration no more than local reserves would be employed to restore the

---

* There were eight machine guns disposed in pairs on the 9th Brigade front, which was supported by one Field Brigade of artillery. Of the Corps heavy artillery, one 6in. Howitzer battery and one 60-pounder battery were in exclusive support of the 3rd Division.

situation. In short, the loss of the 1st System would not constitute a major disaster. It was otherwise with the 2nd and 3rd Systems which together formed the "Battle Zone." A hostile penetration of this would be regarded as so serious a matter, that it was laid down that, should this occur, the Corps or Army Reserve would be employed in a deliberate counter-attack to expel the enemy.*

The Brigade and Battalion War Diaries for the early weeks in March would make dull reading were it not that, for anyone knowing the context, certain passages indicate how, under the outward semblance of normal trench warfare on a "quiet front," there lay the constant and certain expectation of a heavy attack. Reading the day to day entries with the after knowledge of the direction in which they were tending, one feels vividly how suspense must have been intensified by the almost uncanny quiescence which prevailed; but one learns too that the 3rd Division had not been lulled into a false sense of security. On the 9th there was "practically no artillery fire all day," in spite of which intensive work was in progress on the defences of the Division. On the 11th again the enemy was "very quiet," and on this day the "Brigadier explained what was likely to happen in the coming German offensive." Alas! There is no record of this forecast to assist one to judge the extent to which, in the events which followed, the Brigade Commander enhanced or damaged his reputation as a prophet. One learns that on the 13th the weather was very good, and the enemy still very quiet; this, however, was not so much a matter for satisfaction to the Divisional Commander as the good work done on the defences, on which he congratulated the troops. Except for fog and haze, rendering visibility bad, the weather continued fair from the 14th to the 17th, and the inactivity of the Germans amounted almost to lethargy; yet our infantry every day were feverishly at work strengthening their position, while the artillery were busy in practising counter-preparation bombardments†. On the 17th, the FIFTH relieved the 13/Kings's in the front line. The 18th broke as a fine day but turned to rain, and the 19th was very wet. From the entries in the war diaries for the 20th, one gathers that the weather was now causing more trouble than the enemy; for, while that of the FIFTH briefly records "Stand to as usual. No enemy activity at all," that of the Brigade tells us that "the trenches have been reduced to a very bad state by the rain." All, however, knew that an attack was imminent, and doubt only remained as to the date on which it was to be delivered. In the hope of being able to clear this up, the 4/Royal Fusiliers had been ordered to raid the enemy's trenches on the night of the 21st/22nd.

This, then, was the situation at nightfall on the 20th March, when the 9th Brigade was disposed as follows: the FIFTH were in occupation of the 1st System, with "Y" Company (Captain Carrick) and "Z" Company (Captain Chipper) holding the right and left of the front and support lines, and "W" (Lieutenant Allen) and "X" (Captain E. Lawrence) in "Concrete Reserve"; the 4/Royal Fusiliers held the front line of the 2nd System and manned blocks in Shaft and Hind Avenues; the

---

* For reasons which will be apparent, it was not possible, when the attack came to put these plans into execution. It is necessary, however, for the reader of this History to appreciate that the troops in occupation of the 1st System were regarded as being to a large measure self-supporting, and that there would always in the first instance be some reluctance to reinforce them from those allotted to the defence of the Battle Zone, on account of the superior importance attached to this.

† Bombardment of the probable assembly positions of the enemy on indications being given that he is forming up for attack.

21st Mar., 1918 13/King's were in Brigade Reserve. The 101st Brigade of the 34th Division was on the right, and the 8th Brigade of the 3rd Division on the left. At 1.30 a.m. on the 21st a report came from the Third Army that there had been large movements in relief among the German troops opposite the Sector. All, however, remained quiet, and no further indication that the enemy might be preparing for attack came till 5.10 a.m. At this hour the 15th Division, on the left of the 3rd, discharged a number of gas projectors against the German trenches, which immediately brought a bombardment by guns of all calibres, including many gas shells, on the whole area of the 3rd Division. Very heavy artillery and trench mortar fire was brought to bear on the front and support lines of the 1st System, and the 2nd System was also heavily shelled. For weeks past the Germans had borne every sort of provocation with marked forbearance, and it was clear that this bombardment was something more than a mere sudden retaliatory outburst in reply to a few gas shells. This became even more evident when two hours had passed without any sign of slackening in the intensity of the enemy's fire, and it was realised that the long awaited attack had at last opened. At 7.15 a.m. the German artillery lifted and their infantry advanced to the assault against the position held by the FIFTH. The British artillery and machine guns covering the front immediately put down a defensive barrage, but the Germans succeeded in gaining a footing in the front line. Carrick and Chipper at once organised and launched counter-attacks. At 8.40 a.m. Carrick reported that " Y " Company had cleared the front line of the enemy. " Z " Company was faced by a more difficult task, the Germans having established themselves firmly in Lone Sap; and considerable bombing was required to eject them from this position. By 10.25 a.m., however, the left of the front line had been recovered, and the FIFTH were again in touch with the battalions on either flank.

Map No. 29.

The front line had been so badly damaged by shell fire that communication along it had become impossible, and the best that could be done was to establish posts at intervals where this proved practicable. For a time the situation became quieter in the forward system. Then, at 10.55 a.m., a heavy bombardment by trench mortars opened on the front line. Again, our artillery and machine guns with great promptitude replied with counter-preparation fire, preventing the German infantry from developing an attack. The situation once more became gradually quieter till, at 12.55 p.m., all fire had practically died down, except on the left of " Y " Company. The 101st Brigade (34th Division), on the right, reported that all was quiet on their front and that the " Stand down " had been ordered. The same order was then given to the troops of the 9th Brigade in the Battle Zone. At this point the men of the FIFTH may well have wondered if they had seen the end of the Great Attack against which they had been preparing for weeks past. At 2 p.m. the disposition of the troops in the 9th Brigade was the same as at the opening of the attack, except that Lone Sap, having been obliterated, had been evacuated, and some other posts, for similar reasons, had been shifted to one flank or the other of their original positions. Further, a platoon of the Royal Fusiliers had been sent forward to Concrete Reserve in replacement of one of the FIFTH which had been moved forward to assist in counter-attack. Two platoons of the same battalion were a little later sent forward to take up a position on the right of " Y " Company.

But all was by no means over. At 2.45 p.m. the enemy re-opened his artillery bombardment, which, growing increasingly heavy, reached its maximum intensity about 3.25 p.m. Large numbers of Germans were observed moving in Fontaine Wood, and a hundred of these who now attempted to advance were driven back in disorder. Our artillery and machine gun barrages undoubtedly were most effective, and by inflicting heavy casualties on the enemy did much towards completely crushing this fresh attack. The Germans, however, ultimately succeeded in gaining the front line, which by now had been almost completely obliterated, and further in driving the two platoons of the Royal Fusiliers from Dodo Trench, on which they had fallen back. 2nd-Lieutenant Yatman, commanding the right platoon of "Y" Company, with his flank thus exposed, in turn fell back in order to avoid being surrounded. Captain Carrick with great promptitude flung back a defensive flank from Swift Support along First Avenue, bringing enfilade fire on the enemy with such effect as completely to hold up their further advance, and sent orders to Yatman to take up a position in Brown Support. These orders, however, had been anticipated by Lieut.-Colonel Moulton-Barrett, to whom Yatman had reported at Battalion Headquarters in Concrete Reserve. On the remainder of the Battalion's front the attack had been brought to a standstill. At 4.30 p.m. the FIFTH held a line running along Brown Support, up First Avenue, along Swift Support to Wren Alley, thence back to Curtain Support, by which it continued to Foster Avenue; while the Germans were in occupation of our old front line and Tank and Dodo trenches. In short, after close on twelve hours' fighting, which had cost the enemy heavy casualties, the ground gained by them was negligible.

On the other hand, while the attack had been definitely checked on the front of the 9th Brigade, things had assumed a more serious aspect on their right. Here, though the platoons of the Royal Fusiliers which had come up on the right of the FIFTH were in touch at Farmer's and Fuldner Lanes with elements of the 11/Suffolk Regiment, the latter had completely lost touch with the remainder of the 101st Brigade, to which they belonged, and masses of the enemy were now observed moving south and west across the high ground on the far side of the Sensée River. It seemed that the 9th Brigade might shortly have to meet an attack from the south combined with a renewed attempt by the enemy from the east, and in these circumstances the FIFTH were ordered to hold fast to their present position and not to attempt counter-attack for the recovery of the now shattered front line. At 4.53 p.m. an attack against Swift Support was beaten off with further heavy loss to the enemy, and the situation remained satisfactory on the front of the FIFTH. But, as the afternoon drew on, reports came that the Germans were advancing from the south-east and occupying Pug and Shaft Avenues, and the Royal Fusiliers' detachment was warned to keep a look-out in this direction. Later, information came of more enemy movement over the high ground to the south of the Sensée, and it was learnt at the same time that, except for the detached parties of the 11/Suffolk still in touch with the 9th Brigade, the whole of the 101st Brigade was withdrawing to Hill Switch in the 2nd System. No further incident, however, occurred before the day closed, and nightfall on the 21st found the 9th Brigade disposed as follows:—

First System :
(Forward Zone)
Front Line (i.e. the line described above as held at 4.30 p.m.).
Right—$1\frac{1}{2}$ platoons 4/Royal Fusiliers and 2 M.G.
Left—$12\frac{1}{2}$ platoons 1/FIFTH.
Concrete Reserve.
Right—$5\frac{1}{2}$ platoons 4/Royal Fusiliers.
2 M.G. at junction of Shaft Avenue.
Left—$3\frac{1}{2}$ platoons 1/FIFTH.

21st/22nd Mar., 1918

Second System :
(Battle Zone)
    First Line—2 companies 4/Royal Fusiliers.
    Reserve Line—2 companies 13/Kings.

Map No. 29.

1 platoon 4/Royal Fusiliers and 2 companies 13/Kings were in reserve in " The Tunnel."*

During the afternoon of the 21st an attack made against the 8th Brigade in the centre of the Divisional front had been repulsed with heavy loss to the enemy. This, however, represented the northernmost limit of the German's effort on the opening day of their great offensive, and there had been no organised attack against the 76th Brigade on the left of the 3rd Division.

The mist in which day broke on the 22nd March was early dispelled by the sun, and the weather turned fair and bright. The enemy were soon active. At 6.30 a.m. some slight shelling of Shaft Avenue and the front line started; this gradually increased to a more severe bombardment, which extended to Concrete Reserve and Earl's Court, and included many gas shells. At 9.25 a.m. the enemy were definitely located in Pug Avenue, and an attack from here was momentarily expected. None, however, came, the German artillery fire gradually died down, and by 9.30 all was quiet. Later in the morning there were two minor episodes : a small reconnaissance party of the enemy, advancing to Wren Alley, was dispersed by bombs, with the loss of one man captured ; and another party moving up Shaft Avenue to its junction with Brown Support was repulsed by a party of bombers who manned a block at this point. The local situation is all that comes within the view of a trench garrison, and this may well have persuaded the men of the forward companies of the FIFTH to believe that all was well ; for to realise the danger which to an ever increasing degree was now threatening the 9th Brigade, it was necessary to

---

    * With regard to the above dispositions, which are taken from the 9th Brigade War Diary :—

    (i) It will be noted that the forward companies of the FIFTH had been reinforced by those in reserve. It has not been possible to determine the exact time at which this was done. Lt.-Colonel Moulton-Barrett states that it was only after continual " haggling " with Brigade H.Q. that he was ultimately permitted to send forward one company from Concrete Reserve. Captain Carrick, on the other hand, records in a note written shortly after the battle that at one time he had under his command the whole of " W " Company (less Company H.Q.) and two platoons of " X " Company, in addition to his own Company, " Y." It seems probable that the 12½ platoons above referred to represented " W," " Y " and " Z " Companies with ½ platoon of " X," the remainder of " X " being in Concrete Reserve.

    (ii) " The Tunnel " mentioned was probably just in rear of the Second System and close to Brigade H.Q. The old Hindenburg Line, which ran south-east through the 2nd System, and continued under the name of Shaft Avenue in the 1st System, was extensively tunnelled, and this gave rise apparently to different positions in the Defensive System being referred to as " The Tunnel," e.g. the tunnel which will later be referred to as having been destroyed prior to withdrawal from the First System was clearly in Shaft Trench and quite different from that mentioned here.

know what was taking place further south. Here, the withdrawal of the 101st Brigade had completely exposed the right flank of the 9th Brigade, which it was clear the enemy would now aim at turning by an attack from the south. To guard against this, the small defensive flank which had already been formed was extended westwards by bringing forward a company of the 13/King's for the occupation of Hind Avenue between Fuldner Lane and Earl's Court.*

At 11.25 a.m. the Germans opened a very heavy barrage on Brown Support. Later, masses of the enemy were observed advancing opposite this position and from the south through Croisilles. At 11.41 the barrage lifted, and the men in Brown Support, seeing three white lights rise from the enemy's lines, prepared to meet attack. None followed, however, for the German advance had once more been disorganised by the fire of our artillery and machine guns; their attacking masses had been shattered, and by 12.30 p.m. all again was quiet on the right. At 12.45 the enemy opened a bombing attack against " Z " Company on the left of the FIFTH, and succeeded in obtaining a footing in the portion of Swift Support to the north of Wren, which had been re-occupied. Their success, however, was short lived, for within five minutes they were driven back and the trench retaken.

During the whole afternoon large bodies of the enemy, observed concentrating near Fontaine Wood and south of Hind Avenue, were made the targets of our artillery, and from 2 p.m. till dusk rifles and machine guns inflicted heavy losses on the Germans in their repeated attempts against Swift and Brown Supports, those directed against the latter position being caught time and again by enfilade fire from First Avenue. But, though no frontal attack against the trenches held by our men could prevail, the danger to the right flank became hourly more critical, and at 4 p.m. two companies of the 20th (Pioneer) Bn. K.R.R.C., representing half of the whole Divisional Reserve, were placed at the disposal of the 9th Brigade for the further strengthening of this flank.

At 5.45 p.m. our artillery was brought to bear on masses of the enemy observed concentrating due south of the 1st System, but, though their losses must have been heavy they did not prevent the Germans from attacking Hind Avenue in very large numbers at 6.20 p.m. and gaining a footing at the points where Fuldner and Fooley Lanes joined this trench. Counter-attack by the King's and Royal Fusiliers, however, drove them from the positions they had gained and once more restored the situation on the right flank. At 6.45 a heavy artillery barrage placed by the enemy on a block at the junction of Brown Support and Tank Trench forced the withdrawal of a party of the FIFTH in occupation of this point. As the barrage lifted the enemy's infantry attacked but were met by rifle fire and failed to reach our trenches. Later, the Germans renewed their attempts to carry Hind Avenue, but were everywhere beaten off; and at 8.15 p.m. the line held by the 9th Brigade twenty-four hours before was still intact.

The enemy, however, had not yet abandoned their efforts. At 9 p.m. they attacked and occupied a block at the junction of Brown Support with Shaft Avenue. Once again they were ejected; but in view of the increasingly critical situation on the right flank, permission was now granted for troops to be withdrawn from Brown Support to Concrete Reserve if serious danger developed, and a little later the Royal Fusiliers, acting on these instructions, fell back. The FIFTH, however, continued

---

* The elements of the 11/Suffolk who still clung to their position had now been absorbed by the 9th Brigade.

22nd Mar., 1918 in occupation of the north-east end of Brown Support till 10.15 p.m., when the Map No. 29. Division ordered the withdrawal of the troops in this position to Concrete Reserve immediately south of First Avenue. On the completion of this movement the front line of the 9th Brigade, starting from Foster's Avenue, ran from left to right along Curtain Support to Wren, thence forward and along Swift Support as far as First Avenue, along which it fell back to continue by Concrete Reserve to the southern end of Fuldner Lane, whence it turned west along Hind Avenue to join the Second System. The FIFTH were in occupation of the left of this line as far as the junction of First Avenue with Concrete Reserve; three companies of the Royal Fusiliers held Concrete Reserve and Fuldner, supported by their fourth company in Grey Street; Hind Avenue was occupied by two companies of the King's and one company of the Pioneer Battalion.

The repeated desperate attacks made by the Germans throughout the 21st and 22nd March had completely failed to break the front of the 9th Brigade, and their efforts to envelop its flank had been defeated by the skilful manner in which the infantry had been handled and the prompt and accurate fire of the supporting artillery and machine guns. The losses of the Germans opposite the 9th Brigade during these two days must indeed have been stupendous, for only the most shattering casualties could have prevented an attack in such vastly superior numbers by so determined an enemy from overwhelming the defence. On the other hand—and here our troops had reaped the reward for their past labours on the defences—the casualties in the 9th Brigade had been surprisingly light. In the FIFTH, who had borne the brunt of the battle throughout, they amounted only to 1 officer slightly wounded and remaining at duty, 14 other ranks killed, 96 wounded, and 15 missing—a total of 126.

Though the men were desperately weary, their spirit was high, and after the experiences of the past two days all were confident that the enemy could not prevail against them. Lieut.-Colonel Moulton-Barrett, however, had long been conscious that things were going badly to the south, though it had not been till 9.30 p.m. that he became fully aware of how serious the situation was. At that time his transport officer, Captain Guy Allgood, had reported at his headquarters and informed him that the pack ponies, which were bringing up the rations, had come under heavy rifle and machine gun fire when still a mile distant from Battalion Headquarters. One driver had been killed, one wounded, and a third was missing; of the ponies, twelve had been killed or wounded, or were missing, and all rations had been lost. Without any direct information from higher authority as to what was transpiring outside his own immediate surroundings, this had been sufficient to give Moulton-Barrett a fairly close appreciation of the danger in which the 9th Brigade stood. He was, however, ignorant of the action which had been taken to meet the situation. As to this, the 2nd and 3rd Guards Brigades had been brought up during the evening to man the 3rd System of Defence, and the VI. Corps had directed the 3rd Division to fall back on this position in conformity with the 34th Division on their right and the 15th on their left.

Even in the most favourable circumstances the time taken for an order emanating from a Corps Headquarters to reach units in the fighting line must be considerable, but on this occasion transmission was rendered the slower by the fact that, forward of Brigade Headquarters, mention of retirement by telephone was forbidden, for fear of interception of the message by the enemy. Battalion Commanders were, therefore, merely informed that the Brigade-Major was bringing forward certain orders in person. From what he had learnt from his transport officer, Moulton-Barrett had no doubt in his mind as to what would be the purport of these orders, and was keenly alive to the urgent necessity of withdrawal. As hour after hour went by without any sign of the arrival of orders, he became increasingly anxious; more than once he reported by telephone that they still had not reached him, and midnight had long passed when once again he received the only reply that Brigade Headquarters would vouchsafe—" The Brigade-Major is now on his way to you." Then, shortly after 1 a.m., Captain Chipper reported that the Royal Scots of the 8th Brigade on the left of " Z " Company had withdrawn, and it became known that the Royal Fusiliers on the right of the FIFTH had also fallen back. The enemy's Very lights were now rising on three sides of the Battalion's position, which, it seemed, would soon be completely surrounded. Desperately, Moulton-Barrett yet again had recourse to the telephone. On this occasion a voice from the other end inquired: " Do you understand Hindustani? " None, perhaps, but those familiar with the limits of Moulton-Barrett's Hindustani vocabulary could appreciate his dilemma, but boldly he replied " Yes " ! Then came the words " Hamāra pichhe jāo ek dam " (Go behind us immediately). The words were perfectly understood and would have been enough for most men. Typically, however, intensely anxious though he was to escape from a perilous position, Moulton-Barrett was going to run no risk of the FIFTH being accused of retiring without orders. " Is that *official*? " he asked. " Yes," and hurry up ! " came the curt reply. *

One learns from the 3rd Division Narrative that, on the orders which had been issued, the withdrawal of 9th Brigade was in general carried out in three stages during the early hours of the 23rd March. The 1st System was evacuated at 1 a.m., the front line of the 2nd System at 2.30 a.m., and its reserve line at 3.30 a.m., withdrawal in each case being covered by outposts and strongly protected by machine-gun fire. Prior to the troops falling back the Shaft Tunnel was blown up in several places.† " Hamāra pichhe jāo—and hurry up ! " the orders on which the FIFTH had acted, did not, however, indicate any delicate co-ordination of their retirement with that of other units, and all unofficial records show that from a " bad start " they made the best of their way back under their own arrangements. During the morning of the 23rd Major-General Deverell came forward personally to thank all the officers for the good work done by the Battalion in the previous day's fighting, and in his written report of the action of the 9th Brigade he says :—" I wish to place on record the skill of all commanders and the splendid steadiness and discipline of the troops in carrying out this operation. All brought back as much ammunition, grenades and entrenching tools as they could carry."

On completion of the withdrawal of the 3rd Division, the 8th Brigade relieved the 3rd Guards Brigade in and to the north of Hénin, and the 76th garrisoned the line on their left. The 3rd Guards then moved to the right of the 2nd Guards Brigade, which was in occupation of the line to the south of Hénin. The 9th Brigade was

---

* Lt.-Colonel Moulton-Barrett, in communicating the substance of what is related above, states that " the voice " proved later to have been that of the Officer Commanding the Field Artillery Brigade in support of the 9th Brigade front. The 3rd Division narrative states that orders were communicated in Hindustani and Arabic, but does not make it clear whether this was from Division or Brigade Headquarters; it makes no mention of the delay in orders reaching the FIFTH. As to time, Lt.-Colonel Moulton-Barrett is of opinion that the FIFTH did not begin to withdraw before 1.30 a.m. Contemporary records by Captain Carrick and Captain Chipper state that " Y " Company began to withdraw about 1 a.m., " Z " not till 2 a.m.

† See Note * (ii) page 210.

23rd/28th Mar., 1918 — withdrawn to Northumberland and Yorkshire Lines in Mercatel, in rear of the 4th System, where the FIFTH "all grimy, bearded, and dead weary, but absolutely unconscious of any suggestion of defeat," found themselves accommodated in the Nissen huts of their former rest billets.*

Map No. 30.

The 23rd March passed fairly quietly on the 3rd Division front. At dawn the enemy bombarded the evacuated 2nd System, and a small, unsuccessful raid was made against the left of the right brigade, but there was no serious attempt to attack the new position. The trenches which represented the 3rd System had been strongly wired, but dug only to a depth of a few inches. It was impossible with the troops available to deepen them through their whole length, and the best that could be done was to make rifle pits at intervals. While the two forward brigades worked away at this, the 9th was employed in improving the 4th System. On the 24th the enemy grew more active, and a vigorous attack was launched against the right of the Division near Hénin. The attack, which was repulsed, was, however, only a local affair, made with the object of securing a ridge to the south of Neuville Vitasse, preliminary to the German main operation which was now in preparation.

On the night of the 24th/25th, in order to strengthen and deepen the defence, the 9th Brigade, which had now been given 48 hours' rest, was inserted between the 8th and 76th. Two battalions were detailed to garrison the 3rd System, the FIFTH for the present remaining in Northumberland Lines in readiness to take up position in the 4th System. Though the 25th passed without incident on the 3rd Division front, an attack was delivered against the Guards Division on their right, who, owing to the situation further south, were withdrawn during the night to the 4th System. This necessitated the right flank of the 3rd Division being thrown back W.S.W. from the west side of Hénin to the Arras-Bapaume road and a consequent re-adjustment of fronts, whereby the 9th (Centre) Brigade was now given 2,300 yards of line to hold, from just north-west of Hénin to a point 1,000 yards north-west of Héninel.† The disposition of battalions remained as before, and, after two more uneventful days. the FIFTH relieved the 4/Royal Fusiliers on the left of the Brigade front just before midnight on the 27th/28th March. On their right the line was held by the 13/King's, on their left by the 8/K.O.R.L. of the 76th Brigade. On the ridge along which the position lay, "W" and "X" Companies, holding the front line, were on the forward slope and out of sight of "Y" and "Z," who, some 500 yards to the rear, occupied the reserve line on the reverse slope. The trenches were still no more than a foot deep, and rifle pits provided the only protection for the men.‡

"At 3 a.m. on the 28th March heavy hostile artillery fire opened against our back areas, and soon after 4 a.m. the enemy put down a heavy barrage all along our Front and Reserve Lines.

---

* (i) The quotation is from "A Rolling Stone on the Western Front," by Captain C. Chipper, privately circulated.

(ii) The battle honour "St. Quentin" was awarded in respect of the fighting on 21st and 22nd March.

† Though in reserve during the 24th and 25th March, the Battalion was in the area designated for the battle honour "Bapaume 1918" awarded for the fighting on those two days.

‡ Captain Carrick having been invalided, "Z" Company were now under the command of Lieutenant A. S. Greener.

Map No. 30. "The story of the Battle which followed is one of desperate fighting—A 28th Mar., 1918 Soldier's Battle—in which the order 'no retirement' was literally carried out as far as the Centre Brigade was concerned." (3rd Division Narrative Report.)

When the bombardment opened on the front line it was at first confined to the trenches of the 76th Infantry Brigade. But, spreading rapidly from left to right of the British line, it was not long before it reached the position of " X " Company of the FIFTH, and almost immediately afterwards crashed on that of " W " Company. The fire of numerous trench mortars was included, and the infantry in the partially dug trenches of the front line could find scant protection from the bombardment, which continued with unabated fury for 1½ hours. Then, at 5.30 a.m., the German infantry, advancing in dense masses, delivered a determined attack. Opposite the 9th Brigade they were driven back with heavy loss by rifle and Lewis gun fire, but they succeeded in penetrating the front of the 76th Brigade, immediately on the left of the FIFTH. The situation of " X " Company was now critical. Its commander, Captain Lawrence, and his second-in-command, Lieutenant Rose, had been killed, and the casualties caused among other ranks by the bombardment had been terribly heavy. The enemy were working round the company's left flank, and the survivors of its shattered platoons, to avoid being surrounded, fell back along a hollow road to the north-east. Gaining the Support Line, Lieutenant Turnbull set about collecting men to strengthen the threatened flank, but before he could achieve his purpose was severely wounded and placed *hors de combat*. In any case however, such measures would have proved of little avail, for the enemy's penetration had by this time deepened, and it now fell to the two young officers who remained, of whom 2nd Lieutenant Burton in particular " set a magnificent example by his energy and determination " * to fight a rear-guard action with the last remnant of " X " Company, to save it from being overwhelmed by numbers. In the meantime " W " Company, though suffering heavily, had managed to hold its own. In the course of the bombardment, however, Lieutenant Allen, the company commander had with others been buried in the débris of the shattered trenches, and though at length extricated was in a pitiful condition, bleeding from the nose and ears and half-conscious. Lieutenant Finch, his second-in-command had then taken charge, and it is recorded by one who was present how this young officer, standing up, careless of his own danger, had observed the enemy massing for attack and called on the men to resist. Already there were few left capable of defending themselves, and many of the rifles and more than one Lewis gun were clogged with earth and useless, yet such fire as it had been possible to maintain had held the enemy in check. The Germans, however, though stopped in their first attack in front of the centre and right of the 3rd Division, had gained ground further to the south, and now by a second attack drove the troops of the 8th Brigade from the front line and swept in masses behind the two forward companies of the King's. The men of these companies were last seen standing on the parapet of their trench engaged in a gallant but hopeless fight. None returned. In the whole front line of the 3rd Division there remained now only " W " Company of the FIFTH isolated and with both flanks turned. Very shortly the company

---

* Statement of services issued by the War Office, 18th July, 1918, with reference to awards conferred by *London Gazette*, 18th February, 1918. (See *St. George's Gazette* of July, 1918.)

28th Mar., 1918 was surrounded, and to its survivors the only alternative to surrender lay in the forlorn hope of being able to cut their way back to the Reserve Line. Lieutenant Finch with 2nd Lieutenant E. Lawrence and a handful of men made the attempt by a sunken road leading back from Company Headquarters but they were immediately caught by machine-gun fire, the gallant Finch was killed, Lawrence fell wounded by his side, and of the whole party Serjeant Lewis of No. 4 Platoon, which had been holding the right of the company front, alone escaped. Now, where numbers in defence are being constantly and rapidly diminished, automatic weapons—so long as they remain in action—are invaluable. In this respect 2nd-Lieutenant Joss, whose No. 1 Platoon held the left of the company's line, was favoured by possessing two Lewis guns as against one only allotted to each of the other platoons. Although of his 36 men there were now only 9 survivors, this small party, with the help of their Lewis guns, managed for a time to hold their own, till first one gun, and shortly afterwards the other, ceased to work. Realising that further resistance was hopeless, Joss, supported by "a very gallant corporal," * now instructed his men to rush back individually from one shell-hole to another, hurling Mills' bombs as they went, to clear the way and keep the enemy at a distance. Slender as were the chances of the ten who set out on this desperate venture, the corporal and three men, together with Joss himself, eventually reached safety under cover of the machine-guns of the Reserve Line and passed unscathed through the rear companies of the Battalion. In addition to those already mentioned, only four others of " W " Company—making a total of 1 officer and 9 other ranks in all—escaped death or capture. Of those who fell into the hands of the Germans there were few who had not been wounded and rendered helpless.†

Map No. 30.

Immediately on the opening of the bombardment all forward telephone communication had been cut by shell fire, and while the events which have been narrated above were in progress Battalion Headquarters and the companies in the Reserve Line could only guess at what was happening beyond the crest. They concluded that the front line had been subjected to a bombardment no less severe than that from which they themselves had suffered, but for a while remained in ignorance of the full extent of the storm that had broken over their forward companies. At length Captain Chipper, growing anxious as to what was occurring in the front line, instructed Sergeant Mantle, in whose cool courage and resource he had great faith, to take forward a section of men to reconnoitre the situation. It was, perhaps, a quarter of an hour later that Mantle returned with the alarming news that the Germans had

---

* Captain W. T. B. Joss, M.C., M.B. (R.A.M.C., T.A.), to whom the writer is indebted for the details of this incident, has expressed his regret at not being able to recall the name of this corporal. He states that the N.C.O. referred to was promoted serjeant very shortly afterwards and was wounded in the following April.

† In a letter addressed in 1920 by 2nd-Lieutenant H. P. Mullen (now deceased) to Major E. G. Finch, describing the circumstances in which his son, Lieutenant P. Finch, met his death, the number of men left capable of action when the end came is put at " some 20 odd all told." These, it seems, were men of Nos. 1, 2 and 3 Platoons, who had closed to the right and taken up a position near Company H.Q. The total given would not have included the remnant of No. 4 Platoon under 2nd-Lieutenant Joss.

Lieutenant Finch, through his mother, was a grandson of Major J. W. D. Adair, who joined the FIFTH in 1846 and was noted for gallantry in the Indian Mutiny. The record of Major Adair's service will be found on page 482 of H. M. Walker's " History of the Northumberland Fusiliers." (John Murray.)

overrun the front line and were following hard at his heels. Scarcely had this report been received than the artillery barrage lifted from the Reserve Line, and the enemy's infantry were seen advancing in swarms over the crest of the ridge, soon to be sent to ground by rifle and Lewis gun fire.

The first attack on the Reserve Line of the 9th Brigade is recorded in the 3rd Division Narrative as having been delivered at 8.40 a.m. Rumour arose that the enemy had penetrated the right of the Brigade, and a company of the 4/Royal Fusiliers was sent forward to reinforce the 13/King's. In fact, the attack had been everywhere repulsed on the front of the Brigade. The situation on the left of the Division, however, soon became serious. The troops who flanked the Division to the north, after having their trenches demolished by shell fire, had been forced to withdraw, and the 76th Brigade, with their left flank thus endangered, had to conform. At 9.30 a.m. their right was still holding the Reserve Line on the left of "Z" Company of the FIFTH, but later the whole brigade was withdrawn a distance varying between 700 and 1,500 yards to a switch line. 2nd-Lieutenant R. Brown of "Z" Company, wounded in the head and with blood streaming down his face, was the first to acquaint Captain Chipper of the danger which now threatened his company, round the rear of which, it was said, the enemy were attempting to work. Chipper promptly ordered his left (Brown's) platoon, which now came under the command of Serjeant Mantle, to withdraw to a communication trench facing north and form a defensive flank. Mantle, handling the platoon with great skill, disposed it in the position indicated just in time to repulse a determined attack.

The Battalion Headquarters of the FIFTH and the King's were situated alongside in the Reserve Line in the centre of the Brigade front. They were in communication with Brigade Headquarters by visual signalling, and by now the whole of their personnel was manning the defences. Shortly after the repulse of the attack on the left flank, the German artillery, in response to three green lights fired by their infantry, once again opened on the Reserve Line. The S.O.S. signal was sent up, and our guns immediately brought down a barrage across a sunken road in front of battalion headquarters. After fifteen minutes fire the enemy's artillery lifted and his infantry advanced to the attack. Again they were everywhere beaten off with heavy losses, suffering in particular from the fire brought by the two battalion headquarters, of which those of the FIFTH had already sustained many casualties, including two officers who could ill be spared—Captain Partington, the Intelligence Officer, and 2nd Lieutenant Colton, M.C., the Bombing Officer—both killed, one after the other, when running forward to report to their Commanding Officer. Twice again the Germans renewed their attack—each time after three green lights had brought a fresh artillery barrage to precede the infantry assault—but they failed to break the front of the 9th Brigade. Then, at mid-day, a fourth attack, delivered further to the right, forced the 8th Brigade to withdraw some 600 yards, half way to the Arras-Bapaume road. Shortly afterwards a party of some forty Germans, who had worked round the now open flank of the King's to within 200 yards of the battalion's headquarters, opened fire from the rear. Lieut.-Colonel Lawrence of the King's was fortunately at this time with Lieut.-Colonel Moulton-Barrett, and the two commanding officers rapidly formed a plan to deal with this most critical situation. It was obviously urgent that the right of the King's should be thrown back to form a defensive flank, and it was arranged that Moulton-Barrett should engage the German riflemen while Lawrence made the necessary dispositions. The fire brought by the men of the FIFTH quickly subdued that of the German intruders, who were ultimately completely wiped out, but not

28th Mar., 1918 before Lieut.-Colonel Moulton-Barrett, on turning to deal with a fresh attack from the front, had his right arm shattered and an artery severed by a bullet. Command now fell to Major Buckle, with whom, of all the officers of Battalion Headquarters, there remained only the Adjutant, Captain Ellison, whose coolness was never more marked, or more needed, than throughout this critical day.

Map No. 30.

In the meantime the right company of the King's having been successfully drawn back, the position of the 9th Brigade was for the time secure, but, with the left platoon of the FIFTH already disposed in like manner on the northern flank, the Brigade was now fighting on three sides of a square. The headquarters of the Battalion were about one thousand yards distant from those of "Z" Company, and the curve of the ground made visual communication between them impossible. A runner, however, now succeeded in reaching Captain Chipper with a message informing him of what had occurred on the right. The situation on the left is best recounted in his own words : " On the left we could see up the valley for a couple of miles, and it was full of movement. Near by, the hillside teemed with field-grey figures in coal-scuttle helmets dodging from shell-hole to shell-hole as they closed in on our flank. Our riflemen and Lewis gunners were kept busy snap shooting at these moving targets of short exposure. Further away through my field glass I could see at first waves and then columns of infantry advancing down the valley apparently unopposed. At the time we did not know that the Division on our left had withdrawn to the 4th System, and it was to me unaccountable and certainly not encouraging.* Presently, as the enemy closed in, standing up had to be sparingly indulged in. The least exposure was greeted by rifle shots from three sides at point blank range, and the deafening crack of the bullet as it passed close to one's ear from behind showed that it would not do to take chances."

In the meantime a company of the 4/Royal Fusiliers had been sent forward to reinforce the FIFTH and word was sent to Chipper that two of its platoons were being sent to his assistance. The left of "Z" company, however, was now practically surrounded, and it seemed they must be overwhelmed before the arrival of this help. The enemy were attacking both by bombing down the trench and by charging over the the top, but the men of the FIFTH remained steady and took a heavy toll of the attackers. One one occasion, it is related, some twenty Germans seemed suddenly to rise from the ground at a distance of under thirty yards and make a wild rush forward ; a Lewis gunner opened fire and before they had advanced ten yards, every man was down. " The exultant cheer they had raised died away in a fashion really pitiful." To obtain a better field of fire for his Lewis Guns, Chipper now decided to withdraw his defensive flank some forty yards to a position in which he had already instructed the remains of a Vicker's gun detachment to establish themselves. 2nd Lieutenant Simpson, standing close to his company commander, was now shot through the chest and was breathing his last, when news came that 2nd Lieutenant Richards had also been mortally wounded. At last the reinforcing platoons of the Royal Fusiliers arrived, but the subaltern in command, running forward to report to Captain Chipper, was immediately shot through the head from close range. Until this poor lad could be led away, for he was still capable of walking, the terrible nature of his wound added for the men close at hand a crowning horror to the nightmare scene through which they were passing. For a time the Germans remained inactive and made no attempt against the new position

---

* Actually the troops on the left of " Z " Company belonged, not to another Division, but to the 76th Brigade of the 3rd Division.

that had been taken up. But now trouble came from a fresh and unexpected quarter. The reserve battalion of a flank brigade some 500 yards to the rear, in front of Neuville Vitasse, believing that all in advance of them must be Germans, opened fire on the sorely afflicted " Z " company. Signals failed to stop this, and a volunteer to run back to them was called for. Immediately a gallant fellow sprang up and set out at his best speed towards the firers, dodging from shell-hole to shell-hole, and waving as he went. Spurts of dust all round him showed that he was under fire from both friend and foe, yet miraculously he got through untouched to achieve his mission.*

It seemed that it could only be a matter of time before the Germans got round the small defensive flank of " Z " Company to attack the 9th Brigade in rear, and it now occurred to Captain Chipper that, if he could swing his whole company back to face east along a sunken road which led into Neuville Vitasse from St. Martin, and gain touch in front of the former village with the British troops who had recently brought him under fire, he would be in a good position for defence and the whole flank would be secured. To accomplish this change in dispositions meant trickling the men by groups down a trench, of which a portion was so shallow that protection could only be obtained by crawling on the stomach. It was a slow process, rendered the more unpleasant by a German machine gun firing in enfilade on the trench. One of several hit at this period was Serjeant Mantle, whose services on this day and in the raid at Arras in March, 1917, have been recorded on previous pages. He was shot between the shoulders, but, fortunately, though seriously wounded, could still crawl down the trench and was later safely evacuated. At length the new position was reached and proved excellent in every respect. Not only did it constitute a shorter line, which, with the added platoons of the Royal Fusiliers, could be strongly occupied, but control was rendered easy by the cover afforded by the sunken road to within fifty yards of the troops on the eastern outskirts of Neuville Vitasse. The field artillery maintained a steady protective barrage in front of this position, which the enemy, as worn out as those who held it, made no attempt to attack.

The action of the enemy had not been confined to efforts to envelop the flanks. While the events described above had been occurring, repeated attacks had been made against the centre of the Brigade, where the two battalion headquarters with " Y " Company of the FIFTH and the left company of the King's stood at bay on a total front of not more than 600 yards. Every attack, however, was repulsed, though not without heavy loss to the defenders.

> " At 5 p.m. the FIFTH and the King's with flanks thrown back still faced the enemy in the 3rd System."
> (3rd Division Narrative Report).

The troops had now been fighting continuously since dawn, darkness was approaching, rain had begun to fall, and orders were issued by Major-General Deverell for the 9th Brigade to be withdrawn after dark behind the 4th System, which, after

---

* This incident is related in " A Rolling Stone on the Western Front," to which reference has already been made. After an interval of nearly twenty years Major Chipper is unfortunately unable to recall the name of the man who performed this great service. He was awarded the Military Medal in recognition of his gallantry.

THE FIFTH IN THE GREAT WAR. 211

28th Mar., 1918   units had re-organised and re-formed, they were to be prepared to man. The with-   Map No. 30.
drawal of the FIFTH, beginning with "Y" company on the right, was made by a
trench leading back to Neuville Vitasse. It was not yet so dark that the enemy did
not detect the movement and press forward to harass the retirement. The
rear detachments of "Z" company were brought under the fire of a machine gun,
and had to move at their best speed; but, thanks, to the failing light and the rain that
was now falling, the gun was unable to range on them with sufficient accuracy to do
any material damage, and they passed through the defences of the 4th System to join
the remainder of what was left of the 1/FIFTH at the Battalion's rendezvous just west
of Neuville Vitasse. It was pitch dark and raining hard when Major Buckle summoned
Captain Chipper and Lieutenant Greener to Battalion H.Q. where, "in a dug-out
about six feet square and five feet high," they assembled with the officers of the Headquarters of the 13/King's and, each with a mug of whiskey and water miraculously
produced by someone, discussed the events of the day and took stock of the situation.
No man, perhaps, realises all that life means to him until, like these, he has for long
hours been faced with death, and it would be natural to suppose that there cannot
have been one of them who was not filled with thankfulness for being still alive. But
above such personal considerations there must have come to them, when reflecting
on all that they had passed through, a sense of great pride in their men and of
gratitude for their devotion. One may believe, too, that a point on which all were
agreed at this dug-out conference was the one made by the Divisional Commander
later in his official report that "again the artillery had been most skilfully handled
and their support throughout the day was the admiration of the infantry." It is
probable, however, that these survivors were as yet unconscious of the magnitude of
their achievement, though, now that the roll had been called, they cannot have failed
to grieve for their losses. The FIFTH had done all that had been asked of them, and
knew that the enemy had been made to pay dearly for what he had gained, but it had
cost them the following casualties :—

OFFICERS.

Killed	..	Captain E. Lawrence, M.C., D.C.M.
		Captain L. Partington.
		Lieutenant S. A. Rose.
		Lieutenant P. G. Finch, M.C.
		2nd-Lieutenant S. E. Colton, M.C.
		2nd-Lieutenant J. J. Simpson.
Wounded	..	Lieut.-Colonel E. M. Moulton-Barrett, D.S.O.
		Lieutenant S. A. Turnbull.
		2nd-Lieutenant R. Brown.
Prisoners of War	..	Captain W. R. Allen (wounded).
		2nd-Lieutenant E. I. Lawrence (wounded).
		2nd-Lieutenant H. P. Mullen.
		2nd-Lieutenant J. C. Thompson.
		2nd-Lieutenant J. Richards (died of wounds in German hands).

OTHER RANKS.

Killed 29.   Wounded 107.   Missing 149.*

---

* "Arras 1918" is the honour held by the Regiment for the fighting on 28th March.

The trials of the Battalion, however, were not yet over. A telephone message from Brigade Headquarters announced that touch with the neighbouring troops about Neuville Vitasse had been lost, and that it was believed that some of the enemy had got through. " Z " Company was ordered to take up a position facing Neuville Vitasse and endeavour to clear up the situation. There followed what Captain Chipper describes as the most miserable night of his life. The exhausted men were collected from a tumbledown trench in which they were crouching to get what shelter they could from the pouring rain, and the company after being formed into groups, was spread out to face the village, with the men in shell-holes or small hollows, where they could huddle together for warmth and companionship and yet be in a position for defence. Patrols, for the most part, got lost in the inky darkness and wandered round in circles ; and those that searched the village and the ground in front of it could find no sign of either friend or foe. Actually, it seems, there was no foundation for the rumour of a penetration by the enemy, who in truth were utterly exhausted. During the night many of our wounded made their way through the German troops without interference, and, in the opinion of the Divisional Commander, the punishment which the enemy had received had so disorganised them, that had fresh troops been available for counter-attack it would have been certain of success.

By dawn the weather had cleared, and the morning of the 29th was bright and sunny. Though there was no attempt by the enemy to renew the attack, shelling continued, and the FIFTH suffered some further casualties. Then, at last, in the afternoon came the welcome news that the 3rd Division was to be relieved by Canadian troops. On the arrival of their relief after dark, the FIFTH moved back to Monchiet, where by 1 a.m. on 30th March the Officers, having seen their men accommodated in huts and served with a hot meal, were themselves sitting down to a sumptuous repast of eggs and bacon.

Those who have read the earlier chapters of this history will doubtless have seen in the fighting in which the 1/FIFTH were engaged from the 21st to the 29th March, 1918, a reproduction on a larger scale of the part played by a detachment of the 2/FIFTH at the Battle of St. Julien, for the situation in which " Moulton-Barrett's Detachment " made its stubborn stand to the east of Ypres had much resembling that in which Lieut.-Colonel Moulton-Barrett's battalion had faced and held the German attack to the south of Arras in these later days. As on the former, so on the latter occasion, the character and inspiration of the commander had been in no small degree responsible for what had been achieved, as may be learnt from the official statement of the services of Lieut.-Colonel Moulton-Barrett in the battle which has been described in this chapter :—

> " Throughout two day's fighting his courage and resource were an example to all. On receipt of orders he cleverly withdrew his battalion from close contact with the enemy without a casualty. Some days after, he was wounded while holding his headquarters in the support-line against heavy hostile attacks, using a rifle himself."

RUINS OF NEUVILLE VITASSE.

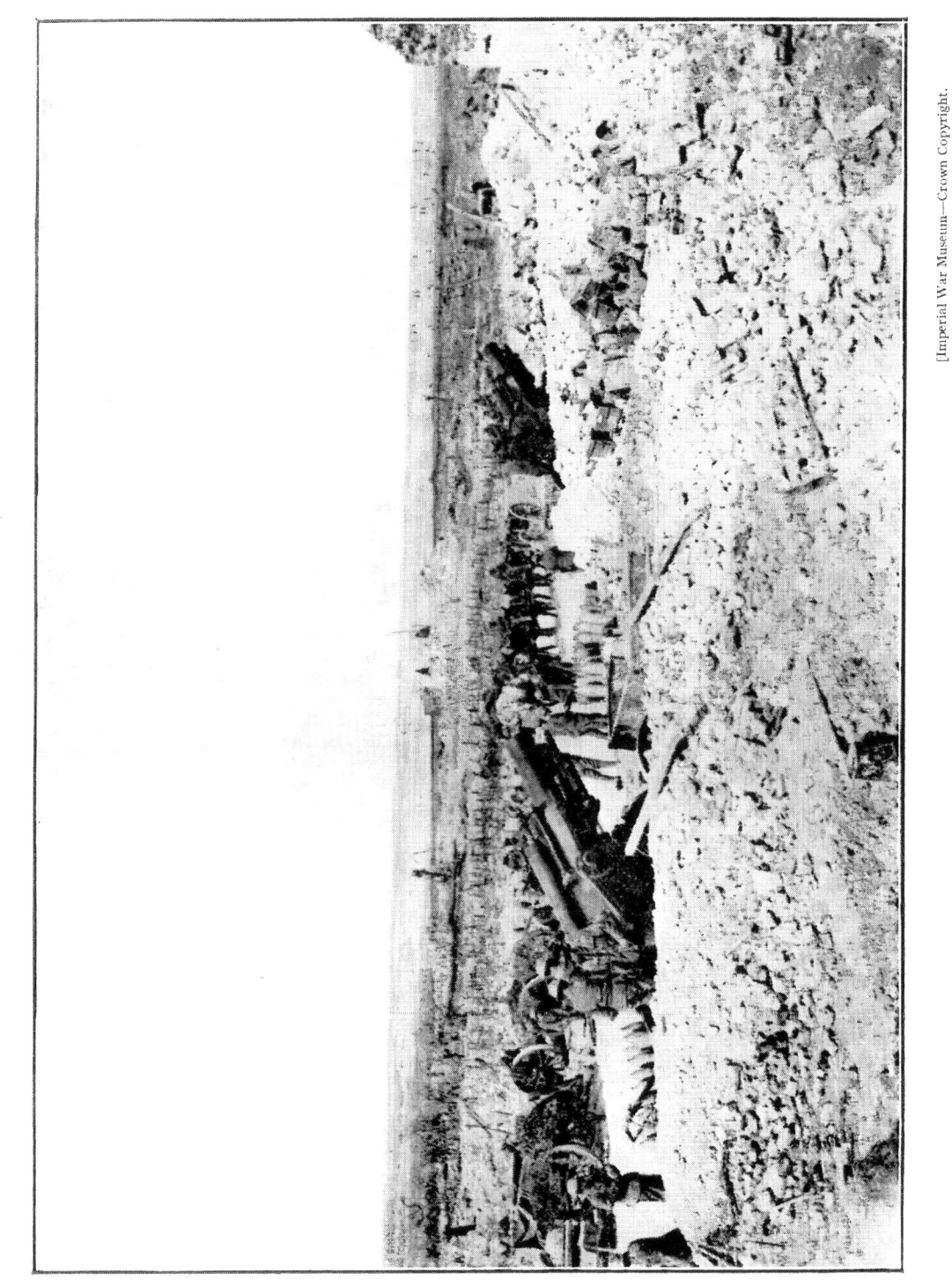

(Taken during the British offensive, April, 1917.)

[Imperial War Museum—Crown Copyright.

NOTE A.—So far as can be ascertained, the following officers were present with the 1st Battalion during the period 21st–28th March :—

HEADQUARTERS.

Lieut.-Colonel E. M. Moulton-Barrett, D.S.O., commanding.
Major D. F. de C. Buckle, Second-in-command.
Captain T. F. Ellison, Adjutant.
Captain L. Partington, Intelligence Officer.
2nd-Lieutenant S. E. Colton, M.C., Bombing Officer.

"W" COMPANY.

Captain W. R. Allen (Commanding).
Lieutenant P. G. Finch, M.C.
2nd-Lieutenant W. T. B. Joss, M.C.
2nd-Lieutenant E. I. Lawrence.
2nd-Lieutenant H. P. Mullen.
2nd-Lieutenant J. C. Thompson.

"X" COMPANY.

Captain E. Lawrence (Commanding).
Lieutenant S. A. Turnbull.
Lieutenant S. A. Rose.
Lieutenant D. S. Rowe.
2nd-Lieutenant W. O. Burton.

"Y" COMPANY.

*Captain C. B. Carrick, M.C.
*Lieutenant A. S. Greener
2nd-Lieutenant W. Blenkinsop.
2nd-Lieutenant J. B. Casse.
2nd-Lieutenant A. W. Davidson.
2nd-Lieutenant R. Hastie.
2nd-Lieutenant D. H. Yatman.

"Z" COMPANY.

Captain C. Chipper (Commanding).
2nd-Lieutenant R. Brown.
2nd-Lieutenant P. S. Cull.
2nd-Lieutenant C. Grant-Ross.
2nd-Lieutenant J. Richards.
2nd-Lieutenant J. J. Simpson.

* Greener replaced Carrick in command of "Y" Company on the 24th March, when the latter was admitted to hospital.

NOTE B.—The following awards were made to officers and other ranks of the Battalion in recognition of their services during the same period :—

Bar to Distinguished Service Order.

Lieut.-Colonel E. M. Moulton-Barrett, D.S.O.

Bar to Military Cross.

Captain C. B. Carrick, M.C.
2nd-Lieutenant W. T. B. Joss, M.C.

Military Cross.

Captain C. Chipper.
Captain T. F. Ellison.
Lieutenant A. S. Greener.
2nd-Lieutenant W. O. Burton.

A bar to the Military Medal was granted to two other ranks, and the Military Medal to 42 other ranks.

In the *St. George's Gazette* of July, 1918, will be found the statement of services for which the awards were made to the officers. In the same number a list of 46 other ranks is given, which undoubtedly includes the names of the 44 mentioned above. Since, however, the War Diary refers only to the number of awards made, without giving the names of the recipients, this is a matter of conjecture.

CHAPTER XV.

The Battle of the Lys.

" Lys " — " Estaires " — " Bethune."

FIRST BATTALION—1ST APRIL TO 8TH AUGUST, 1918.

Map No. 31

1st April, 1918

It is indisputable that in the fighting on the Western Front the weather, which may prove such a valuable ally in war, generally favoured the Germans. Rain, as we have seen, interfered with the concluding phase of the Somme offensive of 1916; and in the following year it had affected even more seriously the attacks at Paschendaele at the close of the Third Battle of Ypres. Now, when rain would have been welcomed by the Commander-in-Chief, an abnormally dry Spring had come to upset his calculations. As early as the 21st March it had been reported that the Germans were making preparations to the north of the La Bassée Canal which seemed to point to their intention of opening an offensive in the valley of the Lys; but it had been reckoned that in that low-lying area of dyke-drained land no large scale operations would be possible till well on in the year. As it proved, this northern front by the end of the year was rapidly drying, and it had become urgent that such precautionary measures against attack as were possible should at once be adopted.

The problem was no easy one. Although by the 5th April the great German offensive on the Somme front, against which 46 out of Sir Douglas Haig's 58 divisions had been engaged, had exhausted itself, the possibility of its being renewed still remained; nor could the British centre about Vimy be safely weakened. In the circumstances, it was decided that the best that could be done was to reinforce the First Army on the northern front with certain divisions, including the 3rd, which, after the recent fighting, had been withdrawn to rest and re-organise, and to arrange for the relief by the 10th April of the Portuguese divisions of the First Army, which for a considerable period had been in occupation of a central sector in the Lys valley and would, it was thought, benefit by a few weeks' rest.

It was thus that the 1/FIFTH, on withdrawal to Ivergny after their desperate and successful resistance to the German attack to the south of Arras, had had but two nights' rest, when on the 1st April they were moved north with the 3rd Division to the Bruay area, in reinforcement of the First Army. Here the Battalion, which was billeted first in Houdain and later at Ourton, spent the next few days in re-organising and re-equipping its greatly reduced companies. At the beginning of March the strength of the 1/FIFTH had, fortunately, totalled no less than 49 officers and 1,020 other ranks. But although all of these had not been engaged in the recent fighting, the total had now, through battle casualties and sickness, been reduced to 34 officers and 634 other ranks. Drafts on the 3rd and 4th April, totalling 430 men, numerically more than made up for the Battalion's losses in Other Ranks. They were composed, however, almost entirely of young soldiers who had as yet seen no fighting, and included no officers. Over a week was to pass before the Battalion was to receive officer reinforcements; and during the most critical period of the battle

6th/10th April, 1918 — in which the FIFTH were shortly to be engaged, the responsibility of command was to remain with Major Buckle.

Map No. 31

In his despatches Sir Douglas Haig states that the divisions sent north from the Somme were moved behind the Lys front. In the first instance, as has been seen, this was not altogether the case. It seems, in fact, that an attack on the Hulluch-Loos front was regarded as scarcely less probable than one to the north of the La Bassée Canal. It was for this reason that the 3rd Division had been placed in reserve to the I. Corps, which held this portion of the line; and that the FIFTH, having completed their re-organisation, were moved forward on the 6th April to Hersin for work on the rear defences known as the I. Corps Defence Line. The Battalion was employed on this work during the 7th and 8th, which passed uneventfully. On the 9th, while two companies continued the strengthening of the defences, another was firing on the range, and the fourth enjoying the all too rare luxury of baths, when, at 12.30 p.m., orders were suddenly received for the Battalion to "stand to." As no further orders were received, however, during the afternoon, all were persuaded by the evening that they were to be allowed at least one more night's rest. The manner in which they were disillusioned as to this may be learnt from the sad tale of an interrupted dinner party, which the officers of "Y" Company had declined to cancel on mere "rumours of war." We are indebted to a guest for an account of how the "really civilised dinner" to which he had been invited, after justifying his hosts by its first two courses, came to an abrupt end. "At 7.45 p.m.," he tells, "we had consumed soup (cube) and fish-cake (tinned salmon), when orders came for the Battalion to fall in at once . . . we were to embuss at Noeux-les-Mines."

To see how it had come about that the FIFTH's programme of bathing and training has thus been interrupted, and "Y" Company's dinner party wrecked, it is necessary to turn to events which had occurred on the 9th April in the Lys valley; and in particular to study how these had affected the 55th Division, which was holding a sector immediately to the north of the La Bassée Canal on the right of the Portuguese. The relief of the latter, which, it will be remembered, was to be completed by the 10th April, had barely begun when the Germans, at 4.15 a.m., opened a terrific bombardment on a front of over ten miles from the La Bassée Canal to the Bois Grenier, 2½ miles south of Armentières. This was followed by a determined attack against the centre, which drove the Portuguese from their trenches, entirely disorganised their defence, and, creating a huge gap in the front of the XI. Corps, left the 55th and 40th Divisions, on the right and left of it, with their flanks completely exposed. The 55th Division, with its right on the Canal to the north of Cuinchy, was holding the line with two brigades, the 164th and 165th, and had its third, the 166th, in reserve in the Locon area. Space cannot be found here to describe in detail the gallant and stubborn resistance put up by the troops of the 55th Division throughout the 9th April. At the close of the day, of its two forward brigades, each reinforced by a battalion from the Divisional Reserve, the 164th still held the whole of its original front line; and the 165th, slightly withdrawn, was in occupation of the *Line of Resistance*, which covered the villages of Le Plantin and Festubert and had in addition thrown back a defensive flank at right angles for a distance of 2,000 yards from Cailloux Keep to Loisne Central Keep. Thence the line was continued by the 166th Brigade (less two battalions) to the Lawe Canal north-east of Locon, where they gained touch with troops of the 51st Division, which, together with the 50th further to the north, had been hurriedly thrust forward to close as best they could the breach that had occurred in the XI. Corps front through the collapse of the Portuguese.*

<small>Map No. 31</small>

<small>10th April, 1918</small>

The situation resembled that in which, to check the encroachment of a flood, there has been thrown up a loosely constructed dam, which it is necessary to consolidate throughout, concentrating firstly on the weakest points or on those where pressure is greatest. It was thus that the 9th Brigade had been detached from the 3rd and placed at the disposal of the 55th Division, and that orders had come to the FIFTH to embuss at Noeux-les-Mines. The Battalion was the last unit of the Brigade to move; and when, just before daybreak on the 10th April, its companies passed through Béthune to debuss outside the town, the 4/Royal Fusiliers and the 13/King's had already been despatched to reinforce the 164th and 165th Brigades respectively. In the lovely dawn of a perfect Spring day, the country—green and blooming—presented a striking contrast to the mining district which the Battalion had just left. It could, indeed, have been termed "peaceful," but for the shells which were seen bursting from time to time in Béthune and on the roads leading forward to the British positions. The town, however, had long since been within the range of the enemy's guns, and its bombardment did not necessarily suggest any change in the situation. But evidence of a deep penetration by the enemy was soon given by the sight of a sad procession of old men, women and children, struggling back with such of their worldly goods as they had been able to save from their abandoned homes.

In the haste with which the Battalion had been moved, lorries as they became available had been immediately filled and despatched, without any very definite instructions as to rendezvous. As a result, on debussing it was some time before all companies could get in touch with Battalion H.Q. At length, however, they received orders to concentrate at Essars, where the FIFTH were to be held with 9th Brigade H.Q. in reserve to the 55th Division.

At 7.40 a.m. the Germans resumed their operations by delivering a heavy attack against Loisne Central Keep and Le Touret,† and at 9.55 a.m. the FIFTH received orders to move forward to Croix de Fer in support of the 166th Brigade. Actually, however, though the news had not yet reached them, the attack had been beaten off by 9.30. Consequently, on arrival at Croix de Fer, the Battalion was instructed to stand fast there, in readiness to move forward to Le Hamel or Loisne, as circumstances might demand. A further heavy attack against Le Touret was repulsed, but the position of the left battalion of the 166th Brigade had by now become so precarious that the line they held was later withdrawn some 200 yards. At 3.30 p.m. the FIFTH came definitely under the orders of the 166th Brigade and were ordered forward in support of the 1/5th King's Own, who were holding out in a line of shell holes 1000 yards to the north-east of Le Hamel. At 7 p.m. a determined attack on Loisne Central at first gained some success, but ultimately the Germans were once again driven back, leaving a number of prisoners and a machine-gun in our hands.

Although at nightfall the situation of the 166th Brigade had greatly improved,

---

* The 1/4th Seaforth Highlanders, to whom reference will later be made, was at this time placed at the disposal of the 166th Brigade by the 51st Division.

† This attack is so described in the report of the 55th Division. By the situation maps, which illustrate the report, it seems, however, that both here and later "Le Touret" refers to the Keep of that name, and not to the village.

REFUGEES.

". . a sad procession of old men, women and children. . ."

[Imperial War Museum—Crown Copyright.

11th/12th April, 1918

the danger of the enemy collecting an overwhelming force to batter their way down the Rue de Bois, and on to Le Hamel, Essars, and Béthune, was still present. To resist this possibility fresh troops were necessary, and amongst the reliefs that were ordered to meet it, " X " Company of the FIFTH at 10 p.m. replaced two exhausted and depleted companies of the 1/5th King's Own on a line running roughly north-west from Loisne West Keep to the Rue de Bois. " Y " Company took up a position in immediate support; and " W " and " Z," further to the rear, occupied a wired line between the Rue de Bois and the Lawe Canal to the north-west of Le Hamel, where Battalion H.Q. were now situated. By dawn on the 11th April the whole front of the 166th Brigade was held by fresh troops, the 1/4th Seaforth being on the left of " X " Company, and the 1/4th South Lancashire on the left again between the Seaforth and the Lawe Canal.

Map No. 31

At 11 a.m., after a very heavy bombardment, the enemy attacked the whole front of the 166th Brigade, from Loisne West to the Lawe Canal, forcing the centre and left back to a line Mesplaux-Le Casan. Later, the situation was partially restored; but a gap of some 500 yards had developed between the inner flanks of the Seaforth and South Lancashire about midway between the Rue de Bois and Mesplaux, and " Y " Company of the FIFTH was ordered forward to attack from Les Façons and fill this gap. Though the operation was most skilfully carried out, with the loss of hardly a man, the company suffered severely from machine-gun fire after occupying the position, Lieutenant D. H. Yatman being killed, and 2nd-Lieutenants Hastie and Casse wounded. Writing of this small operation, in which a company of the Pioneers, under command of the Brigade-Major, had co-operated, the Brigadier states: " The net result was that a very dangerous gap in our line was filled at a critical moment by these troops."

At 6 p.m. orders were issued for " Z " Company to move up on the left of " Y " to strengthen the line on that flank, which the greatly reduced numbers of the South Lancashire by themselves were too weak to hold, and for " W " to relieve the Seaforth Company which till now had been holding the line between " Y " and " X." In the face of many difficulties these dispositions were made during the night; and dawn of the 12th April found all four companies of the FIFTH in position side by side, with all their platoons in the front line, with the exception of one of " W," which was held in immediate support. There was practically no cover for the troops on taking over the line, but by strenuous work they had secured for themselves by daybreak a trench 2 feet deep by 2 feet wide, which gave them some slight protection.* An amusing, if not very heroic, episode occurred on the front of " Z " Company while they were employed in this work. An enemy scout, who blundered noisily into their line, on being seized and conducted to Company H.Q., was found to be a lad of 18, dripping wet, and shivering with cold and fright. The only information that could be got out of him was an explanation of his indifferent scout-craft. This he attributed to having fortified himself before setting out on patrol, with a bottle of

---

* Captain Chipper, in referring to the relief carried out by " Z " Company, writes : " To show how the troops we were relieving had indeed fought to the last man, I may mention that I found the line held by a mixture of sappers, infantry, and even oddments of an entrenching battalion. The " line " was simply a succession of men of mixed units strung out at wide intervals, who had scratched themselves into the ground with their entrenching tools under heavy rifle and machine-gun fire." (For later generations it may be explained that the " entrenching tool " was a small implement carried by the infantryman as part of his equipment).

Map No. 31   *vin rouge*, with the not unnatural result that he had pitched head first into the first ditch that crossed his path !

On the 12th, Lieut.-Colonel Herbert returned to resume the battalion command, which he had so recently handed over after holding it for over twelve months. The day passed quietly for the FIFTH, and is summed up in the War Diary by the brief entry : " No change in the situation." On the left of the 166th Brigade, however, an attack by the enemy, following the usual heavy bombardment, penetrated the line between Mesplaux Farm and the Lawe Canal. The ground gained here by the Germans was later recovered, but their thrust to the westward was still progressing, and the British troops on the left flank of the Brigade were slowly forced back to the line Le Casan-Locon. At 11.30 p.m. a renewed bombardment by the German artillery was followed by yet another attack against the left of the 166th Brigade, but once again the enemy was driven back, leaving a few prisoners in our hands and several dead in the vicinity of Mesplaux Farm.

On the 13th, shelling of Mesplaux Farm, which began at dawn, developed at 3.30 p.m. into a heavy bombardment of the whole front of the 166th Brigade, by both light and heavy artillery. At 4.30 p.m. Brigade Headquarters, from which the whole Front, Support, and Reserve Lines could be seen enveloped in the smoke of bursting shells, itself became included in the bombardment, and an infantry attack seemed certain. But if this had been the enemy's intention, it was not carried out, and at 5 p.m. the shelling died down. Our infantry, who had stood fast in their trenches throughout this fierce bombardment, had, however, suffered severely. In the FIFTH, 2nd-Lieutenant P. S. Cull, of " Z " Company, had been killed and Captain A. Rochell, the commander of " W " Company, mortally wounded, and the losses sustained by " Y " Company made it necessary to reinforce it now with the platoon of " W " Company which had hitherto been held in support.

The scattered units of the 9th Brigade were now gradually to be brought together again. On the night of the 13/14th, the Seaforth in support were relieved by the 4/Royal Fusiliers, and two platoons of this battalion were placed at the disposal of the FIFTH and moved up in rear of " W " Company. On the following night the 55th Division was withdrawn, its right (164 and 165) Brigades being relieved by the 1st Division, and the 166th by the 9th Brigade. In this relief the FIFTH stood fast on the line which they had taken over on the 11th and since held intact.*

A slight alteration in the dispositions of the FIFTH was now made. The Royal Fusiliers, coming up on the left, replaced the two companies on that flank, which were withdrawn to a support position, leaving two companies on either side of the Rue de Bois, of which that on the right was required to extend its front slightly to the south. The 15th and 16th passed quietly, and orders were issued for the relief of the FIFTH by the 13/King's on the following night. Later, however, on news being received that the whole 9th Brigade was to be withdrawn on the night of the 18th/19th, it was decided that the Battalion should remain a further 24 hours in the line. This alteration, as it proved, was to cost the FIFTH dearly. At dawn

---

* During their period of attachment to the 55th Division, the Fifth and other battalions of the 9th Brigade had earned the highest praise from the Divisional Commander and the G.O.C. I Corps. The casualties of the 55th Division between the 9th and 15th April amounted to 163 officers and 2956 other ranks. No less than 14 guns of the Divisional Artillery were put out of action by shell fire during the same period. On the other hand, the Division captured 900 prisoners and 70 machine-guns in the course of their stubborn and gallant defence.

18th April, 1918

on the 18th, the enemy opened a very heavy bombardment on the trenches of the brigades on either flank of the 9th Brigade, whose front, however, was not itself affected till shortly after 9 a.m. At this hour the German artillery fire, which included a large proportion of gas shells, began to spread to the front of the FIFTH; considerable enemy movement was observed to the east of Loisne Central Keep, and a little later white lights were observed rising from the same quarter. When informed of this, the Brigadier, fearing that the enemy might attempt to work round the right flank of the FIFTH, ordered a company of the 13/King's to take up a position about 700 yards to the west of Gorre Wood. At 9.30 a.m. the Germans were seen definitely to be collecting to the east of Loisne Keep, and our artillery was immediately turned on to this concentration, with the result that no attack developed on the front of the FIFTH. Some slight success, however, was obtained by the enemy against the troops of the 1st Division on the right, and for a time the situation gave rise to some anxiety, as the FIFTH, having lost contact with their neighbours on this flank, were compelled to extend their line southwards. Later in the day, the 1st Division, having recovered the ground lost, re-established themselves in their original position; and by the evening the enemy's efforts had died down. On the relief of the 9th Brigade after dark, and its withdrawal to Divisional Reserve, the FIFTH were moved back to Vendin-les-Béthune. In the course of the day Lieutenant A. S. Greener, M.C., had been mortally wounded, and 2nd-Lieutenants Joss, M.C., and Burton, M.C., had also become casualties, bringing the total losses in the Battalion since the 10th April to 3 officers and 39 other ranks killed, and 7 officers and 190 other ranks wounded. As against the loss in officers, three subalterns had joined the Battalion on the 16th April, and four more were to report before the end of the month, but of these all but two were joining on first appointment and had no experience of active service.*

Map No. 31

Of the enemy with whom the FIFTH had been engaged at this time, Captain Chipper writes: "The German opposite this particular sector was certainly quite a sportsman. Although any fighting man who moved in or near the line became immediately the target of many rifles, stretchers bearers were permitted to come and go in broad daylight." He relates, too, how on one occasion he saw a party of peasants enter a farm in full view of the enemy, and return with a cart loaded with household goods without a shot being fired. The abandoned farms were full of live-stock, and at night, in the intervals of digging, our own men used to search the farm-yards for the animals which had been left behind; such as were brought in being sent to the rear for restoration to their owners, if they could be found. Among the beasts recovered in this way was a tiny donkey, which could only be induced to leave its stable in the battle area after much coaxing. As it was claimed by nobody, it was taken on the strength of the 1/FIFTH as a regimental mascot and ultimately accompanied them to England.

After four days in reserve the 9th Brigade relieved the 76th between the Lawe Canal and Pont Levis, on the La Bassée Canal, a front which represented the left

---

* The names of officers who joined during the period dealt with will be found at the end of the Chapter. Lieutenant A. S. Greener, whose death is recorded above, joined the 1st Battalion with his brother Lieutenant H. M. Greener, in September, 1916, and after being wounded opposite Serre in November of that year had rejoined in July, 1917, since when, except for 14 days leave, he had served continuously with the Battalion. Both brothers rendered conspicuous service to the FIFTH, in respect to which they were alike awarded the Military Cross. Arthur Greener, however, it would seem, may possibly never have known of the award made to him, since, though earned by his conduct on the 28th March, 1918, it was not gazetted till the following July.

Map No. 31 — 23rd Apr./4th May, 1918

Section of the line held by the 3rd Division, to which all its brigades had now reverted. On the 23rd April, the FIFTH were moved to a support position at Long Cornet. Alas! this year, owing to some hitch, the St. George's Day roses did not arrive in time for the regimental festival. One learns, however, that there were sufficient left over from the previous years stock to adorn a favoured few. Later, the Battalion, after another brief tour in the front line, was moved back on the last day of April to billets at Chocques, where it was held with the 9th Brigade in Divisional Reserve. Here, two days later, it was reinforced by a draft of 3 officers and 101 other ranks.

The penetration of the British line, which had followed the opening of the Lys offensive, had reached its furthest limit. But although, with the holding up of the enemy's advance, the situation was now stabilising, there had not yet been time to establish the solid defences which create the complete stalemate of trench warfare. Active operations were dying down, but with the positions of the opposing forces not yet definitely fixed, the relief of a unit in the line, as the FIFTH were now to experience, proved often to be a difficult and hazardous undertaking. In the replacement of the 76th by the 9th Brigade, which was to be carried out on the night of the 4th/5th May, the FIFTH were to take over from the 8/King's Own a sub-section which represented the extreme left of the 3rd Division's front, where the line crossed the La Bassée Canal at Pont Levis, and was continued thence along its south-western bank. Forward posts, however, had been established to the north east of the canal, and on the left were situated near an orchard.

At 8.30 p.m. on the night of the 4th May, the FIFTH moved forward for the relief. "Y" and "X" Companies were to occupy the front line on the left and right respectively; "Z" was to take up a position in support, and "W" to be held in Battalion Reserve. At 2 a.m., before "Y" Company had completed the relief of the left company of the King's Own, the enemy opened a heavy bombardment of both banks of the canal. There were many casualties; particularly at the crossings, which the German artillery had apparently registered with great accuracy. Fortunately, 2nd Lieutenant Blenkinsop's platoon, which had been detailed to occupy the most advanced post, at the southern edge of the orchard, was already in position; but before the platoon that was to take over the post on its left had reached it, its commander, 2nd Lieutenant Roblin, a young officer who had joined less than a week before, was killed, the guide who accompanied him wounded; and the sections, left in the darkness with no one to direct them, lost their way. From the scattered firing in the orchard it was realised at 2.45 a.m. that it was occupied by the enemy, and at this time a wounded N.C.O. managed to get back to Battalion H.Q. with the report that Blenkinsop's platoon had been outflanked and surrounded, the supporting artillery was immediately requested to put down a barrage to the north of the orchard, and 2nd Lieutenant Davidson of "Y" Company was ordered to lead his platoon across the canal and clear it of the enemy. When, after some delay and with great difficulty—for the shelling was still heavy—he managed to get two of his sections across the canal, he saw the S.O.S. signal fired and deemed it better to go forward at once with the men he had with him than to wait till the remainder of his platoon had crossed. He had with him as guide Pte. Brown, 2nd Lieutenant Blenkinsop's servant, who had returned with a message. In the darkness, and dazzled by the blinding flashes of the shells, the men, all of whom were young and inexperienced, failed to keep touch with their officer; and the guide lost direction.

Suddenly, the two latter, advancing by themselves, encountered a German post at the corner of a wood some distance to the north-west of the orchard. The

5th/14th May, 1918

surprise was mutual. Brown immediately bayonetted the nearest German, Davidson shot another, and others of the enemy, believing themselves about to be overwhelmed by numbers, were seen to be throwing up their hands in token of surrender, when a machine gun at close range suddenly opened fire, forcing the officer and his guide to seek cover. Not knowing how many of the enemy he had to deal with, and realising that he had lost direction, Davidson now withdrew and later reached the orchard, where shortly afterwards both he and his guide were wounded by shell fire. In the meantime Blenkinsop, cut off from his supports, had been putting up a gallant fight. At one time the enemy had actually gained a footing in his post, when, collecting a handful of men, he counter-attacked with such effect as to drive them back in confusion and discourage them from risking a second attempt. "Z" Company, in support, was now ordered to push forward a platoon across the canal. By this time, however, Davidson's remaining sections, together with two of "X" Company, had already advanced through the orchard unopposed, and unable to subdue Blenkinsop's post, the enemy, rather than risk the danger which daylight might bring, had withdrawn. Thus, in the end, the relief was successfully completed. It had, however, cost the Battalion some 38 casualties in all.*

The special nature of the dispositions taken up by the Battalion makes it simpler to give these in terms of platoons than of companies. Seven were in position on the north-east side of the canal, with four disposed in immediate support, in two posts on the south west bank, in rear of the right and left centre of the line. Of the remaining five, three formed a general support further to the rear, and two were held in Battalion Reserve. While establishing three new posts on the night of the 5th/6th, "Y" Company captured four prisoners, who are recorded as having been Hessians and "friendly people." On the same night, however, the FIFTH lost yet another officer in 2nd Lieutenant A. R. Brown, who was severely wounded. During the week that the Battalion remained in the line a hostile attack was regarded every day as imminent. Though none materialised, the German artillery fire, which included a large proportion of gas shells, was incessant. Our own artillery policy at this period, which was mainly directed to harassing the enemy's infantry and communications, is criticised in the Battalion War Diary as unsound, since it induced the hostile guns to retaliate in like manner; and it is suggested that counter-battery work would have produced better results. Though it is highly probable that a precisely similar comment would have been found in the diary of the opposing battalion commander—indicating the natural desire that the rival gunners should fight out their own battle between themselves—there would seem to have been much in the situation to support Lieut.-Colonel Herbert's criticism. The restriction imposed by the canal crossings on parties moving up for the relief or supply of our front line troops made the task of harassing fire a far simpler task for the German artillery than for ours; and in such circumstances the punishment of the enemy's guns was, perhaps, more likely to reduce their activities than chance shelling of his infantry and communications.

After suffering another officer casualty in 2nd Lieutenant T. C. Bullen, the FIFTH were relieved on the night of the 13th/14th May, and returned to Chocques. Later, following a period in Brigade support, they took over trenches in the right section of the Divisional front. The luck of "Y" Company, who in the course of the German attack in March had suffered less than any other, seems to have changed

---

* For the details of the action of 2nd Lieutenant Blenkinsop on the night of the 4th/5th May, see *St. George's Gazette* of September 1918 page 113.

on the Lys front. Already the company had here sustained very heavy casualties, and on the 22nd May it lost 9 men from the burst of a single shell. The only other incident of the tour was an encounter in No Man's Land, in which a patrol of " W " Company, under 2nd Lieutenant Hunter, accounted for two of the enemy. On the 28th, the Battalion was withdrawn to Brigade support, and the end of the month found it once again in reserve at Chocques. The total casualties sustained during May had amounted to 1 officer and 25 other ranks killed, 4 officers and 137 other ranks wounded. Reinforcements of 13 officers and 395 other ranks had, however, brought the strength of the Battalion on the 1st June to 38 officers and 935 other ranks. At this time the 1/FIFTH was deprived of the services of Major Buckle, who on the 26th May had left for a six month's tour of duty in England. No officer had more thoroughly earned the rest which was now to be granted to him.

Heavy as the losses during May had been, they compared favourably with those of the previous month, at the end of which the Lys offensive had been definitely held up. Following this, both sides had been occupied in adjusting and consolidating their positions. As will be related later, the Germans at the end of May had turned south to make their last great effort against the French ; and for the next nine weeks, during which the 3rd Division was to remain in position covering Hinges, there was, except for the steadily increasing strength of the British forces, particularly in guns, no change in the local situation on this northern front. For the FIFTH, life relapsed once again into the routine of trench warfare, with its periodical tours of duty in the front line and support, or in reserve at Chocques. The need for finding working parties while in reserve, however, gave little rest to the Battalion ; and it was while employed on these duties that Captain A. Mackenzie was mortally wounded on the 1st June. Though things in the line were now generally quieter, carrying parties bringing rations and stores to the trenches suffered many casualties from the harassing fire that was constantly directed on back areas and communications. On the 5th June, for example, a carrying party of the FIFTH lost 4 killed and 16 wounded.

On the night of the 8th/9th, a sharp bombardment of our trenches, brought in retaliation for a raid by a neighbouring division, resulted in two men of the Battalion being killed and Captain T. E. Heron, M.C., who had joined but three weeks before, and 10 other ranks wounded. On the night of the 15th/16th the 3rd Division carried out a very successful surprise attack, which resulted in the advancing of its line to a depth of 450 yards on a front of two miles and the capture of 200 prisoners. The FIFTH, as a battalion, took no part in this attack, but two platoons of " Y " Company, under 2nd Lieutenants Wailing and Regan, were attached to the 4/Royal Fusiliers, who were engaged in it. In the report of the action of his battalion, the O.C. 4/Royal Fusiliers states : " I am very thankful for the assistance of the 1st Northumberland Fusiliers, and all ranks appear to have behaved with a great gallantry."

Though a continuous toll had been taken of the ranks of the FIFTH during June, the battle casualties, amounting to 30 killed and 84 wounded, again showed a decrease on those of the previous month. One finds, however, that evacuations to the Casualty Clearing Station for sickness suddenly rose to 80, a figure just twice the average of the eight preceding months. The reason for this can be found in the War Diary of the 20th June, which records that a considerable number of men are going sick with " Three Day Fever." This was, in fact, the date at which the FIFTH were attacked by an influenza epidemic, which, at different periods and with varying intensity, ravaged the armies of all belligerents throughout the world during the closing months of the Great War.

THE RUINED BELFRY AND SQUARE AT BÉTHUNE.

[Imperial War Museum—Crown Copyright.

July, 1918　　　Till the last days of the month there is little to record of July. The duties　　Map No. 31
of the Battalion were a repetition of those of the previous month, but the enemy was far less active, and the total battle casualties dropped to less than one-third of those sustained in June. It is pleasant to find " Y " Company—so prominent in less happy respects in the War Diary of recent months—recorded as the winners of the Paget's Horse Football Cup. One wishes that this and similar entries made in the preceding years of the War could be seen by the donors of the Cup, that they might learn how it served, despite the shattering casualties of the Western Front, to preserve the tradition of a friendship formed in a lesser war in days long past. On the 26th July, a patrol consisting of 2nd Lieutenant W. L. Nimmo, a young officer who had but recently joined, and Serjeant Molyneux, failed to return, and it was later learnt that both of them had been killed.

Just after midnight on the 30th/31st July, a minor raid was carried out against an enemy post about 800 yards west of Locon. The report of the operation states that it was " carried out according to orders submitted," but as these are no longer extant, there is no record of the strength of the raiding party or of its leader. The garrison of the enemy's post appears to have been on the alert, and as the raiders approached, hurled some fifteen grenades, which fortunately burst short. On the opening of our artillery barrage, which was most accurately placed, the post was rushed and four Germans were seized. Two of these, who resisted capture, were killed, the others were brought back as prisoners to furnish the identification which had been the object of the raid. This very successful minor operation was carried out at the slight cost of six men very slightly wounded.

While, on a front where the stagnation of trench warfare had set in after the critical days of April, the raid referred to above represented at this time the most outstanding incident in the immediate experiences of the FIFTH, events had been occurring further to the south, which, by producing a complete change in the situation on the Western Front, were directly to affect the employment of the Battalion in the near future. With the collapse of Russia and the entry into the War of the United States, it had been the policy of the Allies to play for time ; for their opponents, more than ever, to strive for an early decision. The Germans, after the ultimate failure of the great attacks of March and April, which had come so near to attaining their object, relaxed their pressure against the British front and massed their forces for an offensive against the southern portion of the Allies' line, held by the French. On the 27th May, they had attacked to the north-west of Rheims on a front of 35 miles, with something of the initial success which had attended their March offensive against the British. On the 9th June, they had extended their operations by opening an attack between Noyon and Montdidier, but here they had failed to effect a surprise, and gained little beyond adding to the strain put on the French armies. On the 15th July, they had renewed their attack on the Rheims front and succeeded, as in 1914, in forcing the French to withdraw south of the Marne. Then history repeated itself, for the Germans had once again over-reached themselves ; and the French, who had been awaiting their opportunity, counter-attacked. In the same manner as the enemy nearly four years before, when seemingly on the point of a great victory, had been suddenly and dramatically thrown on the defensive, so now, in the Second Battle of the Marne, was he finally robbed of the initiative, and the way prepared for his defeat and the end of the World War.

Echoes of these events came to the FIFTH as they went in and out of the line, helping to hold the enemy in the salient in which he now found himself so uncom-

224   THE FIFTH IN THE GREAT WAR.

Map No. 31   fortably confined as a result of his early success in the Lys Battle, and whence he was   1st/6th August,
so soon to be exerting every effort to escape. But to the regimental soldier who had   1918
lived, if not fought, through close on four years of a seemingly unending war, the full
significance of what had occurred was not yet apparent. Indeed, without a full
knowledge of the internal conditions in Germany, even the better informed could
not forsee how near was the end. By the Higher Command, however, it was realized
that the initiative had definetly passed to the Allies, and for this moment they were
prepared. Plans had already been made for the Fourth Army to open, on the 8th
August, the first phase of a great British offensive, with the object of freeing Amiens.
Should this opening attack prove successful, an advance further to the north against
Bapaume was to be made by the Third Army, which the 3rd Division was now under
orders to rejoin. In order to be in readiness to participate in these later operations,
the Division was withdrawn from the Hinges area on the 5th August, and the FIFTH,
after being relieved in the line, were moved on the 6th to billets in Auchel, a village
some eight miles west of Béthune.

In this chapter we have seen the end of that critical period in which the
British Army on the Western Front had stood fighting with its back to the wall, and
the Allies preparing for what was to prove the final phase of the War. In the meantime the 2nd Battalion of the FIFTH had returned to France, and the point reached in
the history seems to be that at which it is most fitting to go back some years and take
up the threads of their story, before relating the events of the Advance to Victory,
in which both battalions were to play a prominent part.

NOTE.—During the period 1st April—8th August, 1918, the Battalion lost 17 officers killed or
wounded, 7 invalided, 7 transferred, and received the following reinforcements :—

April.
Lieut.-Colonel W. N. Herbert.*
Lieutenant R. S. F. Pattenden.*
2nd-Lieutenant P. C. Bullen, W.
,, G. R. Hunter.
,, R. Elliott.
,, A. R. Brown, W.
,, J. W. M. Anderson.
,, L. G. Robbin, K.

May.
Captain T. E. Heron, M.C., W.
,, A. Mackenzie, K.
Lieutenant C. H. Steele.*
,, T. M. Scanlan, M.C.
,, J. G. C. Brady.
,, N. R. Futers.
2nd-Lieutenant C. G. W. Wailing.
,, J. H. Regan.
,, H. T. Green.
,, J. Steel.
,, G. W. Wightman.
,, W. B. Pitkethley.
,, J. C. Bell.
,, F. Hall, W.

June.
Lieutenant D. Hewitt.
,, G. M. Lamb.*
2nd Lieutenant T. A. C. Holmes.
,, N. P. Sellick, M.C.
,, H. Nicholson.
,, R. Brown.
,, J. H. Carswell.
,, W. H. Polley, W.

July.
Captain F. A. Hobbs.
,, H. M. Greener.*
,, R. Lord.*
2nd-Lieutenant H. A. Ingledew.
,, W. L. Nimmo, K.
,, J. G. Brown.
,, D. S. Rowe.
,, J. Cannon.
,, D. Story.
,, J. C. Bell.

August 1st–8th.
2nd Lieutenant R. Lynes.
,, R. F. Ritchie.
,, W. Dunglinson.
,, R. W. H. Fryer.

* = re-joining.   K. or W. = Killed or wounded during same period.
Strength of Battalion, 1st August, 1918 = 37 officers, 936 other ranks.

CHAPTER XVI.

Second Battalion—25th October, 1915—26th June, 1918.

"Macedonia, 1915-1918"—"Struma."

While concerned in the past few chapters with the actions in which the 1st Battalion was engaged in the Somme Battles and at Ypres and Arras, the reader of this history may have wondered what, during this period of close on three years, had been the experiences of the 2/FIFTH, whom we left many pages back aboard H.M.T. *Invernia*, in which they had sailed towards the end of October, 1915. The contrast between the life that had been led by them during this time and that of the 1st Battalion was, perhaps, no less than between the nature of the country to which they had been called and that of the Western Front. This chapter, in which we return to their doings, unlike those that precede it, will be concerned comparatively little with active fighting, and but remotely with large scale operations. As will be seen, the 2/FIFTH while in Macedonia were engaged in only two attacks, and these, though one was costly, were but minor and subsidiary operations. At no time were they called on to defend themselves against an organised attack on any position they held. For the most part the tale to be told is one of constant watchfulness and patrols; of incessant labour on defences and communications in a mountainous and undeveloped country, and of service under climatic conditions which not only by extremes of temperature brought great hardship to the troops, but caused losses from malarial fever far in excess of those arising from battle casualties.

But though, as the reader may recollect, the 2/FIFTH on sailing from Marseilles had learnt that their destination was to be Salonika, where British troops had already been landed, some weeks were still to elapse before they reached Macedonia.* Their first destination proved to be Alexandria, where they disembarked on the 29th October and moved into camp at Mundara. Here they were joined by Lieut.-Colonel A. C. L. Hardman Jones, who had been sent out from England to assume command. He was accompanied by 2nd Lieutenant W. H. Griffiths, on first appointment, and Captain E. L. Salier. The latter officer resumed the duties of Adjutant, which, as may be remembered, he had performed in the Battalion for twenty-four hours in the previous May, before being wounded on the Bellewaarde Ridge. While in camp at Mundara and later at Aboukir, to which the Battalion moved on the 10th November,

---

* The entry in the War Diary of the 2/FIFTH under 24th October—"Destination is stated to be Salonika"—was at the time well justified. But, owing to the uncertainty that existed as to the policy to be adopted with regard both to Macedonia and the Gallipoli Peninsula, the Battalion's destination later became more doubtful. The plan that had been formed as an alternative to the evacuation of Gallipoli is outside the scope of this History, but it was in consequence of the possibility of its adoption that the 28th Division, which would have been made available for the proposed operation, was retained in Egypt until the plan was abandoned and the evacuation of the Peninsula decided on.

life was uneventful, time being divided between training and inoculation for cholera. After rather over three weeks had been spent in Egypt, orders having been received for the 28th Division to move on to Salonika, the Battalion on the 21st November embarked on H.M.T. *Kalyan*.

Following the first outbreak of war, and before the British Army itself had become engaged, Serbia for a brief period had been in the forefront of the news in England. Events in that country, however, had long since been eclipsed by those in France and Flanders; and to the soldier on the Western Front little was known of what had been passing more recently in the Balkans, where the first spark had started the world conflagration. Yet many British units were to be profoundly affected by a course of events which had now drawn the 2/FIFTH from the fighting for the Hohenzollern Redoubt in France to embarkation for Macedonia. Here it is possible only to give the briefest outline of what had occurred in the Balkans during 1914 and 1915, based on the Official History,* to which all who wish to read a fuller story of Serbia's heroic struggle should turn. Incidentally they will learn, too, something of the fatal weakness which afflicts all allied operations.

At the outbreak of war the Serbians were gradually forced back by superior numbers, till at the end of November, 1914, it seemed that the end had come and that they must capitulate. At this juncture the aged King Peter, who had abdicated in favour of his son, suddenly appeared from retirement and, armed with a rifle and fifty rounds of ammunition, went forward to the trenches among his men, so inspiring them that they turned against the Austrians and, fighting desperately, drove them back with the stupendous loss of 227,000 men out of a total of 450,000. The Serbians themselves were exhausted by this tremendous effort; and with the Austrian army for the time crippled, the War in the Balkans had remained stagnant for close on a year. Then once again, early in October, 1915, the Austrians, now reinforced by Germans, advanced in greatly superior numbers. In the meantime, the despatch of troops to Salonika had been the subject of discussion between Great Britain, France and Greece since the beginning of the year; but diplomatic differences had been the cause of constant postponements. Throughout, Great Britain had been opposed to becoming involved in a campaign in the Balkans save for one purpose, viz. the direct support of the Serbian Army; and had ultimately agreed to participate only on the understanding that if communication could not be opened up with the Serbians, the allied forces should be withdrawn. At long last, on the 5th October, two days after the 2/FIFTH had been withdrawn from the fighting in the Hohenzollern, British and French troops landed at Salonika. They were, however, too late. The Serbians were being gradually forced back; and although the Austro-German armies were unable to bring them to a decisive battle, the Allies were not yet in a position to move to their assistance. Then, on the 13th October, Bulgaria, who since the outbreak of war had been sitting on the fence, judged that it would best suit her interests to throw in her lot with the Central Powers, and declared war against Serbia. The Serbians, now threatened with encirclement, were doomed. There followed what may rank

---

* Military Operation—Macedonia (compiled by Captain Cyril Falls).

[Imperial War Museum—Crown Copyright.

SALONIKA.
(July 1916—the troops are Russians.)

as the most tragic and heroic episode of the World War, when the Serbians, rather than submit to Austria, abandoned their starving women and children, and set out to cross the Albanian mountains by narrow tracks, deep in snow. " Slowly this army of misery drifted to the coast, bestrewing the tracks as it went with frozen corpses." (Official History.) Only a remnant of those who set out on this terrible journey, finally reached Scutari on the Adriatic ; and, of these, many, having gained their goal, died of the privations they had endured. In the meantime, General Sarrail,* with such French and British troops as were immediately available, had pushed north in the vain hope of gaining contact with the Serbian Army, and covering its retreat to some position on which it could stand in defence. Too late to save the Serbians, he found the safety of his own force threatened, and ordered a withdrawal to the Greek frontier, preparatory to taking up a position for the defence of the town and harbour of Salonika.

Map No. 32

Thus, a situation had arisen in which, by the declared policy of Great Britain, the allied forces should now have been withdrawn from Macedonia. The Government, however, found that, having once become committed to sending troops to Salonika, it was not only impossible to withdraw those already landed, but necessary to reinforce them. They still remained firm, however, in their intention not to become involved in an offensive, and in insisting that the rôle of British troops should be limited to the defence of Salonika.

The events briefly related above are those which led to the 2/FIFTH being despatched to a theatre of war in which they were to be employed, with thousands of other British troops, in little more than passive defence for over $2\frac{1}{2}$ years, while the question of the reinforcement of our Armies on the Western Front was ever becoming an increasingly serious problem.

Nov./Dec., 1915

H.M.T. *Kalyan* dropped anchor at Salonika at 10 a.m. on the 24th November, but it was not till 8 p.m. that H.Q. of the FIFTH and two companies disembarked, and marched to Lembet, a village $4\frac{1}{2}$ miles north-west of Salonika, near which the infantry of the 28th Division were to camp. The remaining companies, having off-loaded the baggage, joined H.Q. on the following day, and the whole Battalion then marched off to pitch camp two miles to the north of the village. The weather was bitterly cold, and the march was made in the teeth of a snow storm, driven by a gale that was blowing down the Vardar valley. The experiences of the 2/FIFTH during the next few weeks were in many respects similar to those which they had undergone twelve months before, when they had returned from India to camp in an English winter, in that the heat during their recent brief sojourn in Egypt had been very severe, and now for three days their camp was swept by northerly gales and driving snow. The weather then cleared ; but the intense cold continued.

In the meantime reconnaissance for the defence of Salonika had been undertaken, and by the 14th December the general line to be occupied had been determined. The following description of this line and of what is referred to as " the outer perimeter " is taken from the Official History.

" It (the line now to be taken up) ran from the village of Tumba, on the south-

---

* The French Commander-in-Chief in Macedonia.

western shore of Lake Langaza, through Aivatli, Balcha, Dautla, and Naresh, to the Vardar about Kara Oghlu, and thence down to the left bank to the bridge which carried the Monastir road over the river... The line just mentioned may be called the inner perimeter, and runs along the forward slope of a sharp ridge, which has in front of it a fosse in the form of a wide, gently-curving basin. The ridge is connected south of Lake Langaza with the mountainous peninsula of Khalkidike, while the fosse is is continued eastward ... by Lake Langaza itself, by the Eiri Dere valley between that lake and Lake Beshik, by Lake Beshik, and by the Rendina Gorge running down to the Gulf of Orfano...

The natural outer perimeter of the fortress could not at this period be occupied by the Allies, but as it was to be their main position at a later date it may also be described here. From the Gulf of Orfano to Lake Dojran it consists of a mountain ridge—the Beshik Dagh rising out of the gulf, continued north-west by the Krusha Ridge—again fronted by a great fosse: first Lake Tahinos, then the valley of the Struma, then Lake Butkovo and the river of the same name, then the Hoja, running westward into Lake Dojran..."

We shall be concerned only with certain portions of the lines described above; and it is unnecessary here to follow the "outer perimeter" beyond Lake Dojran. The sector of the inner perimeter allotted to the 28th Division, which with the 22nd and 26th Divisions now composed the XII. Corps, was due north of Salonika, from which its forward line of defence, running from Aivatli to Balcha,* was distant between 8 and 9 miles. The 84th Brigade was detailed for the occupation of the right of the two sections into which this Sector was divided. In order to undertake the organisation of this position for defence—work on which they were to be almost exclusively employed for the next $4\frac{1}{2}$ months—the FIFTH left Lembet Camp on the 13th December and moved forward with the 84th Brigade to Aivatli, which was reached two days later in heavy rain and bitter cold. Since, during the whole period that the FIFTH were in the Salonika Defence Line, the enemy remained on the far side of the Greek border, 55 miles distant, no purpose would be served by giving a detailed description of the defences or of the disposition of troops in the event of attack. On the map of the Sector the area allotted to the FIFTH can be immediately identified by such homely names as St. George's Redoubt, Newcastle Dug-outs, or Hexham Cutting. The Battalion was never in permanent occupation of its defences, but was concentrated near its Headquarters at "Hardman Place."

How uneventful, from the point of view of the military historian, were the months spent by the 2/FIFTH in the Salonika Defence Line may be judged from the single entry in the 84th Brigade War Diary, which deals with the whole period:—
"The Brigade was employed in 'D' Sub-section of the Salonika Defence Line. Latterly battalions were struck off two days (later three days) a week for Field Training. The training of specialists, especially bombers and signallers, continued during the whole period 15th December—3rd May. Regimental tours and staff rides lasting about five days were also carried out latterly. Finally each battalion, the Brigade, and Division moved out of the lines for manoeuvres lasting about five or six days each. On the termination of the Divisional Exercise on the 10th May the Brigade moved to the 42 kilo stone† on the Salonika-Seres road to repair the same."

---

* Aivatli is just west of the Seres road, and Balcha about $2\frac{1}{2}$ miles north-west of it.

† Near Likovan.

Jan.-May, 1916

There had, however, been a good many changes among the officers of the Battalion during this period. At the end of January, Captain Heyder, who had been twice severely wounded—in February 1915 with the 2nd Battalion, and again in the following June when with the 1st—joined for duty. On 18th February Major Cruddas left, on appointment to command the 8/Oxfordshire and Buckinghamshire L.I. Early in April, 2nd Lieutenants Hill, Rogers, Donaldson and King arrived from the Special Reserve Battalion, and a few days later Captain Rushbrooke, together with 2nd Lieutenants Garrard, Garner-King, Hutchinson, and a draft of 82 other ranks joined. On 25th April Major W. Gibson reported and took over the duties of Second-in-Command, and on the 8th May, Captain C. R. Freeman replaced Captain Salier as Adjutant, on the appointment of the latter as Brigade Major to the 12th Australian Infantry Brigade.

There had been changes, too, in the dispositions of the Allied forces. Early in March, French troops had been pushed up the valley of the Vardar towards the Greek frontier; some weeks later a British mounted brigade and infantry brigade were moved forward to take post on the right of the French to the south of Lake Dojran, and by the beginning of May had been joined by the bulk of the 22nd Division. By this time all four French divisions had left the Salonika Defence Line, and, in addition to the troops in position astride the Vardar, had established outposts on the line of the R. Struma and the Constantinople railway to the east of Lake Dojran. Except for the 22nd Division, however, all British troops were as yet still in the Salonika Entrenched Camp.*

It will be seen that the Allies' forces, which had now been strengthened by the re-constituted Serbian Army, had already in part pushed forward to the line which has been referred to as the "outer perimeter." But, while General Sarrail regarded this forward move as being preliminary to active operations, it was still the policy of the British to stand strictly on the defensive. If troops were to be pushed forward to the Struma, however, the question of their supply, apart from that of their subsequent action, made the construction of communications a matter of extreme urgency; and this consideration was to rule the employment of the FIFTH for the next $2\frac{1}{2}$ months. Apart from the Salonika-Seres road, itself little better than a rough cart-track, there was no other which could take wheeled traffic. While work was to be immediately started to make the Seres road fit for motor traffic, a reconnaisasnce of the hill tracks in the country to the north-west of Likovan was to be carried out with a view to selecting a line on which a track for limbered wagons could be constructed as a secondary communication.

Reading the diary of the younger of the two officers of the FIFTH who were detailed for this reconnaissance, one sees something of the brighter side of campaigning in Macedonia. This was his first campaign, and he had not suffered the disillusionment as to the romance of war brought by long tours in the trenches on the Western Front. So, on the eve of setting out on what he regards as a great adventure, he is found gleefully anticipating: "We may meet some *Uhlans* with luck." As to this; since the party accompanying the officers consisted of 2 mounted grooms, 2 soldier servants, an interpreter, and 2 led mules, one cannot but reflect that such an encounter could

---

* In May 1916, General Sir Bryan Mahon having been replaced in command of the British Salonika Force by Lieut.-General G. F. Milne, the latter was succeeded in command of the XVI. Corps by Major-General C. J. Brigges, and Major-General H. L. Croker was appointed to command the 28th Division. The 84th Infantry Brigade was commanded by Brigadier-General G. A. Weir.

230   THE FIFTH IN THE GREAT WAR.

Map No. 33   more rightly be regarded as luck for the *Uhlans* had such existed! In truth, however,   June, 1916
the enemy proper were still many miles away, on the far side of the Greek frontier.
Nevertheless, there was some real danger of meeting *Comitadjis*—bands of irregulars,
many of whom had been born and bred as bandits, and who could at any time conceal
their rifles in some local village and pose as peaceful peasants. None of these gentle-
men, however, were encountered, and reading the description of the three days'
reconnaissance, with its "perilous ascents and descents of slopes covered with stunted
oaks"; of a bivouac established by the side of a stream under the shade of trees (for
the weather was now getting very hot); of the view obtained of the Struma valley
and the hills ten miles beyond, where the Bulgar positions lay, one feels that there
were compensations in this rugged and beautiful country for the drudgery of road
making and the monotony of life in the trenches.

On the 6th June the Battalion was withdrawn with the 84th Brigade to
Guvezne, 13 miles north of Salonika, to undergo a few days' training. This, however,
was only a brief respite from their labour on communications. On the 10th they
moved forward again to Likovan, preparatory to undertaking the construction of
limber tracks in the hills, as planned by the recent reconnaissance. On the 11th, the
companies, moving north-west across country, climbed 1,000 feet to Mirova, where
they were joined later in the day by the transport, which had to make a longer journey
via Lahana, whence a track had already been constructed. The line selected for the
limber track on which the Battalion was now to set to work ran by Mozgall, Paprat,
Hamzali, Gurlemeli, Ortamah, to the right bank of the Struma. During the next
few weeks, its bivouac was moved forward by stages as each successive section of the
track was completed. Interference by *Comitadjis* had to be guarded against, piquets
being posted for the protection of working parties, and houses in suspected villages
being searched for arms and ammunition. The heat by day was now very severe,
but rapid progress was made. By the 14th June the track had been carried forward
to Hamzali, by the 21st to Gurlemeli, and by the 13th July it had been pushed forward
through Ortamah to the plain. The first of the many entries in the Battalion War
Diary with regard to malaria appears on the 7th July. At this time the FIFTH were
near Ortamah, and it is stated that "several cases of slight fever are beginning to
appear." On the 8th over 100 men reported sick; and on the following day 70
were detained in hospital.*

It is necessary at this point to refer to events which, though of little concern
to the 2/FIFTH at the time of their occurrence, can now be seen to have been definite
steps leading up to a situation which was later to rule the manner in which the Battalion
was to be employed. The first episode, related here in the words of the Official History,

---

* It would be tedious to repeat in this History the figures that appear periodically in the
War Diary in connection with malaria. It is important, however, that the reader should bear in
mind that the 2/FIFTH while in Macedonia were the constant victims of what the Official History
describes as "the most formidable, the most unconquerable foe" of the British Salonika Army.
It is recorded that between 11th October and 14th November, 1917, a period at which the total
strength of the Battalion was 850, the number of men reporting sick with malaria (in addition to
those already in hospital from the same cause) averaged 66.5; the greatest number in any one day
being 120. Captain G. E. Fenwick recalls an occasion when, owing to the ravages of malaria, his
company on parade consisted of himself and two lance-corporals.

will incidentally give some idea of the difficulties presented to the Allies by the doubtful attitude of Greece.* "Hitherto—the enemy had crossed the Greek frontier only to obtain observation posts just beyond it. On the 26th May a force of Bulgarians and Germans suddenly advanced down the Struma towards Fort Rupel. The Greek garrison opened fire, whereupon the column retired without casualties. In the afternoon the Greek troops received orders from Athens not to oppose the advance, the Greek divisional commander at Seres being forbidden to inform the French or British of what was happening. Next day the enemy, in strength about a division, occupied not only Fort Rupel but the villages on a line some ten miles south of the frontier, thus covering the mouth of the pass and blocking the chief gateway to Bulgarian territory from the Struma valley . . . the Bulgarians had now closed the pass against invasion, and were also free to make any further advance with the certainty that it would not be opposed by the Greeks.

Map No. 33

June–July, 1916

Before the above incident had taken place it had been decided to make considerable alterations in the British dispositions, and these were carried out in the first week of June. With the exception of the 84th Brigade, which was left to work on the Seres road and other communications, the whole of the 28th Division was moved up from the Salonika Defence Line to a position in support of the 22nd Division on the Dojran front. Scarcely, however, had these fresh dispositions been taken up, than a difference arose between the French and British commands, which made further moves necessary, when General Sarrail informed the British Commander-in-Chief that he had received orders to attack. General Milne, who, as has been indicated, had strict instructions from his own Government not to allow his troops to become involved in an offensive, saw no alternative to disengaging from contact with the French and asking that a definite zone of operations should be allotted to the British Army. On agreement being reached that the British should take over an area south-east of Lake Butkovo and the R. Bashishli, the 28th Division was made responsible for the defence of the line of the Struma between Orlyak and the left flank of the British front. The 2/FIFTH, as we know, were at this time still at work in the hills to the west of the Struma, but the remainder of the 84th Brigade were brought up from the Seres road to take over, on the 24th June, the left section of the divisional front between the Cavaldar-Bursuk road and the Kranmah nullah, 1½ miles to the west of Lozista.

To return to the 2/FIFTH. The Battalion, having now completed its work on the limber track, was to take its place in the defence line. On the 14th July it was moved forward to Lozista, and on the following day relieved the 2/Cheshire in the left sub-section of the Brigade front, between the southern end of Lake Butkovo and the Kranmah nullah. The defence depended on two *points d'appui*, to each of which a garrison of one company and one machine-gun was allotted, with a wire entanglement filling the intervening spaces. The Battalion remained in occupation of this position for the next fortnight. During this period the front was watched by posts and patrols by day, and at night protected by outposts. Patrols were also sent north to Butkovo village to keep touch with the French, who were in position

---

* With the entry of Bulgaria into the War there remained now, of the Balkan nations, only Rumania and Greece left "sitting on the fence." The decision of the former of these will be related in due course; of Greece it can only here be said that her attitude seems to have changed with each successive change in her Government.

along the line of the railway to the west of the northern end of the lake. There was a certain amount of activity on the French front, and the shelling of Poroj was observed on most days; but opposite the FIFTH all remained quiet,, and our fire-eating 2nd Lieutenant records in disgust on the 18th July: " Dogs trip over ' B ' Company's trip-wire and send up flares. They shoot two in the marshes next morning. Some war ! " This, it seems, was the only out-standing incident and, after an otherwise uneventful tour in the line, the FIFTH were relieved on the 29th July, and moved into Divisional Reserve with the 84th Brigade to a position on the Seres road south of Orljak, which was reached on the 2nd August.

It has been explained that hitherto Rumania had remained neutral. As time passed, however, she inclined increasingly towards the side of the Allies, and this consideration caused a modification in the attitude of Great Britain to the campaign in Macedonia, which in turn was to bring about a change of dispositions during the period that the FIFTH remained in reserve with the 84th Brigade. One learns in the Official History that, on the 10th July, the British Government agreed that " if Rumania definitely intervened, they would be prepared to co-operate in an offensive from Salonika, with the object of holding the largest possible proportion of the Bulgarian Army on the Greek frontier, *on a scale commensurate with the strength and equipment of their force."*

The latter condition, so far as equipment was concerned, was based on the consideration that to engage in active operations in the Balkans it was essential that a force should be equipped for mountain warfare. For the infantry this was a question of transport. We have seen how the FIFTH, by being required for work on communications, had not been available for duties more appropriate to trained infantry; and what a vast amount of labour and time had been needed for the construction of a track for wheeled transport covering a distance of no more than a day's march. For a force with such limited mobility and so large a proportion of its fighting troops absorbed in road construction, to embark on an offensive was out of the question. The solution lay in the conversion of transport from wheel to pack. It was, however, no simple matter to convey from overseas the thousands of mules required, when British shipping was already strained to the utmost. None the less the War Office, on the 11th July, had given approval to the introduction of a pack transport establishment in the units of the Salonika Army.*

Later, the entry of Rumania on the side of the Allies became certain; and it was agreed that, in order to cover her mobilisation, an offensive should be opened from Salonika at least eight days before her declaration of war. The XII. Corps was ordered to send two divisions once more to the Dojran front, and the 28th Division was transferred to the XVI. Corps, with orders to extend southwards in defence of the Struma. No serious offensive was to be undertaken on this front, owing to the great prevalence of malaria in the Struma valley, but an active defence was to be maintained, infantry patrols being sent across the river to the left bank, and the

---

* The French, who had secured 12,000 mules at Salonika, had been able to re-organise all their divisions with pack transport in April 1916. The British, on the other hand, in addition to their own requirements, were expected to find and transport to Salonika 4000 mules for the re-constituted Serbian Army !

THE FIFTH IN THE GREAT WAR. 233

Aug., 1916 — ground further forward patrolled by troops of the 7th Mounted Brigade. Furthermore, a French force of all arms, under General Frotiée, sent up from Salonika, was to cross to the far side of the Struma in front of the 28th Division and demonstrate towards Rupel, which still represented the limit of the enemy's advance in the Struma valley. — Maps Nos. 33 & 34

We are not here concerned with all the shuffling and re-shuffling of troops necessary to complete these new dispositions, as during this period the FIFTH remained in reserve with their Brigade in the camp on the Seres road to which they had been withdrawn, spending the time in training. It will be sufficient to define the front for which the 28th Division had now become responsible, and describe briefly the system of defence. It was holding a line from (excl.) Sakavca to (incl.) Butkovo village, a distance of 20 miles. Although, as a temporary measure, only two brigades took over this front, the defence scheme arranged for its eventual division into three brigade sections, the centre brigade holding from Dragos Ferry to the junction of the Butkovo and Struma rivers, those on its flanks occupying the line from these points to those which marked the right and left flanks of the Division. Owing to the great length of front to be held, and to the extent to which infantry units were under establishment, the defence relied principally on an artillery barrage and mutually supporting machine-guns. A series of localities on the right bank of the river, constructed for all-round defence by garrisons of one company or less, formed the *Line of Resistance*, with strong bridge-heads established opposite Orlyak and Kopriva; while observation over the whole of the Butkovo and Struma valleys was obtained from a chain of posts sited on the heights further to the rear.

In view of the great distance at which the enemy still remained from the 28th Division, there seemed to be no urgent need for closing down the training of the 84th Brigade, merely to bring all three brigades into the line and so conform with the defence scheme. In the third week of August, however, complacency on the Struma front was shaken by a sudden and somewhat dramatic change in the situation. About the middle of the month General Sarrail, against his will, had become involved in fighting on the Dojran front. He had planned an offensive further to the west, but was not yet fully prepared to deliver it. Then, on the 18th, he learnt that at long last a convention had been signed with Rumania which required the Allies to open their proposed offensive on the 20th. Simultaneously, however, he received news that was far less to his liking. It was that the Bulgarians, anticipating the Allies' action, had advanced on both flanks; had driven in the Serbian posts on the left of the French; and on the right—the flank with which we are more closely concerned—had pushed forward from the Rupel Pass, surrounded Demir Hissar, and gained the outskirts of Barakli Jumá.

In face of this threat, Frotiée's detachment hurriedly withdrew to the right bank of the Struma, and patrols of the 7th Mounted Brigade were fortunate in being able to regain their lines. On the 20th August Frotiée's force re-crossed the Struma, but encountered greatly superior numbers, and after being roughly handled, fell back across the river at Orlyak. Troops of the 7th Mounted Brigade found Kumli and Bairakli Jum'a strongly held, and after being in some danger of being cut off from Kopriva bridge, were withdrawn after dark to the right bank, having suffered 24 casualties. The defence of the 20 mile front of the 28th Division by two brigades now constituted too great a risk; and the 84th Brigade was ordered to send forward the 1/Suffolk to Orlyak bridge forthwith, and to hold the remainder of its battalions in immediate readiness to move.

General Sarrail now put before the allied commanders a revised plan of campaign. By this he proposed to attack on the left flank, mainly with Serbian and Russian troops, and to stand on the defence on the Vardar and Struma fronts*. It was important to his plans, in the first place, that they should not be prejudiced by any penetration of the right of the allied line by the Bulgarians who had advanced down the Struma valley; and accordingly, that the line of the river should as far as possible be made impregnable. When this had been achieved he desired that the descent of the enemy from the Rupel Pass should be turned to his own advantage by action which would hold them to their position, and so prevent them from reinforcing the front which was the objective of his attack.

It was now arranged that the 84th Brigade should take over the right Section of the Divisional front, with two battalions in the forward defences, and the remaining two in reserve half a mile north-west of Orlyak village; and late on the evening of the 21st, the FIFTH received orders to march to Orlyak, preparatory to taking over the left sub-section. The night march which followed will not soon be forgotten by those who took part in it, and least of all by the battalion transport officer. Only ten days had elapsed since 127 unbroken mules had joined the Battalion for the conversion of its transport to pack. In this brief period all that was possible had been done to fit these untrained animals with pack-saddles and to induce them to consent to loads being placed on their backs; but few if any of them had as yet seen a motor vehicle at close quarters, even in the daylight. When, therefore, a string of French motor ambulances, evacuating the wounded of the previous day, approached the marching column from the opposite direction with glaring head-lights, a scene ensured that can be more easily imagined than described. The task of handling mules was as strange to many of the men as that of carrying loads was to the animals they led. The first of these to break away from its guardian and take to flight bore with it the new Officers Mess paniers; and in a short space of time a number of the unfortunate transport men were lying knocked-out in the ditches which lined the road. When, on arrival at Orlyak, the mules were counted it was found that no fewer than 50 were missing. In the circumstances, however, the Battalion could be regarded as fortunate in having retained as many as it had, and with its reduced transport it continued the march to Idris Mah, which was reached at 3.30 a.m. on the 22nd.

The front allotted to the FIFTH extended from a point 800 yards north of Orlyak bridge to Dragos ferry, and faced the village of Nevolyen, which lay 1½ miles back from the left bank of the Struma, opposite the centre of this line. During the morning of the 23rd the Battalion's camp at Idris Mah was sniped by the enemy from the opposite bank of the river, C.S.M. Pattison being wounded by a missile of the primitive type fired in the old days from Afridi *jezails*. A few days later, when fifteen shells were fired into the camp, a second casualty occurred, and it was decided to move the rear companies to a more sheltered position. Generally, however, the situation remained quiet. The scouts and patrols who crossed the river to reconnoitre towards Cuculuk and Nevolyen rarely encountered the enemy, an exception being an officer's patrol which engaged a party of Bulgars on the 3rd September and came under machine-gun fire from the direction of Nevolyen. For the rest, time was taken up with work on wire entanglements and in generally strengthening the defences, with the result that by the beginning of September it was felt that the line of the Struma was secure against attack, which, in truth, the enemy gave no evidence of any desire to open.

---

* The allied forces in Macedonia included British, French, Italians, Serbians and Russians.

Sept., 1916   An incident which occurred at this time will recall a solemn warning that is   Map No. 34
always given on the N.W. Frontier of India to those who are responsible for selecting
the site of a camp in the hills. When seeking a safer position to which to shift their
camp on the 23rd August, the FIFTH, like many others before them, had been tempted
to choose a site on the bank of a dry nullah; the inducement to this being the cover
and concealment afforded to their transport lines, which were disposed in the nullah
bed together with large quantities of stores and ammunition. For a fortnight everyone
felt very secure and comfortable in their new camp, until on the 8th September, a
violent thunder-storm, accompanied by torrential rain, burst over the hills and lower
slopes. Instantly, the " dry nullah " was transformed to a raging torrent, which
swept away mules, pack-saddlery, stores and all else that had been seemingly so safely
disposed. Of the long suffering mules, one was drowned, but the remainder were
rescued; and as the stores were, fortunately scattered about the plain without being
washed into the river, the bulk of these was also recovered. There was, however, one
grievous loss. Material for the red puggarees to which the Regiment is entitled had
but recently arrived from England. Now alas! £40 worth or red puggarees, destined
for the helmets of the FIFTH, were strewn far over the Struma valley.

The first requirement on the Struma front—the establishment of a secure line
of defence—had now been satisfied; and the time had come to carry out the second—
the holding of the Bulgarians to the positions to which they had descended opposite
the front of the XVI. Corps. This could only be accomplished by persuading the
enemy to anticipate an offensive which, as the reader knows, it was contrary to the
policy of the Allies to open; in other words, by bluff. The principal part as decoy
in the action to be taken to this end on the front of the 28th Division was to be played
by the FIFTH.

Orders were issued for the Battalion to cross the Struma on the 10th September
for the attack and temporary occupation of Nevolyen village. The object of the operation was stated to be twofold: firstly, to test the strength of the hostile forces in the
Struma valley, concerning which there was still considerable uncertainty; secondly,
to convey to the Bulgarians the impression that the attack was preliminary to a
big offensive against the left wing of their Army. Further to encourage the enemy
in this idea, simultaneously with the FIFTH's attack, troops of the 84th Brigade, acting
the part of a " stage army," were to show movement and activity on the hills to the
rear without descending to the river. It was reckoned that if the operation were not
carried out till late in the afternoon, and came as a surprise, the Bulgarians would not
have time to bring forward superior forces to overwhelm the small attacking force;
furthermore, that if the FIFTH could hold on to their captured objective till dusk, the
enemy would not be able to form a true estimate of the scope of the operation.

The attack that had been planned was to be directed by Battalion Headquarters from the high ground in rear of the right bank of the Struma, from which
a perfect view of the area of operations could be obtained. The four companies
which, together with two Lewis guns attached from the 2/Cheshire, were to cross the
river and advance for the capture of Nevolyen, were, however, to be under the
immediate command of Captain Rushbrooke. In co-operation whith the attack of the
FIFTH, a company of the 2/Cheshire and one machine-gun were to take up a position
on the left flank. in order to deal with any attempt that might be made by the enemy
to counter-attack from the direction of Cuculuk. Despite the heavy rain which had

236   THE FIFTH IN THE GREAT WAR.

Map No. 34   recently fallen, the river was everywhere easily fordable, and though rafts had been   9th/10th
constructed by the Royal Engineers, their main purpose was to be the evacuation of   Sept., 1916
the wounded. The attack was to be supported by the 31st Field Artillery Brigade.

On the 9th September the FIFTH were relieved in the defence line by the 2/Cameron Highlanders, temporarily detached from the 27th Division; and during the night the batteries which were to support the attack took up forward positions near Dragos and at Idris Mah. At 11 a.m. on the following morning, the companies of the FIFTH moved to a rendezvous in rear of the right of the front now held by the Highlanders, and half an hour later " D " Company, the first to cross, began to ford the river.* The crossing was a somewhat slow process, but by 2.43 p.m. the four companies, and the two Lewis guns of the 2/Cheshire had assembled on the left bank, and at 3 p.m. began to take up dispositions for attack under cover of the maize crops, which extended for a distance of 1000 yards from the bank of the river towards Nevolyen. " B " and " A " Companies, the former on the right, were to form the centre of the Battalion's attack, with " D " and " C " échelonned slightly in rear on the outer flanks. In the meantime the Cheshire company, crossing the river on the left of the Camerons' front, had moved to their appointed position. While these dispositions were being taken up, and during the advance of the FIFTH under cover of the standing crops, the fire of the supporting artillery was directed on the Bulgarian gun positions; and at this stage there was no indication that the enemy suspected what was afoot. The attack, however, could not be long concealed from him, for the last 1,000 yards of the advance lay over ground completely devoid of cover; and it had, accordingly, been arranged that the artillery should bring a concentrated bombardment on Nevolyen when the infantry were on the point of debouching from the crops. It was well that this was done; for scarcely had the companies of the FIFTH emerged into the open than they were brought under fire by the Bulgarian artillery and by riflemen who had hastily manned the defences of the village. Fortunately the enemy's artillery was for the most part directed to the rear of the attacking troops, but considerable casualties were incurred by his rifle fire. Losses, however, would undoubtedly have been far greater had it not been for the accuracy of our bombardment.† As it was the advance of the FIFTH was carried forward without check. By 4.45 p.m. " A " and " B " Companies had reached the outskirts of the village, and

---

* The total strength at which the Battalion went into action was only 360. Companies were commanded as under :—

" A " by Captain H. U. Scrutton.
" B " by Captain G. E. Fenwick.
" C " by Lieutenant F. A. Price.
" D " by Captain P. E. Johnstone (3/D.L.I.).

It was in consideration of the shortage of regular officers with the British Salonica Force that the officers of Battalion H.Q. were not permitted to cross the river.

† The occasions on which individual casualties occurred on this day have always been difficult to determine. The narrative of the 84th Brigade describes the enemy's fire in opposing the advance as not very effective. Major Redwood, however, is emphatic in stating that by far the greater number of casualties sustained by " A " Company occurred as this stage; and it was at this time that 2nd Lieutenant R. Parish, a very fine officer, who had been commissioned to the FIFTH from the Lincolnshire Regiment, in which he had held the rank of Regimental Serjeant Major, was killed. His death was witnessed by Lieut.-Colonel Rushbrooke, who holds that the losses sustained by the companies as a whole during the advance were severe. Captain Fenwick, on the other hand, states that the fire directed at " B " Company was wild and did little harm.

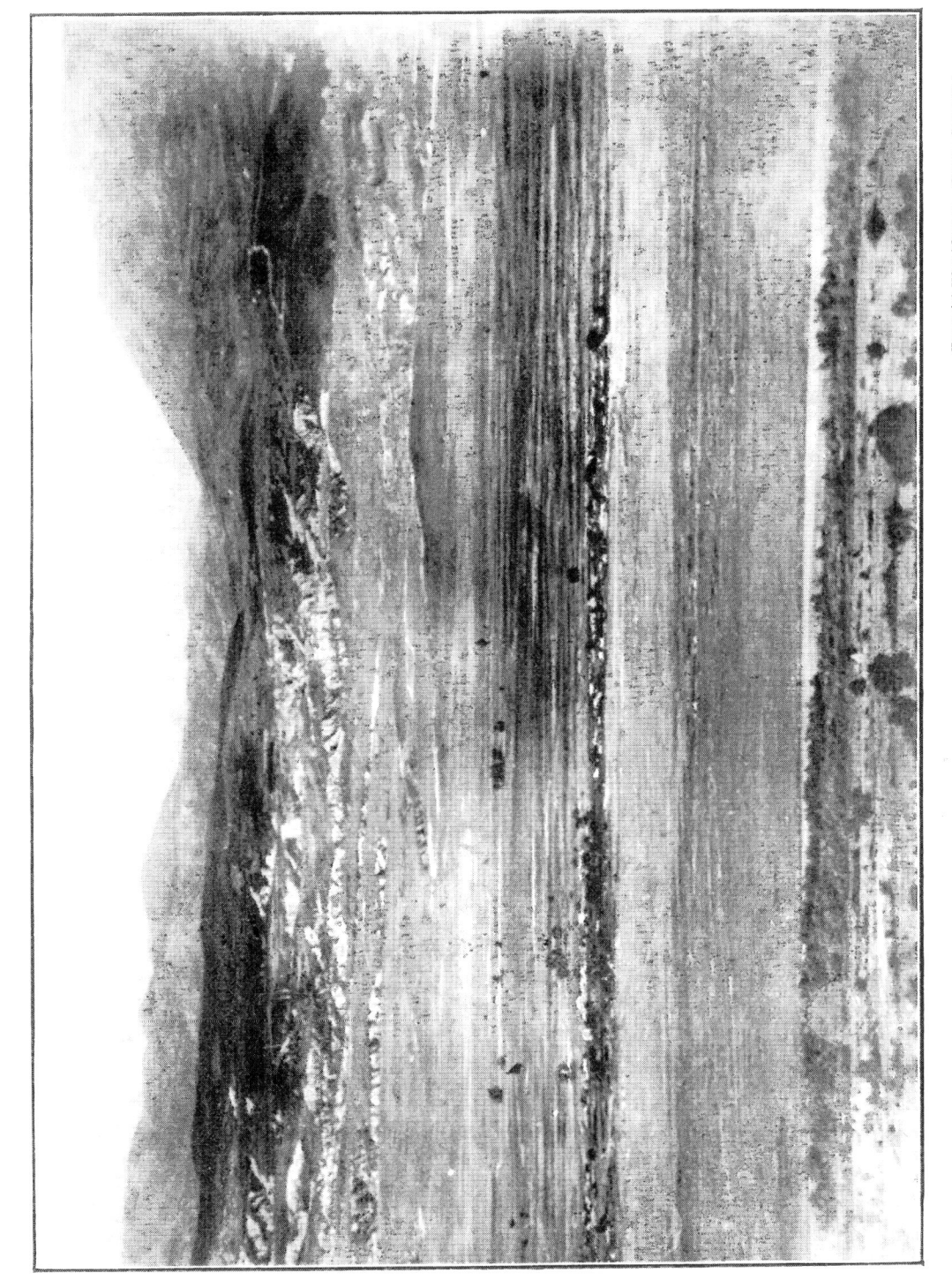

[Imperial War Museum—Crown Copyright.

NEVOLYEN.

The R. Struma is seen in the immediate foreground, and the village of Nevolyen stretching roughly parallel to it across the centre of the picture.

10th Sept., 1916

in less than fifteen minutes had forced their way against half-hearted resistance to its centre, while the flank companies, pushing forward, came into line very shortly afterwards. At this point the enemy garrison, estimated at about 200, abandoned all effort to maintain their position and, but for an officer and 29 men who surrendered, fled in confusion to the N.N.E., suffering heavy losses from the fire of our guns, which had now established a protective barrage just beyond the northern edge of the village.

So far the operation had proceeded according to plan and had been completely successful. But, if the resistance of the enemy holding Nevolyen had been less than had been anticipated, it was now to be found that the Bulgarians' ability to organise an immediate counter-attack by their reserves had been sadly under-estimated. The intention, it will be remembered, was for the FIFTH to remain in Nevolyen till dusk and to withdraw under cover of darkness. About 5.45 p.m. a very disturbing development was observed from the hills to the rear of and high above Battalion Headquarters, where the Corps, Division and Brigade commanders had taken their stand and been able to view every movement of the attackers after their emergence from the crops. Now a Bulgarian battalion was seen to be moving against Nevolyen from the northeast, and very shortly afterwards a second was observed advancing south from Topalova. The Brigadier, realising the danger which threatened the FIFTH, immediately sent word to Captain Rushbrooke, instructing him to exercise his own discretion with regard to retirement, and warning him not to allow his troops to become so closely involved as to be unable to extricate themselves without assistance. These orders, however, never reached their destination;* and though, as the advancing Bulgarians began to throw out wings to either flank, their intention of enveloping the village became ever more evident to those watching from the hills, the movement was concealed from the FIFTH, who had now completed the occupation of Nevolyen, and for some time yet were to know nothing of the danger in which they stood. It was not, in fact, till the enemy were actually closing on the village that Rushbrooke became aware that a situation had arisen which had been unforeseen by those who had planned the operation, and from which escape could be effected only by an immediate withdrawal. This he ordered, and thereby at a most critical moment extricated the bulk of the Battalion from the perilous situation in which it was placed. Casualties, however, had already been heavy; and the killed and wounded, among whom was a large proportion of officers, had perforce to be abandoned. Immediately he observed that the companies were in motion, Rushbrooke fired a pre-arranged signal for the artillery to cover the retirement. By 6.35 p.m. the FIFTH were clear of the village, and a barrage had been placed on its southern edge by the guns, which had answered the call for covering fire with great promptitude. In the course of the withdrawal the Battalion suffered further losses from an attack against its left flank. This, however, was successfully repulsed, and under cover of the artillery, whose accurate and deadly fire inflicted heavy casualties on the enemy, the survivors of the four companies at

Map No. 34

---

* Captain (now Lieut.-Colonel) Rushbrooke was unaware that these orders had been sent to him until he was informed, 20 years later, by the present writer that their despatch is recorded in the War Diary of the 84th Inf. Brigade. That he did not receive them is explained by the following facts:—(i) there were no means by which Brigade H.Q. could have transmitted a message, except through Battalion H.Q., with which they were connected by telephone; (ii) communication forward of Battalion H.Q., from which a line had been run out, for some reason completely broke down. From start to finish Rushbrooke received no message of any kind from the rear, and in so far as he was compelled to depart from the formal orders given to him, he acted throughout on his own initiative.

length gained safety in the concealment of the crops. At 7.40 p.m. they began to re-cross the Struma, but the search for wounded men was continued for some hours, and it was not till 10.45 p.m. that the last of the unwounded reached the right bank and companies re-formed to return to their headquarters.

Thus, owing to an under-estimate of the enemy's organisation, an operation which had opened brilliantly had narrowly escaped ending in complete disaster. Those who from the hills had watched the advance of the FIFTH on Nevolyen, witnessing the steadiness with which the men moved forward under fire, and the perfect formations maintained by the companies, had felt that they were looking down on some peace manoeuvre. Had timely warning been given of the enemy's counter-attack, the Battalion could have withdrawn in equally perfect order, bringing with them their killed and wounded, and the total of their casualties would have been far less. Yet, though the plan had miscarried, the operation had gone far towards attaining its main object. To the Bulgarians it doubtless appeared to be a reconnaissance in force preliminary to an attack on a larger scale. However, this may be, it is certain that there was no weakening of the enemy forces on the Struma front after the FIFTH's attack on Nevolyen.

The losses sustained by the Battalion on the 10th September, 1916, were as under :—

OFFICERS.

Killed or Died of wounds	Captain H. U. Scrutton, " A " Company. Captain P. E. Johnstone, " D " (Company. 3/D.L.I. (att.) 2nd Lieutenant J. Dingle, " B " Company. 2nd Lieutenant J. Garner King, " A " Company. 2nd Lieutenant R. Parish, " D" Company.
Wounded	Lieutenant F. A. Price, " C " Company. 2nd Lieutenant J. A. Tiswell, 16/Royal Fus. (attd.).
Wounded and P. of W.	2nd Lieutenant S. C. Barber, " A " Company. 2nd Lieutenant H. G. Taylor. 2nd Lieutenant I. A. McGregor, " C " Company.

OTHER RANKS.

Killed, Wounded and Missing = 119.

The above casualties represented roughly 50% of the officers and 30% of the others ranks who had taken part in the operation.

After two days' rest the FIFTH relieved the Camerons, who had been in temporary occupation of their defence line during their attack on Nevolyen. It was now decided that the British line should be advanced by the occupation of the villages on the far side of the Struma. As a first step towards this, demonstrations and

Sept.–Oct., 1916

reconnaissances in force were carried out by the 28th Division during the remainder of September; and on their right a brigade of the 27th Division on the last day of the month attacked and occupied certain villages to the south of the Orlyak-Seres road. October was to see a gradual extension northwards of these positions, and the end of the month to find the British firmly established on the left bank of the river.

Winter was now approaching, and it was bitterly cold at night and in the early morning. The weather, however, remained fine, and there was as yet no sign of the mosquitoes relaxing their activities. On the 5th October, in a raid on Nevolyen, the 2/Cheshire captured 16 prisoners; but the time had not yet come for its permanent occupation, and the battalion later withdrew. On the following day cavalry patrols reported that the enemy had vacated the more advanced villages and fallen back on an entrenched position between Kalendra and Topalova, covering the railway. On the 10th the FIFTH were detached to the 85th Brigade, and relieved the 2/Buffs in the village of Mazirko, which they had occupied a few days earlier. And on the same day the 2/Cheshire also crossed the river and pushed patrols forward to Topalova, which was found deserted, and Prosenik, which was cleared against slight resistance. This situation remained unchanged till the 25th October, when the 84th Brigade, on relief by troops of the 10th Division was withdrawn to Turica, where it was rejoined by the FIFTH.

While, during these days, the right and centre of the 28th Division had thus been advanced, the 83rd Brigade on the left had crossed the Struma and occupied the line of villages, Elisan–Ormanli–Haznatar. This line was now to be temporarily taken over by the 84th Brigade, preliminary to an attack by the 83rd on the 31st October for the capture of Bairakli Jum'a. In the relief, which was carried out on the 28th, the FIFTH (less one company) were held in reserve at Cavdarmah, and one company placed in a forward position between the two battalions in occupation of Elisan and Ormanli. From a private diary one learns that duty in reserve at Cavdarmah was not without its excitements. Under 29th October one reads: "All sitting about in new camp when two shells come over and land slap bang amongst the men. Not big and only one man grazed." It seems, however, that certain amenities could be enjoyed in the village, for the diarist also records that he slept the same night "in a room which is quite comfortable though only made of mud and sticks."

The 84th Brigade was required to co-operate in the attack of the 83rd on the 31st October, firstly by covering the flanks of the advance as far as Elisan and Haznatar, and secondly by the capture and occupation of Dolap Ciftl, a farm situated east of the Dolap stream and about 1200 yards south of Bairakli Jum'a. The latter task was allotted to the FIFTH, who, having carried their objective, were to gain touch with the 1/K.O.Y.L.I., the right battalion of the 83rd Brigade, near Trench 10 at the north end of Dolap Wood. By the original plan the FIFTH were required to cross the Dolap stream to the west of the farm, and to attack from that direction. To this, however, Lieut. Colonel Hardman Jones put forward the objection that the enemy's defensive artillery barrage had been observed to fall on that side of his position, and he urged that a more favourable line of advance would be from the south.* The suggested alteration in the plan having been sanctioned, arrangements

Map No. 34

---

* This point is mentioned as it has been found that in the 84th Brigade's report on the action it is erroneously stated that the FIFTH deployed to the west of Dolap Ciftl. The error, however, has not been repeated in the Official History.

were made for the construction of a foot-bridge across the Dolap stream at a point about 1500 yards north-east of Cavdarmah, by which the FIFTH were to cross under cover of darkness and advance north for the clearing of Dolap Wood and the capture of the farm. The nature of the operation, which had little in common with the trench to trench attacks of the Western Front, demanded the tactics of open warfare. There was, for example, to be nothing in the form of a creeping barrage to cover the infantry advance, artillery support being rendered in the first place by a sharp bombardment of the enemy's positions, and later by observation. Following the preliminary bombardment, companies and platoons, giving mutual support, were to gain ground by fire and movement till within assaulting distance of their objectives. One section of the 84th M.G. Company was attached to the 2/FIFTH for the attack, which was to be carried out by "B" Company (Captain Fenwick), on the right, and "A" Company (Captain Dodd), on the left; the remaining companies were to follow in reserve with Battalion H.Q. in readiness to support the forward troops as required.

The weather during the night preceding the attack was appalling; and when, in the small hours of the morning of the 31st October, the Battalion moved out of Cavdarmah, torrential rain was falling, and the troops had to grope their way forward to the foot-bridge in inky darkness, broken by occasional blinding flashes of lightning. Conditions for an approach march could, indeed, have scarcely been worse; but the two leading companies, under Major Gibson, were none the less across the bridge in good time, and by 6.30 a.m. the whole Battalion had been transferred to the east bank of the stream and deployed for attack about one mile south of Dolap Ciftl.

Rain was to continue intermittently throughout the day, and though at daybreak, it had for a time ceased, the sky remained overcast, mists hung over the distant hills, and haze in the valley made artillery observation difficult, if not impossible. At 7.15 a.m. the British bombardment opened. Opposite the 83rd Brigade, the enemy's outposts, having sought shelter from both weather and artillery fire, were taken by surprise, and within thirty minutes the troops of the main attack had entered Bairakli Jum'a without encountering any serious opposition. It was otherwise with the FIFTH, who in their subsidiary attack met with stiffer resistance. On approaching their objectives, the leading companies came under heavy fire from the enemy's riflemen, many of whom had climbed the trees of the orchards surrounding Dolap farm, in order to obtain a better command over the ground over which the attackers were advancing. At this point 2nd Lieutenants Redwood, Rogers and Hills were wounded, and many casualties were sustained among the other ranks.* The advance, however, was continued slowly and methodically, and by 8 a.m. the FIFTH had secured a footing in Dolap Wood. The enemy now abandoned all effort to oppose the advance and fled to Bairakli Jum'a, where they fell into the hands of the 83rd Brigade; while the FIFTH, following up through Dolap Wood, by 9 a.m. had carried the whole of their objectives, and shortly afterwards joined hands with the 1/K.O.Y.L.I. at Trench 10.

In this very successful operation the Battalion lost, in addition to the three officers already mentioned, 11 other ranks killed or died of wounds, and 20 wounded—casualties which greatly exceeded the total number sustained by the whole of the 83rd Brigade. 300 prisoners in all were taken, and though few, if any, had surrendered to the FIFTH, who had driven them into the hands of others, this was

---

* 2nd Lieutenant J. M. Hills died on the 10th November, 1916, as a result of his wounds.

but a reversal of the fortunes of war which had favoured the Regiment on a previous occasion in its history.*

The line now taken up by the 28th Division ran from Elisan, by Dolap, Bairakli Jum'a, and Haznatar to the junction of the Struma and Butkovo rivers, and thence along the south bank of the latter to Akbusalik. The 84th Brigade, occupying the right of the three sections of the Divisional Front, held a line from Elisan to just north of Bairakli Jum'a—a frontage of nearly five miles. The defences, covered by a continuous belt of wire, consisted of 25 self-contained posts at an average interval of 300 yards, each garrisoned by a platoon or half-platoon. The three battalions allotted to the defences each held two companies in the line and two in reserve in Elisan, Ormanli, or Bairakli Jum'a. Two trench-mortars were attached to each battalion, and three sections of the Brigade M.G. Company were distributed along the defence line. For the next four months the FIFTH, when actively employed, were to do duty in one or other of these three battalion sub-sections. In this more advanced line that had now been taken up beyond the river, the British troops in the Struma valley were in a more favourable position for holding the Bulgarian forces opposed to them. Though the task of keeping the enemy in constant suspense as to our intentions allowed of little rest for the troops, it provided no outstanding episode; and there was little variety in the work of the FIFTH while in the line. Reconnaissance was carried out from day to day towards the opposing villages of Kumli, Kyupri, and Bairakli† either by infantry patrols or cavalry supported by infantry; and from time to time when it was found that the enemy had occupied some village, stronger parties would be sent out to clear it, and a company or platoon left to occupy it during daylight, or sometimes for a day or two. Though there were frequent encounters with the enemy, our casualties were insignificant; the FIFTH losing no more than two or three men wounded or captured during the whole period. On the other hand, the enemy at times suffered considerable loss, as for instance on the occasion of a raid on Kyupri carried out by a troop of Yeomanry and two companies of the 1/Suffolk, supported by " D " Company of the FIFTH. The complete success of this operation, in which 30 prisoners were taken at the cost of one man of the Suffolk killed and one of the FIFTH slightly wounded, owed much to the action of a platoon under the command of Lieutenant Clive Smith, which by a skilful demonstration against the south-west corner of the village held the enemy to an advanced trench, and so prevented them from opposing the advance of the Suffolk.

The mosquitoes had now retired to winter quarters, and malaria was no longer depleting the ranks as it had done during the summer and autumn; but, though rid of these pests, the troops—who, be it marked, had not had a roof over their heads since landing in the country—suffered great hardship from the bitter cold and frequent heavy snow-storms. Here was an essential difference between the

---

* Professor C. T. Atkinson, the eminent military historian, recently pointed out to the present writer that the capture of a large number of prisoners at Wilhelmstahl, which won for the FIFTH a hitherto unique battle honour, was, in fact, due chiefly to the exertions of others. "On that occasion Guards, Grenadier, and Highland battalions (8 in all), at a cost of close on 600 casualties, drove the enemy into the arms of the FIFTH, who received them with so fierce and effective fire as to make it clear that there was no chance of escape, whereupon they surrendered, over 2,700 of the choicest troops of France laying down their arms." The total casualties of the FIFTH, however, amounted only to 13.

† About 1½ miles east of Bairakli Jum'a, with which it should not be confused.

lot of the soldier in the Struma valley and that of his comrade on the Western Front. The latter could often look to a considerable degree of comfort when in reserve; the former to none. Moreover, great as was the value of the "Kopriva Palace Theatre" as relief to the monotony of life in the Defence Line at Elisan or Bairakli Jum'a, it could scarcely be comparable to the entertainment organised for the troops at rest in France or Flanders in the year 1917.

Hitherto the wide extent of front for which the 28th Division was responsible, combined with the weakness of its units through sickness, had made it impossible for infantry brigades to be withdrawn for the purpose of rest and training. Towards the end of 1916, however, the War Office, having regard to the special conditions prevailing in Macedonia, decided that the "Garrison Battalions" in that theatre— units recruited from men who by reason of age or other disabilities were normally regarded as fit only for employment in back areas—should be formed into the 228th Infantry Brigade and employed on defence duties in the line. In March, 1917, this brigade was placed at the disposal of the G.O.C. 28th Division, who was thereby enabled to arrange for each of his active brigades to undergo in turn a period of training for operations which were now in contemplation. General Sarrail was still determined to pursue the policy of a strong offensive in the Balkans, and April and May were to see the opening — and, as it was to prove, the collapse — of a large scale attack. Though the XVI. Corps in the Struma valley was to take no direct part in these operations, which were to be carried out on and to the west of the Dojran front, it was required to embark on a minor offensive for the capture of limited objectives, with the object of holding the Bulgarians on its front, and thereby indirectly assisting the main attack. In the first phase of these subsidiary operations, the 85th Brigade was to capture a group of trenches to the north-west of Bairakli Jum'a, known as Ferdie and Essex, which were held by the enemy as an outpost position. After these forward trenches had been carried and consolidated, preparations were to be made for the capture by the 84th Brigade of Ernekoj and Spatovo in the Bulgarian main line of defence.

Although, as will be seen later, the final phase of these operations was never to mature, it was in order to practice its part that the 84th Brigade, on the 15th March, was relieved in the line and moved to Orlyak. On the 21st the FIFTH marched thence to Ferry Hill, three miles north-west of Kopriva, in order to rehearse an advance under a creeping artillery barrage. This somewhat hazardous exercise, which was carried out with live shell, and in full view of the enemy, was rendered the more realistic by the bewildered Bulgarians adding their quota of artillery fire before it was concluded. It was, however, completed without any untoward incident. Further practice for the attack was carried out during the last few days of the month with the help of a replica of Ernekoj—Spatovo position, which had been constructed near Orlyak.

On the 2nd April the 84th relieved the 85th Brigade in centre of the 28th Division front between Baraikli Jum'a and Alipsa, the FIFTH taking over the right of the section. The tour was, however, a brief one, as at the end of a fortnight, occupied mainly with active patrolling, the 85th Brigade returned to the line, and the 84th Brigade withdrew once again to Orlyak. After celebrating St. George's Day here, the FIFTH on the 24th April set out on a four days' trek in the hills round Mirova. Daily battles were fought against the 2/Cheshire, who played the part of "Comitadjis."

April-May, 1917

The object of the expedition was to re-condition the men, and the general health and fitness both of the FIFTH and their "guerilla enemies" had greatly benefited when they declared peace and returned together to Orlyak to resume training in "civilised warfare."

Maps Nos. 33 and 34

In the meantime General Sarrail's projected offensive had opened with attacks by the British divisions on the Dojran front, which had made little progress, and had been followed by operations by the French and Serbians to the west of the Vardar which had fared no better. The disappointing results of these initial efforts, however, in no way dissuaded Sarrail from continuing the offensive; and his decision to renew the attack required that the 28th Division should now carry out the subsidiary role allotted to it.

On the evening of the 14th May the FIFTH were moved to Ormanli, where they came into reserve to the 85th Brigade, which, it will be remembered, was to carry out the first phase of the operations against the enemy's outpost positions to the north of Bairakli Jum'a. The attack, which was launched at 6.30 p.m. on the following evening, proved a complete success; Ferdie and Essex trenches were carried without the FIFTH being called upon, and 80 prisoners were captured. Some days were to elapse before the 84th Brigade was brought up to continue the attack for the capture of the enemy's main position; and during this time the FIFTH, still attached to the 85th Brigade, were employed in assisting in the consolidation of the captured position, making preparations for the second phase of the operations, and practising their own deployment by dark for the part they were to play in this. But before the 84th Brigade had been brought forward, news came that a final attack opened by General Sarrail on the 17th May had ended disastrously. "The Franco-Serbian offensive, to which all the British operations had been subsidiary, had, in fact, resulted in total failure." (Official History.) From the first the task allotted to the 84th Brigade had been regarded as one which could be accomplished only at heavy cost, and as it now could serve no useful purpose, General Milne ordered its cancellation.*

It has only been possible to give a vague outline of the general situation on the front of the Allies; but this should be sufficient to satisfy the reader as to the wisdom of General Milne's decision. To the troops in the Struma valley, however, with little knowledge of any but local events, the reason for the cancellation of the attack was by no means clear. For months past they had been manning defences, which the enemy seemed quite content to let them hold; in such encounters as they had had with the Bulgarian troops they had proved their own superiority; and it was but natural that, from time to time, they had wondered what purpose they were serving towards ending the War. During their recent training, however, it had seemed that at last they were to be given the opportunity of engaging in an operation, the object of which was clearly defined. With its cancellation, accordingly, there came a sense of anti-climax and disappointment in feeling that they were to be thrown back on the same monotonous and seemingly purposeless existence, with its

---

* The view that the attack of the 84th Brigade would result in heavy casualties was chiefly based on the belief that the enemy's main position was protected by heavy wire. After the armistice Lieut. Colonel Rushbrooke had the opportunity of viewing the position from the enemy's side, and found that actually the wire in front of it was by no means a serious obstacle. He formed the opinion that the 84th Brigade would have had little difficulty in carrying the position. This, however, does not alter the fact that the operation had lost its whole object.

everlasting patrols, which had been their lot for so many months. If this was their expectation, it was, indeed, to prove well justified; but they at least had the satisfaction of learning now that they were for a time to leave the Struma valley. General Milne had long since decided that he would not leave his troops in this malarious region during a second summer. As it had proved impracticable to quit it by a forward movement, he now adopted the only alternative, and ordered a withdrawal to the hills which overlooked the valley. In preparation for this, the next few weeks were to be spent in dismantling defences and evacuating stores to the right bank of the Struma.

It has been suggested above that the British troops were occasionally puzzled as to the reason for their having been sent to Salonica and their retention in Macedonia. The following propaganda pamphlet, preserved in the records of the 84th Brigade, may be of interest as purporting to show that there were others who shared their bewilderment :—

> " Good Englishmen
>
> We the Bulgarian soldiers wonder why you people stand opposity us, when the end of this war will be desided to some other front not here. . . .
>
> You left your own fatherland and came here to fight with people who has nothing to divide with you.
>
> We simply are waching our dear home, and never had enny intention to disturb you.
>
> You came here to protect the grandomaniac ideas of the bloodthursted and discontented Servian poeple, who are looking to grab lands which do not bllong to them.
>
> By the way you are geting deseived and misleaded by your officers. . . .
>
> Your allys did not have and will not have the slightes success nowhere. Their failors and smotes (?) they show to you as their victory, but they have never made a headalong nowhere.
>
> We take pleasure to inform you that the Italians are resieving what they deserve. They have lost in three days what they gained in three years. . . . Why do you not go, O ! you brave and noble Englishmen to save your poor ally Italy ? "

Though the intention of the above address to the British soldier was, of course, deliberately subversive, evidence was not lacking that the Bulgarians in truth not only favoured a policy of " live and let live," but had the qualities of sportsmen. A game of football, for instance, could be played in full view of the enemy without fear of molestation—unless it was being watched by a *very* big crowd ; nor was hunting ever interfered with. A drill parade, however, was more than they would put up with : once one was observed, shells were sure to follow.

On the 26th May, the 84th relieved the 85th Brigade in the captured position of Ferdie and Essex trenches; and the FIFTH, on reverting to their own brigade, replaced the 2/East Surrey in the line. Shortly before this relief, Major W. Gibson, who had been acting as Second-in-Command for just over twelve months, left the Battalion, on appointment to command the 2/21st London Regiment, and was replaced by Captain W. L. P. Rushbrooke.

May-June, 1917

A withdrawal in the face of the enemy, such as was now contemplated, is always a difficult and delicate operation; but fortunately the Bulgarians showed little enterprise. Our patrols occasionally came under fire, and a few shells were directed against our positions, which were also sniped by riflemen or machine-guns from time to time. Generally speaking, however, demolition of the wire entanglements and evacuation of stores proceeded from day to day without serious interference or evidence that the enemy suspected a withdrawal. On the 2nd June a raid by the 1/Welch, who were on the right of the FIFTH, secured 20 prisoners and inflicted heavy loss on the enemy, who was thereby induced to concentrate on measures for his own protection rather than for informing himself of our activities. By the 12th June everything was in readiness for evacuation, and shortly after midnight "C" and "D" Companies, under Captain Rushbrooke, withdrew across the Struma to bivouac in the Gumas Dere nullah, just west of Kopriva. In wretched weather—for heavy rain had now set in—the remainder of the Battalion continued in occupation of the outpost line throughout the following day till darkness fell, when they withdrew without molestation and, crossing to the right bank, reached Gumas Dere without incident. On the 15th June the FIFTH concentrated at Paprat, to which "C" and "D" Companies had already moved, and on the same day the Bulgarians opened a bombardment of the positions which had been evacuated 36 hours before. Thus the Battalion came again to Paprat, to camp within 400 yards of the site it had occupied twelve months before, when constructing tracks leading to the Struma, from which they had now been withdrawn.

In the "Summer Line" the 28th Division was responsible for a frontage of 18 miles, from Lozista to the eastern shore of Lake Dojran at Surlovo. The "Line of Defence," which was also defined as the "line of resistance," consisted of a chain of detached works, established along the 1000 foot contour on the northern slope of the Krusha Balkans, running in a curve roughly parallel to the Dojran-Rupel railway, which faced it to the north. The system included advanced defended localities embracing Dova Tepe Fort and Dova Tepe East. The front was divided into two sections, each garrisoned by one Infantry Brigade Group, with the Todorovo Rieka as the central boundary. The third Brigade Group was held in Divisional Reserve at Paprat and Karamatli.* The Policy was one of active defence; the line of resistance being held as lightly as possible, in order that local reserves should be available if required. Constant patrolling was to be carried out, minor enterprises organised, and all means taken to harass the enemy and prevent his patrols from crossing the valley which separates the Krusha Balkans from the Belasica plateau.

After ten days at Paprat the 84th Brigade, having received orders to relieve the 228th in the right section of the 28th Division front, made a four days march by Mirova, Krusova, and Petkovo, to Bashanli. In the relief which followed, three battalions only were required for the Defence Line, and the FIFTH were held in reserve at Baili.† Though the Battalion had left the Struma valley, it was not yet rid of

---

* Infantry Brigade Groups, which included R.A. and R.E., were, it seems, generally kept intact. In referring to reliefs, etc., the term "Brigade" has been hitherto employed for the sake of brevity, when "Brigade Group" would have been often more strictly accurate. The dispositions of the Division in the Summer Line as given above are based on a Defence Scheme dated July 7th, 1917; actually, on first taking over the line, the 228th Brigade was still with the 28th Division, and *two* brigades were in reserve.

† Baili is not shown on Map 33. It was situated west of Bashanli and about 3¼ miles south of Todorovo.

246   THE FIFTH IN THE GREAT WAR.

Map No. 33   the curse of malaria, to which no fewer than 148 casualties which had occurred during   July–Oct.,
the march from Paprat were attributable.   1917

Of the next three months, during which the 28th Division remained in the Summer Line, there is little to record. Even with the forward battalions few incidents occurred to break the normal routine of patrolling; and with the FIFTH, in reserve, time was taken up with training and the everlasting, if important, work of road construction. The heat in August was severe; and during the two months ending the 10th September no rain fell. With this drier weather the health of the Battalion greatly improved, malaria cases dropping by over 50% within a week or two of the cessation of the rains, and thereafter steadily diminishing.

At the beginning of October preparations began for the troops to descend again for the winter to the Struma valley and the lower slopes of the Krusha Balkans. The sector allotted to the 28th Division in the "Winter Line" ran from the junction of the Struma and Orlyak rivers to Hodza Dere, just north of Akbu Salik, and was divided into three parts—the Struma, Butkovo Marsh, and Krusha Balkan Fronts. The 84th Brigade was to be responsible for occupying the last-named of these three fronts for the greater part of the time that the FIFTH remained with it in Macedonia, but as it was to take its place on the line of the Struma shortly before the Battalion left the country, a brief description of the whole Divisional Sector may be given here.

Starting from the right; on the Struma front, permanently occupied bridgeheads, linked by works which could be manned at short notice, were together to form the line of resistance. These defences on the line of the river were, however, to be covered by outposts on the line Jenikoj-Nevoljen-Cuculuk-Elisan-Cavdarmah. To the north of Kopriva the line was drawn back to the right bank of the Struma, to pass south of the Butkovo Marsh (or Lake).* In this central portion of the Sector, protected as it was by the marsh, the only measures that it was necessary to take in defence were for the prevention of the passage of spies. This was to be guarded against during daylight by military patrols furnished by the units on each flank, and at night by Divisional "agents."† The defence line on the Krusha Balkan Front was to run from Lozista to Akbusalik, just in advance of and lower than the Summer Line; and the duty of the troops holding it would be, not only to keep the enemy on the far side of the Butkovo stream, but to patrol across the stream and clear the villages to the north of the railway of any parties that might descend to them from the Bulgarian main position, which here ran along the crest of the Belasica Range.

The FIFTH had now been detailed for the occupation of the left sub-section of the Krusha Balkan Front, with boundaries, defining the flanks of their position and of the area they were to patrol, which ran, on the right, from Matnica to Tchaouchlou (1 mile S.E. of Todorovo), and on the left, from Globostica to Akbusalik—a frontage of roughly two miles. The line to be taken up in defence included three main spurs, which were to be strongly held by rifle posts protected by the cross fire of Vickers and Lewis guns, and three re-entrants, which were each to be blocked by a central work. Three companies were to be disposed in defence of the line, and the fourth held in reserve with Battalion H.Q. at Todorovo.

---

* Like other lakes in Macedonia, e.g. the northern part of Tahinos, Butkovo at certain seasons of the year could be more aptly termed a *marsh*.

† The name given to *Comitadjis* in the service of the British.

Oct., 1917

By the 9th October reconnaissance of the winter position had been completed, and the work of establishing forward dumps of stores began; the parties employed on this being covered by scouts. On the 11th, the enemy, having observed the movement that was in progress, laid an ambush of some 25 men among the scrub and thorn bushes which covered the hill side. As our scouts went forward to search some old trenches and dug-outs they were suddenly received by a volley of bombs. These were wildly thrown and caused no damage, but as a result of a final discharge, hurled as a Parthian shaft by the Bulgarians before they fled to the shelter of the woods beyond the Butkovo stream, Lieutenant Clive Smith, the Scout Officer, and three of his men were slightly wounded.* Fire opened by the scouts inflicted several casualties on the enemy before they made good their escape, and later a wounded man was found and brought in as a prisoner.† From the 12th to the 14th the Belasica Range was shrouded in heavy mists, which concealed all movement from the enemy's observation posts; and on the latter date, all arrangements having been completed, the FIFTH took up their position in the Winter Line.

Map No. 33

The Battalion was to remain in defence of this position for rather over four months, during which patrolling was continually carried out across the stream to the line of the railway. Contact with the enemy was rare, but had always to be anticipated, as from time to time his patrols descended from the Belasica to the lower slopes just north of the railway, and on occasion would be found in temporary occupation of the villages in that region. During the first four weeks, although enemy movement had been reported by our observation posts, no patrol of the FIFTH was engaged. Information then came that the Bulgarians had established themselves to the south of the village of East Sugovo; and Captain G. Clarke, attached to the 2/FIFTH from the 3/North Staffordshire, was ordered to patrol towards the village in the early hours of the 5th November and endeavour to locate the enemy's posts. Setting out shortly before midnight with one platoon, Clarke crossed the Butkovo stream and the railway, and by 3 a.m. came to within close distance of the village without any sign having been given of the presence of the enemy. He then decided to make a personal reconnaissance of the village, and, keeping with him his orderly and two scouts, ordered the platoon serjeant to withdraw the remainder of the party to the cover of a bank a short distance in rear. The serjeant, it seems, misunderstanding his orders, withdrew the whole way back to the bank of the Butkovo stream. Clarke, unaware that he had been thus left unsupported, was now working his way forward through the scrub, which surrounded his objective. On approaching the village, he suddenly came under heavy rifle fire from a house that stood in a semi-circular clearing

---

* Lieutenant Clive Smith was awarded the Military Cross in recognition of his courage and resource in many patrol incidents. In 1920, while serving with the 2/FIFTH in Northern Iraq, he was assassinated at Tel Afar, together with the crew of an armoured car of which he was in charge.

† Major Redwood relates that, though several of the enemy fell to our fire on this occasion, others met their death in more tragic circumstances. Several bombs were heard to burst from the direction in which the enemy had fled, and it was later found that these had been exploded by certain wounded *Serbians*—men who had earlier in the war been captured and forced to fight on the side of Bulgaria. These unfortunate men regarded a self-inflicted death as preferable to the fate they thought would be theirs if, by falling into our hands, they were found to be fighting for the enemy. Major Redwood says that the prisoner was himself a Serbian, and that the terrible wound which he survived had been, by his own confession, self-inflicted. He is of opinion that the greater number of the men forming the ambush were Serbians.

on its outskirts. Hastily withdrawing to cover, he found that of the three men who had accompanied him, one had been wounded in the leg and another was missing. He immediately went forward again to search for the missing man, whose groans he presently heard; and whom a little later he saw lying within twenty yards of the house. He then began to crawl forward with the intention of assisting his wounded comrade and endeavouring to bring him in. His movements, however, were observed by the enemy, who once more opened fire and wounded him, breaking his arm in two places. Thus disabled, he was forced to abandon his efforts; but, despite his shattered arm, assisted the other wounded man back over a distance of nearly three miles to the Butkovo stream, where he rejoined the main body of the patrol.*

Rather more than a week after the incident related above, the Bulgarians in their turn crossed the Butkovo, and at 1 a.m. on the 16th November made an attempt to raid one of our posts. The raiders, however, who numbered about 30, in trying to get through our wire obstacle, fell into a trap which had been set all along the line. Stumbling against trip wires, they released flares and bombs which gave the alarm to the garrison. Finding themselves immediately subjected to rifle and machine-gun fire and a hail of rifle and hand grenades, they paused only to fling a number of bombs, which effected nothing, before retiring. A patrol, which crossed the Butkovo at dawn, found that they had abandoned six rifles, a stretcher, and a telephone apparatus, which, together with a large number of caps, gave evidence of the confusion into which they had been thrown and the severe casualties which they had undoubtedly suffered. The sharp lesson taught to the Bulgarians in this, their first attempt against the front of the FIFTH, resulted in it being also their last. Throughout the whole subsequent period spent by the Battalion the enemy never again approached its trenches. Nor did their artillery show any greater enterprise than the infantry. On one day only during December is it recorded that they shelled the front; and in January, though their guns were a little more active, no harm was done by their fire.

But, if the life of the Battalion was devoid of such incident as can find a place in this history, it was by no means one of ease and idleness. All with experience know the danger there is of daily patrols from a fixed front being allowed to become a matter of routine; and how easy it is, when for days on end no sign is seen of an enemy, for patrol leaders to grow careless and consequently liable to be ambushed. The work was always dangerous; and that the casualties in the FIFTH amounted during this period to no more than 1 officer and 4 other ranks wounded testifies to the skill and care with which it was carried out. It may even be held that this less spectacular work of the 2nd Battalion in Macedonia was in some respects better calculated to

---

* The account given of the above incident is based for the most part on the official report which accompanied the recommendation of Captain Clarke for the award of the Military Cross, which was granted to him in recognition of his gallantry on this and two previous occasions. The point concerning the misunderstanding, by which the main body of the patrol was prematurely withdrawn to the Butkovo, has, however, been communicated by Major Redwood, who also gives a slightly different account of Clarke's action. According to this, the man fell wounded among the scrub. The nature of his wound meant that it would be fatal to carry him any great distance, and Clarke conceived that the only chance of saving his life would be to carry him *forward* to the clearing, where he would be found and, it was hoped, attended to by the Bulgarians. Whichever be the true version of the incident, it remains clear that this officer risked his life in an attempt to save that of one of his men.

develop initiative in junior leaders than that in which the 1st Battalion was at this time engaged at such heavy cost on the Western Front.

On the 25th February the FIFTH were relieved in the line and withdrawn to Radile, whence they marched on the following day to Tile Spur,* where they were engaged in training till the 10th March. Orders were now issued for the 84th Brigade to change places with the 228th, which had hitherto occupied the right section of the Struma Front.† In this the Brigade was to be disposed in depth, one battalion being in occupation of the outpost line, one placed at Dragos in readiness to garrison the river line, and a third held in Brigade Reserve. The fourth battalion was to be in Corps Reserve. Under these arrangements the FIFTH were ordered to take over the outpost position from the 22/Rifle Brigade, and on the 11th March left Tile Spur for Dragos, which was reached the following day. The relief was completed on the 13th; "B," "C," and "D" Companies taking over a line from Nevolyen, by Cuculuk, to the eastern edge of Elisan, while "A" was held in reserve with Battalion H.Q. at Cuckoo Bridge. The forward companies were disposed in six works, each constructed for all round defence and occupation by two platoons. These works, of which some were as far apart as 1100 yards, were connected by telephone; and the whole front was protected by a continuous belt of wire, which was patrolled by night.

Shortly after the move to the Struma front, Brigadier-General G. A. Weir, under whom the 2/FIFTH had served for the past 2½ years, was transferred to Egypt, being replaced in command of the 84th Brigade by Brigadier-General R. C. Nisbet.

The six weeks spent by the FIFTH in the outpost line were uneventful. The enemy remained inactive, and it seems from the number of deserters from their ranks that are recorded at this time in the War Diary of the 28th Division, that their morale was steadily declining. That a sense of humour, none the less, still survived among the Bulgarians is shown by an incident that is related in the same records. In a pantomime, which had been staged by the Division for the amusement of the troops, a song entitled "Boris the Bulgar" had made a great hit. On a night in April notices were left on our wire by an enemy patrol, quoting two verses of the song, stating that it had been translated into their native tongue, and requesting that the music should be supplied!

After spending St. George's Day in the outpost line, the FIFTH were relieved and withdrawn to Dragos.‡ On the 9th May, Major Rushbrooke left the Battalion on appointment to command the 2/D.C.L.I., and the duties of Second-in-Command were taken over by Captain Freeman, who was replaced as adjutant by 2nd Lieutenant W. Pattison, an officer who had been commissioned from the ranks of the FIFTH.

Preliminary to the withdrawal of the troops on the Struma to the Summer Line, Battalion H.Q. and two companies were moved on the 16th May to Ferezli, where they were joined on the 12th June by the remaining companies. The actual

---

* Below Bashanli.

† See p. 256 for the defensive organisation of this Front.

‡ Mention of this last St. George's Day cannot pass in this History of the FIFTH without gratefully recording the name of Sister Augustine (by birth a Fenwick of Northumberland), the Mother Superior of St. Paul's Hospital, Salonica. It was due to the kind interest taken in the Regiment by Sister Augustine that the 2nd Battalion during their service in Macedonia could each year wear their St. George's Day roses, made by refugee Bulgarian children under her care.

taking up of the "Summer Line" in 1918, however, has no place in this history; for news now came that the 2/FIFTH had been selected for service in France. Sad as it was that the Battalion would have to leave the Division with which it had returned from India in 1914 and passed through 3½ years of war, there was little else in the prospect of leaving Macedonia, but the keenest satisfaction. This is not the place to discuss the justification for the maintenance of a British force on the Salonika front; but it is relevant to this History to suggest that, for the regimental officer and man in the ranks, who were not directly concerned with wider strategical considerations, Germany always stood as the one essential enemy in the War. It was, accordingly, on the Western Front, where the Germans were massed, that they could best appreciate the need for the sacrifices they were required to make.

On the 14th June, orders were received for the FIFTH to move to Guvezne, which was reached on the 17th after a three days' march. On the 19th, the Battalion furnished a guard of honour to General Franchet d'Espérey, who had just arrived to assume command of the Allied Armies in Macedonia;* and on the next day it was inspected by the C-i-C. of the British Salonika Force. After his inspection General Milne complimented the Battalion on its fine turn-out, and expressed his pleasure at finding the men so fit after their long stay on the Struma. Later, he presented the riband of the Military Cross to Captain G. E. Fenwick and Lieutenant D. Scott.

On the 22nd and 23rd the FIFTH were moved by half-battalions to a rest camp at Bralo, and on the 25th transferred by motor-lorry to the port of Itea, on the Adriatic. Here, at midnight, they embarked on the French transport *Odessa*; and at dawn on the 26th set sail for Taranto, in southern Italy.

Though the Second Battalion's association with the British Salonika Army was at an end, it was far from having seen the last of "the most formidable, the most unconquerable foe" it had encountered in Macedonia. Some years, indeed, were yet to pass, before the men of the FIFTH who had served in the Struma valley were free from the fever that had been their scourge in that unhealthy theatre.

---

* In relief of General Guillaumat, who had replaced General Sarrail in the preceding December.

CHAPTER XVII.

The Advance to Victory.

"Somme 1918" — "Hindenburg Line"

"Bapaume 1918" — "Canal du Nord."*

FIRST BATTALION—9TH AUGUST TO 29TH SEPTEMBER, 1918.

Aug., 1918.

Map No. 35

On withdrawal from the line on the Hinges front, preparatory to re-joining the Third Army, the 3rd Division remained for some days in the First Army Area, re-organising and preparing for the next great task that lay before it. Its move south began on the 13th August, when the 9th Brigade was transferred by rail to the Le Souich area, just north of Doullens. Here the FIFTH were billeted once more in Ivergny, the little village to which, it may be remembered, they had been withdrawn to rest after the heavy and costly fighting at the end of March. But the situation on the Western Front was now far different from that which had prevailed in those critical days. For, on the 8th August—described by General Ludendorff as "the black day of the German Army in the history of the war"—General Rawlinson's Fourth Army had opened its attack astride the Somme; and in five days the Germans had been driven back a distance of over 12 miles, 22,000 prisoners and 400 guns had been captured, and Amiens freed from the danger in which it had so long stood.

Following this great success, the time had now come for the next stage of the British offensive—the advance of the Third Army on Bapaume—in which the 3rd Division was to participate. The operations were to open on the 21st August with an attack by the IV. and VI. Corps on a front of nine miles to the north of the R. Ancre, for the capture of the line of the Albert—Arras railway, which here formed the enemy's main line of resistance. The 3rd Division, as the right division of the VI. Corps, was to capture a portion of this line; but not till an earlier objective known as the Blue Line, which included the enemy's forward defences, had been carried by the 99th Brigade (2nd Division). It was further planned that, if all went well, success should be exploited by pressing forward beyond the railway for the capture of the village of Gomiecourt and a line running north and south of its eastern edge, known as the "Green Line." This further advance, in which the 3rd Division would be responsible for the capture of the village itself, was however only to be undertaken if it could be covered by whippet tanks. The commanders of leading battalions, on gaining the railway, were accordingly to report as to whether there were places at which it could be crossed by these. Although, as will be seen later, this final phase was not to be carried out on the first day, it was considered in the 3rd Division's plan, and had a direct bearing on the dispositions for attack. With these it is necessary for the reader to be acquainted, if he is to understand the circum-

---

* The battle-honour "Canal du Nord" was awarded in connection with the fighting east of Havrincourt, 27th September 1918. The honour "Havrincourt," which is not held by the Regiment, was granted for the capture of the Hindenburg Front Line at that village, in which the 1/FIFTH took no part.

Map No. 36 stances in which certain units of the several brigades came into contact with the Aug., 1918
FIFTH in the course of the action which is to be described.

By the divisional orders for attack, the 9th and 8th Brigades, with the former on the right, having passed through the 99th Brigade on the Blue Line, were to advance for the capture of the railway. Each brigade was to be disposed with two battalions in line, and the third echelonned in support, in rear of its outer flank. The 76th Brigade was to advance in rear of the centre, with two battalions forward and level with the two supporting battalions of the leading brigades. These four battalions together were to be prepared, on the capture of the railway line, to advance on Gomiecourt, covered by whippet tanks, if this should prove practicable. The diagram below, which shows the position of the FIFTH and certain other battalions, may make the dispositions of the Division clearer.

	1 Bn.	R.S.F.	King's	Fifth	
8 Bde.					9 Bde.
	1 Bn.	1 Bn.	Suffolk	Roy. Fus.	

76 Bde.

1 Bn.

In addition to eight field artillery brigades supporting the Division, one mobile field battery was to be allotted for the close support of each of the three infantry brigades, to which a proportion of machine-guns and R.E. was also attached.*

In the early hours of the 19th August the 9th Brigade left its billets and moved forward to the Hannescamps area, and on the following night was assembled for attack in rear of the 2nd Division and at a distance of some 2,400 yards from the Blue Line. The position allotted to the FIFTH lay between Ablainzeville and Ayette.

†At 4.55 a.m. on the 21st, when the attack opened, the whole country was

---

* Operation Orders leave no doubt that it was intended that the infantry attack should be preceded by heavy tanks. But though their co-operation is mentioned in the 8th Brigade's report of the attack, it seems that, presumably owing to the weather conditions later described, none *covered the advance* of the 9th Brigade, whose Narrative makes no reference, positive or negative to such action. Mention, however, is made of two " carrier tanks," each equivalent to a carrying party of 400 men, which were employed for taking forward tools, stores, etc.

† In attempting to give a close account of the events of the 21st August, the writer has encountered greater difficulty than in any action hitherto recorded. In the fog which prevailed, no accurate idea could be obtained of the actual movements of the various units, and for the Brigade to reconcile the conflicting reports of battalions must have been quite impossible. In such circumstances it seems that the reports on the action rendered by the Brigade and Division present it as having proceeded more closely in accordance with *plan* than was justified by fact. While following the general substance of the " official narrative," the present writer has departed from it in dealing with certain points, which seem to be definitely established by battalion narratives and the statements of company officers. He has had the advantage of far more time to study these than can have been available to the staff officers who were responsible for compiling the official reports.

Aug., 1918 shrouded in mist. Fog, as the British had experienced on more than one occasion during the War, is a severe handicap to the defence; but, as was to be seen to-day, the advantage which to that extent it confers on the attack, is largely discounted by the difficulty found by advancing troops in maintaining touch and direction, and also by the impossibility of their obtaining the assistance of batteries detailed for their close support. When the 99th Brigade advanced for the capture of the Blue Line, visibility was less than 20 yards; and, though very little opposition was encountered before the objective was carried, many parties of the enemy were inevitably over-run. Consequently, a great deal of "mopping up" fell to the troops of the 3rd Division, who, moving on compass bearings, followed close in rear; and it was thus that the FIFTH at a very early stage suffered several casualties from the rifles and machine-guns of isolated parties of Germans, before these, having been located, were rushed and captured. By the time the Battalion closed up on the 1/Berks (99th Brigade) its companies, in these "mopping up" operations, had taken 80 prisoners and several machine-guns. None the less they were well up to schedule, and at 6.25 a.m. the FIFTH passed through the Berkshire on the Blue Line, to advance, as the right battalion of the 9th Brigade, for the capture of their objective on the line of the railway. "W" Company (Captain C. H. Steel) and "Z" Company (Captain Scanlan) led the attack; "Y" Company (Captain Newstead), advancing in support of "W," was to be prepared to form a defensive flank on the right; and "X," (2nd Lieutenant Dunglinson) moving in rear of "Z," formed the Battalion Reserve. The "Anson" Battalion of the 63rd (R.N.) Division moved forward on the right of the FIFTH, and the 13/King's on their left. In the blind advance, which now followed, the dispositions of the FIFTH, as will be seen, were to undergo a radical change. Map No. 36

Scarcely had the companies advanced from the Blue Line, when disorganised parties of the enemy, who had been driven from their forward trenches, were encountered in the fog and 150 prisoners and several machine-guns taken. In the dense mist which prevailed not only companies but platoons were unable to maintain touch, and their leaders were left to guide their advance as their instincts dictated.* Very little opposition came from the front, but continuous heavy machine-gun fire from the right flank soon indicated that the troops of the 63rd Division had met with sterner resistance and were failing to progress. Before half the distance to their objectives had been traversed, "Y" and "Z" Companies, moving from opposite directions, met face to face. To add to their confusion, one of our own tanks, emerging from the mist and taking them for Germans, opened fire; but fortunately they were able to establish their identity before any harm was done. Newstead and Scanlon, taking off their steel helmets and revolvers, and removing themselves from the neighbourhood of the now stationary tank, took fresh compass bearings and started again. The tank vanished in the mist, and within fifteen minutes the two companies had once more completely lost touch. For a time we will leave "Y" Company groping its way forward, capturing occasional enemy posts on which it stumbled, and will follow the fortunes of "Z." By the general loss of direction of all, this company, which had started as the left of the Battalion, was now on the right. The extent to which fog had hampered the advance has been seen; the manner in which it favoured attack was now to be shown. Scanlan, suddenly finding himself faced by Dorothy Trench, immediately rushed the position with his company, and in the surprise that

---

* To lead by compass bearing, never an easy matter, is not made simpler by the needle being obstinately directed towards the guide's steel helmet.

was effected captured 8 machine-guns, whose detachments were killed, and took 60 prisoners. Without doubt, but for the concealment of its approach, the company must have suffered very heavy casualties from the fire of so strongly held a position. The enemy, however, were now better prepared, and "Z" Company, on resuming its advance, immediately came under very heavy machine-gun fire from the direction of some gun pits and a neighbouring trench,* which made further forward movement impossible unless the troops of the 63rd Division came up on the right, and of these contact patrols could find no trace. Scanlan accordingly disposed his company under the cover of a bank to the south-east of Dorothy and in a neighbouring trench, in which an abandoned field gun was found.

To return now to "Y" Company. While Scanlan with "Z" had been drifting to the right, Newstead, after losing touch with him, had been leading such of "Y" Company as he had been able to keep under his hand too far to the left; until, closing on the artillery barrage, he had found direction by the whistling of the shells close overhead. About 7.45 a.m. he came upon Captain Steel with two platoons of "W" Company, and, joining forces, they continued the advance. Some thirty minutes later, on approaching what in the fog appeared to be a hedge, they suddenly came under the fire of a machine-gun at a range of about 50 yards. If the opening of this fire came as a surprise, its abrupt cessation came as an even greater relief. The gun apparently had jammed, and the whole party, rushing forward, killed or captured its whole crew before they could make good their escape. Then came the greatest surprise of all, when they found that they had gained a cutting on the railway which was the objective of the 9th Brigade's attack; and that, despite the zig-zag course they had taken, they had reached it only ten minutes after schedule time. But, actually, though as yet they did not realise it, the point they had reached was on the front allotted to the 13/King's, of whom nothing had been seen since the opening of the advance. Ignorant of their exact position, Steel and Newstead, turning north, proceeded to lead their men forward astride the railway, clearing dug-outs and capturing 100 of the enemy, together with 8 machine-guns and a trench-mortar. Then, suddenly, other British troops began to emerge from the mist, and, on finding that these were the 1/Royal Scots Fusiliers, they realised that, instead of being on the right of the 9th Brigade, they had gained contact with the right flank of the *8th Brigade*. Thereupon, they handed over the portion of the line they had cleared to the Scots Fusiliers and, turning about, moved south again, with their men still disposed astride the railway, and took up a position in a cutting about the left of the FIFTH's objective.

The fog was now beginning to lift, and patrols which attempted to push forward beyond the railway were met by heavy machine-gun fire from Gomiecourt. The railway line was also under enfilade fire from the direction of Achiet-le-Grand. At this point Major West, V.C., of the Royal Tank Corps, rode up and inquired why the troops were not pushing forward. Steel and Newstead represented that they had with them less than 100 men in all, and that none of our tanks had been seen for over an hour. On learning this, Major West said that he would try to find some tanks to assist them; and, observing how they were under enfilade fire, recommended withdrawal to a line of trench which he had noted some 50 yards to the rear. With this

---

* This trench, of which more will be heard later, was roofed in, and represented the living quarters of the German gunners, as well as a refuge in which they could seek shelter from our artillery fire. It had, however, been adapted for defence by rifles and machine-guns.

Aug., 1918 — he rode off into the mist, and the two officers of the FIFTH, adopting his suggestion, withdrew their men to the trench indicated.* — Map No. 36

In the meantime 2nd Lieutenant Ingledew with his platoon of "X" Company had found his way forward, slightly further to the right, to the German wire covering the railway. Checked by this, the platoon suffered several casualties, but eventually succeeded in getting forward to the railway line. Later, Ingledew met Newstead, with whom he combined in organising a defensive position on the line which the latter had taken up.

It was now after 10 a.m., and though the fog was considerably lighter, it was still impossible for any accurate idea to be obtained by units as to the position of troops on their flanks, or by Lieut. Colonel Herbert as to the general disposition of his battalion. It was clear, however, from the enemy's fire that they were strongly established on the right of the FIFTH's objective, and that the attack of the 63rd Division had been held up. At this point Major Tower of the 4/Royal Fusiliers arrived on the scene with a tank and one company of his battalion; and it was decided to make a combined attack with such troops as were at hand, with a view to subduing the fire that was raking the line from the right. The weather, however, was now rapidly clearing, and in the face of the fire of the German machine-guns the attack could effect nothing. In the meanwhile, Lieut. Colonel Herbert, having satisfied himself that it was feasible for whippet tanks to cross the railway at certain points which had been occupied, fired the pre-arranged signal to notify this to Brigade Headquarters. In the poor visibility which still prevailed, however, it seems that his signal was not observed.

At 11 a.m. the fog completely cleared. The disorganisation of the Battalion that was revealed will, perhaps, be realised from what has been written of the conditions under which its companies had advanced. Captain Newstead relates that he found himself, not only with men of every company of the Battalion, but with a complete platoon of the "Anson" Battalion of the 63rd Division, and also in possession of two German field guns! If confusion reigned among the attackers, however, it seems to have been no less among the enemy. With the sudden lifting of the fog a battery was observed to be limbering up about 500 yards beyond the railway, and the teams and detachments were shot down. Parties of German infantry wandering about, seemingly in complete ignorance of the situation, were also brought under fire and suffered heavy casualties. But the enemy's machine-guns on the right, which even by firing at random in the mist had already given so much trouble, now with the clearing of the atmosphere began to cause severe losses. Two further attempts to secure the right of the FIFTH's objective failed, and finally, with the help of a company of the 2/Suffolk, of the 76th Brigade, a defensive flank was thrown back to switch the captured portion of the railway to the position held by Scanlan to the south-east of Dorothy Trench. On the left of the 9th Brigade, the 13/King's had now occupied their objective except for 500 yards on the right, and were in touch with the 8th Brigade on the line of the railway.

---

* Captain Newstead, who relates this incident, states that Major West fulfilled his promise, but that when, about half an hour later, two tanks approached, the fog had completely lifted and they were driven back by shell fire. As, by the plan, the railway represented the objective of the 9th Brigade, it is difficult to understand the suggestion that "W" and "Y" Companies should have been pushing forward to Gomiecourt. Major West, V.C., D.S.O., M.C., was killed on the 2nd September 1918.

The enemy, though still firmly established on the railway for some 1,200 yards to the north of Achiet-le-Grand, were completely commanded by the position held by Scanlan, who had now succeeded in establishing posts in the gunpits and the trench connected with them, and also by the troops thrown back from the railway. In these circumstances the G.O.C. 9th Brigade decided at noon that, until the troops of the 63rd Division got forward on his southern flank, nothing would be gained by further efforts to carry the right of his objective, and orders were issued for the troops to consolidate and stand on the positions they held. At 3.30 p.m. an attack by the 5th Division, in co-operation with the 63rd, was launched against Achiet-le-Petit and Achiet-le-Grand, but failed, and when darkness fell the situation of the 9th Brigade remained unchanged. During the day the FIFTH had lost four officers wounded—2nd Lieutenants Blenkinsop, M.C., Redpath, Lynes and W. Dunglinson—of whom the last-named died before reaching the Regimental Aid Post; and there had been considerable casualties among the other ranks.

The company of the 2/Suffolk was now withdrawn from the defensive flank; and at midnight on the 21st/22nd, the Brigadier reported that his battalions had re-organised and were disposed as follows. The 13/King's occupied the whole of their objective, with posts on the railway and companies in a supporting position some 200 yards to the rear; on their right, the FIFTH, similarly disposed, held the railway as far as a point 300 yards further south, whence their line was thrown back for a distance of 600 yards. In the sense that it was not in direct contact with other troops, the right of this defensive flank was in the air; but it was to some extent supported by "Z" Company in the position it occupied south-east of Dorothy Trench. Attempts were made during the night to gain touch with the troops of the 63rd Division, but the patrols sent out for this purpose could find no trace of them.*

At 7.45 a.m. on the 22nd, the Germans opened an attack under a heavy machine-gun barrage against Scanlan's position, and succeeded in driving in a platoon under Lieutenant Story, who himself was wounded and captured, and in occupying the Gun Pits Post.† Their attempts to advance beyond this point were, however, checked by the fire of the main position, and it was decided to postpone any effort to recover the post till after dark. The posts on the railway had been withdrawn at daylight, and, apart from continuous harassing fire by the enemy's machine-guns north of Achiet, no action was taken against this part of our line till just after noon, when a party of Germans, advancing from a railway cutting, attempted an attack against "Y" Company. They were met, however, by so heavy and accurate a fire that, of the whole party, the leader alone reached our trench. This man, a N.C.O. whose desperate bravery was the admiration of the defenders, was found to have received no fewer than six bullet wounds. Newstead then assumed the offensive, and, thanks

---

* From the report of the Brigadier that "the re-organisation of units had been completed," it should not be understood that companies were now *intact*. Throughout this battle "W," "Y," and "Z" Companies should be interpreted as the troops under Steel, Newstead and Scanlan respectively. In this sense, so far as can be ascertained, the general dispositions of the FIFTH, starting from the left, were as follows :—"W" and "Y" Companies and Ingledew's platoon of "X" were holding the line of the railway and the defensive flank; "Z" in the position that has been indicated; Taverner's platoon of "X" was, according to Captain Scanlan, definitely some distance in rear of "Z," and it is probable that the bulk of the remaining platoons of "X" were similarly placed, in Battalion Reserve.

† Story belonged to "W" Company, but had been absorbed with his platoon by Scanlan.

Aug., 1918 largely to the gallant behaviour of a corporal of the " Anson " platoon which had been absorbed by the FIFTH, succeeded in capturing 13 prisoners.* The number of both British and Germans who were now lying seriously wounded at this spot was very great. In response to an appeal for assistance, Captain Clarke, the Battalion's Medical Officer, immediately went forward under heavy fire and, having safely reached " Y " Company's trench, remained there till dark in constant attendance on the wounded.

When darkness fell on the 22nd, the Germans opposite " Z " Company were still in occupation of the Gun Pits Post, but Lieut. Colonel Herbert had now made plans for its recapture, which was to be carried out by two platoons under the leadership of 2nd Lieutenant J. Steel. At 9 p.m. this small party, supported by the fire of one trench-mortar, advanced to the attack. Almost immediately, Steel was wounded, and command fell to Sergeant Christmas. Leading his men forward, Christmas rushed the post, and succeeded, after considerable hand-to-hand fighting, in capturing it and securing the surrender of no fewer than 3 officers and 56 other ranks, the greater number of whom had sought refuge from our trench-mortar fire in the dug-outs of the trench which represented their main fire position.† Two of the men of Story's post, who had been made prisoner by the Germans in the morning attack were recovered.

At dawn on the 23rd August, the 76th Brigade, exploiting the success gained by the left and centre of the 3rd Division, attacked and carried the village of Gomiecourt, which lay some 800 yards east of the railway. Further south, however, the 63rd Division had been unable to make any progress; and to deal with the situation in this quarter, a large scale attack had now been planned for 11 a.m.. In this the 2nd Division, passing through the 3rd, was to co-operate with the 37th Division further to the south in completing the capture of the Green Line; and, having carried this, to advance the British line a further 2,000 yards. The FIFTH, however, were left for a considerable time in ignorance of this project. Machine-guns and mortars continued to give them serious trouble from the position the enemy still occupied, to the north of Achiet, and the situation on the Battalion's right flank seemed still to be precarious. There was as yet no sign of the enemy relaxing his hold on the position to which he had clung so obstinately; and, in endeavouring to establish a Lewis gun to close a gap in the defensive flank, 2nd Lieutenant Ingledew was wounded by the machine-gun fire that had been so consistently maintained from this direction. Then, at 10.45 a.m., only fifteen minutes before the 2nd and 37th Divisions were due to advance, Lieut.-Colonel Herbert was informed of the attack and ordered to co-operate by pushing forward in a gap which would exist between their inner flanks, for the capture of that portion of the railway line which he had hitherto been unable to carry. This task was allotted to " W " and " Y " Companies, who were ordered to drive the enemy from the line of the railway and continue their advance to the Green Line south of Gomiecourt.

On moving forward, the two companies encountered very slight opposition

Map No. 36

---

* Captain Newstead, who himself was awarded the Military Cross for his conduct on this occasion, states that he believes that the Military Medal, for which he recommended the corporal, was granted to him. It is pleasing to be able to record that the gallant German survived his wounds.

† For his conduct on this occasion Serjeant Christmas, who already held the Military Medal and one bar, was mentioned in Despatches. Captain Scanlan received a bar to his Military Cross for his services 21st–23rd August, 1918.

258   THE FIFTH IN THE GREAT WAR.

Map No. 36 and had little difficulty in gaining the line of the railway, from which the enemy, Aug., 1918
realising the manner in which their southern flank was now threatened by the 37th
Division, had at last fallen back. But, on continuing the advance, " Y " Company
very soon came under such heavy machine-gun and artillery fire from positions to
the south of Gomiecourt, that to Captain Newstead it seemed that only a miracle
could save his company from complete destruction before it reached its objective.
Then suddenly the miracle occurred. To his relief and amazement all fire ceased, the
Germans began to throw up their hands, and a little later it was seen that six of our
whippet tanks, swooping down from the north of Gomiecourt, had taken the enemy
in rear. Upwards of 200 Germans surrendered, and " Z " Company, which was now
following up to the right rear, had temporarily to halt, in order to organise the
collection of this mass of prisoners. In the meantime " W " Company, separated from
" Y " by a small ridge and unaware of the resistance the latter had encountered, had
advanced unopposed to Gomiecourt. Later, the two companies joined hands on the
line of the road which had been given as the limit of their advance.

The FIFTH were held in a position south of Gomiecourt for the following
twenty-four hours, in readiness, with the remainder of the 9th Brigade, to move in
any direction that circumstances might require. The 3rd Division then having
received orders to withdraw to Corps Reserve, the Battalion, at 4 p.m. on the 24th
August, was moved back to bivouac close to the position in which it had assembled
for attack on the night of the 20th/21st.

Thus ended the part played by the FIFTH in the opening attack of the Third
Army in 1918. In referring to the operations carried out by his Division on the
21st August, Major-General Deverell wrote :—" I consider that great credit is due to
Brigade and Battalion staffs for the approach march, and to all commanders for the
forming up and launching of the attack in a very dense fog. The initiative and skill
shown by junior leaders and the steadiness of the men in advancing and keeping
direction and touch, and regaining it when lost was most creditable. Some confusion
was bound to result, but the ease with which this was remedied as soon as the fog
lifted would have been highly creditable to veteran soldiers." In addition to the
seven officer casualties already mentioned, the FIFTH between the 21st and 23rd
August lost 26 other ranks killed ; 240 wounded ; and 48 missing.

Maps Nos.   The 3rd Division could be allowed only a few days' rest in Corps Reserve,
35 and 37   as the maintenance of a steady pressure against the enemy meant strenuous work for
the forward troops. By the 28th August the Guards Division which formed the left
of the VI. Corps, had gained the line of " Banks Reserve " from a point south-east
of the village of St. Leger to the Mory-Écoust road, and their relief by the 3rd Division
was arranged for the night of the 28th/29th. The 76th Brigade took over the front
line, with orders to continue pressure towards Écoust and Noreuil ; the 9th Brigade
moved to Moyenville in support ; and the 8th Brigade took its place as Divisional
Reserve at Hamelincourt. The 76th Brigade, after making good progress on the 29th,
on the following day attacked and captured the twin villages of Écoust and Longatte ;
but it was unable to maintain its position, and was later driven back to the line
of Écoust Support and west of the Écoust-Vraucourt road. The 9th Brigade (with
the 1/Gordon Highlanders attached) was now ordered to pass through the 76th
Brigade, and attack for the capture of a line Noreuil Switch–Longatte Trench–

Aug., 1918 Longatte Support to its junction with Bullecourt Avenue, gaining touch at the last-named point with troops of the 56th Division, who would be operating on its left.

The attack was to be launched at 5.15 a.m. on the 31st August in co-operation with tanks. During the night of the 30th/31st the 1/Gordons, 4/Royal Fusiliers, and 13/King's relieved the forward troops of the 76th Brigade in the position on which they had fallen back, and were there assembled in readiness to advance at zero hour. The FIFTH, who were to be responsible for supporting the attack, were disposed as follows :—" Y " Company (Captain Newstead) about Mein Lane, with " X " (Captain Lord) some distance in rear; " Z " Company (Captain Scanlan) in a trench some 600 yards to the right rear of " Y " and " X "; " W " (Captain Steel), as Battalion Reserve, in Banks Trench, 1500 yards further to the west.

On advancing to the attack, the 13/King's, on the left, encountering little opposition, swept through Écoust and Longatte, and soon joined hands with the 56th Division in Bullecourt Avenue; but in passing through a tangle of shattered buildings and trenches, this swift advance had over-run certain parties of the enemy; and these were to give trouble later, particularly with a machine-gun at the southern edge of Écoust, which had escaped notice. The Gordons, on the right, also gained their objective without difficulty; but not so the Royal Fusiliers in the centre. Just before the opening of the attack, they suffered severe casualties from an artillery barrage, which fell on their assembly position. Nevertheless the battalion advanced punctually at zero hour, but only to come immediately under a devastating fire from machine-guns sited in a sunken road which faced their advance.* After gallant but fruitless efforts to gain the position of these guns, the battalion fell back to its starting line, having lost all but one of its officers. Now, the position taken up by the FIFTH had been selected in anticipation of opposition proving strongest against the left of the Brigade, and was by no means favourable for rendering assistance to the centre, where the Royal Fusiliers had been held up. Reinforcement of the centre, in no circumstances an easy matter, had, moreover, become the more difficult since the enemy were now able to trickle men round the right flank of the 13/King's to Écoust, from which they could enfilade troops advancing over the northern slope of a valley which lay to the west of the village. " Y " Company, however, by moving in small parties, managed to cross the valley under cover of Écoust Trench and push forward to a point just south of the Longatte-Mory road. Here, however, they were held up by machine-gun fire directed from a sunken road immediately facing them, and by the fire of snipers and machine-guns in Longatte Support.

The difficulties experienced by Brigade H.Q. this day in obtaining accurate reports of the situation in time to take appropriate action were very great. Telephone lines were constantly cut either by artillery fire or the movement of our own tanks, and communication forward of Brigade H.Q. depended almost entirely on runners, whose task was made extraordinarily difficult by the bareness of the country and lack of landmarks.† The order on which " Y " Company had taken action was issued

---

* These guns were in position to the north and south of Point " B " on Map 37. According to officers of the FIFTH who were in action this day, the difficulties encountered by the Royal Fusiliers were due to a breakdown of the arrangements for tank co-operation, which had served the flank battalions well. There is, however, no reference in either the Brigade or Division narrative reports of the battle to a failure of the tanks on the Royal Fusiliers' front.

† As the crow flies, the H.Q. of the FIFTH were 2,000 yards from Mein Lane and 2,250 yards from the position gained by " Y " Company. Brigade H.Q., at Mory Copse, were over two miles from Écoust and 1¾ miles from the H.Q. of the FIFTH.

at 8.15 a.m., but we are left to guess the time at which it was received and acted on. Considering the delay in communication it is at any rate unlikely that it can have been till after noon that the advance of " Y " Company was held up, or till considerably later that Captain Newstead, having satisfied himself that further progress was impossible, reported the situation. On receipt of Newstead's report, Lieut. Colonel Herbert went forward personally to view the situation and plan how best to deal with it. It was not, however, till 5 p.m. that, after returning from the front line, he reported at Brigade Headquarters, in order to submit his recommendation as to the action that should be taken. The Brigadier was most anxious that the FIFTH should as soon as possible renew the attack in the centre, and simultaneously clear Écoust of the hostile elements which had escaped the first attack on the left. Herbert, however, expressed the view, based on his own reconnaissance, that the number of the enemy in Écoust was inconsiderable, and urged that any renewal of the attack in the centre should be delayed till dusk. He held the opinion that to attempt to advance in broad daylight across the open in face of heavy machine-gun fire would lead to almost certain disaster; and ultimately his proposals were agreed to.

In accordance with the decision thus made, it was planned that at dusk " Y " Company should advance under cover of a creeping barrage for the capture of the portion of Longatte Trench that lay between the sunken roads marked " A " and " B " on the map. Simultaneously, " X " Company was to push south and clear the sunken road " B " as far as the fork road " C," where they would gain touch with the Gordon Highlanders. While this attack in the centre was in progress, " W " Company was to obtain contact with the 13/King's in Écoust Support, and advance by platoons through the village, clearing it of such parties of the enemy as might be found to be still lurking there. Later, these platoons were to fill any gaps in Longatte Support which the King's had been unable to occupy.

The operation, which was timed to begin at 8 p.m. proceeded precisely as planned, and proved completely successful. " W " Company, meeting with no opposition in Écoust village, had no difficulty in occupying Longatte Support to the south of the Noreuil road, immediately on the right of the King's; and " Y " and " X " Companies, supported by the perfectly timed and accurate fire of the artillery, carried the whole of their objectives, bayoneting 20 of the enemy, and capturing 50 prisoners, 9 machine-guns, and 3 trench-mortars.

General Potter, encouraged by the success of the FIFTH, now decided to attempt to occupy the final objective of the morning attack, in co-operation with the 76th Brigade, which had now taken over half of the 9th Brigades' front.* As a first step towards this, the FIFTH were ordered to clear Longatte Trench as far as its junction with Noreuil Switch. This task was promptly carried out by patrols of " Y " Company, who found that the enemy had withdrawn. Then, at 3 a.m. the 4/Royal Fusiliers, advancing across the open, took over the whole of Longatte Trench from Point " A " to its junction with Noreuil Switch, which was simultaneously occupied by troops of the 76th Brigade. Thus, the whole objective of the 31st August had been carried before dawn on the 1st September.

In the fighting of these twenty-four hours the FIFTH had suffered but trifling loss. Though the companies on the southern outskirts of Écoust had been under continuous and heavy artillery fire, the men had dug themselves in so well that few casualties were sustained; and in the evening attack, the FIFTH, thanks to Lieut.

---

* The 1/Gordon Highlanders had now reverted to the 76th Brigade.

Sept., 1918   Colonel Herbert's sound appreciation, had been saved by the cover of darkness from   Map No. 38
the heavy losses experienced by the Royal Fusiliers in the earlier attack on the same position.*

In the meantime considerable progress had been made on the left, where the whole of the Noreuil Switch north-east of Longatte Trench had been occupied; and the 8th Brigade had been brought up to carry forward the attack for the capture of further objectives on this flank. On the afternoon of the 1st September the FIFTH, having been placed at the disposal of the 8th Brigade, were detailed to act in support to its attack, which was to be delivered on the following day in a general direction south-east. To carry out its duties in support the Battalion was disposed as follows: " Z " Company was placed in Noreuil Switch west of the Longatte-Noreuil road; to guard the left flank, " W " took up a position astride Dewsbury Trench to the west of the Noreuil Switch, with " X " some distance to its rear; " Y " was held in reserve to the south of Longatte village.

Map No. 38.

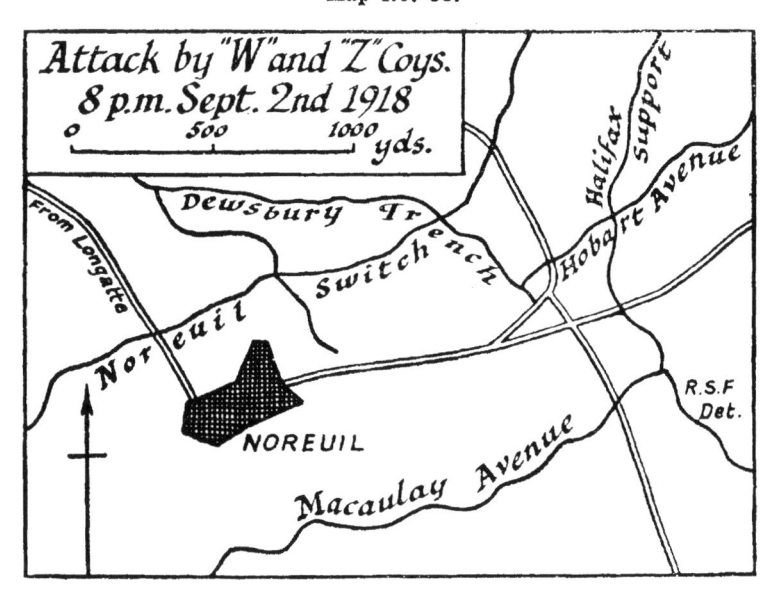

Attack by "W" and "Z" Coys. 8 p.m. Sept. 2nd 1918

In the 8th Brigade's attack, which opened at 5.30 a.m. on the 2nd September, Noreuil was quickly carried, and 2nd Lieutenant Holmes' platoon of " Z " Company was called on to assist in the " mopping up " of its southern quarter. No progress, however, could be made beyond its eastern outskirts; and further north, the centre and left of the attack were held up by fire from Halifax Support and Hobart Avenue. " W " Company brought several abandoned German machine-guns to bear on these positions, but for long it was thought that no British troops had been able to get forward. Late in the afternoon, however, it was learnt that some detachments of the 1/Royal Scots Fusiliers, attacking on the left, had managed to work their way

---

* In a conversation with the present writer nineteen years later, Brigadier-General Potter spoke in the highest terms of the manner in which this operation had been planned and conducted by Lieut.-Colonel (now Major-General) Herbert, who was awarded a bar to the D.S.O. in recognition of his services on the 31st August and 1st September.

Map No. 38 — forward to a point some 1,500 yards to the east of Noreuil, where they were isolated. Sept., 1918 Thereupon orders were issued to the FIFTH to attack for the capture of Halifax Support to the north of the position in which these troops were holding out, while the 1/Royal Scots cleared Macaulay Avenue. At 8 p.m., accordingly, " Z " Company advanced from the eastern edge of Noreuil, and " W " moved forward on the left as " Z " drew level with its position. The main body of the enemy had long since been retiring eastwards; and of his rear-guards, which had put up so strong a resistance during the day, there remained now only certain machine-gun posts covering the final withdrawal. The advance of the two companies of the FIFTH was soon met by the fire of three machine-guns which had been posted for this purpose near the junction of Dewsbury Trench and Hobart Avenue. Captain Scanlan, the commander of " Z " Company, and one of his subalterns, 2nd Lieutenant Sanderson, were wounded; but the company's Lewis guns were quickly brought into action, and under cover of their fire the German guns were captured together with 20 prisoners. After this no serious opposition was encountered, and by 9.15 p.m. the two companies, in touch on the right with the Royal Scots, and on the left with troops of the 52nd Division, had carried their objectives and rescued the Scots Fusiliers' detachments from the danger threatened by their isolation.

Map No. 35. — On the 29th August the enemy had evacuated Bapaume, and the operations in which the FIFTH had been engaged during the following few days marked the conclusion of the second stage of the great British offensive. " The troops of the Third and Fourth Armies, comprising 23 British divisions, by skilful leading, hard fighting and relentless and unremitting pursuit, in ten days had driven 35 German divisions from one side of the old Somme battlefield to the other, thereby turning the line of the River Somme . . . and had taken from the enemy over 34,000 prisoners and 270 guns."—(*Haig's Despatches.*) It was anticipated that the German plan would now be to fight a rear-guard action, retiring from one intermediary position to another till they gained the shelter of the Hindenburg Line. This so-called " Line," which was actually a deep defensive belt running in a general direction south-east, represented the most formidable system of field fortification hitherto known in war. On the First Army front the northernmost portion of the system had already been captured, but opposite the Third Army, where its forward defences ran through Havrincourt, and its Support Line through Flesquières and Ribécourt, it still stood intact.*

On the 3rd September, the 3rd Division, on relief by the Guards, was withdrawn to Corps Reserve; and the FIFTH were moved back to their former bivouac at Moyenneville. A week later, on the Division being ordered to an area in rear of the right of the VI. Corps front, the Battalion marched in pouring rain to a bivouac in Bee Wood near Ervillers, where during the next few days co-operation with tanks was practised. In the meantime the German withdrawal had been closely followed up; the left of the Third Army had captured the Hindenburg Front and Support Lines, and the VI. Corps on the right of the Army had carried the forward defences of the system to the north and south of Havrincourt.

Orders having now been received for the 3rd Division to relieve the 62nd in the right sector of the VI. Corps front, the 9th Brigade moved forward to Beugny on

---

* South of Havrincourt, on the front of the Fourth Army, the Hindenburg Front Line fell back south-east before turning south to follow the line of the St. Quentin Canal.

SENTRY IN SAP-HEAD.

" . . . some speculation as to the enemy's intentions . . "

[Imperial War Museum—Crown Copyright.

Sept., 1918 the 14th September, and on the following night took over trenches from Triangle Wood to Clarges Avenue. The FIFTH, as the right battalion of the brigade, held a position to the south of Kimber Avenue, and were disposed as follows: " Z " Company on the right, in touch with the 1/Hertfordshire (37th Division); " W " in the centre, and " Y " on the left. " X " Company was in a supporting position in the Hindenburg Line to the south of Havrincourt. The 16th and 17th September passed very quietly, and nothing unusual occurred during the morning of the 18th. At 1.30 p.m., however, considerable movement in the trenches opposite the FIFTH provoked some speculation as to the enemy's intentions. Artillery and rifle fire was directed on the area in which the movement had been observed, but nearly two hours passed before the Germans gave further signs of activity. Then, at 3.20 p.m. a very heavy gas bombardment was brought on to our battery positions; and an hour later intense artillery fire was opened on the forward defences of the 3rd Division and the left of the 37th. Fortunately for the FIFTH, this bombardment, which extended to a depth of 800 yards, fell for the most part in rear of their front line. At 5.20 the enemy's infantry were seen to be advancing to the assault. Opposite the FIFTH they were immediately brought under the fire of every rifle and machine-gun in the line, while simultaneously two Stokes mortars from a position in T Wood, deluged Kimber Avenue and Wood Switch with bombs. As a result, the enemy here got little beyond the positions in which they had assembled for attack. On the Battalion's right, however, they succeeded in gaining a footing in the front line of the 1/Hertfordshire; and the right platoon of " Z " Company of the FIFTH, after being forced to withdraw, was completely surrounded by the enemy, and for a time in grave danger of being overwhelmed. Lieutenant Carswell, the company commander, realising that this critical situation demanded immediate action, at once led forward his support platoon and such men of the 1/Hertfordshire as were at hand, and engaging the enemy with bombs, completely routed them, killing 15 and making 30 prisoner.* Similar penetrations at two other points on the front of the 3rd Division were dealt with in like manner; and daylight on the 19th found the line intact and over 100 Germans captured. In the course of the enemy's attack, 7 men of the FIFTH had been killed; and 2nd Lieutenants Wailing, Cannon and Marks and 40 other ranks wounded. The greater number of these casualties had occurred in " Z " Company, and on the 19th September the right flank of the FIFTH was strengthened by the addition of two platoons of the 13/King's, which remained with the Battalion until it was relieved on the night of the 20th/21st and withdrawn to Brigade support. Just prior to this relief a sad event occurred, when two young officers, 2nd Lieutenant J. Greaves and S. Riley, who had joined the FIFTH together little more than a week before, were together killed by the same shell. Two platoons of " Z," which had been required to remain in the line for a further twenty-four hours, were heavily bombed during their withdrawal to the south of Havrincourt on the night of the 21st, with the result that this company, already seriously weakened, was further reduced by the loss of 2 men killed and 7 wounded.

Map No. 39

Lieut.-Colonel Herbert had now served with the 1st Battalion in the War for a total period of just over two years, and during twenty months of this time he

---

* For the particulars of Lieutenant Carswell's action, for which he was awarded the Military Cross, see *St. George's Gazette*, January 1919, page 5.

had, except for one brief period, been continuously in command. His subordinates, than whom none had a fuller opportunity for recognising his high qualities as a commander, had long since realised that promotion to higher rank, which to them seemed long overdue, might at any time take him from the Battalion. Yet, when it came to him, it could have scarcely been at a moment more inopportune for those who had become accustomed to the confidence and sense of security afforded by his leadership, as the Battalion was to be engaged in a large scale attack by the 3rd Division on the 27th September. On the 26th, Lieut.-Colonel Herbert was appointed to the command of the 112th Infantry Brigade. Nor were matters made easier by the fact that the Adjutant, Captain Ellison, was at the time absent on leave. Throughout the War, however, the FIFTH were fortunate in never having to look outside the Regiment for an officer to command either of their battalions; and now no better substitute could have been found for Herbert than Lieut.-Colonel Cruddas, who was detailed to replace him. Cruddas had had varied and valuable experience during the past 3½ years. After serving as adjutant in the 4th (Territorial) Battalion of the Regiment, he had acted as second-in-command for brief periods with both the 1st and 2nd Battalions. In Macedonia, it may be remembered, he had been appointed early in 1916 to the command of a Pioneer Battalion, with which he had remained for over two years before being transferred in June 1918 to France, where he had taken over command of the 4/Royal Scots Fusiliers.*

To command a battalion in an attack of the nature of that in which the FIFTH were now to be engaged, which in the War was always the subject of very elaborate and detailed preparation, required not only an intimate knowledge of the plan, but personal reconnaissance of the ground. Lieut. Colonel Cruddas, who did not arrive at Battalion H.Q. till late in the afternoon of the 26th September, had neither opportunity for reconnaissance nor time for acquainting himself with anything more than the broadest outlines of the plan of attack. The company commanders, moreover, were as yet unknown to him. In these circumstances the Brigadier considered that it would be wiser for Captain C. H. Steel, who had a full knowledge o every detail of the proposed operation, to remain in temporary command until its conclusion. The duties of adjutant were to be performed by Lieutenant Porter-Hargreaves, who was answering for Ellison during his absence.

On the 27th September, the VI. Corps, with the 3rd Division on the right and the Guards on the left, was to attack for the capture of the Flesquières Ridge and the " clearing up " of the Hindenburg Support Line which crossed it. On the capture of Flesquières village, which it was estimated would be effected three hours after the opening of the attack, the IV. Corps, which to the south held a more forward line than the VIth, would join in the advance, with its left (42nd) Division in touch with the 3rd.

Two main objectives were given to the 3rd Division. The fact that these were not parallel throughout their whole length, either to each other or to the Starting Line, was an important consideration in planning the attack. which it was desired to launch simultaneously along the whole front. The relative direction of these several lines should be studied on the map, if the timing of the FIFTH's advance is to be understood. It will be seen that the advance of the Division was to take the form of a wheel, in which the troops on the left would have a considerably greater distance to traverse than those

---

* This battalion, in the inopportune loss of its C.O., was, perhaps, entitled to even greater sympathy than the 1/FIFTH over the departure of Lieut.-Colonel Herbert. The 4/R.S.F. were actually *in action* when Lieut.-Colonel Cruddas was withdrawn from them to take over the 1/FIFTH.

Sept., 1918 on the right. It was on this account that, while the 9th Brigade, as the right of the Division, was to be responsible for carrying both objectives; on the left, after the 8th Brigade had captured the First Objective, the 76th was to pass through it for the clearing of Flesquiéres and the capture of the Second Objective (Station Avenue).

Map No. 39

The 9th Brigade's plan was also influenced by this wheel, which would be pivoting on its right. Two battalions—the 13/King's and the 1/FIFTH—were to carry the attack right through for the capture of the line of Station Avenue. In the initial advance the right company of the King's was to stand fast, while the remainder of the battalion swung forward on to Ravine Avenue as far as its junction with Wood Switch. The latter trench was simultaneously to be captured by the FIFTH, who, with their left on the railway would advance straight forward. Having gained these positions, the two battalions would remain stationary for 96 minutes, in order to allow time for the 8th Brigade to come into line to the north of the railway. Then, as the 76th Brigade passed through the 8th, the FIFTH, keeping touch with them, were to swing right-handed on to the line of Ravine Avenue between the railway and Wood Switch. This movement having completed the wheel and brought the leading battalions into line on the whole front of the Division, all would straightway advance for the capture of Station Avenue, their final objective. If the operation up to this point proceeded in accordance with plan, success would be exploited on the front of the 9th Brigade by passing the 4/Royal Fusiliers through the FIFTH for the capture of the village of Ribécourt.

The FIFTH, on the night of the 25th/26th September, had taken over trenches to the east and north-east of Havrincourt on their front of attack; and at 5 a.m. on the 27th were here assembled in readiness to advance. " W " (Captain Futers) and " X " (Captain Lord), the two leading companies, were lined up just behind the wire; " Y " (Captain Newstead) and " Z " (Lieutenant Carswell), which were to follow in support, were formed up in the front line trench. Although, during the night, occasional bursts of artillery and machine-gun fire suggested that the enemy was uneasy, there was no definite indication that he expected attack until ten minutes before it was due to open. Then, at 5.10 a.m., a very heavy bombardment by artillery and trench-mortars fell on our front line. 2nd Lieutenant Regan of " Y " Company was killed, and numerous casualties occurred among the assembled troops. Such an event has often of itself proved sufficient to crush an attack before it can be launched. But the FIFTH, under the severest ordeal to which troops can be subjected, remained steady; and with the opening of our barrage at 5.20 the Battalion advanced in perfect order, together with the King's on their right. The barrage was to lift from the enemy's trenches to clear the way for the infantry assault at 5.34., and at this time " W " Company, advancing as the right of the FIFTH in the face of very stern resistance, had gained their appointed position. It was not, however, till 45 minutes later that the trenches on its front of attack had been completely cleared of the enemy, of whom 80 together with several machine-guns were here captured; but before this was accomplished, Captain Futers had been killed, and 50 of his men had become casualties. For a considerable time the left of the company had been held up by the fire of two machine-guns sited on the edge of a chalk pit, but had eventually got forward in circumstances which will be related later.

In the course of " W " Company's advance. a gap had developed between its right flank and the left of the King's. Captain Newstead, in support, having observed this, had immediately led forward three platoons of " Y " Company to fill it; and, attacking a quarry on the right of the FIFTH's objective, secured the surrender of 75

Germans and several machine-guns. Touch with the King's, however, had not yet been gained, and in leading forward a party to secure this Newstead was wounded. None the less he continued to exercise command; and when, a few minutes later, the enemy attempted to counter-attack, they were met by so heavy and accurate a fire that they abandoned their effort and surrendered. The position being then secure, command was taken over by Company Serjeant-Major Adlard, and Captain Newstead was safely evacuated to the Regimental Aid Post.* By this time the company had lost, in addition to both its officers, 30 other ranks killed or wounded.

While "W" and "Y" companies had been fighting for the right of the objective, "X," advancing on the left, had come under very heavy machine-gun fire from three points: firstly, from a railway embankment on the left of its objective; secondly, from a point about the junction of Kimber Avenue with Wood Switch, and thirdly from the chalk pit which has been referred to as the site of the guns which were holding up the left of "W" Company. The first of these positions was quickly rushed, and the party which carried it turned right and began to bomb their way down a trench leading to Wood Switch. The other positions, however, gave more trouble, and for a time the centre and right of the company could not get forward. 2nd Lieutenant Fryer, going forward with Corporal Dodd, made a gallant attempt to bomb the enemy from the position at the trench junction, but were unable to silence the guns. In the meantime "Z" Company, suffering very heavy casualties, had pushed forward to the assistance of "X", and Carswell, its commander, arrived at about the point of junction between "X" and "W". Simultaneously, Pte. Buglass, a stretcher-bearer, who had returned to the line after carrying back a wounded man, came on the scene. Seeing how many men were being hit by the fire of the guns from the chalk pit, Buglass tore off his S.B. badge, collected some bombs, and started to creep forward with Carswell towards the enemy's position. They succeeded in getting to within close distance of the guns, when Carswell's hand was blown off. Thereupon, Buglass, hurled a bomb and succeeded in registering a direct hit on one of the guns. He then sprang up, and rushing forward under hot fire, hurled a second bomb, which put the Germans to flight. He was not content, however, to let them escape. Finding the second gun loaded and undamaged, he turned it round and opened fire on its retiring detachment. But Buglass had been trained as a stretcher-bearer—not as a machine-gunner. To quote his own words—" not knowing how to hold the gun, the butt kept hitting me in the shoulder;" and it seems the fire was ineffective. The men on the left of "W" Company whose advance had been held up now got forward; simultaneously the guns in the Kimber Avenue position were rushed by "X" and "Z"; and Buglass went back to resume his duty of collecting the wounded.†

---

* This was the third notable action performed by Captain Newstead in the course of a few weeks. For his services in the operations 21st/23rd August and 31st August/2nd September, he had been awarded the Military Cross and Distinguished Service Order respectively. He had previously been wounded during the operations for the capture of Lonely Trench in August, 1916.

† The Battalion *War Diary* suggests that it was the Kimber Avenue position which was carried by Buglass. 2nd Lieutenant (now Captain) Fryer, however, states that the chalk pit guns were south of this. He also records that Carswell, after being wounded, informed him that a certain Lce.-Corporal Grieves had gone forward with him and Buglass. The *War Diary* makes no reference to Grieves; nor does it mention the action of 2nd Lieutenant Fryer, which will be found recorded in the *St. George's Gazette* of February 1919 in connection with the award of the Military Cross. Pte. (Lce.-Corporal) J. Buglass, who already held the Military Medal, received for his action this day the D.C.M. and the Médaille Militaire, the highest French war decoration.

Sept., 1918 "X" and "Z" Companies in carrying the position had together captured 70 prisoners and 6 machine-guns; but they had suffered very heavy casualties. In "X", 2nd Lieutenant G. B. Sibbit had been killed and 21 other ranks killed or wounded. The losses of "Z" were even greater. Lieutenant Carswell had been wounded, 2nd Lieutenant L. Mayfield, the only other officer, had been killed, and the casualties among other ranks amounted to 40. With the loss of both its officers, "Z" Company had now come under the command of Company Serjeant-Major Archer.   Map No. 39

To sum up: the four companies of the FIFTH in completing their first task had captured 224 prisoners and numerous machine-guns; but of their 9 officers, 3 company commanders and 3 others had become casualties; their weak platoons had been diminished by the loss of 140 other ranks; and the day's work was as yet but half done. An opportunity for reorganisation, however, was now afforded by the pause which had been arranged in order to allow the left of the Division to come forward.

At 7.10 a.m., the hour fixed for the FIFTH to swing on to the intermediate objective of Ravine Avenue, the companies were in readiness to resume their advance. Although at this time the 76th Brigade had not actually passed through the 8th, the FIFTH in accordance with their orders moved forward without further delay. On the right, "W" Company, still supported by "Y," though suffering a few casualties from machine-gun fire from the south, encountered no serious resistance, and shortly after 8 a.m. established itself in Ravine Avenue. A longer advance lay before the companies on the left; and here "X," followed by "Z," had to overcome strong opposition before gaining a footing in Bilhelm Avenue. Over twenty minutes were occupied in clearing this trench, in which 50 prisoners were taken. By then the 1/Gordon Highlanders of the 76th Brigade had come up on the left, and together with "X" and "Z" Companies of the FIFTH, completed the half-right wheel on to the line of Ravine Avenue. Despite the opposition encountered on the left, the casualties during this manoeuvre had been very slight.

The leading troops on the whole front of the 3rd Division having now been brought into line, square to Station Avenue, the advance for the capture of this, the second main objective, began at 8.20. On the front of the FIFTH, "W" and "X" Companies now stood fast in Ravine Avenue and consolidated the position they had gained, while "Y" and "Z," led by their Serjeant-Majors, passed through to carry out the Battalion's final task. The distance to be traversed varied between 700 and 1,000 yards, and as this last advance progressed, the already greatly reduced companies suffered further considerable loss from the fire of machine-guns sited on a ridge to the north of Ribécourt. They succeeded, none the less, in pushing forward by 9 a.m. to within 200 yards of Station Avenue, and here consolidated a position in close touch with the 13/King's on their right. On their left, the 2/Suffolk of the 76th Brigade, having suffered very heavily, had been unable to get quite so far forward. The so-called "companies" of the FIFTH which had reached this final limit of the Battalion's advance now consisted of—"Y" Company, 1 C.S.M. and 32 other ranks; "Z" Company, 1 C.S.M. and 15 other ranks !

At 10 a.m. the 4/Royal Fusiliers and a battalion of the 42nd Division passed through for the capture of Ribécourt, which was successfully accomplished. The FIFTH remained in the positions they had captured and consolidated till 1 a.m. on the following morning, when they were ordered to fall back to the shelter of some dug-outs just east of Havrincourt. Later in the morning they were withdrawn with the remainder of the 9th Brigade to the west of the Canal du Nord, where they came into Divisional Reserve.*

The total casualties sustained by the FIFTH in the fighting of the 27th September had amounted to :—

Officers—4 killed, 2 wounded.
Other Ranks—26 killed, 134 wounded, 35 missing.

The attack of the Fourth Army, on the British right, against the Hindenburg Line to the north of St. Quentin did not open till the 29th September ; and fighting was to continue for several days before the Germans were driven from the entire defensive system, and the " Hindenburg Line " could be declared to have been captured throughout its whole length of forty miles, from east of Arras to the southernmost limit at St. Quentin. The 2/FIFTH were to be engaged in the later stages of the operations by which this was accomplished ; and it is necessary now to return to the narrative of their doings, before resuming the story of the First Battalion, which for the present we may leave enjoying a brief rest with its Brigade in reserve to the 3rd Division.

---

* On the 1st October, articles extolling the recent exploits of the 3rd Division appeared in many of the English papers under the heading of " The Iron Division." That which appeared in *The Times*, in referring to the attack east of Havrincourt, concluded :—" It is known as the ' Iron Division,' and its iron truly entered into the German soul."

CHAPTER XVIII.

The Advance to Victory (continued).

Return of the 2nd Battalion to France and The Final Phase.

"Hindenburg Line"—"Beaurevoir"—"Cambrai."

SECOND BATTALION—28TH JUNE TO 11TH NOVEMBER, 1918.

FIRST BATTALION—30TH SEPTEMBER TO 11TH NOVEMBER, 1918.

2nd Bn.
July, 1918

During the War the experiences of the two battalions of the FIFTH differed widely in one respect. Whereas the First Battalion up till the Armistice was never more than 300 miles from its starting point of Portsmouth, the Second, after its 6,000 mile voyage from India, had already travelled another 3,000 miles in its wanderings by Egypt and Macedonia before landing at Taranto on the 27th June, 1918. These changes of scene, whatever hardships might follow, undoubtedly did much to break the monotony of the War; and the return journey to France which was now to be undertaken by the 2/FIFTH was to be remembered as one of the happiest interludes in four seemingly endless years. Troop trains could travel neither at top speed nor by the most direct routes, and the 1,300 mile journey, which took them through some of the most beautiful scenery of Europe, was covered at an average rate of little more than 200 miles a day. After two days in a rest camp at Cimino, near Taranto, the Battalion entrained late on the evening of the 29th June. The early part of the journey took them up the east coast of Italy to Ancona, where breakfasts were taken on the 1st July. Thence the route struck across to Bologna, and passed by the shores of the Gulf of Genoa to Ventimiglia, where the French frontier was crossed in the early hours of the 3rd. After traversing the French Riviera to Marseilles, the train travelled north by the Rhone valley, Lyons, and Nevers, and reached the outskirts of Paris on the 5th. The journey at length was beginning to be rather irksome, and all were pleased to learn that it was now nearing its end. Late in the evening the Battalion detrained at Forge-les-Eaux, about 15 miles south of Dieppe, and darkness found it settled in camp on the outskirts of neighbouring village of Serqueux.

At the end of April and early in May 1918 certain exhausted British divisions, including the 50th, which had taken part both in the Somme and Lys Battles had been placed at the disposal of Marshal Foch, who despatched them to the Sixth French Army. In Sir Douglas Haig's view, they were, "despite their high spirit and gallant record, in no condition to take part in major operations until they had had several weeks' rest." Nor was it with any idea of their being seriously engaged that these divisions, which together constituted the IX. Corps, were put into the line to the north-west of Rheims. It was in this quarter, however, as related in a previous chapter, that the Germans, towards the end of May, had unexpectedly launched a great offensive. As a result, the IX. Corps, instead of securing an opportunity to rest and recuperate, had been called on to bear the weight of one of the heaviest and most determined attacks of the War. In referring to the events which followed and the achievement of these British divisions, but lately filled up with young drafts, Sir Douglas Haig quotes in his despatches the following words of the French general under whose orders they had come :—" They have enabled us to establish a barrier against which the hostile waves have beaten and shattered themselves. This none of the French who witnessed it will ever forget."

2nd Bn.
July, 1918

But this high tribute had been won at a terrible cost, and the infantry of the 50th Division, than whom none had been more closely involved, had been practically annihilated. Already, and but recently, they had absorbed all available drafts, and it was now decided that the division should be reconstituted by allotting to its commander, Major-General H. Jackson, ten battalions from Salonica and Palestine, including the 2/FIFTH. It thus came about that the Second Battalion of the Regiment, in the closing months of the War, was to fight in the Division whose name its Territorial Battalions had done so much to make famous, and to represent during that time the one connecting link between the original and future composition of the Northumbrian Division.

The re-organisation of the 50th Division, however, was not to be carried out for a week or two yet ; and in the interval those of the FIFTH who were awaiting their turn for home leave, which had been opened on the arrival of the Battalion in France, remained at Serqueux in enjoyment of amenities to which they had long been strangers. It was not till the 16th July that the Battalion was moved to Martin l'Église, where it was formed with the 7/Wiltshire Regiment and the 2/Royal Munster Fusiliers into the 150th Brigade under the command of Brigadier-General C. P. Heywood.

Although these battalions which had been brought together to form the infantry of the re-constituted 50th Division had been drawn from various sources, they had one fatal characteristic in common. The strength and efficiency of all had alike been undermined by malarial fever, and before the Division could be regarded as truly fit for active service in France it was essential that its battalions should be nursed back to health. So, while the training of the troops and their leaders for the varied type of fighting which would arise with the penetration of the enemy's defences was undoubtedly important, an even more anxious concern of the Divisional Commander was the re-establishment of the health of his troops, in order that they should be fit to engage in tasks which would entail as great a physical demand as any hitherto undertaken. Fortunately there was now opportunity for this, for the time had passed when every half-trained recruit had to be flung into the fighting line to avert disaster by stopping a gap : and the 2/FIFTH were accordingly to be occupied during the next ten weeks solely in training and recuperating. Though the weather was not entirely favourable for either purpose, for there was much rain, a great amount of very useful training was carried out, and the health of the men benefited markedly from the change, not only of climate, but of the conditions under which they lived. There was, indeed, a contrast between life at Serqueux or Martin l'Église and that which they had been leading in Macedonia. Whereas, for instance, but a few months since at Butkovo, officers would ride 25 miles and back to attend a divisional pantomime at " The Kopriva Palace Theatre " ; here any man by stepping across the road could be entertained by Miss Lena Ashwell's company of London professionals or the less ambitious, yet wholly enjoyable, Jesmond Jesters. Again, where in Macedonia the dry bed of a river had often done duty as a football ground, at Martin l'Eglise outdoor games were properly provided for. Then there were trips to Dieppe, and, above all, short leave to England for the refreshment of body and mind. For the rest, beyond recording that the day to day training was based on the prospect of the Division being engaged in open warfare, there is no need to dwell further on this period in the rest area, during which units in close association with each other were being prepared to enter battle as a strong and united division.

By the beginning of September the Division was in every respect ready to take the field, and orders were received for it to join the XIII. Corps. On the 15th, the 2/FIFTH entrained with the 150th Brigade at Rouxmenil and moved to the Doullens Area, where they were billeted at Pommera, a few miles from Ivergny, in which the 1st Battalion had been accommodated but a few weeks earlier. Ten days later the forward movement was continued by bus to the Allonville Area, the Battalion going into billets at Cardonnette, 4 miles north-west of Amiens. On the 28th its " Battle Surplus " concentrated with that of the remainder of the 50th Division at the neighbouring village of Coisy, and the Battalion was moved by bus to Combles.

On the 29th the Fourth Army's attack on the Hindenburg Line opened, and the 150th Brigade remained at Combles during this and the following day in readiness to move at a half hour's notice.* Late in the afternoon of the 30th, sudden and unexpected orders came for Lieut.-Colonel Hardman Jones to return to Coisy in order to take over command of the Divisional Battle Surplus, and for Major Freeman to replace him in command of the Battalion.† The XIII. Corps having now been ordered to relieve the IIIrd, the 50th Division moved forward on the 1st October to take over the line from the 18th Division.

In order to arrive at the situation in which the 50th Division was to enter battle, it is necessary to turn to the operations which had been in progress on the Fourth Army front between the 27th September and the 1st October. On the 27th September, when the 1/FIFTH were engaged east of Havrincourt in the Third Army's attack for the completion of the capture of the Hindenburg Defences, the Fourth

---

* On this day Brigadier-General Rollo assumed command of the 150th Brigade on the appointment of Brigadier-General Heywood to the 3rd Guards Brigade.

† DIVISIONAL BATTLE SURPLUS.—A system had been introduced by which, so far as the total strength of a battalion permitted, 50% of the officers and a proportion of other ranks were left out of battle, as a reserve which would be available to enter fresh on future operations. The circumstances in which Lieut.-Colonel Hardman Jones was at this time required at short notice to replace the senior officer who had originally been detailed to command the infantry reserves of the Division were unfortunate. He had attended a conference at which the Divisional Commander had explained the situation in the battle area and the action which would probably be required of the Division. Major Freeman, on the other hand, was in complete ignorance of these matters when suddenly ordered to go forward and take over command of the Battalion.

272   THE FIFTH IN THE GREAT WAR.

Map No. 40   Army to the south, in front of whom lay the most formidable sector of the Hindenburg   2nd Bn.
Line, stood fast in the positions they had gained between Holnon and Gouzeaucourt.   Sept.–Oct.,
An intense bombardment, however, had been opened on the enemy's defences in this   1918
quarter and continued throughout the 28th. On the 29th September, as already
related, the Fourth Army's attack had opened, and by the 1st October had carried
the Hindenburg Line on a front of ten miles to the north of St. Quentin. In the
northern sector, with which we are concerned, the British line had been advanced
some 1,500 yards east and north of Bony, and the village of Vendhuille had been
occupied.

Map No. 41   In the reliefs carried out by the XIII. Corps on the 1st and 2nd October, the
50th Division took over a line from a point 1,000 yards west of Mont St. Martin to
(incl.) Vendhuille, the 151st Brigade being placed on the right and the 149th on the
left. The 150th Brigade marched to Nurlu, where it was held in reserve, and occupied
some iron shelters which had been constructed by the Germans. Orders had now
been issued for the 50th Division, in co-operation with troops of the Australian Corps
on its right, to attack on the 3rd October for the capture of Prospect Hill and a line
running thence roughly west, by the northern edges of Gouy and Le Catelet, to
Macquincourt Farm. The attack was to be carried out by the 151st Brigade, on
whose left the 2/Royal Dublin Fusiliers of the 149th Brigade were to co-operate by
gaining ground to the west of Le Catelet. By the original orders Prospect Hill, the
occupation of which was of the utmost importance, was to be captured by the
6/Inniskilling Fusiliers. supported by the 1/K.O.Y.L.I., who were to advance in echelon
in rear of their right flank and ensure liaison with the Australians. The 4/K.R.R.C.
were to be responsible for carrying Gouy and Le Catelet.

During the afternoon of the 2nd October the 2/FIFTH were moved forward
to May Copse, 1 mile south-east of Épehy, and settled down in the open in expectation
of remaining there throughout the night. At midnight, however, orders came for
the Battalion to march at 3 a.m. to the Hindenburg Line, where they were to come
under the orders of the 151st Brigade. Major Freeman, going forward in advance,
reported to Brigade H.Q. at Bony at 3 a.m., and was here joined by the Battalion
2½ hours later. In the meantime a serious hitch had occurred in the arrangements for
the attack. It was learnt that the assembly of the Innsikilling Fusiliers had been
delayed, and that they would not be ready to advance at zero hour, which had been
fixed for 6.10 a.m. On receipt of this very disturbing report, the 151st Brigade
immediately issued orders for the K.O.Y.L.I. to advance for the capture of Prospect
Hill, and for two companies of the FIFTH to be sent forward to undertake the duties
originally allotted to this battalion, viz. to support the attack and ensure liaison with
the Australians. " A " and " B " Companies, under the command respectively of
Captain King and Captain Fenwick, who were detailed for this task, promptly moved
forward from Bony to take their place in echelon in rear of the right flank of the
K.O.Y.L.I., who, although the alteration in orders had reached them only a moment
before the opening of the barrage, had advanced punctually at Zero hour. Owing
to an error in the compass bearing given to them, Woodroffe's and Snailham's platoons
of " A " Company lost direction from the outset and became completely detached
for the remainder of the day; but the remainder of the two companies of the FIFTH
gained touch with the K.O.Y.L.I. on approaching St. Martin, and thereafter continued

2nd Bn.
3rd Oct., 1918

to move forward in close support of the battalion.* By 7 a.m. Gouy, in the centre of the 151st Brigade's attack, had been captured by the 4/K.R.R.C., but it was not till after 8 a.m. that the K.O.Y.L.I., with twice the distance to cover, approached their objective. In the assault which followed, and swept the Germans from Prospect Hill, certain of the FIFTH participated; Lieutenant Stephenson's platoon of " B " Company alone capturing 36 prisoners and two machine guns.†

Map No. 41

In the meantime the enemy had been driven by the K.R.R.C. from Le Catelet; further to the left the Dublin Fusiliers had gained Macquincourt Farm; and by 8.40 a.m. the whole objective of the 50th Division was reported to have been carried. Though attempts to push north of Macquincourt Farm were checked by heavy fire from Richmond Copse, the Germans for long made no effort to recover the positions they had lost, which they were content to keep under heavy and continuous artillery fire. The K.R.R.C., however, had by now become considerably reduced in numbers, and at about 11 a.m. the FIFTH received orders to reinforce the portion of this battalion which had occupied the northern edge of Le Catelet. First " C " Company (Captain Muir), and a little later " D " Company (Captain Carr-Ellison), were sent forward for this purpose. During the descent of the slope leading to the hollow in which Le Catelet lay, very few casualties were suffered, but before the village was reached a sudden violent counter-attack by the Germans drove the K.R.R.C. back to its southern outskirts, where the reinforcements of the FIFTH on coming to their assistance encountered intense artillery and machine-gun fire. In face of this, recovery of the lost position was impossible, and the best that could be done was to cling to the southern edge of Le Catelet, where with the remnants of the K.R.R.C. the two companies remained engaged in close and heavy fighting till dark.

During the night the 150th Brigade relieved the 151st; the 7/Wiltshire taking over from (incl.) Prospect Hill to the eastern outskirts of Le Gouy, and the 2/Munster Fusiliers relieving the K.R.R.C. and the two companies of the FIFTH in Le Gouy and Le Catelet. The whole of the former village was still occupied, while the southern and western outskirts of Le Catelet were held, with patrols pushed into the interior, where the number of enemy dead gave terrible evidence of the severity of the fighting. Battalion H.Q. had now moved forward to Rue Neuve, where they were rejoined by " C " and " D " Companies after their relief, and later by the two detached platoons of " A," which on failing to get in touch with their company had fallen back on Bony. The casualties sustained by the 2/FIFTH during the day had included Captain H. S. King, M.C., killed, and 2nd Lieutenant Bentley wounded in the attack on Prospect

---

* The loss of direction and detachment of the two platoons of " A " Company, to which no reference is made in any official record, has been communicated by Mr. K. D. Woodroffe. It is important to this history as explaining how these platoons came to be engaged with " C " and " D " Companies in an attack on the following day, which from the Battalion War Diary is quite unintelligible. The adventures of the two subalterns and their platoons, astray on the battlefield, were extremely unpleasant, but they have no bearing on the general narrative.

† Strangely enough, this incident, which is related in the Battalion War Diary, is not mentioned in the " Narrative " preserved in the records of the 151st Brigade, which in referring to the action of the two companies of the FIFTH states :—" These companies moved forward well and maintained close liaison with the 1/K.O.Y.L.I., *but occasion for their employment did not arise.*" In the particulars of the action for which Lieutenant J. Stephenson was awarded a bar to the Military Cross, however, the following passage occurs :—" This officer *in the attack on Prospect Hill* led his platoon with great dash and captured," etc., etc. This is conclusive evidence that the FIFTH did participate in the assault. (The italics in the above quotations are the author's.)

274   THE FIFTH IN THE GREAT WAR.

Map No. 41

Hill ; 2nd Lieutenant Creighton wounded in the fighting at Le Catelet ; and Lieutenant Searles, who had been wounded while performing liaison duties under the direction of Divisional H.Q.

Orders were now received for the attack to be resumed at dawn on the 4th by the 150th Brigade, which, while maintaining a firm hold on Prospect Hill, was to advance for the capture of La Pannerie South and a line running thence towards Hargival Farm. The attack was to be carried out by the 2/Munster Fusiliers, on the right, and the 3/Royal Fusiliers (attached from the 149th Brigade), on the left. The 2/Dublin Fusiliers (149th Brigade) were to co-operate by gaining ground towards Hargival Farm, and the 2/FIFTH (" C " and " D " Companies and 2 platoons of " A ") to move down to Le Catelet in general support of the attack.

At 6.10 a.m. on the 4th, the troops advanced under cover of a creeping barrage. On the right the Munster Fusiliers succeeded in carrying La Pannerie, but the Royal Fusiliers advancing west of Le Catelet, came under intense machine-gun fire from Richmond Copse, Hargival Farm, and a defended locality situated at a spinney immediately north of the village.* This fire, which swept the slopes which rose to the north and west of Le Catelet, completely held up the advance of the Royal Fusiliers. In the meantime the FIFTH, who had found the village clear of the enemy, had reached its north-western edge, but on attempting to debouch were also met by heavy machine-gun fire from the spinney locality. Prospect Hill was still firmly held and the Munster Fusiliers were established at La Pannerie, but the left of the 150th Brigade s attack had for the time been brought to a complete standstill. The FIFTH, under heavy shell-fire, and unable to advance, could serve no purpose in the position they had gained, and were now withdrawn for better protection to the high ground south of Le Catelet.

For the remainder of the morning there was no change in the situation. That it was far from satisfactory was realised by all, but it was not till about noon that it was known who would be called on to take action to remedy it. Orders then came to Major Freeman to lead forward his 2½ companies and capture the spinney position which had been so prominent in bringing the attack to a standstill. The manner in which this should be done with his small force of some 170 men was not indicated, nor was the task made easier by the fact that the position from which the enemy's fire was being directed had hitherto not been very definitely located. The extent to which the Royal Fusiliers advancing in the morning some distance to the west of Le Catelet had suffered was, however, obvious ; and this decided Major Freeman to plan his approach by an old communication trench leading between the village and a stream which ran north, a short distance from its western edge. The troops were directed to advance in single file, the two platoons of " A " Company leading, followed by " D " Company, with " C " in rear. Lieutenant Woodroffe of " A " was at the head of the Battalion with Capt. Carr-Ellison, the commander of " D." It was a hazardous undertaking. The old derelict trench gave direction but little cover ; and the advance for the most part was made by crawling on hands and knees. Just to the north-

---

* It has been impossible to decide with any degree of certainty on the exact situation of this locality, which becomes prominent at a later stage in this narrative. On the independent evidence of three officers of the FIFTH who were in action this day, the writer has become convinced that the map reference by which it is described in the records of the 50th Division is quite inaccurate. Its most probable position was at the point marked " Spinney " on Map 41. A small wood is shown at this point on contemporary maps.

A SHELL-WRECKED HOUSE IN LE CATELET.

[Imperial War Museum—Crown Copyright.

west of Le Catelet the stream which they had kept on their left joined a larger one, the Escaut, which ran roughly from east to west. Here, too, the communication trench turned right along the northern edge of the village. The head of the column, after following the altered course of the trench for some distance, found that it came to an abrupt end. Such scant cover as it had given was now no longer available, and word was sent back to Major Freeman, who came forward to view the situation. This was far from favourable for the task in hand. Between his companies, strung out in file, and the enemy's position ran the Escaut, too wide for men hampered by rifles and equipment to leap. Close at hand a broken bridge had been replaced by a couple of planks, but it could not be hoped that more than the first few leading files would be able to cross by these, since it was reckoned—rightly as events proved—that they would be under the observation of the enemy. Freeman thereupon decided to make a personal reconnaissance, in order, firstly, to ascertain whether the stream was fordable, and, secondly, to locate the exact position of the enemy. A solitary reconnaissance by a battalion commander may, perhaps, be regarded as unorthodox; but the age of this one—25 years—was exceptional for one in his position. In any case, no scout's report could have the same value to him as his own investigations. Screened by some shrubs and trees, he crept to the stream unobserved, and bidding his orderly remain on the near bank, entered the water, which he found to be fordable, though rather more than waist deep. Then, crossing to the far bank, he worked his way across a narrow strip of meadow to gain the cover of an empty communication trench which he had noted ran up the opposite slope. After crawling forward a short distance, he ventured to raise his head over the edge of the trench, but as quickly withdrew it. Quite close at hand, in a trench running at right angles to that by which he had approached, he had observed a German sentry. Having thus located the enemy's position, he lost no time in returning to his companies and issuing orders for attack. By these the troops were to follow him and if possible advance under cover of the communication trench which led to their objective; but if fire was opened, they were to deploy right and left, cross the stream as best they could, and charge the enemy's position.

The precise sequence of events which followed cannot be given in detail, for those engaged in a desperate venture such as was now to be undertaken act by instinct rather than by studied reflection, and in the elation that comes with success recollect little of the means by which it has been attained. Woodroffe, whose platoon of "A" led the attack, together with his leading files crossed by the plank bridge, but several of his men plunged through the stream. Freeman, already across, was seen standing, regardless of danger, directing and urging forward the attack. The enemy, however, had almost immediately opened fire, and he fell wounded in the arm and leg. "D" Company had now spread out right and left along the bank of the stream and, plunging through the water, were hot on the heels of the leading platoons. Muir followed, pausing only for a few moments to collect his men of "C" Company under cover of a building on the far bank, before leading them forward to the assault. The enemy's post proved to be an enclosed work, surrounding the spinney, with extensive dug-outs in the centre. Attacking from the flank, Woodroffe's and Snailham's platoons of "A" had scarcely carried the front face of the work, before "D" and "C" Companies swept round the rear. Though the Germans had been quick to open fire, how completely they had been surprised by the incredible swiftness with which the FIFTH had forded the deep stream and delivered the assault may be judged from the sequel. A few showed fight, more fled up the slope which rose in rear of the work, but the bulk of the garrison, who, had they manned the parapet, could have scarcely failed to shatter the attack by fire, were trapped in the deep dug-outs, from which they had not been given time or warning to emerge. With Freeman *hors de combat* command had now fallen to Captain Muir, by whose orders the rear face of the work was manned and fire opened on those of the enemy who had escaped and were retiring to the north. At this point Captain Carr-Ellison, struck in the forehead by an enemy bullet, was killed, and further casualties began to occur. Not till then was it realised that the heads of our men, silhouetted against the chalk parapet of the front face, were presenting a clear target to the enemy's snipers, and orders were given to cease fire and take cover.

In this attack, delivered by 170 men of the FIFTH, no fewer than 250 prisoners, together with 18 heavy and light machine-guns and several trench mortars, had been captured. It is not surprising that a post of the strength indicated by these figures should have resisted earlier attacks, but rather that it should ultimately have been carried by a force that can have numbered little more than half the total of its garrison. Credit for what must rank as one of the most brilliant episodes in the history of the FIFTH lay in the first place with Major Freeman, who planned the approach and assault; but once his orders had been given and the crossing of the stream begun, the success of the attack had depended solely on the determination of the men and their trust in the officers who led them. In addition to the officer casualties already recorded, 2nd Lieutenants Williams and Phillips of " C " Company, and 2nd Lieutenants Girdlestone of " D " had been wounded; of the other ranks, 2 only had been killed and 45 wounded. Though, in relation to what had been accomplished, these losses could be counted as extraordinarily light, they meant a reduction of over a quarter of the total strength of the companies, to whom it now fell to hold what they had won. It was not long, however, before their position was made secure. Following an intense bombardment of the enemy's positions, the 4/K.R.R.C. and 1/K.O.Y.L.I., attacking at dusk, carried the line forward to within close distance of Richmond Copse and gained touch with the Munster Fusiliers at La Pannerie South, while a simultaneous advance by the 2/Dublin Fusiliers carried Hargival Farm. The capture by the 7/Wiltshire of a line of trench to the north of Prospect Hill further improved the position of the right of the 50th Division.

When darkness fell, the companies of the FIFTH, though now covered by the troops which had carried forward the attack, had but scant knowledge of the situation. All telephone wires had been cut, and in the heavy shelling which continued, any attempt to repair them would have been useless. Thus isolated, without food, water, or ammunition, the troops spent a wretched night in the position they had captured. Against the considerable amount of gas which was included in the enemy's bombardment the box respirators, which had been submerged in crossing the stream, gave inadequate protection, though its worst effects were lessened by its tendency to drift to the valley from the higher ground the companies now occupied. When day broke on the 5th October, the troops, cramped, and worn with hunger and fatigue, were still in position; but the relief of the 150th Brigade (less the 7/Wiltshire on Prospect Hill) by the 115th Brigade (38th Division) had now been ordered; and at 11 a.m. H.Q. and the 2½ companies of the FIFTH were relieved and withdrawn to Rue Neuve, where they were rejoined by the 1½ companies which had remained detached since dawn on the 4th October. At 1 p.m. the Battalion was served with a hot meal. Sorely as this was needed by the exhausted troops after their exertions during a fast of over 24 hours, it was not, as will be seen, to represent merely an appreciation of what had been accomplished, but to form the foundation for further efforts required of at least some of those who enjoyed it.

In the meantime patrols of the 149th Brigade, finding De la l'Eau and Putney evacuated by the enemy, had pushed up the Hindenburg Line for a distance of a mile north of Richmond Quarry without meeting any opposition. The Germans, their line of retreat being threatened, had, it seems, fallen back east across the British front. The direction of attack, hitherto north-east and north, was accordingly now changed to east, and the 7/Wilts swung round on to the Nauroy Line, where they came into touch with the 38th Division on their left. During the afternoon, orders came for the 2/FIFTH to send forward three companies to take over 600 yards of the Nauroy Line to the east of La Pannerie. On arrival they were to come under the orders of Lieut.-Colonel Tonson-Rye of the 2/Munster Fusiliers, whose battalion would be holding the line on their right. "B," "C," and "D" Companies having been despatched for this duty, Battalion H.Q. and "A" Company were withdrawn for the night to Mont St. Martin, which they found being subjected to periodical bombardments by the German guns.

At 8 a.m. on the 6th, "B" and "C" Companies, under Lieut.-Colonel Tonson-Rye, were ordered to deploy to the south of Aubencheul and advance for the capture of a section of the Beaurevoir Line. Little resistance was offered to this attack, but on the objective being carried it was found that the trench had been dug only to a depth of 12 inches. It was, moreover, under the fire of machine-guns sited on high ground to the east, from which several casualties were sustained before the companies were withdrawn to the cover of a sunken road a short distance in rear. At 1 p.m. orders were given for a further attack to be made for the capture of Villers Farm; but on the troops advancing at 2 p.m. they immediately came under the fire of the machine-guns which had previously made the Beaurevoir Line untenable. In the fighting which ensued, 2nd Lieutenant Collings' platoon of "B" Company became closely involved. Collings with a section of six men succeeded in carrying an enemy post, but he himself was killed, and of the remainder all but the section commander, Lce.-Corporal Collins, became casualties. For a considerable time Collins hung on single-handed to the post, and managed to send back a report by one of the wounded to Captain Fenwick, the company commander. Serjeant Tudor, to whom command of the platoon had fallen on the death of 2nd Lieutenant Collings, handled it with great ability in the difficult circumstances which had arisen, and in inspiring confidence in his men he was supported by the fine example set by Lce.-Corporal Mylett. It had, however, become clear that nothing but heavy casualties could result from further efforts to push forward, and the attack was accordingly broken off, and the companies again withdrawn to the shelter of the sunken road. Here they remained till dusk, when, on relief by troops of the 149th Brigade, they moved back to rejoin Battalion H.Q. at Bony, where the 150th Brigade was now held in Divisional Reserve. In addition to 2nd Lieutenant W. N. Collings, the FIFTH during this day had lost 5 other ranks killed, and 2nd Lieutenant Lees-Barton and 12 other ranks wounded.

In view of the failure of this first effort against Villers Farm, the further operations for its capture are of particular interest. During the night of the 6th/7th October an attack by the 149th Brigade failed to secure it. Yet another attempt was made on the following morning; but though the farm was taken and a number of prisoners captured, the attacking troops were later driven back by machine-gun fire. Orders were then given for the 50th Division to co-operate with the 66th

278 THE FIFTH IN THE GREAT WAR.

Map No. 41

Division on the right and the 38th on the left in a general advance in the early hours of the 8th October. In the course of this operation, which was completely successful, Villers Farm, which for two days had proved so formidable an obstacle, was carried by the 151st Brigade, which had replaced the 149th on the front of the 50th Division. It had been planned that the lines of advance of the 38th and 66th Divisions should converge on Marliches Farm, roughly 1¼ miles east of Villers Farm. On resuming its advance after the capture of the latter, the 151st Brigade was accordingly squeezed gradually out of the battle front, and the whole of the 50th Division came into reserve.

2nd Bn. Oct., 1918

Of the six great battles which come under the general heading of " The Battles of the Hindenburg Line," the fighting in which the 2/FIFTH had been engaged near Le Catelet between the 3rd and 5th October is known as the " Battle of the Beaurevoir Line." The actions which took place on the 8th and the 9th October extended over a far wider area, and are together known as " The Battle of Cambrai, 1918." By their location on these dates both Battalions of the FIFTH became entitled to this battle honour. But while, as has been seen, the Second Battalion on the 8th October was in reserve, the First Battalion was actively engaged on that day on the Third Army front. Sequence demands, therefore, that we should now return to the narrative of the 1/FIFTH; for, as in no previous period of this history, the two battalions, though in different Armies, were closely concerned with the same events.*

Map No. 40

" The enemy's defence in the last and strongest of his prepared positions had been shattered. The whole of the main Hindenburg defences had passed into our possession, and a wide gap had been driven through such rear trench systems as had existed behind them. . . . The threat to the enemy's communications was now direct and instant, for nothing but the natural obstacles of a wooded and well-watered country-side lay between our Armies and Maubeuge."—(*Haig's Despatches*).†

1st Bn. Oct., 1918

Following the fighting on the Third Army front which had culminated in the capture of Ribécourt and the Hindenburg Support Line, the 1/FIFTH, it will be remembered, had been withdrawn with the 9th Brigade to Divisional Reserve. While the long drawn out battle described in the earlier part of this chapter was in progress on the Fourth Army front, they had remained inactive and at rest. Not so, however, the remainder of the 3rd Division, which had been engaged in heavy fighting, and had continued to advance in conjunction with the New Zealand and 2nd Divisions on its right and left. By the 4th October the 8th and 76th Brigades had captured Rumilly and, further to the south, had advanced the line to the road running north from Crévecoeur (now in the hands of the New Zealanders) to the l'Épine cross-roads. This line had been consolidated with a view to its forming the starting-line of an

---

* The brief period during which the two battalions were together in the 28th Division in February 1915 might, perhaps, be taken as an exception to this statement (see Chapter VI.).

† It will be seen in the description of the 1st Battalion's fighting at Seranvillers that actually, as stated later in Haig's Despatches, there were still " certain incomplete defences " to be captured in the opening stage of the concluding phase of the British offensive.

1st Bn.
8th Oct., 1918

attack which had been planned for the 8th October. In the meantime the 9th Brigade had been moved forward to an area south-west of Marcoing.

In the operations about to begin, the Third Army (IV., VI., XVII. Corps) was to continue its advance towards the line Le Cateau—Solesmes. In the opening attack the 3rd Division, as the right of the VI. Corps, was allotted three objectives: (i) A line of trench running north-west on the near side of Seranvillers (ii) The village of Seranvillers and the line of the La Targette—Forenville road (iii) The village of Wambaix and the line of the railway to the north of it. The task of carrying these objectives had been given to the 9th Brigade, strengthened by the 2/Suffolk and two machine-gun companies. Its attack was to be supported by the fire of one Heavy and four Field Artillery Brigades, and further assisted by tanks.

By the brigade plan the 1st Objective was to be captured by the 1/FIFTH on the right and the 4/Royal Fusiliers on the left, supported respectively by the 2/Suffolk and the 13/King's. At Zero plus 130 minutes the Suffolk and King's were to pass through the leading battalions, for the attack on the 2nd Objective. If this were carried, success was to be exploited by pushing forward fighting patrols under cover of an artillery barrage for the occupation of Wambaix and the line of the railway.

The 9th Brigade moved forward during the night of October 7th/8th, and by 3.30 a.m. the FIFTH and Royal Fusiliers were assembled for attack to the west of the Crévecoeur—l'Épine road, immediately in rear of the troops of the 8th Brigade, who were in occupation of the line. At 4.30 a.m. the attacking troops advanced to close on their artillery barrage, which was to remain stationery on a road some 600 yards to the east before creeping forward at a rate of 100 yards in 4 minutes over the further 1,500 yards which would still lie between the infantry and their objective. The 1/FIFTH—though themselves 100 under strength—as the strongest battalion in the Brigade had been allotted a front of no less than 1,300 yards. This length of frontage necessitated their disposition on a three company front—" Z " Company (Captain H. G. Steele) advancing on the right, " X " (Captain Lord) in the centre, and " Y " (Captain Pigg) on the left, with " W " Company (Lieutenant Brown) following in support.* The three leading companies each advanced in two " two platoon waves " at 100 yards distance; platoons being disposed with their rifle sections leading and their Lewis gun sections ten yards in rear. Very shortly after moving forward, Captain Lord † was killed and 2nd Lieutenant Pitkethley wounded by shell fire, but our artillery barrage throughout the advance was perfectly regulated, and casualties in its early stages were not generally heavy. On the left, " Y " Company, which had rather less distance to cover than the right of the attack, encountered no opposition till it came under the fire of an enemy post established in some shell-holes about 300 yards on the near side of the trench which was to be carried. This post was quickly overcome, and several prisoners and machine-guns were captured. The company now experienced the disadvantage which infantry must sometimes suffer

Map No. 42

---

* Captain C. H. Steel, the commander of " W " Company, was on this day acting as 2nd-in-Command to Lieut. Colonel Cruddas, who had for some days been suffering from malarial fever but had refused to report sick lest he be ordered to hospital.

† Captain R. Lord had served during the War with both battalions of the FIFTH. Severely wounded in 1915 at Frezenburg with the 2nd Battalion, he later joined the 1st in August 1916, but in the following March had been invalided on account of his old head wound. He had rejoined the 1st Battalion in July 1918. He was mentioned in Despatches in April 1917.

when the rate of their advance is regulated by the movement of an artillery barrage working to a time-table. Its platoons were in position and ready for assault, but were held to the ground they had gained by their own barrage, which had not yet lifted from the objective. At this juncture a machine-gun, sited at the point at which the opposing trench crossed the Rumilly road, opened heavy fire on the leading troops of the now stationary " Y " Company. Fortunately the position of the gun was quickly located, and the concentrated fire of the company's Lewis guns quickly silenced it, but not before casualties had occured and Lieutenant Davidson had been temporarily stunned by a bullet which struck his steel helmet. In the meantime " Z " Company, on the right, had been opposed at a much earlier stage. Scarcely had its platoons closed on the barrage and continued their advance as it moved forward than they came under fire from a point on the road from which it had lifted. This forward post of the enemy, however, had been immediately rushed, and ten prisoners and a machine-gun were captured. After this they had not again been checked until, when within 300 yards of the German main trench they were held up by very heavy machine-gun fire directed from a point on the left of their objective. The situation of the Company was serious. It was now after six o'clock and the barrage was shortly due to lift and clear the way for the assault; but it was clear that to attempt a further frontal advance in the face of this fire, if possible at all, must result in heavy casualties. A small party was, therefore, directed to endeavour to work its way forward to a point on the Seranvillers—Crévecoeur road, from which the guns that were causing the trouble could be rushed as the barrage lifted. While the two flank companies had thus got forward to within assaulting distance of the German position, " X " had advanced steadily in the centre without meeting any opposition until close on its objective. At 6.10 a.m. the barrage lifted. " Y " Company, who had been waiting impatiently for this moment, immediately swept forward and carried the trench; but not without loss, Lieutenant Potter, who was killed as he reached the enemy's position, being among those who fell at this point.* Such of the enemy who here remained to face the assault were killed or captured, but the greater number had already fled to the shelter of the village. In the meantime the party sent forward by " Z " had succeeded in reaching its appointed position on the Seranvillers-Crévecoeur road, and at the given moment assaulted and carried the post on the left of the company's objective, killing a number of the enemy and capturing 8 prisoners and 3 machine-guns; while, under cover of this diversion, the remainder of the company flung forward, capturing a further 2 machine-guns together with 8 prisoners, and shooting down many of the enemy as they fled back to Seranvillers. To " X " Company, whose advance had never faltered, fell yet another machine-gun and several prisoners. Punctual to the minute the FIFTH had carried their whole objective, and found themselves in touch on the right with the New Zealanders, and on the left with the 4/Royal Fusiliers whose advance had been practically unopposed.

It was now about 7.50 a.m., and a half hour remained before the Suffolk and King's were due to pass through for the attack on the 2nd Objective, during which our artillery barrage, which had lifted forward 300 yards, remained stationary. As yet the forward situation was not clear enough to the enemy's headquarters for them to bring artillery fire to bear on the captured position, but their infantry and machine-guns very soon began to give serious trouble from the village on which they had fallen

---

* Lieutenant R. W. Potter was attached from the 16th Royal Warwickshire Regiment.

back. It was at this point that 2nd Lieutenant Walker of "Y" Company was killed, and the company threatened with heavy casualties by a machine-gun sited at the base of a road-side shrine some 200 yards from their position. Lieutenant Davidson, now the only subaltern left with Captain Pigg, realising the danger in which the company stood while this gun remained in action, gallantly volunteered to attempt its capture. With Corporal Jewell and three men he succeeded in creeping forward to within close distance of the shrine and then rushing the gun, which he captured and brought in together with two of its detachment. This action, in the words of Captain Pigg who witnessed it, was "a splendid achievement and saved many casualties." * Patrols were now pushed forward into the south-western quarter of Seranvillers, where they remained till the 2/Suffolk advanced for the second phase of the attack at 8.20 a.m., when they withdrew, bringing with them twelve more prisoners.

The attack on the 2nd Objective did not meet with the same immediate success as the earlier phase of the operations. The right of the Suffolk gained the line of the Forenville-Esnes road, but La Targette could not be carried; and on the left of the 9th Brigade's attack, the King's, after securing the centre of their objective, were taken in enfilade by fire from both flanks, and forced by a counter-attack by a tank to fall back on their starting line. Nor did the enemy content himself with repulsing these attacks. At 9 a.m. he brought the position captured by the FIFTH under a heavy bombardment which was to continue for the remainder of the day. At 10.30 a.m. two platoons of "W" Company were sent forward to reinforce the Suffolk and took up a position in a sunken road running south-east from the centre of Seranvillers. Later, the remainder of the company was ordered to join them for the purpose of assisting in a further effort against La Targette at 1 p.m., which it was planned should be made after a preliminary bombardment of 25 minutes and in conjunction with an attack by the King's and Royal Fusiliers further to the North. Owing, it seems, to some misunderstanding of orders, this operation proved a costly fiasco. No bombardment was put down; and an isolated attack by "W" Company and 15 men of the Suffolk was repulsed with heavy casualties.†

In the struggle for the capture of the 2nd Objective, which continued for the remainder of the day and was still in progress when darkness fell, the FIFTH took no further part, as they were given the task of clearing Seranvillers of parties of the enemy who still remained concealed in the cellars and dug-outs of the village. This proved to be beyond the powers of the patrols which were in the first place detailed for the purpose, and it was not till a methodical search had been made late in the evening by six platoons under Captain Steele that the village could be declared completely

---

* The shrine at the base of which the gun was sited sheltered a crucifix. Lieutenant (now Doctor) Davidson states that, prior to the capture of the gun, one of our tanks had charged the shrine, but failed to put the gun out of action and moved off to other tasks. A photograph of the shrine, taken by him at a later date, clearly shows the hole made in it by the tank. This and an aeroplane photograph, showing "Y" Company's objective and the position of the shrine, are unfortunately too faded for reproduction.

† The Brigade Narrative, which refers to this attack as having been made by "the 2/Suffolk (plus 1 company 1/Northd. Fus.)," makes no mention of the absence of the bombardment, which is revealed in the 1/Fifth War diary. The result of the attack was not learnt at Brigade H.Q. until 3 p.m., when a report was received from the 2/Suffolk that La Targette was still in the hands of the enemy.

clear of the enemy. Even so, Divisional H.Q. were not satisfied until after a further search at 11 p.m. this report was confirmed.

Arrangements had now been made for the Guards to pass through the 3rd Division during the night; and the 9th Brigade, who had at length secured and consolidated the line of the Forenville-Esnes road, was for the most part withdrawn between 2 a.m. and 5 a.m. The FIFTH, however, were required to remain forward for some hours longer, in order to guard against the enemy again filtering into Seranvillers, by patrolling the village until the Guards had passed through it; and it was not till daylight that the Battalion joined the remainder of the 9th Brigade at Rumilly, where breakfasts were taken before moving back to an area to the south of Havrincourt.

The 1/FIFTH, whose losses had been more severe than those of any battalion in the 9th Brigade, sustained the following casualties in the attack of the 8th October:—

OFFICERS.

Killed	Captain R. Lord.
	Lieutenant R. W. Potter.
	2nd Lieutenant S. R. E. Walker.
Wounded	2nd Lieutenant W. B. Pitkethley.
	2nd Lieutenant T. W. Butcher.
	2nd Lieutenant J. D. W. Mills.

OTHER RANKS.

Killed 22.   Wounded 111.   Missing 27.

As a result of the attacks by the Third and Fourth Armies on the 8th October the enemy's resistance temporarily gave way. Cambrai was evacuated, and so rapid was the pursuit of the disorganised forces of the Germans that by nightfall on the 9th the British were within two miles of Le Cateau, and Caudry was being attacked from the south. In this pursuit the 3rd Division took no part, and the 1/FIFTH were not again to be engaged with the enemy for a week or two following their withdrawal to rest in the Havrincourt area. The 50th Division, on the other hand, as reserve to the XIII. Corps, was following up the advance; and our interest is accordingly once more centred on the Fourth Army front, where the 2/FIFTH was very shortly to come into action.

On the night of the 6th October, it will be remembered, all four companies of the 2/FIFTH had concentrated with Battalion H.Q. in the Hindenburg Line at Bony. On the following day Lieut. Colonel Hardman-Jones, relieved at length of his duties with the Divisional "battle surplus," had arrived to take over the Battalion from Captain Muir, who for a time was to revert to the command of "C" Company. The forward move of the 50th Division began on the 9th. Roads had to be left clear for the transport, and on this and the following day the infantry, moving in parallel columns across country, were passing through the wreckage of the German retreat. On all sides lay abandoned machine-guns, artillery pieces, and the bodies of those who had but recently manned them. That the pursuit had not been without casualties to the cavalry which led it was also evident from the dead bodies of their horses, which here and there were lying on the fields. The Battalion was once again in inhabited country, and the billets at Serain, where the night of the 9th was spent, were in welcome contrast to the discomfort of the Hindenburg Line bivouac at Bony. At Reumont, where the following night was passed, the troops were again in comfortable billets, but no longer undisturbed. For, on the line of the R. Selle, less than 1½ miles distant, the enemy, reinforced from the rear, had called a halt and once more stood on the defensive; Reumont was under shell fire, and our own guns, in action close at hand, combined with those of the enemy to render sleep impossible. Early in the day Le Cateau had been cleared of the enemy, but the attack had been held up to the north and south of the village, and the troops who had effected this had been later forced to withdraw to its western outskirts. It had become apparent that the running fight which had been in progress for the past three days was at an end, and that a strongly organised attack would be needed to force the passage of the Selle. This meant some days delay, for the Germans had covered their retreat by extensive demolitions of road and rail communications, and the British armies, as a result, had for a time outrun their supply services.*

The 50th Division, having now received orders to relieve the 25th Division in the right sector of the front line of the XIII. Corps, the 150th Brigade on the 11th October took over the whole front allotted, which ran southwards, on the left bank of the Selle, from the Cambrai-Le Cateau road to a point about 700 yards south of St. Benin. The 2/FIFTH, who were detailed for the left flank, relieved the 9/Manchester on a ridge immediately facing Le Cateau.† Here, covered by posts established on the forward slope, the companies in the front line were disposed under shelter of a bank on the reverse slope, in the face of which holes had been excavated by the troops they had relieved. The disadvantage of the position lay in its being regarded by the enemy as one under cover of which his opponents could concentrate for attack, and so as one to be kept under constant shell fire. Lieutenant Gardner, the acting adjutant, was wounded while visiting the companies in the front line with the Commanding Officer shortly after taking over, and three men were killed and eight wounded on the first day. Further casualties were sustained from artillery fire on the following day, when 2nd Lieutenant Lumsden, who had joined the Battalion only two days before, and two of his men were killed by a shell when returning from patrol duty. The general conditions under which the next few days were passed, and the duties required of the FIFTH in preparation for a renewal of the attack, may be gathered from the following extracts from the diary of a company commander, written up by him a few days later when at rest:—" Scott, Bird and Macdonald were for ever on patrol, on bridge reconnaissance and river soundings, and the rest of us were always on the move, dodging 5.9's and whizz-bangs ‡. . . . and deepening our cubby-holes in that Heaven-provided bank." As to the part played by Lieut. Colonel Hardman-Jones in these strenuous days, one reads:—" The C.O. was about everywhere

---

* On the 10th October 2nd Lieutenants Welch, Atkinson, Bird Lumsden and Macdonald joined the 2/Fifth.

† The 9/Manchester were actually the right battalion of the 66th Division, which was in occupation of the left sector of the XIII. Corps.

‡ Field Artillery high velocity shells.

arranging for patrols and the posts of night and day. The weather was wet and cold, and he is far from well, but he's a regular hero in the line, with every detail at his finger ends." None of this work, however, was directly to serve the 50th Division, as a re-adjustment of fronts was now ordered for the 14th October, by which the S. African Brigade of the 66th Division would relieve the 2/FIFTH, and the 50th Division extend its line southwards to just north of St. Souplet. Before relief, a final reconnaissance of the crossings of the Selle was made during daylight by Lieutenant Stephenson, who succeeded in obtaining all the information required, at the cost of one man of his patrol killed by machine-gun fire. At 9 p.m. the Battalion was relieved and withdrawn to a supporting position south of Reumont.*

Of the twenty officers who had gone into action at Le Catelet, three had now been killed and nine wounded. Of the eight who remained, only one, Lieutenant Rogers, the signalling officer, was to be actively employed with the Battalion in the forthcoming operations, the others being relegated to the battle surplus and replaced from the same source. By this arrangement, "A" Company was now commanded by Captain Dodd, "B" by Lieutenant Wilson, "C" by Lieutenant Wardlaw, and "D" by Captain Price. The adjutant, Captain Pattison, having returned from leave, was again with Lieut. Colonel Hardman-Jones at Battalion Headquarters.

The objectives laid down for the attack by the IX., II American, and XIII. Corps of the Fourth Army, which had been arranged to open on the 17th October, might at first sight seem to have been rather ambitious. But the amount of resistance that a retreating enemy will show—particularly one of the quality of the Germans—is always an unknown factor. The plan of attack cannot ignore the possibility of an early collapse in the defence, and in anticipation of this must prepare for its exploitation.† Although, as will be seen, the task allotted to the 50th Division in its attack as the right division of the XIII. Corps was to be completed neither in the time nor by the methods laid down, the action that the 2/FIFTH were ultimately to be called on to take will be made clearer by a rough outline of the original plan. For reasons

---

* The narrative reports of events between the 11th and 19th October are missing from the War Diaries of the 50th Division and 150th Brigade, and the writer has relied for much, on the record found in "The Story of the Fourth Army" by Major-General Sir A. Montgomery (now Field-Marshal Sir A. Montgomery-Massinberd). A statement is found in this, which, if taken as being applicable to the 2/Fifth, would be misleading. It is said that prior to the 11th October the 50th Division had received strong reinforcements to replace the casualties suffered in the fighting at Gouy and Le Catelet. Actually the 2/Fifth remained very weak in numbers, and it is clear from the Battalion War Diary that no reinforcements of "other ranks" arrived till drafts totalling 8 officers and 245 O.R. were received between the 22nd and 24th October. This is confirmed by a private diary, which records the fighting strength of "C" Company as having been reduced to 49 on the 14th and to 33 on the 20th October. This company had left Cardonette on the 28th September at a strength of 127. From the Battalion War Diary it seems that battle casualties, which are alone recorded, account for roughly 50% of these losses; the remainder were presumably due to sickness—notably malaria, from which the Battalion continued to suffer severely.

† It had been estimated that the Fourth Army, which attacked at the outset with 7 divisions, would be opposed by 4 fresh and 2 exhausted divisions in the line. Actually it was to be opposed by 5 fresh and 3 fairly fresh divisions, and another fresh division was to be brought forward for counter-attack. A severe resistance was expected, but it was to prove even more obstinate than was anticipated.

THE FIFTH IN THE GREAT WAR. 285

2nd Bn.
17th Oct.,
1918

Map No. 43

which will later be apparent, particular note should be taken of the parts to be played by the *left battalions* of each of the two leading brigades. The attack of the 50th Division, which held a line from (excl.) St. Souplet to a point ½ mile north of St. Benin, was to be directed in a general direction north-east, for the capture of three objectives: (i) the line of the Arbre Guernon road as far north as the Le Cateau railway station, which itself was included; (ii) a line along the high ground south-west and west of Basuel, from a point north-east of La Roux Farm to the Basuel-Le Cateau road, and thence by this road to Le Cateau; (iii.) the village of Basuel, and thence a line running roughly W.N.W. to the Pommereuil-Le Cateau road. The initial advance of the 151st Brigade, which was to be responsible for forcing the passage of the Selle and carrying the 1st Objective, was to be made on a narrow front of 600 yards for the capture of the railway embankment south of St. Crépin. Its two right battalions were then to fan out and direct their advance on the Arbre Guernon-Le Cateau road, while its left battalion, the 6/*Royal Inniskilling Fusiliers*, was to turn north along the line of the railway and, taking the enemy in flank, seize the extensive buildings and goods-sheds about the railway station. In the 149th Brigade, which was detailed for the capture of the 2nd Objective, the two right battalions were to pass over the Selle by the St. Crepin crossings and, passing through the right of the 151st Brigade, to advance north-east. Its left battalion, the 13/*Royal Highlanders (Scottish Horse)**, was to act in a manner somewhat similar to the Inniskilling Fusiliers in the first phase. Crossing the Selle at St. Benin, it was to pass through the 151st Brigade on the 1st Objective and then turn north for the capture of the Railway Triangle. On the completion of the first two phases, the 150th Brigade, who would have been assembled west of St. Benin, was to pass through for the capture of Basuel and the line of the 3rd Objective. It is, perhaps, well to note that, though the plan on paper was simple and straightforward, it entailed a total advance of some four miles, in which each successive brigade would be operating on a front of roughly two miles.

At 5.20 a.m. on the 17th October the 151st Brigade advanced to the attack. The Selle was successfully crossed, but immediately afterwards very stiff opposition was encountered both from the line of the railway and the high ground to the east of it. By 8.45 a.m. the right of the attack had progressed little further than the line of the railway, the centre was still fighting for some orchards on the crest of a ridge due east of St. Benin, and the Inniskilling Fusiliers on the left, after advancing north, were meeting strong opposition from the station buildings. The 149th Brigade had now moved forward in accordance with the programme to carry out its allotted task. But in the situation which had arisen, its two right battalions by 9.30 a.m. became embroiled in the fight of the 151st Brigade for the 1st Objective, and the Scottish Horse turned north, not for the capture of the Railway Triangle as had been planned, but to assist the Inniskilling Fusiliers in their struggle for the station buildings. In short, instead of advancing on the 2nd Objective, all three battalions of the 149th Brigade had been absorbed as reinforcements to those of the 151st, with whom they were now intermingled.

It is time now to return to the 2/FIFTH and their movements during the events which have been related above. At 4.45 a.m. the 150th Brigade had been assembled west of St. Benin, where it remained inactive till 9.30, when orders were

---

* This yeomanry regiment converted to infantry will be referred to on later pages as The Scottish Horse.

received for it to move forward and cross to the east bank of the Selle by the bridges between St. Souplet and St. Crépin. On approaching the latter village, the FIFTH came under shell fire, but were fortunate in escaping with very slight casualties— 2nd Lieutenant Atkinson and two men being wounded. Having crossed the stream, the Battalion took up a position on the railway due east of St. Crépin, The 7/Wiltshire and 2/Munster Fusiliers being placed about 500 yards further south. The situation on the right of the attack had now improved; the troops of the 151st and 149th having here gained a position just west of the Arbre Guernon road, with their right flank thrown back towards Bandival Farm, which was held by the Americans. But the centre of the attack was still held in check by the enemy in the orchards; and the Inniskilling Fusiliers and Scottish Horse had not yet carried the station buildings on the left.

Orders were now issued for the 150th Brigade to undertake the capture of the 2nd Objective, and in preparation for this an intense bombardment of the station buildings and the Railway Triangle was put down between 3 p.m. and 3.30 p.m. Before this fresh plan could be put into execution, however, it was completely upset by two heavy counter-attacks, which forced back the right of the 50th Division and recaptured Bandival Farm from the Americans. In consequence, previous orders were cancelled, and at 4 p.m. the 150th Brigade was required to regain the lost ground and make good the *1st Objective*. This task was successfully accomplished by the 2/Munster Fusiliers and 7/Wiltshire, who swept forward and, carrying with them the troops who had been driven back, established themselves on the line of the Arbre-Guernon road. The FIFTH, who took no part in this attack, had in the meantime been employed in the consolidation of their position on the railway.

By this time the battalions of the 50th Division had become mixed up to an extent that rendered brigade control impossible. The divisional front was accordingly now divided into three sections, each to be held by a "group" of three battalions. The 2/FIFTH, who under this arrangement were placed at the disposal of Brigadier-General Robinson (149th Brigade), appointed to command the "left group," were ordered at 5 p.m. to move north in support of the Inniskilling Fusiliers and Scottish Horse. After advancing as required, the Battalion was halted just south of the railway buildings, which now at last had been captured. About 7.30 p.m. orders were issued for the Battalion to engage in an attack on "The Triangle," a very strongly defended position in which the enemy were offering a stubborn resistance. Owing, however, to the late hour at which the orders were received, the FIFTH were unable to advance till 9.45 p.m., and since a considerable distance lay between them and their objective, the orders for the attack were cancelled. At 3 a.m. the Battalion moved to the railway station, to which rations had been sent forward, and later took up a position as the right battalion of the "left group" on the Arbre Guernon-Le Cateau road, which the 50th Division now held from their right boundary to its entrance into Le Cateau.

Orders were now issued for the attack to be renewed at 5.30 a.m. on the 18th for the capture of the 2nd and 3rd Objectives of the previous day. The first of these was to be carried by the three groups into which the Division was now organised, and the final objective, including the village of Basuel, by the 75th Brigade attached from the 25th Division. In the "left group," the Scottish Horse were to be responsible for storming "The Triangle," while a railway embankment situated a short distance from its eastern apex was to be captured by the FIFTH on a front of roughly 700 yards. "A" and "B" Companies, which had been detailed for the attack,

2nd Bn.
18th Oct.,
1918

advanced at zero hour, supported by "C" and "D." Captain Dodd, who had been placed in command of the two leading companies, had no easy task. It was still quite dark, he had had no opportunity of viewing the ground over which the advance lay, and the enemy's artillery, in reply to our barrage, immediately put down heavy concentrations of 5.9 and 4.2 shells, which included a considerable amount of gas. The FIFTH, however, continued to move forward slowly but steadily over the 1,200 yards that lay between them and their objective. But, though the enemy's artillery were still able to respond to the desperate exhortations of their higher command, their infantry, whose numbers and morale had now been greatly reduced by the fierce fighting and constant bombardment of the past twenty-four hours, were no longer in condition to withstand attack.* As the FIFTH closed on the position and rushed forward to the assault, little attempt was made to resist them, though Lieutenant Wilson, the commander of "B" Company, fell mortally wounded just after the position was won.† By 8.30 a.m. the whole objective, together with 29 heavy and light machine-guns, had been captured, and 1 officer and 30 men made prisoner. This formidable position had been carried after a long advance under shell-fire at the comparatively slight cost of 1 officer and 5 other ranks killed and 28 other ranks wounded. The success of the operation owed much to the skilful leading and fine example set by Captain Dodd, who was awarded the Military Cross for his services on this day.

In the meantime the 50th Division's objective in this first phase of the attack had been carried all along the line; and at 8.45 a.m. troops of the 75th Brigade passed through the FIFTH for the completion of the day's operations. "A" and "B" Companies remained in the position they had captured, and "C" was moved forward at 6 p.m. to act as a close support to them during the night.‡

On the 19th October the 50th Division, on relief by the 25th, was withdrawn to Corps Reserve, and the 2/FIFTH went into billets at Maretz, where they rejoined the 150th Brigade. As they were not to be in action again for over a fortnight, we will turn now to the narrative of a battle which was to prove the last in which the First Battalion was to be engaged in the Great War.

Map No. 43

1st Bn.
Oct., 1918

The rapid pursuit by the Third Army, following the fighting in which the FIFTH had been involved at Seranvillers, had, like that of the Fourth Army further to the south, been checked on the line of the Selle. But the passage of the river had been forced on the 20th October; and to the north, east of Solesmes, the line had been

---

* Two captured orders addressed to the German artillery are given in "The Story of the Fourth Army" (p. 225). The following extracts from the first of these, issued on the 12th October, may here be quoted:—

"The Higher Command states that the possibility of an armistice being brought about depends on the battle being brought to a standstill . . . The English must not cross the Selle on our front. The artillery must prevent them."

† Lieutenant J. B. Wilson was the last officer of the 2nd Battalion killed in the Great War.

‡ A map in the "Story of the Fourth Army" shows the FIFTH at 6 p.m. as having been pushed forward 1000 yards to a position on the final objective of the 50th Division. There is, however, no mention of this either in the Battalion War Diary or in that of the 149th Brigade, which deals with the action of the "left group."

carried forward to the outskirts of Romeries. While these operations were in progress, the 3rd Division had remained in III. Corps Reserve. On the 13th the 1/FIFTH had moved with the 9th Brigade from the Havrincourt area to billets in Marcoing; and on the 20th, when it became necessary to bring the Division closer to the fighting line, to Bévillers.

In a further advance that was now ordered to start on the 23rd, the VI. Corps, as the centre of the Third Army, was to attack with the 3rd and 2nd Divisions on the right and left respectively. Four objectives were allotted to the 3rd Division; (i) the villages of Romeries and Vertain; (ii) the line of the road running north-east from le Trousses Minon, and the village of Escarmains; (iii) the far bank of the R. St. George; (iv.) the line of the Beaudignies-Escarmains road (the "Brown Line"). It will be noted that after the capture of the first two objectives, the left of the attack would be pivoting on Escarmains. The 76th and 8th Brigades were to capture the first three objectives, and the 9th Brigade, following in Divisional Reserve, was then to be prepared to pass through and carry the fourth. If, however, opposition proved slight during the early stages of the advance, the leading brigades were to go straight through to the final objective, and the 9th Brigade to continue to follow up in reserve. The insertion of a provisional clause of this nature tends to complicate orders, as these operations were to prove. In the later phases of the attack, with which we are most closely concerned, the New Zealand Division of the IV. Corps would be on the right of the 3rd Division.

The IV. Corps, which had a much greater distance to advance than the VIth. fixed an earlier time—3.30 a.m.—as its zero hour. The G.O.C. 3rd Division, however, who wished to secure the advantage of darkness in his attack on Romeries and Vertain, decided to adopt the hour of the neighbouring corps for his first advance, although it would mean a pause of $3\frac{1}{2}$ hours after the villages had been captured, in order to allow the divisions on either flank to come into line. The early start, however, did not affect the 9th Brigade, which was not required to move until the leading troops advanced from the 1st Objective, and the FIFTH accordingly were able to look forward to the supreme advantages of a full night's rest and a good breakfast before going into battle.

In the late afternoon of the 22nd October the two attacking brigades moved forward to their assembly positions, and the 9th Brigade marched to night billets at Quiévy, three miles south-west of Solesmes. The opening attack in the early hours of the 23rd more than justified the decision of the Divisional Commander to advance under cover of darkness. Little resistance was offered, Romeries and Vertain were captured without difficulty, and close on one thousand prisoners were taken. Shortly after 6 a.m. the FIFTH left their billets and marched to the west of Solesmes, where they assembled with the remainder of the 9th Brigade. Orders had been given that, if required to carry the final objective, the Brigade would attack with the FIFTH on the right, the Royal Fusiliers on the left, and the 13/King's in support; and units were now instructed to take up their appropriate positions during the preliminary advance. At 8.40 a.m. the hour at which the leading troops were due to move forward from the 1st Objective, the battalions of the 9th Brigade resumed their march, and threading their way between Solesmes and its northern suburb of St. Python, reached Romeries without suffering a single casualty. It was necessary, however, to avoid the village, which was now being heavily shelled; and the FIFTH, skilfully led by Lieut.-Colonel Cruddas, passed to the south of it and escaped the worst of the enemy's fire, though at this point one man was killed and 2nd Lieutenant Collins, the acting adjutant, wounded.* By 11 a.m. the 9th Brigade, formed for attack, had reached its forward assembly position, the FIFTH being disposed just in rear of the crossroads to the south of le Trousse Minon, " W " Company (2nd Lieutenant Dignen) in position to the south of the Romeries road, " Z " Company (Captain H. G. Steele) to the north of it, " Y " Company (Captain Pigg) in support, and " X " Company (Captain Hobbs) in reserve. There were still three objectives to be carried, but the feeble resistance hitherto encountered pointed to the enemy being thoroughly demoralised. There was further evidence of this, when in Escarmains, which contained numerous machine-guns, 200 prisoners surrendered to the 8th Brigade, and the whole of the 2nd Objective was captured at a total cost of only 50 casualties. The enemy seemed so little disposed to stand in defence of his positions, that it was now decided to put in force the alternative plan by which the 76th and 8th Brigades, after carrying the 3rd Objective, were to continue their advance for the capture of the Brown Line. The orders which conveyed this decision gave a fresh task to the 9th Brigade, which was required to pass through the Brown Line, and, under cover of the Corps Cavalry, secure (i) the line of the R. Écaillon; (ii) the high ground on its north bank; (iii) the village of Ruesnes; and (iv) the line of the Le Quesnoy-Valenciennes railway, 1,000 yards beyond Ruesnes. The FIFTH at 12.10 p.m. had resumed their advance in support of the 76th Brigade; and it was not till 1 p.m. that these fresh orders reached Battalion H.Q. and were passed forward. The difficulties of conveying orders to troops already deployed and moving forward are, however, very great; and up to the time that these were to be acted on, the Commanding Officer had received no acknowledgement from his forward companies. In fact, however, they had reached all companies of the FIFTH, though subsequent events seem to indicate that the battalions of the 8th and 76th Brigade remained in ignorance of the change of plan until considerably after the time at which it was to be put into execution. However this may be, it was the FIFTH who, finding that no attack was being delivered on the right flank, themselves advanced and captured the Brown Line; and it was with the 4/Royal Fusiliers, not the 8th Brigade, that their left gained touch on the Beaudignies-Escarmains road after the objective had been carried. Little resistance had been offered from the position itself, but several casualties had been sustained from machine-guns firing from the north bank of the Écaillon. On the right, the flank of the FIFTH was thrown back to gain contact with the New Zealanders at a point 500 yards south-west of Beaudignies.†

Even though the enemy's resistance had hitherto been feeble, an advance to the line of the Écaillon could not be blindly thrust forward, and cavalry reconnais-

---

* Captain Ellison had but recently been attached to Brigade H.Q. with a view to permanent appointment to the staff. On 2nd Lieutenant Collins being wounded, the Brigadier permitted him to return to the Battalion and resume the duties of adjutant, which he carried out for the remainder of the operations.

† The official report of the 3rd Division stated that the Brown Line was captured by the 76th and 8th Brigades *supported by the 1/Fifth and 4/Royal Fusiliers.* As shown above, that was the *later intention*, but that it was not the fact is proved by a message despatched by Captain N. B. Pigg, D.S.O., M.C., at 6 p.m. on the 23rd October, of which the carbon copy is now before the present writer. It runs as follows:—

To KUVO (*code name of* 1/FIFTH).

All coys on Brown Line aaa Order left to right is Y Z W X aaa Royal Fusiliers on our left are retiring to reorganise aaa W X Z coys attacked owing to the fact that the 76 Bde. did not appear to be advancing aaa Objective was reached and held at least one hour before Suffolks appeared

sance patrols were now sent out. Before their reports were received, however, darkness had fallen, and the 9th Brigade was ordered to establish a line from which an advance under cover of an artillery barrage could be made on the 24th, for the capture of the further objectives that had been given. Ultimately a line running north-west and south-east just beyond the village of Ruesnes was to be occupied as a *Line of Resistance*, covered by patrols pushed forward to the line of the railway. The cavalry, supported by the 8th Brigade, were then to pass through and establish an *Outpost Line* north-east of the railway.

In addition to 2nd Lieutenant Collins, 2nd Lieutenants Carey, Robson, Caldicott, and Jenkins had been wounded during the attack on the 23rd. The last-named, unfortunately, died of his wounds three days later.

At 4 a.m. on the 24th October the artillery barrage opened on the line of the Écaillon and the 9th Brigade advanced to the attack. The FIFTH were on the right, the 4/Royal Fusiliers on the left, and the 13/King's, in support, followed in rear of the FIFTH. At the outset no opposition was encountered; and the FIFTH descended to the valley, crossed the stream, and climbed the steep wooded slope which rose from the far bank, without suffering casualties other than those caused by our own artillery barrage, which throughout this day was somewhat ragged. But the companies had barely reached the crest of the far slope of the valley, when a machine-gun opened fire, wounding Captain Steele and several others. Its position had, however, been located by Captain Pigg, who immediately led forward a small party and with great gallantry captured it. A greater surprise was to follow. Suddenly five field guns, sited at close range to the south of Ruesnes, opened fire over open sights at the FIFTH and Royal Fusiliers. The moral effect on less steady troops of this point blank artillery fire might have been very great; but the Germans had others to reckon with. Almost immediately, the battery found itself under the concentrated fire of fifteen Lewis guns, and Captain Pigg, leading forward his men, charged and captured the guns together with such of the gunners as had not already fallen or fled.* At 8 a.m. Captain Pigg reported that the Royal Fusiliers were clearing Ruesnes village, and that all the companies of the FIFTH had reached their objectives. The latter statement, however, was challenged by Lieutenant Williams, the Battalion Intelligence Officer; and Lieut.-Colonel Cruddas, going forward, confirmed his view that, owing to an error in map reading, the FIFTH were still some 600 yards short of their objective. At 10 a.m., accordingly, he gave orders for the companies to push forward. They now came under very heavy machine-gun fire, and it was in the course of this

---

in driblets aaa Y Coy. reached the objective at 15.35 aaa Patrols are being kept out all night aaa Y Coy. frontage approx. Q 36 d 7.8. to R 31 c 3.9.
23–10–18

N.B. Pigg Capt.

18.00 hours

The message book in which the above is included contains the copy of every message sent by Captain Pigg during the operations, 23rd/27th October. As senior company commander he was exercising a general supervision over the four companies, and the very clear situation reports rendered by him have been of immense help to the writer in compiling this narrative.

* Captain N. B. Pigg, who had already earned the Military Cross and two bars, was awarded the Distinguished Service Order in recognition of his fine leadership during the operations 23rd/26th October, 1918. The two actions related above were specifically mentioned in the *London Gazette*, which, in referring to the second, stated :—" This fine act of gallantry undoubtedly saved the battalion many casualties."

final advance that the greater number of casualties occurred. The companies, however, steadily worked their way forward, and by 1 p.m. Cruddas was able to report that he was firmly established on his objective, in touch with the Royal Fusiliers on the left, and on his outer flank with the New Zealanders, who had advanced level with the FIFTH throughout.

During the afternoon, while the 9th Brigade continued to consolidate the position it had occupied, the 8th Brigade was brought up in rear, in readiness to pass through under the cover of cavalry patrols, which had now been pushed forward. These latter, however, came under such heavy fire that they were unable to progress; and ultimately orders were issued for the 8th Brigade to withdraw, and for the FIFTH and Royal Fusiliers to patrol after dark to the line of the railway and maintain contact with the enemy. The latter battalion found that the line of the Precheltes stream was held by machine-guns; but on the front of the FIFTH the earlier patrols found no trace of the enemy, whose presence was only revealed by Very lights rising from beyond the railway. Orders were now received from the Brigade for the FIFTH to send patrols northwards along the railway, with a view to cutting off the enemy opposed to the Royal Fusiliers. At 9.40 p.m. 2nd Lieutenant Cockerell and 9 men of " Y " Company worked their way forward to a point south-east of Belle Vue Farm, and then turned north-west along the railway. At the farm five prisoners were taken, one blundering into the patrol in the dark, two being found in a waggon, and the remaining two discovered in the farm-house. A further search of the house revealed 20 French civilians cowering in its cellars. Beyond Belle Vue Farm the railway was found clear, and it seems that by this time the enemy had withdrawn from in front of the Royal Fusiliers. After being out for two hours, Cockerell's patrol returned just before midnight. During the fighting on the 24th October 2nd-Lieutenant G. W. Dignen had been killed and Captain F. A. Hobbs wounded, which, with Captain Steele a casualty in the early morning, left Captain Pigg as the only remaining company commander.

At dawn on the 25th it became evident that no enemy remained on the line of the railway, on which posts were now established on the whole front of the brigade. The Germans, however, had not as yet withdrawn to any great distance, and of the, three posts found by the FIFTH, of which the central one occupied Belle Vue Farm, that detailed for the right came under machine-gun fire from the north-east and was unable to gain its position until these had been silenced. At 1.30 p.m. cavalry patrols were pushed beyond the railway; but there was little change in the situation until an hour later, when the 8th Brigade at last passed through and, under cover of the cavalry, established an outpost line some 200 yards to the north-east of the railway. The FIFTH and Royal Fusiliers then recalled their forward posts and undertook the organization of a *Main Line of Resistance* covering Ruesnes. Under considerable gas shelling this work continued throughout the 26th, when the FIFTH suffered another officer casualty in 2nd Lieutenant Ennis, who was wounded. Then, at last, relief came; and late on the afternoon of the 27th October the 1/FIFTH were withdrawn with the 9th Brigade to Divisional Reserve at Escarmains, having, though they knew it not, fired their last shot in the Great War.

The total casualties sustained by the Battalion between the 23rd and 26th October had amounted to—

	Killed.	Wounded.	Missing.
Officers	2	7	—
Other Ranks ..	25	170	27

While the Third Army, on whose front the 1/FIFTH had been engaged, had been fighting its way eastward from between Solesmes and Valenciennes, the Fourth Army further south had by the 24th October advanced its line, on the right, to the Sambre Canal, and on the left, to a line west of the Landrécies-Englefontaine road, where it was now faced by the southern half of the Forêt de Mormal. During these operations the 50th Division had remained in XIII. Corps Reserve, with the 2/FIFTH quietly at rest in billets at Maretz.*

On the 28th October orders were received for the 50th Division to move forward for the relief of the 25th Division in the front line. On the following day the 150th Brigade marched to Le Cateau, where the Battle Surplus of the 2/FIFTH was to remain under Lieut.-Colonel Hardman Jones during the forthcoming operations. On the 29th a further march of five miles brought the Brigade to the front line, where it took over positions from the 25th Division from the south-east corner of Fontaine-au-Bois to (incl.) the village of Robersart. All three battalions were placed in the line, the FIFTH being in the centre about Les Grands Chênes. Later, the flank sections were taken over by battalions of the 149th and 151st Brigades, and on the 2nd November the FIFTH were relieved in the centre and withdrawn to reserve.

The operations which had now been planned for the 4th November were divided into two phases. In the first of these, while the passage of the Sambre was forced south-west of Landrécies, the 149th and 150th Brigades, advancing as the right and left of the 50th Division, were to secure a footing in the Forêt de Mormal and occupy the high ground running from Haute Cornée towards Locquignol. In the second phase the 151st Brigade was to continue the advance of the 50th Division north of the Sambre to a line between Hachette Farm and the Carrefour de l'Hermitage.†

The 150th Brigade was to attack with the 7/Wiltshire on the right and the 2/FIFTH on the left, for the capture of two objectives; (i) a line running north-west through the forest about 1,000 yards from its western edge; (ii) the "Red Line," which ran north and south at a distance of some 1,200 to 1,500 yards east of (i). The portions of these objectives allotted to the FIFTH lay; (i) between the Route de Fontaine and the Laie de la Carrière du Vivier; (ii) astride the Route de Fontaine on a frontage of 1,000 yards. In conjunction with this attack, the 2/Munster Fusiliers were to advance north, and in co-operation with troops of the 18th Division clear the ground about Le Preux and capture that village. A complete change in the nature of the ground would occur before the 1st Objective was reached, demanding a change both in the tactics of the infantry and in the character of the support given to them by other arms; and the advance up to that point was, accordingly, to be made in two "bounds." In the first bound, which would represent an advance of some 1,200 yards across very close and difficult country to the western edge of the forest, the infantry, moving in artillery formation, were to be covered by a creeping barrage and assisted by tanks. Once the forest was entered, co-operation by tanks would no longer be possible, and owing to the extensive areas which were rendered almost

---

* Here the Battalion had received greatly needed reinforcements. On the 22nd October Lieutenant Clive Smith had rejoined, bringing with him 2nd Lieutenant Brown and a draft of 115 O.R., and on the same day 2nd Lieutenants Patterson, Appleby, Firth, Shields, and Cotton joined the Battalion. Two days later a further draft of 130 O.R. arrived. The total strength of the Battalion on the 24th October is recorded as:—Present—27 officers and 631 O.R. Absent (hospital, courses, leave, etc.)—11 officers and 223 O.R.

† On the Locquignol road 1 mile north of Hachette Farm.

2nd Bn.
4th Nov.,
1918

impassable by dense undergrowth, the infantry advance would be largely restricted to roads and tracks. In this second bound, companies, moving in such formations as their commanders regarded as most suitable, would be covered by advanced guards, and the supporting artillery would concentrate its fire on roads and tracks 500 yards in front of the infantry. The ordinary creeping barrage, however, would be resumed when the troops moved forward from the 1st Objective for the capture of the Red Line.

Map No. 43

At 3.45 a.m. on the 4th November the 2/FIFTH, under command of Major A. W. Muir,* assembled for attack at Les Grands Chênes; " C " and " D " Companies, commanded by Lieutenant Snailham and Captain Price, were in readiness to lead the advance; " B " Company (Lieutenant W. H. Barrass) to move in support, and " A " Company (Lieutenant Redwood) to following reserve. The 7/Wiltshire were formed on the right, and the 10/Essex (18th Division) on the left. Of the two tanks allotted to the FIFTH, one was ditched on the way up to the assembly position, but the other was in its appropriate place. At 6.15 a.m. the artillery barrage opened, and in a heavy ground mist the FIFTH, preceded by their tank, advanced to the attack. The fire of the German guns in reply to our barrage was wild and scattered, and as it was directed mainly on Fontaine-au-Bois and Robersart, interfered little with the infantry advance. The enemy's machine-guns, on the other hand, which were difficult to locate in the close ground intersected by hedges, caused many casualties. These, however, were gradually overcome, and by 7.45 a.m. the FIFTH and Wiltshire, well served by their tanks, had crossed the Landrécies-Englefontaine road, and the 150th Brigade could be reported as making good progress. The strongest opposition, however, had been encountered on the right of the 50th Division, and it was not till an hour later that the 149th Brigade reached this line. By that time the FIFTH and Wiltshire had gained the line of the Ruisseau d'Hirondelle, and the 2/Munster Fusiliers had carried Le Preux.†

With the crossing of the Hirondelle stream the activities of the tanks were at an end, and at about 9.30 a.m. the FIFTH entered the dense Forêt de Mormal. Slowly but steadily working their way forward, the companies without great difficulty reached their first objective; and continuing the advance, were by 11 a.m. within 500 yards of the Red Line. In the meantime it had been decided to take advantage of this slighter opposition to the left of the attack, and the 151st Brigade was ordered to move forward by the Route de Fontaine, pass through the 150th Brigade, and advance with all possible speed for the capture of the final objective. By 11.15 a.m. the FIFTH and Wiltshire had established themselves on the Red Line; the 149th Brigade was making better progress, and the 151st Brigade had entered the forest. By now all organised resistance had broken down, and the only opposition offered was by machine-guns at long range. By 12.30 p.m. the 151st Brigade, with its three battalions in line, passed through the Red Line, and by dark were within a short distance of the Hachette Farm-Carrefour de l'Hermitage road. Here it was necessary

---

* The former commander of " C " Company, promoted Major 23rd October, 1918.

† The question of time is one of the greatest difficulties with which the writer of a narrative like this has to contend. From this point forward discrepancies of as much as four hours are found on comparing the war diaries of the 50th Division and the 2/FIFTH, the latter generally recording events as having occurred much later than the former. The times given are those recorded in the divisional war diary. On the *sequence* of events, as distinct from the exact hour of their occurrence, the two diaries are in agreement.

to call a halt for the night; for though the Brigade had met with but slight opposition, its supply had been seriously hampered by the craters in the roads and other obstacles created by the enemy to cover his retreat. While the second phase of the attack was in progress the FIFTH had been withdrawn with the remainder of the 150th Brigade to bivouac in the neighbourhood of the first objective of the morning attack. In the course of the fighting on the 4th November the Battalion had captured 150 prisoners; 1 field-gun (taken by "D" Company), and numerous machine-guns. Lieutenants Barrass, Snailham, and Mouat had been wounded, and casualties among other ranks totalled 85. These losses, which had for the greater part been sustained n the first stage of the advance, would undoubtedly have been far heavier but for the fog, which had favoured the opening attack.

On the night of the 4th November, the 25th Division, which had carried Landrécies and forced the passage of the Sambre Canal, was in touch with the right of the 151st Brigade. The objective now given to the 50th Division for the 5th November—the line of the Chaussée Brunehaut—entailed the crossing of the Sambre and an advance of over six miles. It was planned to carry out this task as follows:—The 150th Brigade was to cross the river by a pontoon bridge at Hachette Farm and move by Rue des Juifs and Noyelles* to Haute Noyelles. On arrival here the Wiltshire were to move east to the road junction 1,000 yards north of Le Cattiaux, the Munster Fusiliers north-east to Petit Landrécies, and the FIFTH to stand fast in reserve. The 149th Brigade, following close on the heels of the 150th, was then to move to a position on its left on the Le Cattiaux-Leval road. The two brigades, having been thus assembled for attack, would then advance for the capture of the day's objective. The 151st Brigade was to be held in Divisional Reserve.

These operations, which failed to accomplish their full object, can be briefly told. At 9 a.m. the FIFTH marched in pouring rain to a position west of Hachette Farm to await their turn for passage of the river, which was not undertaken by the leading battalion till 12.50 p.m. As this proceeded, the approaches to the bridge over sodden ground gradually became deep in mud, and the condition of the bridge increasingly unsafe. As a result the FIFTH, forming the rear of the column, experienced the greatest difficulties, and did not gain the far bank before some of their vehicles had fallen into the river. These, however, were successfully salved, and by 3 p.m. the whole Brigade had reached Rue des Juifs. The Wiltshire were now pushed forward towards Basse Noyelles, which, despite some slight opposition, they reached at 4.30 p.m. The most important tasks that now lay before them were the seizure of the crossings of the Grande Helpe at Haute Noyelles and Champ du Parc. But, though the latter was secured, the battalion could make no headway against the very determined resistance of the enemy who had withdrawn to the houses in the southwest of Haute Noyelles; and when darkness fell the Wiltshire were here no further forward than the line of a small stream some 300 yards west of the Grande Helpe. As a result of this check to the advance, which had followed the delay in crossing the Sambre, the FIFTH moved no further forward than Rue des Juifs, where they were ordered to billet for the night. The inhabitants, overjoyed at the sight of British troops after four years of German occupation, did all in their power for the comfort of the troops.

Operations were to be continued on the 6th on the same plan that had been

---

* This was the village in which the 1st Battalion had been billeted in August 1914 on the concentration of the B.E.F. (see Chapter II.).

The Fifth in the Great War.

2nd Bn.
6th Nov., 1918

made for the preceding day, except that the FIFTH, instead of acting in reserve, were to assemble on the right of the 7/Wiltshire on the Le Cattiaux-Leval road, and the 150th Brigade to attack with its three battalions in line. The objective given to the FIFTH on the Chaussée Brunehaut was a frontage of 700 yards a short distance to the north of Lobiette cross-roads. At daybreak heavy rain was falling, with every prospect of its continuance throughout the day. At 7.30 a.m. the enemy, of whom the bulk had withdrawn, blew up the bridge at Haute Noyelles. The Wiltshire, however, effected a crossing by the lower bridge at Le Champ du Parc, and were closely followed by the Munster Fusiliers and the FIFTH, who had in the meantime moved up from Rue des Juifs. Their advance from the Grande Helpe was opposed only by long range machine-gun fire, and by noon the whole of the 150th Brigade was assembled on the line of the Le Cattiaux-Leval road, with the 149th Brigade in position on its left.

Map No. 43

At 12.15 p.m. the two brigades advanced for the capture of the line of the Chaussée Brunehaut. In the FIFTH, " A " and " B " Companies led the attack, with " D " in support and " C " in reserve.* In the early stages of the advance very little opposition was encountered; but as the attack approached the railway, resistance stiffened, particularly against the FIFTH on the right. By 3.30 p.m. the Munster Fusiliers and Wiltshire had succeeded in gaining the railway; but the FIFTH, under heavy fire from an embankment south of Jean Ledoux, were for a time held up and forced to throw back their right flank to gain touch with the 29/Manchester of the 25th Division, whose advance had also been checked. The check, however, was not for long; fire concentrated on the embankment drove the enemy from his position, and the FIFTH reached and crossed the railway in time to continue their advance in line with the Wiltshire. The country now to be crossed was very difficult, with thick hedges and orchards concealing the German machine-gun positions; increasing opposition along the whole front gave evidence of the enemy's intention of resisting the capture of the line of the Chaussée Brunehaut, and the day was drawing to a close. Continuous pressure and bold leading, however, succeeded by degrees in driving the Germans from their machine-gun nests with heavy loss, and when darkness fell the FIFTH were within 200 yards of their objective. In the heavy rain, which had been incessant throughout the advance, patrols now had the greatest difficulty in finding their way through inky darkness over the enclosed country, and it was not till 3 a.m. that the Battalion was finally established on the line of the road. Soaked to the skin, the troops must have looked regretfully back to the comfortable billets of the previous night. There was never an occasion when a hot meal would have been more welcome. But, for the first and last time during the rapid advance of these days, the battalion transport had been defeated by the tremendous difficulties with which they had to contend, and the men had to fall back on their emergency iron rations. As a set-off to the recollection of these hardships, however, the 2/FIFTH were to have the satisfaction of recalling in later days that, thanks to skilful leading, they had carried their last objective in the Great War, against considerable opposition, at the astonishingly slight cost of eight men wounded.

At 8 a.m. on the 7th November, the 151st Brigade passed through to continue the advance on the front of the 50th Division; and at 10 a.m. the FIFTH marched into billets in St. Remy-Chausée, where they were to remain resting and cleaning up for

---

* Snailham and Barrass having been wounded on the 4th. " B " and " C " were now under command of 2nd Lieutenants Woodhead and Houston respectively.

the next forty-eight hours. An incident—tragic in the circumstances of the date and the fact that the Battalion was at rest—occurred on the 8th. A long range shell struck one of the houses occupied by " D " Company, killing one and wounding 11 men who had passed unscathed through the close fighting of preceding days. These were the last of the many hundreds of casualties sustained by the 2/FIFTH in the War.

In the meantime the 151st Brigade, advancing on the 7th for the capture of the line of the Maubeuge-Avesnes road, had met with stiff resistance, and it had become clear that the enemy had received substantial reinforcements, particularly of artillery. As a consequence, the brigade, though making considerable progress, had been unable to reach its final objective that night. When the advance was resumed on the 8th the Germans made a most determined counter-attack, but were repulsed with heavy loss. After this despairing effort by the enemy, there were signs that his resistance was weakening along the whole front. The 50th Division was now ordered to carry its advance forward for the capture of the high ground in the Bois de Beugnies,* and at 2.30 p.m. the 149th Brigade passed through the 151st to carry out the allotted task. Dark despair by now must have filled the hearts of the Germans, and it is impossible to withold one's admiration for the fight that their rear-guards continued to put up, or one's pity for their troops—many mere boys—who were being sacrificed to no end. Throughout the whole afternoon they continued to make a most stubborn resistance; but towards evening it slackened, and by midnight entirely ceased. By then the 149th Brigade had established itself on the western edge of the Bois de Beugnies, and at 2 a.m. the brigadier reported that the whole front was quiet and that, in his opinion, the enemy had completely withdrawn.

This news came as no surprise, for recent statements by prisoners had consistently pointed to the enemy's intention of embarking on a large scale retreat on the 9th November; and his whole action during the 8th had seemed to be in accord with such a plan. Major-General Jackson had therefore prepared for such an eventuality by the formation of a Mobile Force, equipped and rationed for a rapid pursuit under his personal command. The force, which was provisioned for four days, on each of which it was to be capable of a march of eight miles, was composed of the 150th Brigade and certain divisional troops, and organised in three columns of similar constitution. " Muir's Column," for instance, consisted of :—

    2/FIFTH,
    1 section field artillery,
    1 section Royal Engineers
    1 section trench mortars,
    1 section machine-guns,
    1 platoon pioneers,
    Some cyclists.

On receipt of the report from the 149th Brigade, cavalry patrols were at once sent forward to Solre-le-Château, which they reached without gaining touch with the enemy's rear-guards; and orders were issued for the Mobile Force to prepare to move. At 8 a.m. Major Muir paraded his column—a fine command for an officer of 27 years of age—and marched to Lez-Fontaine, just west of Solre-le-Château. The enemy had done all in his power to delay pursuit by blowing craters in the

---

* Two miles east of Dourlers.

THE FIFTH IN THE GREAT WAR.

2nd Bn.
9th/10th Nov.,
1918

roads and destroying bridges, but large dumps of wagons and ammunition left by the roadside gave evidence of the sore straits in which he was placed; and at Sars-Poteries nine fully loaded trains had been abandoned at a siding. The Mobile Force had now covered from 9 to 10 miles, and it was necessary to call a halt. The enemy's rear-guards, with a start of eight hours and no obstacles to hamper their retirement, had probably covered more; but, weighted with the sense of defeat, their disorganisation was likely to increase, and the 2/FIFTH were in expectation of bringing them to battle on the morrow. This, however, was not to be. During the afternoon it was notified that a force composed of cavalry and units of the 66th Division would take up the pursuit, and the 50th Division was ordered to stand fast. In the early hours of the 10th November, this force, under Major-General Bethell, passed through, and at noon the 2/FIFTH were withdrawn to billets in Dourlers.

Map No. 40

Thus "Muir's Column" never went into action, but its commander, who in 1914 had enlisted as a private soldier in the 16th Battalion of the Regiment, was awarded the Distinguished Service Order in recognition of his services in command of its 2nd Battalion between the 4th and 10th November, 1918.* Major Muir, however, has never failed to testify to all he owed to the advice and guidance of Lieut.-Colonel Hardman Jones, who, after having commanded the 2nd Battalion with distinction for three years, had been deprived by circumstances from leading it into battle in these last decisive days.

1st Bn.
3rd/11th Nov.
1918

While the 2/FIFTH had been engaged in the momentous events related above, the 1st Battalion had continued to enjoy a well earned rest. On the 3rd November, after three days at Cattenières, they had moved once more to Quiévy, where they remained quietly in very comfortable billets till the 8th. News of victory came from all quarters. Bulgaria, with an armistice signed on the 9th September, had long since ceased to count. Turkey had held out for a month longer, till admitting defeat on the 30th October; and the final collapse of Austria followed five days later. But though all knew that the surrender of Germany could not now be much longer delayed, that the end was imminent was—at any rate with the regimental soldier—still a fervent hope rather than a settled conviction. When, therefore, on the 8th November the 1/FIFTH moved to Romeries, and on the 10th continued its forward move to Frasnoy, it was in the expectation of being engaged once more with the enemy. Coincidence ruled that their next destination should be determined as La Longueville, that very village to which, on the 21st August, 1914, the Battalion had marched on first moving forward to meet an enemy of whom as little was then known as of the realities of modern war. The 1/FIFTH had indeed marched far, learnt much, and lost many before completing this circle on the Western Front! On the 11th reveillé sounded at 5 a.m. Rumour which had spread through the billets that the War was at an end was strengthened at 7.30 by an order for the Battalion to stand fast; but it was not till 9.5 a.m. that news came that an Armistice had been signed, by which hostilities were to cease at 11 a.m.

---

* Major Muir had already been awarded a bar to the Military Cross for the part he played in the fighting at Le Catelet.

So ends the story of "The FIFTH in the Great War." The two old battalions, which at its outbreak had been separated by 6,000 miles, were at its close, to the north-east and south-west of the Forêt de Mormal, but 15 miles apart. With them and their sister battalions of the Territorial Army lay the great task in years to come of preserving the name of a Regiment, already high, which had been enhanced during over four years of hardship and sacrifice. But it was not they alone who had upheld that name in the greatest war the world had ever witnessed. Throughout the whole 50 miles of the British Front, from east of Oudenarde to south of Malplaquet, and away down in Italy, were battalions which bore as their motto, "Quo Fata Vocant." Very soon these were seemingly to vanish, but their spirit and deeds are not forgotten. Should the British Empire ever again stand in the same dire peril as in August 1914—which God forbid—one may be confident that the sons and grandsons of those who fought in those battalions will be found as ready to rally to the call as did their forebears to "THE FIGHTING FIFTH."

CASUALTY CLEARING STATION.
(From a painting by A. K. Lawrence, R.A.)

APPENDIX A.

OFFICERS WHO SERVED WITH THE FIFTH IN THE GREAT WAR.

The main purpose of this Appendix is to recall to readers who served with the FIFTH during the War the names, some perhaps since forgotten, of officers who were their comrades during that period. The granting of temporary or acting rank resulted in officers so frequently changing their designation between 1914 and 1918 that it has been considered best, except in a few cases where initials cannot be determined, to omit rank. A certain number of those who appear in the lists were attached from other regiments, but the names of over one hundred officers posted to the 1st Battalion merely "for record purposes" are not included.

(K.) indicates those who were killed or died of wounds received while actually serving with the FIFTH. It is not shown against the names of the many who met their death later in the War with other units.

(i) OFFICERS WHO SERVED WITH BOTH BATTALIONS.

Booth, R. M. St. J.	Hamilton, C. E.	Moulton-Barrett, E. M.
Buckle, D. F. de C.	Hardman Jones, A. C. L.	Rose, S. A. (K.)
Bucknall, W. H. C. (K.)	Heyder, H. M.	Scrutton, H. U. (K.)
Cruddas, B.	Hoffman, R. H.	Steel, C. H.
Dodd, T. C.	Hogshaw, J. H.	Stephen, H. C.
Fenwick, G. E.	Lord, R. (K.)	

(ii) OFFICERS WHO SERVED WITH THE 1ST BATTALION.

Ainslie, H. S.	Bell, J. C.	Caldicott, L.
Alexander, R.	Bending, H. A.	Cannon, J.
Allen, W. R.	Blayney, O. G.	Carey, F.
Allgood, G. H.	Blenkinsop, W.	Carrick, C. B.
Anderson, J. W. McL.	Bodey, F. W.	Carswell, J. H.
Apps, J. H. (K.)	Boyd, E. F. (K.)	Carter, H. (K.)
Appleby, A. H.	Bowman, C. S.	Casse, J. B.
Archer, R. H.	Bradford, S. V.	Chipper, C.
Arkwright, C. G.	Bramwell, G.	Cockerell, P. C.
Arnold, W. W.	Brew, G. I.	Cogan, C. T. S.
	Brown, A. R.	Coles, D. M. (K.)
Bagshawe, L. V. (K.)	Brown, J. G.	Collins, H. F. G.
Barber, B. K. B.	Brown, R.	Collinson, M.
Barnes, H. S. (K.)	Brown, R.	Colton, S. E. (K.)
Barnsley, A. (K.)	Bullen, T. C.	Condon, D.
Barrett, L. A.	Burdon, N. E.	Cooper, C. M.
Bastow, N.	Burton, D. C.	Cull, P. S. (K.)
Bateman, J.	Burton, W. O.	Cunningham, R.
Belchem, H. M. (K.)	Butcher, T. W.	

Appendix A.

Dalbiac, C. J. S. (K.)
Davidson, A. W.
Dent, W. H. N.
Dignen, G. W. (K.)
Dinning, W.
Donald, H.
Dorman-Smith, E. E.
Downing, P. H.
Dunglinson, W. (K.)
Dwelley, W. E.

Edwards, C. J.
Elliott, R. C.
Ellison, T. F.
Ennis, E. R.
Evans, D. (K.)

Fearnley-Wittingstall, G. E.
Festing, F. L.
Finch, P. G. (K.)
Firth, D.
Fisher, H. B.
Fletcher, R. S. (K.)
Forster, E. L. D.
Fox, D. C. (K.)
Fraser, P. C. (K.)
French, H.
Fryer, R. W. H.
Futers, N. R. (K.)

Gatehouse, A. H.
Gatehouse, R. F. (K.)
Geddes, A. F.
Gordon, E. B.
Grantham, E. R. H. (K.)
Grant-Ross, C.
Greaves, J. (K.)
Green, H.
Greener, A. S. (K.)
Greener, H. M.
Gunner, B. G. (K.)

Hadow, D. P.
Hall, F.
Hall, R. M.
Hamilton, C. E.
Handcock, R.
Hardy, M.
Harland, E.
Harper, W. E.
Hastie, R.
Haworth, C. B.
Herbert, W. N.
Heron, T. E.
Hervey-Bathurst, B. E.

Hill, R. C.
Hobbs, B. G. C.
Hobbs, F. A.
Hodgson, C. L. C.
Holmes, H. J.
Holmes, T. A. C.
Hopkinson, R. C.
Hornby, J.
Howgill, J. F.
Hunter, G. R.

Ingledew, H. A.

Jacques, J. (K.)
Jeffreys, E. G.
Jenkins, E. G. (K.)
John, H. G.
Johnstone, R. Edgeworth-
Jones, M. G.
Joss, W. T. B.
Jung, H. A. (K.)

Keatinge, E. G.
Kingdon, L.

Laing, J.
Lamb, E. J. (K.)
Lamb, G. M.
Lamb, R. M. R.
Lambert, J. M. (K.)
Landen, A.
Lawrence, E. (K.)
Lawrence, E. I.
Laws, A. (K.)
Lawson, J. O.
Leather, C. E. J. (K.)
Lee, D. S.
Linzell, E. L.
Lloyd, M. (K.)
Lowther, T. B.
Lyde-Malcolm, S. M.
Lynch, A. C.
Lynes, R.

Mackenzie, A. (K.)
Majoribanks, M. E. (K.)
Marks, H. V.
Marrs, L. G.
Marr-Baker, H. W. C.
Martin, D. F. de R. (K.)
Matthews, J. H. (K.)
Mayfield, L. A. (K.)
Miller, J. E. H. (K.)
Mills, J. D. W.

Mitford, Hon. D. B. O.
Moore, A. L.
Mortished, L. R.
Mullen, H. P.
Murdock, A. J.
Myers, W.

Newstead, B. R.
Nichol, A. T. (K.)
Nichols, H. L. F. (K.)
Nicholson, H.
Nimmo, W. L. (K.)
Nunneley, C. F. (K.)

O'Dowd, R. E. D.
Ovans, H. L.

Parkinson, G. M.
Partington, L. (K.)
Passingham, E. G. (K.)
Pattenden, R. F. S.
Pease, E. G.
Phelan, A. E. (K.)
Pigg, N. B.
Pilling, D.
Pitkethley, W. B.
Platt, W.
Polley, W. H.
Porter Hargreaves, A. H.
Potter, R. W. (K.)
Potts, J. R.
Powell, H. I.
Powell, N.
Prideaux, H. H.
Probert, A. J.

Radcliffe, J. F. E.
Rayner, J. W.
Rea, F. N. (K.)
Redpath, G. E. (K.)
Redpath, H. E.
Regan, J. H. (K.)
Reveley, D. F. P.
Richards, J. (K.)
Richardson, A.
Richardson, W. E.
Rigby, H.
Riley, S. (K.)
Ritchie, R. F.
Robertson, R. R.
Roblin, L. G. (K.)
Robson, J.
Rochell, A. (K.)
Roddam, R. C. (K.)
Roderick, W. B. N.

APPENDIX A.

Routledge, J. F. (*K*.)
Rowe, D. S.
Rutledge, C. J.

Sanderson, T.
Sandilands, H. R.
Salt, W. H.
Scanlan, T. M.
Schofield, R. S.
Scott, A. F.
Selby, B. H. (*K*.)
Sellick, N. P.
Short, E. L.
Sibbit, G. B. (*K*.)
Simpson, J. J. (*K*.)
Skey, R.
Sloper, G. O.
Smith, H.
Smythe, R. C.
Somerset, J. H.
Steel, J.
Steel, J. R.
Steele, H. G.
St. John, B. T.

Story, D.
Strong, C. H.
Sutherland, H. O.
Surtees, A. B.
Sydney, P.

Tait, J. T.
Tavener, L. A.
Taylor, R.
Thompson, C. J. McK. (*K*.)
Thompson, J. C.
Thorp, R. O. V.
Todd, J. C.
Toppin, H. S. (*K*.)
Tottie, E. H. (*K*.)
Travell, N. E.
Turnbull, S. A.
Twigge, F. (*K*.)

Vachell, R. T.
Van der Merwe, J. J.
Van Neck, C. H. (*K*.)
Vernon, R. D.

Waddilove, G. E. D.
Wailing, C. G. W.
Walker, E. J.
Walker, J. W.
Walker, S. R. E. (*K*.)
Ware, A. F.
Watkins, F. E. (*K*.)
Watson, B.
Waud, E. H.
White, J. P.
Wightman, G. W.
Wiles, H.
Wild, W. H.
Willans, R. St. J. (*K*.)
Williams, T.
Williams, T.
Wilkinson, F.
Wooldridge, J. A.

Yarrow, C. A.
Yates, J.
Yatman, C.
Yatman, D. H. (*K*.)
Young, F. I. (*K*.)

(iii) Officers Who Served with the 2nd Battalion.

Allan, W. M.
Allgood, N. J.
Appleby, J. D.
Appleyard, H.
Armstrong, C. A. (*K*.)
Atkinson, J. C.
Auld, R.

Bacon, D. F. C.
Baker, 2nd-Lieut.
Barber, S. C.
Barkworth, H. R.
Barrass, J. H.
Barrass, W. H.
Baxter, E. H.
Bentley, R.
Bird, R. J.
Bogle, D.
Bramwell, G.
Brown, 2nd-Lieut.
Burgess, L. G.
Burhouse, E. S.

Cardew, E. B. A.
Carpenter, P. V.
Carr-Ellison, O. F. G. (*K*.)
Clarke, G.
Collings, W. N. (*K*.)

Cooper, C. H.
Cotton, O.
Coulson, C. B.
Crabbe, C. H.
Craig, C.
Craig, 2nd-Lieut.
Cramsie, A. B. (*K*.)
Crawford, R. B.
Creighton, T. S.
Crew, B. D.

Dawe, G. M.
Dingle, J. N. O. (*K*.)
Dodd, A. H.
Donaldson, 2nd-Lieut.
Dunlop, R.
Dunn, N. A.

Enderby, S. H.
Elders, C.
Elston, J. L.

Firth, C.
Fontaine, L. A.
Fordham, J. M. G.
Freeman, C. R.
Friend, L. H.

Fulton, E.

Gardner, H. E.
Garner-King, H. (*K*.)
Garrard, W. G. B. (*K*.)
Gibson, W.
Gilchrist, J. H. L. (*K*.)
Girdlestone, C. J.
Griffiths, W. H.

Hardy, B. C.
Hart, A. C. (*K*.)
Hills, J. M. (*K*.)
Hobbs, H. E. (*K*.)
Hobley, 2nd-Lieut.
Holmes, H. S.
Hopkinson, A. G.
Houston, A. G.
Howell, R. B.
Hutchinson, 2nd-Lieut.

Jardine, T.
Jenkins, W. E.
Jones, B. H.
Jones, C.
Johnson, P. E.
Johnstone, P. E. (*K*.)

Appendix A.

Kerrod, J.
King, H. S. (*K*.)

Lamb, R. M. R.
L'Amie, H. St. C.
Lee-Barton, J.
Legard, G. P. (*K*.)
Longdon, F. C.
Lumsden, J. C. (*K*.)

Macdonald, A. F.
Mahon, B. E. S.
Manger, J. K. (*K*.)
Markham, C. H.
Maxwell, E. C.
Maynard, J. H.
Mc. Dool, E.
McGrgeor, I. A. (*K*.)
Molineux, G. K. (*K*.)
Morgan, A. M.
Mouat, B.
Muir, A. W.
Muir, N. H.

O'Dowd, M. V. (*K*.)
Oldfield, A. E.

Parish, R. (*K*.)
Parkin, A.
Patterson, J.
Pattison, W.
Phillips, A. K.
Phillips, E. R.
Pollock, C. W.
Poole, 2nd-Lieut.
Price, F. A.

Redwood, T. C. L.
Ritchie, F. A.
Rogers, R. J.
Ross, P. A.
Rushbrooke, W. P.

Salier, E. L
Scott, D.
Searles, N. A.
Sellars, J. H. (*K*.)
Shann, K. (*K*.)
Shaw, S. H.
Shiel, G. G.
Shields, J.
Sidston, S.
Sims, A. W.
Smith, C.
Smith, W. D.

Snailham, J. J.
Stephenson, J.
Sweet, G.

Taylor, G. G. C.
Taylor, H. G.
Taylor, R. V.
Taylor, W.
Tiswell, J. A.
Tuke, A. H.
Tuke, H. S. (*K*.)
Turnbull, S.

Wallin, J.
Walsh, R. W.
Walton, J.
Ward, L. A.
Wardlaw, J.
Watmough, J. C. (*K*.)
Watts, F. G.
Wilkins, G. (*K*.)
Williams, E. J.
Willson, J. B. (*K*.)
Woodhead, A.
Woodroffe, B. C.
Woodroffe, K. D.
Wreford-Brown, C. W. (*K*.)
Wright, C. C. G.

APPENDIX B.

The total of "Other Ranks" of the FIFTH who died in The Great War was as under:—

	Killed or Died of Wounds.	Died from other causes.	TOTAL.
1st Battalion	1337	405	1742
2nd Battalion	392	317	709
	1729	722	2451

The above figures have been obtained from the official publication, "SOLDIERS DIED IN THE GREAT WAR, 1914-19—Part 10. The Northumberland Fusiliers," which can be purchased through any Bookseller or directly from H.M. Stationery Office. (Price 7s. 6d.) In it, under the headings of the various Battalions, will be found the regimental number, rank, name, place of enlistment and date of death of every man of the Regiment who died in the War.

INDEX.

A. NAMES OF INDIVIDUALS.

His Majesty the King, 66.

Adlard, Coy. Serjt.-Major, 266.
Adair, Major J. W. D., 207 (*f.n.*).
Ainslie, Lieut.-Colonel H. S., 4, 38, 39, 40, 66, 107, 110.
Alexander, 2nd-Lieutenant R., 194.
Allan, Captain W. M., 93–4, 99, 100, 109, 122, 129.
Allen, Captain W. R., 175, 178, 198, 206, 211.
Allenby, Major-General E., 47.
Allgood, Captain G., 129, 134, 203.
Apps, 2nd-Lieutenant J. H. M., 190.
Archer, Lieutenant R. H., 194.
Archer, Coy. Serjt.-Major, 267.
Armitage, Serjeant, 132.
Armstrong, Major C., 122, 126–8.
Arnold, 2nd-Lieutenant W., 78.
Atkinson, Professor C. T., 241 (*f.n.*).
Atkinson, 2nd-Lieutenant J. C., 286.
Augustine, Sister, 250 (*f.n.*).
Auld, Captain R., 74, 91, 97–9.

Bacon, 2nd-Lieutenant D. F. C., 128.
Bagshaw, Captain L. V., 112–3.
Banks, Serjeant, 185.
Barber, 2nd-Lieutenant B. K. B., 130.
Barber, Lieutenant S. C., 238.
Barnes, Lieutenant H. S., 174.
Barkworth, Lieutenant H. R., 123.
Barnsley, Captain A., 51–2.
Barrett, Captain L. C. A., 50, 60.
Barrass, Lieutenant W. H., 293–4–5 (*f.n.*).
Bateman, 2nd-Lieutenant J., 150.
Baxter, Captain E. H., 84–6.
Belchem, Lieutenant M., 81.
Bending, 2nd-Lieutenant H. A., 179, 181.
Bentley, Corporal, 66.
Bentley, 2nd-Lieutenant R., 273.
Bethell, Major-General, 297.
Bird, 2nd-Lieutenant R. J., 283.
Blayney, Captain O. G., 159, 162–6.
Blenkinsop, 2nd-Lieutenant W., 220, 221, 256.
Bogle, Major B., 128.
Bols, Brigadier-General L., 78, 96, 103.
Bonham-Carter, Lieutenant I. M., 35.
Booth, Captain R. M., 45, 60, 100, 101–2–4.
Boyd, 2nd-Lieutenant E. F., 16, 39, 41.

Bradford, 2nd-Lieutenant S. V., 169, 174.
Bradley, Lieutenant, 88.
Brew, 2nd-Lieutenant G. I., 183–5.
Briggs, Major-General C., 128.
Brown, Lieutenant A. R., 221, 279.
Brown, 2nd-Lieutenant R., 208, 211.
Brown, Private, 220–1.
Brownlow, Lieutenant W. H. C., 76.
Buckle, Major D. F. de C., 48, 100–2–4, 194, 209, 211, 215, 222.
Bucknall, Lieutenant W. H. C., 104, 145, 176–9.
Buglass, Private, 266.
Bulfin, Major-General E. S., 70, 90, 128.
Bullen, Lieutenant T. C., 221.
Burdon, Lieutenant, 139.
Burton, Lieutenant W. O., 206, 213–9.
Butcher, 2nd-Lieutenant R. W., 282.

Cannon, 2nd-Lieutenant J., 263.
Caldicott, 2nd-Lieutenant L., 290.
Carey, 2nd-Lieutenant F., 290.
Carlin, Serjeant W. P., 144.
Carr-Ellison, Captain O. C., 273–4–6.
Carrick, Captain C. B., 140–1 (*f.n.*), 144–9, 173 (*f.n.*), 174, 197–8–9, 200–1 (*f.n.*), 204 (*f.n.*)–5 (*f.n.*), 213.
Carswell, 2nd-Lieutenant J. H., 263–5–6–7.
Carter, 2nd-Lieutenant H., 113–5.
Casse, 2nd-Lieutenant J. B., 217.
Chenevix-Trench, Captain J. F., 132.
Chipper, Captain C., 198–9, 204–5 (*f.n.*), 207–208–9, 210–1–2–3, 217 (*f.n.*).
Christmas, Serjeant, 257.
Clarkburn, Serjeant J., 107.
Clarke, Serjeant, 110.
Clarke, Captain G., 247.
Clarke, Captain (R.A.M.C.), 257.
Clarkson, Serjeant, 110.
Clive-Smith, Lieutenant, 241, 247, 292 (*f.n.*).
Cockburn, Serjeant, 163.
Cockerell, 2nd-Lieutenant P. C., 291.
Cogan, Lieutenant C. T. S., 33.
Coles, Lieutenant D. M., 53.
Collings, Lieutenant W. N., 277.
Collins, Lance-Corporal, 277.
Collins, 2nd-Lieutenant H. F., 288, 289 (*f.n.*), 290.
Colton, 2nd-Lieutenant S. E., 192, 208, 211.

Comerford, Private J., 83 (*f.n.*).
Cooper, Lieutenant C. M., 148, 153-4.
Cooper, 2nd-Lieutenant G., 82.
Cooper, Coy. Serjt.-Major T. F., 144, 149.
Corbet-Singleton, 2nd-Lieutenant F. B., 72.
Crabtree, Regtl. Serjt.-Major, 137.
Craig, 2nd-Lieutenant, 123.
Cramsie, Lieutenant A. B., 98.
Creighton, 2nd-Lieutenant T. S., 274.
Crouch, Serjeant, 62.
Cruddas, Lieut.-Colonel B., 128-9, 133, 229, 264, 279 (*f.n.*), 288, 290-1.
Cunningham, 2nd-Lieutenant R., 117-8-9.
Cull, 2nd-Lieutenant P. S., 218.

Dalbiac, 2nd-Lieutenant C. J. S., 113.
Darley-Waddilove, Captain G. S., 185.
Dashwood, Captain C. B. L., 132.
Davidson, Lieutenant A. W., 220-1, 280, 281.
Dawson, Serjeant, 110.
Day, Corporal, 144 (*f.n.*).
Dent, 2nd-Lieutenant W. H. N., 179.
Deverell, Major-General C. J., 156, 167, 194, 204, 210, 258.
Dignen, 2nd-Lieutenant G. W., 289, 291.
Dingle, 2nd-Lieutenant J., 238.
Dinning, 2nd-Lieutenant W., 156.
Dodd, 2nd-Lieutenant T. C., 147.
Dodd, Captain U. H., 240, 284-7.
Dodd, Corporal, 266.
Donald, 2nd-Lieutenant H., 190.
Dorman Smith, Captain E. E., 25, 64, 68, 108, 112, 116-7-8 (*f.n.*), 119, 120, 130.
Dunglinson, 2nd-Lieutenant W., 253, 256.

Edgeworth-Johnstone, 2nd-Lieutenant R., 179.
Edmonds, Brigadier-General J. E., 20 (*f.n.*).
Ellingham, Private, 110.
Ellison, Captain T. F., 183-8, 209, 213, 264, 289 (*f.n.*).
Enderby, Lieut.-Colonel S. H., 74, 85 (*f.n.*), 91, 96-8.
Ennis, 2nd-Lieutenant E. R., 291.
Evans, 2nd-Lieutenant D., 185.

Fearnley-Whittingstall, 2nd-Lieutenant G. E., 115.
Fenwick, Captain G. E., 129, 230 (*f.n.*), 236 (*f.n.*), 240, 250, 272-7.
Festing, Captain F. L., 64.
Finch, Lieutenant P. G., 188, 206-7, 211.
Finch, Major E. G., 211 (*f.n.*).
Fishbourne, Lieut.-Colonel C. E., 132 (*f.n.*).
Fisher, Lieutenant (R.A.M.C.), 40.
Fisk, Corporal A. J., 52, 64.
Fletcher, Captain R., 56-7.
Foch, Général, 92, 269.
Fordham, 2nd-Lieutenant H. A., 128.
Forster, Captain E. L. D., 37, 75-9.

Foster, Captain O. B., 75-6, 84-5, 90-1-2.
Fox, 2nd-Lieutenant D. C., 133, 156.
Fraser, 2nd-Lieutenant P. C., 156.
Freeman, Major C. R., 101-2-4, 229, 249, 271-2-4-5-6.
Freeman, Captain (Cheshire R.), 127.
French, F. M., Sir John, 20, 31, 50-5-6, 64, 92.
Frotiée, Général, 233.
Fryer, 2nd-Lieutenant R. W., 266.
Futers, Captain N. R., 265.

Gardner, Lieutenant H. E., 283.
Garner-King, 2nd-Lieutenant J., 238.
Garrard, 2nd-Lieutenaut W. G. B., 104.
Gatehouse, Captain R. F., 36, 41.
Geddes, 2nd-Lieutenant A. F., 38.
Geddes, Lieut.-Colonel (Buffs), 74.
Gibbon, Lieut.-Colonel (King's), 148.
Gibson, Major W., 240, 244.
Gilchrist, 2nd-Lieutenant I. H. L., 101, 122, 126-7-8.
Gillborn, Coy. Serjt.-Major, 61, 64-6-8.
Gillespie, Lieutenant (R.A.M.C.), 104.
Girdlestone, 2nd-Lieutenant C. J., 276.
Glynn, Captain A. S. (R.A.M.C.), 159 (*f.n.*).
Gordon, Captain E. B., 51-2-7-8, 60-1-2-3.
Grantham, 2nd-Lieutenant E. R., 171.
Greaves, 2nd-Lieutenant J., 263.
Greener, Lieutenant A. S., 166, 205 (*f.n.*), 211-3-9.
Greener, Lieutenant H. M., 173, 219 (*f.n.*).
Grew, 2nd-Lieutenant B., 128.
Grieves, Lance-Corporal, 266 (*f.n.*).
Griffiths, 2nd-Lieutenant W. H., 225.
Gunner, Captain B., 60, 131 (*f.n.*), 133-4.

Hadow, Lieutenant D. P., 163.
Hague, Serjeant, 97.
Haig, F. M., Sir D., 146, 167, 178-9, 184, 214-5, 269, 270, 278.
Haldane, Major-General A., 64, 143, 156, 196.
Hall, 2nd-Lieutenant R. M., 182.
Halliday, Serjeant, 97.
Hamilton, Major-General H., 3 (*f.n.*), 45.
Hardman-Jones, Lieut.-Colonel A. C., 225, 239, 271, 282-4, 292.
Hardy, 2nd-Lieutenant B. C., 98.
Harland, 2nd-Lieutenant E., 182.
Harper, 2nd-Lieutenant W. E., 131.
Hart, Captain A. C., 76, 84-5, 91, 97-8.
Hastie, 2nd-Lieutenant R., 217.
Heathcote, Corporal, 163.
Herbert, Lieut.-Colonel W. N., 5, 21 (*f.n.*), 44, 81, 117, 131 (*f.n.*), 133, 162-7, 176 (*f.n.*), 177, 182-3-9, 192-3-4-6, 218, 221, 255-7, 260-1-3-4.
Heron, Captain T. E., 222.
Hervey-Bathurst, Lieutenant B. E., 109.
Heyder, Lieutenant H. M., 72, 112-3, 229.

Heywood, Brigadier-General C. P., 270, 271 (*f.n.*)
Hill, Lieutenant R. C., 150.
Hills, 2nd-Lieutenant J. M., 240.
Hobbs, Lieutenant B. G. C., 48.
Hobbs, 2nd-Lieutenant H. E., 102, 104.
Hobbs, Captain F. A., 289, 291.
Hoffman, Captain R. H., 128, 145.
Hogshaw, Captain J. H., 102 (*f.n.*), 104, 144, 176-7.
Holmes, Captain H. J., 128, 139, 144-9, 159 (*f.n.*).
Holmes, 2nd-Lieutenant T. A. C., 261.
Homer, Private, 116.
Hopkinson, Lieutenant A. J., 123, 128.
Horne, General Sir H., 160.
Hornby, 2nd-Lieutenant J., 196.
Houston, 2nd-Lieutenant A. G., 295 (*f.n.*).
Howell, 2nd-Lieutenant R. B., 128.
Hunter, 2nd-Lieutenant G. R., 222.
Hutton, Q.M. Serjeant J., 132.

Ingledew, 2nd-Lieutenant H. A., 255-7.
Ives, Private, 97.
Iveson, Corporal, 144 (*f.n.*).

Jackson, Major-General H., 270, 296.
Jaques, 2nd-Lieutenant J., 186.
Jenkins, Captain W. E., 75, 128.
Jenkins, 2nd-Lieutenant E., 290.
Jewell, Corporal, 281.
Joffre, Général, 28, 30.
John, 2nd-Lieutenant H. G., 115-7-8 (*f.n.*), 119.
Johnstone, Edgeworth—*see* Edgeworth.
Johnstone, Captain P. E., 129, 236 (*f.n.*), 238.
Jones, 2nd-Lieutenant M. G., 132, 142, 144.
Joss, 2nd-Lieutenant W. T. B., 182-3, 207, 213-8.
Joyce, Private, 97.
Joynson, Corporal, 121.
Jung, 2nd-Lieutenant H. A., 109.

Kelrsey, Corporal, 139, 144.
Kelly, Bandsman, 110.
Kentish, Brig.-General, 151.
King, Captain H. S., 272-3.
King, 2nd-Lieutenant Garner, 238.
Kitchener, Lord, 7, 8.
Knox, Serjeant, 144.
Kluck, General Von, 28, 30, 34.

Lamb, Lieutenant E., 57.
Lamb, 2nd-Lieutenant G. M., 185.
Lamb, Captain R. M., 76, 123-6-7-8.
Lambert, Captain J. M., 39, 53.
Landen, Major A., 23, 60, 122, 133, 180.
Lane, Serjeant, 97.

Lawrence, Captain E., 198, 206, 211.
Lawrence, 2nd-Lieutenant E. I., 197, 207, 211.
Lawrence, Lieut.-Colonel (King's), 208.
Laws, 2nd-Lieutenant A., 51.
Lawson, 2nd-Lieutenant J. O., 64 (*f.n.*), 110, 116.
Leather, Captain C., 40, 52.
Leckie, Captain M. (R.A.M.C.), 22.
Lees-Barton, 2nd-Lieutenant J., 277.
Legard, Lieutenant G. P., 76, 92, 98.
Lewis, Serjeant, 207.
Lewis, C.Q.M.S., 17.
Lloyd, Captain M., 79.
Logue, Private, 97.
Longden, Coy. Serjt.-Major, 37, 41.
Longden, Captain F. C. (D.L.I.), 128.
Lord, Captain R., 97, 98, 259, 265, 279, 282.
Ludendorff, General, 251.
Luke, Coy. Serjt.-Major, 37, 42.
Lumsden, 2nd-Lieutenant J. C., 283.
Lynes, 2nd-Lieutenant R., 256.

Macdonald, 2nd-Lieutenant A. F., 283.
McGregor, 2nd-Lieutenant I. A., 238.
Mackenzie, Major-General C., 45.
Mackenzie, Captain A., 222.
McMahon, Lieut.-Colonel (R. Fusiliers), 44, 62.
McQuade, Private, 144 (*f.n.*).
Mahon, Lieutenant B. E. S., 74, 85, 98.
Manger, 2nd-Lieutenant J. K., 98.
Mantle, Serjeant, 171, 207, 208, 210.
Marden, Lieut.-Colonel (Welch R.), 76-8.
Marjoribanks, 2nd-Lieutenant M. E., 190.
Marks, 2nd-Lieutenant H. V., 263.
Markham, 2nd-Lieutenant E. H., 85.
Marsden, Private, 116.
Martin, 2nd-Lieutenant D. F. de R., 159, 177.
Matthews, Captain J. H., 38, 41.
Maunoury, Général, 30, 34, 43.
Mayfield, 2nd-Lieutenant L., 267.
Maxwell, Captain E. C. (Cheshire R.), 128.
Mellish, Captain The Rev. E. N., 144.
Miller, 2nd-Lieutenant J. E., 138 (*f.n.*).
Mills, 2nd-Lieutenant J. D. W., 282.
Milne, General G., 231, 243, 244, 250.
Mitford, Lieutenant Hon. D., 41, 93-4.
Molineux, Captain G. K., 98.
Molyneux, Serjeant, 222.
Montgomery - Massingberd, F. M. Sir A., 284 (*f.n.*).
Mortished, 2nd-Lieutenant L. R., 72.
Mouat, Lieutenant B., 294.
Moulton-Barrett, Lieut.-Colonel E. M., 74, 87-8-9, 90-1-2, 197, 200, 201 (*f.n.*), 203-4-8-9, 211-2-3.
Muir, Major A. W., 273-5-6, 282, 293-6-7.
Mullen, 2nd-Lieutenant H. P., 207 (*f.n.*), 211.
Myers, Lieutenant W., 122, 180.
Mylett, Lance-Corporal, 277.

INDEX.

Newstead, Captain B. R., 159 (*f.n.*), 253-4-5-256-7 (*f.n.*), 258-9, 260-5-6.
Nichol, 2nd-Lieutenant A. T., 177.
Nicholls, Captain H. L. F., 79.
Nimmo, 2nd-Lieutenant W. L., 223.
Nisbet, Brig.-General R. C., 249.
Nunneley, Lieutenant C. F., 51.

O'Dowd, 2nd-Lieutenant M. V., 102-3-4.
O'Dowd, 2nd-Lieutenant R. E. D., 174.
Ouzman, Regtl. Serjt.-Major, 83.
Ovans, Lieutenant H. L., 17, 18, 37.

Panter, Serjeant, 14, 16.
Parish, 2nd-Lieutenant R., 236 (*f.n.*), 238.
Partington, Captain L., 130, 208, 211.
Passingham, Captain E. G., 132, 170-1, 179.
Pattenden, 2nd-Lieutenant R. F. S., 174.
Pattison, Captain W. (formerly C.S.M.), 234, 249, 284.
Pearce, Brig.-General, 128.
Pease, Captain E. G., 183.
Pereira, Brigadier-General, 125.
Peter, King of Serbia, 226.
Phelan, Lieutenant A. E., 155, 179, 188-9.
Phillips, 2nd-Lieutenant A. K., 276.
Pickering, Corporal, 66.
Pigg, Captain N. B., 279, 281, 289 (*f.n.*), 200-1.
Pilcher, Major-General T. D., 132 (*f.n.*).
Pitkethley, 2nd-Lieutenant W. B., 279, 282.
Platt, Captain W., 44, 50.
Pollock, 2nd-Lieutenant C. W., 123.
Porter-Hargreaves, Lieutenant A. H., 264.
Potter, Brigadier-General H. C., 138, 155, 187 (*f.n.*), 193, 260-1 (*f.n.*).
Potter, Lieutenant R. W., 280-2.
Potts, 2nd-Lieutenant J. R., 174.
Poulter, Regtl. Serjt.-Major F., 132.
Powell, Captain H. I., 166, 176-7.
Price, Lieutenant F. A., 236 (*f.n.*), 238, 284, 293.
Prideaux, Captain H. H., 136.
Prince of Wales, H.R.H., 66.

Radcliffe, Lieutenant J. F. E., 79.
Rawlinson, General Sir H., 3, 47, 146, 251.
Rea, Lieutenant F. M., 142.
Redesdale, Lord—*see* Mitford.
Redpath, 2nd-Lieutenant H. E., 150.
Redpath, 2nd-Lieutenant G. E., 256.
Redwood, Lieutenant T. C. L., 129, 236 (*f.n.*), 240, 248 (*f.n.*), 293.
Regan, 2nd-Lieutenant J. H., 222, 265.
Reichwald, Captain, 4.
Richards, 2nd-Lieutenant J., 209, 211.
Riddell, Brigadier-General J. F., 91 (*f.n.*).
Riley, 2nd-Lieutenant S., 263.
Roberts, 2nd-Lieutenant A. J., 132.
Robinson, Brigadier-General, 286.
Roblin, 2nd-Lieutenant L. G., 220.

Robson, 2nd-Lieutenant J., 290.
Rochell, Captain A., 218.
Roddam, Captain R. C., 106-7, 112-3, 115.
Roderick, Lieutenant W. B., 106.
Rogers, Lieutenant J. R., 240, 284.
Rollo, Brigadier-General, 271 (*f.n.*).
Rolph, Corporal, 185.
Rose, Lieutenant S. A., 128, 137, 206, 211.
Routledge, 2nd-Lieutenant J. F., 185.
Rushbrooke, Captain W. L. P., 76, 122, 229, 235-6 (*f.n.*), 237, 243 (*f.n.*), 245.
Rutledge, Captain C. J., 148-9, 174.

Salier, Captain E. L., 101, 102 (*f.n.*), 103-4, 225-9.
Salt, 2nd-Lieutenant W. H., 156.
Sanderson, 2nd-Lieutenant T., 262.
Sandilands, Captain H. R., 19, 20, 112, 114-5-117-8.
Sapte, Lieut.-Colonel D., 4.
Sarrail, Général, 227-9, 231-3-4, 242-3, 250 (*f.n.*).
Scanlan, Captain T. M., 253-4-5-6-7 (*f.n.*), 259, 262.
Scott, Lieutenant D., 250, 283.
Scrutton, Captain H. U., 115-7-8-9, 121, 236 (*f.n.*), 238.
Searles, Lieutenant N. A., 274.
Selby, Captain B. H., 39, 41.
Sellars, 2nd-Lieutenant J. H., 102, 104.
Shann, 2nd-Lieutenant K., 98.
Shaw, Brigadier F. C., 3, 5, 7, 27, 34, 46, 56-7, 58-9, 61-2.
Shiel, Lieutenant G. G., 129.
Shoolbred, Lieut.-Colonel (Queen's Westminster R.), 117 (*f.n.*).
Sibbit, 2nd-Lieutenant G. B., 267.
Sidney, Captain, 81.
Simon, Soldat, 9.
Simpson, Coy. Serjt.-Major, 107.
Simpson, 2nd-Lieutenant J. J., 209, 211.
Sloper, Captain G. O., 37, 108, 115-7-8-9, 121 (*f.n.*).
Smith, Lieutenant Clive, *see* Clive
Smith, Brigadier-General Douglas, 62, 138.
Smith, Lieut.-Colonel (Lincoln R.), 39.
Smith-Dorrien, General Sir H., 5, 23-4, 58-9, 66-8, 83, 143.
Smythe, Major R. C., 150.
Snailham, Lieutenant J. J., 272-5, 293-4-5 (*f.n.*).
Sockett, Serjeant, 144 (*f.n.*).
Spencer, Serjeant, 95.
Squires, Serjeant, 66.
St. John, Captain B. T., 16, 17, 46, 57.
Steel, Captain C. H., 122, 188, 190, 253-4-6-9, 264.
Steel, 2nd-Lieutenant J., 257.
Steel, 2nd-Lieutenant J. R., 159 (*f.n.*).
Steele, Captain H. G., 279, 289, 290-1.

INDEX.

Steinhardt, Soldat, 9.
Stephen, Captain H. C., 99, 100–1–2–4.
Stephenson, Lieutenant J., 273, 284.
Stevens, Captain (Bde.-Major), 25.
Story, Lieutenant D., 256–7.
Sutherland, Lieutenant H. O., 36, 37.
Sweet, 2nd-Lieutenant G., 128.

Tait, 2nd-Lieut. J. T., 170, 174.
Taylor, 2nd-Lieutenant H. G., 238.
Taylor, 2nd-Lieutenant R. A., 98.
Taylor, Captain R. V., 150.
Taylor, 2nd-Lieutenant W., 98.
Taylor, Serjeant, 95.
Tedstill, Serjeant, 144 (*f.n.*).
Thomas, Colonel H. St. J. (9th Bn.), 132.
Thompson, Lieutenant C. J. McK., 142.
Thompson, 2nd-Lieutenant J. C., 211.
Thompson, Serjeant (No. 1629), 110.
Thompson, Serjeant, 163–4.
Thorp, 2nd-Lieutenant R. O. V., 163–4–5.
Tiswell, 2nd-Lieutenant J. A., 238.
Tonson-Rye, Lieut.-Colonel (Munster Fus.), 277.
Toppin, Captain H. S., 25, 37, 41.
Tottie, 2nd-Lieutenant E. H., 40, 41.
Tower, Major (R. Fusiliers), 255.
Travell, 2nd-Lieutenant N. E., 186.
Trobe, Private H., 144.
Tudor, Serjeant, 277.
Tuke, 2nd-Lieutenant H. S., 85, 92, 95.
Turnbull, Lieutenant S. A., 206, 211.
Turner, Lce.-Corporal M., 85.
Twigge, 2nd-Lieutenant F., 174.

Vachell, Lieutenant R. T., 48.
Van Neck, 2nd-Lieutenant C. H., 48.
Vernon, Lieutenant R. D., 142.

Waddilove, Darley—*see Darley.*
Wailing, 2nd-Lieutenant C. G. W., 222, 263.

Walker, 2nd-Lieutenant S. R., 281–2.
Wallace, Lieut.-Colonel (Suffolk R.), 88.
Walton, 2nd-Lieutenant J., 85, 123.
Wanless, Corporal, 163.
Ware, Lieutenant A. F., 142.
Wardlaw, Lieutenant J., 284.
Watkin, Captain F. E., 27, 64–7–8.
Watmough, 2nd-Lieutenant J. C., 123.
Watson, 2nd-Lieutenant W., 97–8.
Weir, Brigadier-General G. A., 128, 249.
West, Major (R.T.C.), 254.
Westmacott, Major G. R. (9th Bn.), 132.
White, Captain J. P., 144–9, 150.
Wild, Lieut.-Colonel W., 116 (*f.n.*), 132, **133,** 143–9, 150–1–2–3–4–5–9, 162, 183, 196.
Wilkins, 2nd-Lieutenant G., 128.
Wilkinson, Major-General P. S., 144.
Wilkinson, Coy. Serjt.-Major, 38, 42.
Wilkinson, Serjeant S., 144 (*f.n.*).
Willans, Lieutenant R., 56, 60.
Williams, 2nd-Lieutenant E. J., 276.
Williams, 2nd-Lieutenant T., 197.
Williams, Lieutenant T., 290.
Wilson, Lieutenant J. B., 284–7.
Wing, Major-General F. D., 45, 64.
Wintour, Brigadier-General, 70, 76–8.
Woodhead, 2nd-Lieutenant, 295 (*f.n.*).
Woodroffe, Lieutenant B. C., 129.
Woodroffe, Lieutenant K. D., 129, 272–3–4–5.
Wreford-Brown, Captain, 100–1–2–4, 112 (*f.n.*).
Wright, Lieutenant T. (R.E.), 17.
Wright, 2nd-Lieutenant C. C. G., 129.

Yates, 2nd-Lieutenant J., 178.
Yatman, Lieut.-Colonel C., 11, 12, 13, **14, 16,** 17, 18, 24 (*f.n.*), 41, **60–3–6,** 110–2, 116 (*f.n.*), 117–8, 120, 130, 133.
Yatman, Lieutenant D. H., 200, 217.
Young, 2nd-Lieutenant F. I., 155-6.

B. MILITARY UNITS.

9th Infantry Brigade—

1/Fifth ; 4/Royal Fusiliers, 71, 17, 18, 19, 34–6–7, 45–6–7–8, 51–2–3–9, 61, 111–5–8, 139, 140–2–3–7, 152–3–4–5, 163, 172–3–6–8–9, 187–8–9, 190–1–4–8–9, 200–1–2–3–5–8–9, 210–6–8, 222, 252–9, 260–1–5–7, 279, 280–1–8–9, 290–1 ; 1/Lincolnshire Regiment, 11, 17, 18, 19, 20, 21 (*f.n.*), 34–6–7–9, 47–8, 51–2–3–6–7–8–9, 60–1–2–7, 111–5–8, 120, 133–6 ; 1/Royal Scots Fusiliers, 11, 17, 18, 19, 32–4–7, 44–7–9, 51–2, 62–3–7, 111–112–5–8–9, (252–4, 261–2–4)* ; Liverpool Scottish, 80, 106–7, 111–4–5–7–8–9, 120 ; 12/West Yorkshire Regiment, 136, 147–8–9, 151–2–4–7, 172–3–6–8, 186 (*f.n.*), 187–8–9. 192–3–4–7 ; 13/King's Regiment, 142–7–8, 151–2–4–5, 167, 172–3–6–8–9, 184–7, 192–193–9, 201–2–5–6–8–9, 210–6–8–9.

*After transfer to 8th Inf. Brigade.

84th Infantry Brigade—

2/FIFTH; 1/Suffolk Regiment, 74–6, 88, 95, 101–3, 233, 241; 2/Cheshire Regiment, 72, 76, 87–8, 91–5, 101, 127–8, 231–5–6–9, 242; 1/Welch Regiment, 72–6, 86, 91–5–6, 101–3, 127, 245; 12/London Regiment, 88, 96; 1/Monmouthshire Regiment, 87–8, 95–96–7, 101–3.

150th Infantry Brigade (from 16th July, 1918)—

2/FIFTH; 7/Wiltshire Regiment, 270–6–7, 286, 292–3–4–5; 2/Royal Munster Fusiliers, 270–3–4–6–7, 286, 292–3–4–5.

Other British Army Units—

Cavalry.—2/Life Guards, 72; 3rd Hussars, 57; 12th Lancers, 58; 16th Lancers, 58.

Infantry.—Grenadier Guards, 62; 2/Royal Scots, 120, 262; 2/Buffs, 74, 239; King's Own, 2nd Bn., 76; 8th Bn., 151–2–4, 185, 205, 220; 1/5th Bn., 216–7; 3/Royal Fusiliers, 84–7–9, 274; Suffolk Regiment, 2nd Bn., 172–5, 186; 11th Bn., 200, 202 (f.n.); 1/West Yorkshire, 119; 8/East Yorkshire, 157; 2/Royal Irish, 47–9; 10/R. Welch Fusiliers, 186; 6/R. Inniskilling Fusiliers, 272, 255–6; 2/Worcestershire, 19; 1/East Lancashire, 98; 2/East Surrey, 74, 89, 244; 2/Duke of Wellington's, 61–2; 2/R. Sussex, 62; 1/Hampshire, 89, 90–1; 1/4th South Lancashire, 217; 10/Essex, 293; 2/Sherwood Foresters, 132; 1/Berkshire, 253; K.O.Y.L.I., 1st Bn., 239, 240, 272–3–6; 2nd Bn., 63; 7/K.S.L.I., 159; Middlesex, 3rd Bn., 72; 4th Bn., 67; K.R.R.C., 3rd Bn., 103; 4th Bn., 272–3–6; 20th Bn., 202; 1/Wiltshire, 52, 115–8; 9/Manchester, 283; 1/York and Lancaster, 126; Durham L.I., 8th Bn., 88, 90; 9th Bn., 176 (f.n.); 2/Highland L.I., 65; 1/4th Seaforth Highlanders, 216 (f.n.), 217–8; 1/Gordon Highlanders, 44–5, 67, 175, 185–6, 258–9; 2/Cameron Highlanders, 85, 236–8; 2/R. Irish Rifles, 51; 2/R. Dublin Fusiliers, 272–3–4–6; Rifle Brigade, 4th Bn., 103; 22nd Bn., 249; Queen's Westminster Rifles, 117 (f.n.); 1/Hertfordshire, 263; Anson Bn. (R.N.D.), 253–5; Scottish Horse, 285–6.

Indian Army—

20th and 21st Coys. Sappers and Miners, 14th Sikhs, 2/Gurkha Rifles, 53.

Dominion Forces—

Canadian, 123, 145; New Zealand, 280–288–9, 291; South African, 284.

LIST OF MAPS.

- Map 1 "Quo Fata Vocant"—Mons to Ypres, 1914.
- ,, 3 Mons, 22nd—24th August, 1914.
- ,, 4 Battle of Le Cateau-Cambrai, 26th August, 1914.
- ,, 5 Actions of 8th, 9th, 10th September, 1914.
- ,, 6 The Fighting on the Aisne, September, 1914.
- ,, 7 "La Bassée, 1914."
- ,, 8 Ypres. General Map, November, 1914—March, 1915.
- ,, 11 Positions of the two Battalions in the Ypres Salient, April to August, 1915.
- ,, 12 "Ypres, 1915." The Stages of the Battle.
- ,, 13 Attack by 1/Fifth on Bellewaarde, 16th June, 1915.
- ,, 14 Situation at Loos and The Hohenzollern Redoubt, 28th September, 1915.
- ,, 15 The Attack at St. Éloi, 27th March, 1916.
- ,, 16 Opening Phases of the Somme Battle, 1916.
- ,, 17 Assembly Positions and Objectives of the 9th Inf. Brigade in the Attack on Bazentin Ridge, 14th July, 1916.
- ,, 18 Distribution of 9th Inf. Brigade prior to Attack on Longueval, 23rd July, 1916.
- ,, 22 Area East and South of Arras. For reference Chapters XII., XIII. and XIV.
- ,, 23 The Advance of the British Line between Lens and the R. Somme, 30th June, 1916—29th June, 1917.
- ,, 25 Attack by 1/Fifth on Guémappe, 13th April, 1917.
- ,, 26 Area of 3rd Division's Attack on Zonnebeke, 26th September, 1917.
- ,, 27 The Attack North of Bullecourt, 20th November, 1917.
- ,, 29 The 9th Brigade Front, 21st and 22nd March, 1918.
- ,, 30 The Attack against the 3rd Division, 28th March, 1918.
- ,, 31 The Battle of the Lys, 1918.
- ,, 32 The Macedonian Front.
- ,, 33 Area of Operations of 2/Fifth in Macedonia, 10th May, 1916—21st June, 1918.
- ,, 34 The Struma Valley.
- ,, 35 General Map. The Advance to Victory. 8th August—28th September, 1918.
- ,, 36 The 3rd Division's Attack, 21st—23rd August, 1918.
- ,, 37 The 9th Brigade Attack, 31st August—1st September, 1918.
- ,, 39 Operations on 3rd Division Front, 18th to 28th September, 1918.
- ,, 40 General Map. The Advance to Victory. 29th September—11th November, 1918.
- ,, 41 Operations of 50th Division, 3rd to 7th October, 1918.
- ,, 42 The 9th Brigade Attack, 8th October, 1918.
- ,, 43 The Crossing of the Selle, and the Last Phase—showing areas of operations of the 3rd and 50th Divisions.

For Maps 2, 9, 10, 19, 20, 21, 24, 28, 38, see Table on page 10 of the Volume, which gives the pages of the History on which they will be found.

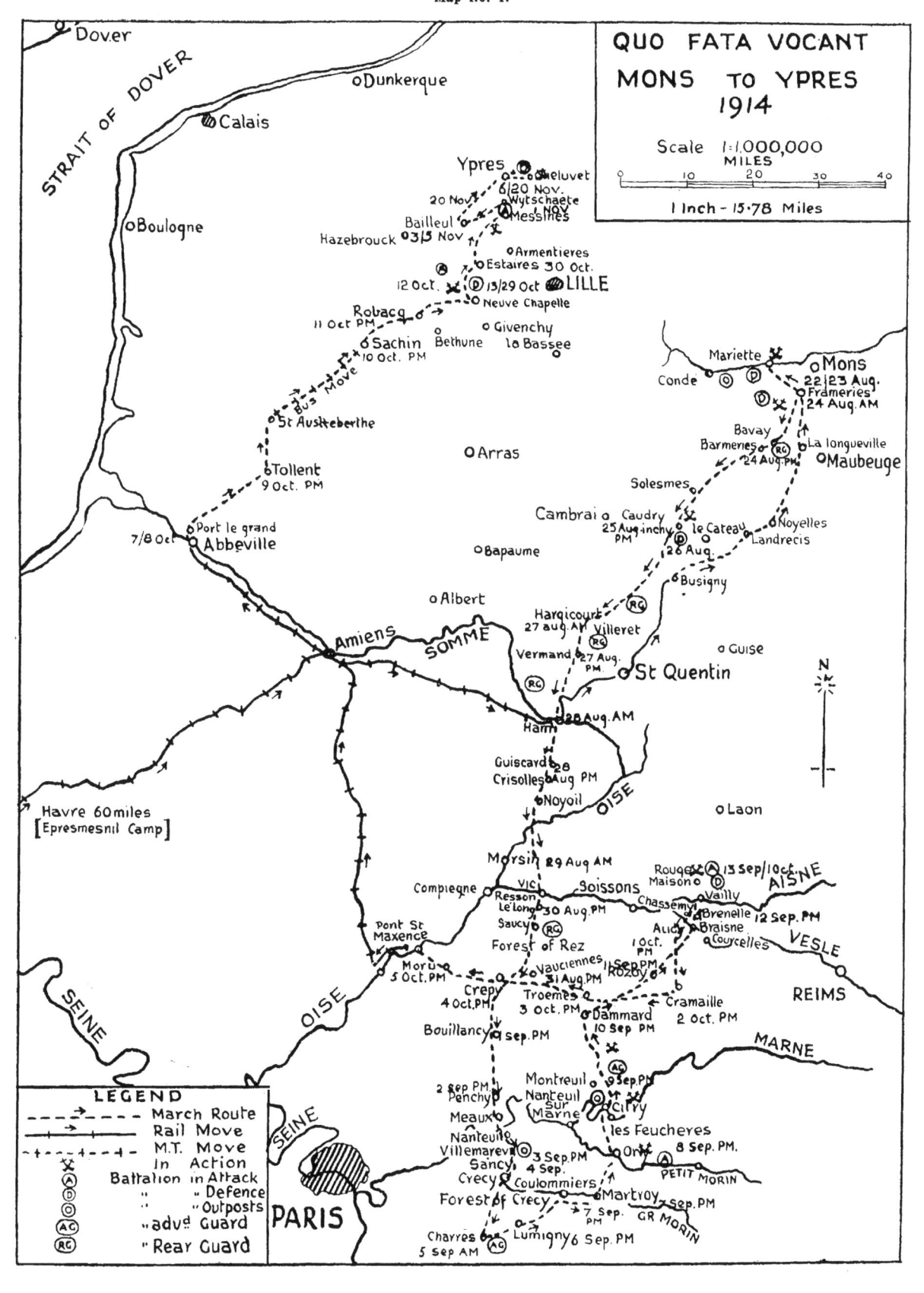

Map No. 1.

Map No. 3.

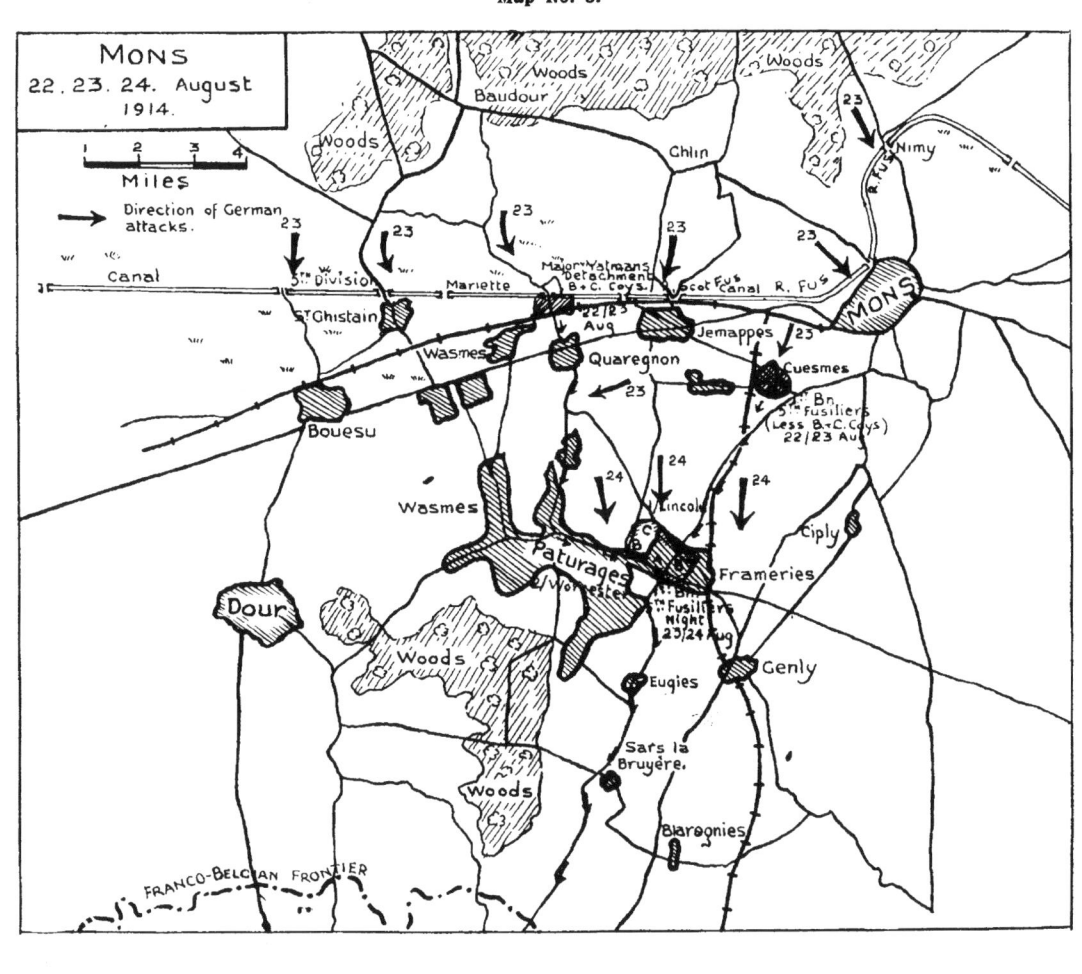

Map No. 4.

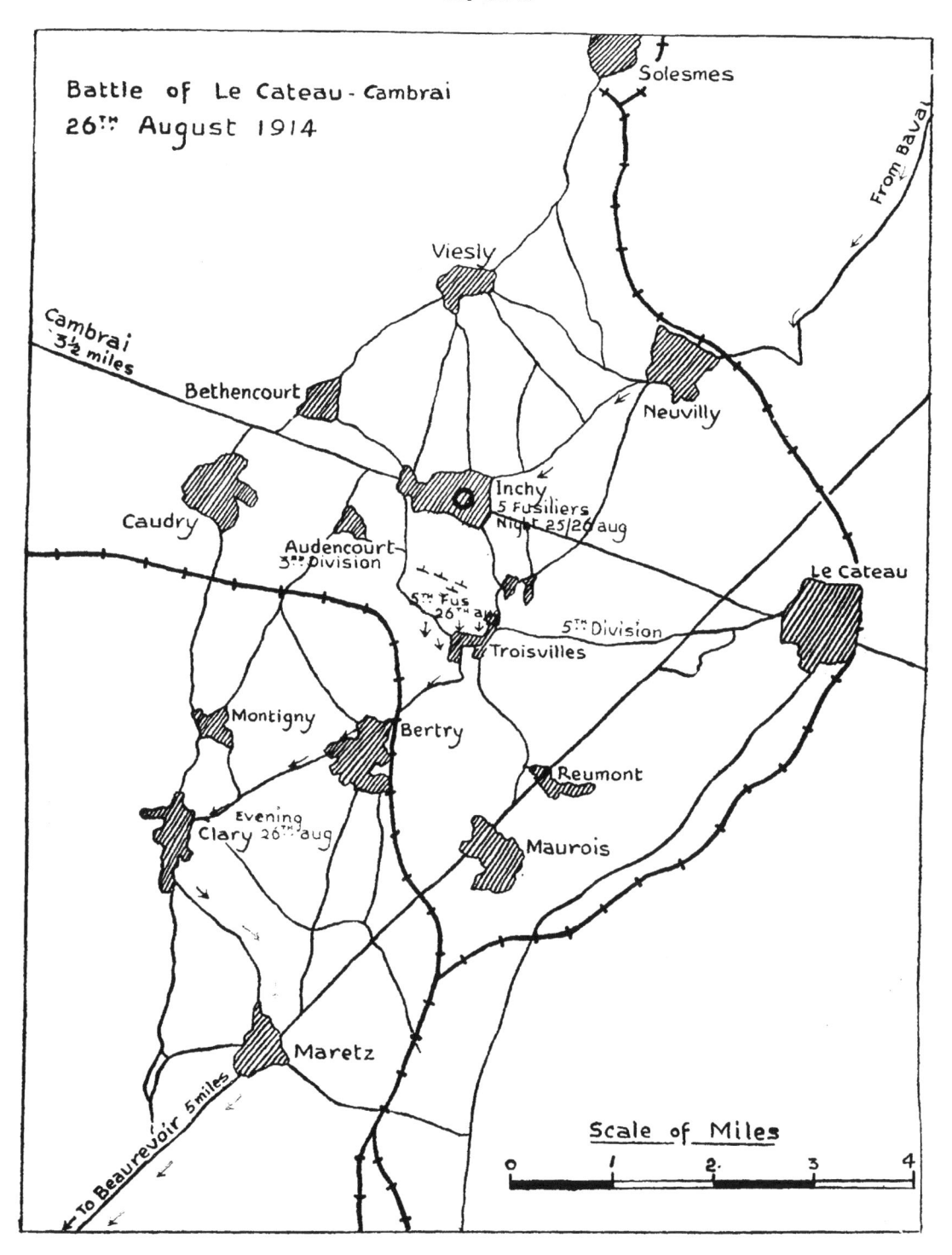

Map No. 5.

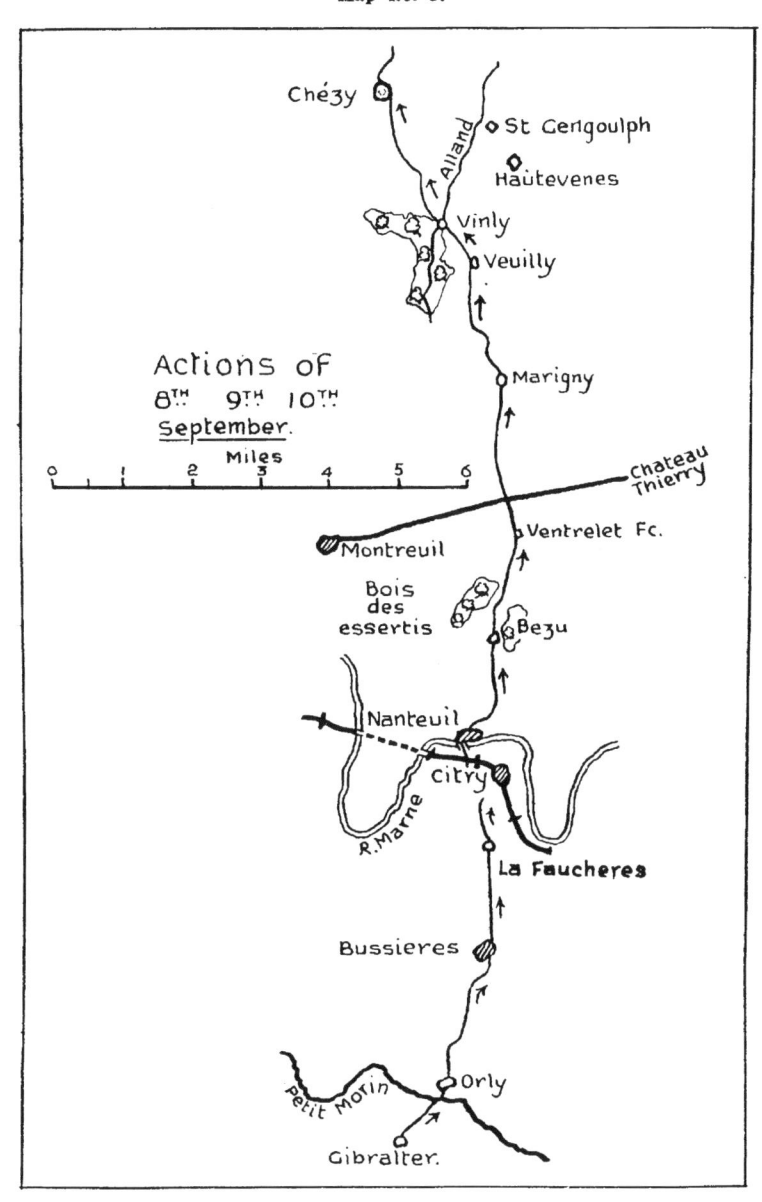

Actions of
8TH 9TH 10TH
September.

Map No. 6.

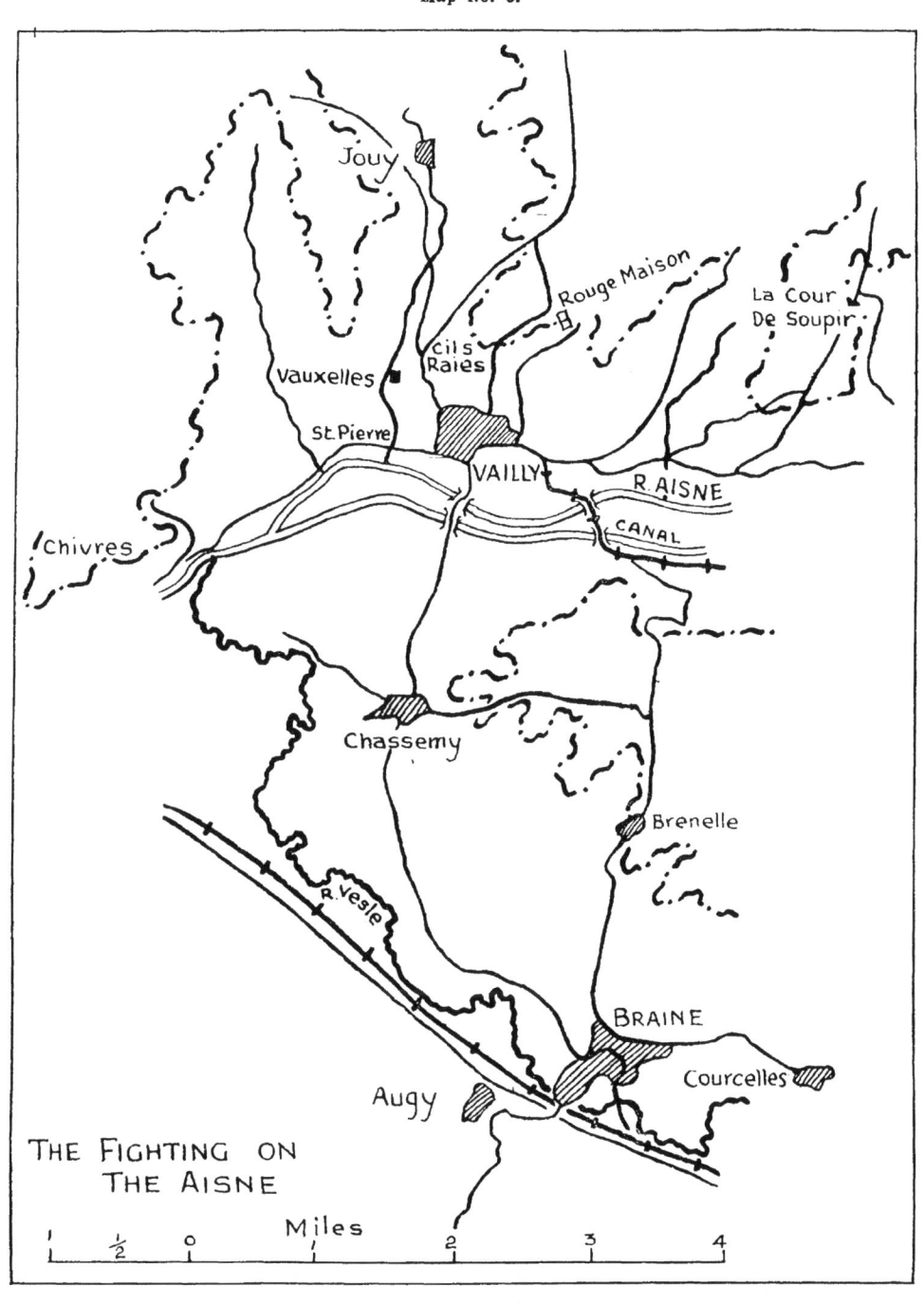

THE FIGHTING ON
THE AISNE

Map No. 7.

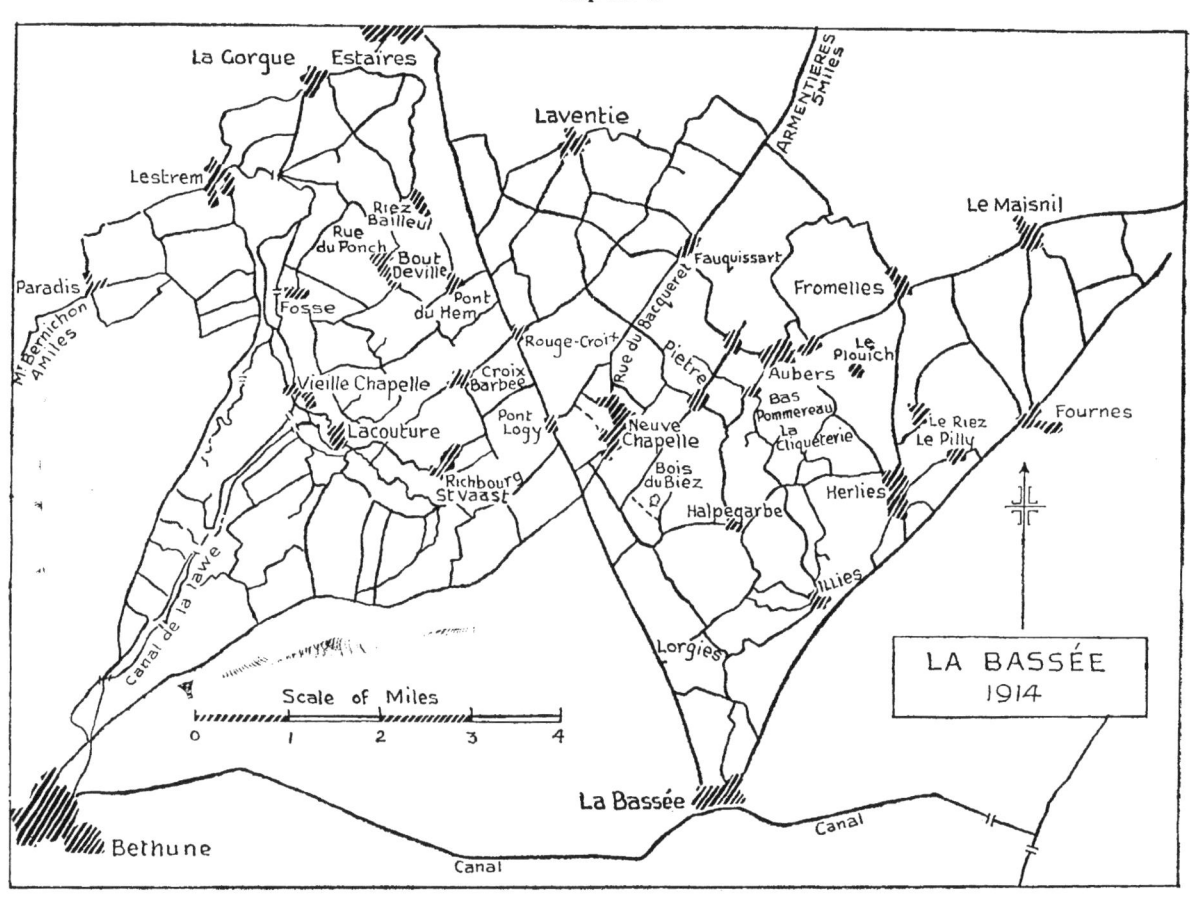

LA BASSÉE
1914

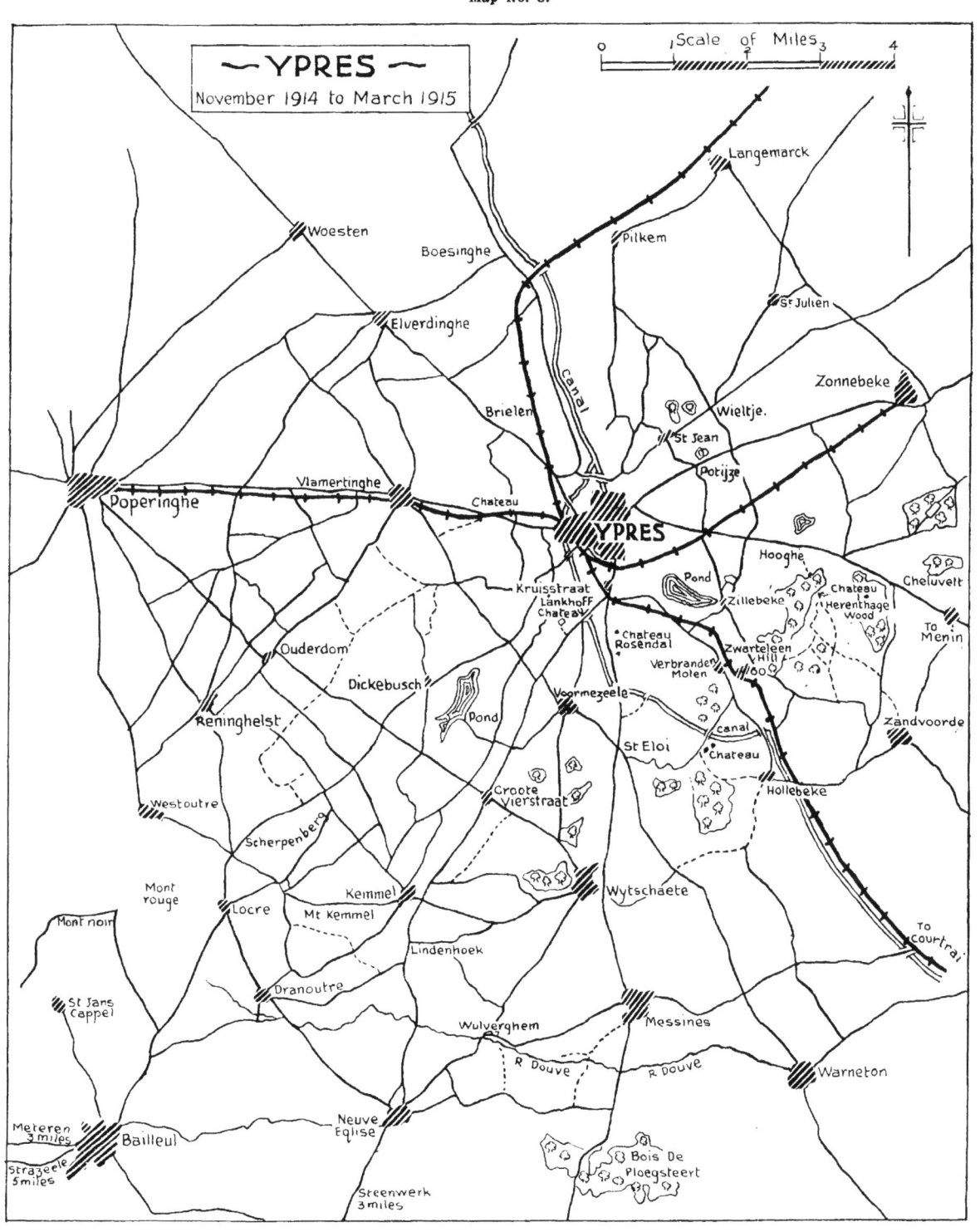

Map No. 8.

YPRES
November 1914 to March 1915

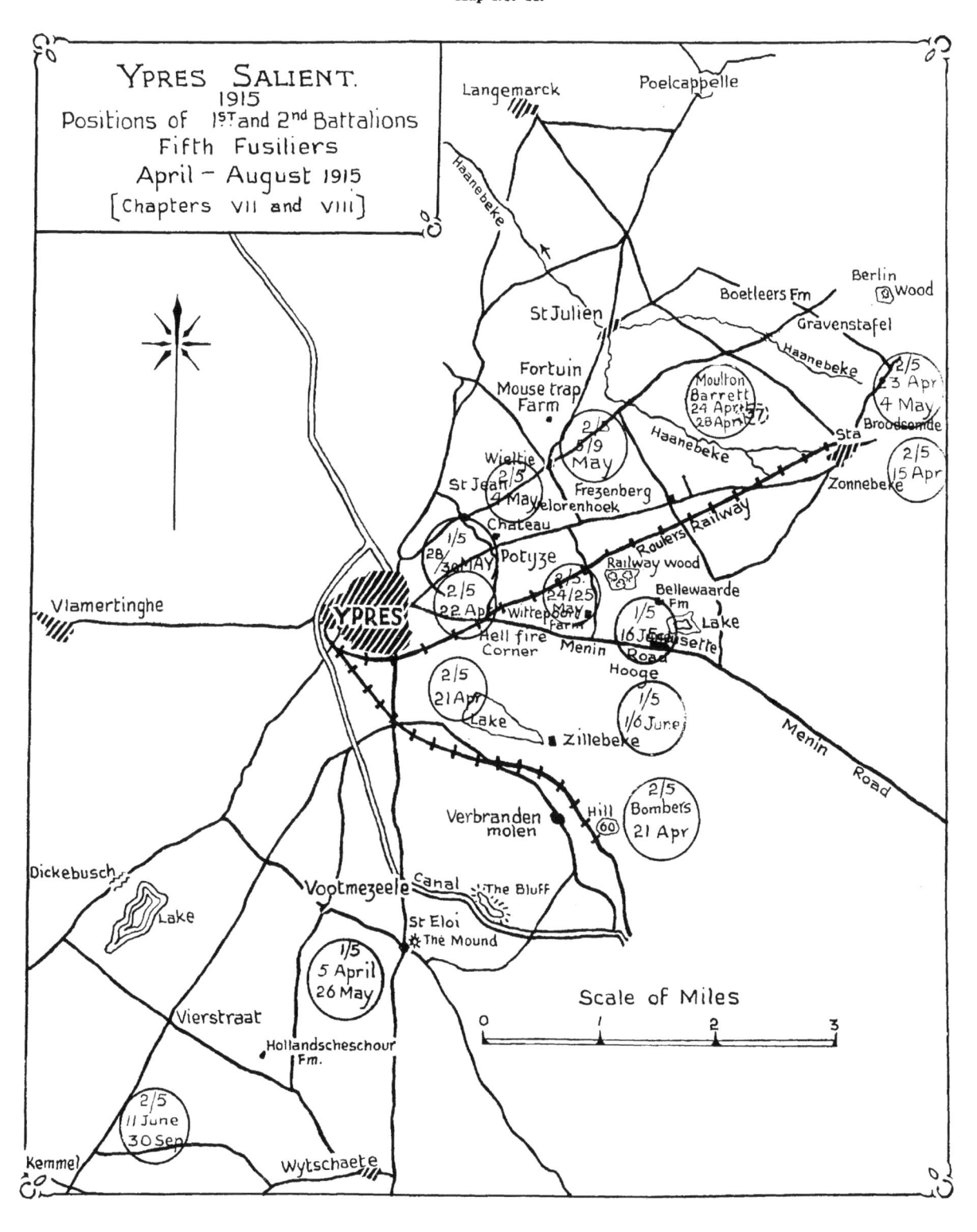

Map No. 11.

Map No. 12.

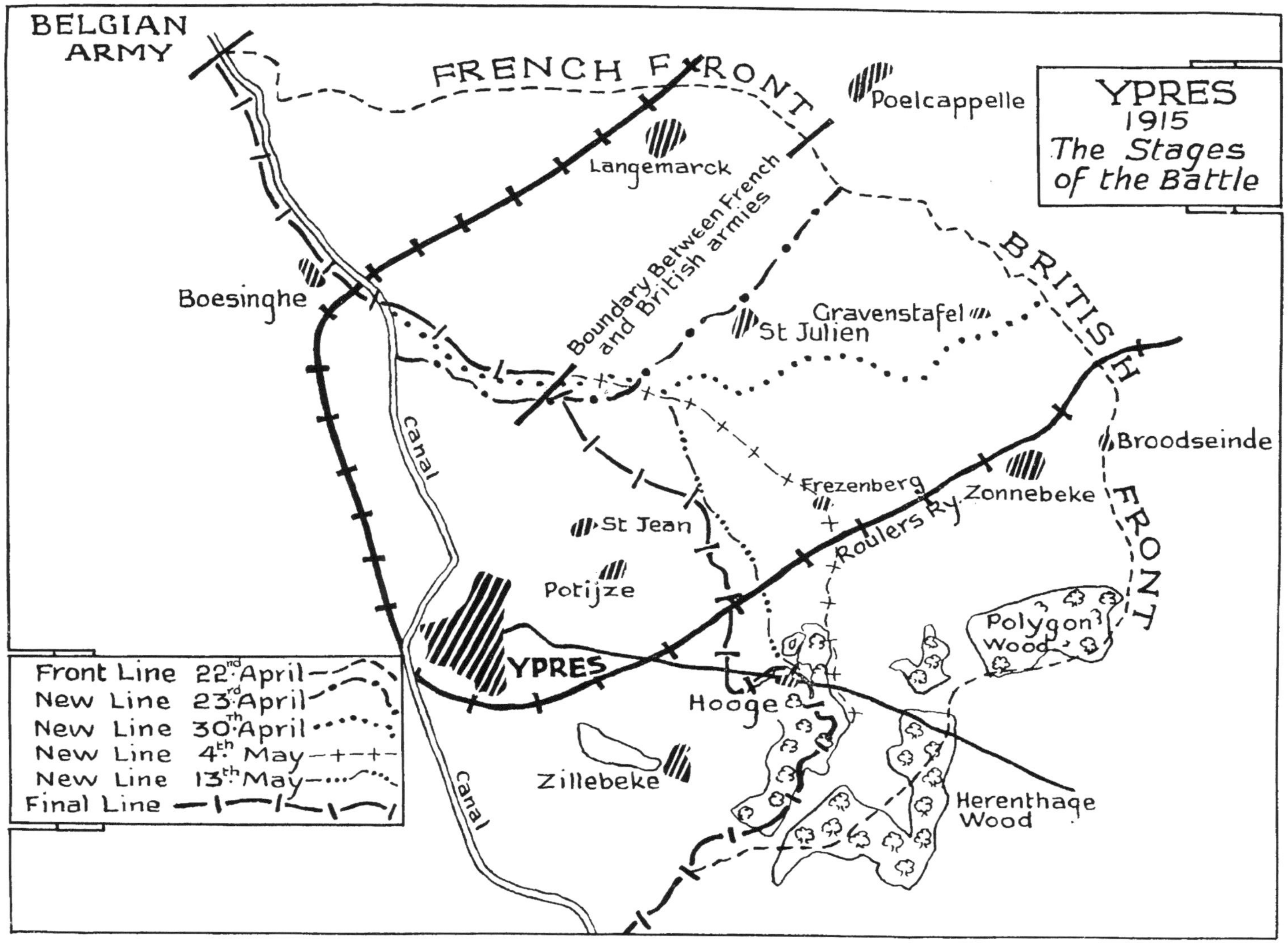
YPRES
1915
The Stages
of the Battle
BELGIAN
ARMY
FRENCH FRONT
BRITISH FRONT
Poelcappelle
Langemarck
Boundary Between French
and British armies
Boesinghe
Gravenstafel
St Julien
Broodseinde
Frezenberg
Zonnebeke
Roulers Ry
St Jean
Potijze
Canal
YPRES
Hooge
Polygon
Wood
Zillebeke
Herenthage
Wood
Front Line 22nd April
New Line 23rd April
New Line 30th April
New Line 4th May
New Line 13th May
Final Line

Map No. 13

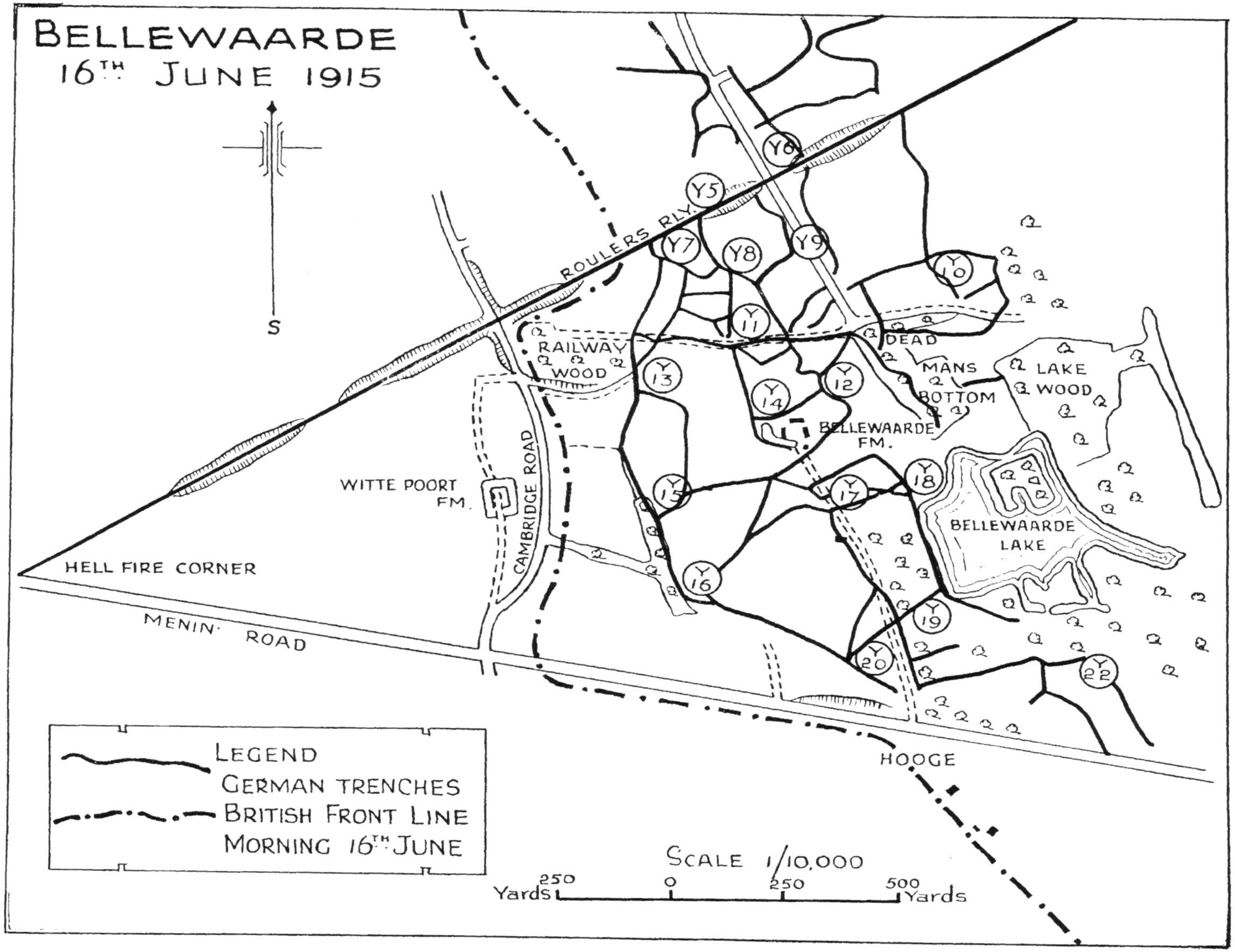
BELLEWAARDE
16TH JUNE 1915
S
ROULERS RLY.
Y5
Y6
Y7
Y8
Y9
Y10
Y11
Y12
Y13
Y14
Y15
Y16
Y17
Y18
Y19
Y20
Y22
RAILWAY WOOD
DEAD MANS BOTTOM
LAKE WOOD
BELLEWAARDE FM.
BELLEWAARDE LAKE
WITTE POORT FM.
CAMBRIDGE ROAD
HELL FIRE CORNER
MENIN ROAD
HOOGE
LEGEND
GERMAN TRENCHES
BRITISH FRONT LINE
MORNING 16TH JUNE
SCALE 1/10,000
250 Yards
0
250
500 Yards

Map No. 14.

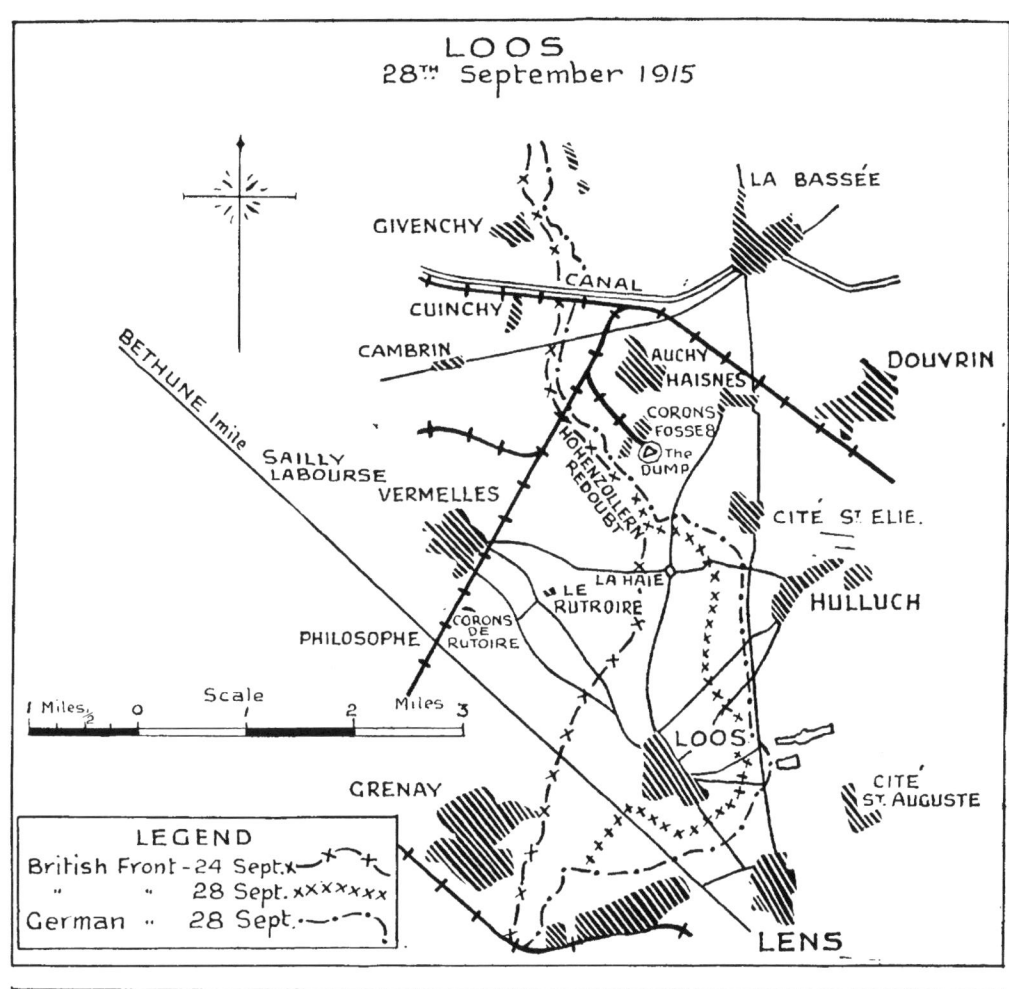

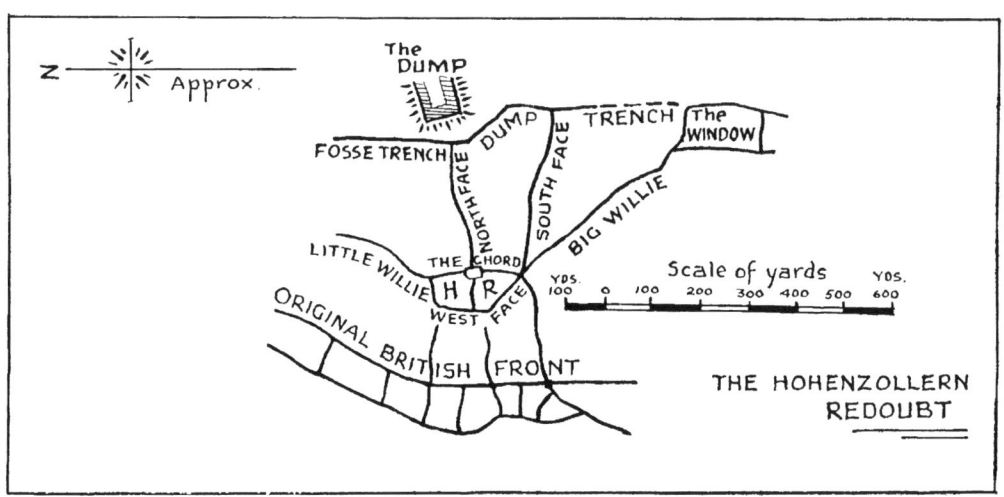

LOOS
28ᵀᴴ September 1915

LEGEND
British Front – 24 Sept. ×—+—×
   "   "   28 Sept. ××××××
German   "   28 Sept. —·—·—

THE HOHENZOLLERN REDOUBT

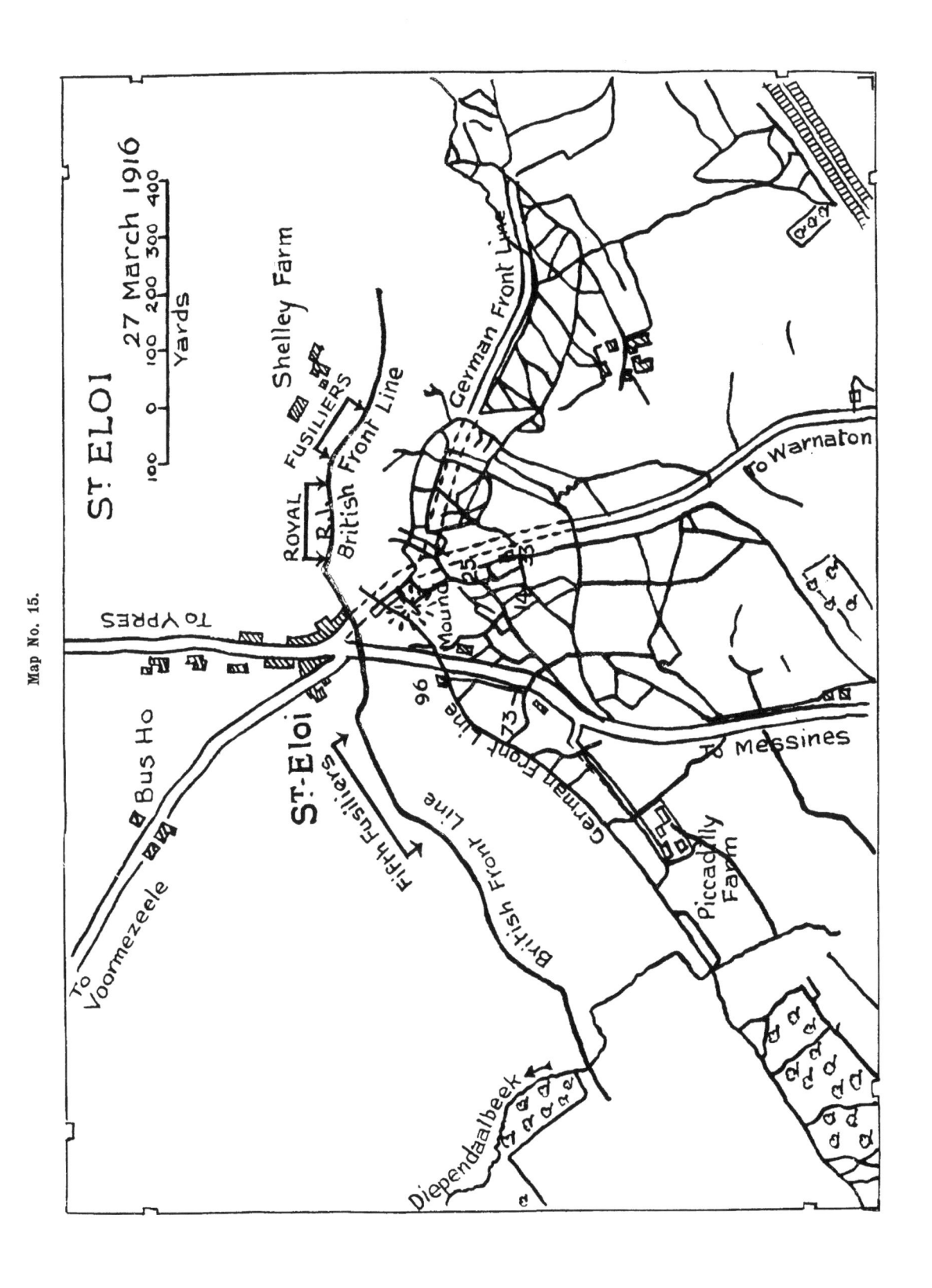

Map No. 15.

St. ELOI
27 March 1916

Yards: 100 0 100 200 300 400

- Shelley Farm
- Royal Fusiliers
- British Front Line
- German Front Line
- To Ypres
- To Warnaton
- To Voormezeele
- Bus Ho
- St-Eloi
- Fifth Fusiliers
- British Front Line
- German Front Line
- To Messines
- Piccadilly Farm
- Diependaalbeek

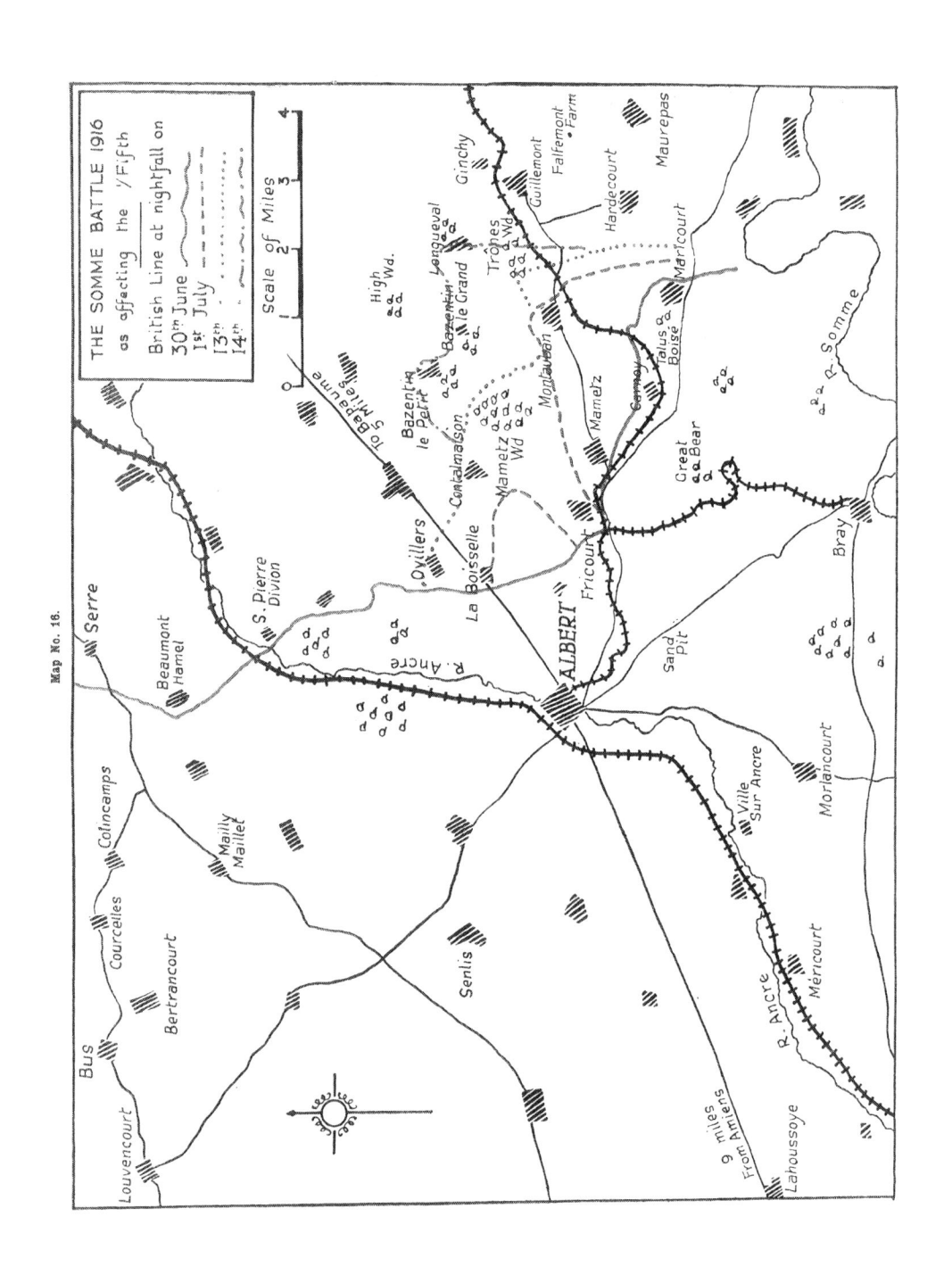

Map No. 18.

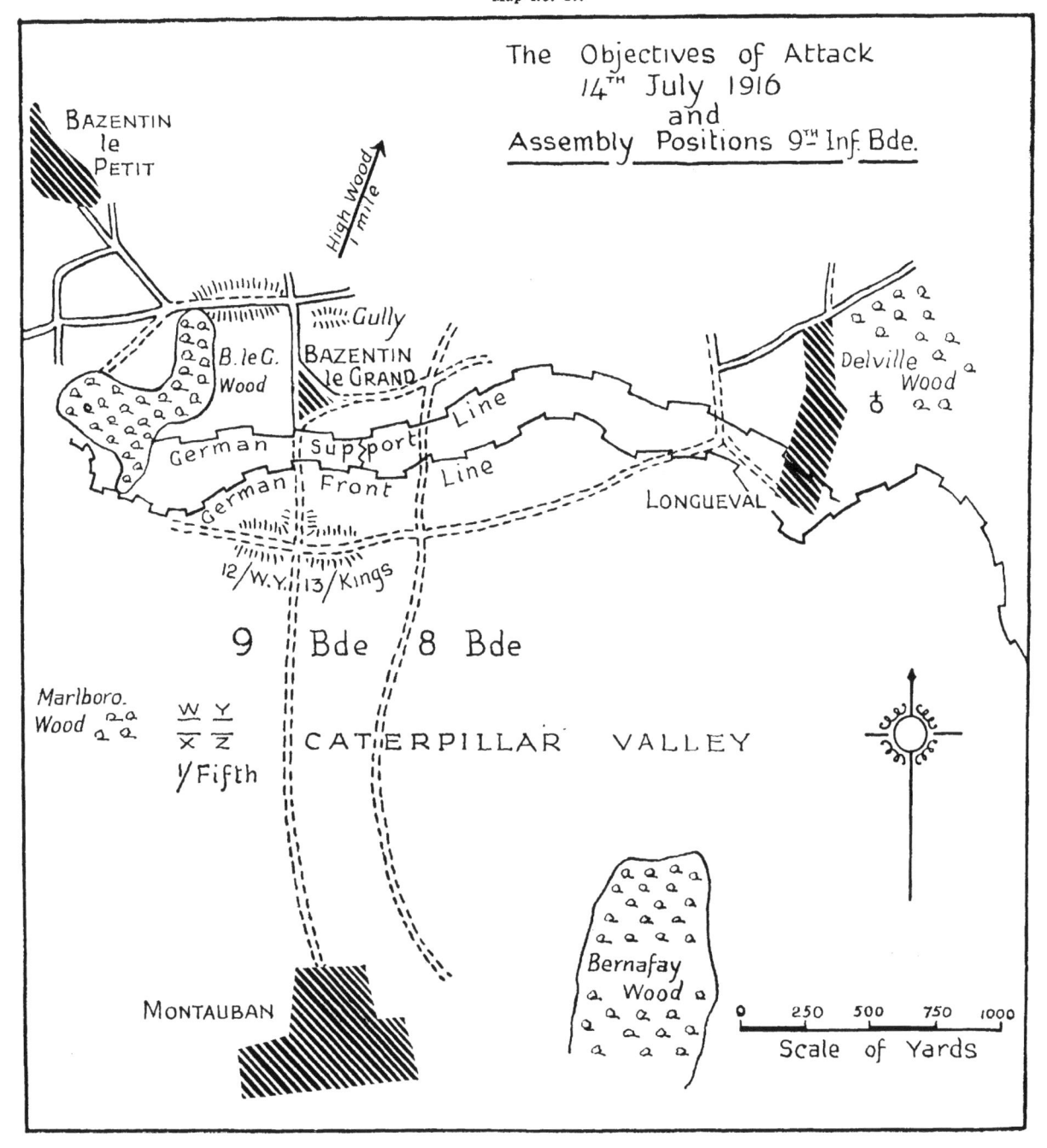

Map No. 17.

The Objectives of Attack 14th July 1916 and Assembly Positions 9th Inf. Bde.

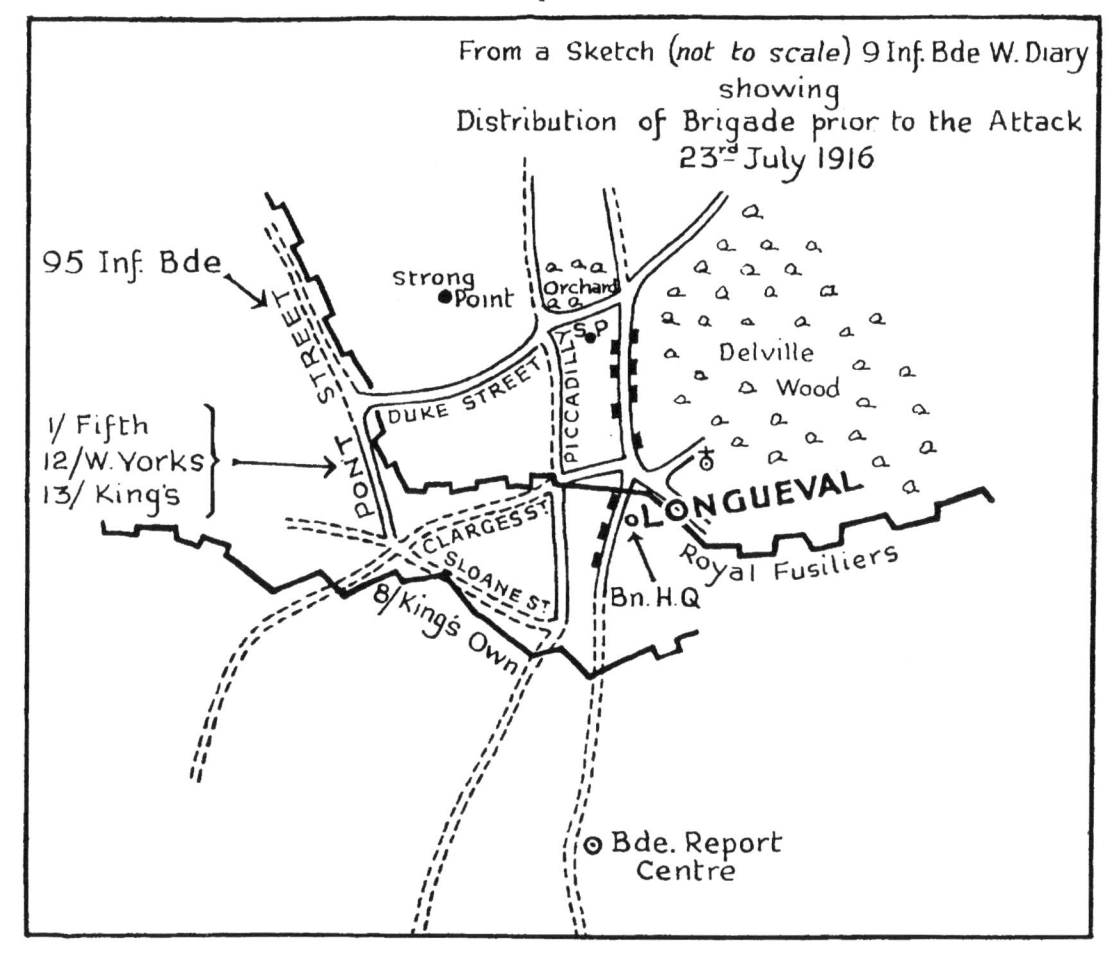

Map No. 18.

From a Sketch (*not to scale*) 9 Inf. Bde W. Diary showing
Distribution of Brigade prior to the Attack
23rd July 1916

Map No. 22.

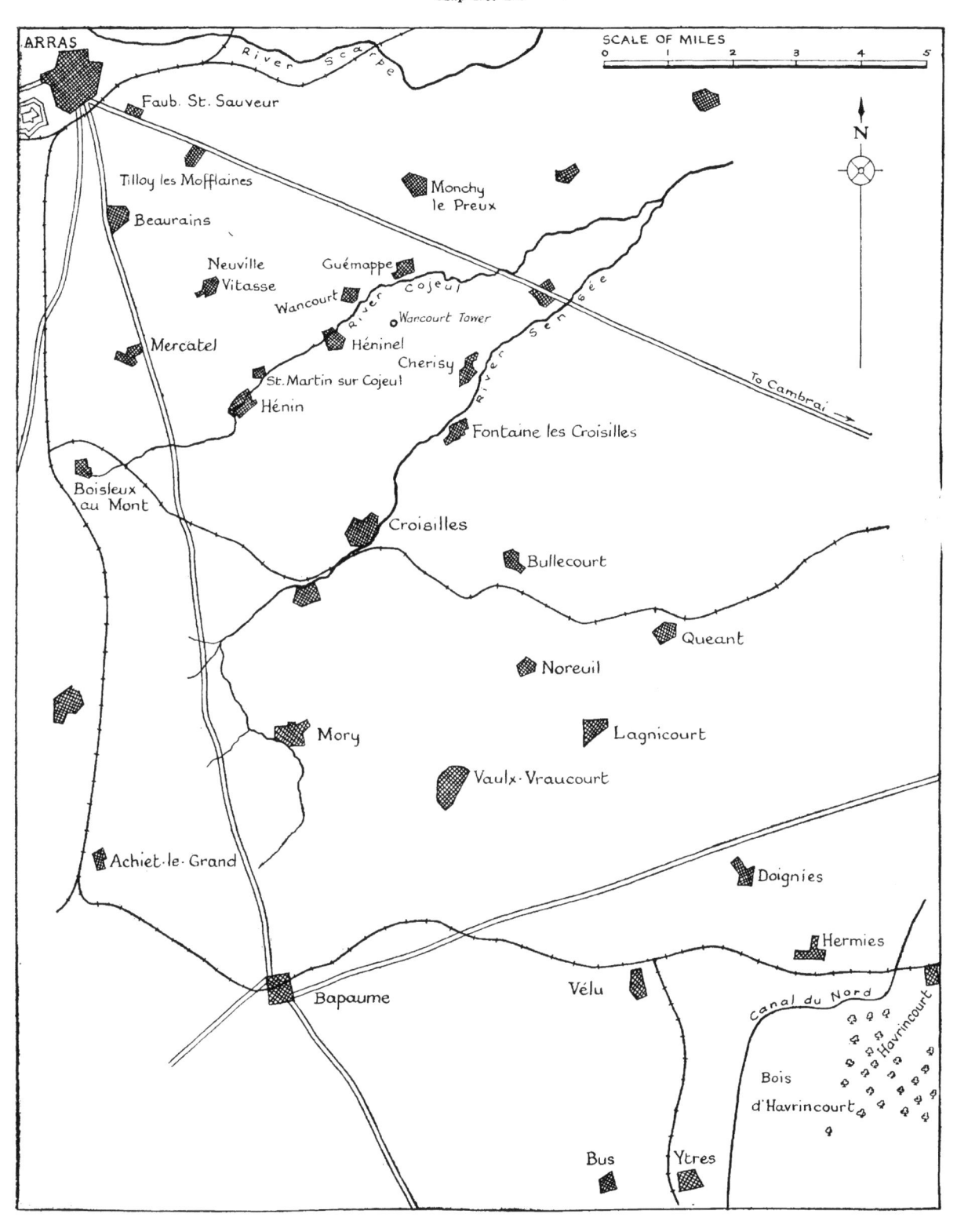

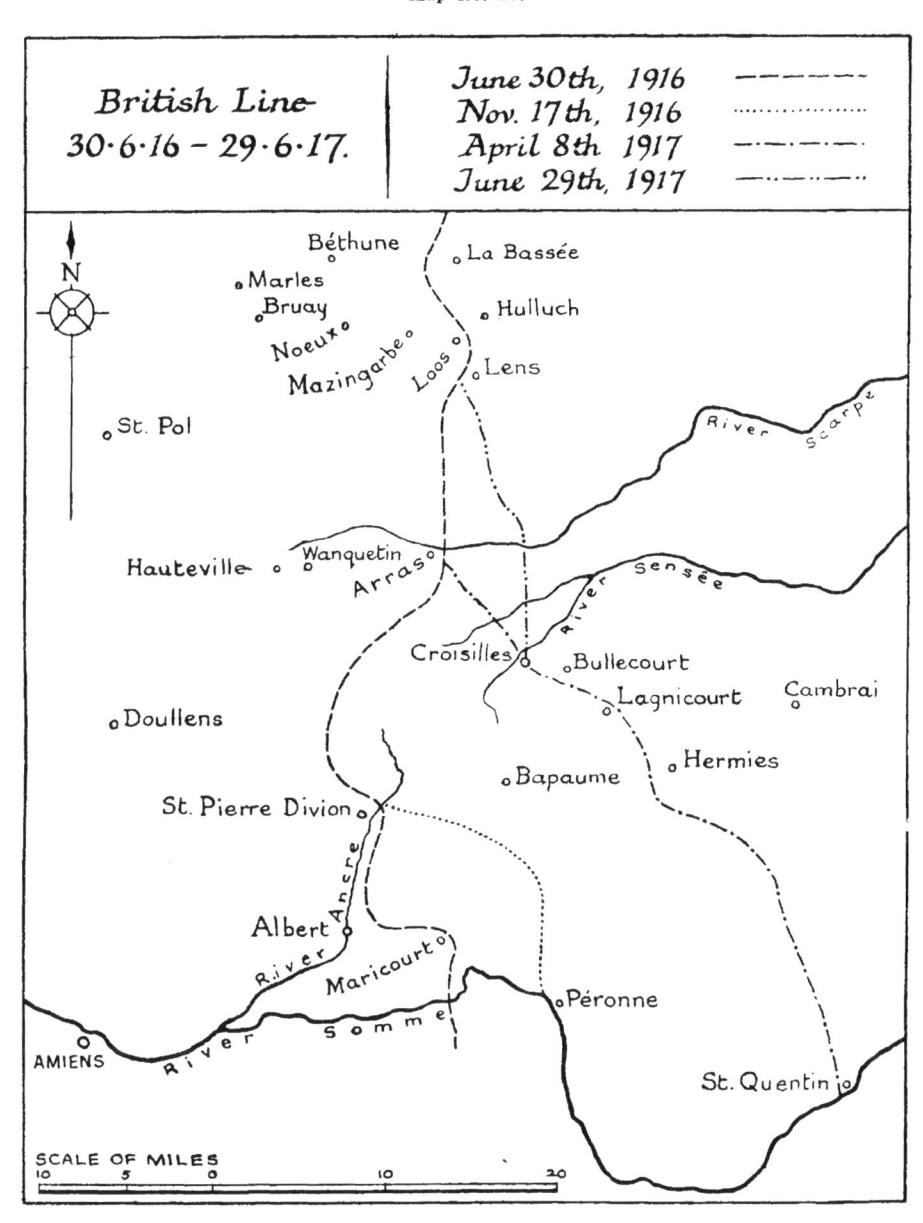

Map No. 23.

British Line 30·6·16 – 29·6·17.

June 30th, 1916	————
Nov. 17th, 1916	············
April 8th 1917	—·—·—·—
June 29th, 1917	—··—··—··

SCALE OF MILES

Map No. 25.

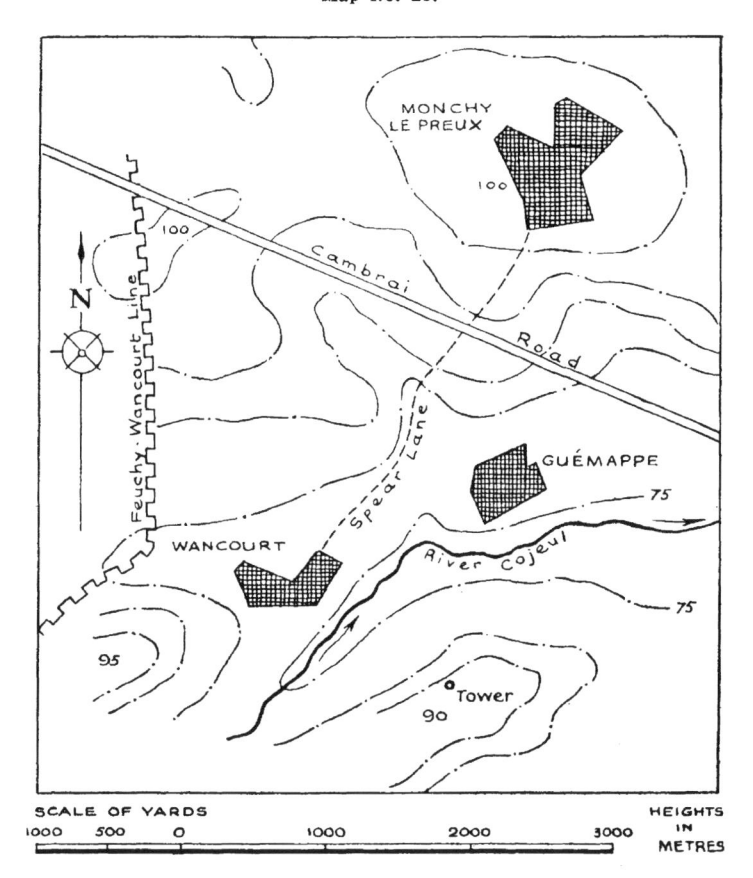

Area of 3rd Division Attack showing Dispositions of 1/Fifth (in Reserve) at zero hour on 26th September, 1917.

Map No. 26.

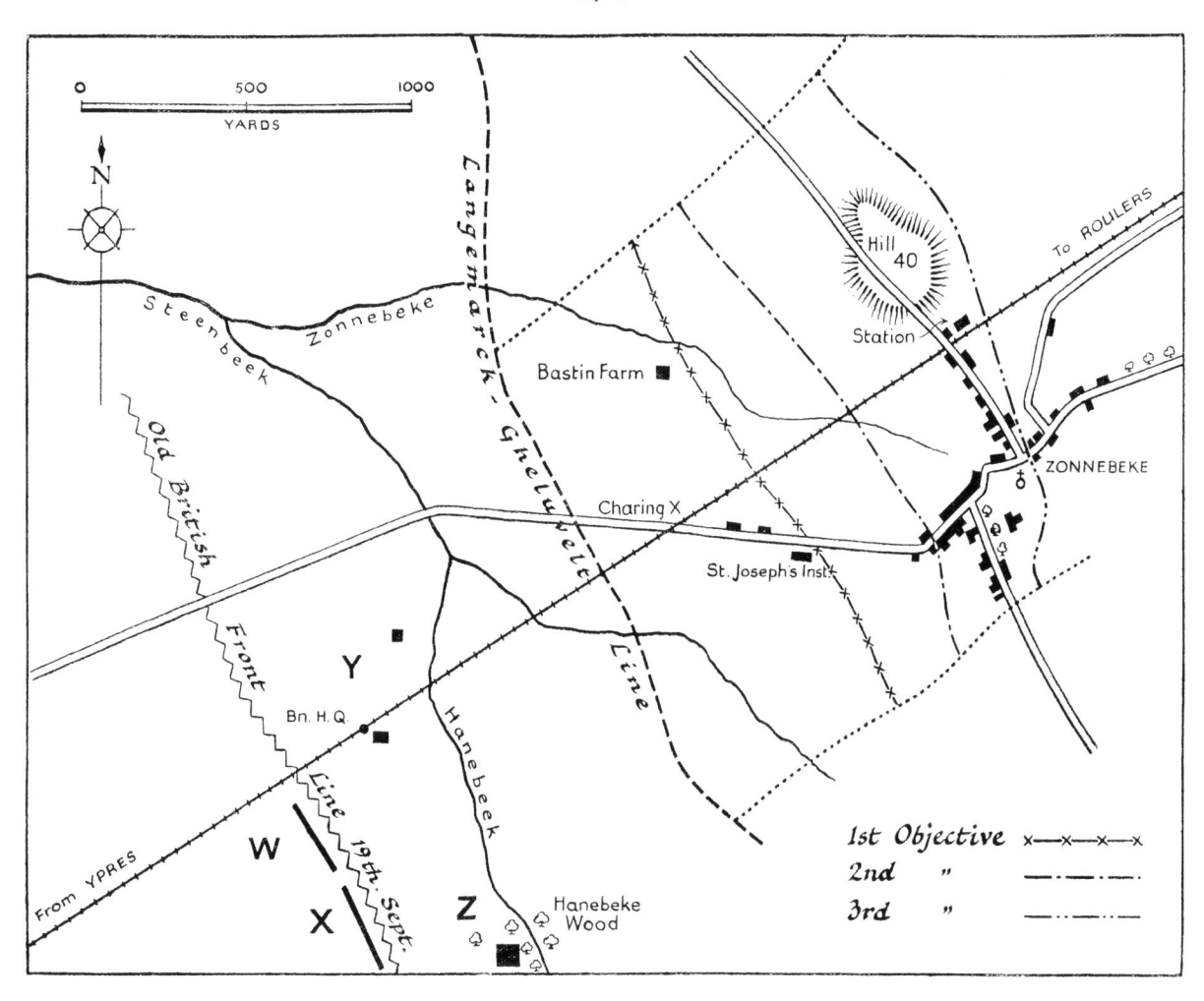

Attack north of Bullecourt, 20th November, 1917.

Map No. 27.

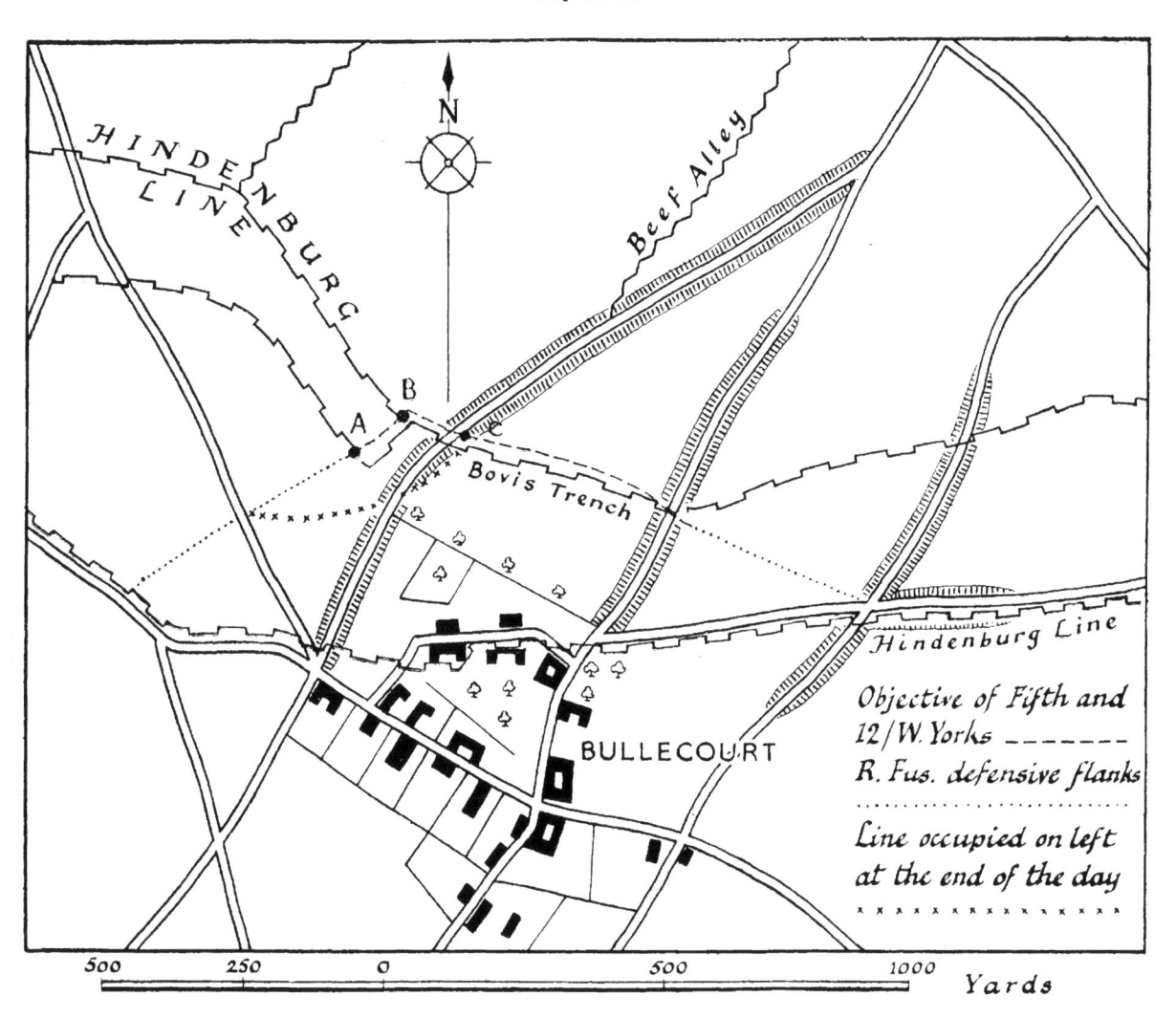

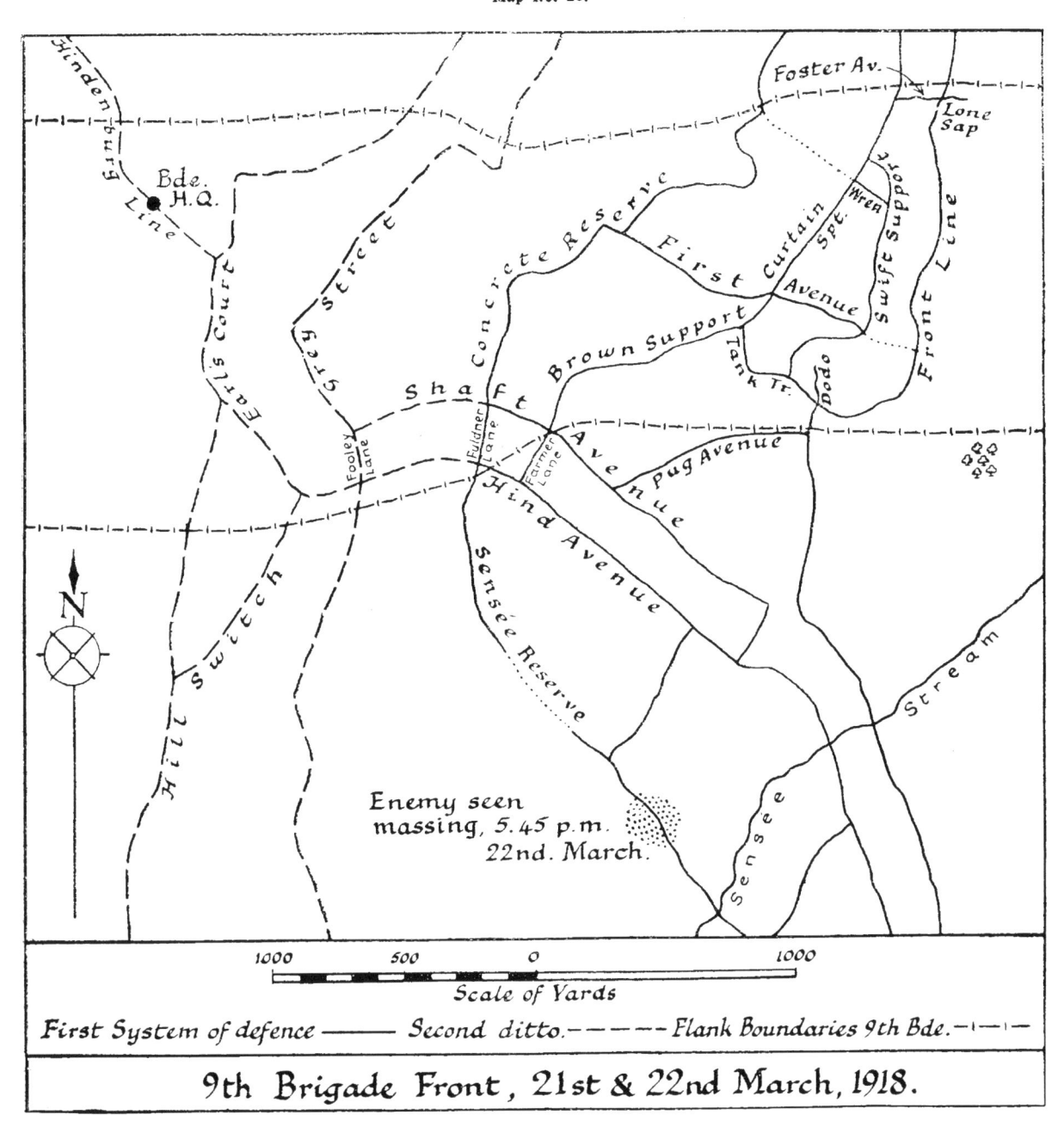

Map No. 29.

9th Brigade Front, 21st & 22nd March, 1918.

Map No. 30.

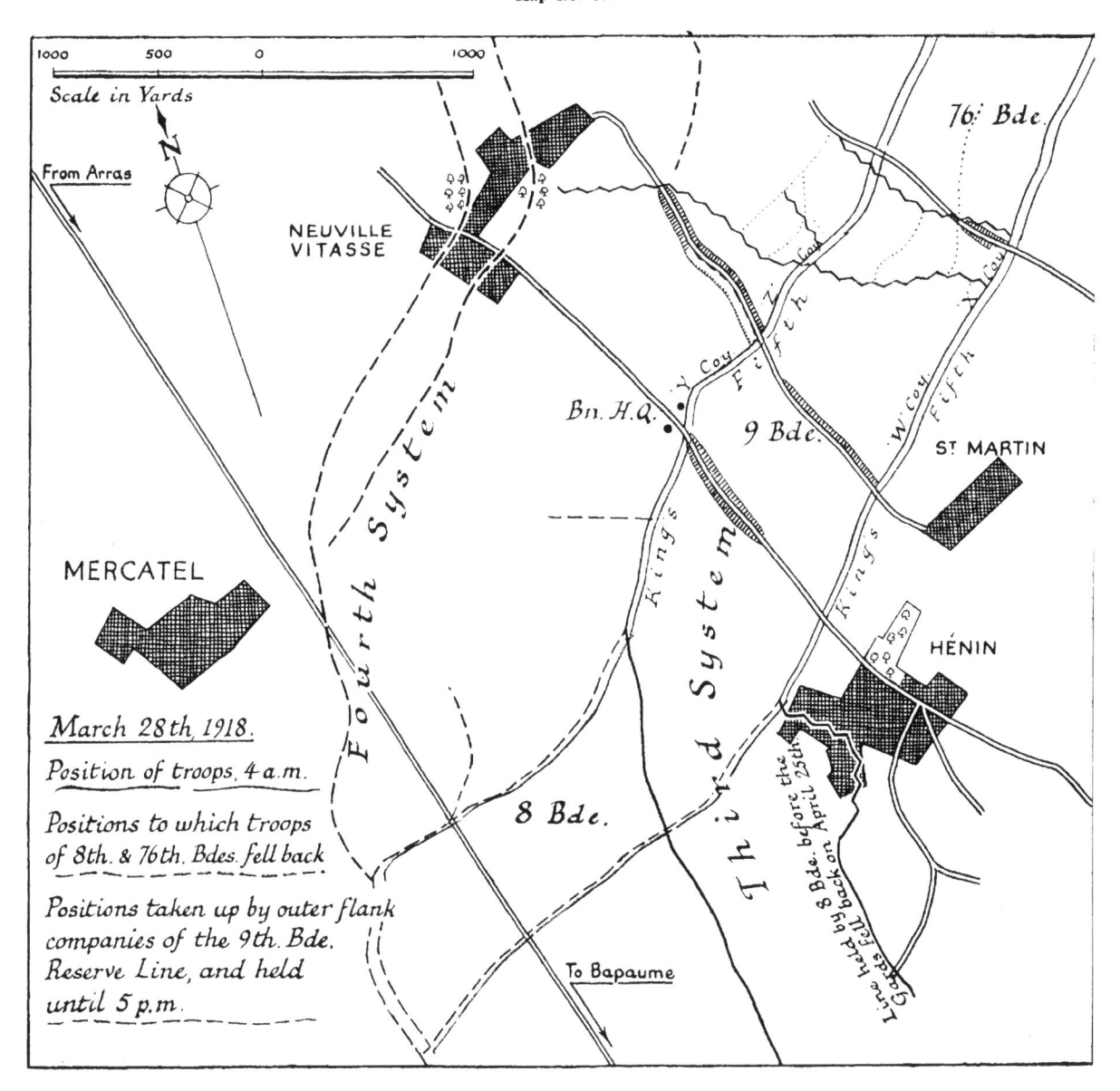

March 28th, 1918.
Position of troops, 4 a.m.

Positions to which troops of 8th. & 76th. Bdes. fell back

Positions taken up by outer flank companies of the 9th. Bde. Reserve Line, and held until 5 p.m.

Map No. 31.

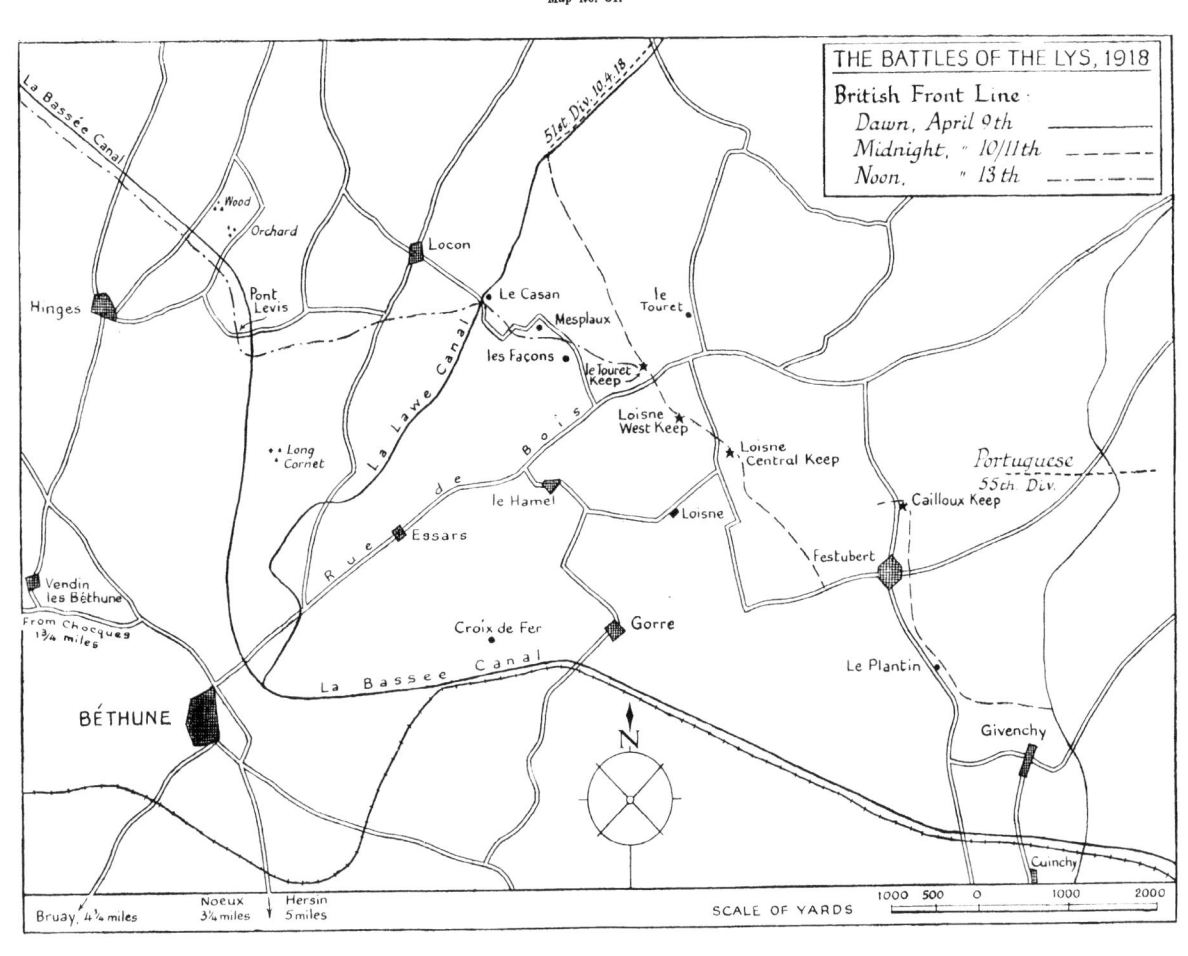

Map No. 32.

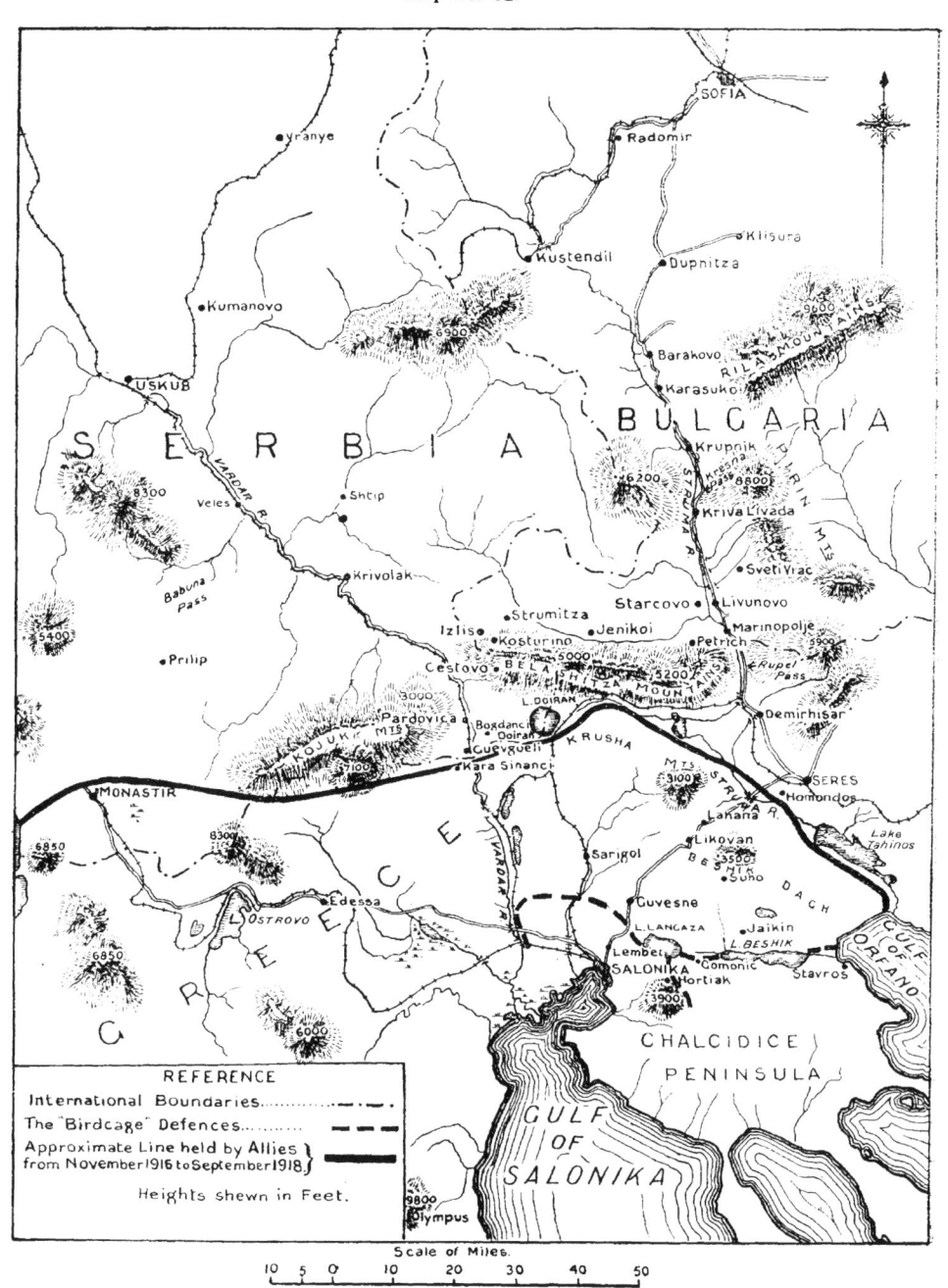

(From "The Historical Records of the Cameron Highlanders" (Wm. Blackwood and Sons), by kind permission.)

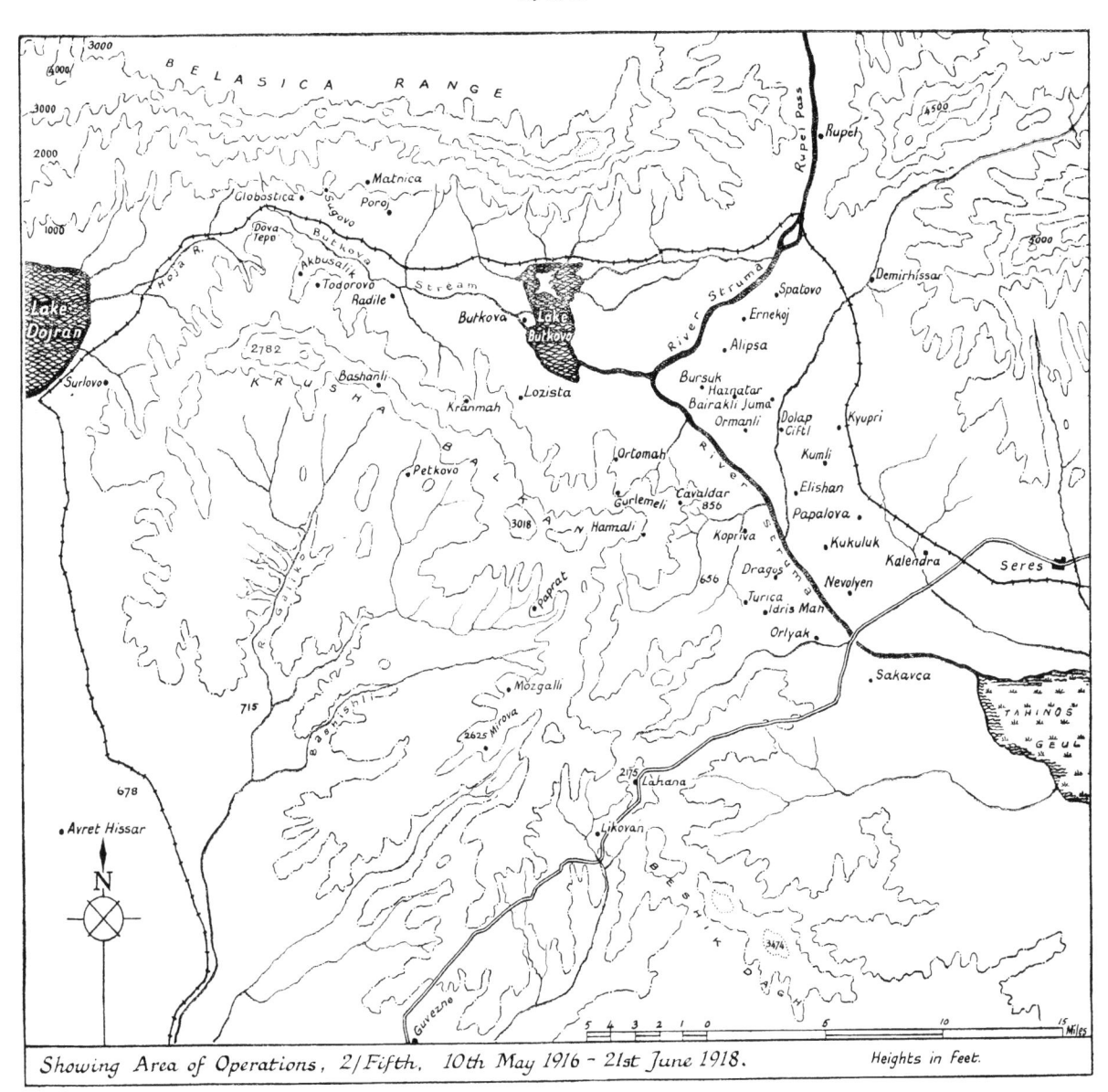

Map No. 33.

Showing Area of Operations, 2/Fifth, 10th May 1916 – 21st June 1918.   Heights in Feet.

Map No. 34.

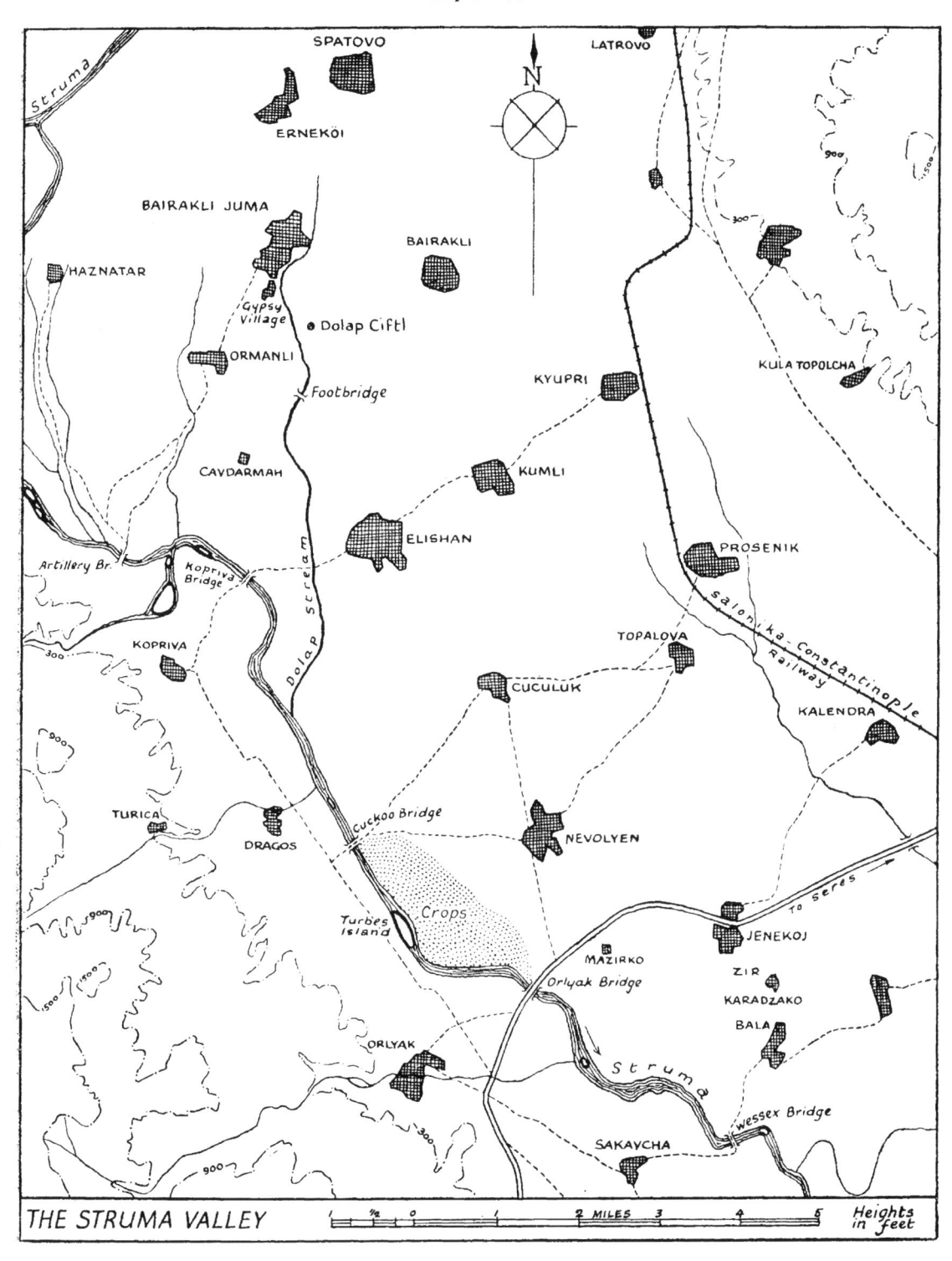

THE STRUMA VALLEY

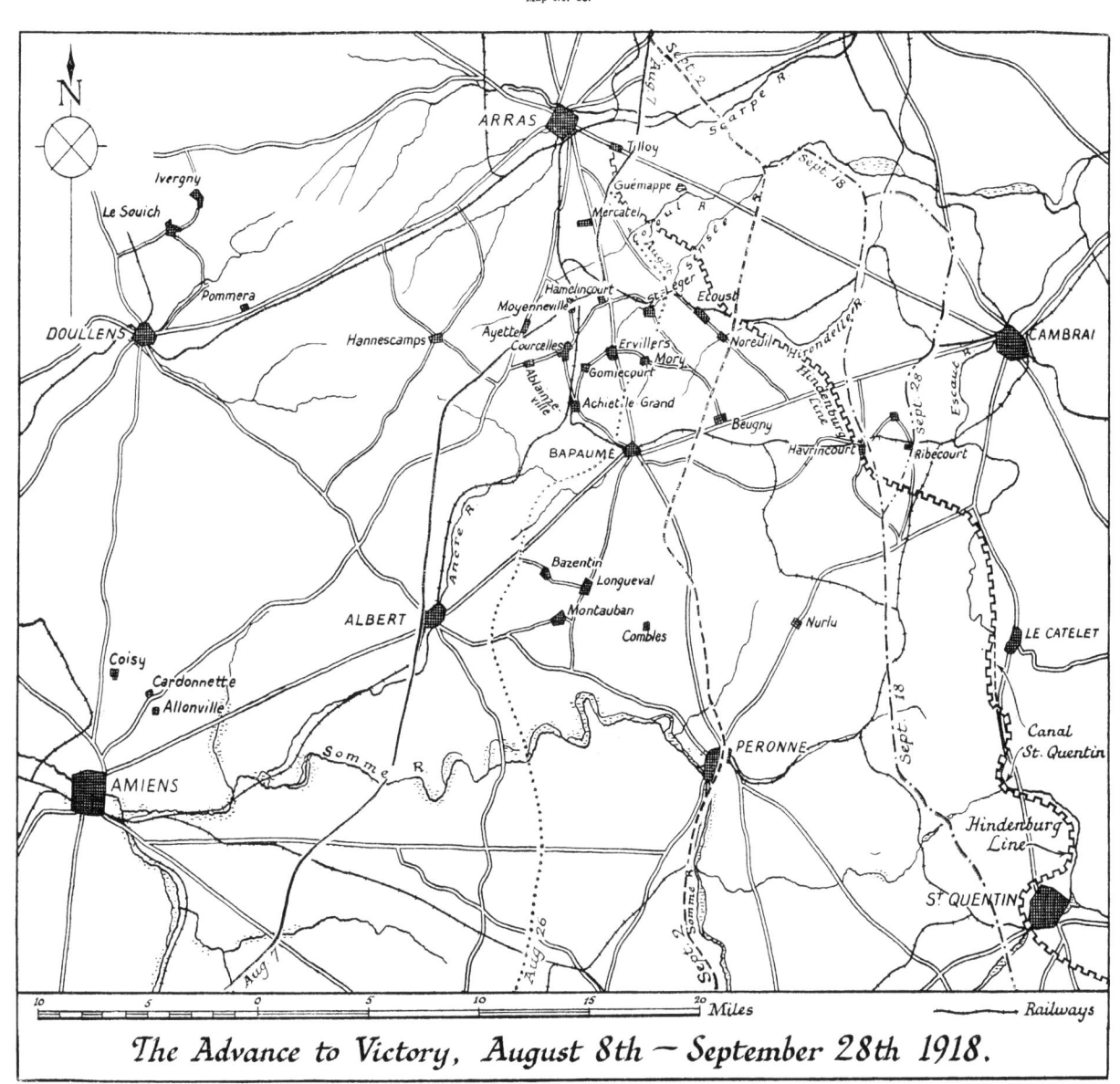

Map No. 35.

The Advance to Victory, August 8th — September 28th 1918.

Map No. 36.

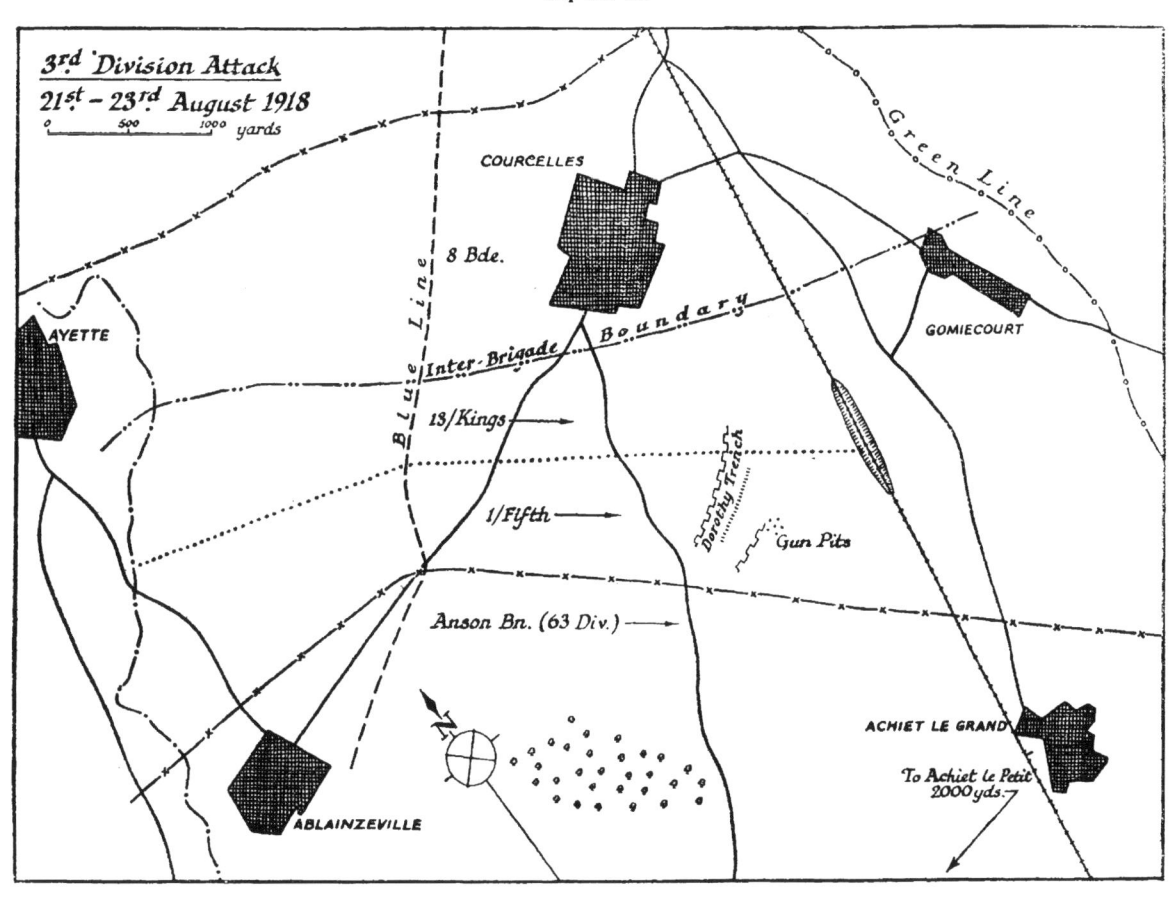

Map No. 37.

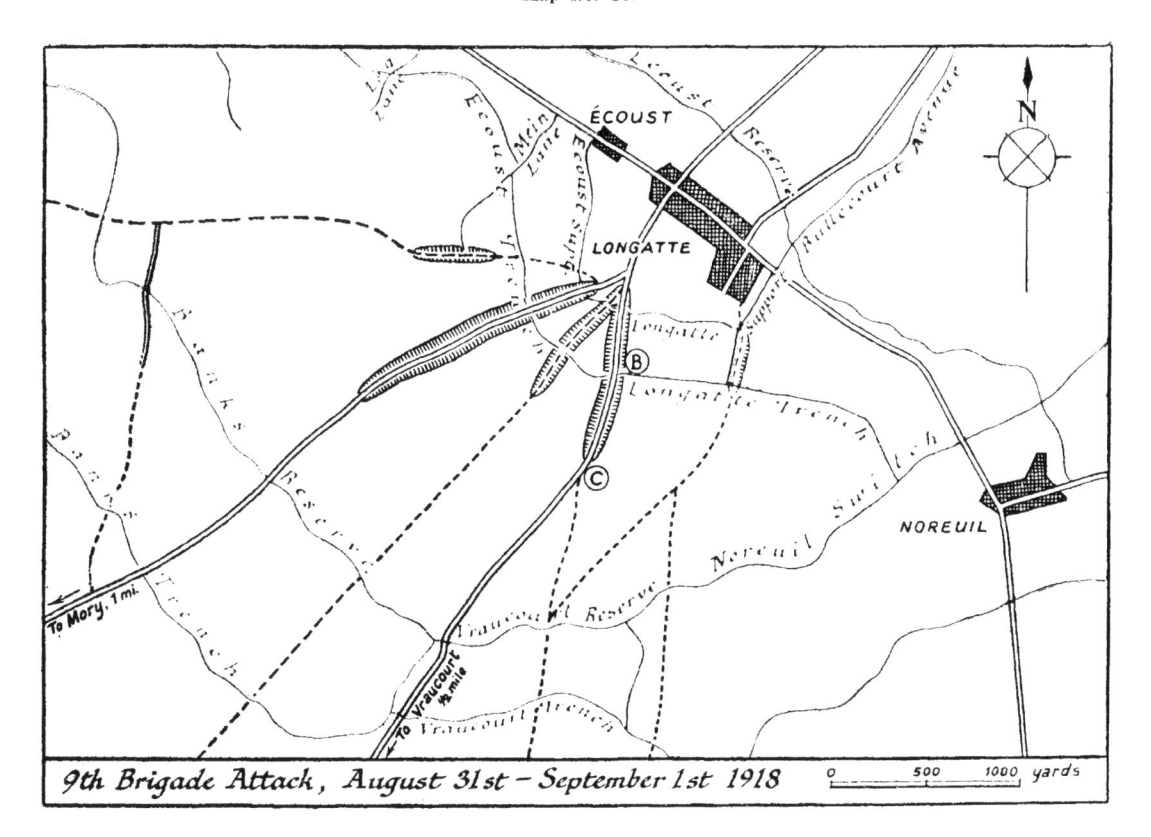

9th Brigade Attack, August 31st – September 1st 1918

Map No. 39.

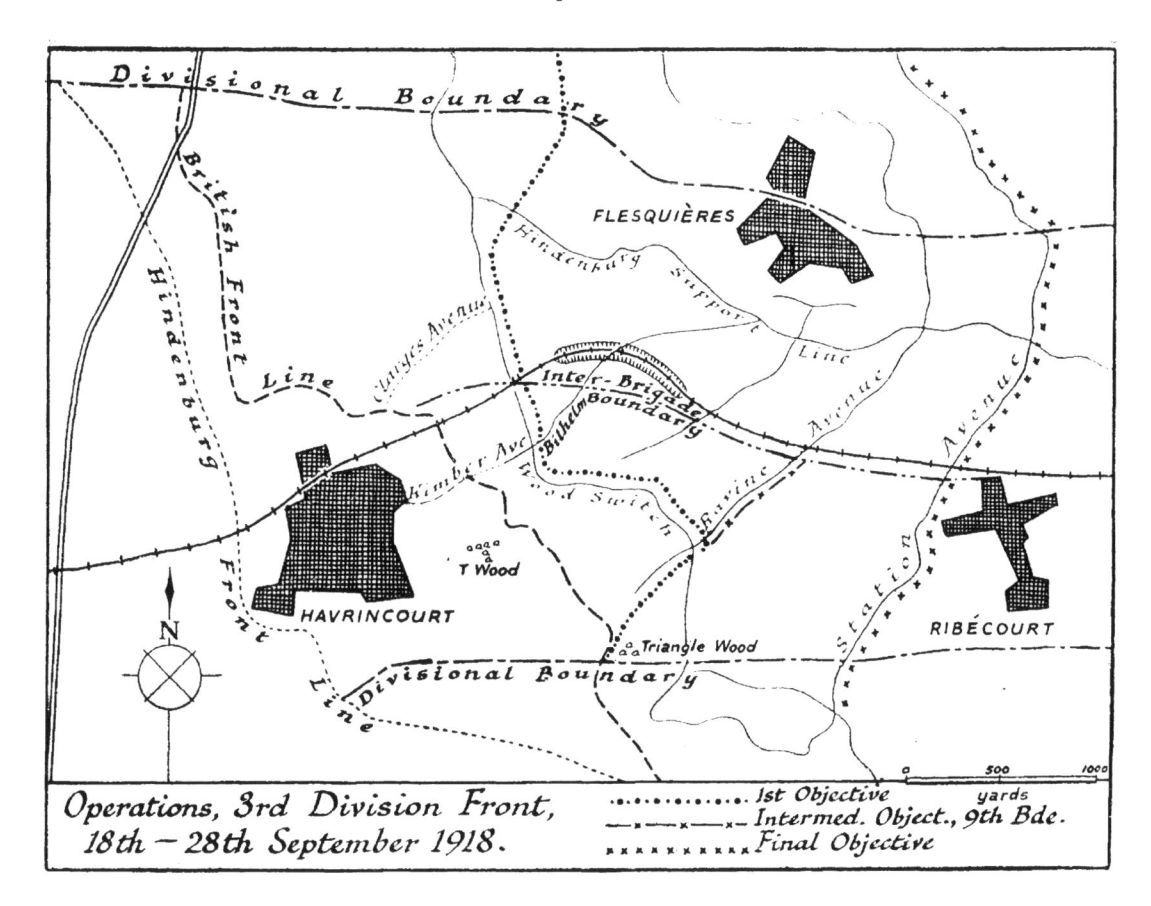

Operations, 3rd Division Front, 18th – 28th September 1918.

· · · · · · · 1st Objective
— × — × — Intermed. Object., 9th Bde.
× × × × × × Final Objective

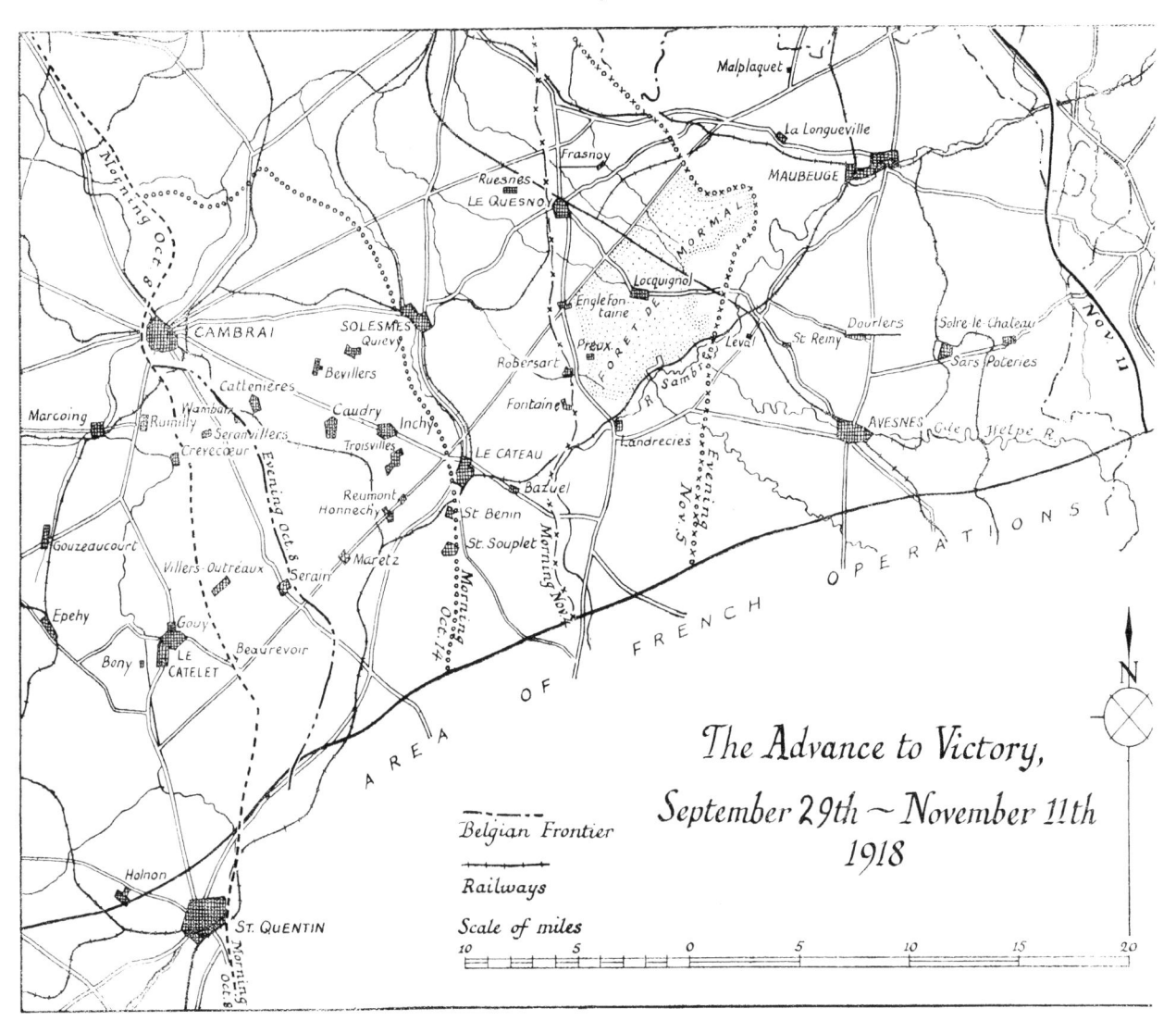

Map No. 40.

The Advance to Victory,
September 29th — November 11th
1918

Map No. 41.

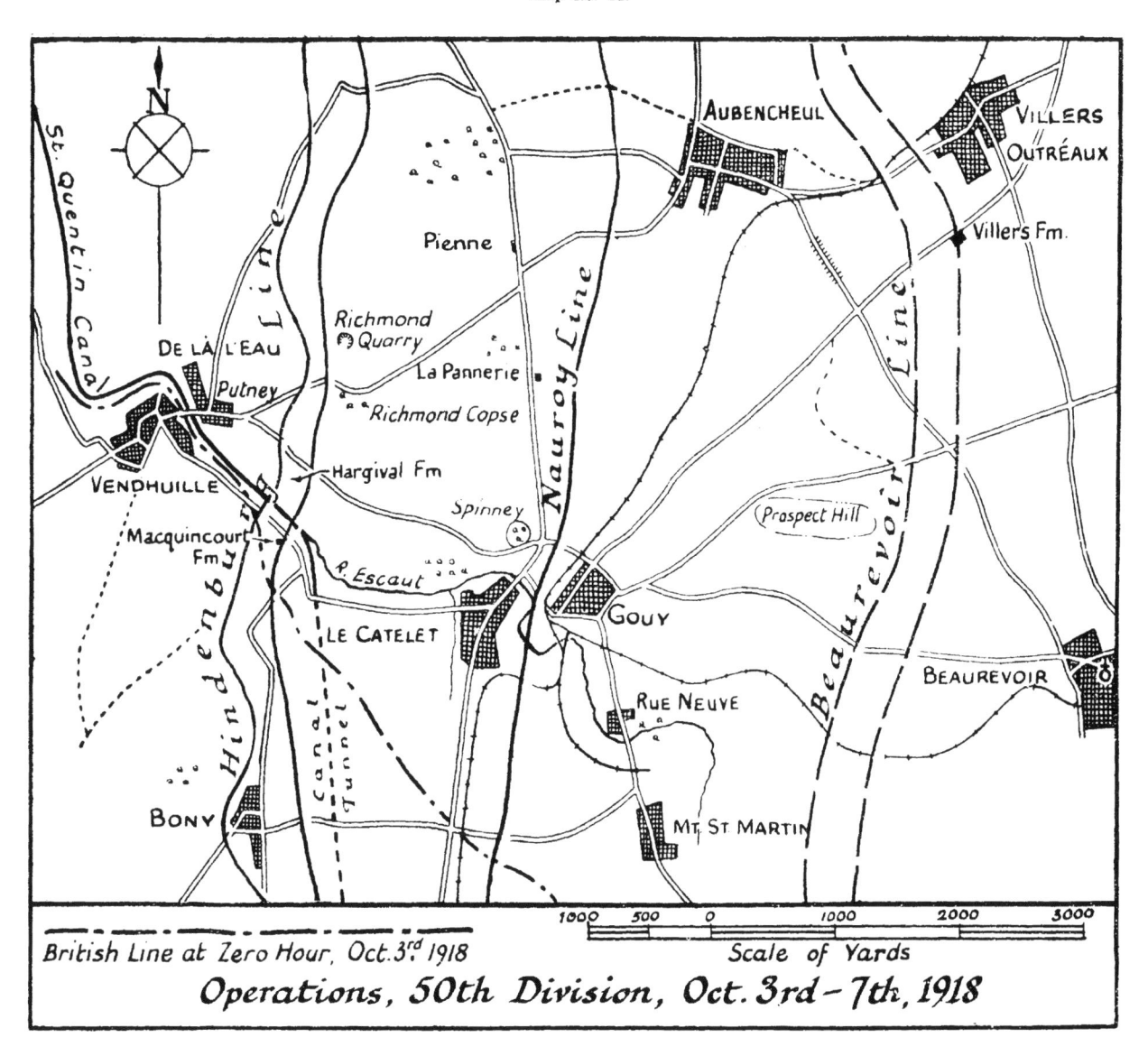

British Line at Zero Hour, Oct. 3rd 1918

Scale of Yards

Operations, 50th Division, Oct. 3rd – 7th, 1918

Map No. 42.

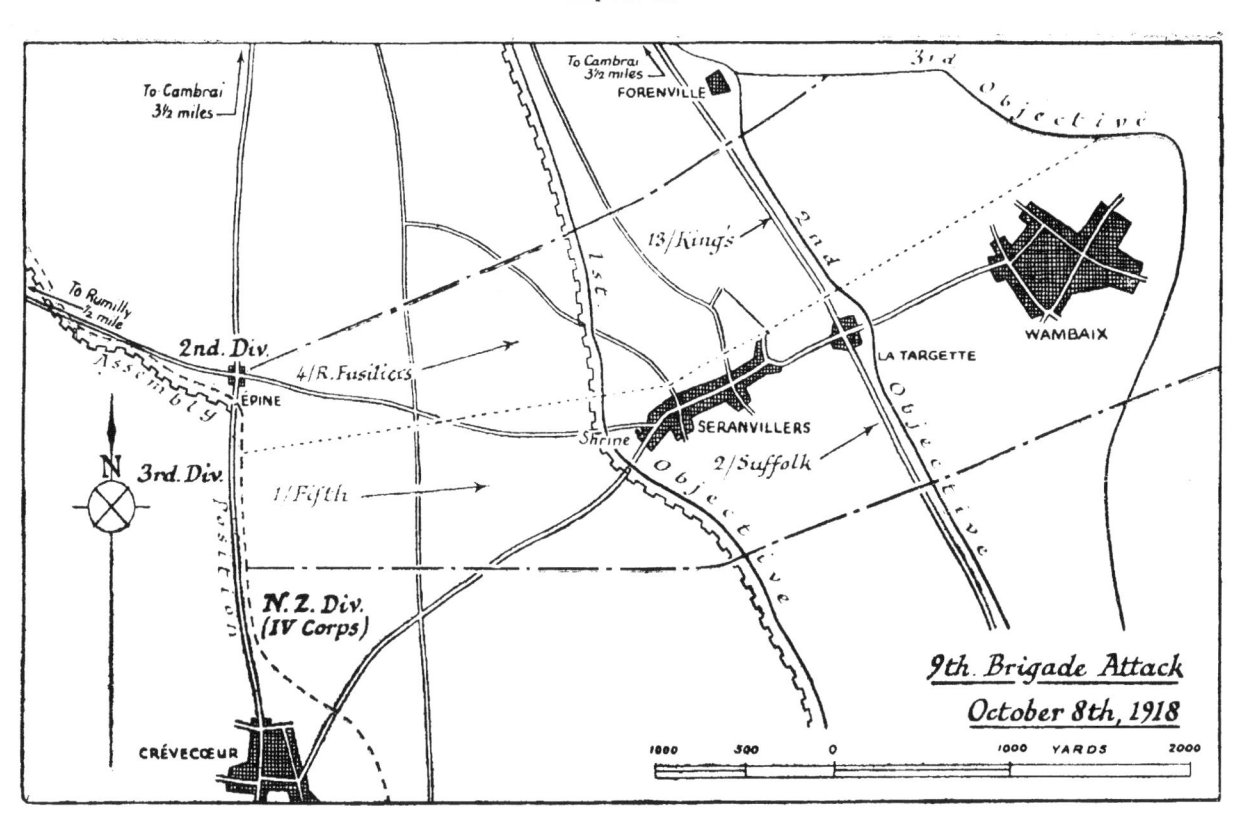

**9th Brigade Attack
October 8th, 1918**

Map No. 43.

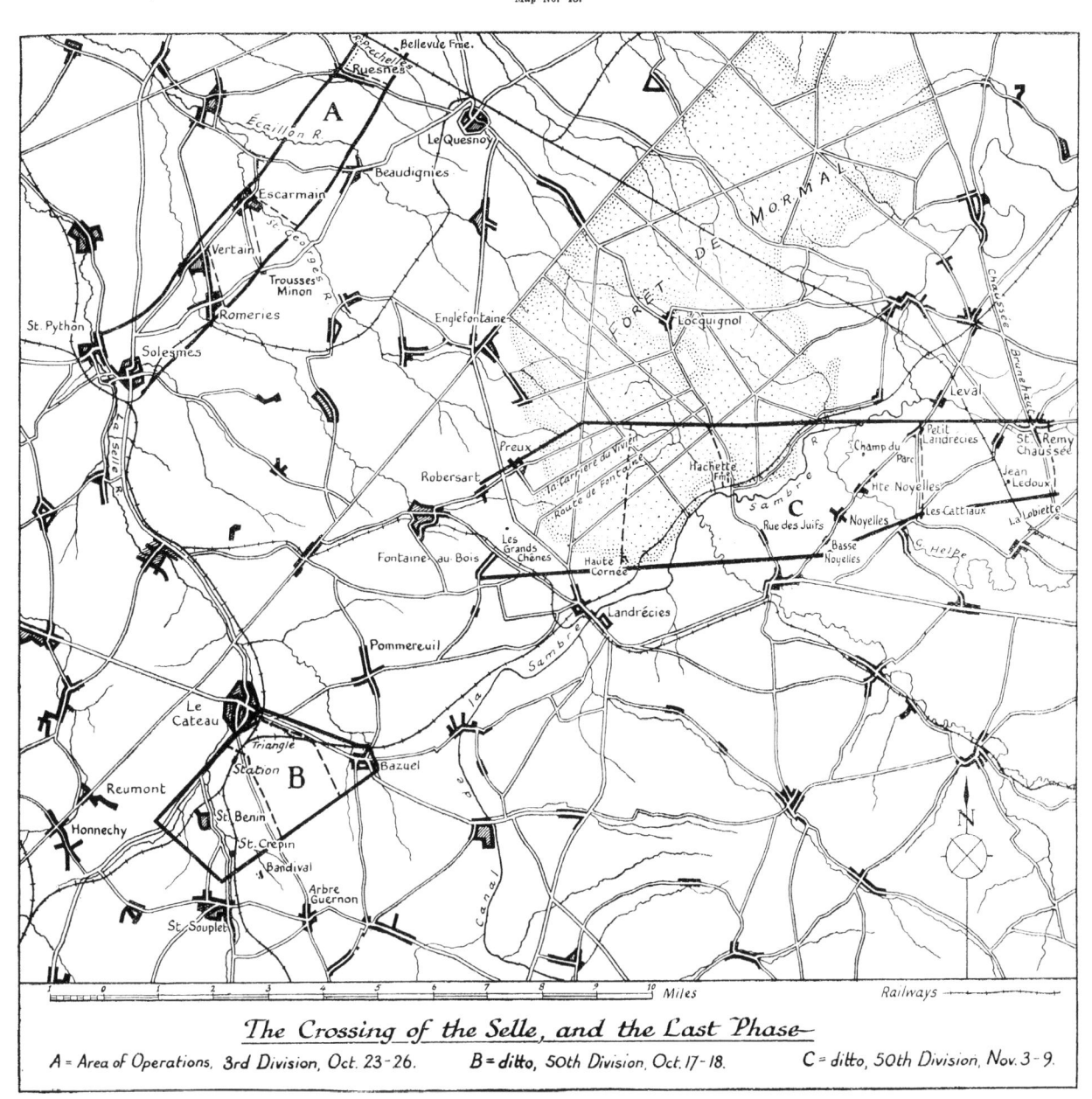

The Crossing of the Selle, and the Last Phase

A = Area of Operations, 3rd Division, Oct. 23-26.   B = ditto, 50th Division, Oct. 17-18.   C = ditto, 50th Division, Nov. 3-9.

Printed in Great Britain
by Amazon